D1505649

Contemporary Authors®

Autobiography Series

ISSN 0748-0636

Contemporary Authors

Autobiography Series

Joyce Nakamura
Editor

Shelly Andrews
Motoko Fujishiro Huthwaite
Associate Editors

Marilyn O'Connell Allen
Editorial Associate

volume **17**

Gale Research Inc. • DETROIT • WASHINGTON, D.C. • LONDON

EDITORIAL STAFF

Joyce Nakamura, *Editor*
Shelly Andrews and Motoko Fujishiro Huthwaite, *Associate Editors*
Michael J. Tyrkus, *Assistant Editor*
Marilyn O'Connell Allen, *Editorial Associate*
Laura Standley Berger and Laurie Collier, *Contributing Editors*

Victoria B. Cariappa, *Research Manager*
Mary Rose Bonk, *Research Supervisor, Biography Division*
Reginald A. Carlton, Clare Collins, Eva Marie Felts, Andrew Guy Malonis, and Norma Sawaya,
Editorial Associates
Patricia Bowen, Rachel A. Dixon, Shirley Gates, Sharon McGilvray,
and Devra M. Sladics, *Editorial Assistants*

Peter M. Gareffa, *Senior Editor*

Mary Beth Trimper, *Production Director*
Shanna Philpott Heilveil, *Production Assistant*

Cynthia Baldwin, *Art Director*
C. J. Jonik, *Keyliner*
Willie Mathis, *Camera Operator*

Donald G. Dillaman, *Index Program Designer*
David Jay Trotter, *Index Programmer*

The paper used in this publication meets the minimum requirements of American National Standard for Information Sciences—Permanence Paper for Printed Library Materials, ANSI Z39.48-1984. ∞™

Library of Congress Catalog Card Number 86-641293
ISBN 0-8103-4514-5
ISSN 0748-0636

Printed in the United States of America

Published simultaneously in the United Kingdom
by Gale Research International Limited
(An affiliated company of Gale Research Inc.)

10 9 8 7 6 5 4 3 2 1

Contents

Preface vii

Brief Sampler ix

Acknowledgments...xi

Victor Hernández Cruz 1949- 1

Philip Dacey 1939- 19

Robert Flanagan 1941-..37

Joseph Hansen 1923- 59

Hugh Hood 1928- 75

Gerard Malanga 1943- 95

James A. McPherson 1943- 121

Jessica Mitford 1917- 137

John Frederick Nims 1913- 153

Al Purdy 1918- 195

Nahid Rachlin 215

James Still 1906- 231

Tomas Tranströmer 1931- 249

Anne Waldman 1945- 267

Cumulative Index 297

Preface

A Unique Collection of Essays

Each volume in the *Contemporary Authors Autobiography Series (CAAS)* presents an original collection of autobiographical essays written especially for the series by noted writers.

CA Autobiography Series is designed to be a meeting place for writers and readers—a place where writers can present themselves, on their own terms, to their audience; and a place where general readers, students of contemporary literature, teachers and librarians, even aspiring writers can become better acquainted with familiar authors and meet others for the first time.

This is an opportunity for writers who may never write a full-length autobiography to let their readers know how they see themselves and their work, what brought them to this time and place.

Even for those authors who have already published full-length autobiographies, there is the opportunity in *CAAS* to bring their readers "up to date" or perhaps to take a different approach in the essay format. In some instances, previously published material may be reprinted or expanded upon; this fact is always noted at the end of such an essay. Individually, the essays in this series can enhance the reader's understanding of a writer's work; collectively, they are lessons in the creative process and in the discovery of its roots.

CAAS makes no attempt to give a comprehensive overview of authors and their works. That outlook is already well represented in biographies, reviews, and critiques published in a wide variety of sources. Instead, *CAAS* complements that perspective and presents what no other ongoing reference source does: the view of contemporary writers that is shaped by their own choice of materials and their own manner of storytelling.

Who Is Covered?

Like its parent series, *Contemporary Authors*, the *CA Autobiography Series* sets out to meet the needs and interests of a wide range of readers. Each volume includes essays by writers in all genres whose work is being read today. We consider it extraordinary that so many busy authors from throughout the world are able to interrupt their existing writing, teaching, speaking, traveling, and other schedules to converge on a given deadline for any one volume. So it is not always possible that all genres can be equally and uniformly represented from volume to volume, although we strive to include writers working in a variety of categories, including fiction, nonfiction, and poetry. As only a few writers specialize in a single area, the breadth of writings by authors in this volume also encompasses drama, translation, and criticism as well as work for movies, television, radio, newspapers, and journals.

What Each Essay Includes

Authors who contribute to *CAAS* are invited to write a "mini-autobiography" of approximately 10,000 words. In order to give the writer's imagination free rein, we suggest no guidelines or pattern for the essay. We only ask that each writer tell his or her story in the manner and to the extent that feels most natural and appropriate. In addition, writers are asked to supply a selection of personal photographs showing themselves at various ages, as well as important people and special moments in their lives. Our contributors have responded generously, sharing with us some of their most treasured mementoes. The result is a special blend of text and photographs that will attract even the casual browser. Other features include:

Bibliography at the end of each essay, listing the author's book-length works in chronological order of publication. Each bibliography in this volume was compiled by members of the *CAAS* editorial staff and submitted to the author for review.

Cumulative index in each volume, which cites all the essayists in the series as well as the subjects presented in the essays: personal names, titles of works, geographical names, schools of writing, etc. To ensure ease of use for these cumulating references, the name of the essayist is given before the volume and page number(s) for every reference that appears in more than one essay. In the following example, the entry in the index allows the user to identify the essay writers by name:

> Auden, W.H.
>> Allen **6:**18, 24
>> Ashby **6:**36, 39
>> Bowles **1:**86
>> etc.

For references that appear in only one essay, the volume and page number(s) are given but the name of the essayist is omitted. For example:

> Stieglitz, Alfred **1:**104, 109, 110

CAAS is something more than the sum of its individual essays. At many points the essays touch common ground, and from these intersections emerge new patterns of information and impressions. The index is an important guide to these interconnections.

For Additional Information

For detailed information on awards won, adaptations of works, critical reviews of works, and more, readers are encouraged to consult Gale's *Contemporary Authors* cumulative index for authors' listings in other Gale sources. These include, among others, *Contemporary Authors, Contemporary Authors New Revision Series, Dictionary of Literary Biography,* and *Contemporary Literary Criticism.*

Special Thanks

We wish to acknowledge our special gratitude to each of the authors in this volume. They all have been most kind and cooperative in contributing not only their talents but their enthusiasm and encouragement to this project.

A Brief Sampler

Each essay in the series has a special character and point of view that sets it apart from its companions. A small sampler of anecdotes and musings from the essays in this volume hint at the unique perspective of these life stories.

Victor Hernández Cruz, observing the dualities of culture in the United States: "English was like a new coat which didn't fit but had to be worn. In the New York City public school system, the speaking of Spanish was strictly forbidden.... I was beginning to feel like a stereo system, speaking Spanish on one side and English on the other. It was not only speaking these two sets of sounds, it was also listening to them, thinking in them, feeling.... The language of my home, the Spanish of my parents, tenderness and discipline, the proverbs of advice and consolation. The Spanish of Andalusia animated and possessing flesh, here Taino sentiment, there Gypsy sway, here African beat, all the ancestral maneuvers depositing into an instant of street. On the streets of the Lower East Side, there was a chop-suey English lingering in the neighborhood from the Jewish and Irish past.... As if a peacock with feathers of sound fanned out in front of me, the center of a spinning wheel.... I exchanged Spanish with Afro-American friends. The English was bending, twisting and diving, new spices were seasoning the tongue, which was like a magnet drawing to it the music of talk, the tempo and the flavor of the city. Mixing it all with the language of my birth, the Romantic Spanish that crossed the Atlantic with the sails of the Renaissance. It in itself showing the scars of one invasion after another."

James A. McPherson, on overcoming life's opposing forces: "As for myself, I have survived. I know there are still, and will remain, obstacles and traps for black males who demonstrate intelligence and ambition. But I also know that places like Charlottesville, Virginia, are no longer representative of the evolving South. And I know that the world is a very large place. Because I know these things, I now believe that, in the authentic sense, in terms of the real meaning of my own life, it was necessary for me to enter Charlottesville so I could reclaim a deeper understanding of the lives of my mother and father. I also believe that I would not have been given the traits that were limitations in my parents if it had not been the fate assigned to me to transcend them. I have found that public displays of intelligence, even in black males, is not a 'sin,' as my mother might have thought. I have also found that the forces that conspire to destroy such intelligence are not always successful. The fact that they do exist should not be used to justify what can ultimately become a self-defeating stasis in the self. People do survive. They do proceed in the face of, and in spite of, the worst that can be done to them."

Al Purdy, providing a glimpse of the man who appears in many of his poems: "Grandfather was slightly over six feet tall. He weighed 260 pounds. His nose was a parrot's beak; his face still had the remains of youth—not of happy and carefree childish days, but the bullmoose time of being a lumberjack and backwoods wrestler, barnraiser and don't-give-a-damn-about-anything stud and hellraiser. He was. Grandfather tolerated me. And all the time something smoldered and burned inside him, which I felt too—something out of the far-distant past. He was eighty years back of me in time, and seemed less a relative than a queer aging animal from the forests, where other animals wisely avoided him. My parents had been old when I was born, and my own connection with these people seemed many generations distant. All the world was old, this very world that was closest to me. My grandfather's ferocity, that smoldering and burning self, concealed or half-concealed in rotting flesh! His talk about wrestling the woods bully; and no doubt he was a bully himself, although that thought never occurred to me then. Barn raisings and booze, and 'I wanted to get into her pants.' Nothing softened or euphemized for me; he said what he thought and felt. Death became, 'I'll turn up my toes.' About life: 'You don't dast stop,' or everything would fall down."

Tomas Tranströmer, sharing a nine-year-old's perspective of World War II Sweden: "My 'political' instincts were directed entirely at the war and Nazism. I believed one was either a Nazi or an anti-Nazi. I had no understanding of that lukewarm attitude, that opportunistic wait-and-see stance which was widespread in Sweden. I interpreted that either as support for the Allies or as covert Nazism. When I realized that some person I liked was really 'pro-German,' I immediately felt a terrible tightening over my breast. Everything was ruined. There could never be any kind of fellow feeling between us. From those close to me I expected unequivocal support. One evening when we were on a visit to Uncle Elof and Aunt Agda, the news inspired my generally taciturn uncle to comment that 'the English are successfully retreating...' He said this almost with regret yet it struck me there was an ironic undertone (on the whole irony was foreign to him) and I suddenly felt that tightening. The Allied version of history was never questioned. I stared grimly up at the roof light. There was consolation to be found there. It had the shape of a British steel helmet: like a soup plate."

Anne Waldman, upon realizing her life's true calling: "I think of myself as a kinetic writer, thinker: amazed at the places writing originates from. Not just a conceptual place. Is it 'voices' in the head? Emanating from all sense perceptions in concert? Is it innate psychophysical-personal rhythm? My own sound? The gestures and sounds of the phenomenal world? Do I write the way I think—ungrammatically? Do I write the way I move? Found language? I'd felt, from my first reading at St. Mark's Church, where I sat, head bowed to page, that the voice coming out of me was only partial, and that I had a bigger sound to exhibit and explore. A sound that I would literally 'have to grow into.' But I was nervous. Next time, I stood positioned to honor the poem, to let it guide me. I saw how the text demanded a particular rendering, and it was often close to how I heard it, how words sounded in my ear. A particular kind of resonance increased after chanting mantra, I noticed as well. And since I'd had some early experience with theater, I appreciated the way voice could carry, inflect, conjure up various psychological and emotional states. How the words carried very particular and expressive energy pulses in its minutest forms—phones, phonemes. And although I couldn't pinpoint the effects of such experience of poetry, I knew I felt something 'awakening' in my body..."

These brief examples only suggest what lies ahead in this volume. The essays will speak differently to different readers; but they are certain to speak best, and most eloquently, for themselves.

Acknowledgments

Grateful acknowledgment is made to those publishers, photographers, and artists whose works appear with these authors' essays.

Photographs/Art

Victor Hernández Cruz: p. 16, © C. DeVault.

Philip Dacey: p. 19, W. Patrick Hinely; p. 35, Barb Skoog.

Robert Flanagan: p. 45, U.S. Marine Corps.

Joseph Hansen: p. 67, Frank Baker.

Hugh Hood: pp. 75, 88, Noreen Mallory; p. 92, Sam Tata.

Gerard Malanga: Essay photos largely by Archives Malanga, © Archives Malanga. p. 95, Artwork © Gerard Malanga; pp. 96, 97, 116, 118, © Gerard Malanga; p. 100, William T. Wood/Archives Malanga; pp. 106, 108, Gerard Malanga/Andy Warhol; p. 113, Diane Dorr-Dorynek/Archives Malanga; p. 114, Richard Ballarian/Archives Malanga; p. 119, Anne Wall/Archives Malanga.

James A. McPherson: p. 121, Kio Ono; p. 132, Olan Mills © 1991.

Jessica Mitford: p. 137, Mayotte Magnus; p. 138, Gilman & Co. Photos; p. 148, Bob Treuhaft; p. 149, People Weekly.

Al Purdy: p. 206, © Eurithe Purdy; p. 209, Julia Ashberry.

Nahid Rachlin: p. 215, Howard Rachlin; p. 225, Diana Photography.

James Still: p. 231, painting by Sam McKinney; p. 236, Van Dyke Studio; p. 241, Dean Cadle.

Tomas Tranströmer: p. 249, Oklahoma University News Services.

Anne Waldman: p. 278, Bill Yoscary Photography; p. 281, © Gerard Malanga; p. 284, Rachel Homer; p. 285, Louis R. Cartwright; p. 286, Wayne Padgett; p. 290, Dan Wilcox; p. 292, Cindy Dach.

Text

John Frederick Nims: All poems reprinted with permission of the author, John Frederick Nims. Credit is supplied for the following: Lines from "The Child," in *Selected Poems*, University of Chicago Press, 1982./ Lines from "Dedication," first published in *American*, October 11, 1941./ Lines from "The Library," first published in *American Libraries*, February

Contemporary Authors®
Autobiography Series

Victor Hernández Cruz

1949-

THE RHYTHMS THAT MOVE YOU
AN AUTOBIOGRAPHICAL AND CRITICAL SKETCH

Victor Hernández Cruz

The tropical morning with its orchestration of sounds and melodies. The aroma of café like a song permeating the air. Dancing in the memory the coquís who through consciousness and deep sleep print their Morse codes upon the inner drum. A dog barking on a distant mountain. The hot dark air has wings for sound. The pores of the molecules stretched. Night musicalities. When the sun rises all material follows.

Island of images, island of sounds.

Balconies which are as if stages onto the streets, platforms that make the town accessible, where speech crisscrosses with wind, where bird songs collide with vision, aroma integrates with thoughts. Separating the ether, the river distinguishes itself as it rolls into the belly of the mountain, towards the spectacle of the coast, what

is not tied down doing somersaults, tumbling through its wet power.

The river made a path through my ears, another color to the music of the insects, layers of sound poetry inhabiting horizontal and vertical planks of space. As far away as the word *gone* can get there were mountains dancing danza, danzon of courtesy and fragrance, movement of controlled passion, flirtation of eye and elbow, forestry of choreography, tilts of wind, ceiba trees bowing, suggesting hidden Taino grace. Plenas lifting out of the coast, frame that supports the cadence of Africa raining upon the red soil. Gypsy flamenco, transported heels tapping through the pineapple fields, each frog with its own guitar, serenading lizards that dash with sun glasses, the yellow rays of the sun turning amapolas into trumpets, centipedes playing bongos into the tamarindo flavor, azuzenas turning off the stars which migrate towards the verses of the mountains, for the troubadours to wear in their eyes, memory that keeps the stories stored in the rhyme of dream, falcons with fire in their beaks, bringing in the day, as the curtain of darkness rises upon the Andalusian tiles on the balcony of time.

Outside the little streets were being paved with cement, red dirt disappearing under the grey. Before, when the streets were all earth, the rain water used to run down the sides of the streets like guayava juice. Progress was coming in on the wings of time. My childhood was a stage where I witnessed the transformation of humanity.

As a young child one doesn't separate dream from reality, we are too immersed in time to know or even to care of its passage. We had entered history. Petroleum was coming in through the tropical vapors, the landscape was being stretched like a hive, it was polluted with tractors and diesel trucks, bringing and taking cement, throwing the mix in every direction of yonder and beyond.

Seducing mountains, raping them right through the middle. Upon the lips of the population a new word was being pronounced which sounded like: Nujol. A place far away that one can go to, another world, where jobs played like music. Migration is the story of our age. People folded up and jumped into suitcases, huge Packards took them off over the mountain, where they vanished forever.

We are born into a place and a time, a province, it begins to mold us, the language of the region makes footprints in our hearts. The flora and fauna enter our souls through our eyes. The trees, the mountains, the sounds of the coquís, space music that originates in the vast darkness.

I remember walking to a river with my mother, where she and the other women of the town washed clothes along the bank of the river upon the rocks. When they were finished they would hang the clothes on nearby bushes to dry. Children played amist wandering cows, picking immediate fruit, listening to the tales of the women. Sometimes as a way of caressing the labor at hand, they would hum and sing songs. Singing

A tropical river

boleros, the songs of lost love, of sadness, tragedy, the songs made popular on the island by singers like Felipe Rodriguez. The sound of Spanish landing like birds into my ears.

Languages also migrate, conquer, and marry one another. When in 1492 the Christians of Spain reconquered their territory back from the Arabs, who had occupied it for over eight hundred years, Arabian words remain standing like tents all over the Iberian landscape. The lament of the Arabian-Andalusian songs echoed through the Moorish structures that were recycled with Christ and Castilian. The vibrations of the guitar drank milk at the breast of the la'ud, its Arabian mother. Migrating on the ships of the colonization of the new world were the swords of language upon the lips of the people who are poetry. It was those songs which the women hummed by the river.

Poets are travelers out of curiosity and many times for outright survival. Many poets had to take flight out of Franco Spain. Federico Garcia Lorca was found by Franco's soldiers and used as a notebook, they wrote with bullets the sonnets of fascism. Pedro Salinas, Luis Cernuda, and Juan Ramon Jimenez heard the flow of the Spanish river on the other side of the world.

Juan Ramon Jimenez lived in many places of the Americas, including New York, but it was in Puerto Rico where he most felt at home. He heard the sounds of Andalusia in the talk of the Puerto Rican people. His words were full of the light of the island sun. In a book of conversations with Juan Ramon Jimenez, Ricardo Gullon, a Spaniard who was a professor at the University of Puerto Rico where he taught alongside the poet in the early fifties, reminisced about a trip they both took to the mountains of Jaqueyes, which is in my hometown of Aguas Buenas. They went to a small hotel which is set cozy in the tropical scenery. Could it be possibly within chance that they drove down the principal street of this small enclave and passed the wooden house wherein I dwelled deep in the mist of play? Resounding in the poetry of Juan Ramon Jimenez is the conference of the birds and the color of the flowers of my childhood island.

Luis Muñoz Marín, Puerto Rico's first elected governor, was born in 1898, the year of the North American invasion. I was born in 1949, one year after he took office—a child of a government of experiment, within a Caribbean culture comprised of aboriginal elements mixed with Spanish, which in turn is mixed with Arabian, permeated through-

out with African. That was the inside and the outside.

Our first governor was known as El Vate (The Bard), for he was also a poet. He frequented the cafes of Old San Juan in the 1920s, considered himself a socialist, a bohemian, and proclaimed the independence of Puerto Rico. He wrote proletarian verses and some which were fused with a Whitmanesque spirit. In Ricardo Gullon's memoirs he speaks of the fine receptions at the Governor's Jajome residence, where industrialists, intellectuals, and poets met. The gamut of the conversations must have run from literary anecdotes to the political future of the island. The poet Luis Pales Matos was a close friend of the governor. They even once wrote a poem together by each contributing alternating lines. As the liqueur passed around in these sessions, the island convulsed and struggled to get out of its eternal poverty. Many islanders gathered their past and stuffed them into suitcases to ship them into the future. Muñoz Marín, with a fiery poet's oratory, gave speeches in mountain towns to the Jibaros. Vegetation was listening to the drums of industry. His campaign of the late forties used Lenin's revolutionary slogan: *Pan, Tierra y Libertad* (Bread, Land, and Liberty). In the acquisition of his political power, the muse abandoned Muñoz. His new verses were factories on the landscape. His metaphors were petrochemical installations broadcasting sonnets of pollution. His coplas the machinery of industrialization. Smoke pipes littering the countryside the imagery of his new poetry. Westinghouse popping out of the banana leaves.

As the island of Puerto Rico industrialized and progressed, the exodus of the *campesino* (Jibaros) intensified. Turmoil in their culture. You would think that progress would do the opposite, keep people striving in their own land.

Through the tropical electricity of the radio, the music and the songs perfumed the bombs of progress. From my childhood, mountains had the awesome grandiose qualities of gods. Tremendous productions of nature emitting from their bowels a sound. Wooden houses lined the street where I lived, painted in colors that would impress the impressionists. Lizards, which Federico Garcia Lorca described as drops of crocodiles in one of his poem-paintings, were speeding through the walls and trees faster than the speed of bullets, almost as fast as the speed of thought.

Roosters were always chasing chickens. Bewildered cows would stroll into town as if looking for someone to talk to. When children played in the streets, goats would crisscross through the games. Singsongs and guessing games, our toys manufactured by the imagination. Once there was a great commotion created by a horse that went berserk, supposedly after bestowing its own image in the mirror of a house into which it had popped its head.

The television was the mountain tops, the flamboyant trees featuring the passion of their red flowers, the birds flying in unison towards the river through the blue silk of the firmament. Balconies had mouths and ears and told stories that went back towards Taino bones or upon the palms of the Spanish, back to Andalusian angels, who blew the wind for the sailboats of the epoch of exploration. In the town of my birth, language was a fertile rain storm, inundating, sliding, riding, bouncing, curving, surprising, synchronizing, as happens many times when you pass by a stranger and they shout out information which connects with the things you were puzzling in your head, becoming random advice. Proverbs preserved by grandmothers from generation to generation. Refrains bopping down Antillean street. Courtesies of speech and manner that fascinate and inhabit the total expression of the people. Television was a line of lips attached to a series of buttons located in the panels of memory. It was once upon a time and two makes three. The telling of stories was a cultivated pastime. Family incidents got swollen after each sip of coffee. Notorious occurrences, especially those related to love scandals, were seasonal reruns, sometimes with fresh information added to the stew. Everyone had a list of what today would be considered paranormal phenomena, but within that dwelling of a natural alphabet, within that space of the people who herbal and listen to the whispers in the wind, it was as if to say merely, look it's going to rain.

Sometime in 1952 or '53 Jorge Luis Borges, the Argentine writer, was teaching at the University of Puerto Rico in Rio Piedras. Perhaps he played with some of the ciphers of his mathematical propositions there, within that Carib moisture. Could it be that he met Juan Ramon Jimenez and toasted with a piña colada, as they weaved through the movements of Modernism? Aguas Buenas, hidden in the mountains some forty-five-minute distance away from this literacy, within the same breath of existence, marched in a slower syrup, as many families who were in the agitation of migration waited for their airline tickets to fly towards the word Nujol, tickets that would blast them into a foreign epoch. Their prose technique was all-enpackaging a venture off to a Borgenian library of buildings, to splatter onto the pavement of endless metropolis.

My grandfather made cigars; he was a tobacconist. He was also a fabulous singer of boleros and was hired to bring serenades to the balconies of maidens by their lovers. He knew hundreds of songs by memory. The place where cigars were made was known as El Chin-chal. Tobacco is the gift of the Tainos to the Spaniards. It was used by the medicine shaman to cleanse people of evil drifts, it creates aroma to facilitate the communication with spirits. The cigarette arises from a much more primitive rolling of leaves. Modern day tobacconists roll with the ancient music in their fingers, with a humming, with a swaying. Throughout the Caribbean it was a tradition for cigar makers to accompany the routine of work with singing, reciting of poetry, and the reading out loud of books. As if it were a library, a place where the popular meets the text, where words of a book are spoken by a reader, an orator of great charm. It was within that Chin-chal that I first heard a poem recited, in this case it was my uncle Carlos, who proclaimed the famous declaimer's poem "El Brindis Del Bohemio," decorated with his dramatic hands, inflamed with the passion of one who was living the words he was speaking. The Spanish coming out in jolts as if from the throat or the center of the chest, the pores of my small body swallowing the melancholy sense, trembling to the point of tears. When the recitation ended, I walked out and stared down the tropical street.

As my grandfather Julio El Bohemio rolled the leaves of tobacco into cigars, singing the romances of one bolero after another, the gestures of his hands in conjunction to palm rhythms, Luis Muñoz Marín entertained the literati, advanced Hispanophiles, and third-world scientists, who came to marvel at the miracle, the showcase of democracy, which Puerto Rico was in the Caribbean. As one more cigar was accomplished and Muñoz showed off the fine books in his library, we packed our lives away, getting ready for the trip to heaven.

Over the radio we listened to el Duo Irizary y Cordova, a man and a woman singing duet, the Trio San Juan with Johnny Albino, the plenas of Canario. My uncle Carlos went to the Korean War, because that was one of the privileges of North American democracy. His body vanished over the mountain onto the other side where there seems to have been a carnivorous mouth swallowing whole families. Lovers were separated, their kisses and

*Victor as a child about four years old
in Aguas Buenas*

caresses had to be continued in the penmanship of letters. On a corner of a street that bowed into verdant vegetation, there used to be a group of young men who quickly dissolved like ice cream being eaten by the sun. More than rumor was that they were shooting rifles in Asia. Many soldiers coming back were seen marrying their sweethearts sporting the khaki uniforms of the army.

The island was jumping like a frog across a frying pan. We were fricassee upon a burning stove. Puerto Rican coffee once used to be top choice in world markets. The Dutch would import it by the crate, sipping the island flavor before going through the frozen canals to post themselves in front of Rembrandt imagery. It was the favored coffee in the court of kings. The island was getting ready to blast off in a rocket. The earth was abandoned, the newly planted crops were heavy metal making terrible sounds as they gasolined through mountain vistas. Everywhere there was a come and go, a Ven y Go which wasn't a Starry Night. The mountain became a divinity to worship, an object of long mementos of moist contemplation. Families took turns leaping over its plantains to plant somewhere else.

One day my father disappeared. There was no doubt that the mountain had swallowed him, for it was the path to the airport and on into the clouds. He left for the syllables Nujol. The plan was for him to go up ahead and scout the place out. Get a job, acquire a dwelling for the family whereupon he would send for us. I was a child in a tropical dream and knew nothing as to how time transpires, with the Mexican poet Jose Emilio Pacheco I repeat *No Me Preguntes Como Pasa El Tiempo* and continue to acknowledge along the road of his poetry that for many who left the isle of enchantment it was *Iras Y No Volveras*. We were like shrimp in the hands of Chronos, taken by the river of history. The motion of time and history that brought the Arabs to Spain to make gravel out of the rock of Gibraltar, also wavered the Spaniards to these isles. Now it was time for us to feel the strong directional pull of destiny and leave with it to unknown terrain, history guiding us away from our homeland, without pity or shame.

On the day that my family left from our interior mountain town towards the San Juan airport, there must have been many a festival alit across the country's plazas. El Trio Mayari could have been doing a rosary of love lyrics in the plaza of Cayey. Did I hear Mon Rivera doing Dada surrealism in Dulces Labios, Mayaquez? Was Ramito singing under a tree of fresh gourds a decimal to the East Trade winds? Was the plaza in Manati full of white Panamas dancing plenas and fending off solar heat? In stereo with our exit, in some remote corner, tractors and construction crews descended upon a row of flamboyant trees, cutting them at the root, preventing the destined red flowers from ever seeing the light of day. Since everything is simultaneously in motion, as the car spun us through the mountain road, could Juan Ramon Jimenez, the "Andaluz universal," conducting a conference on the politics of poetry in Rio Piedras, hear the propelling engine of a plane ascending through the clouds of his inspiration? At the very moment of our take-off, could he have been explaining to the class that in Spain the popular classes play an influential role in the development of literature, that they broadcast a strong radiation into the content, that people who do not read say the lines of Cervantes, without any awareness as to where they come from? The refrains, songs, and proverbs rise from the belly of the people into the most gifted cultured pens, who style a language of high architectural splendor. Taking what they have heard into the regions of their dreams, giving birth to a never before tasted *paella.* At the very moment the Spaniard weaved with voice and hands his anecdotes of Ruben Diario, we were migrant swans, nouns which had become verbs, in motion to imaginary Cibolas, where who knows what beautiful princess awaited, dreamy-eyed upon red Italian sofas within a marble of a room. Off we went. Evicted songs of the mountains upon H. G. Wells's *Time Machine,* peeling space towards another age, a new dimension.

The first thing that struck me, that I could distinctly recognize, was the odor of the cold. A process that felt like this: after having jumped from the frying pan into the fire, we dove towards the refrigerator, falling into the center of the freezer; for of all seasons available, we chose the middle of winter to make our big jump to the states, November to be exact. November is truly the cruelest month, which puts me at odds forever with T. S. Eliot. The smell of this different atmosphere called New York is frozen cement and steel printed in the soul of my nostrils.

English was a sound, another sound like the racket of cars, sirens, and cans rolling on the street. Still in childhood I merely thought it was some unopened door of the Spanish, some back alley I didn't know about, another side of the language. My sister Gladys and I found a way of saying Spanish words in what we thought was an English fashion: "La Casin," "Dinerolis," "El Policin," "La Escuelin." Some other island kids who had arrived before us into the big orb of Manhattan were already scattering lip in this "Englishni."

My mother stood by the radio from which a Spanish language station sprayed the songs of the island into the falling snowflakes. She also followed a radio "novella" that was aired everyday at the same time. She always sang as she accomplished the chores of the house, the new language never even saying a thing to her.

The great invasion of English into our house was when my father showed up out of the cold with another man carrying a big box. "Es una televisión," he announced. It was our first television. This box brought the world into our provincial transplanted Aguas Buenas that we were still living, in our newly adopted home. Hopalong Cassidy, Claribel the Clown, Groucho Marx all started weaving through our living room minds, crisscrossing with the stories told in Spanish, blending with the singing, the guitar and güiro scratching of relatives

A Taino ceremonial park

and neighbors, our laughter and dancing in front of the sobriety of President Eisenhower.

English was like a new coat which didn't fit but had to be worn. In the New York City public school system, the speaking of Spanish was strictly forbidden. English ink was quickly spreading through my being, I was beginning to feel like a stereo system, speaking Spanish on one side and English on the other. It was not only speaking these two sets of sounds, it was also listening to them, thinking in them, feeling. Each language had its area. The language of my home, the Spanish of my parents, tenderness and discipline, the proverbs of advice and consolation. The Spanish of Andalusia animated and possessing flesh, here Taino sentiment, there Gypsy sway, here African beat, all the ancestral maneuvers depositing into an instant of street.

On the streets of the Lower East Side, there was a chop-suey English lingering in the neighborhood from the Jewish and Irish past. Working-class bark. As if a peacock with feathers of sound fanned out in front of me, the center of a spinning wheel. Walking the streets of the Lower East Side, I exchanged Spanish with Afro-American friends. The English was bending, twisting and diving, new spices were seasoning the tongue, which was like a magnet drawing to it the music of talk, the tempo and the flavor of the city. Mixing it all with the language of my birth, the Romantic Spanish that crossed the Atlantic with the sails of the Renaissance. It in itself showing the scars of one invasion after another.

The metropolis of New York was like a work of art, with sound and motion. As a young man I took to walking the streets way beyond the borders of my own neighborhood. I became friends with Picasso's *Guernica,* which was hanging at the Museum of Modern Art. Van Gogh, Velázquez, Degas, Renoir, Matisse all ran through my pupils minutes before I went underground to catch a subway back home, where perhaps there would be some singing or, if my uncle Carlos was in the mood, the recitation of poetry.

My spiritual grandfather, a Cuban, Arturo Vincench, whom I have remembered in a series of poems that start off "Don Arturo says," was a classical guitarist who would for periods of time sit up on the roof and finger-pop Segovia melodies through the murmur of the tenements. The tune swept through the hallways like a distant light of a past moon. On those afternoons I would place a chair by the window and read the gypsy ballads of Lorca, transporting myself from the Nuyorican barrio to a view of the streets of Granada. The sirens of police cars passing below piercing like etchings onto the movements of a culture.

As a teenager, the only way to travel was through the pages of a book. Reading books was like taking boats. I read all the seafaring stories and accounts of other lands, other times and people, that I could find at the Thompkins Square Branch Library. The words that were entering were giving birth inside, divorcing themselves from their original meanings and walking new paths of invention, exploding into imaginings that opened upon an exit where they started to pour back out, especially onto a plastic loose-leaf notebook which I had found somewhere on the streets, the lettering on it told that it belonged to an insurance company. I filled it up with fresh sheets and started to keep a journal. At that youthful intersection, language stood up inside of me and pronounced the word: POET. With the words giving birth in my interior, I made a mask in space, and on it I placed a Spanish eye and an English eye—so that I could see the duality of the world.

Papo Got His Gun

My first book of poems was done on a mimeograph machine. A friend who lived in the neighborhood made a woodcut to resemble bricks, which we impressed onto paper to create the cover. The bricks were blazing red. The poems were angry, revolutionary. I wanted to knock buildings down. They did not reflect the poets I was privately reading. It was an immediate urban language. The poems were blasted off the top of my head. I was still not learning from the methods of other poets, that is, I still did not know how to read them. Enthusiastic about the content, overwhelmed with what was being said, I missed the features of their style, their temperament. I was reading poets like Federico Garcia Lorca, Cesar Vallejo, Pablo Neruda, Luis Pales Matos. It was the poetry of youthful fire which exploded out of my pen. Though language was beginning to grow inside of me, horizontally and vertically, my poetry was still issue oriented, it was full of passion for an ideal, momentary convictions. I thought the world could be reprimanded for its injustices, scolded into shape. It was 1966 and I wanted to eat and feel the world.

The Beat poets were important to me: Ginsberg, Corso, LeRoi Jones (Amiri Baraka), and others. Their influence was mostly grammatical and not philosophical. It showed up in the construction of free verse.

Some of my first poems were done in rhyme, because I grew up around the tradition of popular poetry, which is declaimed, and the rhymes are an aid to memory. The repetition of a refrain is part of this poetic style. It goes all the way back to Moorish Spain, when certain Arabian and Jewish forms entered the Castilian. The form which carried refrains was from the Moslems and is known as *zejeles,* Mozarabic songs whose structures were taken over by cultivated poets. A lot of Spanish popular poetry flourished out of these forms and have been handed down for generations, all the way to the Latin American popular masses. There I was writing in this fashion in English, which is a terrible language for rhymes.

Reading Lorca's "Poet in New York" freed me from these strictures. He was very traditional, yet free to experiment, making him utmost contemporary. There is always more inside than what comes out. Those early poems clearly show this. My cultural resources were inside of me dormant. I felt I had to document what was around me, bestowing opinion upon everything that moved. Still there was something developing which I liked, quick images charging out of the page, a razor swiftness cutting the thoughts.

We did the book ourselves from scratch. We typed the poems onto stencils, rolled them out on the mimeograph machine, and stapled them together. Rolling red ink onto the wood block, we pressed cover after cover. We cut out the letters on cardboard, placed the cardboard over the woodblock bricks, and sprayed the titles on each book individually. We took the books around to every bookstore that was within walking distance. A batch was left at the old Eighth Street bookstore in Greenwich Village.

It was 1966 and I was a Latin from Manhattan. I wanted to dance. Putting a couple of my self-published books in my back pocket, I went to places like the St. George Hotel Ballroom in Brooklyn, or up to the Bronx Music Palace, showing the book around and spinning around the dance floor listening to Ricardo Ray and Tito Puente. The music dismantled my anatomy into parts and classified them. I couldn't believe the speed that Tito Puente achieved with his timbale sticks—so fast, they disappeared in front of you. I listened to the beats he was making, then turned quickly around and looked at what the dancers were doing with their feet. I would sit at such an angle that I would only see the dancers from the

knees down across the whole floor. It was such a zigzagging cartoon, scissor work, knee bends, shoes flying. Right there and then I would jot down fleeting poetic thoughts on the back of the colorful flyers that were passed out when you entered the dance.

The music that I wanted to hear was a combination of jazz and Latin. Symphony Sid, a New York DJ, used to have a late-night radio show which featured a lot of the innovative contemporary Latin music. Everyday I was anxious for night to fall so that I could stuff my ears with what they wanted to hear. I would put the Symphony Sid Show on before the Latin switch at 11 P.M. and listen to straight jazz. John Coltrane, Miles Davis, Oscar Brown, Jr., Nina Simon. Sometimes he would mix it all up. Play Eddie Palmieri's "Azucar Pa'ti" after John Coltrane's "My Favorite Things."

My poems were dancing to all these rhythms, in a very unconscious way. It was the mold I was in without awareness. The music of Afro-Caribbean rhythms and the romantic boleros lived side by side, without any contradiction. They were decorations in the living room of a family. Sentiments of love coming through voice, guitar, and drum. In the city of the Empire State Building, I was still connected to the songs that my grandfather mellowed out in the Aguas Buenas that was melting in my snow-covered dreams.

The city was spinning and I was divided into Spanish and English, the Latin and Germanic substratum, as if universes distributed through channels of thought and emotion, mental and physical. My friends were being eaten by the streets or disappearing to the Vietnam War which was raging in Asia. Sadness in the eyes of my mother. My father was gone. Upon them came the indifference of destiny, the toll charged by the migration. History has no heart; it is all drama and action, colonization, relocation. I loved knowledge but hated school, the language spirits inside of me made no compromises with the disguise of society. A bridge made of words across the rooftops of the city was my walkway. Everything within the air was enlarged or reduced with words. Experience was linguistical motions, polyrhythmic phrases. Living is reading the books of the faces, the chapters of the features, the sentences of feeling that flow out of the eyes. One book led to another. Everything is energy and nothing remains the same. After *Papo Got His Gun,* the poems were speaking more. I was living inside of them. The private persona began to explore the terrain of the historical being, the

"In the locale of my birth"

cultural rhythms materialized in the experience of daily living. I was not just thinking of an issue or a specific opinion. A sense of how I was attached to the past through my words was beginning to crystalize, especially in Spanish, which is ridiculous because I was writing mostly in English.

It was around this time that I read William Carlos Williams. A direct language opening episode, feelings peeling right onto the page. As the language of Williams cleared linguistic smoke, as if going towards a core of spoken psychology, verbal immediateness, Manhattan was feeling like the end of the world. I wanted to leave to a slower space. I thought of Puerto Rico. I longed for the island. My poems were planting fruits I was not seeing. *Papo Got His Gun* was picked up by *Evergreen Review.* They did a spread with photographs. My new poetry was read by Allen Ginsberg and Robert Lowell. After I signed with Random House, I met Lowell and he accompanied me to my high school. Our conversations now dissolve into the urban fantasia of bricks and windows. Random House wanted to do a major collection. The poems were

giving birth to themselves, churning with laws of expression hidden even to the vehicle which became a victim of their production. Leaving the book in the hands of an editor at Random House, I made plans to leave the space of my upbringing for the first time. Language was in my feet when in 1968 I danced in California, which used to be Mexico.

Snaps

Snaps was the first major collection. I really consider it my first book. *Papo Got His Gun* was like a demonstration of passion, the flashing of energy. Some of the poems were written all in capitals. It was like billboard art.

Snaps is a walking and running book. Urban life bursting, accumulating, and detonating. The streets of New York splicing by, the frenzy of a young man running through them, involved with the content yet detached, episodes of the streets without any coloring. Despair and the quick-moving images of reality in flight, an emergency, a departure, an escape. I wanted to clear the buildings, the structures, out of the way and see what was beyond them, anticipating a change in landscape.

It was a poetry very close to the events of my life. Instant autobiography. The element of the city, the outside pointing in, towards the interior of the person living this adventure. More and more the man inside was standing up, using available experience for ulterior motives. A searching coating the purpose of the language, a life claiming itself through the distress. The light of possibilities was bright. The contents of a personal life joining the jewels of research. The recognition that in writing something far more important than the details of a singular life is in operation. The truth of one's interior obstructed by the organized forces of a city, a mental layout, a physical bondage.

Some of the pieces I remember writing at the Village Gate: Symphony Sid used to have Monday night presentations there of the Latin musicians who were pumping the city with rhythm and flavor. Trying to capture Eddie Palmieri's keyboard, orchestrating gardens in the air, I would fill pages of a notebook. The first things that came to mind filtered through the plumbing system of specific concerns that were permanent features of an outlook, to which random flurries of words had

to be submitted. The Village Gate dancers whirling like Rumi's dervishes, while the pen which was the first object to come from heaven deciphered bone and joint connections to Arawak ceramic patterns and Yoruba *mofongo* meshings. Ismael Quintana, Palmieri's vocalist, singing songs about yucca, mangoes, and pineapple while outside snow-covered streets were a testament to our Northern displacement. The ice of the outside contrasting with the inner humidity of sunshining mountains.

After reading *Snaps,* Allen Ginsberg wrote a note in which he said I was using language "the way Williams wished." In those days I was reading a lot of Williams, so his statement said a lot to me. I did not know then that William Carlos Williams was half Puerto Rican. His mother was born in Mayaquez, which is on the western coast of the island. She was born to a well-to-do family, but after her father passed away they went through some hard times. After studying art in Paris she moved to Rutherford, New Jersey, where Williams and his brothers were born. She never learned the English diction and had a way of talking which fascinated Williams. Reading Williams's biography of his mother, *Yes, Mrs. Williams,* I learned that this poet whose work I admired had grown up listening to the same refrains and proverbs as I had— proverbs which mothers and grandmothers are notorious for using, as ways of giving advice to

Cruz (left) with Luisa Valenzuela and Jose Emilio Pacheco, 1981

their children. Her manner of being, of speaking, and storytelling entered his poetics. Like many Spanish and Latin-American poets who have been inspired by rivers, the structure of "Paterson," William's long poem, flows along the Passaic River. His poetic dissection of that city is a total holistic endeavor.

Many writers are embarrassed by their first book. After publishing his first book, Juan Ramon Jimenez tried purchasing every single copy and destroyed them as they came into his hands. The Cuban novelist Alejo Carpentier "disowned" his first literary manifestation *Ecue-Yamba-O* (the word is from an Afro-Cuban religious cult and means: Praise Jesus Christ). Looking back on *Snaps* I am disgusted at the amount of coarse words. How one shoots off at the mouth without regard for the audience. A lot of the content of the book is distant from me. As I have mentioned, it is an escape book, a dispossession of the imagery and metaphors of New York. The galleys for *Snaps* were corrected in a Mel's Drive-In restaurant on Shattuck Avenue in Berkeley.

In California I ran smack into the university students getting beat up. As a matter of fact, on the first day that I chose to go up by the campus and visit the famous Cody's bookstore, I got caught in the street ruckus and had to flee from baton-wielding police. I was working with Herbert Kohl and Allen Kaprow on a project called Other Ways, working with teachers of the Berkeley Unified School District. The program sought to bring poets and artists into the classroom to liven up the public school experience.

California was opening up like a tortilla for the ingredients of a burrito, but I was also homesick. I don't know why I was missing New York. Home there had not been like real earth to step on. My real home was the birds of my memory flying to the flowers of my island childhood. In New York my home had been halfway up into the sky, in a village which was vertical. What I still longed for was the movement of the streets and the music. I was music sick in California and rhythmically isolated. For the local record stores, Latin music was Herbie Mann and Cal Tjader. There were also some of those records which Willie Bobo made for college students. I was hungry for the source, the root, the *clave*. After some eight months in California, I was back in New York.

Walking on the continent of language which was rising from the water of my being, I continued to make discoveries of new nations and cities of expression. I like the structure of *Snaps*. I began in this book to write about the tropical past, to recognize the importance of my mixed racial blood. Spanish melodies sprinkling onto dried goatskin which has been tightened onto wood, indigenous harmonics rushing through the strings of the guitar. I saw the flesh of my bones connected to the drama of history. The radio signals put out by Cesar Vallejo were coming in strong. The Incas were over Manhattan turning the buildings into syllables, the junctions of their consciousness visiting the Spanish. The Spanish inside of me was giving the English lessons in courtesy. The first linguistic base was churning in the deepest chambers, where sound takes its shape. Like a rose shedding petals, I kept undressing the language. I wanted to get to some core, to the matrix. The buildings in New York were sticking out like pimples. Once again the clamor of the city was getting to my nerves. In order to pursue my poetic and personal vision, I felt the urge to migrate south like a bird. On a cold morning of 1971, I got a flash that involved the better part of the horizon. The mountains had sent a telegram. I never doubt those flashes and went for my suitcase.

When I went back to the island for the first time since the migration, I took a small amount of luggage with me. The rest of what I took was an invisibility which wanted to visualize.

Mainland

Mainland is the book that embraces my return trip to the island of Puerto Rico in the early seventies. Most of the poems were written there or right after my return to New York. The visit helped me recharge the Spanish. I stayed near the university in Rio Piedras and was able to visit the library and the surrounding bookstores. Along with the morning cafe and bread, I was devouring Spanish and Latin-American literature. The theater of the university featured concerts, plays, and film festivals. There was a corner cafeteria called La Torre where students, professors, poets, and painters gathered and exchanged caffeine, dark espresso of the thoughts sweetened with cane. Just seeing structures and going on voyages into the islandscape was enough for me. I was filling in many of the empty squares.

With my father I visited Aguas Buenas for the first time since I left at age five. Entering the town we took the breathtaking curves of the mountain road, a sensation of endorphic experience stronger than all the drugs you can come across in California.

I went down the streets I used to play in as a child and into the house where I once lived, where I was born as well, for in 1949 it was much more rural and all births were by midwife. The house seemed so small. Did it shrink or did I grow? The surrounding mountains kept their overpowering splendor of deities. All over I was getting whiffs of fragrances which were helping to recuperate memory. Some of the children were still eating the same homemade candies. Guayava, tamarindo, and passion fruit were playing maracás in the wind. My uncle Jose Antonio was still making cigars the same way my grandfather Julio El Bohemio did. Like his father, Jose Antonio was a great singer. He and his friends would get together on Friday afternoons and with the poetry of the boleros create a halo over the town.

Some friends of mine lived in the very Afro-Puerto Rican coastal town of Loiza Aldea. I went there to stay during carnival. This town is very important for the traditions of rhythm and spirit, which have been preserved within its territory. The festival of the Catholic Saint El Apostol Santiago is really the festival of Ogun. A special poem in *Mainland* called "Loiza Aldea" is dedicated to the meter and Antillean spirit of this town. Not only has "Loiza Aldea" preserved African forms intact, it has also maintained many Taino methods of cuisine and fishing. There was much communication between the Tainos and the Africans the Spanish brought over to do the labor for them. Attempts were made to enslave the Tainos. Many committed suicide rather than work for the Iberios. Many took off for the interior of the island to still standing ancestral villages. The African slave heard the native drum descending from the mountain tops, integrating its Morse code into a map for liberation. Between the African and the Taino, two world views which danced in the round, ceremony and food was exchanged. Rebel communities formed in the secrets of the jungle. Dissident and bohemian Spaniards also heard the melody and took off for the coffee brewing in the hills. In *Mainland* I was searching for these affinities, the movements and struggles of the Caribbean peoples, within the island that I knew. How history flowered out of the windows of a campesino house. How a musical structure contained both beauty and imperialism. Cultural narratives flowing out of facial features tumbling down Santurce streets aflame.

Luis Pales Matos was and is important to my poetic luggage. This great island poet was in the grain of the Antilles. In his language the island is in motion, panoramic views of our soul carrying its load towards the eternal waves of the ocean, mountain flowers the letters of his poems.

He was among the first poets of the modern era to see the importance of living the full Caribbean, of recognizing the expressive potential of this racially mixed region of the world. We cannot live in denial of who we really are. We must integrate all our components into a larger frequency. He was the first poet in Puerto Rico to sing our Africanness. Despite this I am not impressed with his so-called Negroid poems. These supposedly Negroid poems of Pales Matos are full of voluptuous Black women, sensual dances, and onomatopoetic words which are meant to represent African vocabulary and sounds. Some of it is outright silly, some borders on racism.

Africa permeates and runs through the whole fabric of Caribbean society, Puerto Rico not excluded. To me our gestures, cuisine, music, language, and spirituality are all impregnated with African tonalities. It runs through all colors and social classes. What need was there for him (and the critics) to say that a group of poems are of "Negroid" sentiment and others not? In the Caribbean everyone has of everyone. It is the racial melting pot of the world, a confluence of tones and timbres, on the planet earth the highest manifestation of cosmopolitism. What isn't available?

A quote from a Pales Matos poems hangs at the entrance to *Mainland,* as respect for the poet and to focus light upon Puerto Rico as inspiration. Book covers are important because they are like the doors of the house you are about to enter. Quotes are like names on the door, welcome mats, that invite us to think and introduce us to some of the elements that live within.

One of the wonders of the world is a flowing tropical river. Poems about rivers are among my favorites, for poetry is like a river flowing in the language, the eternal current of words curving through the flora and fauna to reach the immensity of the sea of expression, an uttered phrase, a written poem, a group of words swimming together like a school of fish, which otherwise would be lost.

Before leaving the island I made a special trip to the mouth of El Rio Grande de Loiza in a ceremonial farewell. When I was there the poetry of Julia de Burgos was in the saltine air. She wrote

The author with his daughter, Rosa Luz,
about 1984

one of the greatest poems ever written to a river, "Rio Grande de Loiza." If in it she saw the arms of a man lift out of the river and caress her, I felt her lyrics walking up my flesh. I could never look at a river without thinking of her. Her final years were tragic. She died after walking the streets of Spanish Harlem. She was heading towards Central Park, as if she wanted to die within proximity of the verdure of the trees. She collapsed across the street around 104th Street, her final strength setting in motion the task of clearing the cement of the city, to deposit her in the park's semblance of nature, so that her soul could better make it back to her island river. Dropping a white flower into the river in her honor, I parted towards San Juan. On the plane back to New York, I thought of California. After Puerto Rico, New York was too strong a pill to drop for a full year. I dreamed of the many people there that I wanted to see. Something was calling me, something pacifical, celestial, and sweet. Through the massive Carib clouds, the whispering of a woman's voice. I wanted to get back West which is closer to the East.

Tropicalization

Everywhere in New York there were people mumbling to themselves. In subways and on the streets words were pouring out of mouths like on automat. The minute you lose your mind, language takes you over. Given that language is a strong force of nature, it overwhelms any forces that might stop it. It is for that reason that poets should treat language with utmost respect, like a loved one, with tender, loving care.

In Puerto Rico I gained a lot of enthusiasm, a lot of spirit which I felt had to be grounded, imagination which had to make itself available. *Tropicalization* is the musings of this period. Caribbean Spanish was dancing everything from danzon to mambo in my skull. It was like a Rolodex plugged to an electrical outlet. One of the books I read on the island was the novel *Très Tristes Tigres* by the Cuban G. Cabrera Infante. It was a total linguistic invasion, a seance possession, Cuban Spanish conjured by drums, candles, cigars, and chants. Metaphor and conversation extending themselves like rubber bands, each word exhausted for all its possible meanings, reverberations, permutations. Entities of technique taking total control of the writer (vehicle), staying in command until its purpose is accomplished, until it has molded and twisted itself through the whole color spectrum, trying out all the tempos and rhythms that the moment of the content calls for. *Très Tristes Tigres* is Havana speaking.

Tropicalization is Caribbean Spanish in English. The ideas, especially in the second section of the book which is called "Electricity" to denote the volcanic energy issuing out of collective speech, were mostly embodied in a series of prose poems. It is more in the tradition of Spanish and Latin-American literature to use the designs of popular talk, feeling, color. The Spanish language changes from the bottom up, the people dictate its course. Verse pours down from the mountains, a way of thinking that verbalizes. Walking down the street suddenly one hears a fleeting *satori,* a tropical *haiku.* The writer creates from the given and adds to it personal magnifications, deduces, enlarges, reduces based on ingredients at hand. *Tropicalization* is like the greenhouse effect, a warming of the Northern latitudes, bringing writing concepts into the English from my other language. Importation of fruits and vegetables, vistas, mixing and confusing geographic locations. Racial and cultural miscegenation episodes jumping the monism of the

States. A wind which to me comes in from the Modernist movement of the Spanish.

Modernism opened up a third rail for the Spanish language, commencing with many different poets catching the same wave, like lightning that flashed through the ether of an epoch. There were many poets who fueled its initial appearance: Mexican, Cuban, Peruvians. I believe it was Jose Marti leading into Ruben Dario that truly blew the embarkation whistle. Dario was born in 1867, a man with Spanish, Indian, and African blood renovated the poetic language of his times. This is the way it had to be for it is in the Americas where the Spanish spirit continues to grow, having moved away from its original sources, distancing itself from its grammatical rules, from customs and those things which tie it down. Like a person, language escapes from the provinces with only the best humor, leaving behind the phobias. In the Americas it reaches the highest plateaus, it improvises, receives new words. In the prose poems of *Tropicalization* I took the English syntax to the point of destruction. The result of having heard the contents with two different systems of sound reception. It is something actually beyond myself and out of control, that is conscious direction, the talk sense in the poems creating their own style and

even shapes. The collective voice of the folk re-inventing itself, with its own equipment. I was creating new metaphors and imaginings massaged by the invisible hands of spontaneity. I am merely another victim of the language, which was around before and will be around after we abandon our body cabinets. Sparks of chatter coming down the mountains and the streets like molasses.

It has always been interesting to be part of alternating periods between rural island towns and advanced urbanity such as New York, something about the contradiction which keeps you alert. Manhattan a merry-go-round, imposing upon one's attention. Back from mountain tranquility I saw more and more the pressing accumulation of heads, popping, bopping, all ready to explode. I wanted to write a long poem about the city, which would express the way the city came at me, a gallery of voices, a montage of episodes. New York is one scene after another, like a long-playing record of endless sides. "New York Potpourri," the extended poem that opens *Tropicalization*, was like open windows, small glimpses that gathered together to form a larger mural of how I was filtering the city. Small lyrical side/slides that were mentally or physically in the city.

Later in '73 or '74 when I went to read in Europe to the One World Poetry Festival of Amsterdam and at the American Center in Paris, I ran into a lot of international poetic information. My work started to be translated into other languages. I wanted to take my historical/cultural information and innovate with it. Do like a folkloric avant guard. I was interested in doing *haiku*, not in their usual setting of nature but have them take the train into the city. I was even writing Elizabethan-period type sonnets as spoofs on the form. Fill them all up with plantains, guayavas, and boleros in the courts of kings. This creative research went on towards my next book which was published in San Francisco. Within it I practiced many different techniques, escaping definition, having a fear of being pinpointed and classified. I had relocated back to the Bay Area. I was also now the father of two children. It was truly a creative and productive renaissance.

With the Puerto Rican poet
Clemente Soto Velez, 1991

By Lingual Wholes—1982

Living in the Mission District of San Francisco during that period when one thinks one is a mature adult because of age, but really isn't because of lack of experience, there are so many things that one has to ride out or write out of the system. Spin, make a circle, and come back to the same point several times before jumping off the wheel. It was a living that I was writing, and a writing that I was living.

Ishmael Reed and David Henderson, original poet and writer friends of mine from New York, had also been living on the West Coast for several years and there was in a way a literary social community amongst us and other writers. Ishmael Reed had come in with some ideas that were talked about in New York and this was the seed for the Before Columbus Foundation. Bob Callahan, David Meltzer, Simon Ortiz, Shawn Wong and myself were all founding members of this organization which hoped to promote literature that was being ignored by the New York establishment. They have since gone on to give the annual awards, known as the American Book Awards. Because the judges are also poets and writers, this tribute has gained in popularity and respect and is considered quite prestigious.

In California I met Latino writers and artists from just about every country in the Americas. I began to explore different dialogues of the Spanish and the way to use them within writing. I was seeing how racial and cultural *mestizaje* has affected the entire continent. Despite the painful origins of the Latin American republics, the Spanish conquistadors raping the land and the indigenous women, somehow we are all a product of that collision, and must survive and evolve, inventing hybrid psychologies and technologies for our cultural fluids.

By Lingual Wholes was an attempt to write a language that was neither Spanish nor English. Some of the work in *Wholes* is outright visual. The letters were perceived as sculpture. Influenced by some Brazilian concrete poets, I wanted my visual experiments to be rooted in some purpose, a concept, to have meaning and not be mere decorations. That was an important criteria for all the energy, painting and sculptural calligraphy, bilingual ink which was let loose within that book.

In San Francisco a group known as the Contemporary Music Players was putting on a production of Hans Werner Henze's *22 Voices,* which was poetry selected by the composer and set to music and song in an operatic mode. When the director/conductor called me, a French fellow, it was the first time that I had ever heard of Henze's creative project and that it involved some of my work. The famous German composer had used two of my poems. One of the poems served as an introduction to the entire text, the other was set to music and performed by a soprano. It was a spectacular experience to hear Caribbean slang words which I had forged into the English being stretched out by a high pitched soprano voice. I couldn't believe my ears. It was the second time that my poems had been set to music. Years earlier, in the '70s Ray Barretto had done a poem which I dedicated to him in the album *Headsounds.* Using congas, timbales, and bongos, and turning off all studio lights, he and the other musicians went after my poem with percussive improvisations.

San Francisco was getting to be one ridiculous search for a parking space. On certain nights people just got eaten by a chill as they stared up at palm trees which produced no coconuts—they were constipated. I was tired of the Bay Area and the endless rotation within traffic. I felt that I had learned and developed as far as I could go in California and the United States. Once again the urge to go back to Puerto Rico was all over my mind and soul, but this time with a strong sense of not just going for a period, but to totally re-migrate, go back home for good. I wanted to go back to a rhythm, to a culture, to a language. I was longing for warm weather and to be bitten by insects. To see my hometown of Aguas Buenas, to speak to the people of my grandfather's generation that were still around, to hear with my grown ears the stories emanating from balconies, to integrate my thoughts with the nightly singing of the coqui-coki-coqui-ki-kikiki-coqui—to write the aroma of the past into fragrances of the future. When in 1989 I left California for Puerto Rico, I made a full circle in my life. Back to the geography of my birth and the nature of tropical rhythms that move. Once again I was in the hands of motion.

Red Beans

Translation is not simple transportation of one word into its equivalent in the other language. What if the word does not exist? Sometimes it's a matter of arrival and departure. The way I left in Spanish is not the way I returned in English. Even the way you sit, stand, or walk has a relationship to your language, the language you are doing it in. Senses operate differently. You see in Spanish you would move your whole body into it, and here is what I am touching upon as I listen to the local conversation about taste. "I like my rice slightly burned, the bottom of the pot, toasty, crispy, even hard.'' Listening I understood there is no translation of experience. Only the representatives of life, words, are open to interpretation. Everything else is not lying, is not fiction. When you sit down to read, you're removed some twofold. In English there could be a yakkity yak of the mind that could put it out of business. It has to put the other half on patrol, otherwise it might blow up trying to analyze some fussing. Spanish has more outlets to the holy spirit. This rush could save you the burning of cells. Just relax, don't insist, otherwise you might bend iron with your looks. Just look at the way it comes to you in dream, without discussion, debate, essentially variable, kaleidoscopical. Looking everywhere for the word omnipresent. It's no use to flip the eggs over, or backward. You couldn't do it in Spanish without getting the mothers of invention involved. The atmosphere is weaved with saltine mist.

Landing in San Juan, the tourist strip known as El Condado looms to my left from the airplane window. So much riffraff has gathered there that it might as well be an international bastion for cheap manufacturers, their products, and the worst class on earth, the merchants. Quickly to the right you can get a peek of the first session of mountains on the outskirts of the metropolitan area. From it came the echoes of the *areyto*, a Taino celebration involving poetry singing and dance, maraca and drum, and also the rhyming of Spanish coplas, *paso fino* verse strutting by the side of purple orchids.

The Caribbean is rhythm from light to dark. Everything is in motion in steady flux. The East trade winds brushing the trees as if they were hair. The sky is a museum for the clouds. Within this thoroughfare of history, I live and write, rising early with the clear singing of the roosters. The earth is red.

Red Beans is a significantly different book. Between its covers I included both poetry and essay, dance and instruction. Much of the prose was written while I was still in California. The poetry was written in Puerto Rico. In one sense it is a history book. More than ever I poeticize the forces of history. The poems set up a telescope at the intersection where civilization encounters the person, whose interior is nowhere on the societal program. It is a hybrid cuadra-cultural communication where the creative surges pursue their stimulus, to engorge them with self-awareness. Selfs meeting selfs.

Sinking into the caves as far as possible with the light of Germanic English, passing the torch over to the Latin Spanish. Writing in Spanish is

Cruz and Allen Ginsberg at the Naropa Institute, Boulder, Colorado, 1992

seeing the scars of the body, its lyrics full of swords and whips. Merely to speak it is an act of violence, it bellows out with much more force than the English can ever gather up. As I vaporize into the meaning, into the patterns, each day I feel more at home. There is a lot to do. Writing is a responsibility to self and to the epoch. There are so many circles, squares, pyramids, ovals, pentagons, lines, and colors making up the mandala—that there is no time to waste. We need to start tracing the etchings on the *quiros* (gourds). Listening to it—dancing. That is Life. *Eso es la vida.*

BIBLIOGRAPHY

Poetry:

Papo Got His Gun, Calle Once, 1966.

Doing Poetry, Other Ways, 1968.

Snaps, Random House, 1969.

(Co-editor with Herbert Kohl) *Stuff: A Collection of Poems, Visions, and Imaginative Happenings from Young Writers in Schools—Open and Closed*, Collins & World, 1970.

Mainland, Random Rouse, 1973.

Tropicalization, Reed & Cannon, 1976.

The Low Writings, Lee/Lucas Press, 1980.

By Lingual Wholes, Momo's Press, 1982.

Rhythm, Content, and Flavor: New and Selected Poems, Arte Publico Press, 1989.

Red Beans, Coffee House Press, 1991.

Work has been included in anthologies, including *Giant Talk: An Anthology of Third World Writings,* Random House, 1975. Contributor to numerous publications, including the *Berkeley Poetry Review, Down Here, Evergreen Review, Image, Life, New York Review of Books, Ramparts, Revista del Instituto de Estudios Puertorriqueños,* and *Village Voice.*

Philip Dacey

1939-

*Philip Dacey reading at Washington and Lee University, Lexington, Virginia,
about 1986*

1

My earliest memory is that of my parents fighting in bed. I had to have been quite young, as I was standing up in a crib, holding on to the metal guard railing, my face at about the level of the horizontal bar at the top. I was crying as I shouted at them to stop. During my early years, my parents were forced to share their bedroom with me because the apartment, in St. Louis, Missouri, my city of birth, had only one bedroom; my two siblings—an older sister, Joan, and a brother older than she, Owen—slept on a daybed in the dining room and a couch in the living room. I lived in that apartment, which never once as I was growing up seemed to me to be too small, until I went to high school.

Nor do I recall the presence of any books there, except for the ones I borrowed from the nearby Sherman Park branch library. Especially appealing to me was a series of biographies for young people, a distinguishing feature being its illustrations—all of them silhouettes. I felt not deprived of color as I turned the pages but both charmed by the simplicity of the graphics and moved by the drama of the black and white. My father read the newspaper each evening as he lay on the living room couch after his day on the

19

assembly line at the airplane factory; by managing to stay thoroughly conversant with current events, he partially compensated for the fact that his formal education ended when his foster parents— both of his natural parents were dead by the time he was five, his father, an Illinois coal miner, having been killed by black lung disease—pulled him out of grade school in order to use him as a laborer on their farm. To give himself an education into at least the ways of the world, he ran away from home as a teenager and joined the navy during World War One, lying about his age to gain admission.

An insurance salesman by trade, my maternal grandfather, Owen McGinn, who was born in County Cavan, Ireland, regularly wrote sentimental verses and recited them at family gatherings. On one occasion, he chased out of the house and down the street a son who had the audacity to laugh at one of the more maudlin stanzas or perhaps at the grandiloquent delivery of his father. Upon her death at twenty-one of heart failure,

Owen's daughter and my aunt, Eileen, by all accounts a beautiful and kind young woman, left a thick stack of verses as sentimental as her father's. Almost as soon as I could write sentences, I began writing stories and expecting my relatives to read them; I told everyone that I intended to be a writer. My mother, Teresa, a secretary by trade and an inveterate letter-writer at home, always owned a typewriter, and I very early began typing my stories on her machine. I never consciously thought of my grandfather and aunt as models, since writing was not something they pursued as a career; besides, my aunt died before I could know her personally, and my grandfather was a distant figure whose verse meant nothing to me.

2

My formal education was heavily Catholic, including eight years of grade school with nuns and eight years of high school and undergraduate college with Jesuits. The nuns, members

*Dacey (front) with his brother, Owen, father, Joseph, sister, Joan,
and mother, Teresa, in St. Louis, about 1945*

of the Order of the Incarnate Word, required that pupils passing them on the street always greet them with, "Praised be the Incarnate Word, good morning, Sister"—or "afternoon" or "evening," depending on the time. A too hurried or mumbled recitation of the formula would result in detention until the greeting was repeated slowly and clearly. For eight years of my youth, then, and with at best minimal consciousness of what I was saying, I daily praised the word, albeit the word embodied in human flesh and not in sound and syllable. Another daughter of Owen, Margaret, became a nun herself, a Dominican, and my sister entered our aunt's order but only proceeded as far as her noviceship before returning to secular life. Strangely, given my environment, I never seriously considered the priesthood as an option for me; perhaps I thought that a vocation as a writer precluded one as a priest. I served throughout my education, however, as an altar boy, and for a while in college even had a private confessor, to whom I would bravely announce my name before I began confessing. I must have assumed he kept a running, mental account book of my soul's state. I was, I realize now, what was technically known as an overscrupulous Catholic, worried about the smallest or nonexistent infractions; my confessor, unfortunately, was underscrupulous and failed to point out to me that I should relax and enjoy my life at least a little more than I was obviously doing.

By the time I was in high school, my parents were divorced, and my mother could not afford to send me to St. Louis University High School, even though my father faithfully paid child support, which was minimal in those days. She was determined that I be admitted, however, for the sake of the education I would get there, and talked the school's rector—equivalent of superintendent in a public high school—into letting me work off my tuition with a job, which turned out to be that of a switchboard operator on weekends. As the majority of the faculty were Jesuits, all of whom lived on the school grounds, I retain a strong image of black-robed young men standing around the switchboard and chatting informally with each other—entirely in Latin. I studied Latin for four years there (plus one year in college), as well as Greek for a year or two. I consider myself fortunate to have received such a classical education and owe it directly to my mother's assertiveness. One of my English teachers, a Jesuit, who had read some of my essays, once took my mother aside and said, "Your son is going to be a writer." My father, to whom my studies must have seemed as

foreign as life on the moon, said to me when I was in college, "No matter how educated you become, don't forget how to talk to ordinary people." I realized years later that the "ordinary" person he most did not want me to lose touch with was of course himself. He is, in this year 1992, ninety-two years old, and we exchange letters weekly.

At St. Louis University—not formally affiliated with St. Louis University High School but also a Jesuit institution—I participated in the cult of the Blessed Virgin Mary through membership in the school's sodality, an organization devoted to devotion to the Mother of Jesus. At the all-male high school, my socio-sexual development was slow or nonexistent; at the coeducational university, that development was accelerated but not dramatically so, given the braking effect of both my membership in Mary's sodality and my insufficiently jolly private confessor. Progress had to wait until I attended graduate school at Stanford; the air of northern California acted to dispel much of what had been circulating in my head for the previous twenty or so years: as an outward sign of the changes effected in me during my stay in that western outpost, I stopped going to church. I do not recall feeling particularly guilty about the development.

While still a student at St. Louis University, I sold my first piece of writing. Although I had published nonfiction features in my high school paper (I was one of the editors, appointed by the paper's Jesuit advisor) and short stories in the college literary magazine, my first professional publication took place in the *Sentinel of the Blessed Sacrament,* a commercial religious magazine I had seen listed in an annual of literary markets. A piece of fiction I submitted to them brought me a check for $35, an amount that must have seemed surprisingly large in 1960. Mercifully, the name of the story escapes me, but it told of an altar boy who assists at Mass one morning while keeping rolled up in his back pocket what was known in the immediately post-war years as a "girlie magazine." After Mass, while both helping remove the priest's special outer garments—alb and chasuble—worn during Mass and removing his own cassock and surplus, the boy gradually dislodges the magazine until it falls to the floor in view of the priest. A kind but stern lecture from the priest follows, and the story ends with the boy dropping the offending publication into a trash can as he walks home. It was the kind of pious story I had been brought up on, particularly in grade school; miracles, it seemed, were hardly miraculous but cheap and abundant. I was proud of the puerile fiction and of my sale—until I showed the published story to my creative writing instructor, Dr. James Cronin. Expecting to receive praise for what I had done, I eagerly watched him as he read the story, in no way prepared for what he told me upon finishing it: that the story was shamefully bad and I should take no pride in having written or published it. Many years later, I could gratefully appreciate the honesty and accuracy of his response and see him as model of kindness for his refusal to participate in my flattering self-delusions. He was a teacher who deserved the name.

3

The literature I remember encountering at St. Louis U. High School was the Homeric epics, Virgil's *Aeneid,* Caesar's *Gallic Wars,* and Ernest Hemingway's *Old Man and the Sea,* which an English teacher read to us word-for-word out of the issue (or issues) of *Life* magazine in which it first appeared. My most fortuitous encounter with literature took place, however, at St. Louis U., where I first read Dylan Thomas. His brand of pagan religiosity appealed to me, perhaps especially because I met his work not in class but outside it, through conversations with my peers in the university's honors program, into which I had been placed, without any request from me, as a freshman. In high school, I was a loner; at St. Louis U., I enjoyed the community of the honors program for the entirety of my four years there. I had never before encountered excited and exciting intellectuals—I think that's the right term—my own age. Picnics, parties, and field trips forged bonds between members of the program, some of whom—including myself—even for a period made forays into the sewers of St. Louis. Such descents no doubt were a way of declaring our independence from the obsessions of the hoi polloi. They also may have carried Dantesque significance for some of the more feverish Catholic imaginations in our group. I came to see them as a way we so-called "brains" had of maintaining our equilibrium: always in danger of floating off into the stratosphere, we kept ourselves earthbound by exploration of the low, the hidden, the discarded. The sewers of St. Louis were our own version of the "foul rag-and-bone shop of the heart." Savoring our lawlessness, we had to time our entrance through a grating in Forest Park—not too far

As an altar boy, about 1950

from the school—to avoid the eyes of policemen cruising at night in their patrol cars.

Enter Dylan Thomas, himself hardly law-abiding. At an honors gathering, I first learned of the Welsh poet when someone, no doubt one of the upperclassmen, read aloud the whole of *A Child's Christmas in Wales.* The charm worked instantaneously. In those days, other books by other authors competed with the Thomas work for the allegiance of the honors students—particularly Antoine de Saint-Exupery's *Little Prince,* to name one, although the writings of French thinkers like Gabriel Marcel and Jacques Maritain were also highly valued in the late fifties at a Catholic university—but I proved loyal to the famous boyhood memoir and soon began to read the author's poetry. Thomas himself, of course, had died about five years earlier as he was touring America. His fame had posthumously peaked during my undergraduate years. Soon, however, his connection to me was to take a more personal turn.

A St. Louis U. English professor and mentor to many of the honors students, Dr. Albert Montesi, had begun organizing during my time at the university annual evenings devoted to poetry and music, usually jazz. The linkage of jazz and poetry was experiencing considerable national popularity in those years, and I was then a devotee of West Coast jazz musicians Gerry Mulligan and Chet Baker, proponents of "cool" as opposed to "bop." At one of the earlier annual events sponsored by Montesi, having been allowed or asked to perform, I did so quite poorly, though no Dr. Cronin seemed to be around to tell me so at that time—the poem I wrote and read was no doubt not a poem, and I am afraid I acted out, foolishly, a kind of parody of a hipster as I read the words from a conspicuous sheet of paper, evidence of my place among the brotherhood (this was the fifties, before personhood) of writers; in short, neither the poem nor the performance was genuine. Leading up to jazz-poetry night the following year, however, I conceived the notion of putting Dylan Thomas's poem "Fern Hill" to music, specifically for a small choir of voices, accompanied by a piano. I set about writing the piece and, largely because I was ignorant of just how ignorant of music I was, finished it in time to begin looking for a choir to perform it at the upcoming show. I wanted eight singers, two female sopranos, two female altos, two male tenors, and two male basses, and posted a notice to that effect in the music building.

The point of this story of musical folly is that Florence Chard, the future mother of my three children but a young woman at the time little known to me—although a member in the honors program, she was a sophomore, while I was a senior, eyes forward—was one of the eight who, betraying an innocence equal to my own, signed up to perform the number. We rehearsed for weeks, I conducting the eight as if I knew what I was doing. A piano had always been present in the one-bedroom apartment I grew up in, as if in absolute defiance of the dictates of common sense: since there was already not enough room for the five people there, why worry about taking up more space with something as big as a bed? After all, wasn't the piano an upright? My mother loved to give parties for lots of people, nor did it take many people to fill the rooms where we lived. My most vivid memory from those parties is that of my mother at the piano, playing and singing current hits as well as old favorites—including, naturally, sentimental Irish standbys—as a small crowd of friends forming a semicircle around her sang along. I had taken piano lessons—"You'll be popular at parties if you do," I was told—but did

not persist. Nevertheless, for years after quitting lessons, I entertained myself by sitting down and improvising or by employing a method of trial and error to play recognizable songs. Thus I had composed the music for "Fern Hill" on the omnipresent piano—it followed my divorced mother and me (my siblings were now gone off into their independent lives) when we moved from my first home at 5210 Northland Avenue into another rented apartment, this one with a separate bedroom, amazingly, for each of us.

My musical setting for "Fern Hill" was over-long, especially considering that during the performance I interspersed between sung stanzas of the poem lengthy, incompetently rendered improvisations by me. They must have seemed interminable to the audience, a large one that with the collective patience of a saint did not boo me. The only part of the score I can still remember and sing is that for stanza four, which begins, "And then to awake, and the farm, like a wanderer." I got lucky and developed a lyrical, singable line that I can still, in weak moments, bring myself to inflict upon people. Not long after the performance I asked Florence Chard out to dinner with me. Before bringing her back to the women's residence hall after our evening together I recited to her another poem by the poet who had connected us, "In My Craft or Sullen Art." During the next two years, after an engagement, a broken engagement, and a re-engagement, we were married in May 1963. In 1965, as part of a longer trip, we made a pilgrimage to Wales, including visits to Swansea, where Thomas was born, and Laugherne, where he lived the final years of his life. Near Laugherne, we picked fern from a hill apparently the inspiration for "Fern Hill." That fern remains pressed behind glass in my possession to this day and, along with a bust of Dylan Thomas recently acquired, will be passed down to my children to remind them of the power of poetry generally to create community through language and of one poet specifically to engender, by means of comings together of one sort or another, beauties such as the three of them.

4

It was at St. Louis U. that I attended my first reading devoted solely and seriously to poetry, not counting the special musical and poetic bacchanals annually overseen by Montesi. The reader was John Logan, whose visit would have been blessed by not only Montesi but also two other writers associated with the school at that time, the poets John Knoepfle and Pete Simpson. If St. Louis had a literary Mafia in the late fifties, these three were members in good standing. I, however, outside of my regard for Thomas, had little interest in poetry and attended the reading only because it was required; my dream was still to be a writer of prose fiction: short stories first and then novels, including The Great American Novel (my version of it would define and embody some form of domestic love—my knowledge of which probably vied with my knowledge of music).

With the auditorium full of students, I had to stand at the back. Logan onstage in my memory is small and uncommanding, but his appearance obviously had no bearing on the impact he made on me, or the impact his words made on me, for what I remember most strongly or solely from that hour more than thirty years ago is Logan's presentation of a particular passage of a dozen lines or so. And that one passage is enough.

I no doubt had heard in a class of mine before the reading that Logan was a preeminent Catholic poet. Anyone who could bring national attention to Mother Cabrini, as Logan had done through his first book, was a cultural hero at St. Louis University during this anesthetized decade. The universal validation of our parochial icons validated us as well.

But it is not anything about Mother Cabrini that I remember. Rather, what I can still see is Logan saying the passage from "To a Young Poet Who Fled" about "the gift of the poet's jaw." I did not know I still carried that experience with me, however, until about ten years later—after I had begun, for reasons largely mysterious to me both then and now, pursuing with some seriousness the writing of poetry myself—when I first came across that very poem in print. I would have been living in either Palo Alto, or St. Louis, or Iowa City, or Cottonwood, Minnesota, but wherever I was at that moment hardly mattered, for suddenly— much to my amazement—I remembered myself back in that auditorium, listening to Logan's words:

> The gift of tears
> is the hope of saints, Monica again and Austin.
> I mean the gift of the structure of the poet's jaw,
> which makes the mask that's cut out of the flesh of
>   his face
> a megaphone—as with the goat clad Greeks—to
>   ampli-

fy the light gestures of his soul toward the high
    stone seats.
The magic of the mouth that can melt to tears the
    rock
of hearts. I mean the wand of tongues that charms
    the exile
of listeners into a bond of brothers, breaking
down the lines of lead that separate a man from a
man, and the husbands from their wives, in these
    old, burned glass
panels of our lives.[1]

Those words performed the action they describe. The seats weren't stone in that auditorium, but I was at the back, among the "high" seats, and Logan's poet's jaw acted as a megaphone—I almost wrote "metaphor"—to amplify the light— weightless and light-bearing—gestures of his soul toward me, an unenthusiastic (as in, "rock of hearts") but apparently not entirely impervious listener. The words spoke to me beyond my knowing; I heard them and then forgot them, or forgot I knew them. He reached across space, literally and figuratively, to give me a gift—a poem, himself, himself in the form of a poem, something spiritual that obviously stayed with me.

I don't know what to make of the importance to me of that experience. I know I don't wish to make too much of it. It's tempting, for example, to say that Logan called me to poetry, although my sixteen years of Catholic education, besides guaranteeing much talk of calls to service, also created considerable skepticism in the face of what's tempting. Anyway, if it was a call, it was certainly a delayed one, suggesting that if "God works in strange ways," so does, or did, Logan. Maybe that reading was a kind of secular Mass: like a priest holding up the Host at the Offertory, Logan was in some way holding up an ideal, and, as far back as I was in that auditorium, I could see it.

5

But the call I answered most immediately was President Kennedy's. After graduating from St. Louis U. in 1961 and working toward an advanced degree in English at Stanford for a year, I joined the Peace Corps, with my bride of about one month, and was sent off in 1963 to teach English as one of the first volunteers in Eastern

---

[1]*Only the Drummer Can Change the Dream: Selected Poems*, by John Logan. Ecco Press, 1981.

Nigeria. In those early years of the new administration's brainchild, the idealism was not always matched by an appropriate level of bureaucratic competence—for example, volunteers fluent in French were just as likely to be sent to a Spanish-speaking country as not—and as a result the failure of certain medicine to arrive at the right place at the right time meant I contracted malaria soon after landing in the country and spent the first couple of weeks in a hospital in the bush, near the town of Ikot Ekpene, where we were stationed. Two years later I weighed considerably less than I did when I arrived in the country. To go newly married may not have been the best idea: one can adjust to just so much at one time. The teaching was draining, partly because of the weather: when we first arrived, an Irish priest working in the area told us that we should take a nap each afternoon in order to preserve our strength in the face of the constant and intense heat and humidity, but we two Americans aged twenty-four and twenty-two refused, convinced that such literal lying down on

Philip and Florence Dacey serving as Peace Corps volunteers in Eastern Nigeria, 1963

the job was not only a sign of weakness but also an expression of the dregs of colonialism—refused, that is, for about a month or two, until we began to appreciate the wisdom of that retreat practiced by not only the Irish father but also all of our students and the villagers in the compounds surrounding our house. We accomplished no revolution; we aimed at preparing secondary school students to take, in their final year, the national exams, administered by the Ministry of Education in Lagos, the passing of which meant jobs and the improvement of living standards. The system of external exams, based on the British educational pattern, satisfyingly united the teacher and student against the distant, impersonal examiner in a way I had not experienced in the United States. Retrograde tribalism was supposed to wither away under the strong light of education and training based on information and skills, although in January of 1966, just a few months after our departure, the Biafran War bloodied that place which had impressed us upon first flying in and last flying out as the greenest we had ever seen.

The rains, when they came during the season named for them, were beautiful. The house we lived in had a tin roof upon which the spectacularly heavy rains drummed to make one of the most memorable sounds of my entire life. I have said more than once since then that to hear that sound again—to fall asleep to that thunderous and oddly soothing rattling—would be reason enough to go back to West Africa. I survived an attack by soldier ants one night, though I had to strip from the waist down to pick the nibblers all off of me. I still regret the many praying mantises I killed needlessly: as I read by oil lamp near an open window, they would fly in and land in my hair, from which I frantically plucked them before throwing them to the floor and stomping on them (nothing was wasted in the bush: insects who lived in our house's foundation would sense the presence of the larger, dead insect and come out, dismantle its entire carcass, then carry it away in little pieces into their holes, leaving the floor exactly as it had been minutes earlier). We took the presence of deadly snakes for granted: I recall a dinner party where a group of us sat talking casually about the day's events as we watched a poisonous green mamba a few feet away writhe on a window screen that was the only thing separating him from us. The dinner plate-sized spider I found and killed in our bathtub may have grown an inch or two over the years, but maybe not. And I loved to see the brightly dyed wash of our next-door neighbors as they spread it out to dry on the grass between their compound and our house: they, like all Nigerians, daily wore a rainbow of primary colors. We felt a little drab.

I kept a journal of my two years there but burned it before I left because I believed, probably correctly, that it was sophomoric and badly written. I also produced about fifty pages of a novel that shamelessly imitated William Faulkner. Those pages also suffered, even more deservingly, the fate of the journal. For the next twenty years or more, until the late eighties, I made occasional forays into the world of prose fiction, attempting to claim some territory there; each such attempt resulted in frustration and abortive work. Finally, in 1988 or 1989, I made a vow to myself, as solemnly as I could, never to try to write prose fiction again. I therefore entered into my sixth decade free of the elusive and illusory dream that had nagged me since boyhood. I attribute some of my happiness in recent years to the firm keeping of that vow.

In retrospect, I see as a kind of coda to the years in the Peace Corps the teaching Florence and I did for about six months in Birmingham, Alabama, at Miles College during 1966. Dr. Lucius Pitts, the president of the school, which served primarily or exclusively students who were black, was at the time trying to solve his institution's financial problems by hiring teachers who were willing to work as volunteers in exchange for room and board. We had apparently heard of the school through some network of service organizations and decided to spend the time between our return from overseas late in 1965 and my return to graduate school at Stanford in the fall of 1966 living and working in the city made notorious two years earlier—on September 15, 1963—when a bomb exploded during Sunday school at the 16th Street Baptist Church and killed four children while injuring fourteen others.

Birmingham in 1966 was witnessing conspicuous and frequent protest marches, in which Florence and I participated; in that place at that time, the sight of whites and blacks riding in the same automobile was the occasion for jeers and shouts from white youths in other cars or on street corners. I don't believe we felt our physical safety was threatened, but we knew that our behavior— the marching, the teaching at Miles—was a social anomaly and, as such, a reason for us to feel generally conspicuous; we had been outsiders in Nigeria and were, though closer to home, outsiders still in Birmingham. Our experience in the Deep South recalled to me some of the racism that

was part of my early years: a little African-American boy's expulsion from my childhood backyard by a next-door neighbor shouting ugly racial epithets at him (he had wandered in to play with me while his mother apparently cleaned the house of someone in the neighborhood, which, lower middle-class at best, must have had its pretensions and needed to reassure itself of its superiority), and, many years later, while I chatted with a younger, black Peace Corps volunteer I had just met, the shock of recognition and moral confusion I felt when, upon learning that he had grown up not only in St. Louis, as I had, but also on my block and just a house or two away from the one in which I had grown up, I began to exclaim happily of the coincidence until I quickly realized that it was he, or his family, or other families of his color, from whom my family had moved away in order for us to escape from a neighborhood changing from white to black (while no doubt fully understanding the social significance of the intersection—or non-intersection—of our local histories, he graciously chose to make nothing of it, and we continued chatting of our current life as overseas representatives—representatives, indeed; more so, for better or worse, than we had at first thought— of our native land).

6

It was at Stanford, in 1966, that I wrote the poem with which my career as a professional poet began. Somewhere in the middle of the fall quarter of that year I dropped out of graduate school, gave up my teaching assistantship and pursuit of the Ph.D., and took a menial job in the library to help me make ends meet while I tried to salvage my academic future by aiming to pick up a master's degree the following June. A Woodrow Wilson fellow at Stanford in 1961, I was now both a promising scholar—H. Bruce Franklin had recommended a paper of mine on Hawthorne be published—and, to my dismay and puzzlement, a miserably unhappy person, so much so that I suffered a crisis of confidence and felt I could not continue with my teaching of undergraduates or my studies. The sudden move precipitated fear in my wife; I was a confused person, too confused to understand what was happening to me. Florence continued her own work toward a master's degree in education while I shelved books in the library— I wanted a simple task, and my humiliation was real and serious when I found myself picking up after students who just a week or two before had been my charges in the classroom—and consulted a psychiatrist at the university's medical school. I saw a documentary film about a new poet named Anne Sexton, who had emerged from a tunnel of mental illness as a poet, and was unable to explain why the film affected me so strongly. I began writing a master's thesis (on James Dickey—I had accidentally stumbled upon his work while I was shelving books and immediately loved it, unaware that *Life* magazine had already discovered him) under the direction of Diane Middlebrook. (Only in the early nineties, when Middlebrook published her biography of Anne Sexton, did I realize that God, if she exists, must be the ultimate contriver of improbable plots.) And then one day, with my dream of writing prose fiction more than likely stronger than ever, with the idea of writing poetry nowhere in sight, I wrote a poem.

I was sitting at my desk in the library, looking through a stack of books I needed to process in some way. One of the books I was handling fell open to reveal a picture, a medieval woodcut, of King Mark killing Tristan in the presence of Ysolt. A triangle. Violence. (Only now, writing long afterwards, do I recognize the congruence of the woodcut and my first memory as indicated at the beginning of this autobiography.) The rendering was quaint, delicate, oddly out of sync with the content of the picture. I was moved. And I was further moved to pick up a pen and write down some words to describe the picture. The words fell into lines, twenty-five of them, and I discovered I had written what looked like a poem, which I unimaginatively called, "After a Fifteenth Century Miniature Showing King Mark Stabbing Tristan in the Presence of Ysolt." I knew of the *Beloit Poetry Journal* and within a few days had sent the poem off to that little magazine's editors. After a few weeks an acceptance letter came back; in the summer of 1967 the poem was published. (Early in 1992, I was both shaken—I was getting old—and pleased—I was approaching a milestone—to notice that the twenty-fifth anniversary of my first published poem was fast approaching. I sent off a few poems to the still-going-strong *Beloit Poetry Journal,* without indicating in my cover letter that I was offering them with an ulterior motive in mind. "Recorded Message" was thereafter accepted and appeared in the fall 1992 issue. The fiftieth anniversary will roll around when I am seventy-eight. I'm aiming to celebrate it as I celebrated the twenty-fifth.)

Another poem followed a week or so later, then another a few days after that, and by spring I found myself regularly engaged with the writing of poetry. The myth I have created to explain what happened to me at Stanford that year goes like this: the picture of King Mark *et al.* appealed to me because it told my story; I had been wounded—that is to say, I had suffered some pathological development of a radically private nature—and, in the same way that the blood of Tristan fell with some charm and grace from his side, words arose out of my wound and took the form of a poem; the stream of words was like a little miracle, water (blood; there's that Mass again) from dry ground (Bergman's *Virgin Spring,* more violent wounding); in the weeks following that initial appearance, I began to tend and husband my little natural force, clearing away the ground in order to strengthen the flow, directing it, over the years building beside the waterway that came to develop there a large-scale, consistently productive, and rationally organized waterworks, all the while hoping never to fail to honor the original personal ignorance and modesty with which the undertaking began at that desk in the Stanford University library as I was wondering what had become of my life.

The lesson of those days for me was the opposite of the lesson in *Field of Dreams:* if you tear everything down, She will come. In a "hard time," as Roethke puts it in "The Lost Son," poetry, unasked, rescued me. And as far as I knew I had done nothing to deserve the rescue. My later poem "How I Escaped from the Labyrinth" must have been looking back to this period: "It was easy. I kept losing my way." I have therefore carried with me for the last twenty-five years a sense of gratitude toward poetry for giving me the life I have had; I see that life as a gift, an unpredictable outpouring of good news. My vow never to try to write prose fiction again was a rededication of myself to my benefactor/-tress.

7

After a year of teaching at the University of Missouri at St. Louis, a kind of interim period during which I was building a whole new frame of reference by which to understand my journey after the simultaneous debacle and renewal that took place at Stanford—I had taken a course from Wallace Stegner there but not from Yvor Winters, as if to prove my failure to appreciate my needs—I was admitted to the University of Iowa's program in creative writing. To say that the high point of my stay there was the birth of my first son, Emmett, is not to indulge in a fashionable put-down of The Mother of All Workshops but to define my life in accordance with my major joys. Iowa treated me well. The curricular experience that has remained most strongly with me over the years was Jon Silkin's seminar in British World War One poetry. The course occupied ground that merged both moral and literary concerns, as when Silkin taught me to distrust irony if it blunts outrage at human injustice.

I may have learned from Iowa that the literary world was breachable; that, if these teachers and students represented "the best and the brightest," I could hold my own. I may also have learned that that world was not as attractive, now that I was seeing it up close, as I had originally thought, or even that that world was a fiction, a mutually agreed upon—believed in—social construct that carried less weight than any single writer sitting at any desk anywhere writing anything, so that when in 1970 I moved to southwestern Minnesota to teach and write I could feel that I was not withdrawing from a matrix that mattered (I think, unwillingly, of Jeffers's "thickening center") but moving toward a space free of distracting voices. In fact, many years after publishing my first book of poems in 1977 I was surprised to realize that the book contains poems written before and after going to Iowa but none while there. Upon further reflection I began to see the logic of the fact: at Iowa I was trying on hats, writing a New York School poem one week (Ted Berrigan was one of my teachers) and a W. S. Merwinesque poem the next, with the end result being that my two years there were negatively instructive: I learned who I was not. Finally in Minnesota, I may have felt, not entirely consciously, "Well, I've done that, checked out the competition, or paid a few dues to the union, or had a good time for a while with some folks afflicted by a madness similar to my own, but now it's time for me to get back to work, and I have the isolation—it's not easy to get to Marshall, Minnesota—to allow me to do so."

8

Austin was born in 1972, three years after Emmett. He was born at home, by design, in Florence's and my bedroom, with an old country physician, Dr. Borgeson, who had no qualms about house calls and home deliveries, by his side. Even

in the seventies, Borgeson was a rare bird. I phoned him prematurely and he came immediately, showing nothing but calm and goodwill as we sat and talked for a few hours, drinking coffee, before the process of parturition had actually gotten under way. Emmett stayed with a neighbor, lest any unforeseen complication in the birth cause him anxiety. But things went smoothly and I wish now we had let Emmett watch; maybe his earliest memory would be that of his guitarist brother's first stage entrance. Cottonwood then was a town of 600 people, thirteen miles north of the school where I taught, Southwest Minnesota State College (later changed to Southwest State U.). But, as if we were sailors who knew that progress required tacking against the prevailing wind, the family of us four, just as we were settling into our corner of Minnesota, decided to take to the road.

I took the first of my many leaves from the college in Marshall, and we headed for Spain for a stay of six months, three in Cordoba, inland, and three in Altea, on the coast. The professional justification for the leave—a quite genuine justification I did not have to manufacture—was the need to complete a writing project that required considerable uninterrupted time and had grown out of my developing sense of something missing from my—well, not training, but, rather—education at Iowa. In fact, it was precisely training of a certain sort I began to feel I could have used more of in Iowa City.

Gone several years from the place that acted to confirm or help to confirm my idea of myself as a writer, I nevertheless began to develop quite deliberately the idea of myself as an apprentice; the very word "apprentice" appealed to me, perhaps suggesting an earlier world in which highly valued skills and workmanship of quality were nurtured and communicated. I saw quite clearly that for centuries traditional form—meter and rhyme, for example, and certain fixed structures for poems—had been the *sine qua non* of almost all achievement in poetry. Yet the subject of the uses of such form never came up once during my two years there, from 1968 to 1970, neither in nor out of class, at least not that I could recall. Free verse versus traditional form was not an issue, and all the poems on the worksheets had favored the former rather than the latter. I began, thinking back, to feel cheated. Even quite different moderns such as Stevens and Frost, not to mention more recent poets like Plath and Roethke, had absorbed and reshaped and put to their own uses the formal practices of a long line of earlier poets. Before leaving for Spain, then, I made a list of various forms I wanted to experience as a poet. My joke to myself was, "If it was good enough for poets X, Y, and Z, it's good enough for me"; I figured they knew something I didn't know, something they had learned from submitting their talents to a certain kind of discipline, and I wanted to find out what it was. The list was a way for me to further my apprenticeship, or possibly even pass out of it.

I wrote myself through almost all of the listed forms by working just about every morning during our six-month visit; in the afternoons, I joined my wife and sons in simply enjoying where we were. I considered the project a success at the time, and the years since then have strengthened the conviction that those six months provided me with an experience of considerable significance to me as poet. As a rule, anywhere between a fourth and a third of the poems in each of my books embody traditional forms. The percentage of such poems in the book devoted to Gerard Manley Hopkins, in fact, is nearly one hundred. I am pleased to say that more than once poems of mine in traditional forms have passed as free verse among even discerning readers, including the editor of a widely circulated poetry textbook that shall here remain nameless.

Naturally, for the first several years after those six months, I tended to notice and appreciate poems by my contemporaries that used traditional forms in handsome ways. During the late seventies, however, Robert Bly and Galway Kinnell, among others, regularly took cheap shots at meter and rhyme, Kinnell, for example, recommending to young poets "no external guide at all, only your impulse to go on." I belatedly began to learn of Yvor Winters's skepticism in the face of various Romantic principles that too frequently received unquestioning loyalty. I regretted, while understanding, my decision not to take a class from him at Stanford, but tried to make up for my immaturity by learning from his writings what I could during this later period. My frequent discoveries of fine contemporary poetry that continued to honor, in fresh ways, traditional ways of writing which I had begun to value made me realize that while the bully boys got the headlines with their crowd-pleasing put-downs of anything not in lockstep with their notions of literary truth, many poets, young and not so young, but all excellent, not versifiers and poetasters, were quietly extending a long tradition, almost heroically keeping alive in their own underground what the poetry power brokers were mocking as they promoted themselves as The Real Thing. I think the Deep Image set and certain other adherents to the need for radical literary change at the time tended to transfer the moral superiority of their position vis-à-vis the United States government's conduct in Vietnam to their position vis-à-vis aesthetics other than their own.

By the early eighties, I began to notice how often people asked me, "Why don't poets use rhyme and meter anymore?" I had to answer, of course, that the perception behind the question was wrong, that in fact many poets still used them, although perhaps in a fashion that tended to downplay rather than highlight the formal qualities, but that those poets tended to go unsung by prevailing critical voices when they did. I realized that Bly and company had won the battle over principles of form not in fact but through propaganda. What bothered me was both the overshadowing of so much praiseworthy achievement and the consequent deprivation of the young, who did not know what they were missing, either as readers or, perhaps more importantly, as writers. Somebody needed to put together an anthology that would highlight contemporary traditional form poems, gathering into one book a sampling of the poets at work in the underground I had observed, even though in this case, inverting the usual order of such things, the traditionalists were the underground while the self-styled rebels were the establishment.

In the spring of 1982 I taught at my school an advanced poetry workshop that featured the practice of traditional forms. A look now at the syllabus for that course provides a startling reminder that no textbook or anthology existed at that time that promoted exclusively and emphatically the work of living poets who had not abandoned traditional forms. Teaching that course, I sharply felt the need for such a book.

Earlier, from 1974 to 1977, one of my colleagues in Marshall had been David Jauss, a student of mine in 1970 who had come back to his alma mater to teach between stints in graduate school at Syracuse and Iowa. Even as early as the mid-seventies, after my time in Spain, I had speculated with David on the possibility of an anthology of current poems in traditional forms, and we had started collecting ones we liked. By the early eighties, given the existing vacuum we could hardly help but fill, the possibility had become a commitment. Thus, in 1986, about a decade after David's and my first talk on the subject, Harper & Row published our *Strong Measures: Contemporary*

American Poetry in Traditional Forms. I was lucky that Jauss happened to be in my vicinity at the right time. I could not or would not have taken on and completed the project by myself, and no one could have been a better partner than Jauss; in fact, I'm sure few could have been as good a one, and I don't know who those few are. He carried the lion's share of the arduous task and equally importantly beyond that made such contributions to the ongoing and difficult decision-making process that the shape and character of the book owe much to his sound, informed judgment, his combination of sophistication and good sense.

Since the publication of that book, something called The New Formalism has emerged and struck a dominant pose on the poetry scene. *Strong Measures* has been associated with that movement in the eyes of some readers and critics. But Jauss and I took great pains in our jointly authored introduction to distance ourselves from any reactionary and exclusivistic evaluation of traditional forms. We knew the clock could not be turned back, nor did we wish to do so. The achievements of so-called free verse were there for everyone to see, and were glorious. Our aim was only to bring forward something forgotten or neglected, obscured by buffeting in the literary wars. We pointedly were not seeking the inauguration of a new movement of formalism, precisely for the reason that it was our contention that the practice of formalism had not stopped, had just gone underground because of the unfavorable climate, and was now due for a dose of tolerance or even encouragement. Some of those who chose to be known as New Formalists, however, had in effect taken up the bully-clubs from the weakened grips of the earlier reigning regime. Authoritarian regimes in one country after another fall to the liberators, who themselves turn into authoritarian regimes, and the literary world, mistakenly thought by many to be a removed and protected enclave of the effete, repeats the pattern.

In Spain, beginning my explorations of a tradition I longed to get inside, I never imagined the ultimate fruition of that trip would be the book that has fulfilled or perhaps even exceeded the expectations Jauss and I entertained for it.

9

A post-Spain baby, Fay Dacey was born in 1975, shortly after a kind neighbor drove Florence and me to the Marshall hospital in the middle of the night in his four-wheel-drive pickup truck through a storm against which the Minnesota State Patrol had been advising no travel. There was no longer a Dr. Borgeson alive to assist at a home delivery of our third and last child. The name Storm temporarily appealed to the infant's parents; a blessedly strong and independent seventeen-year-old girl today suggests that that name would not have been inappropriate.

The arrival of Fay began the decade from 1975 to 1985 on the highest possible note, followed soon by a celebratory trip of the now five-member Dacey family to Mexico for several months, but personal loss brought the decade to a close with the death of my sister in 1983 and the end of twenty-two years of marriage for Florence and me in January 1986.

My sister had worked overseas for several years as embassy secretary to United States ambassadors in Oslo, Norway, and Dublin, Ireland. Her wanderlust satisfied, she returned to St. Louis

Owen Dacey, "the Dancing Policeman of St. Louis," on his corner at North Broadway and Grand, about 1970

Joan Dacey, about 1950

around 1970 to continue working for the federal government, this time as secretary to army generals posted to a supply depot at the edge of the city. Meanwhile, my brother had begun a thirty-year career as a policeman in St. Louis, from 1958 to 1988. During half of those years, from 1962 to 1977, Owen became famous as the Dancing Policeman of St. Louis, featured on *Candid Camera* as well as in various other television shows and even in a short movie called *Pop Cop*. As part of a three-man team, he had been assigned in 1962 to North Broadway and Grand, a notoriously bad corner at which to direct traffic. Prior to the assignment, various systems of expensive lights had failed to untangle the traffic caused by several streets angling in to one place as well as by entrance and exit ramps for a nearby highway and a number of factories disgorging large numbers of workers and cars in the late afternoon. On the fateful day my brother's two partners called in sick, Owen's station chief, in desperation, assigned Owen by himself to the impossible corner, expecting nothing. And nothing was what he got: no jam, no honking horns, no cursing drivers. Like an understudy long waiting for the time the star would take ill, Owen stepped into the role he seemed to have been waiting his whole life to fill. By an extraordinary and graceful display of body movements,

including pointing or whirling arms, a jabbing head, swinging hips, and legs constantly bending and shifting, he moved the traffic as smoothly as if the cars were skaters on ice. His fame quickly spread. Crowds would gather to watch, thereby increasing the local traffic, which he handled with his usual style and command. He was indeed in charge: drivers who did not want to follow his benign directorial signals quickly chose to rethink their stubbornness. *Candid Camera* filmed him with a musical soundtrack that revealed an almost balletic flow. When twice he was hit by cars (like a great bullfighter working close to the bulls, Owen worked close to the cars), his times in the hospital were big news and his return to his corner—*his* corner—was greeted by a steady stream of welcoming honks and slaps on his back from passing motorists.

The point of this seeming digression from my sister's fate is that, although in 1977 Owen moved inside to a desk at the precinct station, requiring the city to redesign the streets at his old corner in order to achieve some semblance of the harmony he had achieved, he seemed to me to resume his place at a difficult crossroads when he became my sister's primary caregiver during her final days in 1983 as a victim of cancer. Knowing she had months or weeks in which to live, Joan chose to come out of the hospital and die at home. Owen took a leave of indeterminate length from his job in order to be with Joan as much as possible in her apartment and do for her what she could not do for herself. I was able to come down from Minnesota for some of her final days, during which I observed Owen's devotion. She died one morning in his arms. The example of his devotion was equalled only by the example of her courage: she had made peace with her approaching death in a way none of her family or friends had, and she spent the last month or so of her life consoling those around her, caring for the feelings of us, who had arrived to care for hers. My life is not the lives of my brother and sister, but I was given by my sister the gift of a lesson in how to die well and by my brother the gift of a lesson in compassion and tender solicitousness, this latter from a "tough cop" who knew how to keep things moving.

Even he, however, if he had tried, could not have kept moving the marriage of mine that ended in the mid-eighties. Nor could I tell, if I wanted to, the story of that end; more than twenty years of intimacy naturally created such thickly entwined, even grafted-together lives that the process of dissolution was complicated and obscure beyond

Daughter, Fay, 1992

the ability of my intelligence to grasp it. An unfortunate and wrenching disagreement over the custody of the three children, a disagreement that had to be adjudicated, was the final guarantee that the end of the marriage would be an unhappy one, with senses of violation on both sides that were slow to heal. Fay, who had given the ten-year period such a promiseful start, because she was the youngest of us five perhaps suffered the most. Her journey during the course of about the next five years from low-spirited pre-teenager to vibrant high school cheerleader, instilling spirit, gave further evidence that our lives are being authored by someone not above manipulating the plot toward improbably pat ends. The boys found a new spiritual family temporarily in a local fundamentalist Christian church—their world shattered, they clung to a handy coherent one that seemed to provide answers to every question. Long after they outgrew what gave them comfort for a while, they carried with them a certain legacy which their church must be given credit for having nurtured in them—their music-making.

10

In retrospect, my own response to the dissolution of the family as we had known it, and perhaps of our idea of family, too, seems to have been one of fairly constant motion, as if I thought that whatever pain and bewilderment I was subject to at that time could be lessened by packing and unpacking suitcases.

The travelling binge began in 1984; Joan had been dead a year and the marriage had begun seriously to unravel. I went with Emmett to Ireland, where we caught up with my mother (one generation from Ireland and a great lover of that troubled but beautiful land, she travelled there a total of about fifteen summers until the trip became too much for her aging frame) and where I read from my book of poems about Gerard Manley Hopkins at a conference in Dublin to honor the English priest. (Travelling home from Nigeria, Florence and I had visited Ireland and my Irish relatives, as well as England, Germany, France, and Italy in the course of a four-month trip we awarded ourselves for the purpose of decompressing after our two years in the bush—and also, I seem to remember, as a way of putting off the expected culture shock of our return to the United States, a shock that did in fact materialize.) In the summer of 1985, I took Austin and Fay to Ireland, again for a couple of weeks, with no professional obligation this time. In the fall of 1985, I spent a month in Wichita, Kansas, as the annual writer-in-residence sponsored by the English department at Wichita State University.

My perhaps somewhat driven mobility was climaxed by the three months I spent in the spring of 1988 as a Fulbright Lecturer in Creative Writing in what was then Yugoslavia. Aside from Ireland, which I cannot see straight because of my sentimental ties to it, and aside of course from my own native land, Yugoslavia was the most interesting country I have ever lived in. The city, in fact, that drew me back three times to it was Sarajevo, now reduced apparently to barely habitable near-rubble. The Adriatic coast cast a spell over me like no other. Part of the appeal of the country was its checkered nature. Hopkins might have called Yugoslavia "dappled," an example of "pied beauty." But—here's that clever Author again—the checkered nature which gave it such beauty is the very source of its fatal tensions. While in Yugoslavia, I began work on a series of between twelve and fifteen poems to be called *Cycle for Yugoslavia*

(John Logan's first book was *Cycle for Mother Cabrini),* completing and publishing about half of them before the political and social situation in the country—or, more accurately, what had been a single country—became so bad that I had to shelve plans to return and finish the cycle. History has been too quick for me, and the half-finished cycle is now about a ghost, though it did not begin as such.

I stayed in motion locally also; during the years from 1985 to 1990 I had five different residences and obviously was engaged in some kind of search, a search precipitated by the changes in the family structure. All this motion, inside the country, outside it, and locally, came to an end in March of 1990 when I bought a home in the country near Lynd, Minnesota, not far from Camden State Park, a park whose first name derives from the last of the homes of Walt Whitman, the city in New Jersey. The move to the rural acreage definitely ended one period in my life and began another, one still extending itself

and showing no sign of coming to some kind of closure.

11

The purchase and move to end all moves occurred during the second half of a full sabbatical for the academic year 1989–90, the nine months actually extending to fifteen because of a free summer at each end. At the completion of the sabbatical period, knowing I loved the wooded and secluded place in which I had come to live—my nearest neighbors were three horses in the pasture next to my property—and loved even the trains that ran atop the hill behind my house, and having accomplished a great deal of writing that I was pleased with, I was encouraged by my circumstances and most recent experience of productivity to make what seemed to me to be the momentous decision to resign from full-time teaching at the school which had hired me twenty years earlier. I arranged with the administration to teach a maximum of six months a year, usually fall and winter quarters, in order to have available to me a minimum of six months each year in which to write poetry, with the understanding that if I chose to teach still less than the maximum arranged for, I could do so, by taking further leaves of absence. The arrangement proved suitable to me, and the department benefitted by its ability now to bring in a guest teacher each year with funding provided by some of the salary I was choosing no longer to draw. That arrangement continues to the present. Five members of the current English department were on staff in 1970 when I was hired: Leo Dangel, Jack and Mary Hickerson, Perry Lueders, and Eileen Thomas. These, along with Carol Hirmer, our secretary all these years, constitute a kind of second family for me, more than co-workers only and something like brothers and sisters after twenty years of close cooperation and shared experiences. My decision to begin to reduce my teaching time in the department brought home freshly to me the importance of these people in my life, the continuity and support of their presence.

Making possible the success of my new arrangement was a physical environment that seemed designed to encourage work. Always steadily prolific—probably to a fault—I now began to devote even more, and more regular, time to writing. (One of my fundamental beliefs is that there's no such thing as a writer's block, that the concept is a cover used by writers who choose not

"Feeding my next-door neighbor," near Lynd, Minnesota, 1990

to write.) I brought no television into the house and discovered in that place, in one of the few valleys in southwestern Minnesota, one in fact visited in the nineteenth century by the painter George Catlin after he had heard of its beauty, an experience of solitude I had never before known. I began to think of the house, with its openness, its airy and light spaces, and its fertile and spacious grounds that included a stream along one side, as a kind of secular monastery. While there I continued to work on my series of poems about Walt Whitman and began writing another series about Florence Nightingale. I was struck to notice that, along with my earlier subject Hopkins, the three historical figures I have written most about chose to live lives of productive singleness, each maintaining if not isolation then at least independence in the face of various social pressures. That I would both be drawn to these three people and begin to thrive in a special, new way at what one of my children called "Dad's Lynd Hermitage," I took to be no coincidence. Turning fifty in 1989, I predicted to myself and friends that my sixth decade would be, all told, the best one yet, and that prediction has so far been proven true.

12

That my new situation and arrangement agreed with me and was not a retreat from a full life—I had asked myself when I moved to the country if in fact I was engaged in a kind of wounded withdrawal—became clear to everyone in 1992 when I formed, with Emmett as percussionist and Austin as guitarist and keyboardist, the successful music and poetry performance trio called Strong Measures.

Among the roots of the concept were no doubt the days of jazz and poetry with Dr. Montesi. Later, as a faculty member at Southwest State University, I organized within about a ten-year period three week-long literary festivals, at the last of which, in 1989, I hired The Swoon, the rock and roll band of whose four members two were my sons, to play music behind certain selected poets as they read poems pre-chosen and prepared for by the band. As organizer, I did not participate in the event, which climaxed the week on Friday night and drew enthusiastic praise, but harbored a wish to have my own work so given a musical context. In the fall of 1991, I approached the boys with the idea of a trio—their band by coincidence happened to be breaking up at that

time, after a life of seven years, a good span for a group of quite young musicians—that would consist of their music, written and performed by them, and my poetry, along with the work of a few other poets. I was afraid they would laugh, call me sentimental, and suggest I "get a life." Instead they were taken by the idea and we began planning and rehearsing immediately.

They both lived at the time in St. Paul, Minnesota, while I lived close to three hours away, on the opposite side of the state. For six months, every other Sunday, I arose at 4 A.M. in order to be ready to leave my house at 5 A.M., so as to arrive at the boys' apartment at 8 A.M., in order to rouse them for a day of rehearsal at a basement music studio we rented, after which I would leave at 5 P.M. so as to arrive back in Lynd at 8 P.M., in time to begin to get ready for the upcoming school week. We rehearsed intensively for six months— about one month developing generally what we wanted to be up to, two or three months creating the numbers, and another two or three months drilling over and over, with an eye toward public performance, what we had created—for we wanted to avoid any taint of amateur night, or anything that smacked embarrassingly of horsing around that should have been kept in the family rec room. We knew the combination of father and sons would play a part in the audience's response, but we also knew we wanted in no way to exploit that combination and therefore never chose poems I had written about the children, although such poems were legion. We also knew of a history of excruciatingly bad combinations of some form of music and poetry, and very much wanted to avoid the various pitfalls typical of the association.

Early in rehearsal I realized that my plan to read from a book or sheaf of poems throughout each hour-long performance would guarantee a certain artsiness, and that I had no choice—if I wanted the hour to achieve a special success, and I did, as much for the boys' sake as my own—but to memorize an hour of poetry. I panicked and then submitted. The decision was a salutary one. The most salutary element in the whole mix, however, was Emmett's and Austin's music, which seemed to fit the poetry—mine, as well as Walt Whitman's, Theodore Roethke's, and Leo Dangel's—seamlessly. It was impossible to tell if the music was arising from the words or if the words were arising from the music, so intimately were the two media wed. The audience response was gratifying, to say the least. An opening performance at an art gallery in Duluth, Minnesota, in March 1992, inspired a

Strong Measures: Austin, Philip, and Emmett Dacey, 1992

standing ovation that seemed more like a kind of eruption. Three subsequent performances with their attendant word-of-mouth advertising drew bigger and bigger crowds—up to two and three hundred people—and equally enthusiastic responses from audiences. Asked by many people even after our first show for audiocassettes of our work, we produced such a tape in the summer of 1992 so that it was available at performances the following fall.

Audiences attest to compelling entertainment, an unexpected intensity that issues in both laughter and tears, and it has occurred to me that one explanation behind the audience's experience is a kind of hidden agenda for the boys and me, one that pervades and colors everything we do onstage. The custody dispute in 1985 resulted in a considerable loss of time shared by the three children and me. The recognition of that fact, a recognition not entirely unconscious in Emmett and Austin, nor, of course, in me, gives to our work together, at some level, the sense of a reunion as well as an affirmation or reaffirmation of a strong connection.

When, at a performance of Strong Measures one day after Fay's seventeenth birthday, we dedicated the show to her, the affirming nature of the band's hidden agenda was complete.

I believe that with Strong Measures, the band, I climbed, with my sons, a kind of mountain. At the moment, I am at a loss for an encore, for a project to commit myself to equal in challenge and significance to the one recently realized.

Coda

Early in my sixth decade, I have told many people, quite sincerely, that I believe I am living a charmed life. The charm extends to my mother and father, ninety-two and eighty-seven, both of whom are enjoying remarkably alert and active lives. My father's second wife, Rose, and her daughter, Joan Jackson, have brought him much happiness during the latter half of his life. I consider myself fortunate to have more friends than I can easily keep current with. Poetry has provided me with considerable opportunities to travel and enrich my life accordingly, particularly through the new people I meet that way. The manuscript for my sixth book of poems, tentatively called *Death and Television,* is presently under review by publishers, and the manuscript for a seventh book, tentatively called *Florence Nightingale's Rat,* is taking shape. Finally, I enjoy my time in the classroom more, and probably do better work there, than ever before. Unlike most English professors anywhere with my seniority, I take special pleasure in teaching freshman composition and choose to teach a greater share of such classes than I am expected to, as I agree with Joe David Bellamy that, "If our citizens become dead to language, it is not healthy for our democracy."

BIBLIOGRAPHY

Poetry:

The Beast with Two Backs (pamphlet), Gunrunner Press, 1969.

Fish, Sweet Giraffe, the Lion, Snake, and Owl (pamphlet), Back Door Press, 1970.

Four Nudes (pamphlet), Morgan Press, 1971.

How I Escaped from the Labyrinth and Other Poems, Carnegie-Mellon University Press, 1977.

The Condom Poems, Ox Head Press, 1979.

The Boy under the Bed, Johns Hopkins University Press, 1981.

Gerard Manley Hopkins Meets Walt Whitman in Heaven and Other Poems, Penmaen Press, 1982.

Fives, Spoon River Poetry Press, 1984.

The Man with Red Suspenders, Milkweed Editions, 1986.

The Condom Poems II, Spoon River Poetry Press, 1989.

Night Shift at the Crucifix Factory, University of Iowa Press, 1991.

Editor:

(With Gerald Knoll) *I Love You All Day: It Is That Simple,* Abbey Press, 1970.

(With David Jauss) *Strong Measures: Contemporary American Poetry in Traditional Forms,* Harper & Row, 1985.

Contributor:

Daniel Halpern, editor, *American Poetry Anthology,* Avon, 1975.

Lucien Stryk, editor, *Heartland II: Poets of the Midwest,* Northern Illinois University Press, 1975.

David Rigsbee and Ellendea Proffer, editors, *Ardis Anthology of New American Poetry,* Ardis (Ann Arbor, Mich.), 1977.

Edward Field, editor, *A Geography of Poets,* Bantam, 1979.

David R. Pichaske, editor, *Beowulf to Beatles and Beyond,* Macmillan, 1981.

Jim Perlman, Ed Folsom, and Dan Campion, editors, *Walt Whitman,* Holy Cow! Press, 1981.

X. J. Kennedy and Dorothy M. Kennedy, editors, *Knock at a Star: A Child's Introduction to Poetry* (illustrated by Karen Ann Weinhaus), Little, Brown, 1982.

Roger Gaess, editor, *Leaving the Bough,* International Publishers Co., 1982.

Paul B. Janeczko, editor, *Poetspeak,* Bradbury, 1983.

Ronald Wallace, editor, *Vital Signs: Contemporary American Poetry from the University Presses,* University of Wisconsin Press, 1989.

Recordings:

"Strong Measures" (audiocassette), EMC Productions, 1991.

Contributor of poems to more than fifty additional anthologies. Also contributor of poems to more than two hundred periodicals, including *American Review, Antaeus, Esquire, Hudson Review, Nation, New York Quarterly, Paris Review, Partisan Review, Poetry Northwest,* and *Shenandoah;* and more than thirty articles, essays, and reviews to periodicals and books.

Also editor, *Crazy Horse,* 1971–76; contributing editor, *Pushcart Prize: Best of the Small Presses,* 1983—. Manuscript for Hopkins book at Harry Ransom Humanities Research Center, University of Texas, Austin.

Robert Flanagan
1941-

LIFE'S FICTION, FICTION'S LIFE

Attention

Writing is a matter of attention. At the simplest level this means getting attention. Like children, writers want people to notice them. Look, look at what I made!

The people in my family were talkers. Their lives pared down by hard times, they entertained themselves by playing word games, mocking their supposed betters with sly jokes, and recounting past family exploits to a point that they took on mythic status. If you wanted to hold your own at those late night boozy kitchen table confabs, you had to know how to tell a story. When you had judged your listeners' interest and patience correctly, dropping the punch line at just the right moment, your reward was a burst of laughter. And family pride. An uncle might clap you on the shoulder and compliment your grinning father, "Red, this kid's no dummy."

At a deeper level, writing is a way of paying attention to the world. Translating the coded messages behind the slogans we live by is hard work that requires conditioning the self to be acutely and painfully conscious.

As a boy in Catholic schools I was forever being told to "Pay Attention." It seemed that frequently I would float off somewhere in my head. At the end of my teens I was called to attention—"Ten-hut!"—in the Marines. There, the veil of familiarity stripped from things, I began to take notice, and to question.

At still another level, writing is a way of deflecting attention from the performing self onto the subject. In fiction, since subject matter most often is character, this may mean calling attention to others.

When I was younger I wrote to escape my reality and to parade my talent. Sinking deeper into fiction over the years, I became less concerned with self-display and more interested in calling attention to those who commonly go unnoticed by society. "Attention must be paid to such a man,"

Robert Flanagan

I'd say, quoting Miller, although it was my father's fate, not Willy Loman's, that spurred me to work.

Writing holds surprising rewards. The act of creation which spirits you away from family and community may in time return you to them as you learn to pay better attention to things beyond the self. But there are costs as well. Fiction that aims at truth is very demanding of the writer. It calls everything into question. It requires a balancing act between the private and public self. Like the writer, it contains its opposite and is created at tension.

The Glass Center of the World

I was born and raised in the Ohio city that makes the scales used to weigh-in prizefighters ("He tipped the Toledo's at 159 and ½"), the home of Owens-Illinois and Libbey-Owens-Ford, companies that owed their success to old Mike Owens, my Dad liked to point out, an immigrant Mick who taught the high muckety-mucks a thing or two and made a bundle in doing it; the Glass Center of the World, as its billboards bragged, where the AAA ball club for a time bore the bizarre moniker, the Glass Sox; an industrial town of workers' neat houses clustered feudally about Willys Jeep and Auto-Lite, Spitzer Paper Box and Pinkerton Tobacco, and the Champion Spark Plug plant where my mother worked as a machine operator for twenty-five years.

My father's father John and his father Thomas came to America from Aghoo village, County Roscommon, Ireland, in 1890. They left behind John's sister Bridget to scrabble a living out of the eight acres that was insufficient to support them

Robert, aged two

all. I don't know how long the farm had been in the family, but it was a long time. When I went to Ireland in 1978 to see the stone homestead, now tumbled and roofless and part of the Martin dairy farm, I was moved to hear the Martin brothers remark that some of their cows were up in "Flanagan's field." John, son of Thomas Flanagan and Honorah Mattimoe, married to Mary Cody of Hugginstown, County Kilkenny, set up residence on City Park in Saint Patrick's parish, a Toledo neighborhood crammed with Irish who kept a goat in the backyard and a bin full of potatoes in the cellar. Thomas took his shovel and got work on the streets and John joined the police force. My father, Robert, was John's second son. Hard times ended his education at the sixth grade. He went to work as a bellhop at the Boody House hotel to help his father support a family of nine on a policeman's pay. The oldest child, Mayme, had died suddenly of pneumonia, and Jim, the older son, couldn't be looked to for help; despite the Captain's frequent use of the razor strop, Jim ran with a bad crowd of corner boys and Earl, the youngest son, was a precocious drunk. But no one worried much about Rob's missed schooling; a flame-haired bundle of energy, quick-witted, skilled at tap dancing, acrobatics, and boxing, he was a go-getter sure to make his mark in a land of opportunity.

My mother's family came from Redruth, Cornwall. Her grandfather Samuel Treloar was a tinsmith with an attached cottage on Foundry Row. He emigrated to Canada where he started up his own foundry. His son Charles left Canada for the States and became a traveling insurance salesman; in Georgetown, Ohio, he met and married a schoolteacher, Almona Robinson. They settled on a sixty-acre farm on Summerfield Road near Petersburg, Michigan, struggling to provide for their six children. Despite persistent poverty, Charles Treloar thought of himself as an aristocrat whose talents and abilities went unappreciated by his country neighbors. His youngest daughter he named Minnie, after a prosperous sister who failed to reward her brother with a monetary gift for the honor. Devilish and lively, Minnie seemed unafraid of the tyrant father the rest of the family shied from. She tried to cure his stiff neck by sneaking up behind him and giving it a sudden jerk. She substituted sand for sugar in his coffee to see if he could tell the difference. Hearing a new phrase at school one day she skipped all the way home past neighbors' houses chanting at the top of her lungs so as not to forget it: "Son of a bitch, son of a bitch!" Minnie began high school but collapsed with a severe case of tonsillitis. A bleeder, she was sick for months after her tonsils were removed, at times coughing up blood so thick it looked like chunks of liver. In those days if you didn't pass the year-end tests you were charged a fee for the otherwise free schooling; the Treloars couldn't afford to pay, so upon recovery Minnie left school for good in the seventh grade and stayed at home to help her mother with housework. Resenting her father's heavy drinking and bad temper, she refused to surrender to his rule. She dropped what she felt was a rube's name, Minnie, in favor of her middle name, Jane. She shocked the family by getting her hair bobbed. Finally she packed her things, and in a new flapper dress caught the interurban train to Toledo where a red-headed tap dancer offered to help carry her bags.

Our family rented a one-bedroom apartment on Monroe Street near Detroit Avenue. It was above Maloney's Bar and Grill, which stood between the Do-All machine shop and Ideal furniture store. "Here we are," my father would joke, "living on the far side of Ideal." He took the bedroom because his nerves had him up and down all night long, my mother slept with my sister Mona Mary, ten years older than I, in the Murphy bed that pulled down from the living room closet, and my bed was against one wall of the small dining room which also held my desk and toys. Swayne Field, home of the Mud Hens, was a half block away and we could see most of the playing field from our back porch. Many summer nights I stood out on Detroit Avenue waiting for home-run balls to sail over the right-field fence.

Dad was a disabled veteran, a shell-shocked World War I U.S. Marine Corps machine gunner, one of the Devil Dogs who'd broken the German advance at Belleau Wood and Chateau Thierry. His veteran's compensation check barely paid the rent. Sometimes he held down a sort of job, part-time or short-term. When he was short order cook downstairs at Maloney's, we had jumbo pickerel for supper on Fridays; he'd run it up the back stairs wrapped in his apron. But it was Mom, ten years younger than Dad and tall and wiry where he was short and stout, who supported us. Soon after I was born, when we were without light and heat due to unpaid bills, she got hired on at Champion Spark Plug as part of the World War II industrial effort. As Dad said, or I think I remember him saying, "Best thing that ever happened to this family was the Japs hitting Pearl Harbor." She worked second trick, making 5000 aviation plugs every night, and came home about midnight five

"At age ten, with Mother, Aunt Nora, and Uncle Frank"

nights a week completely exhausted. I waited up her for. "Oh Laws," she would say, "I'm so tired I could just die." Dad never cracked any jokes right then, and was quick to pour her a beer. In the afternoons when he was sleeping, I sat with her at the kitchen table as she got ready for work, watching her tape her fingers to keep them from getting cut up by the freshly tooled cores. I took pride in her endurance, and in her ability to handle such demanding work. Years later when I learned how to tape my hands for boxing, making sure to pad the knuckles and to cross over to support the thumb, it was my mother I thought of, hoping I'd prove to be as brave as she was.

But this was long before it became chic for women to drive bulldozers and men to be liberated to laundry, and my dominant feeling was one of shame that my father stayed at home, jobless, while my mother headed off to the factory. At school a nun scolded me in front of our class because on the student information form in the space provided for *Father's Occupation* I had written "Housewife." She thought I was being a smart aleck, and maybe I was. I learned early on to use a stinging wit, like a jab, to keep the nuns and my fellow parochial school inmates at a safe distance.

At times Dad crawled under the table if a car backfired in the street. When he was in the veterans' hospital at Brecksville his hands shook constantly; to drink coffee without spilling it he held one end of a towel with the fingers that gripped the cup's handle, then with the towel looped about his neck he'd tug on it with the other hand, guiding the cup to his lips. Once when he'd lost still another job he came home and locked himself in his room and plucked out his eyebrows and the front locks of his red hair. For some time after he covered his head with a white kerchief knotted at the four corners.

Rarely did I bring a friend to the apartment. I didn't want anyone to see my father walking around in his old blue robe dusting the furniture with wadded tissues or burning canned soup for our supper. Mom and Mona had jobs, so mostly it was just Dad and me at home. All the while he cooked or cleaned he was telling me, or maybe himself, stories of the heroic past. My grandfather Captain John Flanagan once shook hands with the great John L. Sullivan himself and was in the police cordon about the ring at the Dempsey-Willard fight, July 4, 1919, in Toledo's Bay View Park. Helping the bloodied Willard from the ring, he had to beat back sore losers trying to sucker-punch the man they'd bet on. My uncle Francis Delora, Lieutenant Detective, kicked down a door in a hail of tommy-gun fire to shoot it out with the notorious Cowboy Hill.

Not very often, but sometimes, Dad talked about his own neighborhood scrapes and boxing matches, but never about the war. It was hard for me to imagine him in combat, although I'd seen for myself his Purple Heart and Presidential Citation and, in the bottom drawer of his dresser, the gas mask and the dented green helmet with a red Indian head on the front, an insignia he had painted on the helmets of his whole platoon. My father was nearly fifty when I was born, an old and broken fifty, and seemed more like my grandfather. Listening to the tales of his past, I'd try to match up the pot-bellied, skinny-armed man before me with the battler in the story. Sometimes I thought he was making it all up. Generally though I believed his story because it was so clear that he believed it. And because I wanted to believe it. I was hungry for a sense of personal history, as if that might confirm my worth, of which I was in grave doubt.

One of the things I learned at home was that although our people hadn't come up in the world, we were a damn sight more interesting and had a helluva lot better stories to tell than the bloodless types who were better off. Another thing I learned, a teaching confirmed later by church and military, was that I was special because I was part of a select unit of mankind; yet I was a very undeserving part of that unit and could be expelled.

When he wasn't talking about the grand past, Dad was whipping up visions of a wonderful future. One of us would do something to hit it big and we'd all be on easy street. I was clever, it could happen to me, I could be the one.

As a young boy I wanted to be a cowboy or a priest, a cop or a boxer. While entertaining such fantasies, I spent my time, a fat kid with a hernia, constant throat infections, a heart murmur and touch of rheumatic fever, drawing and coloring and modeling clay. When Mom went to the bank she would bring home in her big purse thick packs of white Toledo Trust checking deposit slips. I used the blank backs to make cartoon books filled with bright colors and stories of miraculous rescue or heroic violence. I spent whole days making clay figures—usually cowboys and Indians, I was no great shakes at originality—and using them to act out adventures I made up as I went along, saying my characters' lines aloud. Dad spoke with pride of my artistic talent. But I caught the doubt in my mother's eyes. I knew she worried that my "art" was only a way of hiding from the world, and that she feared I would turn out like my father, a man too afraid of life to go out into it, hiding behind an unprovable illness, sleeping away the day in a small airless bedroom with blankets tacked over the windows, and prowling the apartment at night like something caged.

I'd be a success at something, I told her, although secretly I felt sure to fail at anything I tried. How could I hope to match my grandfather and my uncle Frank for courage? What could I hope to do to strike it rich and save our family? And, at another level, I wasn't even sure how hard I was supposed to try. The message I got was mixed. On the one hand we Flanagans were nobodies in a world where being somebody meant that you were corrupt. Our poverty and obscurity were proofs of our virtue. "Look at *her*," my mother would say of someone dressed too fancily at Sunday mass, dismissing the pretender with a sniff. She scorned the man who owned our building, a fellow whose only interests were money and lording it over others. Her goal for me was that I'd hold a steady job—at Champion Spark Plug if need be, though maybe I could get in at Owens-

Illinois where my sister Mona worked, or better yet at the post office where you didn't get laid off. On the other hand our family played Monopoly with a passion, Mom and Dad bet the slots and numbers in hopes of making a killing, and Dad's chatter was filled with envy of those in power. "I'll bet you that you might turn out to be rich and famous," he'd say to me, always when Mom wasn't home, and usually when he wanted me to feel better about some trouble at school or an argument we'd had that he couldn't patch up by giving me a bowl of ice cream, his standard remedy. "No, really, it could happen, Bobby. You just have to have an idea. Like the Parker Brothers." Over the years that became his repeated hope for me: "Maybe someday you'll have an idea."

Back then I never thought of being a writer. Dad had been a writer, briefly: a crime reporter for the old *Newsbee* and, partly due to his flowing Palmer method handwriting, an executive secretary to the *Toledo Blade* editor. Where had it gotten him? (Of course, where had anything gotten him? He'd been a salesman for a meat company, a used furniture store owner, a bankrupt, a dock worker in a tobacco warehouse, a short-order cook, a patient in a veterans' hospital, and finally a recluse. It was not a history to give his son confidence.) And although we were a talky family, we weren't literary. We told jokes, we played word games, Twenty Questions and What's Your Trade, we recited Thomas Moore songs my father had learned from his father and I from him, "Oh believe me if all those endearing young charms," and we admired the newspaper columns of Jim Bishop and the delivery of Don Dunphy doing the Friday night fights. The only reading materials in the apartment were *Ring* magazine and *Police Gazette,* Dad's paperback copy of Dale Carnegie's *How to Win Friends and Influence People,* and Mom's *Laugh with Leacock,* a hardcover which I think had belonged to her father. How religiously we took Carnegie's American principles of business success. How hard we laughed at the Canadian Leacock's parodies, from which Dad might read aloud some nights when he'd had a few, as in "Gertrude the Governess" when the romantic Lord Ronald, rebuked by his father, Lord Knotacent, the Earl of Knotacentinum Towers, pronounced Nosham Taws, "flung himself from the room, flung himself upon his horse and rode madly off in all directions." "Oh Laws," my mother would cry, wiping away tears and struggling for breath, "that darn fool!"

I did some reading on my own, mostly *Men at War* and *Classic* comic books. I owned two real books. My aunt Margaret, a schoolteacher, gave me the first one for Christmas when I was nine, *Boru: The Story of an Irish Wolfhound,* and I read it again and again. On my tenth birthday in April, maybe because I'd been begging for a dog despite the rule against pets in the apartment, Dad gave me *Wild Animals of the World,* a large-size dictionary of wildlife with beautiful, realistic illustrations, many in color. I'd never seen anything like it. I just about memorized the book. Dad liked to quiz me on it to impress my uncles. Quagga? "This partly-striped animal believed to have been related both to the zebra and to the wild ass is now extinct." Tapir? "The Tapir has been picturesquely but unscientifically described as a pig that started out to be an elephant and then changed its mind." Seeing me reading and rereading the same two books prompted my sister Mona Mary who studied art at Notre Dame Academy, was the proponent of higher culture in our family, and was often put in the role of mother, to lead me to the Dorr Street branch library. There I found books that fed my desire to escape into dreams of power: Jack London's *The Call of the Wild* and *White Fang,* Rudyard Kipling's *The Jungle Book,* Mark Twain's *A Connecticut Yankee in King Arthur's Court,* and,

Robert at eighteen

"With my sister Mona," July 1960

one of my favorites, Henry Gregor Felsen's *Street Rod*. Some years later I picked up the family Bible which I'd never seen anyone open, and got lost in Old Testament battles. I would lie on my bed reading Judges and Samuel and Kings. My father kept asking me if everything was all right; behind my back he told my mother he was afraid I'd gone off the deep end.

It wasn't only my Bible reading that worried him. If I wanted to buy a paper route, or to join the Boy Scouts, he immediately sensed danger and predicted disaster. "Now why do you want to start something like that?" he'd complain. "Why can't you just leave well enough alone?" Out of fear, he actively encouraged me to do nothing. Because things were sure to turn out badly, the safest tactic was to keep still. Part of me came to believe that, and often I felt nailed in place. But another part of me resented and resisted inaction. In my late teens, to my father's dismay, the active part of me more and more took over. I sent away for Charles Atlas's *Dynamic Tension* body-building book, and ordered correspondence courses in cartooning and gun

repair; I took up the guitar; I won a Saint Genesius medal (the patron saint of actors) for Best Actor in a Catholic Youth Organization drama festival; I did sit-ups until my hernia was declared healed and I could throw away the hated leather truss; I practiced with handgun and rifle and became a crack shot; I thumped the heavy bag and made the light bag dance; I drag-raced "borrowed" cars like a maniac.

Yet the fear was there, all the same. Especially if I let myself think about Uncle Frank.

Francis L. Delora was six-feet-four-inches tall and weighed over 250 pounds. Retired from the force after forty-six years of service, 1908 to 1954, he still was a formidable figure. In fact, he was my image of God. He had a huge lionlike head with silver hair brushed straight back, a broad leathery red face, and hands that would make two of mine. He wore gold-rimmed glasses, a gold wedding band, and his gold retirement watch. Even in retirement he often packed his service pistol, a 32.20 Colt Police Positive.

The events that follow still confuse me, as they did when they occurred. I can't say for certain what happened; I only know what I think I remember, a memory distorted by pain.

One night when I was sixteen and had just come home from a high school dance, Dad got a phone call from his sister Nora. A great-hearted, fat-billowing woman, who suffered from cataracts and hardening of the arteries, Nora was upset because she "couldn't get Frankie to wake up." Dad began hunting his car keys and fumbling around for a pair of trousers. Mom was due home from work at any minute. I went on ahead, running up to Frank's and Nora's apartment on Lawrence Avenue. When I knocked, Aunt Nora opened the door a crack and said to come in. I pushed on the door but it stuck. Finally I squeezed through, stumbling over Uncle Frank. He lay on his back just inside the door, his neck bent and head propped on the baseboard. Aunt Nora had wedged a pillow behind his head to make him comfortable. She moved off down the hall, saying that she was cooking Frankie a hamburger; he'd feel better if he'd only eat a little something. I could smell whiskey on him. I called to him and pulled on his wrists to get him to sit up. He was so heavy I couldn't move him. His big hands felt cold. Greasy smoke and the smell of charred meat floated in from the kitchen. My fingers touched the back of his head. It felt pulpy, like a smashed melon. My hand came away covered with blood.

Dad and Mom showed up, and the police. Frank had been in a fight with his brother Hank in a bar. Hank was every bit as big as Frank and they were tearing up the place. It took a half-dozen officers to get them calmed down. Then, as a courtesy to Frank, a squad car had run the Delora boys home. Both brothers were banged up, the Polish police captain told us, but Frank must have been hurt a lot worse than he looked. It was a terrible thing, though it'd be best to call it a fall, an accident. We wouldn't want to start something that could get the man's own brother charged with manslaughter, would we?

At home Mom and Dad phoned Hank who said that the cruiser had dropped him off first, and that Frank had been okay then, except for a couple of scratches. After the call, we sat at the kitchen table, Dad saying how it had to have been the cops. Everybody knew the way Frank bullied patrolmen, and how hard he was to handle when he was on the sauce. One of those rookies, Dad said, had used a sap harder than he'd meant to, that was the truth of it, then they panicked and dumped the body and got the hell out of there, the lousy lying murdering bums. There wasn't one damn thing we could do about it either.

For some time after, I lay awake nights imagining myself tracking down the rookie to ambush him with Frank's own pistol. In school I'd daydream about getting the Polish captain too, making sure he recognized me before I let him have it. But finally I just tried not to think about Uncle Frank. Whenever I let myself dwell on it— so much power so easily destroyed!—I'd feel my father's paralysis creeping over me.

After high school I went to work. I worked as night watchman at the Family Fair department store at Bancroft and Auburn, 10 P.M. to 7 A.M., Monday through Saturday. I liked the job because I was left alone and got to carry a gun; it was a .38 American Bulldog, one of Uncle Frank's revolvers that Dad had handed on to me when Aunt Nora died. I worked as janitor at the truck terminals out on Tractor Road, day laborer for a landscaper, and utility man at Republic Steel. I worked as dishwasher at the Waffle Inn downtown by the Town Hall Burlesque. The strippers would come in for coffee and donuts in the afternoon, sexy, scary women with hard faces and harsh, smokey laughs. They called me Kid and said why didn't I drop in and catch their act. I wanted to, but was way too leery of them.

When my daily dish-washing stint was finished, I'd walk to the YMCA to work out. Having

shed enough fat by diet and *Dynamic Tension* to make middleweight, I had taken up the sweet science as a manly alternative to the neighborhood street fights I dreaded. There was no official boxing club at the Y, just a group of guys who skipped rope and hit the bags and sparred with one another under the squinty eye of a big man in grey sweats who claimed to be a professional heavyweight getting ready for a comeback. Some doubted him, but I don't recall that I ever did. He was black, his nose had been flattened, his upper arms were the size of my thighs, and he banged the heavy bag like a champ. If he was willing to take me seriously, I was willing to do the same for him, and I took to calling him Coach, which he appeared to like. He thought I had a snappy jab, and showed me how to double it up and hook off it. When I sparred, he kept urging me to get in range, get in range. How could I tell when I was in range, I wanted to know, and he said, "You'll get hit." I soon learned that he was right. More importantly, I learned that the fear which threatened to freeze me in the corner on my stool got knocked loose by the first good sock I took. I'd been nailed, yet I hadn't broken, so my feeling of being made of glass was only a fantasy. Your eyes might water, your nose bleed, your ribs stab as you sucked air, but you were still on your feet. And you could give as good as you got. You just had to throw yourself forward into that no-man's-land of ring center, tossing everything you had at your opponent, trusting that your energy and need and apparent bravery would be enough to see you through. I even began to think that maybe I'd found my calling, and that it wouldn't be long before I could strut around town in one of those Golden Gloves jackets I admired so. This despite the fact that I had no power, possessed a suspect jaw, soft belly, and small brittle hands, and had worn glasses since the fourth grade, seeing my opponent in the ring as a moving blur. Running into a couple of gym rats who bulled right through my windmilling to coldcock me cleared my head of that fiction. I came away from my six or seven gym bouts with partial hearing loss in my left ear, but not with the broken nose I longed for, believing as I did then that it would provide visible proof that unlike my father I was someone who dared to meet life head-on.

When I'd quit a handful of dead-end jobs in the year since graduating from high school, and when I had no idea what I was doing or where I was going, and was scared that I was proving to be just like my father, I had a beer with a high school

"With my mother and father, just before leaving for the Marine Corps," 1960

buddy in a bar on Toledo's east side. He told me that first thing in the morning he was going downtown to join the Marines. I said, "Pick me up."

It seemed to me that I was doing something to show how different I was from my father, the ex-marine, by joining the Marines. Why I thought that then I don't know now.

At Parris Island I got to talk to guys who'd gone to college (because my friend and I had joined the reserves) and I noticed that they didn't seem that much smarter than I was. As soon as I finished my six months active duty, I enrolled at the University of Toledo, the only college I'd heard of except for Notre Dame, home of the Fighting Irish, whose fight song we'd copied for ours at Central Catholic High.

It was then that I began reading seriously. The works which most influenced me at that time were the stories of Frank O'Connor, so natural sounding I might have been hearing them told around our kitchen table, the plays of Eugene

O'Neill, which seemed to spring right out of the Old Testament, and James T. Farrell's Studs Lonigan novels: *Young Lonigan, The Young Manhood of Studs Lonigan,* and *Judgment Day.* In Farrell's work I recognized the characters I saw around me every day and it struck me that I might write about the people in my own life, even in Toledo.

At twenty-one, I started writing some poems and stories of my own. I didn't write many because I was going to college days and working nights and spending as much time as I could with a great girl I'd found, someone who was good-looking and spunky and took me seriously.

I read Jack London's *Martin Eden,* the story of a tough sailor who by sheer force of will becomes a famous writer, and it excited me so much that I decided then and there to make my living writing. I knocked out a dozen stories and rushed them off to men's magazines and they bounced right back. For the most part the stories were accounts of things I'd seen, like a guy in a diner smacking somebody with one of those heavy glass sugar dispensers. I'd never thought of using something like that as a weapon and I wrote about an unarmed man trapped in a diner by a punk with a knife. I got John Brick, a visiting instructor at U.T. and a published novelist, to read it and he said "Okay, but the only thing that happens in this story is that one fellow hits the other with a sugar jar." I said, "Right! Like it?" He suggested that I sign up for his fiction writing course the next semester which, thank my lucky stars, I did.

Also in those first bursts of work I wrote a play and got the chance to put it on at the university. *The Discontent* was imitation O'Neill with some Ibsen tossed in, and presented as the symbol of a family's despair an heirloom music box that had been wound so tight that it finally snapped. I directed the production as well as played the lead role of the father, a failed artist. I also helped to build the set, a kitchen, and hauled in a real sink as a final, convincing touch. The play, which dealt with art, history, war, love, courage, the family, and alcoholism, ran a bit long for a one act. The action consisted mainly of declamatory speeches which sounded like blank verse and gave the work, I thought, a certain tragic dimension. After the performance, the doyenne of the theatre department stopped by to say "Well, Flanagan, you put in everything *and* the kitchen sink."

My first published work, a poem entitled "The Rift," was inspired by a break-up with my new girlfriend. I'd written it in the middle of the night in a Bancroft Avenue laundromat, conditions which struck me as romantic and artistic. That the poem depended on a metaphor based on cows, animals I knew nothing about, didn't matter. My girl and I got back together and the poem was published in *The Small Pond,* a little magazine in the east. Such publication, I thought, confirmed my calling.

In my junior year of college, at twenty-two, I quit breaking up with my girl and married her. Kathleen Rose Borer was from Ottawa, Ohio, where she'd grown up poor in a family with a troubled, troublesome father, and had come to Toledo to take her nurse's training at St. Vincent's Hospital on Cherry Street. At the time she had it in mind to become an Air Force nurse and see the world. I'd met her on a blind date arranged by some friends who'd gone to Central Catholic with me and were in training with Katy at Saint V's. Maybe they thought I needed a nurse to care for me; in those days, and for too long after, I acted as though I did. I'd ride around nights with two other

amateur actors and aspiring writers from Irish families, Tom Gavin and Mike Harrah, talking literature and drinking and looking for trouble; one night we took a tiny Fiat cross-country over the Ottawa Park golf course as I fired my .38 revolver at trees. Whatever the nursing students' motives, they did me a great favor. I've never known a person of deeper patience or more genuine independence of spirit than Katy; her understanding of people has helped give some depth to my fiction's characters.

Two years after our wedding, expecting our first child in three months, we left Toledo for Chicago, the literary turf of James T. Farrell and Nelson Algren and Richard Wright and Theodore Dreiser, writers I regarded as gods, and of a fairly new guy I thought showed promise, Saul Bellow. Why would *anyone* ever go to New York when there was Chicago? I could not believe my good luck. I had won a full fellowship in Theology and Literature because George Guthrie, my philosophy professor at Toledo, had taken me aside one day

Corporal-E4 R. J. Flanagan, U.S. Marine Corps,
Twentynine Palms, California, 1964

after class to inquire about my future. I thought I'd stay on at the city streets department, I told him, driving weed mowers and trucks, and would write at night. It shouldn't be long before I made some money; I'd already had a poem published. He told me that I ought to consider graduate school. I said okay, and applied to the one place he mentioned, his alma mater, the University of Chicago.

When Katy and I drove out of town in a U-Haul truck, we passed a billboard proclaiming The Glass Center of the World. Despite the promise of our future, I felt the impact of truth in that phrase. It was what I had learned growing up and, despite my reckless efforts to disprove it, still believed. Everything about you was breakable.

It's that knowledge which informs my fiction.

Writing Life

A young marine from Detroit wrote to me about my novel *Maggot:* "Sir, thank you for having the balls to tell the truth!" That's the greatest praise I've ever gotten for my work.

Yet if at times I find truth, I more often lose sight of fact. I confuse what actually happened with what I've imagined or feared. Like a scavenger at a community dump, I'll pick up something from another's life that seems too good to waste. Saving it means putting it into fiction. To do that I need to emotionally live through the incident or anecdote, often to the point that it takes on the feel of personal experience. Sometimes my father's or grandfather's doings, which I've heard recounted in such vivid detail so often, seem to be my own. Or, if what I'm writing is based on something I actually was part of, I'm likely to forget that it didn't happen to the extreme that it does in the story.

For instance, I was only a "summer marine" yet I got more out of the experience by brooding about it afterward than did many marines who lived it for a four-year hitch or longer. The fact that I wrote about it to such an extent, as with my meager boxing experience, or my erotic fantasies, may lead one to imagine me to be more marine, boxer, or Casanova than in fact I am. By "one" I don't mean only my reader, whoever that may be. Often I'll catch myself feeling depressed or excited, or generally guilty, about something that upon reflection I realize exists only in my fiction. Yet it felt so real. I have to remind myself: Look, you just *write* this stuff; you make it up out of things you wish or fear you might do.

Sometimes I ask why I tell stories at all. I'm a fairly healthy, passably competent person. Why don't I just live life? This question most often occurs to me when I'm stuck on something I'm writing. Suddenly the entire enterprise of literature seems suspect. Why should I hide away in a little room making up adventures like some kid with plastic soldiers? Although unlike my father's bedroom it has no blankets over the windows, my study can come to seem a sanctuary unfit for a man who claims an interest in real life.

Maybe I should peddle my bike downtown to Delaware's Hamburger Inn (Olentangy's Swope's Cafe in my short stories) to drink coffee and catch up on local gossip, overhearing perhaps some farm woman remark of her recently passed-away father (as one does to the lawyer Owen Moore in "Local Anaesthetic"), "Things just wore him to a fragile"; or a father-in-law complain about the abusive bum his only daughter married (as handyman Dewey Grooms does in "Father's Day"), "The thing of it is you can't talk to the boy." Or I could take a ride in my truck along the back roads flanking the Olentangy River (past the limestone millworker's cottage where wild Shelly Gold lives alone in "All Alone and Blue"), or head north on Route 23, making the two-hour drive to Toledo to stir bittersweet memories by looking at the place that once held Maloney's and our family's apartment, the landscape of the heart, now an on/off ramp for I–75 North.

Then again I may as well stay at my desk and hope to fill some pages. Because even when I'm not writing I'm thinking about writing. Although I would wish this not to be the case, it's generally not enough for me to live in the present. I want life to be narrated, to be witnessed. The lived moment has a felt value in itself, of course, but it has added value and the pleasure of form when it becomes something written.

Not that there are no rewards to life as lived. There are many times when I don't give a thought to writing. Playing handball, or jogging with my dog Murphy are not things I do in order to fashion narratives from them. When I'm teaching, which I enjoy, although I'd enjoy it more if I could do it less, I'm thinking of my students' work or the work we're studying, not mine. I like my job, the college, the town, and our old house. I count myself lucky to have a marriage that has not only endured over the years but also has grown, lending structure and interest to daily life. I take pride in going to New York City to act as audience for the talents of our daughters, Anne's in a play or Nora's in a photography exhibit. None of these experiences derive their essential value from being potential subject matter for fiction.

Nor has my life lacked dramatic conflict. There was a time, after a long and painful, failed biracial adoption, when it didn't look like our marriage would last. There were other times, during my drinking days, when it didn't look like I'd last. I went roaring and swinging after four Puerto Rican teenagers one night in New York when they passed a remark I took as an insult. I flew a car off the road into a cornfield at ninety miles an hour. These incidents aren't fictional, although I wish they were.

But no matter how dramatic or tawdry, it's not the event that most interests me as a writer. What I want is for language to become style and so to work the magic of transformation on raw experience, to validate it, even to redeem it. This is a childish expectation, perhaps, or a residual Catholic habit. Loving word power, however, is a major part of what it means to be a member of the tribe of writers.

As far back as I can remember I have delighted in language. At home my father's stories were punctuated by phrases that served as refrains in a formal verbal performance: Oh for crying out loud, Not for all the tea in China, As God's my witness, Mark my words, He's only small potatoes. At church I was a willing altar boy because I loved the sound of the Latin mass: *Introibo Ad Altare Dei, Dominus Vobiscum, Ora Pro Nobis.* Not that I was overly solemn about it. I joked that I knew the Pope's phone number, *Et Cum Spiritu Tuo,* and in choir for *Ora Pro Nobis* sang "All blow your noses." But on the altar, in a setting of marble pillars and white candles that made me think of the art museum, I took pride in being prompt with my responses, keeping pace with the priest, matching him line by line in an incantatory dialogue that approached drama. (When the English Mass came in, the magic was gone and so was I.) In the gym, I loved the mix of archaic formality and salty tang in boxing speech: Pronate the blow!, your coach might shout (meaning, Turn the punch over from the shoulder to gain power); Lift it up and knock it off! (meaning, Raise your opponent's head with an uppercut and follow with a hook); and that gem of a maxim on handling an adversary: Make him miss and make him pay. In the service, I discovered the poetry of profanity, how a simple four-letter vulgarity could be used like salt in cooking to

flavor any saying, and how richly metaphorical ordinary speech could be. A drill instructor warning me that the next time I lipped off he was going to punch me would say, "I'm gonna put out your running lights," meaning, the eyes in the Jeep of my head, or in other words knock me out. "You didn't stand close enough to your razor this morning," a sergeant would tell a grunt with five o'clock shadow; "Put some glass in that hole," one boot would yell at another to get him to close the window. On a morning run, our platoon would chant, "I gotta gal who lives on a hill, if she won't then her sister will; You hadda good home but you left, you're right." As clearly as any image of these experiences, the sound of them stays with me.

Often I will say my work aloud as I write. I listen for pattern and tone. The first paragraph of my story "Close Dancing," for instance, works at least in part on tone. The narrative's conflict is between institutional power and the individual conscience. The power is the Catholic Church, represented by a formidable nun, and the individual is a fatherless, scrappy boy who refuses to take the blame for something he has not done.

> Word came down from Sister Mary Annunciation, their eighth grade teacher and principal of Saint Sebastian's. As usual, it had to do with trouble and Doolan.

What pleases me about this is that it opens on *word;* in the beginning was the word, in this case literally so; also that Sister Annunciation is the moving power at the start of the paragraph and moves that power through Saint Sebastian's on down to Doolan who, coming last, bears the weight of the paragraph. And as I said it aloud I was aware of choosing low frequency vowels: word, down, from, Annunciation, usual, do, trouble, Doolan. This gives a blues note to the story's music. Someone told me at a conference that they liked how the boy's name signified his combative nature, his *dueling* with the church. I had to admit I'd not thought of that. I'd gotten the name from a fishing village on the west coast of Ireland where I once waited out a storm before catching a boat to the Aran Islands. Doolin: I liked the sound of it, quiet, with sort of a mournful softness to it, yet solid and enduring, like stone in rain.

Language tone is one thing, emotional tone another.

Many times I've had it pointed out to me, by reviewers or concerned friends, that I most always write about defeated people and that even those works of mine that are comic, are darkly so.

Why do I tell the stories I tell?

It's not my habit to ask myself this. It makes me very uneasy to start digging around the springs of my inspiration for fear that they may dry up. Although a quick look might do no harm.

There was so much horseplay and laughter in my family, why are my stories so dark?

Maybe because my father's family had such a knack for loss. None of them made money or a name for themselves. Dad's mother died young, as did three of his four sisters, his police captain father turned to drink before his heart gave out, his uncle Tom late one night mistook a bottle of carbolic acid for his whiskey pint hidden atop the medicine cabinet and died screaming and kicking on the bathroom floor, his brother Jim, drug addict and armed robber, was shut up in the Ohio state pen, and his other brother, Earl, a wino who walked out on his wife on their wedding night, took a nap on a flattened cardboard box in the basement of a neighborhood shoe repair shop and never woke up. And there was also the memory of Uncle Frank's brutal end. Although Dad was never without a joke at the ready, beneath his sustained patter—Frick and Frack routines, Johnny Juniper jokes, Burma Shave recitations—there lurked a view of life as a losing game.

Then why aren't all my stories grim? Why do they hold so much humor, verbal and physical?

Maybe because of my mother's high-spirited high jinks. Although she might refer to herself as the dummy in her family, she did so with a devilish grin that told you she knew darn well that she was the liveliest and best-looking one of the bunch. She refused to admit that she'd made a mistake in picking a husband. When he was right, she told her schoolteacher sisters, Red was the life of the party. Mom was a practical joker who'd dump ice water down your shirt or jump from the closet to scare the living daylights out of you. A fierce competitor, she played tag with me, frantically racing through the apartment, dodging, laughing, knocking things off tables, anything to keep me from catching her, as Dad stood at the door to his room, calling at us to know when to quit. She and I entertained ourselves on some Saturday nights by making prank phone calls. I usually settled for corny jokes: "Hello, is your refrigerator running? Then you better go catch it." "Eagle Laundry? How much to get my eagle cleaned?" Mom did

characters in various dialects, Polish, black, Irish, Jewish; she'd call bars, asking for someone we'd made up, Stanislaus Coleslaw Horsinkowski or George Washington Lincoln Roosevelt Jones, giggling with me when we heard the bartender call out the ridiculous name, then threatening him when he told her that no one there had answered to it. "Listen, buster, I know he's in there," she'd say. "Put him on the phone this minute or I'm coming down there with my baseball bat and knock some sense into his head *and* yours." Irresponsible, but a world of fun.

Yet Mom's humor could take a bitter twist if she thought someone was laughing at her or her family. She really did think of herself as "just another dumb factory worker," and was fiercely protective of her poor sick factory worker brothers, Hume and Fenn, who even though they weren't Irish could not stay off the bottle. Her loyalty to family was absolute. Find fault with any one of her relatives, and she was your enemy for life. Our high school basketball coach once made a slighting (but true) remark to one of our cousins about me being a lackluster student, and it got back to Mom. From that day forward she would scan the papers for news about the coach and his team, root for his opponent, and never let pass an opportunity to blame him for any loss his team might suffer. Even when the man went on to coach college ball, Mom followed his career; I recall her nodding her head with satisfaction over a news report that his team had been knocked out of a big tournament in the first round. "Good," she said, "maybe it will teach him a lesson."

Growing up, I was given to feel that if life is sad it's comically so, or sadly comical, and that most people are fools, God bless them, so there's no reason to be too hard on them. Yet I also sensed that our family's laughter often sprang from mockery or envy. The point of a joke would be to bring down the smug or pompous with a snide crack. With some discomfort I recognize this trait in myself, a chip on the shoulder about social class, pretension, and wealth. It stands out clearly in "Self-Defense," one of my Toledo stories. The story's narrator, a married student going to college part-time while working full-time as a campus police dispatcher, envies his friend Larry's relative freedom as a fellowship-supported graduate theatre student. Resenting the way Larry wastes time playing around with Glenna, the culture-hungry wife of a well-to-do car dealer, the narrator steps in to help free his friend of the relationship.

And then, Larry having gone inside to cry over her, I stood watching Glenna drive off, heading home to poor dumb Sid the Saab seller who probably was wondering why his wife stayed out so late with her artsy friends.

A yellowish streetlight buzzed overhead. Both sides of the narrow way were lined with fake brick twinplexes and hunkered down white frame cottages. All of their windows were dark. Larry's was the only place lit up like a carnival. Most people had more sense than to stay up all night yapping about romance and heartbreak. They got their sleep so they could hack another shift at Libbey-Owens or Champion or Jeep.

I didn't think Cassie would really leave me, not just because she thought I wasn't sensitive enough. Where would she go? We didn't make enough money to split up. And really I didn't think Sid would risk his nice set-up by beating up Larry. What I thought was that pretty soon Glenna would find somebody more interesting or less serious than Larry, and that Larry would get over her and maybe go back to his paralegal, and that things would go along pretty much the way they had before. That was just the way life was, at least in Toledo.

A certain resentment is evident too, I think, in "Comedy of Eros," my take on a Hemingway fan living the singles' life in New York City, a stalwart male doing front line duty in the battle of the sexes. The story's opening parodies that of *A Farewell to Arms.*

> In the late summer of that year I lived in an apartment on the West Side that looked out over Columbus Avenue. On the avenue there were yellow cabs and gassy busses and platoons of cyclists with whistles in their mouths and roller skaters along the curb. They streamed toward midtown where business towers stood like fortresses. Dust, stirred by the traffic, rose and fell. Secretaries and receptionists and editorial assistants marched past on Adidas and Nikes, their office heels stowed in nylon backpacks.

Smart-alecky, but not necessarily a cheap shot. Papa leaves himself open for such jabs by his stiff-lipped elegiac tone, so self-consciously brave, that nearly conceals his incurable sentimentality. Whether it be stoic or madcap, I don't care for fiction with an overly simplified emotional tone. I tire quickly of the sad, silent, manly American loner. I want fiction to give me a full range of emotions and values, from the serious to the ludicrous, from the sacred to the profane, the way that writers like Ernest Gaines, J. F. Powers, Flannery O'Connor, and Saul Bellow manage to do. Sometimes it's when a writer risks seeming the fool that he's being most courageous—like the heroic Samuel Beckett daring to admit that he doesn't know what he doesn't know, and to show how slippery and shifting identity is, and how uncertain are all our certainties.

My own experience has given me to understand that each of us contains his or her opposite, and I believe it's the writer's task to get in touch with all the elements of the self. Despite the darkness of much of my work, I don't see my characters as losers. They have hard times, true, and they are not always the most upbeat people, but I think that they win more often than not, although they may not win in the most obvious or worldly ways. In "Smoker," my story about boxing in the marines, Billy Troy, a reluctant combatant, loses a smoker bout in which he was way overmatched, but summons the courage and skill to go the distance. Afterwards, as he is being chewed out by Sergeant Schramm, a drill instructor who believes only in winning, Troy is unexpectedly cheered by a recognition regarding his late father, a gutsy, all-offense prizefighter who took fearful beatings for little money, for which his son pitied him while feeling guilty for doing so.

> Schramm starts in on me again. He's got so many words for loser, he must sit up nights studying his Thesaurus. But it all blows by me. Now I know why Dad could grin. He kept his own score.
>
> To think of all the yapping I did back then. Tell them how it is, make them see, yap yap yap. And when Dad held his peace, I'd been foolish enough to think he was a fool.
>
> "You think you're really something, don't you, Troy?"
>
> Light and bouncy, I show the sergeant my bloody teeth.

If I'm to learn anything from my writing, I'd have it be this: to behave in times of trouble like Billy Troy, a character I made up out of my own actions and wishes. I want to keep my own score. Faced with defeat and rejection, life's hard shots, I hope to keep smiling.

Loving Power

The title novella in a recent collection of my fiction is a black comedy about a professor of religion who sees himself as a loving power, but who in fact is in love with the power he has over others. The creator of fictional characters also loves power. As Jean-Paul Sartre, the philosopher whose works I read in college to the exclusion of most others, and whom I was pleased to learn had boxed a bit as a young man, discusses in *The Words,* writing is a god-like act as it gives the writer a godly power over his seemingly alive creations, his characters, and in that act lies the discovery and consequent fear of the self's possibility.

On one level the writer's desire may only be to rescue and preserve people and memories from the wash of time. In a novel I'm working on, *The Beginnings of Charity,* I've tried to fix in print the image of my uncle Francis L. Delora in the figure of Frank Dolan as viewed by his idolizing nephew, eight-year-old Patrick McCandless.

Uncle Frank was so big he took up the whole door. He had a big voice too, like God's. "Patrick!"

Patty ran right into his uncle like he wanted to knock him down, but it didn't hurt him, it only made him laugh. He swung Patty up as easily as if he were a baby and hugged him with powerful arms that nearly crushed the breath out of him. Frank's broad chest felt as hard as a board and his ironed white shirt was stiff with starch. He smelled of pipe smoke and whiskey. His wide hands were hot on Patty's legs and back. His close-shaven face looked as big and pink as a ham.

Frank set Patty on his own two feet, then let himself down into the red leather easy chair, the seat wheezing as the air was squeezed from it. He ran a heavy hand back over his steel-gray hair. There were deep folds and wrinkles in his leathery skin. Just above his left eyebrow lay a bullet-long scar as silver as a dime. Part of it was hidden by the gold rims of his glasses. He wore a gold wrist watch on a brown leather strap and a gold wedding ring with a big rock of a diamond on top. His gold Detective shield he kept in a polished brown leather holder and wore in the outside left breast pocket of his gray suit coat. He lit a fat-bellied brierroot pipe, and lifted his glass of whiskey from the tray.

Patty stood beside the tiled fireplace.

When the glass was empty Frank looked at Patty. "Well, what are you waiting for?"

There was always room on Frank's lap, even with him holding a glass and a pipe and his hard belly bulging and with the Colt Police Positive holstered on his belt.

I believe that it's honorable work to honor your dead by preserving their memory, and that it has its emotional rewards. My play *Jupus Redeye* deals in a comical way with my mother's life growing up on a sandy and unproductive farm ruled by her traveling salesman father. Its humor, I believe, derives from her irrepressible spirit and her refusal to be defeated by events. Like my father, she delighted in stories, although the ones she told were less prone to stressing heroics and more likely to highlight the melodramatic. This seems to have been a life-long habit of hers, and my play takes its title from the name of an imaginary creature she'd made up as a child; for the thrill of scaring herself and her brothers she would relate bloody accounts of this magical red-eyed monster who hungered for a meal of unprotected children.

The first time I saw the play performed was in a production put on by our community theatre, and the role of Minnie Jane Wing, my fictionalized mother, was played by my real-life daughter, Nora Jane Flanagan. Although it pleased my ego to see an audience emotionally moved by actors saying my words, what struck me more forcibly was to witness my daughter acting the part of my mother, doing so in such a convincing way that it seemed she was becoming the character, and displaying in her behavior—perhaps discovering in herself—those traits that made my mother such an admirable person: courage, tenacity, generosity, and that startled, helpless outburst of liquid laughter that seemed to come from an overflow of the soul. I felt as if I were watching my mother deep in the pleasures of her childhood, as yet oblivious to the hard demands that the future would make on her. But of course I knew that the Minnie Wing before me was the product of my informed guesses about her life as a girl, my laborious construction and revision of a difficult script, the theatre group's many rehearsals, and night after night of Nora reciting her lines in bed before going to sleep. And I knew full well that the beings named Minnie and Nora remained separate from one another, as they both did from that being bearing my name. Yet for a short space of time, witnessing the fleshed word, I had an inkling of what it might be like to have that power which Victor Frankenstein sought for the betterment of humanity.

Your mother comes alive in your play, one of my cousins told me, and I thanked her for the compliment. However, I was aware that the image I'd managed to preserve in words had been drawn from my memory and imagination, based upon my partial view of the subject, and strained and colored by my personality with all its impairments and capabilities. As much or more than she, it was I who was revealed in the play. To lean on Sartre again: You can write anything you choose—it's an act of freedom—but you learn that in the act of writing you are defining yourself, and that your new creations are unrecognized projections of your self, serving as both masks for and clues to that self. So one of the joys of writing, bringing characters to life, is closely linked to one of the fears, dredging up things from the depths of imagination and memory, and giving objective form to these found parts of yourself for others to see, for yourself to see.

A few years ago I sat in a cramped and dingy, urine-scented off-off Broadway theatre as part of a tiny audience watching a performance of another of my plays, *Volleys,* a black comedy about an inept firing squad in a state-sanctioned execution. I was very nervous. Now I am usually uneasy when presenting my work to the public, and *Volleys,* subtitled "A Cruel and Unusual Comedy," is a play that strives to affront just about everyone. At this particular production, however, I was suffering the added anxiety of watching our older daughter Anne play a part in my script. Not that she wasn't doing a good job as Fox, the activist actress who cracks under the group's pressure to conform and her own desire to be accepted, and had the role been better written she could have done a better job. But as I watched the staged action, I became aware of an unforeseen danger in her performance. When Anne had been cast, I'd mentioned to her that she shouldn't have too hard a time getting into the part as the character was an actress of about her own age. And now, watching her play Fox, I could see that she had managed to identify to some degree with her fictional counterpart, and was drawing upon the resources of her own personality to bind together the disparate and at times contradictory elements of the role. That was what troubled me. How fully was she absorbing the mind set of a play which, as I had come to recognize not long after the excitement of writing it, amounted to little more than verbal tap dancing at the brink of the abyss, a script containing more denial, than discovery, of meaning? Exactly to what degree was she identifying with Fox, a self-destructive personality? Might Anne come to feel that the role represented something of the way in which I saw her? And might that feeling stay with her on a deeper level than my disclaimer could reach? Would my brittle little fiction in some way *script* her behavior, and not for the better? Define her or help her to define herself in a darker way? Nudge her toward acting out the role off stage as well as on?

At first, I felt surprised that I hadn't foreseen such psychological jeopardy. Then again, as a writer I habitually run this risk of identification. My own emotions serve as yeast activating the doughy fictional characters formed from my observation of others' behavior and habits; in my novel *Maggot* I identify with all three main characters, the idealist Adamczyk, the cynic Waite, and the ambivalent Midberry, because in some ways they each represent me at different stages of my life, as does perhaps the harsh, dark-hearted Sergeant Maguire. I'm used to exaggerating the flaws or contradictions I find in myself as a way to create conflict in the narrative. It's a risk become so familiar that it has faded into the background of my creative activity, like a dangerous, chained dog one passes each day on the walk to work. But there are moral stances and psychological attitudes I allow myself in my work which I do not let into my family life, recognizing as it were a division between the real and the imagined, the lived and the written. As I've said at times in arguing with some writer about an extreme stance or thesis: You can *think* that, but you can't *live* it.

Since the NYC run of *Volleys,* however, I have seen no signs that Anne was damaged by her brief stint as Fox. Overall, I judge the experience to have been a positive one: father and daughter acting as independent adults collaborating on a work of dramatic art, and one which managed to keep a large part of its small audience awake. Yet it served to remind me once again of the dangerous power one wields as a writer, and as a parent.

We all are conditioned by our pasts and have received messages, overt and covert, intentional and unintentional, from our parents. One of the reasons that writers write is to discover what role they play in the story of their life, and what the shape and meaning of that story might be. Making fiction of your past is a way of coming to terms with it, of coming to understand it in a new way, of cracking the code.

One of the earliest poems I published, although not one of my most accomplished, expressed in metaphor a situation I would come to understand psychologically only many years later.

Memories of an Obedient Childhood

My father in his scar-tissued wisdom
warned me never to walk away from a fight.
My mother, her thin lips tight,
believed each sin held its moment of choice.

My father, urging me to get ahead,
recounted the lives of Carnegie and Ford.
Greed was the cruelest sin: Charity
the chief virtue, my mother said.

Fixed in my dreamings, my father complains
from under the old Dodge he kept running
  somehow.
My mother peels potatoes at the sink;
cautions my life with one cocked eyebrow.

For years, in the pendulum arc of my will,
I've been walking away and walking toward;
never before now have I seen so clearly
how for years I have stood perfectly still.

Conditioned by their own pasts, my parents passed on conflicting messages to me, and I took them in without recognizing on a rational level the conflict or its effect. But I had registered it on another level, one that a poem could reach. Because in poems sometimes, as with hypnotism, you allow yourself to know what you didn't know you knew. I've had this happen many times; a poem's images will open up new views and stances, discoveries which later I find informing the projects and attitudes of my narrative fiction, and sometimes those of my life.

My mother, prankster and storyteller, feared art was a way to escape responsibility and the necessity of work. My father, the most unworldly, kindly man, sang the praises of ruthless business success. For my part, I always have had a hard time accepting myself as a literary person, and too easily fall into the pretense of seeming a real-world kind of guy, a genial roughneck who every so often tosses off some bit of writing just because it seemed the thing to do at the time, though it's nothing that anyone needs to take seriously. When the truth is, writing is what I have in place of religion. It's the form of meditation I depend on to help me find a pattern amid the chaos. I story the world in order to make sense of it. Again and again I run up against my own limits, and at times stretch them, in making stories that attempt to express the whole of any one given situation. It's hard to figure out the hidden patterns though, and impossible to see things whole, as I suggest in this scene from *The Beginnings of Charity.*

That night they went out back of the apartment to sit on the roof of the Ideal Furniture store. The Mud Hens were at home against the Louisville Colonels, and the McCandlesses sat looking out over Detroit Avenue to where Swayne Field was shining under the high bright lights.

"Look at that," Dad said, "look how green! The way they take care of that field—boy, you could play pool on that grass, I bet." He put a hand on Patty's head. "And we're up here in our box seats, watching it free for nothing."

"Half of it anyway," Mom said, but she smiled at Dad. She didn't really care about baseball anyway. She hummed "Sheik of Araby" and "I Found a Million Dollar Baby in a Five and Ten Cent Store."

From where the McCandlesses were, you couldn't see the whole field from the roof because the grandstand got in the way. You could see the pitcher all right in his wind-up, but lost him in his delivery. You couldn't see the batter at all. But the third baseman, shortstop, and second baseman, the left and center fielders, you could see them fine.

Patty watched the pitcher wind up and then disappear behind the grandstand. The fielders jumped and then he heard the crack of the bat. The left fielder ran back to the fence, reached up with his glove hand, and there was a cheer from the crowd.

"Wait till the home team gets its turn at bat," Dad said.

No matter how closely I focus on them there are things that to this day I cannot see clearly or whole, experiences I'm not sure if I remember or only think I remember because I have reconstructed them, like fiction, from my own scraps of recollection and imagination and from what others say happened, such as the night of Uncle Frank's death. I believe that I once told a bartender who had a shotgun leveled at me that he didn't have the guts to pull the trigger. My line in the scene is exactly the one my father delivered on the night he stood blocking the door as his brother Jim, hopped up on heroin and gripping a loaded pistol, tried to force his way into our place. Did I unconsciously repeat my father's dauntless remark, which my mother and father told me he said, and which I am assuming he actually did say, or did my memory later rearrange the shotgun scene to include it? I no longer know.

Flanagan coaching boxing, 1976

Nor am I sure how or why boxing ever became such a big part of my life. My writing about it has been based more on my interest than on my experience—after the Toledo Y, I sparred a bit at Camp LeJeune and at the University of Chicago, and in my mid-thirties coached and boxed with college students in training for the area Golden Gloves. I'm nearly as horrified as I am fascinated by the sport. I watched, shocked and depressed, as Duk Koo Kim took a terrible, fatal beating at the hands of Youngstown's Ray Mancini. How can we in a civilized country, I have to ask myself, pay to see two men beat on each other? Although another part of me asks, why does that first fight between Joe Frazier and Muhammad Ali still seem to possess as much dramatic power as a Greek tragedy? And doesn't prizefighting, although brutal and frequently destructive, provide one with discipline, structure, and meaning—in much the same way that writing, another lonely and often unrewarded pursuit, does?

Of course a lot of my interest in boxing is part of my tendency to identify with the underdog, a role my family identified with, and which my father linked to being Irish. And much of my interest is simply a result of conditioning. Sometimes with my uncles present, or more often with just the two of us there, my father would rehash the old stories of the great boxing matches and great fighters—John L. Sullivan, James J. Corbett, Jack Dempsey, Gene Tunney—as if such talk linked us to heroes and in some way made us heroic as well. It seemed a harmless thing to do, and in the welter of that manly chat it went unnoticed—or at least unnoted—that the person telling the stories was my disabled veteran father, still in his old bathrobe at mid-day, a man too nervous to sleep nights, and who couldn't hold a job. On some level I registered the contradiction, even as a boy, yet willingly went along with the talk—as I eagerly went along with Dad when he felt up to going out to watch the Friday Night Fights on a bar's TV set, or to make the rare trip to the Toledo Sports Arena to see Carmen Basilio or Archie Moore. Why? Because our interest in boxing made us seem a more normal American father and son team; it was something I shared with him that we didn't need to feel ashamed of. "Fight Night" was an important part of our time together, as it is for Patty McCandless and his father in *The Beginnings of Charity.*

When the bell rang the men at the bar shouted and whistled. Now we'll see who's top dog!

Walcott came out of the corner, rocking his shoulders from side to side like a man walking a heavy chest of drawers into place. He flicked out a jab, another, bobbed and rocked, then turned sideways to Charles, moving off in kind of a waddle, like a strut, looking back over his shoulder to see if the other man was going to come along. When Charles followed, Walcott spun around and threw a right.

Patty chewed at his fingernails. He looked at the fight, then looked away. Dad was staring at the television, his face hot. He whistled and grinned, then groaned and shook his head. The men all shouted at once and Patty looked to see the fighters close together in a corner, their arms swinging. He turned around on the stool. On the wall across from the bar was a painting of a fighter getting knocked through the ropes and out of the ring. The other fighter stood with his legs spread wide and his left arm thrown across his body just finishing the punch. Patty spun on the stool. Dad lay a hand on his shoulder, saying Hey, hey. Patty tried to sit still. Listening to a fight on radio was exciting, it was like a story you were imagining, but seeing it really happen was scary. Somebody might get hit and go down and not get back up, ever.

In the mirror Patty saw the men at the bar looking up to the television set, like the people in the street when Mr. Pike had climbed onto the roof and said he was going to jump. The men's hands lifted bottles and glasses, cigarettes and cigars to their mouths. Smoke floated up in the light the way incense did at Sunday Benediction. The men told each other what the fighters ought to be doing, and how bad the fighters looked doing what they were doing. You call *that* fighting? They couldn't break an egg with either hand. All they wanna do's play pitty-pat! In the big mirror Patty looked at all the faces, his own soft pink one and his Dad's red puffy one and Sherm's bony yellow one and Sni's lumpy, leathery one, face after face on down the bar, all them looking serious, like the apostles in pictures of the Last Supper. Except for Sni's, none of them looked like fighters.

Patty looked back to Charles and Walcott. He knew they wouldn't cry like a kid, getting hit, but he was surprised to see that they didn't flinch or duck or back away. They acted like they were used to it. They stayed where they were and hit back.

When he wore his Lone Ranger mask, Patty made believe that it protected him and made him brave. The fighters looked like that was the way they felt. But they didn't wear masks over their faces, they made their faces into masks. It was like a fighter using another name to keep himself a secret, except this was another face. You kept it stiff and still. Whatever you were feeling, no one could tell.

Ezzard Charles won the decision, 78–72, 78–72, 77–73.

As a boy I pulled for Ezzard Charles, soulful as a jazz artist, or the monkish grand old man of pugilism, Archie Moore, wanting them to triumph over the raw natural force of Rocky Marciano. Dad called me a traitor to my race, and it surprised and disappointed me that he could let such a superficial thing as color influence him. As I saw it, the battle was not between white and black, but between the artist and the brute world. I see now that my father in his self-hatred and need to disguise himself as the American go-getter couldn't vote his conscience. The shouting matches we had over Marciano—a fighter I feared and despised! And Dad couldn't see that in arguing with him I really was defending him. *He* was the

aged Archie Moore unable any longer to keep the pace; *he* was the artistic Ezzard Charles ignored by the world in its rush to praise the crude but triumphant Rocky. What Dad and I really shared was a love of form, of art, of poetry. But I couldn't tell him that then because I hadn't come to understand it yet. If I'd understood it, I'd have never tied on a pair of gloves myself.

In my teens I took to boxing, I think, to prove myself tough and worldly, like my father before me being eager to fit in, to be known as a regular fellow, to avoid being defined as refined or artistic. Yet on a deeper level what interested me in the sport was precisely that it *was* an art, the manly art as it's been called.

Maybe boxing for me was a way to be an artist yet still be a man. Because somehow I'd learned, not so much by what was said as by attitude, that art was suspect. A man was a soldier, a husband and father, someone who could handle his dukes, and who went out into the business world and made a killing. My father had tried to do all these things and was a failure. But that never seemed to lead him to question his belief in the proper role of a man in the world, or his own suitability for that role. I had many doubts about *my* suitability for such a role, though I kept them to myself. Without thinking about it, sometimes as though following a script memorized so long ago and performed so many times that I'd forgotten it *was* a script, I went about acting out the various prescribed roles— boxer, marine, drinker, husband, father.

On still another level of self, a darker level, I think that my boxing was an attempt to deny and even destroy the artist in myself, an attempt not to open myself to my fears and face them, but to deny them by throwing myself into the teeth of danger, much as my father had done in charging off to war and thereby shattering the possibilities of the rest of his life.

In time I learned that I was trying to be something I wasn't. To again lean on Sartre, in boxing I was experiencing a desire for heroism which in effect is an attempt to escape the self, as later in my drive to become a writer (the refined Sartrian hero, the writer as knight or priest) I was drawn by the lure of the future to become something other than I was, to make my life a book, better yet to *become* a book, something more stable and permanent than fleshly existence, and to escape the fear of death by a premature embracing of the death of the self; in Sartre's words, to commit by a "flight forward" into the future "a simple-minded kind of suicide." Well, maybe. But

I know this much. What I loved in boxing, besides power, was the art, although it took me time to realize that, as it took me time to admit to myself that I loved what I found in art and literature even more than what I'd found in boxing, although that might have seemed weakness or disloyalty to my grandfather The Captain or my uncle Lt. Detective Francis Delora. I wished to live in the richness of literature, and to re-create myself in the creation of stories. Which in the Toledo frame of mind is okay if, like Hemingway, you get rich and famous by doing it. Then you're a regular guy who knows what makes the world go round and people will accept you as being as real as any sports hero or movie star. You knew what you were doing all along, didn't you? Folks just didn't get it until they read about you in *Time.* On the other hand, if you spend your days making up stories or drawing pictures and don't make a name for yourself or a living at it, then really you're sort of an odd ball, aren't you, just a little bit touched maybe? Because, let's face it, what kind of life is that?

Small Potatoes

When *Maggot* was published in 1971, I hailed myself at the start of a great career and went on to write three big novels which now occupy Hefty bags in my garage loft. The widely rejected manuscripts contained worthwhile sections, but so overreached themselves that they had collapsed under the strain. (The title of one, *More More More More,* provided an editor with an opening to say that as he'd read the work he'd kept wishing for "Less, less, less, less.") Such rejection was hard to reconcile with my expectations. "Brilliant! Unflinching! Epic!," I had imagined the blurbs declaring, and a jacket photo revealing me as woodsy and natural, casually cradling a shotgun in one arm, my golden retriever obediently at heel, my look directed away from the camera to the far horizon. Although now I can find the humor in such grandiose dreams, at the time repeated rejection pushed me to the edge of despair. Beginning to flinch, I switched agents. Then I wrote, or to word it more accurately *typed,* two thrillers I thought to

The Flanagans: (from left) Murphy (dog), Nora, Katy, Anne, Bob with Thelonious (cat), Christmas, 1990

be calculatingly commercial, and they too were turned down. Ten years had slipped past since my first novel appeared, and in that time—except for some poems, and a slim chapbook of stories from a small press run by my fellow writer, former student, and good friend Scott Sommer—I had published nothing. Considering *Maggot* mere meat and potatoes narrative, I'd brushed over it as only a precursor to bigger things. Yet the lowly original paperback managed to stay in print year after year, despite its lack of a classy jacket photo of the author. Events mocked any notion I'd had about my progress as a writer. I was turning out to be what every serious writer fears becoming: the one book author. What I wanted from writing was fame and power, what I got was rejection and depression. Fed up, I quit. For months I just *lived,* going about my daily life as a normal person might, and looking into possible hobbies; maybe model trains, I thought. Soon though, I found myself sneaking off to my study to sketch a brief scene or two from my mother's life, glimpses of her as a young girl that had started occurring to me after her death; the images and narrative fragments no doubt were prompted by grief, but also by my sister Mona's recounting of stories she'd heard about life on the Treloar farm, and by her persistent nudging me to write something about Mom to help us remember her. When my notes ran fifty some pages, I began to get cold feet. Not another novel, not more rejection! Besides, the narrative consisted mostly of dialogue, and all the scenes seemed to cluster about one weekend in 1912. Hardly the sweep a novel needed. About that time, some people from our community theatre asked me if, as the local writer, I'd be interested in writing a play for them to put on. Well, I said, though I'd written a couple of plays in college, I was no playwright, but thanks anyway. The next day as I looked over my scenes, I realized I was looking at a play. Since I had never set out to become The Great American Playwright, I felt free to try my hand at a play, and in writing *Jupus Redeye* I rediscovered the pleasure of creative work. Imagining my mother's life from the inside out in some way allowed me to see my own life from the center toward the edge rather than the other way around.

A few years after that, I put in a garden in our backyard. On a walk along the tracks I'd come upon a jumble of hard-used, apparently abandoned railroad ties, and with a friend's help loaded some into my rusty Chevy Luv truck and hauled them to my yard. I spaded up a space, boxed it in with stacked ties, and added clean fill. Later I drove out to another friend's farm where the horse stalls needed mucking out. An English professor used to such labors, I shoveled up a heaping load of manure, trucked it home, tilled it into the ground, and planted potatoes.

The garden occupied the rear of our yard, near to a black walnut tree and hard by a playhouse I'd built for our children. Put together from salvaged boards and bargain plywood, the playhouse was a slapdash affair nailed to the side of our garage like a squatter's shack. Little about it was level or plumb. Two squarish glassless holes served as windows, and a skewed opening in the front seemed an impressionist rendering of a door. Since the playhouse was no longer used, and its shadow encroached on the new garden, I set about taking it down. As I did so, I saw where our children had painted their names—Anne, Nora, Joe—in green house paint along the two-by-six headboard I'd used to support the plywood roof. I recalled then that for a space of seven or eight years, our daughters and their adopted brother had spent day after day playing in the little shack, and how in those days it had served as their clubhouse, hideout, castle, fort, steamboat, and spaceship, as solid a building as they ever could want. As was the case with *Maggot,* still in print, the playhouse's importance had become apparent to me only years after its construction. No longer did it seem scrap lumber tossed together to make do until such time that I could afford something better. Now, it appeared to have been a solid, though imperfect, piece of work that had lasted long enough to serve its purpose. I had been good enough as a carpenter for the needs of my children, I saw, a realization that gave me a delayed sense of satisfaction in my skill and achievement. I also saw that had I not suffered so much literary rejection, I might never have found the time to build the playhouse. What had seemed a roadblock proved to be a detour along the scenic route. And I recognized, as I do from time to time, that your life is a story you tell yourself as you go along, and one that you continually edit and revise. Regarding our lives we all are revisionists. When I took down the playhouse, for instance, our adopted and then unadopted son had found a home with another family, our daughters had gone off to college, and I was getting used to the fact that they were becoming the major characters of narratives in which I would play a minor, supporting role. It was an experience I'd prepared myself for years earlier in a poem.

Bob and Katy Flanagan, 1992

For Birds

Born beside an aviary,
our first child's talk
began as crow *caaas*.
Now three, she flies
about the yard
while her sister tries
to escape her walker,
flapping her arms
like a frantic gull.

With our care
and watching outward
we help them choose
the flight we made;
teach them to use
wings to accept the air,
and this picked branch,
the wide sky's root,
for jumping off.

What strange birds we seem—
sheltering from cats and wind
in a nest all openings.

At the end of that first season of gardening, I carried a colander of potatoes up to the house. Most of them were about the size of a handball, although one was nearly as big as a Grade-A egg. Maybe the black walnut tree's roots poisoned the ground, or maybe I used too much manure. "Ah, he's only small potatoes," my dad would say of someone whose achievements fell short of the grand and heroic.

That evening I boiled the new potatoes and served them in their skins with butter and salt. They made a delicious meal. And I felt then, as I still feel, that I no longer hunger to escape my known life for the illusory salvation of fame. I've come through to a point where I can say that it's all right if the world regards my work as small potatoes. What's important is that the potatoes are cared for, are not let go to rot, and offer you nourishment.

Another thing Dad used to say was, "Bobby, maybe someday you'll have an idea."

Maybe I have had one. Maybe this is it.

This essay was expanded from a piece published in *My Poor Elephant: 27 Male Writers at Work,* edited by Eve Shelnutt, Longstreet Press, 1992.

BIBLIOGRAPHY

Fiction:

Maggot: A Novel, Paperback Library, 1971.

Three Times Three: Stories, Ithaca House, 1977.

Naked to Naked Goes: Stories, Scribner's, 1986.

Loving Power: Stories, Bottom Dog Press, 1990.

Poetry:

Not for Dietrich Bonhoeffer, Crossing Press, 1969.

The Full Round, Fiddlehead Poetry Books, 1973.

On My Own Two Feet, Fiddlehead Poetry Books, 1973.

Once You Learn You Never Forget, Fiddlehead Poetry Books, 1978.

Plays:

Jupus Redeye (professional production), Contemporary American Theatre Company, Columbus, Ohio, 1985.

Teller's Ticket (screenplay), produced and directed by Sheldon Gleisser, 1990.

Volleys (professional production), American Theatre of Actors, New York City, 1991.

Contributor:

Ray Freed, editor, *Doctor Generosity's Almanac: 17 Poets,* Doctor Generosity Press, 1970.

Lucien Stryk, editor, *Heartland II: Poets of the Midwest,* Northern Illinois University Press, 1975.

Jim Perlman, Ed Folsom, and Dan Campion, editors, *Walt Whitman: The Measure of His Song,* Holy Cow Press, 1981.

Larry Smith, editor, *Best Ohio Fiction,* Bottom Dog Press, 1987.

Peter S. Prescott, editor, *Norton Book of American Short Stories,* W. W. Norton, 1988.

X. J. Kennedy, editor, *An Introduction to Poetry,* Scott, Foresman/Little, Brown, 1990.

Eve Shelnutt, editor, *My Poor Elephant: 27 Male Writers at Work,* Longstreet Press, 1992.

Contributor of stories and poems to numerous periodicals, including *Chicago, Fiction, Kansas Quarterly, New England Review, New York Times, Northwest Review,* and *Ohio Review.*

Joseph Hansen

1923-

"The cowboy," South Dakota, 1929

Aberdeen is a railroad town in the flat northeast corner of South Dakota, and I was born there on a hot July afternoon in 1923, in a spindly frame house on Fourth Street, across from a livery stable. My pretty sister, Louise, eighteen, a reader of novels and a writer of moody verses, hated the stink of that livery stable. I suspect my brother, Bob, age nine, had too much else on his mind—every kind of sport in its season, a sandlot baseball game on the day I came squalling into the world—to fret much over horse smells.

My father, Henry, born forty-one years before in Des Moines of Norwegian immigrant parents, was short, bald, devoted to awful cigars, and ran a shoe store on Main Street. He had a sweet tenor voice, and often sang solos at the First Methodist Church. He could play any musical instrument he picked up. He made up funny rimes on the spur of the moment, was clever at drawing, and was a marvelous mimic, especially hilarious with foreign accents, which were then fair game for comedy. He also built elegant kites and taught me to fly them. There was always plenty of wind in South Dakota.

My mother, Alma, aged thirty-nine when I arrived, was a small, dark woman with soulful brown eyes and a pensive mouth. She sang alto, played the piano, and taught all of us children to sing—church music but also tearful Irish tunes like "Mother Machree" and "Bendameer Stream," such Carrie Jacobs-Bond hits as "Just a-Wearying for You," and parlor favorites like "Somewhere a Voice Is Calling," whose writers' names I now forget. The attic of my memory echoes with dozens of treacly songs from those far-off days.

In 1927, we moved to a newly built house on the south edge of town—this time across from an apple orchard. Painted slate blue, with dark woodwork inside, it seemed cozy to me then. Old photographs I have looked at since show a gaunt barn of a place. Soon, I started school. Somewhere I have a photograph of that foursquare brown brick building, taken on a winter day, and it looks bleak. But I liked it, earned good grades, appeared in patriotic playlets and tangle-footed Maypole dances, and made friends.

I learned to read with great suddenness. I have never understood why. South Dakota was among the first states in the nation to embrace Progressive Education, a product of the solemnly lunatic mind of John Dewey. We were taught to read not with phonics but with flash cards. As we sat in a circle on little red chairs, a teacher would hold up a card with a picture of a horse on it, then turn over the card where the word HORSE was printed.

This was no way to teach reading, almost everyone had an awful time learning from it, and some did not learn at all. But it was fine for me. I saw some method in the madness which I could not then, nor can I now, explain. In *Colloquium on Crime,* edited by Robin Winks (Scribners, 1986), I've told how at age seven I was sick for many months, and how, alone for long hours every day, I chanced to read my first adult book, *Abraham Lincoln: The Prairie Years,* by Carl Sandburg. Not a bad writer for a youngster to start off with, who would in time become a writer himself. I would follow Sandburg with Jack London and Mark Twain, but not until a few years later.

In 1932, the Great Depression and the dust-bowl winds swept away the shoe store, the house, the car, and scattered our family. My sister, a graduate of Northern State Teachers College, who had for a time worked there as secretary to the president, went to try her luck in California. My father headed for Minneapolis to look for work. My brother thumbed his way from small college to small college, sleeping the nights in barns and haystacks. He had won medals in regional contests

"Me in my father's arms, my sister, Louise, my mother, and brother, Bob," Aberdeen, South Dakota, 1923

for his singing, and he hoped for a music scholarship, but his high school grades weren't good enough—he'd spent too much time on sports, playacting, and music.

My mother and I hung on in Aberdeen, moving from one dismal spare room to another—no doubt because my father couldn't send money for the rent. At one of these stops, seated by a window outside which bees tumbled in the blossoms of a lilac bush, I did my first writing. In an old stenographer's notebook of my sister's. It was plain to me that something had gone wrong with the country and, in a series of essays, I offered my ideas on how to put it right again. I titled this sage work "Philosophy from a Boy to Older Folks," and illustrated it with drawings in colored crayon.

In the summer of 1933 I got the surprise of my life when I stepped into the tiny grocery store near where we lived, to pick up a bottle of milk and a loaf of bread. "Charge it, please," I said. I always said that. The grocer, a skinny bespectacled man in a white apron, grabbed me by my shirt front, lifted me right off my feet, and told me he'd heard we were leaving town, and if my mother didn't pay him what she owed, he'd set the police on her. I was scared. And maybe my mother was scared too, but I doubt the grocer got his money. Where would it have come from?

Still, he was right—we did leave town. To me it was a fairy-tale flight. A beautiful, modishly dressed young lady drove us to Minneapolis in a new cabriolet with red leather seats and red wire wheels. Who was she? A stranger, at least to me. But with a kind heart. Glinda the Good? Why not? Minneapolis, however, was scarcely the Emerald City. We dwelt in dreary apartments and ate oatmeal. My father heaved coal into the vast basement furnace of some towering downtown church. With frostbitten fingers, my brother clambered around the outside of Sears Roebuck's upper stories, stringing festive SALE banners in the snow.

Minneapolis had many lakes that of course froze in winter when, to the delight of my father and Bob, who had feared I was hopeless at sports, I learned to skate. I was good at it, and spent every free hour I could on the ice. To my joy, I found that a couple of bullies who'd been making my life hell in the halls at school had weak ankles and could only flop around on the ice, helpless and red faced, shaking futile fists at me while I breezed circles around them, grinning. I could easily have knocked them down, and they knew it. They stopped calling me sissy after that.

Yet sometimes the snow piled up to the windowsills, and it was impossible to get to even the nearest lake—Powderhorn, it was called—and this was when I happened upon *White Fang* in our modest bookcase, and read it over and over again. Its only characters were dogs, which somehow comforted me. It wasn't dogs that had wrecked my world.

Still, after I'd pondered it doubtfully many times, the front illustration in a book of my brother's at last lured me away from *White Fang.* The drawing showed a fierce-looking bearded man in ragged clothes climbing in the window of a bedroom where a frightened boy cowered in a corner. I had to learn what that was all about. And thus began my reading and rereading of *Huckleberry Finn,* surely the best of all American novels.

It's not a book for boys, but Twain's disgust at the casual viciousness of white people toward blacks was clear to me from my first trip on that raft with Huck and Jim down the Mississippi. *Huckleberry Finn* is not only a stunning piece of writing, but a good book by a good man about a world that needed then as it still needs all the goodness it can get. I expect I took in this lesson unawares, but when I began to write novels myself I found I expected this stress on goodness from them too. I hope it sometimes shows.

After three hardbitten winters in Minneapolis, my mother and father decided between themselves to sell whatever they still had, including my mother's beloved piano. With the money, they bought a stately if mortally wounded old Marmon automobile. The plan was to go to California, where if we continued to starve, at least we wouldn't freeze. Instead of alerting me to this plan, they shipped me off to stay with cousins in Duluth. Bob was kept in the dark as well. He was on the road with a down-at-heel theatrical company that mostly performed in barns, and rarely got paid.

When the wife of the company's owner began to breathe passionately in his ear, Bob fled. He arrived home in Minneapolis to find no one there. The folks had written him a letter, but too late. He didn't know where they'd gone. They had gone to Owatonna, a German-speaking southern Minnesota town, my mother's birthplace, where her older sister Edith still lived, with a gawky son, my cousin Galen, half-blind, but a whiz at things electric and mechanical. (I loved their house, and moved it to California in my novel *Job's Year,* where it becomes Oliver Jewett's boyhood home.)

Because Tony Erchul, my Duluth cousin, worked for the county, when the folks sent for me, he arranged for me to get halfway to Owatonna in a limousine filled with crippled charity children on their way to therapy in Minneapolis. I sat in front with the chauffeur, who scared me with how fast he drove. He was a great kidder, and when he put me on the bus, knowing how nervous I was about traveling alone for the first time in my life, gravely charged the driver not to forget that I was to be dropped in—Mankato.

The driver, of course, dropped me in Owatonna, where I belonged. Bob at last arrived there too, and as soon as Galen was able to get the Marmon into running condition, we tied cartons and suitcases all over her, and set off in the furnace heat of July 1936, for California. We had enough money for gasoline and food but little to spare for overnight stops, and we slept in ancient, gone-to-seed hotels, or shacky tourist cabins, four to a room. In one such place, the only water came from a leaky tap outside the cabin door.

As the majestic old Marmon rolled westward along the scorching highways, my mother slumped in the backseat, sweating and moaning. I was afraid the heat was going to kill her. But I was the one who passed out, to be shocked awake by water from a garden hose splashing over me. I lay on my back on a small patch of grass, and a sunburned farmwife in a J. C. Penney housedress stood over me, laughing easily, hosing me down, and saying, "Come on, now, sonny. Wake up, boy. You're all right." Where was that? Nevada? Possibly. If so, our nightmare in the sun was almost over.

My beautiful sister, Louise, who was a typist for a bank, lived with her foundry-worker husband, Joe Hubbard, among ten acres of grapefruit, lemons, limes, in Altadena. Joe kept bees that produced magnificent honey, dark and heady with sage. But however charitably and cheerfully the scheme began, moving three more adults (Bob was by now twenty-two) and a child into a one-room cabin led to friction. I was enchanted by the place, where deer sometimes peered in at us through the windows at night. I spent hours outdoors shooting at tin cans with the BB gun Joe Hubbard had given me, reading, daydreaming, playing with a trap-door spider I located under a hulking old pepper tree. In Minneapolis, I had written stories. Here I wrote poems.

But Bob, though he'd been working at some pretty dreadful jobs, was appalled when Joe Hubbard demanded he hire on among the hellish fires of the foundry, and moved out. When winter came, with its rainy nights, and the porch proved unsleepable, my father and mother and I left too—for spare rooms in the wisteria-covered cottage of one Miss Criss (she looked exactly like her name) in Pasadena. Here I labored earnestly at putting the Psalms of David into modern English. I don't know why. Perhaps as a form of prayer. God seemed to be ignoring us.

My father found occasional work as a shoe clerk, but the pay was poor, and the jobs chancy, so we were soon again, and often afterwards, on the move, in search of cheaper rent. This meant making shift in the cheerless brown rooms of other people's houses, but it was surely harder on my parents than on me. Humiliating, hopeless. I was a child. I got used to it. It was simply how things were.

I joined a boy choir at an Episcopal church, where I learned plainsong and the glorious English of the Book of Common Prayer. The choirmaster-organist was Raymond Hill, charming, humorous, gifted, who took special interest in me. I was often at his house, where he saw to it that I heard a wide range of good music. His collection of records was fabulous—almost every week new shipments arrived from England, Germany, Italy. Browsing his shelves of art books, I began to learn something about painting, sculpture, architecture. He wangled me into a private school for brilliant boys where, with my stunted background, I was instantly lost, and survived only one wretched term.

Raymond sailed off to Rome to study Gregorian chant, and I returned to public school, where I soon became a chorister again—this time with a boy choir drawn from schools all over town, and shepherded by John Henry Lyons, a gigantic man who never wore any color but green. Even his shoes were green. The choir had three hundred members, but a core of thirty boys sometimes used to travel to nearby towns for recitals, usually at Christmastime. We were forbidden to sing on our way to these events, but on the way home in the bus, we sang our hearts out. The exuberance of those nighttime shouts of song echo among my happiest memories.

When we staged an all-boy version of "Pinafore," I was inspired to try my hand at writing a comic opera just like it, words and music—but my invention flagged after a lively opening chorus about sailing on the Tappan Zee. Soon I was eagerly typing out reportage with two fingers for the John Marshall Junior High School paper. Later, I was proud to be named its editor. I appeared in school plays, and won a gold medal for

dramatic recitation and a silver one for public speaking—or was it the other way around?

The reason fundamentalist Christian characters sometimes figure in my novels and stories is that for a couple of years in my teens I fell among these people, at one point stooping so low as to become president of my Christian Endeavor group, a Sunday school teacher, and the lead singer in a gospel quartet. I attended vast evangelical youth conventions, and went to summer camps in the mountains where these sanctimonious children gathered in God's Great Outdoors not simply to hike, swim, ride horses, but to pray, sing, study the Bible, and be preached at without ceasing.

To try to snap me out of this unattractive phase, Raymond Hill—back from Rome with Doctor tacked to the front of his name—gave me *Elmer Gantry* to read. It didn't turn the trick. But when I reached such a peak of hysteria that I announced to my parents I had been called by God to become a minister, they did something they'd never done to me before, no matter what wild career—artist, actor, singer, symphony conductor—I'd proposed for myself. They laughed. And that brought me to my senses. They were good Christians both, but they saw that I'd gotten in too deep and that the time had come to drag me ashore.

Someone long ago posited a connection between religious mania and sex. And at this point, sex was plaguing me. My suddenly lanky, six-foot-tall body was giving me surprises I didn't know what to make of. To that point, I must have been the most completely asexual child who ever lived. Now, suddenly, here came rushing at me a whole new set of impulses I didn't want and couldn't handle. This was almost certainly why I fled to the arms of Jee-zuss. Other boys at that church, I now realize, were also scrambling to escape their homosexuality, though I didn't know it then.

In the midst of this confusion, in 1939, I started at a new school, Pasadena Junior College, which offered the last two years of high school and the first two of college. I met a set of shiny new friends, some of them two or three years older than I. With my smalltown, Midwest origins, I was not sophisticated. These youngsters dazzled me with what I took to be their maturity and worldliness. To my delight, they accepted me in spite of my rusticity, and I hurried to adopt their attitudes. Luckily I had a talent for mimicry.

I reported for the school newspaper and acted in stage and radio plays. For one of these, Dickens's *A Christmas Carol,* I wrote the script, with George Hodgkin, the most dazzling of my new chums. I hung out with them in cafes near the campus, talking, smoking Domino cigarettes, drinking coffee, listening to the jukebox. On sunny afternoons when we ought to have been in classrooms, we might pile into cars and head for the beach, or up into the rugged canyons above town, to read poetry, or hold grave adolescent discussions about the meaning of life. I worked after school as a page in the public library, so sometimes I had enough money to join them at movies in the evenings, and afterwards for hamburgers at drive-ins.

By now, my father had found a steady job selling shoes in a department store, and we were living in a small house by ourselves, on a run-down little street shaded by old pepper trees. For that house, that street, forty years later, I wrote an elegy in *A Smile in His Lifetime.* I had my own room, at last, but I'd seen the large, handsome houses of my new friends, and met their prosperous parents, and I was ashamed for them to see how shabbily I lived with parents who were old and poor. This was not only mean-spirited toward my parents, but shows how little I knew the good hearts of my friends. I had a lot of growing up to do.

With Robert Ben Ali at a play in Pasadena, 1942

As best I could with the small money that came my way, I began to fill my room (and my head) with books—Shakespeare's plays, Poe's tales, Walt Whitman's *Leaves of Grass,* Thoreau's *Walden* and Emerson's *Essays.* Whitman startled me by writing of feelings I had supposed doomed me. I had dreaded being classed with the mincing men my cruder schoolmates jeered at on the streets, or with a willowy distant uncle of mine, who in simpering middle age wore rouge and lipstick at his job behind the counter where customers paid their bills at the Pasadena gas company. Whitman's manly ease with his sexuality eased my worries, and Emerson's "Self Reliance" urged me to be myself, no matter what the world might think.

But books, however wise, weren't enough. And for all the friends I had, I still felt lonely. Robert Ben Ali took care of this. Portly, and as Arabic in looks as his name suggested, he was a local *wunderkind,* whose play *Manya,* written at age seventeen, had been staged to nationwide publicity: one of its student actors, Bill Beedle, was given a movie contract that launched his career as William Holden.

Ben Ali's play was about Marie Curie, and for a while he and his mother clung to the hope that the studios would buy it to turn into a picture. Marie Curie's story did reach the screen, but not in Ben Ali's version. As to Holden, after his early success in *Golden Boy,* Ben Ali, with a car full of other youngsters who'd been in school plays with him, drove over to his Beverly Hills mansion to congratulate him. Holden refused to see them. Ben Ali was philosophical about it: "I suppose he was afraid we'd come to ask favors." But I could see that he was hurt.

He was more than lover, he was mentor, counselor, comforter, a spellbinding talker who flung open doors for me into the worlds of Homer and Socrates, of James Joyce and Jean Cocteau, of Rimbaud and Baudelaire, the music of Eric Satie and Igor Stravinsky, and Lord knows what and who else. I've been lucky all my life in my friends. They have been my university—the only one I was to have or to want.

Ben Ali lived with his mother in a tiny book-filled house on Allen Avenue, and was finishing up his studies at PJC. He continued to write plays and to direct plays at school and at the Pasadena Playhouse, where he saw to it that I got an education in theatre—there was a summer festival of all the Shakespeare comedies, another of famous American stage hits of the past—*Clarence,*

The College Widow, The Baby Cyclone. All lavishly mounted, with first-rate professional casts. There were Ibsen and Strindberg and Chekhov. There was Onslow Stevens as a hulking Richard III, and a rumbling-voiced, gold-helmeted Odysseus in a play by Emil Ludwig. There were Restoration comedies dressed in velvets, lace ruffles, and silver shoebuckles. There were funny, sentimental Saroyan plays—*Jim Dandy* and *My Heart's in the Highlands.*

Lucille Ben Ali, a short, fat woman with a splendid nose, worked as a performer with delightful marionettes that she made herself. Her parks and recreation department paychecks kept food on the table, but it was not until Ben Ali took a night job at Lockheed Aircraft that they could afford a car, a wooden-sided station wagon. America was in the war by then, my brother, Bob, was in hazard day and night on a Navy minesweeper, my shining friends had scattered, to the army, navy, air force, Coast Guard. I dealt with the draft as did Oliver Jewett in *Job's Year,* and I won't repeat the story here.

I drifted restlessly from job to job—midnight want-ad tallyman for the *Los Angeles Times,* announcer for a tiny Pasadena radio station, page at the Henry E. Huntington Library and Art Gallery in San Marino, and in Hollywood at the Pacific Aeronautical Library. Still living with my parents, I wrote poems and plays. My heart lifted when a friend promised to get a play of mine produced at Christmastime on the new LA television station. Titled "I Have Been Here Before," it was about Jesus returning as a man to Bethlehem, and to the stable behind the inn, where he'd been born. That there were as yet few if any television sets in the city for anyone to see my play on didn't worry me. And it needn't have—the play was never produced.

In February 1943, I got a job clerking, for eighteen dollars a week, at the Pickwick Bookshop on Hollywood Boulevard. The bus ride from Pasadena took an hour, so with my typewriter, books, and clothes, I left my parents' roof in favor of a rented room on Yucca Street, a block from the store. I was thrilled to be living on my own at last, and immediately began to write a novel. Hell, wasn't it about time? I was nineteen. I had a lot to say, didn't I?

The cavernous bookstore and my dusty work there I have described in *Living Upstairs.* I've put into that novel also the wonderful jazz clubs that flourished along the shadowy night boulevard in those times, and the immortal performers—Jack Teagarden, Erroll Garner, Jimmy Noone, and

others—I got to hear when for the price of a watery highball I could buy an enchanted hour on a wobbly stool at the bar. I was too young to drink legally, but so were most of the servicemen on leave who crowded these places, kids from the sticks, most of them, wide-eyed at being in fabulous Hollywood.

Now and then some non-hick would sit next to me and try to coax me to take him to my room for sex, but I was leery of strangers. For sex I wanted a friend, and I already had one. Ben Ali and I saw each other every weekend, driving in his trusty bangwagon to restaurants, galleries, concerts, ballets, the beach if there were gasoline coupons. But our time together—three years of it—was running out.

One Saturday morning, a young woman called Jane Bancroft came into the shop, saw me carrying an armload of books up an aisle, and for reasons still mysterious to me decided I was the boy for her. At that time, Jane was operating a router, a messy and dangerous job, at the Vega aircraft plant, and in her off-hours at home was designing glorious patterns for textiles. Slender, narrow-hipped, tall for a girl, she wore bell-bottom jeans and cut her hair short like a boy's. I found her a treat to look at.

A Boston Brahmin, descended from the Massachusetts Bay Colony's first governor John Winthrop, she'd passed much of her childhood with her mother's family in Texas, where they also were old blood. Her self-assurance bespoke aristocratic heritage, all right, but her arresting vocabulary suggested the stables of Fort Bliss, the Army cavalry post at El Paso, where she'd spent a girlhood among horses, and the stockyards, where she'd worked cattle from horseback.

My single experience on horseback had resulted in a misunderstanding between me and my glum old mount, and I'd lost interest in riding then and there—so that side of Jane's experience didn't draw me, but she had a lively mind, had read widely, retained what she read, and could talk about it glowingly. Here was a bright new friend to learn from. Her interests ranged from the war news on the radio (and the political motives behind it) to the ancient Chinese poetry of Tu Fu and Li Po, from T. S. Eliot's theology to that of Boethius—she was reading *The Consolation of Philosophy* when we met—from Leonardo's drawings to those of Paul Cadmus, from Wanda Landowska's Bach recordings to the conductor Frank Black's current broadcast series of Mahler symphonies. If Ben Ali

With daughter, Barbara, and wife, Jane, in Hollywood, California, 1945

had read to me with vivid excitement all the Socratic dialogs, Jane had in her memory every myth in Ovid's *Metamorphosis*. My head grew dizzy, and my heart soon followed. We were married on August 4, 1943, at Los Angeles County courthouse, ate lunch in Chinatown, and rode home by streetcar. I had been given a whole day off for my honeymoon.

Our odd apartment I've described in *Living Upstairs*. We were lucky to get it—housing was hard to find during the war. And at first, fate smiled on us there. My account of the courageous struggle of Esther Takei, a Japanese-American girl, to return from internment camp to go on with her schooling in bigoted Pasadena, was published in a national magazine, *Common Sense*. Houghton Mifflin optioned a new novel I'd begun, after I'd scrapped the first one on Jane's advice. And in July of 1944, our daughter, Barbara, was born, one week short of my twenty-first birthday.

Then as surprisingly as it had struck, luck deserted me, at least so far as writing went.

Houghton Mifflin didn't want the novel once it was finished. And though I kept writing, nobody would buy a line I wrote, not articles, not short stories, not poems, not plays, and not novels. The publisher's enormous $500 advance was long gone, and I was back working.

Sometimes, to give me more time to write, Jane would take jobs at the Pickwick and other bookstores along the boulevard, while I kept one eye on the typewriter and the other on the baby. Except for our love for each other, these were years when it seemed always to be raining. It grew hard to keep believing in myself. I took to starting new novels, plays, stories, and not finishing them. What was the use? They all came limping back.

I missed singing, making music, and scraped together enough pennies to buy an autoharp. In the late 1940s, Burl Ives, Richard Dyer-Bennett, and Susan Reed had begun to sing folk songs, and I was fetched by their recordings and worked up a batch of songs on my own. Not that I craved a career in music. Writing was still my aim. But my generous friend from high school, George Hodgkin, now working at a big LA radio station, heard me sing and decided I ought to have a program on the air. He named it "The Stranger from the Sea," wrote the introductory copy, and produced and directed it.

It aired every week from December 1951 to December 1953. A small record company, Tempo, issued a couple of albums that sold well in and around LA. But they and all the broadcasts put together had earned me very little money for all my time and effort. And so I was relieved when George left radio for television, and "The Stranger from the Sea" was canceled. All my spare hours had gone into researching songs, arranging and memorizing them, and writing copy about them for the broadcasts, so for two years, I'd had no time for writing—or trying to write. I was glad to have that time restored.

Back in 1951, Jane's mother had made us the gift of a small house in the Hollywood hills—it figures in *A Smile in His Lifetime*. We had good times there. We added some interesting new members to our cat population, and Jane, in return for looking after a neighbor's horse, got to ride him whenever she wished. There was enough wilderness around us in those days to make riding a pleasure. Little Barbara had taken a liking to reptiles, and had as pets a handsome brown-and-yellow-banded king snake and a dignified desert tortoise who enjoyed Mozart. Then came a young horned owl with a broken wing whom we all took turns looking after until he mended. Cuthbert matured into a magnificent specimen, and after he soared off to live on his own in our wooded canyons, I wrote an article about him for *All-Pets* magazine.

But it grew clear to Jane and me that if we three were going to eat and have clothes to wear, one of us had better find steady work. I had been trying to sell encyclopedias door to door, but my heart wasn't in it. A friend of ours at the Technicolor plant in Hollywood got me a job there as a clerk-typist in the shipping department. It was dreary, but it meant a paycheck every week, so at the same desk, in the same windowless cinder-block room, I kept at that job for ten long years, writing when I could, but with dimming hopes.

In 1954, at my sister's house in Pasadena, my father died of pancreatic cancer, aged seventy-one. He was a sunny man and always good to me. I still dream of him. And only the other evening, when I stepped into the kitchen for something, I smelled smoke from his cigar. It was as if he'd left the room only a moment before.

Tom Lengyel, a young Hungarian with illustrious screenwriter relatives but whose own luck at the studios had been spotty, asked me for help in 1955. He had an in with the story editor of the television series "Lassie." If he could come up with scripts, he was sure she would buy them. The hitch was, he knew nothing about American farm life. This was where I came in. Jane furnished the story ideas, and between us—Tom standing at my shoulder teaching me scriptwriting as we went along—he and I turned out two episodes, "The Greyhound" and "The Hungry Deer," that were, for a fact, accepted, filmed, and broadcast. But I hated the writing process—everybody interfered, producer, advertising agency, sponsor, even Lassie's trainer—and I swore I would never again write for television. I was happy for Tom to have the screen credit—and most of the money, since he needed it worse than we did. After all, I was working.

Then, in 1956, I had some real luck with my writing. John Ciardi bought a poem of mine for the *Saturday Review* about a childhood episode in South Dakota. I wrote another with the same setting right away and the *New Yorker* bought it. And another, and another. The small checks didn't mean I could quit my job, but they were useful. For a year earlier, we'd taken in to live with us a recently divorced and penniless young woman friend and her three little kids.

"The Stranger from the Sea," 1952

This required more room than the small house in the hills afforded, and in 1957 the crowd of us moved into the low-roofed, green-sided, French-windowed house in southwest Los Angeles where Jane and I still live. By 1961, Jane was teaching steadily, and our friend Froncie, whose kids were now in school, also had found a job, so I was able to quit Technicolor and take a four-hour night job at a bookstore. This gave me more time to write, but still it was 1964 before I managed to sell a novel, and that to probably the least-distinguished publisher in the United States—or the world, for that matter. But before we get to that, let me outline what led up to the novel.

A year or two earlier, Wayne Placek, a friend and lover, alas now dead of AIDS, had introduced me to Don Slater, a feisty little Navy veteran, a gay activist long before the term was coined. He edited a small magazine for homosexuals called *ONE,* and soon he began publishing my short stories. Though by today's standards as chaste as a Sunday school paper, yet simply because of its subject matter, *ONE* sometimes ran into trouble with authorities, postal and other. So the paper's policy was that all its writers use pen names, to protect them from arrest and prosecution, possibly even jail. I protested, but Don was adamant, so I became James Colton.

And when, after publishing a handful of stories, I decided to try a novel along the same lines, figuring I might have a fan or two, I stuck with James Colton. Now, there was no graphic sex in "Valley Boy," but it shunned the tacitly agreed-upon formula of earlier homosexual novels—sin, suffering, and suicide—so no one in New York would touch it, not even the reputedly fearless Harlan Ellison, then head of a paperback imprint called Lion Books.

Finally, in desperation, I sent the tattered manuscript to Les Aday, who issued pulp-paper pornography from, of all unlikely places, Fresno, California. He gave it a soppy title, *Lost on Twilight Road,* and chose cover art featuring, unaccountably, a naked woman, but he did have the guts to print the book, and so, however humbly, I was a published novelist at last.

If this account of a *New Yorker* poet unable to find a decent publisher for his novel seems unlikely to you, you came into the world too late to know the fear and loathing a writer faced who, thirty

Barbara with Cuthbert, 1953

years ago, treated homosexuality as simply another element of everyday life.

In 1965, Don Slater made me an editor of *ONE* magazine, and I soon saw that it urgently needed to change. The homosexuals who were our readers already knew what we were telling them. The straight world did not. If things were ever to improve for us, it was the straight world we must educate. This caused a rift at the magazine, with the result that one midnight, Don Slater, aided by a tough, wiry friend who owned a furniture van, stealthily whisked *ONE*, lock, stock, and barrel, out of its old headquarters to a place miles away, in Cahuenga Pass.

Threatened with lawsuits, we changed the magazine's name to *Tangents.* With no money, but with a smart, new design, sometimes even a dash of color, and with a lot of hard work, we kept it going for five years. I wrote editorials, articles, stories, book reviews, and a monthly column based on news clippings sent in by readers from around the country. Jane designed striking covers, drew graphics for the inside of the book, wrote reviews and an advice column. But by 1970, large circulation magazines like *Cosmopolitan* and *Playboy* had begun treating homosexuality candidly and sometimes even with goodwill and common sense. We had become redundant. Subscriptions dried up. We couldn't pay our printer. And we folded.

In the midst of all this, I kept writing novels, not ambitious in scope, but aimed at telling the truth. I was exploring what I had begun slowly to realize was my subject. *Strange Marriage* appeared in 1965 from the mail-order wing of Sherbourne Press, a new Los Angeles publisher. A collection of the stories I'd published in *ONE* and *Tangents* followed from Evergreen Classics, a busy San Diego publisher of gay pornography.

Then in 1966, I wrote a novel that I sensed was better than the first two by quite a stretch. But again, New York wanted nothing to do with it, nor did a swishy but firmly closeted editor at Sherbourne Press. And the novel ended up two long years later as a paperback from Brandon House in North Hollywood, whose editors insisted I add graphic sex scenes, and called it *Known Homosexual.* It is in the shops these days as *Pretty Boy Dead*—without the sex scenes.

Also in 1966, Jane, working at a newsstand, came upon a magazine called *South Dakota Review* and brought a copy home to me. Some years before, I'd written a story called "Mourner." Like several of my poems, it was based on a Dakota childhood memory, but though I'd sent it around, no editor had wanted it. John R. Milton at *SDR* liked it, and soon printed it. I've recounted the thrill of that in *SDR*'s twenty-fifth anniversary issue (winter 1988), where the story makes a reappearance. John Milton not only founded and edited a first-rate literary magazine in an unlikely place, he kept it going through thick and thin, gave a lot of writers breaks, and I'm proud to call him my friend.

In *Pretty Boy Dead* I'd tried on for the first time the murder mystery form, and I felt I'd been less than successful with it. So I tried again. My aim was to write a book about a homosexual that heterosexuals would want to read, and there's no form that keeps readers turning pages like a mystery. But it must hew to the expected lines. I worked hard at this, and the result was *Fadeout*, featuring an insurance death-claims investigator, Dave Brandstetter, whom the *New Yorker* would later call "thoroughly and contentedly homosexual." I knew it was the best book I'd yet written, but again no establishment publisher would accept it. The year was 1967.

The two novels that followed I wrote hastily. I had lost my bookshop job, and I felt, having wasted months on a novel no one would buy, that it was past time I brought some money into the household. Jane and Froncie were both working. So was Barbara by now, at a nearby electronics plant. I owed it to them to do my part. So I'm afraid there's not a lot of literary quality to *Cocksure* and *Hang-Up*. While they have some serious things to say, both are melodramas overloaded with pornography. But they did find publishers, of a sort, and the money did help.

I had begun writing another such novel, *Gard*, when life took a surprising new turn. Without warning me, a young New York writer, Leo Skir, who had sent me outstanding stuff when I was editing *ONE* and *Tangents*, showed my books to his agent, Oscar Collier, who then wrote offering to represent me. He sold *Tarn House* right away, a little Gothic novel I'd written in 1967, when such stuff was crowding the supermarket racks. I'd submitted it to eight or ten publishers, but hadn't been able to sell it on my own. On the strength of some chapters and an outline, Oscar sold *Gard* as well, to Michael de Forrest, at Award Books. As to *Fadeout*, he asked me to have patience. I knew what that meant, but wondered bleakly if he did.

Michael de Forrest, himself a novelist, advised me to scrap the melodrama and murder I'd had in mind for *Gard*, and simply write the story of the two main characters, a thirty-something writer of

children's books, and a supposedly retarded seventeen-year-old neighbor boy, as their relationship develops through a seaside summer of loving and learning. I saw this as a chance to challenge the straight world's notion that homosexual men only exploit and abuse youngsters. Often they do, which is criminal. But sometimes they understand where others cannot or will not, and give unselfish help—emotional, educational, material.

But writing this nearly plotless kind of novel marked a change for me, it was difficult, and took time. When I had finished, I was pleased and moved by what I'd done. But by then, de Forrest had been fired and replaced by an editor who, without consulting me, gutted the novel, so I scarcely recognized it when the printed book arrived. I was outraged, but I had no money for lawyers, and no time for lawsuits.

It stuns me to realize now how I crowded my time in the 1960s, and how much energy I had. Not only was I working at the bookshop (until March 1966), editing *Tangents*, writing novels, playing the guitar, composing songs, singing on Saturday nights at a little restaurant, and painting

Being James Colton, 1969

pictures (a couple of which actually sold), but in October 1967 I began conducting weekly poetry workshops at the Bridge, a hippy bookshop in East Hollywood. I've described the place, its flower-child denizens, and their dreamy, drugged-out life-style in *A Smile in His Lifetime.*

The Bridge's life was brief, and in February 1969, a poet friend, John Harris, discovered George Drury Smith's Beyond Baroque gallery and printshop in Venice Beach, and we moved the poetry workshop there. I left in 1974, but the workshop persisted for at least a decade more, always open to all comers, always free of charge, sometimes argumentative, even explosive, but often good-humored and funny, and sometimes genuinely productive. Some good poets—James Krusoe, Lee Hickman, Kate Braverman, many others—took part, all of us teaching each other, learning from each other.

Toward the end of 1969, Oscar Collier telephoned me from New York—Joan Kahn, the Great Lady mystery editor at Harper and Row had accepted *Fadeout*. Jane was teaching in her class-room in Santa Monica, Froncie was typing in an office near the airport, Barbara was assembling electronics at the Avnet plant, the youngsters were in school. I told our dog, Bantu, who lifted her head, wagged her tail once, lowered her chin between her paws, and went back to sleep. I told such of our snoozing cats as I could locate. Then I began ringing up anyone I figured there was a chance of reaching. This was the biggest and best news I would ever get in my life, and I simply had to tell someone, anyone. No one answered.

Alma Rosebrock Hansen died in February 1970 in the intensive care unit of a San Diego hospital, after a massive heart attack. She was eighty-six years old, and had outlived my father by sixteen years. These years she had spent with my sister, Louise, also a widow now, in a city whose glorious climate gave her back her health. Later, after an engineering career with various aircraft companies that took him from LA to Tucson to Pascagoula, Bob also settled with his wife, Hannah, and their children in San Diego, so though I never visited my mother there—we didn't get along—she had a loving family around her. I flew to San Diego to be with her at the end, but her mind was jumbled, and she didn't know me.

My reaction to having, after years of struggle, at last gained a first-rate book publisher was in some ways sensible—I hung up my guitar, I put away my paints and brushes, I was about to have a

With friend and writer Beryl Bainbridge, London, 1975

career. But then how can I explain to you or to myself plunging ahead in a kind of panic to write, this time for Olympia Press, two more sexually graphic James Colton novels? Part of the answer must be that deep down I didn't trust my good luck. I feared the Harper and Row connection was a fluke, and would never repeat itself.

The Outward Side was written in fifteen days, and shows it. Its subject—a young, married minis-ter in a small town, trying to cope with his homosexuality—deserved better treatment. In *Todd* I tried to make up to Frances Green, my very nice editor, for such a rackety first book with a better one. The concept for *Todd* came in a rush late one night, when the house was asleep. I sat alone leafing over a favorite anthology, and chanced to read again John Crowe Ransom's moving lines, "A cry of absence, absence in the heart / And in the wood, the furious winter blowing," and saw a whole novel in those lines. I could hardly wait till morning to begin to write it.

Todd gives glimpses from inside of the boister-ous gay liberation movement in the LA of the

1960s, but more interestingly to me, in the character of Todd, when he flees in fear from the chance to have a career as a concert pianist, and settles for playing "Stardust" in gay bars, I realize now I was depicting my own failure of nerve about tackling another book for Harper and Row. I had panicked. I couldn't remember how I'd fitted together the mystery plot of *Fadeout.* I was sure I couldn't manage it again. I used still another dodge. I took to broadcasting on the local Pacifica radio station a program called "Homosexuality Today" that popped the eyes and strained the tolerance of some of the left-liberal old guard at the station.

Then came *Fadeout*'s publication day, and good reviews, and I felt better. *Death Claims* was slow going, but in the end it proved to me I needn't worry about plotting. I had the knack. What I didn't have a knack for was making money. However good the press they received, the Brandstetter novels sold poorly. And paperback publishers had at that time stopped issuing reprints of any mysteries not by Agatha Christie. So when Oscar Collier telephoned one day to say he could get me three thousand dollars fast from some paperback outfit if I'd send him the outline of another Gothic novel, I did as he asked. And started writing the book.

But Oscar decided on his own that my proposal was too good for paperback, and showed it to Joan Kahn, who bought it at once. Now, my reading had equipped me with enough period detail to have written a paperback set in the South in 1880 without taking time out for research. But for a hardcover novel? From a major publisher? Jane brought me stacks of books from the library. I groaned, but to my surprise, I enjoyed the research. Harper and Row packaged the book handsomely, it sold well, and brought me letters from New Orleans readers praising how well I'd pictured a place I'd never seen.

By this time, the autumn of 1974, I was living in London on a grant from the National Endowment for the Arts. I'd completed the third Dave Brandstetter adventure, *Troublemaker,* just before I got the astonishing news about the grant. I'd scoffed at the idea that a mystery writer stood a chance, but I'd applied at the repeated prompting of Alexandra Garrett, of Beyond Baroque. Sadly, Sandy is no longer living. But I will always be grateful for her cheerful nagging. I had a big novel to write. This grant would buy me the time.

London was terrifically romantic to me, crowded with associations from a lifetime of read-

With editor Ken Thomson, in Aldeburgh, England, 1975

ing. It seemed as if around every corner I ran into some name or sight that evoked a literary past I could link up with in my memory. The present was exciting too. I made friendships I still cherish— with the delightful novelist Beryl Bainbridge; with Ronald Harwood, the playwright who would later triumph with *The Dresser;* with Charles Osborne, biographer of Verdi and Schumann and Wagner, and a witty and erudite companion.

Ken Thomson, my lighthearted editor, whirled me around London in his red mini, visiting all the sights, and into the countryside as well to lunch in thatched villages, stroll through historic churches, climb the towering ruins of castles. With a neighbor, the stately, white-haired, drolly humorous Eric Walter White, retired head of the literary division of the British Arts Council, I saw operas and ballets at Covent Garden, and an awful *Yeoman of the Guard* at Saddlers Wells.

I saw at the Old Vic—of which my Cypriot taxi driver had never heard—Dame Peggy Ashcroft in Samuel Beckett's *Happy Days,* the best of his plays. I tramped through an endless Turner exhibition at the Royal Academy, and a rowdy Augustus John show at the National Gallery, got up by another friend, the biographer Michael Holroyd. With Michael, Beryl Bainbridge, Ron Harwood, and the gifted and personable poet David Harsent, I traveled to England's bleakly beautiful northeast, to make appearances in schools and pubs, reading our stuff and answering questions. On that trip we visited Hadrian's Wall, got a glimpse of Sir Walter Scott's fabled Cheviot Hills, low-lying, hazily blue, and climbed among the rocky ruins of Lindisfarne, the green and windblown Holy Isle.

But alone in my basement flat through the long nights of a London winter, and the brief, gray, rainy days, I wrestled with that wretched novel and got nowhere. I had a stupid love affair, drank too much, got into absurd scrapes, and wanted to go home. Back in Los Angeles, I put away the novel with a shudder, and got cracking on a new Brandstetter mystery. This was *The Man Everybody Was Afraid Of,* and to my stupefaction, Joan Kahn rejected it, claiming the plot was "put together with paperclips and bandaids." Before my luck changed, fourteen more publishers would vote with her. Those were scary months.

Meantime I began teaching weekly night classes in writing, first at Beyond Baroque, then at the Irvine campus of the University of California, and finally at UCLA. I loved teaching, and would go on with it for ten more years, winding up with four summers at Wesleyan University's writers conference in Connecticut. New England was

another land rich with literary associations for me. And again I made new friends, among them the amiable conference director Jack Paton and his dear wife Sybil, the talented poets Dana Gioia and Henry Taylor, and the genial novelist George Garrett.

Henry Holt bought *The Man Everybody Was Afraid Of* in 1977, and began in 1980 to issue the earlier Brandstetter books in paperback, giving them new life. About this time, I chanced to tell a young writer friend, William Harry Harding, about my abandoned big novel. On a trip to New York, he mentioned it to Natalie Chapman, my Holt editor, Holt offered me a contract, and at last *A Smile in His Lifetime* got written. Five years had distanced me from the pain of the events I wanted to recount. I had thought through the point of the story, and how the book should be laid out. Bill Harding helped me generously with money to stretch the Holt advance, I wrote the novel with a high heart, and there were good, if sometimes shocked, reviews.

In 1970, I had written a little novel, *Backtrack,* that had never yet reached print. Sometimes this was because it was rejected, sometimes because managements changed and/or companies collapsed. In any case, twelve years later, it was still on my hands when, out of the blue, Lou Kannenstine of Countryman Press in Vermont wrote asking if I had anything he and his partner Peter Jennison might print. The moral is that a writer must never give up hope. So far as I know, *Backtrack* is still in print in Penguin paperback.

In New York in 1982, I met the handsome and likable Eleanor Sullivan, editor of *Ellery Queen's Mystery Magazine,* with the result that for the first time since *Tangents* folded I began to write short stories again. I've detailed this meeting in the introduction to *Bohannon's Country.* It would later, after years of maneuvering on my part, bring an end to *Ellery Queen's* ban on stories involving homosexuality. That introduction also tells how and why Hack Bohannon came to be, about whom I've now written some ten stories—which suggests that the six-year-old cowboy in that 1929 photo still lurks inside the graybeard he has become.

I met with some bruising reversals in the early 1980s, and my anger resulted in *Job's Year,* the story of an actor who, after a lifetime at his craft, decides he has misspent his life. Still, its first sentence begins with "He hopes . . ." and so does its last, and I think it is perhaps my best novel. For *Nightwork,* as often for the Dave Brandstetter mysteries, I chose a headline subject, the illegal

Jane with Fargo, 1984

dumping of toxic wastes in wilderness places. One reviewer noted that I had in this book come up with a new motive for murder—an uncommon event, if true. I dedicated *Nightwork* to Bob Ben Ali, and I'm glad I did. Grown frail from diabetes, and walking with a cane, he had only a year to live.

Steps Going Down I tackled as an exercise in writing a kind of crime novel different for me— with the killer instead of the detective as the central character. I had thought it would be easy— no complex plotting needed. It was not easy. I struggled with that book and its unsavory cast for fifteen wretched months. Because of the sheer awfulness of the story and everybody in it, it's the one book of mine that always makes me laugh aloud. With *Steps,* and with *The Little Dog Laughed,* I was temporizing. I'd been asked often when I was going to write about AIDS. And I shrank from the task.

But I owed it to my readers and finally steeled myself to read every scrap of paper I could find with words on it about AIDS. Once past the initial revulsion, I was so deeply moved, so emotionally involved, and found so much drama in this grisly situation that when I at last sat down at the typewriter, *Early Graves* wrote itself in five short months. It was a book I felt mattered. My publisher didn't give a damn.

Joseph Hansen with Sherpa, 1990

In January 1986 Louise Hansen Hubbard died in San Diego of emphysema. She was eighty years old, and had been in failing health for some time, though her mind remained sharp to the end. I have a fuzzy color snapshot of her in her last months that moves me, because in it she sits surrounded by copies of my books, clutching *Job's Year* to her breast. Until I saw that picture, after her funeral, I had no idea my work meant anything to her.

All his life, Bob Hansen was active in little theatres, playing parts in comedies, musicals, dramas wherever he lived. He enjoyed it immensely, and with his talent gave pleasure to a lot of people. Recently, he lost his wife, Hannah, and he lives alone now, in San Diego. His daughter and her husband and kids live nearby, and see him often. Sometimes, even at age seventy-eight, he hops into his Volvo and travels to visit old friends around the state. Now and then, he talks of going to see Aberdeen again, but I don't think he will—the high school burned down, so did the First Methodist Church, and all his friends left long ago.

While I was writing *Obedience,* about the Vietnamese community in Los Angeles, an odd

thing happened. People and events from my teen years began invading my mind, clamoring for attention. They wouldn't go away. And once I'd finished *Obedience,* I gave them their head and wrote a sprawling novel called "The Kids at Moon's." The cold reception it got from publishers I've recounted in *A Country of Old Men,* through the character of Jack Helmers, a grouchy old mystery writer.

I later rewrote and shortened "Kids" and, while it went the rounds in New York, I wrote a sequel, *Living Upstairs,* about my early days in Hollywood. It wasn't exactly snapped up, but thanks to thoughtful networking on the part of a caring friend, mystery novelist Michael Nava, it eventually reached the right editor.

Starting with "Kids" and *Upstairs,* I'd planned to write twelve novels about Nathan Reed, from age seventeen to seventy. Unrealistic for a writer crowding seventy himself? I didn't think so. One of my reasons for ending the Dave Brandstetter series was to clear the time. I was going to be writing, anyway, for as long as I could sit up and think, and I wanted to give some shape to my own life and times.

But for now, while I wait to see what happens to "The Kids at Moon's," I've put the third Nathan Reed novel aside, and am having fun writing short stories, trying angles new to me, as in "Molly's Aim" and "McIntyre's Donald." Those appear in *Bohannon's Country,* but I've written two more since, and a third is underway. I mean to have finished off five before 1992 runs out.

For 1993, I have only one plan. On the fourth of August, Jane and I will open a bottle of champagne. It will be our fiftieth wedding anniversary. Will we eat Chinese food? Why not? Hell—if we can find one, we may even ride a streetcar.

BIBLIOGRAPHY

Fiction; under name James Colton:

Lost on Twilight Road, National Library, 1964.

Strange Marriage, Argyle Books, 1965.

Known Homosexual, Brandon House, 1968, revised edition published (under name Joseph Hansen) as *Stranger to Himself,* Major Books, 1978, revised edition published (under name Joseph Hansen) as *Pretty Boy Dead,* Gay Sunshine Press, 1984.

Cocksure, Greenleaf Classics, 1969.

Gard, Award Books, 1969.

Hang-Up, Brandon House, 1969.

The Outward Side, Olympia Press, 1971.

Todd, Olympia Press, 1971.

Fiction; under name Rose Brock:

Tarn House, Avon, 1971.

Longleaf, Harper, 1974.

"Dave Brandstetter" mystery series:

Fadeout, Harper, 1970.

Death Claims, Harper, 1973.

Troublemaker, Harper, 1975.

The Man Everybody Was Afraid Of, Holt, 1978.

Skinflick, Holt, 1979.

Gravedigger, Holt, 1982.

Nightwork, Holt, 1984.

The Little Dog Laughed, Holt, 1986.

Early Graves, Mysterious Press, 1987.

Obedience, Mysterious Press, 1988.

The Boy Who Was Buried This Morning, Viking, 1990.

A Country of Old Men: The Last Dave Brandstetter Mystery, Viking, 1991.

Fiction:

A Smile in His Lifetime, Holt, 1981.

Backtrack, Countryman Press, 1982.

Job's Year, Holt, 1983.

Steps Going Down, Countryman Press, 1985.

Living Upstairs, Dutton, 1993.

Short-story collections:

(Under name James Colton) *The Corruptor and Other Stories,* Greenleaf Classics, 1968.

The Dog and Other Stories, Momentum Press, 1979.

Brandstetter and Others: Five Fictions, Foul Play Press, 1984.

Bohannon's Book: Five Mysteries, Countryman Press, 1988.

Bohannon's Country: Five Mysteries, Viking, 1993.

Contributor:

Different, Bantam, 1974.

Killers of the Mind, Random House, 1974.

Literature of South Dakota, University of South Dakota Press, 1976.

Year's Best Mystery and Suspense Stories, 1984, Walker & Co., 1985.

Murder California Style, St. Martin's, 1987.

Mammoth Book of Private Eye Stories, Carroll & Graf, 1988.

City Sleuths and Tough Guys, Houghton, 1989.

Rotten Rejections: A Literary Companion, Pushcart, 1990.

Under the Gun, Plume, 1990.

Other:

One Foot in the Boat (poetry), Momentum Press, 1977.

Contributor of fiction to *Alfred Hitchcock's Mystery Magazine, Bachy, Ellery Queen's Mystery Magazine, Mystery Monthly, South Dakota Review, Tangents, Trans-*

atlantic Review, and other literary magazines. Contributor of articles to *Armchair Detective, New Review* and *The Writer.* Contributor of poems to numerous periodicals, including *Atlantic, Harper's, New Yorker,* and *Saturday Review.*

Hugh Hood

1928-

Hugh Hood, in the garden at home, about 1990

Every family has four extended myths to choose among for ways to identify itself, the lines of descent of four grandparental surnames. For us the names were Hood, Macdonald, Blagdon, and Sauriol. Three of these lines of descent surface in my own full name, Hugh John Blagdon Hood, quite a mouthful for a young child to master. I got Hugh from my great-grandfather Big Hugh Macdonald of Guysborough, Nova Scotia, a district so full of Macdonalds with the same given names that individuals had to be distinguished by nicknames, as much as by those given in baptism. My great-grandfather was Big Hugh because he was a very tall man. Maggie "the flea" Macdonald weighed in at over two hundred

pounds, while Maggie "in the sky" Macdonald lived on the top floor of the bank, at four storeys the tallest structure in town.

These Macdonalds were Highland Catholics; my grandmother Kate Macdonald Hood could speak Scots Gaelic as well as English, and her mother was unilingually Gaelic-speaking. They were my father's people on his mother's side. The Hoods were something else again, a west-of-England seafaring family whose activities for hundreds of years were focussed on the Royal Navy in all its actions at home and abroad.

On my mother's side we identified ourselves with Blagdons on one side, people with an ostensibly English surname, but in fact French-speaking

Father, Alexander Hood, "in the height of juvenile fashion," Yarmouth, Nova Scotia, 1909

and not much concerned about their English origins. There are several villages called Blagdon in England. Ours was most probably Blagdon Hill, a small place ten miles southwest of Taunton lying under the Blackdown Hills. Blagdon, most probably a local pronunciation of Blackdown, sent its boys to sea from small ports on the Bristol Channel. My grandfather Alfred Esdras Blagdon was a descendant of sea captains from thereabouts, but by the time of his birth in the early 1870s his family was French-speaking, many of them living in the port and shipbuilding center of Lévis, directly across the Saint Lawrence from Québec City. My grandfather Blagdon's mother, Aubéline Lemieux, was *une Québécoise de vieille souche* who spoke only French. He in due course of time travelled as far west as Montana, where as a young man he taught French in a local school, afterwards returning to Toronto where he married my maternal grandmother, Eugénie Sauriol, in the mid-1890s. My mother, their only child, was born in

Toronto in 1896 and christened Marguérite Cécile Blagdon, a name anglicized by herself in early childhood to Margaret Cecil Blagdon.

My mother was a canny child who considered that her future lay in English-speaking Canada, more specifically in Toronto. She expected to live her life in the bosom of the English-speaking community there. She had many French-speaking relatives among the extensive Sauriol family who came to Toronto at the close of the nineteenth century. But when I was a child in the Toronto of the 1930s my mother was reluctant to acknowledge this link. We saw little of our Sauriol cousins, even though my grandmother Eugénie Sauriol Blagdon lived with us, off and on, for many years after Grandfather Blagdon died in 1933.

My French connection, the Sauriols, came to Québec from the city of Rennes in Brittany before 1680, just at the close of the first great wave of immigration from northern France to Québec. They are a numerous clan, easy to trace in the pages of Québec history. A Pierre Sauriol, then a man in middle age, married a young woman in her late teens in Montréal at the beginning of the eighteenth century, and lived there until his death in 1740. His grave can still be identified in the Montréal suburb of Ville Saint-Laurent. His descendants moved to Ontario in large numbers; many of them established themselves as stonemasons in the town of Perth in eastern Ontario, preparing huge stone building blocks to be used in the extension of the Rideau Canal along the Tay River towards Perth. Later, hearing that a similar canal was to be constructed as a freshwater conduit between Lake Simcoe and Toronto, some of these masons moved to Toronto in the hope of long-term employment on the project, which never came to much. These Sauriols—my grandmother Eugénie was one of eleven children—established the Toronto beachhead of the family towards the end of the gaslight era. One married pair of Sauriols, my great-grandparents, had the misfortune to asphyxiate themselves, when they blew out what they thought was the candle in their Toronto hotel room. They had extinguished the gas jet, and were found suffocated next morning. Their grave can still be seen in the earliest Catholic cemetery in Toronto, Saint Michael's, on Yonge Street near Saint Clair Avenue, now at the heart of midtown Toronto.

Sauriols, Blagdons, Macdonalds, Brétons, British, Highland Scots, plenty of variety there, and some complexity of religious belief, a reproduction in miniature of the early social structure of Canada. The final element of our family life, the Hoods whose surname I've borne all my life, are if anything more essentially Canadian even than the Sauriols, Blagdons, or Macdonalds because of their British origins and readiness to unite themselves to Scots or French. I am one-quarter Scot, one-quarter French, half west-of-England. In the year of my birth, 1928, you couldn't get more Canadian than that. Of course the ethnic mix of the population of Canada has altered radically since. There are now substantial Asiatic communities: Chinese, Japanese, Korean, Vietnamese. There is an enormous Italian community; there is a rich and powerful Jewish representation in the Canadian population. In 1928, though, the English, French, and Scots had things much their own way as far as defining what the word Canadian, *Canadien,* meant.

I've always been acutely conscious of the mixed aspect of my family inheritance. My friend Clark Blaise once inscribed one of his books, "to Hugh Hood, *the* Canadian." Elsewhere Clark has remarked, "Hard to be more Canadian than Hugh Hood." Much of the best writing in Canada has been done by people who have come from somewhere else, the enormous body of Canadian immigrant writing. Adèle Wiseman, Clark Blaise, Rohinton Mistry, John Metcalf, Brian Moore, Irving Layton, Audrey Thomas, Nino Ricci, and hundreds more have enriched Canadian literature immensely by the variety and color of their work. Neil Bissoondath, Marlene Nourbese-Philip; the list is very long. The Canadian who was born here of French-Scottish-English stock is no longer *the* Canadian, and hasn't been for two generations. All the same he remembers the very recent past, when to be a Canadian was to be French or Scots or English or all three.

It was the Hoods who were most prominent in my childhood imaginings. We had the usual family myth of the nobleman in the background. For us, Samuel, Viscount Hood, 1724–1814, and his brother, Alexander, Viscount Bridport, 1727–1814, were our *ancestors.* They conferred an entirely fictitious special status on us. I've got a picture of the first Lord Hood in my dining room. It's perfectly true that my father's paternal ancestors were Hoods from Dorset and Somerset. It is also true that they seem to have used the same four male baptismal names for five hundred years: Samuel, Alexander, Arthur, and John. The graveyards of western Dorset are full of Sam and Alex and John and Arthur Hoods. My dad's name was Alexander Bridport Hood, but he was no viscount,

no peer. His name had been a Hood name for two hundred and fifty years *before* the sailor Alexander Hood, a very tough old bird, was ennobled as Viscount Bridport. What was genuinely *ours* was the name Alexander.

My father was Alexander Hood. My brother is Alexander Hood. My brother's son is Alexander Hood. My elder son is Dwight Alexander Hood. My younger daughter is Alexandra Hood, and my new little grandson is Alexander Hood. By the same token my grandfather was John Hood. My uncle was John Hood. My younger son is John Hood, and I'm Hugh John Hood. Somehow or other Big Hugh Macdonald muscled his way into my name. I often wonder who was responsible for the choice.

This custom of taking children's names from a very small repeating lexicon—Alexander, John, Arthur, Samuel—seems to be found all over the world; its origins are easy to guess. There is a remarkable sense of solidarity with family, and of

Mother, Margaret Cecil Blagdon, "taken before her marriage, while she was working in New York City," 1923

personal identity, conferred by the awareness that you are the tenth or fiftieth bearer of a familiar given name.

Growing up in Toronto in the early 1930s, the depression years which came down very heavily on underpopulated and economically dependent Canada, the years depicted in *The Swing in the Garden,* a sense of communion and shared self-knowledge was a bulwark against the overwhelming presence of our neighbours to the south who insisted on describing themselves as *Americans.* They were from the *United States,* which was only the bottom half of North America. We were just as much Americans as they were and, if they only knew it, our country was bigger! That battle was lost somewhere around 1965. The most chauvinistic Canadian journalist now concedes that America means the United States, and neither Mexico nor Canada. The Brits always use America to mean the United States, and now I find myself doing it.

It was a complex fate, in the 1930s, to be a Canadian. We knew that we should hate the Americans; they had such an exaggerated opinion of their national greatness. In the flyleaves of our spelling books there was a full-color illustration of the Union Jack, and underneath it the caption, "One Flag, one Fleet, one Empire." In the third-grade classroom we sang "The Maple Leaf Forever."

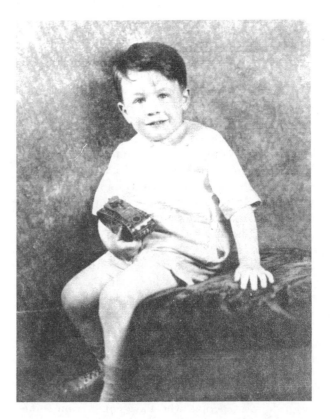

Hugh Hood in a posed child-portrait photograph at the age of three: "I carry a toy tank, perhaps a Christmas present," Toronto, 1931

> In days of yore, from Britain's shore,
> Wolfe the dauntless hero came
> And planted firm Britannia's flag
> On Canada's fair domain.

Forty years later we might wonder jokingly who "firm bra Tanya" was, but as little children our hearts swelled with local patriotism for Canada's fair domain, and we knew that we should have no truck nor trade with the Yankees. Sir Wilfrid Laurier had lost the reciprocity election of 1911 by trying to introduce a modified form of free trade with the Americans, and somehow we all understood why he'd lost.

All the same, in 1935 I addressed my reply to a Quaker Puffed Wheat premium offer to "Babe Ruth, New York" and my letter got there! I didn't think of Babe Ruth as an American, and everybody knew where New York was. Like all Canadians I loved and hated the United States. I did a brisk trade at the age of ten in the *Saturday Evening Post* and the *Ladies' Home Journal.* I earned my pocket money in this way and I knew

that I was just like the kids in Cleveland or Buffalo who delivered the same magazines.

Babe Ruth belonged to me just as much as he did to the boys in Buffalo. When I found out fifty years later that the Bambino actually hit his first home run as a professional ballplayer in *Toronto* on September 5, 1914, as a member of the Providence Grays of the International League, I felt deeply justified in my instinctive childhood feelings that in some way I belonged to a huge continental arrangement—call it a culture if you like—that included all the folks north of the Rio Grande.

I knew nothing about the Hispanic-American peoples at that date, and don't know much more now. Sometimes I think that they must be like our French-speaking peoples, and in the next breath I understand that they aren't. The French have from the beginning been a dominant cultural force in Canada, and I'm part of that force by ancient inheritance. The Hispanics in the United States seem to be in a different position that I don't understand and can't comment on. A different history and a different set of complex social relations.

Membership in the North American community was so easy then! I sold the *Saturday Evening Post*, which never by the slightest accident mentioned Canadian affairs. This ignorance was perfectly acceptable to me, and even reassuring. I felt acceptable to the *Post*'s editors and to the editors of the *New Yorker, Collier's,* and all the other great American magazines that I instinctively turned to later on when I started to write.

I took it for granted that these were the magazines that I should read and understand, more fully than the Toronto newspapers because more attuned to my personal mythology which was largely built up from the American mass media. Radio programs like those of the famous comedians: Jack Benny, Fred Allen, Edgar Bergen, and Charlie McCarthy. Comic books. Batman, Captain Marvel, and that creation of a pair of Toronto boys, Siegel and Shuster, Superman! I knew vaguely that the most powerful of the caped superheros was the invention of a pair of Canadians, but it was the Americans who launched him into the heavens of the mass imagination. America was the land of publicity opportunities. The all-Canadian comic books produced at home during the war years were ill-drawn, cheaply produced, without the profound grasp of the methods of mass communication so powerfully evident in the USA.

What I read in the *Post* were wonderful serials by the likes of P. G. Wodehouse and Agatha Christie. Never mind that both these writers were British-born. When I read *Uncle Fred in the Springtime* or *And Then There Were None* in late 1939, the format of the stories, their illustrations, their production values were unmistakeably those of the American communications network, in no way resembling the magazines published in Britain or in Canada at that date.

In 1939 in Canada there simply was no mass communications network. The audience for network radio was too small to add up to a "mass." Publishing was almost wholly a matter of circulating small Canadian printings of books published somewhere else. Perhaps ten books annually written by English-Canadian writers might be published in Canada without also appearing in Britain or the United States. The sale of these few books would be very small. Canada was a country of one-book authors because these authors' first books invariably lost money for their publishers, and there was no risk-financing available for second

The author's wife, Noreen Mallory, at the same age of three: "She carries a golliwog doll of a kind no longer seen," Brockville, Ontario

books. Much English-Canadian publishing was in part subsidized by a church-related organization, the influential Ryerson Press of Toronto, which was owned by the United Church of Canada and published works of a religious nature, and as well much poetry and a very small amount of fiction.

When there was talk of publication of my first book in 1962, a generation later, no commercial house would touch it. The story collection *Flying a Red Kite*, 1962, appeared from the Ryerson Press, whose senior editor was Dr. John Webster Grant, a distinguished pastoral theologian. When Dr. Grant first read the title story in the collection he smiled and declared, "Ah yes, here we have Hood's defence of natural religion." And how right he was!

At the end of the 1960s the United Church divested itself of its holdings in the Ryerson Press, which then merged with an enormous American publishing house as McGraw, Hill–Ryerson, a

Hugh Hood, at eight years old, his sister, Barbara, at eleven, and his brother, Alexander, at five, "in their Easter finery, standing in the garden that had the swing in it," Summerhill Avenue, Toronto, 1936

striking instance of the secular arm of society supplanting the sacral in a great public work. This is a story so Canadian that only people like me can fully savor all its implications. Canadians have their subtleties and their shared mysteries too; they are as difficult to understand as the Hindu, Sikh, Muslim, or Buddhist inhabitants of the Asiatic subcontinent. This is a fact it has taken me a lifetime to learn.

M y grandfather, John Hood, was raised as a member of the Anglican Church of Canada, an institution of impeccably British allegiance. He must have considered himself an Englishman in pleasant exile. He was the first mayor of Shelburne, Nova Scotia, a place founded after the Revolutionary War by United Empire Loyalists who had come on from New England to preserve their British connections and allegiances. After more than a century as an unincorporated village, Shelburne achieved the status of a town in 1907,

choosing John Hood, always known as "the Squire," as mayor. He was also the town's leading lawyer, a King's Counsel, publisher of the Shelburne *Coast-Guard*, a good Anglican, and much else besides.

When he courted the beautiful Katherine Macdonald of Guysborough in the 1890s, finding in her a redoubtable Scots Catholic, he agreed to what was then known as a mixed marriage, and allowed their three children to be raised as Catholics. My father, my uncle, and my aunt were therefore the first "cradle Catholics" in the Hood family, and I inherited their religious beliefs. When I courted the beautiful Noreen Mallory sixty years later I found that she was an Anglican! I asked her to take instruction in the Catholic faith, which she did. She was received into the Catholic church not long before we were married, in a curious repetition/reversal of something that had happened a long time ago.

Our four children, born in 1958, 1961, 1963, and 1965, might all be described as believing

Christians, but none of them is practising Catholicism as I understood it from the time of my baptism. Looking back over these developments, seeing them as integrally related to modern Canadian history, I suspect that my Catholicism may seem odd and incidental in the main line of development of Canadian social ethics and religious practise across Canada in the twentieth century.

It didn't seem at all incidental in 1940. I would identify my religious education, the movies, and baseball as the three most formative elements of my childhood. Far more than hockey, baseball nourished my imagination and provided me, as an early adolescent, with an epic narrative. I thought of baseball as the sport dedicated to the life of spring and summer, and later found the fine book *The Boys of Summer* expressive of much that I'd felt about the game. I knew that the title came from an unlikely source, Dylan Thomas, who knew nothing about baseball, but I didn't care. The diamond game is the best game for spring and summer, and for October too.

It wasn't just that thousands of Canadians had played minor league or semi-pro baseball, nearly two hundred of them reaching the majors. It was the accessibility, the actuality of baseball as a spectator sport that persuaded me. When Babe Ruth hit his first professional home run for the Providence Grays, at the same time pitching them to a shutout victory over the Toronto Maple Leafs, he did it at the old ballpark on the northwest tip of the Toronto island, in a district that has provided a home for professional baseball for the rest of the century. In the mid-1920s the old island ballpark was superseded by the new steel-and-concrete Maple Leaf Stadium located just across the western entrance to the harbour, at the foot of Bathurst Street on the Toronto harbourfront. Then, when major league baseball arrived in the city in 1977, Maple Leaf Stadium having been demolished a decade earlier, the Blue Jays played their home games for more than a decade at Exhibition Stadium, not much more than a mile west of where Ruth hit that storied homer. Baseball has haunted the Toronto waterfront for nearly a century. Now the wonderful SkyDome is located in almost the same place, about a mile east of the stadium of the 1920s, overlooking the harbour and the Toronto island.

In 1942 and 1943 I could get into the pavilion seating at Maple Leaf Stadium for twenty-five cents. These were the seats in the main stadium structure that lay down the third-base line near the foul pole; the park had no bleacher seats in the outfield. A quarter to get in, a dime for peanuts, and a great afternoon. I used to buy the *Sporting News* and open it ostentatiously in my seat above the Leafs' bullpen, hoping that some member of the relief corps might ask to see it. My patience was rewarded one July afternoon in 1943 when Luke "Hot Potato" Hamlin, with the Toronto club on loan from the Pirates, spied the publication, then still full newspaper size, and said abruptly, "What you got there, son?"

"*Sporting News*, Mr. Hamlin."

"Lemme have a look!"

And he took my *Sporting News* and read it for the final five innings.

That was some kind of a revelation. We were just starting to come out of the worst consequences of the depression. Nobody had much money, and as we used to say, there was a war on. But a quarter and a *Sporting News* could put you in touch with the Immortals! "Hot Potato" Hamlin was a perfectly authentic major league pitcher. He had a long career as a moundsman with the Dodgers and

"All dressed up," spring of 1942, Toronto

later the Pirates. At the beginning and end of his career he made brief stopovers in Detroit and Philadelphia, but his most successful years were with the Dodgers, for whom he won twenty games in 1939! Nine years in the bigs, once a twenty-game winner, he could borrow my *Sporting News* any time.

This whole network of meanings was so darned present and available. I had a series of summer and part-time jobs in downtown Toronto during the war years, and on Saturday or holiday afternoons I could easily walk from there to the ballpark where anything might happen. The high school I attended used to give us a half-holiday for Opening Day. During the season opener of 1942 I saw the young Ralph Kiner, loaned to the Leafs for seasoning by the Pirates, slam the game-winning home run for our guys. He was an untried rookie, soon to disappear into the services, not to be heard from again for a few years. Afterwards he became one of the most feared power hitters in the game. In April 1942, we were the first to see what Ralph could do with one swing of the bat. His later major league career lasted only ten seasons, but oh boy, what a decade. And we Toronto high school kids knew about Ralph Kiner four years before any other baseball fans had even heard of him.

During those years from 1942 through the close of 1945, when I was in high school in my mid-teens, I saw many of my older male friends disappearing like Ralph Kiner into one of the services. Some of them never came back; news of woundings, prisoner-of-war status, losses at sea occasionally filtered back to those of us who were too young to serve. Sometimes I found myself hoping against hope that the war would last long enough for me to get into it. This was a foolish feeling. I was no hero, and would not have enjoyed the conditions of military service, the peculiar hours of sleeping and waking, the enforced obedience to incomprehensible orders. There was a clash in my imagination, not the first and not the last, between wishes and fantasies in which I figured as an adventurous hero, and intimations of chilling reality that revealed me as somebody distinctly unheroic, not very tall, not very strong, unfit to command a younger brother, never mind a regiment.

I was uneasily aware, as the war stretched into its fourth, fifth, sixth year, that terrible things were going on in Europe, North Africa, the Pacific, Southeast Asia, places where I had never been. I knew that Canada was a very comfortable distance away from even the nearest battlefield

and that if I was lucky the war would be over before I was eighteen, the age of enlistment. I often wondered in 1944, the year of D-Day, whether or not I would have the courage to try to enlist while still underage, the next year, say, when I'd be seventeen.

I never met this challenge. I was a very young-looking teenager, short, baby-faced, obviously underage for military service. I recall examining my smooth-skinned features in the bathroom mirror and hoping that I would soon have to start shaving. Then I could trot around to the University Avenue armouries and try to enlist. I used to try to figure out which branch of the forces would provide the smartest uniform and the quickest route to officer status, while at the same time keeping me furthest from any actual shots. The insistent split between romantic fantasy and the dreadful realities of war continued for a long time in my life, and perhaps the lives of millions of others. While the Jewish people were being subjected to race murder in Europe, we in North America knew—or would admit to knowing—nothing about it. We may have heard whispers and rumours of dreadful acts being carried out in eastern Europe but we refused to follow them up.

The first hard evidence I ever saw of the horrors of the death camps came immediately after the end of the war in Europe in May 1945, when *Life* published the first pictures taken in Buechenwald and in other camps immediately after their liberation by the Allied forces. These pictures were horrifying, shocking to a youth of seventeen. So this was what I'd been longing to confront in my fantasies! It certainly wasn't like the movies. I saw that I was lucky not to have been able to sprout a precocious beard. When the Japanese surrender took place immediately after the bombings of Hiroshima and Nagasaki in midsummer 1945, I was seventeen. I had just missed the chance of active service. My war was fought on the screens of the dozens of neighbourhood theatres in Toronto. Errol Flynn bombed the Germans into submission in one film, captured Burma in another. Stiff-upper-lipped British naval officers sank the *Bismarck* or battled U-boats in the North Atlantic, or fought under the improbable command of Noël Coward in his tribute to the Royal Navy, *In Which We Serve.* I think Coward's impressive uniforms in his role as Captain, especially his magnificent officer's greatcoat, did my imagination more harm than any other erroneous flight of self-representation at the time or long afterwards.

It took me half a lifetime to purge my mind of mistaken flights of imagination indulged during the years from 1942 through 1945. No, I wasn't a hero. No, I wouldn't look impressive in naval uniform. Yes, I was frightened of guns and didn't want to handle them. I had never even wanted a Daisy air rifle, no matter how persuasively they were advertised on the back covers of comic books. I'm a person with a peculiarly defined and limited moral courage, and no physical grace or courage at all. There doesn't seem to be much I can do about this.

I never felt guilty about it at the time, but I had a lot of fun during the war. Those years were the most exciting of my life. While other youngsters just a few years older were actually fighting, and homeless children went in search of their parents in bombed-out cities across Europe, I was sitting in Shea's Hippodrome in downtown Toronto watching Bing and Bob and Dottie on the road to Zanzibar or Morocco. I adored Bing Crosby. I admired his singing and musicianship to the point of idolatry, feelings that I've reproduced in those of my fictional character Matt Goderich in the pages of *Black and White Keys,* the "wartime" volume of *The New Age/Le nouveau siècle.* Bing's insouciance, his comedic sense, his effortless relaxed vocal quality, his decent Americanness, all persuaded and charmed me to the point where I accepted them as a set of personal standards for conduct. I imitated Bing. I wanted to have the same sort of career as a band singer and then a radio star. I had no ambitions towards movie stardom, being as I considered myself rather short and funny-looking. But why not radio?

What remains interesting about these personal fables, as the century comes to its end, is their strange blend of absurd fantasy and half-repressed awareness of how things are in fact. I tried out in a few auditions with pianists and small, high school orchestras, and once even in a recording studio, but I could never have performed in public. I had a pleasant singing voice with about the same light baritone range as Bing or Perry Como, another great favourite of those years, but never in a million years could I have got up in public and sung a song in correct pitch and tempo. Too scared. No ability to perform. This perception, which grew on me gradually, has saved me on many occasions over the decades since V-J Day from making an exhibition of myself in public. I no longer cherish any desire to appear as a performer or commentator or professional viewer-with-alarm concerning the state of human affairs. I've been

"A bunch of the boys cruising Yonge Street in Toronto just after the war," (from left) Bill Werle, Hugh Hood, and Ronnie Biggar, about 1946

able to work off all that posturing silliness writing first-drafts and then polishing them for print.

Having fun while faraway people were suffering and dying. This was for four or five years my characteristic conduct. It has taken me just about fifty years, plenty of hard thought, and the writing of thirty books to come to terms with my adolescence. Fortunately for me it reached its final phase in the same summer that the war ended, the period that witnessed the death of Franklin Roosevelt and of Adolf Hitler, V-E Day, the first appearance of the mushroom cloud, V-J Day, and the publication of those pictures of released prisoners, and piles of the dead, in the camps. From the day after the German surrender in Europe until the day of the Japanese surrender on the deck of the USA's *Missouri,* I was fooling around near Collingwood, Ontario, as a not-very-dedicated worker in the Ontario Farm Service Force.

The manpower supply for the Canadian forces in Europe was rapidly drying up in 1945. Underpopulated and overstrained Canadian society was attempting tasks for which it didn't possess sufficient resources. Towards the end of the war, Ontario, and I believe some other provinces, conceived a scheme whereby students in their last year of high school could graduate early without undergoing a tough battery of final exams, if they would agree to serve for thirteen weeks as working members of an organized farm labor force.

This was a heaven-sent opportunity for me because I was close to failing all my math courses, algebra, geometry, and trigonometry, and was unquestionably going to fail the final examination in physics. Without passing grades in these subjects I would be unable to enter the notoriously exigent University of Toronto. When I heard that my high school would accept my grades at Easter for my diploma, rather than the much more difficult provincial Senior Matriculation examinations of June, I leapt at the chance, and the day after V-E Day found myself on a train for Collingwood, a port town on Georgian Bay where there were substantial market garden farms in operation, producing canned goods in abundance, tomatoes, beans, asparagus, rhubarb, the lot.

Five of us from my high school were assigned to room with the same family and work at a farm belonging to one of the major canneries of the region. Contrary to what I'd expected we actually accomplished a considerable amount of productive labor without too much horsing around. We used to rise before six and eat an enormous breakfast. Pie! The only place where I've ever been offered pie for breakfast, together with masses of other food. We would work in the fields from 7:00 A.M. until 5:00 P.M., competing with the four high school girls from Collingwood who were members of the OFSF to see who could best manage the sharp edge of the hoe.

My God, did we hoe? We hoed everything you could think of: rhubarb, tomatoes, potatoes, asparagus, beans, onions, anything you could put in a can. And we sprayed and sprayed. Apple trees, pear trees, you name it, we sprayed it. Sometimes we fed the farm stock, a couple of ancient draft horses and a cow. No pigs, thank God! We battled among ourselves for the attentions of the four Collingwood schoolgirls. With five of us from De La Salle in Toronto in the running, and only four girls, we were one girl short all summer. This caused a certain amount of rivalry and envy, and ended at least one firm friendship, but what the

hell, it was part of growing up, and we weren't going to spend the rest of our lives together anyway. We were to part very soon.

All four girls, and my four buddies, went on to university in the fall of 1945. I got left behind. Even by substituting my Easter grades for the Senior Matric exams I only succeeded in obtaining credit in eight subjects, whereas nine were required for university entrance. I had failed in physics at Easter, with a grade that I'm reluctant to publish even now. This kept me out of university for two years while I sought with increasing desperation to find a physics examination somewhere that I could pass. I tried in 1946, after a winter of highly interesting employment at a fur blender and dyer's establishment, by long odds the smelliest job I've ever had. The work consisted of packing and delivering cheap new fur coats which had just been striped to resemble muskrat or sable or fox. They really were "coney," in the language of the trade, rabbit in fact. The dyes used in the business had the most toxic odor imaginable. I don't know how the dyers survived, and though I seldom went into the dyeing rooms I had a persistent headache all the time I worked in the shipping office. A few months of this convinced me that I had to get into university somehow, and I was mighty dashed when I failed in physics once again in June 1946.

I figured that I could count on one more year of trying. If I didn't make it then I'd have to invent some sort of career for myself that didn't lead through the entrenched, institutionalized system of Canadian social patterns towards secure professional status and a long career. I make no apology for this kind of thinking; most other young men in Canada had similar ambitions that year; the competition for security and position was intense. The high schools and especially the universities were being flooded with returning soldiers who had first claim on professional education because of their wartime service. Special programs were being devised for the veterans of WW II which moved them along in university streaming with as few impediments as possible.

I had no war service, was several years younger than most of the veterans, had seen nothing of the world outside Toronto, and was in fact a very ignorant adolescent. I knew one thing, though. If I didn't get back to school I was effectively blocked off from any improvement in my earnings and any widening of my mental horizons. I had to pass an examination in physics! I had a year to do it in and I had to support myself at the same time. I had the usual string of low-paying routine jobs in that year between 1946 and 1947. I quit the fur blenders because I couldn't stand the poisonous odors of the dyeing vats. I caught on for a while as an office boy in the federal civil service, beginning at fifty dollars a month and gradually rising to seventy. Salaries were very low in the service at the time, and I never achieved permanent status on any nominal roll. I was a temporary office boy the whole time, and you can't get any more temporary than that.

I couldn't teach myself the fundamentals of physics. It was like one of those nightmares about learning where you realize that you simply do not understand what is being asked of you and in the end decide to let it "just flow over your head." I have never mastered the principles of the subject, and to this moment find them mysterious and opaque; that goes for algebra, geometry, and trigonometry too.

I went up to my old high school in June 1947, to give it one last shot. If I failed, farewell any chance of university admission. I wrote the physics exam in the morning of a glorious mid-June day. I knew as I wrote that I was failing. I couldn't give a satisfactory answer to any of the questions. Later on I learned that my grade on the paper was nineteen marks out of a hundred. I must have got that because I folded the paper correctly. I was desperate. I said to the teacher who was supervising the examination room, "Have you got any other exams on this afternoon?"

In those days if you paid a fee of two dollars you could write as many of the Senior Matric exams as you could stand.

"Sure," said the examiner, "there's Canadian History at 2:00 P.M."

"I'll take it," I said. I had never taken a course in the subject and all I knew about it came from a serial in the *Saturday Evening Post* called "Rogers' Rangers" that I'd just finished reading.

I went in and took that history exam without any preparation whatsoever and, by God, I passed with third-class honours. I got sixty-seven out of a possible hundred marks. Now I had the nine passing grades required for admission to the University of Toronto. They were not exactly the nine subjects the calendar prescribed, but they added up to nine any way you counted them. The registrar's office waived this technical objection and I entered the university in the fall of 1947 at the age of nineteen, a year older than most high school graduates and four or five years younger than most of the war veterans who were now in their third year and approaching graduation. Most of my best friends in college were war veterans, with whom I got along much better than with kids my own age.

I hung around the University of Toronto from 1947 to 1955, progressively earning the B.A., 1950, M.A., 1952, and the Ph.D., 1955. I've got the attitudes and the ideas of a U of T man, what we still call a "Varsity grad," in my bones. My mother, my uncle, my sister, my father-in-law, my mother-in-law, my daughter Sarah, and many nephews and cousins attended the University of Toronto from 1912 to 1985, when a last niece graduated. I'm a University of Toronto man permanently, for good or ill, a Marshall McLuhan and Northrop Frye product, not the worst kind of human being.

When I started at U of T, I had no definite career ambitions. Writing was the furthest thing from my mind, although I'd had from childhood a natural ability to tell stories. I was thinking about chemical engineering, an absurd proposal given my defeat by maths and physics. I could never have become an engineer. I then began to think about the law. My grandfather John Hood had been a lawyer, among other things, and was now practising in Toronto with a prestigious firm that still enjoys a great reputation in the legal fraternity. Might I turn into a law student when my Pass Arts B.A. was completed? I had no idea, but it was the only calling that suggested itself. Over the next three years this notion withered up and blew away. Philosophy?

I was enrolled at the Catholic college of the U of T, which is a federated institution composed of many separate but linked colleges: Anglican, Presbyterian, United Church of Canada, Catholic, as well as University College which remained resolutely without church affiliation. At Saint Michael's College I studied a lot of Catholic philosophy centered around the massive systematic thought of Saint Thomas Aquinas. To proceed very far with this study I would have to master the philosophical Latin of the mediaeval scholastics, and I decided to give it a miss. What was left? Graduate work in English literature might postpone a chilly entry into the work force armed with a Pass Arts three-year B.A. I applied for admission to the School of Graduate Studies towards the end of my graduating year, and rather to my surprise I was accepted, on the condition that I put in a year of make-up courses to bring my Pass B.A. up to Honours standards. I was happy to do this, and after I got my B.A. in 1950 I worked off the make-up year of courses, did the three graduate courses and the thesis required for the M.A., and obtained that degree in 1952. I still had no career proposals, and could think of nothing better to do than start work towards the doctoral degree in English literature. I completed my doctoral work over the next three years, almost setting a record for rapidity of execution, and submitted a mammoth doctoral thesis, "Theories of Imagination in English Thinkers, 1650–1798," in the late summer of 1955, receiving my Ph.D. in November of that year. I got engaged to be married to my wife of thirty-five years, Noreen Mallory, on the night I received my Ph.D., a strange and romantic synchronicity. My marriage has been the great circumstance of my life. Next comes the parenthood of four children, writing novels, stories and essays, trying to find out what the world is really like, and in fifth place my university teaching career, begun in 1951 and now in its forty-second year.

While I was working towards my doctorate, and without knowing it towards engagement and marriage, I was slowly realizing that pure scholarly or critical work wasn't what my character and inclinations would allow. I'm simply not a scholar. I don't possess the necessary patience and thoroughness. Nor am I an analytic critic. I don't have the logical power and theoretical consistency for that job.

I was beginning to suspect dimly that I was some other sort of person, the kind that could observe, register, remember, rearrange, play with words, sentence forms, colors, sounds, the design of other people's poetry or stories. I discovered a modest ability to parody people like Hemingway, Henry James, or T. S. Eliot. What sort of person enjoys doing that, and can even make a living at it?

I thought I'd better have a try at Art. At first I guessed that I might become an actor. I appeared in a couple dozen stage productions, always in the smallest parts, and found that although I enjoyed acting I had no gift for it. I did meet many actors. My wife worked for a while at the Stratford Shakespearian Festival, where many of our friends

Wedding party of Barbara Hood Mulroney, the author's sister, Newman Club, University of Toronto, 1951. The author is at left, age twenty-three.

found their first professional engagements. But no, acting wasn't my thing. What kind of art could I produce that didn't require a long period of training, and cost little to attempt?

I began to try to write fiction. My first attempt was 100 percent early 1950s genre stuff, a business novel modelled on *Executive Suite, The Man in the Gray Flannel Suit, The Hucksters, The Big-Company Look,* and other examples of the genre that abounded at that period. It wasn't a satirical criticism of business like *Babbitt,* a book I'd read repeatedly and admired very much, but an accepting and even complacent look at the power relationships involved in the takeover of a big corporation by an even bigger one which we would today call a multinational. I thought my business novel, "The Beginning of Wisdom," 1952, was constructed around a solid, interesting story line, but I really knew nothing about the major corporations, their executives and wives. Especially their wives. I wrote the opening forty pages of the book and then abandoned it. I must have destroyed the manuscript, a foolish thing to do. I wish I could see it now. I had to write two other whole, unpublished novels, "God Rest You Merry," 1957–58, and "Hungry Generations," 1959–60, before a fourth try was completed, revised, much-polished, and finally accepted by E. P. Dutton and Company of New York, the very first publishers who saw it. That would be unusual for a first novel, but it wasn't really a first novel; it was a fourth novel.

If nothing else, I'm a very hard man to discourage. I wrote *White Figure, White Ground* in 1962 and 1963. It appeared in September 1964, simultaneously in New York and Toronto, and it's still in print in a paperback edition in the 1990s. It won me a thousand-dollar prize and had some magazine publication before it appeared as a book. It proved to me that I could write novels, that I might write a whole shelf of them.

Interested people very often ask writers how they learned to write. I have the impression that these inquirers think that there is some sort of collection of practical secrets, techniques which, once mastered, will allow a practitioner to produce finished bits of work in any form. There may be some truth to this conviction; there are schools of writing of every imaginable degree of sophistication, from those advertised in the back pages of magazines—"Learn to Write Easily at Home in Your Spare Time. Send for Free Brochure"—to the schools at Iowa or Michigan State. Nobody ever taught me anything about the way to think up

ideas; what I needed to know were the addresses of editors and publishers, and the format for the submission of material. The process of invention must take care of itself.

There was no community of practising writers in Toronto in the early 1950s, no group of older men and women whom I could consult about these interests, with the exception of Morley Callaghan, who by the mid-'50s was living in the big old house at 20 Dale Avenue that was his home for the remainder of a long and distinguished career. I had become close friends with Morley's son Michael, who was my best man a few years later. I used to go to the Callaghans' home for parties and other get-togethers, and Morley was always ready to discuss his own work, and the ambitions of would-be writers of my generation. It was at a party at the Callaghans' that I met my wife, Noreen Mallory, who was sharing the top-floor apartment at 20 Dale Avenue with two other young women. All three came down to complain about the noise of a party one Saturday night, then stayed to enjoy its closing hours.

I gradually began to see Noreen very regularly, until the November evening in 1955 when we got formally engaged. By then I'd completed my doctoral studies and accepted a teaching job at Saint Joseph College in West Hartford, Connecticut, where I stayed for six years, teaching myself as best I could to write stories and novels. I had to spend my first two years there alone; we couldn't afford to marry until the spring of 1957, when Noreen quit her job as a member of the costume-design staff of the Canadian Broadcasting Corporation's television network. We moved into a place of our own on Hawthorn Street, in an old house not far from Mark Twain's Hartford home. It looked as if we might live in the United States permanently. In fact we lived in Connecticut from the summer of 1957 through the spring of 1961. Our first two children, Sarah and Dwight, were born there and have retained dual citizenship since birth. Sarah, born in 1958, and Dwight, born in 1961, now live in Canada and may never exercise their citizenship rights in the U.S. But the possibility is always there, and it has shaped all our lives. For example, I still imagine a potential dual audience for my work.

I more or less taught myself to write while we were living in Hartford. At the same time my brother Alex was acquiring U.S. citizenship, marrying a woman from Binghamton, New York, and shaping a career that lasted for over forty years with Time, Incorporated, in New York. During my years at Saint Joseph College, I drafted two unpublished novels and nearly forty stories, only two of which had found publication by 1960. Every one of them, however, has since been collected in one book or another. It was those forty stories that gave me an understanding of the basic problems of the fiction writer. Endings, beginnings, titles, anecdotal matter, plot, atmosphere, dialogue, the elements of fiction. I sat down at my worktable in early January 1957 and wrote the first of my hundred and thirty stories, "A Short Walk in the Rain," which is set in downtown Manhattan and is solidly based on an anecdote told me by my brother.

I wrote stories for a year and a half before I had one accepted, by the great Toronto editor Robert Weaver, for the leading Canadian literary magazine, the *Tamarack Review,* which became my best showcase between 1958 and 1975. I had fourteen pieces in the magazine in those years, and two of the magazine's editors arranged the publication of my first story collection, *Flying a Red Kite,* 1962.

When my first published story, "The Isolation Booth," appeared in the *Tamarack Review,* I imagined the way to success as a writer lay open before me, but it was another year and a half before I sold another story, this time to *Esquire.* The story was an account of the aftermath of a nuclear attack on a medium-sized American city about the size of Hartford. It was called "After the Sirens." It appeared in the August 1960 issue of *Esquire,* and must have been about the first anti-nuclear war story to appear in print. It has since appeared all over the world in more than a dozen anthologies, and still seems to strike a nerve in late twentieth-century readers. When the editors at *Esquire* accepted the story, which had been submitted unsolicited, they asked me to drop in and see them if I were ever in New York.

Naturally I wrote straight off to Rust Hills, then the fiction editor at *Esquire,* and made an appointment to see him. This was in the spring of 1960. When I came into the magazine's offices, I was surprised and interested when Rust Hills suggested that I might fill in for a year as their assistant fiction editor, replacing Gene Lichtenstein who was about to spend a sabbatical year in Washington. I was excited and flattered by this tentative feeler, but the very next day I got a job offer from the University of Montréal, the large, private, French-language university where I've been on the faculty for thirty-two years. I asked Noreen if she'd care to live in Montréal, and she

was enthusiastic about the idea. The hinted job offer from *Esquire,* which never matured to the point of a specific proposal, was forgotten in the excitement of planning a return to Canada. It took about eighteen months to complete this decisive move, but we came, wife, husband, two young children, and a big cat, to Montréal in the spring of 1961, and we've been here ever since, except when travelling.

This definitive move concluded the turbulent early years of my life. As soon as I got there I saw that Montréal was the most fertile ground imaginable for the kind of work I might be able to do. I started writing new stories at a furious pace. I wrote fourteen stories in fourteen months; they largely became the materials of *Flying a Red Kite.* I wrote the title story in July 1961, two months after we arrived in Montréal. It's much my best-known single piece of work. It's been reprinted so often that I've had to withdraw it from circulation for

"Holding the first cheque I ever received for writing—$28.00 from the Tamarack Review *for the story 'The Isolation Booth,'" Hartford, Connecticut, 1958*

fear of becoming identified as the author of one story.

Through the 1960s I continued to turn out material voluminously. I published a story called "Cura Pastoralis" in the literary magazine *Contact,* which was being edited in Sausalito, California, by the great Evan S. Connell and his colleague Calvin Kentfield. The story caught the eye of Elizabeth McKee, one of the leading literary agents in New York, at that time the representative of Flannery O'Connor, William Styron, and Connell himself. Elizabeth wrote to me in Montréal and asked if I would like her to represent me! It was Elizabeth McKee who submitted *White Figure, White Ground* to Jim Ellison at E. P. Dutton, where the novel was published in 1964. And it was dear Elizabeth who sent *The Camera Always Lies,* 1967, over to Dan Wickenden at Harcourt, Brace. Dan later told me that he thought I was doing the best fiction writing in North America, pretty heady stuff! I published my first four books in the 1960s, and conceived the idea of my serial novel, *The New Age/Le nouveau siècle,* towards the end of that invigorating decade. I began to make notes for this twelve-volume sequence towards the end of 1966. Our third child, John, was born in 1963, and our fourth, Alexandra, in 1965. I must have been on the lookout for new conceptions. I was closing in on forty, the time of life when, as the French say, a man ranges himself, and accepts the implications of his first four decades.

I remember feeling that *The New Age/Le nouveau siècle* would develop naturally from the optimistic climate of feeling across Canada in 1967, the centenary of the nation's birth. For a year or two afterwards it seemed as if Canada were really "the pacific country." There was Expo 67, the celebrated world's fair. There was the birth of Canada's first major-league baseball team, the Montréal Expos. There was the coming to power of Canada's most celebrated political figure, Pierre Elliott Trudeau. During those years at the end of the sixties and the start of the seventies anything seemed possible, even a twelve-volume epic of modern Canadian life.

And from conception to realization the thing has been proved possible. I'm getting close to finishing it. I began to make written notes for *The New Age/Le nouveau siècle* at the end of 1966. By the early 1970s I had the overall design of the work in my head and had acquired a copious file of notes about it. I continued to write stories and novels, of course, and started to publish collections of essays and articles, like *The Governor's Bridge Is Closed,* 1973. But I could see that if I were to have any hope of completing *The New Age* I would have to produce a first volume in 1975 or thereabouts, aiming at publication of a final book in 1999, just as the third millennium was about to begin, the new age.

On Sunday afternoon, October 15, 1972, at 1:00 P.M., I faced up to the keyboard and typed out, "In those days we used to have a red-and-white garden swing set up in the backyard beside the garage . . ." The opening lines of *The Swing in the Garden,* 1975, the first book of *The New Age/Le nouveau siècle.*

The first four books in the series were dedicated one after another to our children. "For Sarah Hood, with my best love." "For Dwight Hood, funny fingers, much laughter." "For John Hood . . . old soft ears." "For Alexandra Hood, the beautiful model girl." I think most readers could guess the overall dedicatee for the set of twelve. The first four pages of typescript were produced the day before Noreen's birthday, October 16. We're the same age, and we're going into *The New Age* together.

From its first aimless pencil scratchings in late 1966 through the big party my publishers have planned for New Year's Eve, 1999, the production of my serial novel will have occupied just over thirty-three years of my life, a third of a century. I've always conceived the work as representing the twentieth century in structure. Much planning has gone into the execution of this conception. The earliest moment in time described in the work reaches back almost to the year 1900; the last actions depicted will occur as an old age winds down and a new one begins. This is a cyclical pattern found everywhere in our human understanding of the nature of the universe. I wanted to make *The New Age/Le nouveau siècle* a universal history in some way. Nine of the books have been published so far, with *Be Sure to Close Your Eyes,* 1993, the most recent to appear. Three quarters of the work is now complete. As I once wrote, I feel as though I'm trying to drag an elephant out of a darkened room into daylight. When I've got the beast's hindquarters out in plain view we'll see whether I've produced a living leviathan or an extinct woolly mammoth.

Since 1966 I've lived with this project some part of every day. When I wake up in the morning I think first of my wife and children and then of the weather, and then the big book. It's almost like living with two families, or two weather systems.

There's been so much planning, waiting for ideas to mature, that it often seems as if my whole adult life has gone into producing this giant book. Naturally this makes me wonder if perhaps I've wasted my life doing it. I certainly can't stop. I've treated the work in what sometimes seems an obsessive-compulsive way, but I can't walk away from it now.

Living with something like this puts a peculiar spin on your life. You'll be sitting in the bathtub, trying to figure out a narrative pattern for a book you hope to begin in three or four years, and suddenly the inevitable and correct solution of the matter pops into your head. It doesn't simply resolve the imaginative difficulty connected with the book you've been thinking about; it adjusts your approach to intervening tasks, and to the two or three books that will come after the one you've had in mind.

Perfectly ordinary occurrences, in boutiques, malls, offices, that nobody else in the crowd notices, suddenly seem to be lit up with a radiance communicated to you alone, and you say to yourself, "Why sure, of course! That's the end of 'Dead Men's Watches.'" A book you don't plan to write for quite some time. Every artist is familiar with this form of private illumination that means nothing to your nearest and dearest or to the rest of the crowd, but conveys fathomless depths of significance to the lucky artist at the dull end of the pencil. The great danger is that these moments of revelation may become fewer and fewer as time goes on, or may eventually stop coming. When that happens, a writer is usually described as being "written out." Nobody has any guarantee that this won't happen; you have to go on trusting.

There are other lesser sources of invention. I remember vividly the brainstorming session Noreen and I shared when I was trying to choose the most appropriate name for the central character in *The New Age.* It had to be a male name, found in all the major European languages and used in the western hemisphere as well. It had to be familiar, neither dull nor uninteresting, nor comic and outrageously unusual. It shouldn't begin with the letter Z or X or G. I knew the character's last name, "Goderich," and didn't want an alliterative pair of names, like the annoying "Hugh Hood." Eventually we narrowed the range of choice down to the names of Christ's apostles, partly because I write from an explicitly Christian stance, partly because those names are known and used all over the world. One of them was obviously ruled out. I couldn't have called my narrator Judas. John was

too widely used and too familiar in my own family. How about Peter? Put Peter down as a possible. Bartholomew was just a shade offbeat, conveying nuances of the comic and eccentric. Andrew? Certainly usable. So was Philip.

Our final four candidates were Peter, Andrew, Philip, and a late arrival at the post, Matthew.

"I think we're getting close," I said to Noreen. This conversation took place at our summer cottage on Charleston Lake in eastern Ontario in July 1972, three months before I intended to start writing the work. I wanted to get this crucial decision out of the way as soon as possible, so I could live with the character fully present in my imagination. I think most fiction writers will recognize this motive; the character doesn't start to take on flesh, doesn't begin to ground herself or himself in clusters of sensory imagery until you've made a few primordial decisions. You can't write about a character until you know her name, about how tall she is, how old, what color hair, what dress size, all that mass of detailed information that goes into actualizing the person in your meditations about her. What timbre does her voice have? How does she feel about her body? Can she sing a little? Has she been to college, and if so, what sort of college? State university, or one of the seven sisters, or a small Catholic college for women like Saint Joseph College, West Hartford, Connecticut?

Peter, Andrew, Philip, Matthew?

We discarded Peter in the course of this midsummer afternoon chat. There was the merest suggestion of religious reference, "thou art Peter, and upon this rock . . ." I did not want the work to be specifically identifiable as Catholic. We both liked Andrew, and felt that the name was solidly Canadian in its Scottish undertones. There have been an awful lot of Andrews in Canadian public life; it's a common name without seeming banal, and it has the additional virtue of being found in many other languages, as André, Andreas, Andrei, Andrea, Anders, and several other versions. A very strong contender. We felt the same about Philip, but as we went on talking we began to warm up to Matthew, because of some of the subtleties of the name's implications. A tax-collector, therefore not immediately likeable, but necessary all the same. The first of the synoptic gospellers. Matt, nice nickname, good old Matt. Goes well with Goderich. Matthew Goderich.

Noreen and I have been living with Matthew Goderich, his father Andrew, and his uncle Philip, since 1972, in a weird *ménage à cinq.* As soon as I'd decided definitely on my main character's name, a flood of information about him washed through my excited brain. He had an older sister and a younger brother, Andrew was his father, Amanda Louise was his sister, Tony his little brother. He was born two years later than I was, in 1930, not 1928. This served to keep our experiences distinct and distanced from each other. He lived on Summerhill Avenue in north Rosedale, Toronto, the same street that I grew up on, and our houses were strikingly similar. But all the other people in the district that Matt Goderich knew were imaginary people, the most important of them being another small boy called Adam Sinclair, who thrust himself onto the last line of page one of *The Swing in the Garden.*

I'll take my oath that I didn't know anything at all about Adam Sinclair when I sat down on that October Sunday afternoon to start writing the book. There I sat, describing a scene pictured in one of the photographs that accompanies this autobiographical sketch, the back garden with the swing in it as it appeared in the mid-'30s, when all of a sudden this little guy appeared out of nowhere, Adam Sinclair. I shoved him down on the page and discovered to my astonishment that I couldn't let him alone. He took on rounded reality just as fast as the other characters I had in mind. I began to see that if I'd embedded the names of three of the apostles in my narration, I also was using the first human name of all, Adam, whose surname was full of associations. Sin/clair.

The book was called *The Swing in the Garden.* I meant it to begin with a look around Eden, and a story of how Eden came to be lost. Proust's narrator says that all the paradises are lost paradises and with that in mind I made the opening book in my series the story of the 1930s, beginning in the trough of the Great Depression and ending with the first months of the "phony war" on the Franco-German frontier in the autumn of 1939. The book ended with the words, "It made for a long fall." This was of course an intentional reference to the swing away from paradise that supplies the beginning of many narratives, including the book of Genesis. I understood that I absolutely had to have an Adam in the pages of such a work, but only after he'd revealed himself to me when I got to the bottom of the first page. Writing fiction at epic length with epic intentions involves the writer in scriptural, mythic, romantic, and epic structures without her or his knowing it or perhaps even consenting to it. The work isn't entirely in one's control; the narrative has its own integrity which it insists on making known.

Every long work of fiction deals with a central generation, the people about the same age as the author and his main characters, and at least potentially with two other generations, the parents and the children of the central group of personages. Not all such stories arrange the generations with the same prominence. Proust, for example, deals very extensively with his narrator's parents and their contemporaries, Swann, Odette, Oriane de Guermantes, and her circle. He is likewise very thorough in treating people of his own generation, Gilberte, Saint-Loup, Bloch, Albertine, Andrée. But he leaves their children's generation almost wholly out of the picture until the very last pages of *Le temps retrouvé.* Then Mlle. de Saint-Loup makes her dazzling appearance, and ties the whole wonderful work together in an illuminating pattern.

In *The Music of Time,* Anthony Powell handles the parental generation with sympathy but without close identification. Powell's narrator's forte is his own circle of friends and acquaintances, most of them about his own age. Not much is done with the third, youngest generation.

In my own case, as I write this account of my life to date, I have three more books of *The New Age/Le nouveau siècle* to write. They are to be published in 1995, 1997, and at the very end of 1999. I can see that I am going to have to deal with that definitive third generation at some length in the final quarter of the work. Anthony Goderich and his sister Andrea, his brother John Sleaford Goderich, their beautiful young cousin in New York, Emily Underwood; these people are starting to become very familiar to me and very highly coloured. I've already got many ideas about them that I plan to develop as fully as I can in "Dead Men's Watches," 1995, "Great Realizations," 1997, and an unnamed final book in the series, coming at the end of the second millennium.

Mention of Matthew Goderich's lovely young niece Emily Underwood, daughter of his sister Amanda Louise, a New Yorker from birth, makes me think that I'm in the process of inventing a new character in the series who resembles in certain structural properties the lovely young Mlle. de Saint-Loup. This has not been a planned and deliberate parallel conception. As I write these lines I am, as it were, inventing or discovering inferences in my story that I will have to realize in the space and time remaining for the work. What

*Hugh Hood and Noreen Mallory at a conference dedicated to his work; the showcase
displays the author's publications, York University, Toronto, 1979*

to do with Emily Underwood of New York City
who has already made an appearance in *Property
and Value?* Does she have a love affair with a first
cousin? How to resolve that difficult complexity in
an extended family's life? What is this, *Dynasty?
Dallas?*

It seems to me that all long narrative forms
necessarily enmesh themselves in the same entan-
glements of family life. *Finnegans Wake, A la
récherche du temps perdu, Anna Karenina* in which
the narrator tells us in the opening lines that every
unhappy family is so in its own way. In the 1990s it
might appear on the surface as though family life
had lost its central importance to human beings,
but believe me, it ain't so. As one who attaches the
most profound importance to the life of the family,
I'm preoccupied in my long fiction, with the
sequencing of the generations—the dynasties if
you like—that families transform themselves into
after a certain lapse of time. E. M. Forster noted
that hardly anybody can give the full names of his
or her eight great-grandparents; this is a surprising
fact. Most of us can't go back as far as two

generations in our recollections, but what a treasure of discovery lies there waiting for us to
investigate it. The popularity of the three-genera-
tion narrative is self-explanatory.

Grandparents are notoriously more indulgent
than parents. In the last four years, my wife and I
have had our first chance to verify or discard this
popular belief. It seems to us a belief that embodies
a profound truth. We've had the chance to know
our first grandchild, another in the long line of
Alexander Hoods, who was born in July 1989, and
now walks and talks and sings and does all those
things that make your grandchildren enchanting.
Given today's medical technology and a reasonable
break in health, Alexander could be alive in the
year 2070. I find this a date of great significance
because my grandparents were all born around
1870, which means that the lives of people personally known to me from my grandfathers to my
grandchild extend over two full centuries.

The three-/four-generation fiction is becoming a social reality. I can imagine all sorts of things
that my grandchild will live to see; manned space

flight to Mars, perhaps to more distant planets; extension of human life expectancy by another ten to fifteen years; permanently peopled stations on the moon and Mars. My grandson may be the first Alexander Hood on the moon; it's possible.

I wonder whether these technical advances will be matched by progress in human conduct, in morals and ethics and religion. For a long time now it's been clear that technical advance tends to outpace ethical progress. We have achieved immense advances in medicine; soon many of us will live to be eighty-five or ninety. My wife and I, in excellent health at sixty-five, have a good shot at another twenty years of active life. Perhaps we're in the vanguard of medical progress. As I think this over, I grow aware of the striking alterations in human life that I've witnessed directly, or heard about from my grandparents, or can imagine through the person of my four-year-old grandchild.

When John Hood was born in 1870, Queen Victoria was at the midway point in her long reign. There were no automobiles and no airplanes, no telephones, no electric light, no radios. When I was born in 1928 there were no television sets, no jet aircraft, no interplanetary rockets, no photocopiers or fax machines, and no word processors. What will my grandchildren see, that I will not live to see? The elimination of cancer and AIDS? Women and men living on Mars in comfortable, artificially-created atmospheres? Zero pollution from human sources in our environment? A widespread renewal of serious and profound religious belief? The future of humanity still seems to me to be boundless, but certainly there are analysts of human society who don't share my view. To them, the future of our species is gravely compromised; naturally their opinions color what I write.

I hope to live for a long time to come, and I've got work planned that will take me into the third millennium. When I started to write novels and stories and essays forty years ago, I said to Noreen that I had no idea how far I might be able to develop my modest talent. I clearly remember telling her that I would work at this as hard as I could—give it my very best shot—and if I succeeded in a writing lifetime in publishing six short stories, I would feel that I had accomplished what it was in me to do. I felt that failure as an artist can be a dignified fate. I might afterwards turn into a critic or a journalist of some kind. Things didn't work out that way. I've written thirty books and about a hundred and thirty stories, and many, many essays and articles. My stories have been anthologized from Russia to China by way of Croatia and the good old USA. I never expected this to happen. As so many artists will tell you, when you ask them how their careers began, I simply drifted into it.

You really can't plan your creative life. When I started writing *The New Age/Le nouveau siècle* I was perfectly aware that I might not live to finish it. That's the condition of human life; you just never know . . . I've got three more of the series to write and I've got them sketched out in precise detail, but I can only complete them if I'm granted time to do it, say another four to six years. This is a reflection that I awake to every morning. It's only a variation on the fundamental conditions of our lives. As Scripture says, we know not the day nor the hour.

I haven't said much in this sketch about my religious convictions and their corollaries, but I shouldn't walk away from this assignment without specifying them. There's a question of loyalty involved. I'm a practising and believing Catholic, a *Roman* Catholic, my Anglican friends would insist. I subscribe to the beliefs stated in the Nicene Creed, and to the teaching magisterium of the church. I don't see how any reflective human being can avoid Cardinal Newman's conclusion about our moral and ethical predicament, that we are all deeply sunk in the consequences of a terrible aboriginal calamity. I mean that we are fallen beings with darkened reasons and a strong natural inclination to do ill. We are opposed and tempted at every moment by a wicked personal adversary who seeks to turn us from the way of virtue and duty and love. If this be fundamentalism, I will have to live with it. But I don't think it's fundamentalism; I think it's part of the undeniable, evident structure of the real.

Though they are weakened and fallen, our nature and our powers of intelligence and love are not destroyed, and we remain subject to the promptings of Divine Grace. We are not irremediably corrupt, and an infinite future opens before us at every moment. Anything at all may happen to us within the hour. After all, the Toronto Blue Jays won the World Series in October 1992, something unimaginable when "Hot Potato" Hamlin borrowed my *Sporting News* in July 1943. Possibility is heaven.

BIBLIOGRAPHY

Fiction:

White Figure, White Ground, E. P. Dutton, 1964.

The Camera Always Lies, Harcourt, 1967.

A Game of Touch, Longmans, Green, 1970.

You Can't Get There from Here, Oberon Press, 1972.

Five New Facts about Giorgione, Black Moss Press, 1987.

The New Age/Le nouveau siècle serial novel:

The Swing in the Garden, Volume 1, Oberon Press, 1975.

A New Athens, Volume 2, Oberon Press, 1977.

Reservoir Ravine, Volume 3, Oberon Press, 1979.

Black and White Keys, Volume 4, ECW Press, 1982.

The Scenic Art, Volume 5, Stoddart, 1984.

The Motor Boys in Ottawa, Volume 6, Stoddart, 1986.

Tony's Book, Volume 7, Stoddart, 1988.

Property and Value, Volume 8, Stoddart, 1990.

Be Sure to Close Your Eyes, Volume 9, 1993.

Short-story collections:

Flying a Red Kite, Ryerson, 1962.

Around the Mountain: Scenes from Montréal Life, Peter Martin, 1967.

The Fruit Man, the Meat Man and the Manager, Oberon Press, 1971.

Dark Glasses, Oberon Press, 1976.

Selected Stories, Oberon Press, 1978.

None Genuine without This Signature, ECW Press, 1980.

August Nights, Stoddart, 1985.

A Short Walk in the Rain: The Collected Stories II, Porcupine's Quill, 1989.

The Isolation Booth: The Collected Stories III, Porcupine's Quill, 1991.

You'll Catch Your Death, Porcupine's Quill, 1992.

Nonfiction:

Strength Down Centre: The Jean Béliveau Story, Prentice-Hall, 1970.

The Governor's Bridge Is Closed: Twelve Essays on the Canadian Scene, Oberon Press, 1973.

(With Seymour Segal) *Scoring: The Art of Hockey,* Oberon Press, 1979.

Trusting the Tale, ECW Press, 1983.

Unsupported Assertions: Essays, Stoddart, 1991.

(With Noreen Malory) *Watercourses,* forthcoming.

Other:

Friends and Relations, in *The Play's the Thing: Four Original Television Dramas,* edited by Tony Gifford, Macmillan, 1976.

(Editor with Peter O'Brien) *Fatal Recurrences: New Fiction in English from Montréal,* Véhicule Press, 1984.

Contributor of short stories to periodicals, including *Canadian Forum, Exchange, Journal of Canadian Fiction, Queen's Quarterly, Story,* and *Tamarack Review.* Also, a collection of short stories, volumes 10 and 11 of *The New Age/Le nouveau siècle,* and an essay collection are forthcoming.

Gerard Malanga
1943-

NOTES FROM A NON-LITERARY LIFE

WITH LUVB FROM ANDY "PIE" AND GERRY "PIE"

It's a bitter-cold night—new snow blanketing the old snow—early December 1963. Andy and I come out from seeing a double feature at the Empire on Forty-second Street. On the way to hailing a cab, I pull him into the Playland Arcade and suggest we send a photobooth Christmas card to Charles . . . Charles Henri Ford. Andy agrees and I drop a quarter into the slot. Huddled together in the warmth of our coats, changing expressions slightly with each turn of the flash, we stare directly into the camera, like a couple of teenagers. We anxiously wait the three minutes it takes for the finished photostrip to develop. We take turns looking at it, holding it in our hands, joking about each other's expression. My identity (now confirmed by my image with Andy) recalls the way we might have looked to others at the time.

I pocket the strip and take it home; I'm living with my mom in the Fordham Road section of the Bronx. The next day I fasten the strip to a sheet of oaktag and write up along the side, calligraphy pen dipped in red India ink—*With love from Andy "Pie" and Gerry "Pie,"* nicknames Charles had adopted for Andy and me. I seal the strip in a manila envelope and send it off to Charles, not thinking I'd ever see it again. Several months earlier he had brought Andy Warhol and me together in what would amount to a friendship that would forever change my life. The gift is a gesture of thanks.

*

Nineteen fifty-five was a signal year for me in the development of my consciousness. When kids my age were passing time idolizing baseball players, I was discovering Orson Welles, mesmerized as I was by the first telecast of *Citizen Kane* on Channel 9's Million Dollar Movie. An only child, I spent many hours reading *Screen Stories* (a magazine specializing in Hollywood screenplay synopses), and compiled scrapbooks of the *Daily News* Coloroto column, "New York's Changing Scene."

"Last uptown local stopped at 135th Street station in the Mott Haven section of the Bronx facing the three-station backyard corridor before emerging onto Third Avenue. View north—May 12, 1955."

School trips to the Metropolitan Museum of Art didn't hold my attention for long. My earliest recollection of an art that would widen my field of vision was standing before Thomas Cole's sequence of five paintings, *The Course of Empire,* at the New York Historical Society one Sunday afternoon. His vision stimulated me. I would go back several times to see it.

My parents enrolled me in an after-school art class at the neighborhood YWCA, and while students were busy drawing landscapes and still lifes, I would tape sheets of paper into one extended scroll, creating a continuous detailed cross section of New York City's subways and elevated lines from memory.

My art teacher thought I was "overgifted." I didn't know exactly what that meant. A book on her desk caught my eye, *Metropolis: An American City in Photographs.* I would spend entire sessions in a corner of the classroom turning its pages, reading the texts, making elaborate sketches from a few of the pictures, enchanted by a bygone time that somehow didn't seem all that different from the present. At some point (I'm not sure when) I realized the pictures were from the early 1930s,

only twenty years earlier. This was my first aesthetic experience with photography. At the end of the workshop semester I charmed the teacher into letting me have the book. *Metropolis* proudly has its place in my library.

*

For as long as I can remember, I sensed that the experience of my childhood would be ephemeral, so when news reached me that the Manhattan section of the Third Avenue El would be put out of service, I recognized that its passing symbolized the end of a part of my childhood. A few months earlier, I had received a Kodak Brownie 2¼ camera for my twelfth birthday. So I made the decision to imitate the pictures I had admired in *Metropolis,* and set out to preserve what I could on film for my private amusement. I had no idea at the time that such an undertaking would help focus my perception of things to come.

It came as no surprise to my father when I told him of wanting to photograph the El, to remember what it would look like after it ceased to exist. He agreed to accompany me. On the very last day that the El was in service we embarked at Fordham Road and took the ride as far south as 125th Street. I photographed the 125th Street station with its Venetian gables from street level. We then returned to the uptown platform and boarded the train back to the Bronx, not knowing that at that moment it was the last official train in service, closing forever each station it stopped at and passed. As we made our way to the front cab window of the six-car train, we found the aisle crowded with passengers, but for some reason I found myself pressed to the door window next to the motorman's cab, which gave me the perfect vantage point for making my pictures. The train had already pulled out of the station when I realized I would not have much time to photograph all that I remembered from my previous commutes, nor would I be able to make a second trip; the line was officially closed up to the 149th Street station by the time the train pulled out of 125th Street. A group of newspaper photographers crowded and hovered over me taking pictures. They seemed sympathetic to my mission and made room for all four feet, eight inches of me by the window. The first picture I snapped was of a southbound train—the last to make the downtown run. Our train wound its way north through the narrow corridor between apartment tenements in

Mott Haven and I clicked off a twelve-frame black-and-white roll. The last two pictures depicted our approach into the 149th Street station.

*

Whereas Andy Warhol led a sheltered childhood in Pittsburgh, I grew up a street hood in the Bronx. Yet there are parallels here: Both of us had traditional Catholic upbringings. We were first-generation Americans and our parents were considerably older than the parents of our friends. We learned to draw at an early age. We were fascinated by the movies—not just movies but movie posters, movie stars, and movie studios. At one point I even took out a subscription to *Boxoffice,* a trade publication not found on any newsstand. Years later I would give all my back issues to Andy. The first book I remember reading on the movies was Bosley Crowther's *The Lion's Share,* a history of MGM studio.

*

Never had I considered that one didn't make one's living as a poet. I thought it was something that one just did. I continued my interest in poetry as a freshman at the University of Cincinnati, where I first met and studied with Richard Eberhart in the spring of 1961.

I dropped out at the end of my freshman year, unable to return as my father could no longer afford to pay for my schooling. I was eighteen at the time. Not knowing what I wanted to do with my life—except to write poetry—and not seeing much point participating in a structured system of any predictable kind, I occupied my time with just sort of thinking about things, reading anything I could get my hands on that dealt with poetry, exchanging ideas with other people, and sharing poems with friends and poets I came to know along the way. I was without means of support.

Willard Maas, a poet and professor of English at Wagner College in Staten Island, with his wife (filmmaker Marie Menken)—early admirers of my poetry—realizing my plight, were instrumental in securing a fellowship anonymously established to further my literary abilities and education. I was enrolled in Wagner College two weeks after classes began, in early October 1961.

"Last uptown local approaching 143rd Street station. View north at the end of the backyard corridor—May 12, 1955."

*

What to give the poet who has everything? A pair of argyle socks, someone suggests. Argyle socks, it is. As my memory serves me right, the engraved card reads . . . *Chester Kallman requests the pleasure of your company at a 57th birthday gathering for Wystan Hugh Auden, February 21st, 8 pm, at 77 St. Mark's Place.* The year is 1963.

Wystan could probably be considered one of the first modern poets to homestead the East Village in this regard. For a teenager (I would turn twenty a month later) there was nothing more glamorous to my mind than a party filled with poets. But this had to be the exception! You couldn't go much higher. I could only fantasize at who might be present. Charles Henri Ford was there, flitting from room to room, throwing a friendly glance in my direction, but I could not know at the time he would in a few months be the catalyst bringing Andy Warhol and me together.

The one person who did make a lasting impression was William Meredith. Who could not be impressed with "Love Letter from an Impossible Land" . . . opening:

97

Combed by the cold seas, Bering and Pacific,
These are the exile islands of the mind.
All the charts and history you can muster
Will not make them real as the fog is real
Or crystal as a certain hour is clear
If you can wait.

           Write to me often, darling.

I first read this poem in *The War Poets,* so-called "An Anthology of the War Poetry of the Twentieth Century" by its editor, none other than Oscar Williams, anthologist extraordinaire. My copy had been given me by Willard Maas (my English professor at Wagner College), also included. Poems by Rukeyser, Jarrell, Spender and Eberhart, William Abrahams, Dylan Thomas, Ben Maddow, Weldon Kees, and F. T. Prince—favorites I would return to again and again.

The contributor's note listed Meredith, then Lieutenant, USNR, as having entered naval aviation, receiving Navy wings and commission in October 1942, and then serving as pilot in the Pacific area. He had already one book of poems to his credit, *Love Letter from an Impossible Land.* The photo of Meredith, most likely a public relations shot from when he was a noncommissioned officer attached to the Army Air Force public relations, was striking nonetheless. So, here I was sitting at the feet of William Meredith, "war poet" as I had remembered him, now forty-four.

A few weeks earlier I had submitted poems and been accepted to participate in an undergraduate poetry reading competition—the Irene Glascock Memorial Poetry Contest—held annually at Mount Holyoke College, South Hadley, Massachusetts. Judges for the contest were Meredith, then an associate professor at Connecticut College, John Sweeney of Harvard, and Andrews Wanning of Bard College. A press release stated that well-known poets who had read for the prize as undergraduates included Muriel Rukeyser and Robert Lowell. I felt honored to be in such distinguished company. The first prize would be one hundred dollars. The date: 19 April. Meredith said he would be on the lookout for me. I felt reassured.

I'd never been to Mount Holyoke. Even reading a map I had no idea how to get there . . . didn't even have enough money for the bus. Two friends—Mr. Clean (I never knew his real name), a wealthy Argentinean whose visa had apparently expired, and John MacDermott, both looking for adventure—offered to chauffeur me to South Hadley. We tuned up Mr. Clean's 1952

"The freshman Gerard Malanga meeting poet Richard Eberhart (Elliston Poet for 1960) for the first time," Elliston Poetry Room, University of Cincinnati

white Cadillac convertible and off we went. It would be my first time in the Commonwealth of Massachusetts—a kid from the Bronx. We had enough methamphetamine hydrochloride to last us the weekend. I'd packed a three-piece tripler for the occasion, but together we looked anything but presentable. My hair had grown out way past my ears. Mr. Clean wore a sweatshirt with the sleeves ripped out.

We got lost on the way—after taking a wrong turn—and, having arrived late for lunch, I missed out on the group photo opportunity arranged by the *Springfield Union-News.*

I was greeted by my official Mount Holyoke student chaperon, Martha George. Since the rooms for the other contestants had already been assigned, Martha arranged a room for me in one of the girls' dorms—Mandelles Hall, Room 103. The boys and I chuckled at this turn of events, for it was like putting the fox in the henhouse. We proceeded to unpack our bags and relax for a bit before the night's event. We immediately got into our stash, so relaxing was out of the question. We were wired and ready to go.

The contest was to be held at 8:00 P.M., Friday, in the Bookshop Inn, in South Hadley, near the campus. Martha came to escort us to the reading. We arrived at about fifteen minutes prior to the event. The audience consisted mostly of female students and a smattering of teachers. Meredith gave me the nod. As each contestant was allotted ten—maybe fifteen—minutes at most, I'd already timed myself to read only two poems.

Somehow I was last on the roster. The first poem I read, titled "Yellow," was, as I recall, unlike anything else read that night. The poem was an exercise suggested by Kenneth Koch, whose workshop I'd been attending at the New School on a fellowship. The assignment was to write a poem using a comparison in every line—"Yellow is like . . ." or "Yellow is when . . ." For the first time that night the audience applauded between poems. My second poem, much longer, "When Youth Shall This Generation Waste" was both inspired and influenced by the rapid-fire rhetoric I had assimilated from reading Auden's poetry, with a little bit of George Barker thrown in. The poem alluded to a relationship I'd fantasized between two lesbians. (Two years later this poem would appear in the fifth issue of *Art and Literature*, edited by John Ashbery.) The audience response was the most effusive, exceeding any expectation I might have anticipated, clearly demonstrating I was the winner. It was in the bag, as they say.

Martha escorted me and my buddies to a party held in honor of the contestants at the home of an English professor. We made a beeline for the bathroom to give a boost to our nostrils. We were now in high gear. The party was festive enough. I'd spoken a bit with Meredith, reminiscing about Wystan's birthday soiree and getting into a rap with Martha. I noticed that while the students were being served apple juice, the adults were sneaking off into the kitchen and returning with alcoholic beverages. I gave a nod to the boys that we attack the source of supply. We raided the fridge and downed a few beers and stashed a reserve in our duffel bags for when it came time to split.

As the party was winding down, Martha led us back to the dorm. We agreed to meet up next morning for breakfast. Meredith was to give a reading, scheduled for precisely 11:10 and he would also announce the first prize.

We finished off the beers, took a few snorts, smoked some j, and decided to redecorate Room 103. We turned the furniture around, removed the pictures from the walls and threw the mattress on the floor, remembering how the Beats had done it from some photos I had seen published in *Life*. Actually, our real intent was to duplicate the surroundings of the Bond Street loft we'd been living at in the city. We were so much involved in our antics, we didn't take note of the ruckus we were causing. The dorm mother reported the disturbance and within minutes the campus police arrived to investigate—searchlights in hand—and I was told that the room was reserved for me only. They were to escort my friends to the power plant located way the other side of campus. Martha came by in the morning and when we all joined up I discovered John and Mr. Clean were given cots without blankets or pillows. I vowed we'd get even somehow.

After breakfast, Martha took us over to where Meredith would be reading on campus—the New York Room, as it was called. To my utter dismay I learned that I was not the winner of the prize. Bill had voted my work second place and while Andrews Wanning voted me third, Sweeney refused to rate me at all. I was not amused. I gather he

With poet Willard Maas, Jacob Riis Park Beach, Queens, New York, 1960

*"About the time of my first year
at Wagner College"*

wasn't either. Based on the audience's unanimous enthusiasm the night before I felt the prize was stolen out from under me, but I was helpless to turn it around. It made not the slightest difference whatsoever that Auden, months earlier, had remarked of my work: "These are the best poems I have ever read of anyone under twenty-five writing in America today." A lot of help that did. (Ironically, or perhaps not so ironically, not one of the contestants was ever heard from again, in terms of poetry.)

Nearly 1:00 now. A bright, spring breezy day. Martha and I exchanged phone numbers. We would see each other a year or two later in New York when she'd come visit at the Warhol Factory. The boys and I headed for the grassy knoll adjacent to the scene of our ruckus the night before. We took off our shirts and stretched out on the sloping lap. A number of students were spread out on blankets and sheets, with books and clipboards, T-shirts modestly riding up, oblivious to our presence—that is, until I stripped down to my

Rudi Gernrich bikini and suddenly, looking around, all heads turn. The prize was lost but the day was mine. A copy of the *Springfield Union-News* Martha had given me lay by my side—its banner read "Young Poets Compete Friday in Mount Holyoke Poetry Contest." In a day—in a matter of a few hours—the event had become old news, but it would be the first of many, many disappointments I'd experience in the course of my one true vocation at the hands of the poetry elite.

After about an hour of hanging out talking nonstop in what us A-heads called "amphetamine rapture," the speed was beginning to wear off. We decided to chuck it and Mount Holyoke, too, and head back to New York. Along the way, as the sun silhouetted the overall landscape, Auden's adage stuck in my head, "The poem is not completed. It is abandoned."

The Assistant: Working with Warhol

Established as a poet with a string of publications (*Paris Review, Partisan Review, Poetry,* the *New Yorker,* etc.), I was one year short of graduating when I met Andy Warhol, an encounter that was to have a major impact on the direction my life and work would take for the next several years, during which time I collaborated on all major artworks Warhol would produce.

Early on I was busy with the "translation of pictures" in the Warhol Factory, as well as the researching of all photo concepts and the application of the silk-screen process, onto canvas or paper—images for the most part originating from newspapers and magazines.

After working with Andy for nearly a year, I decided not to go back to school for my last year. There was just too much excitement happening for me to suddenly give it up and return to the classroom. Seduced by Andy's access to a world of experience for which no formal education could ever prepare me, I dropped out of school again, to the chagrin of Professor Maas. Ezra Pound has commented about people who make such decisions as "strugglers in the desert"—artists willing to risk everything for what they believe as true to their vision. I agreed with Pound: Being thirsty is better than being bored.

I worked with Andy during inarguably his most important period. The very first painting I screened was a 40″ × 40″ silver Elizabeth Taylor portrait at a shutdown firehouse that Andy rented from the city for one hundred dollars a year. In making the Elizabeth Taylor painting, masking tape was shaped to the contours of the face directly on the canvas to create a stencil that followed the lines of a transfer-rubbing originating from the acetate-positive. Then we would fill in the flesh tones, eyebrows, and lips by hand with Liquitex paint, and when it was dry, the masking tape was peeled off, resulting in shaped colors. Andy remarked to me once that his paintings looked more like Alex Katz paintings before the silk screen was applied. The last step in the process was to screen in the black paint. The paintings were a step-by-step transformation of photography into painting.

Andy loved all sorts of machines and gadgets, embracing new techniques and technologies, working with tape recorders, cassettes, Polaroid, Thermofax, but the heart of all this experimentation had as its central focus photography and the silk screen for making a painting; this was by extension his love for the machine because the screen process was very machinelike. Andy's reasoning was that the silk screen would make it as easy as possible to create a painting. Ironically, the process relied directly on manual application.

When the screens were very large, we worked together; otherwise, I was pretty much left to my own inventiveness. I had a firsthand knowledge of silk-screen technique, having worked for a summer as intern to a textile chemist in the manufacture of men's neckwear, so I knew what I was doing from the start.

Andy and I would lay the screen down on the canvas, trying to line up the registration with the marks we made where the screen would go. Then oil-base paint was poured into a corner of the frame of the screen, and I would push the paint with a squeegee across the mesh surface. Andy would grab the squeegee still in motion and continue the process of putting pressure on pushing the paint through the screen from his end. We'd lift the screen, and I would swing it away from the painting and start cleaning it with paper towels soaked in a substance called Varnolene. If not done immediately, the remaining paint would dry and clog the pores.

With Andy Warhol, "the first day on the job at the firehouse," June 1963

The Warhol Factory, Forty-seventh Street, New York, about 1964

After work was completed, we would go over to Andy's house. The firehouse was three blocks from where Andy lived with Julia, his mother, a seemingly frail but hearty woman who was then in her seventies. She would make lunch for us, which usually consisted of a Czechoslovak-style hamburger stuffed with diced onions, sprinkled with parsley, and always on white bread, and with a 7-Up on ice.

Sometimes, he would have people over to view the work. The paintings were for the most part rolled up in the corner of a very cluttered living room. He couldn't store the art at the firehouse because there was no electricity or running water—no conveniences of any kind. The firehouse was basically a shell of a space. There was an opening in the floor where the slide-pole used to be. However all this would shortly change.

In September of '63, he was notified that the building would be put on the auction block. We went hunting for a space. We spent two months looking for a space throughout the city. We covered Hell's Kitchen and Little Italy. The move

forced Andy to get a better working space. Upon moving into the new studio, which had previously been a hat factory, all socializing at Andy's home pretty much ceased. When this happened, his work schedule changed because once he'd leave the house for the day he was out for good. There was no returning home for lunch or anything. We were now in midtown on the East Side. Andy would arrive at the Factory, as it was now called, noon or thereabouts. We would work on and off until 5:00 or 6:00 P.M. and then go out to party.

The first works created at the Factory were a series of food boxes. Andy was fascinated by the shelves of foodstuffs in supermarkets and the repetitive, machinelike effect they created. Andy wanted to become totally mechanical in his work the way a packaging factory would normally silk screen information onto cardboard boxes. He wanted to duplicate the effect but soon discovered that the cardboard surface was not feasible. I located a carpenter in the East Sixties, and Andy hired him out to build plywood boxes that we would then paint and screen, to create the illusion of the real thing.

The brand names chosen consisted of two versions of Brillo, Heinz Tomato Ketchup, Kellogg's Corn Flakes, and Mott's Apple Sauce. We obtained cardboard-box samples of each of these products either from a grocery store or, in the case of the Brillo box, directly from the manufacturer. I'd deliver the cardboard box, at this point flattened out, to the silk-screen manufacturer Harry Golden, who made all of Andy's screens. Specifications were drawn up according to size and density of the screen. In this case, we went for a total black-and-white contrast to complement the original we were working from.

We'd line up the boxes according to their brand name units of shape and carry the screen across the top side of all twenty boxes, one at a time, and then I'd clean the screen and turn the boxes on their sides and repeat the application until the six sides of each box were screened. We were able to get at least two sides done in a day. A hundred or more were produced in a period of a month. They were literally three-dimensional photographs of the actual products.

The ambiance was one where we talked about registration marks. In making a painting, the conversation would go something like, "Let's move it over this way." When we were working on the Elvis Presley series, I remember suggesting the superimpositions that we tried and successfully realized, and that's why these paintings exist the way they do. It was a very creative period for both of us.

Sometimes, we'd go off-register when making a painting, and there'd be a flaw. Andy accepted all that. I think it can be boiled down to one statement, "Embracing the mistakes"—accepting that which occurs spontaneously.

Andy embraced his mistakes. We never rejected anything. In other words, if we were in the process of making a series of paintings and all of a sudden one painting went off a bit, or the image inadvertently overlapped the previous image, we kept right on moving along. We'd keep it, or, as Andy would say, "It's part of the art." The flaws were part of the art. It was as if he possessed an almost Zen-like sensibility.

Warhol was really one of the first since Duchamp and the Dadaists to embrace this seemingly casual attitude towards art. Rather than create art by hand, he made art by the decision of accepting and discarding. Appropriative selection, as it were. Andy would make decisions about how a

certain thing would go in the screen. We would discuss the possibilities and what they would propose. He would turn the acetate one way, then another. A decision would be reached to go with a halftone or stick with the contrast. We would agree, "Yeah, that's great." The screen would be ordered.

The early paintings from 1961–62 were made from screens absent of any halftone layering. He would draw from actual photos, and the drawing would be converted into a screen that was photographic by nature to recreate the drawing as a photographic image in silk-screen application. But a year or so later, he eliminated the drawing altogether and appropriated the photo head-on and turned it into a screen. I was sometimes Andy's photo researcher. We would discover images in newspapers and magazines, and I would search out photos in out-of-the-way, secondhand bookshops or bring something in from home.

Warhol and Malanga preparing to clean a silk screen at the Factory, 1964

*

He was still making art during the period when he started making films. In July 1963, poet-artist Charles Henri Ford and I took Andy shopping at Peerless Camera and helped him select his first movie camera, a 16-mm Bolex with thru-the-lens focusing complete with motordrive that allowed for a one-shot three-minute take.

Sleep was Andy's first and indisputably his most famous film. Perhaps it was famous, too, as a film that few if any ever sat through. Andy conveyed this idea to me—and this was before he actually owned a movie camera—of wanting to make a film of Brigitte Bardot sleeping for eight hours. He said something to the effect that you could get to know everything there is about a person by watching him sleep. He wanted to know what it would be like to watch a movie star

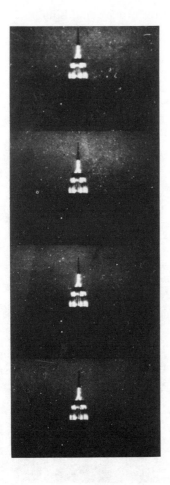

*Film frame
from Andy Warhol's*
Empire, *summer 1964*

sleeping. Obviously the concept was more essential to the realization than was the identity of the protagonist, and knowing Bardot was simply out of his league, he settled for a friend, John Giorno, who was a natural for not waking up.

John gave Andy a key to the flat, and Andy would let himself in. The Bolex was already set up with the lights in place. Andy would turn on the lights and camera, and this activity was repeated for about two weeks.

Sleep runs approximately six-and-a-half hours of equivalent shooting time. Andy duplicated an additional ninety minutes from an equal ninety-minute section of the film to stretch it out to eight hours to approximate the scientifically accepted length of time for normal sleep.

The film *Empire* was also shot mostly at night, in summer 1964. We started shooting around 6:00 P.M.—it was still daylight—and completed around 1:00 A.M. The first two reels are overexposed because Andy was metering for night light, but it was all guesswork. What happens in the course of the first two reels, and partway through the third, is that the building slowly emerges from a twilight haze, balancing out the exposure from the darkness that slowly blankets the sky. The Empire State Building was already a star of sorts when it was featured in *King Kong,* but Andy wanted to make the building an even bigger star!

The films are very similar in style in that they treat time in a one-to-one ratio. Both *Sleep* and *Empire* are in black-and-white, no sound, shot at night, and the camera *never* moves. The only major difference between the two films is that *Sleep* was shot with the Bolex using 100-foot/three-minute film rolls, and *Empire* was shot with a rented Auricon equipped to shoot, 1,200 feet of film for thirty-five minutes nonstop. Andy would have probably filmed *Sleep* with the Auricon had he known of the camera's existence. He was learning as he went along, mimicking the progress of Hollywood without knowing it.

It was John Palmer who came up with the idea for *Empire.* Andy had the resources to get the concept realized finally, so essentially Andy was producer, but he got the billing—Andy Warhol's *Empire.* Andy barely touched the camera during the entire time the movie was being shot. John, Jonas Mekas, and I changed the reels for him. The machine would do all the work, Andy thought. So there's a direct connection between the silk screen, which is a photographic and mechanical process, and the movie camera, which also creates a photographic-type image.

(From left) Malanga and Warhol at the Factory during a film session, about 1964

Photography has always been the underlying theme consistent to Andy's work. If you were to take a strip of 16-mm footage of *Sleep* and examine the frames horizontally, there appears a sameness of repetition that also occurs in his headshot paintings of Marilyn Monroe and Elvis Presley.

I remember once—this happened so many different times and in varied contexts—we were attending the premiere screening of *Empire* at the Bridge Cinema in lower Manhattan near a street that leads onto the Brooklyn Bridge. We were standing in the rear of the auditorium. Andy was observing the audience rather than the film, and people were walking out or booing or throwing paper cups at the screen. Andy turned to me, and in his boyish voice said, "Gee, you think they hate it . . . you think they don't like it?" *Empire* was a seven-hour movie where nothing happened except how the audience reacted.

Andy was not overly conscious of how an audience might respond to one of his films. In his mind, he was realizing a concept that was perhaps less original than the decision ultimately to put that concept in motion. He extended an already minimal and appropriative vocabulary to include the kind of decision making he applied to his painting. The only way his films would be accepted or criticized was through their reliance on an audience to see them; otherwise, they would remain concepts in a can.

Andy is often commented about as being a voyeur. He's generally characterized as someone who liked to watch. Watching takes time. You just don't look and turn away. It's a matter of optic absorption. One of the ways Andy expressed obsessive looking was through the movie camera. His silent films were mostly about approximating the same amount of time it would take to make the film as to watch it. A voyeur needs a window frame, or a blind, as a frame of reference to inhabit a situation in a secretive way, which amounted to Andy's fascination with someone having to sit through it all in the dark. It implies power over a person who is unaware of being watched, like someone sleeping, for instance. Andy's desire for power was initially realized through the voyeuristic tendency of distancing himself from what he was watching with the use of a movie camera.

His desire to make films evolved because he loved Hollywood, and this was his way of getting as close as possible to the allure, magic, and mystery he felt as an adolescent. He wrote to film companies for photos of his favorite stars, which he drew from for hours on end while withdrawing deeper into his fantasies of the rich and famous. So twenty years later in 1965 when Andy met Edie Sedgwick for the first time, it was the closest he'd ever come to someone who possessed the aura of a Hollywood starlet in the flesh.

Edie was not career oriented at the time she met Andy. Edie was a blue blood. She had no active goals other than to enjoy herself to the fullest. Her life imitated art to the extent that it was colorful and ephemeral. She could be very easily molded. She had the one ingredient essential to being a star—glamour. When you characterize someone as glamorous, you're saying that the

person is beautiful. Glamour is not beauty, but it can become that. Glamour is aura. The person who already possesses aura becomes beautiful. Andy was deeply fascinated with glamour on this level. He had an eye for it.

Edie's first starring role in which she talked in a Warhol film was *Poor Little Rich Girl,* shot in her one-room studio. Her close friend Chuck Wein fabricated some notes and coached Edie. The concept of "embracing the mistakes" played an integral part in how the film came to exist in its present form. We shot two reels. When they came back from the lab, we previewed them and, to our horror, found them to be extremely out of focus— not even close to salvageable. After replacing the lens, we reshot the two long takes a week later, and got it right. We took the first reel, from the first version, and sequenced it with the second reel, from the second version, so the film opens with an out-of-focus thirty-five-minute take. That takes a lot of guts.

As the months progressed, Edie appeared in a number of films, some especially scripted for her, the first of these being *Kitchen.* The films would have an instant audience; reviews would appear in the press; and Edie's career was launched, so to speak, but she wasn't getting paid. She thought Andy was making money with the films, because of all the hoopla, but he wasn't. The sales from his paintings were supporting a highly speculative venture into filmmaking. If anything, the films were a drain on him financially. Nevertheless, Edie wanted to get paid, but Andy never indicated that any payment, however small, would be forthcoming, except to say to her ever so often, "Be patient." But Edie's patience had run its course.

Andy assumed, wrongly perhaps, that if he started paying everyone for whatever the work involved, the end result would be of a lesser quality. He was convinced of this. This attitude, ironically, turned on him with the portrait commissions he executed during the '70s.

At around the time Edie was contemplating leaving Andy, an opportunity presented itself. Bob Dylan's confidant and roadie, Bobby Neuwirth, acted as liaison in getting Edie to come over to the Dylan camp. The people advising Dylan had this illusion that they could develop Edie into a singer and in turn capitalize on her already-established reputation in the media. So it was easy for Edie to finally leave Andy. By switching allegiance she became part of a heterosexual milieu. Andy represented every bit a homosexual sensibility and the Dylan group was staunchly hetero. Edie had

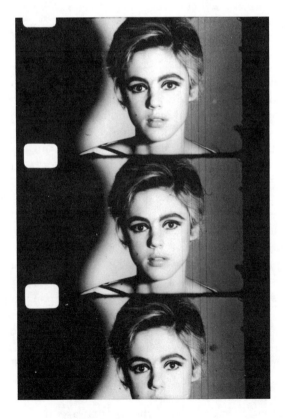

Edie Sedgwick, screen test, the Warhol Factory, 1965

assumed that being promoted as a singer was promised her, but her situation never developed in any viable way because her talent was totally undeveloped. She thought she could further her career by being associated with Dylan, but this was merely an optimism based on hope and dreams. She soon learned that he had been secretly married during this time.

*

There are many different points of view about Andy. Edie somehow came to be a damaging one. A good deal of mythmaking was perpetrated about Andy's association with Edie, as chronicled in the Jean Stein/George Plimpton biography, *Edie.* It was hyped to a certain extent. Andy did not turn Edie on to drugs. She got caught up in the drug scene shortly after leaving Andy. The closest Andy ever came to taking drugs was a prescription for the diet pill Obitrol. At the time, Edie was taking Obitrols to get through the day. Andy was taking them to lose weight. It had much to do with vanity.

What made Andy glamorous was his unique appearance with his silver wig and lack of pigmentation, thus he was instant material for the media. By this, Andy recognized his oddness early on and saw the advantage of using it to gain attention for himself as a public relations ploy. He became his own instant star.

Andy was very simplistic. If he said to me, "Oh, that poem was fabulous, wow!" that was the end of the topic. He didn't get into any in-depth talk about the nuance and function of metaphor. But Andy was more real than his hype because he really was intelligent. He was not an imposter. Reality did cut through on lots of occasions. It wasn't like we got on a bus and took a trip to Des Moines, Iowa, rented a motel room, and conveniently Truman Capote would be there to record all the great remarks. On trips, many a time, we would share the motel room. So that says something about the relationship I had with him. Maybe it wasn't all that verbal, but a sense of trust existed between us in a genuine way. And he was frightfully modest. Not once did I ever see him undressed. Wherever we travelled he always kept a small satchel. Once I took a sneak peek and discovered a roll of Johnson & Johnson adhesive tape, scissors, and hair spray—the apparatus for maintaining his silver bonnet. His trust in me was simply that Andy probably never wanted to be alone. He lived with his mother for the greater part of his adult life, up to the time she died in the late '70s.

This fear of being alone was very much a part of his being an extremely shy and private person. I don't think Andy was consciously trying to hide something about himself as much as attempting to maintain a mystique, as a cover for his own inadequacies. His shyness allowed him to be private. He felt that his sexual preferences were really no one's business, and therefore he didn't go out of his way to make pronouncements like "Here's my new boyfriend."

Many people seem to agree that the '70s were bad years for Andy, but in the '80s he seemed to have made an extraordinary comeback. The '70s were a less urgent period than the '60s. I call the '70s the "Age of Hibernation," and Andy was simply out of touch with those from whom he truly could have benefited creatively, had it not been for his fascination with the so-called rich and famous. Those people never really had anything to contribute to his art except by way of their vanity. They paid dearly for a forty-inch square canvas of themselves—that speaks of the vacuity of their intellect. The vitality of Andy's creativity diminished to the point where all he was making were these ooh-and-ah celebrity portraits, receiving incredible sums of money for them. Who would want those works today? I don't believe for a second that he had any genuine interest in the people whose portraits he made. Friendships like these are created between agents. But the very thing that Andy had identified in his artwork in the '60s became identifiable icons for the '80s. This complete circle of events gave Andy a new surge of optimism and self-confidence . . . and then he died.

Andy could have survived 1987. He should not have died when he did. Unfortunately, much deceit and confusion exist now in his wake. Attributions to several artworks are misleading, improvised. And since estate certification is a way to manipulate Andy's auction and resale value, toes inevitably get stepped on.

Andy's fate is sealed. There's no denying that he is part of the history of art in the modern world. But which amplifies what? Andy Warhol the social phenomenon boosting up Andy Warhol the artist, or the other way around? Some people would say that his greatest achievement was the adage, "In the future everyone will be famous for fifteen minutes." That in itself is a frightening thought because the culture seems to be developing in ways that would allow one to be famous merely on charm.

If you were to meet him for the first time, and Andy liked you, he became your instant fan, and this, in turn, would create in you a feeling of self-esteem. It's as if he were collecting people. He had a hypnotic power to create a personality for someone. This is perhaps connected to Andy's adulation of Hollywood movie stars when, as an adolescent, he would draw from the 8″ × 10″ glossies for hours on end. He would be recreating his daydreams on paper. The secret to Andy's success was his own self-effacement.

Benedetta Barzini

Benedetta Barzini

Benedetta Barzini

Gerard, this is Benedetta. Benedetta . . . Gerard." Leo Castelli completed the triangle and looked at each of us, with generous, fraternal touch of arms outstretched, as if he were bringing us closer together. All else—the swirl of activity at Rauschenberg's loft the night of Saturday, February 6, 1966—seemed to fade in the background.

Of course I'd seen Benedetta before! The beauty mark on her right cheek was her trademark. She was fast becoming one of the most recognizable faces in *Vogue* and *Bazaar,* but here in the flesh she transcended all expectation of being perceived otherwise.

Benedetta was wearing a velvet dress—burgundy hue—with embroidered trim. She had an inch over me, standing about five feet, seven-and-a-half inches tall. Her black hair, pulled tight in a bun, accentuated her chiseled features and a delicate, aquiline nose. Her complexion, the color of pearl—warm, translucent. But it was her eyes, like two emeralds, unflinching and deeply soulful . . . those wide, startled eyes, that gave total absorption. The lyrical lilt of her voice. Refinement, discretion, understatement, nobility. Her intricate intellect was what magnified her beauty even more.

She was cultivated, smart as a whip, with a no-nonsense approach. She said she grew up in Manhattan, enrolled at Lycée Français, East Ninety-fifth Street at about the same time I was attending PS 46 in the Fordham section of the Bronx. We joked how we could easily have played together as kids in a Central Park playground. We talked poetry. Her tastes were eclectic—from Dante and the Greek and Latin classics and Apollinaire, to Rilke, Yeats, Pavese, Voznesensky. I was impressed.

Had anyone told me then she was one of the world's great beauties, it would have been a gross understatement and misleading besides. It was as if Benedetta's inner beauty had emptied my consciousness, causing my sight of her to become pure, mirror-like. I was momentarily mesmerized, and though everything from that moment on would no longer be the same for me, the significance of that change would not be felt for quite some time—several months, in fact.

Robert Rauschenberg—as reported in the next week's edition of the *Village Voice,* under a photo by Fred McDarrah—at exactly 12:18 A.M. of a Sunday morning, balanced himself atop a ten-foot ladder, "unscrewed a 500-watt lightbulb, held his arm outstretched momentarily, and descended—thus completing his rarely performed Statue of Liberty happening. Removal of the bulb was the signal for spontaneous dancing of the frug in the dark by such luminaries as Lawrence Alloway, Leo Castelli, Barnett Newman, Dennis Hopper, Larry

Poons, Tom Wolfe, Clay Felker, Andy Warhol, and Gerard Malanga." Where was I? I was in a state of reverie, as if hit by a thunderbolt from the gods. I had met a young woman; I was attracted to her; my emotions were moved, my sensitiveness increased, my intellect excited, and that dim state of being which we call the soul purged and cleared. That pretty much summed it up.

*

Paul Blackburn, poet-impresario, had scheduled a reading for me at St. Mark's Church In-the-Bowery, for March 24, a Thursday. The theme of the reading centered around my father, when—shortly after arriving in New York in the mid-1920s, living alone and barely speaking the language—he'd had a photo of himself made, which formed the centerpieces for my design of the flyer, with the banner "THE GERARD MALANGA STORY." Three hundred flyers were clandestinely run off by Marie Menken at her office at Time-Life and mailed out two weeks in advance of the event.

Shortly after, I would encounter Allen Ginsberg at a party in Elaine de Kooning's loft. He was astonished to learn that my reading coincided exactly the same day and hour as Andrei Voznesensky's first public appearance in America at Hunter College. Allen insisted that I cancel my reading and attend Voznesensky's instead. When I told him that the flyers had already gone out, he urged me to print up a cancellation announcement and dictated how the copy should read: "In honor of the Soviet poet Andrei Voznesensky, reading at Hunter College, Thursday, March 24, Gerard Malanga has cancelled his reading at St. Mark's Church." Allen even handed me a twenty-dollar bill to cover postage. Ideally, as he had theoretically surmised, anyone planning to attend my reading might likely want to come hear Voznesensky.

But my reason for cancelling was altogether not entirely altruistic. I remember Benedetta mentioning Voznesensky as one of her favorite poets. I rightly intuited that she would be at his reading. It would be to my advantage to make my presence felt, even if only affording me a glimpse of her at a distance.

On the morning of March 24 I would run into Blackburn on St. Mark's Place. I couldn't ascertain for sure whether he was red in the face from a late-niter at McSorley's, the local pub a few doors from his flat on East Seventh, or just plain ripped at my

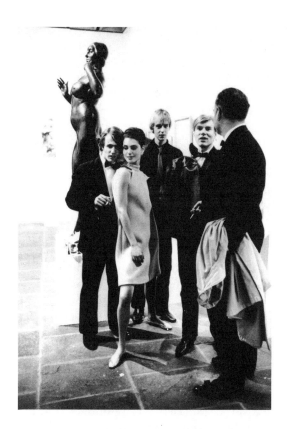

At the inaugural opening of the Whitney Museum of American Art, October 1966: (from left) Gerard Malanga, Benedetta Barzini, Rene Ricard, and Andy Warhol

fait accompli. His attitude was abrupt and we went our separate ways. At that moment all else didn't much matter. My sights were elsewhere. Not even my own reading could prevent my being in Benedetta's sphere.

As it happened, Andy and I were only two rows behind from where she was seated with friends, so in exiting we rushed up to each other, hugging and kissing. Mission accomplished. I had a foot in her psyche, so to speak. I was testing my power, but I would not see her again until the coming fall.

*

What are the images that I can recall now? I begin about Benedetta in the present tense of our lives with each other as they were then. I'm reading through "The Secret Diaries"—a notebook I maintained during much of this time—

from where Benedetta re-emerges as a real presence to the point where a rapport soon develops.

September 27, Benedetta is back in New York after a summer spent at Williamstown Theatre Festival—"I can build sets—run the light board—make costumes—fly in the flats—work the Follow Light and the whole thing was an illuminating experience. I acted—I also sang in *Annie Get Your Gun,* of all things! . . ."[1] We're to attend the Whitney Museum inaugural.

I purchase formal slippers and a tuxedo shirt at Brooks Brothers. Marie Menken supplies me with her black tie-jacket and trousers. It's arranged that Benedetta meet me at the Factory so she can change from blue jeans to evening clothes, but Billy Name locks the downstairs door and she spends fifteen minutes in the garage across the way trying to reach me by phone, but Andy's on the line, so she finally heads home and gets through—she'll come by and pick me up by car. Andy is also planning to attend the opening, so—why not—I invite him to join us.

Andy, Benedetta, and I arrive as a trio through the doors of the new Marcel Brauer edifice. Fred McDarrah is positioned inside the lobby and takes our picture. Looking at the photo now, Andy and Benedetta focus their attention on me. Was I the boy of the hour, or did I just crack a joke?

Benedetta without question is the most beautiful woman at the opening. She's wearing a stunning, shocking-pink wool Cardin dress and ruby studs. I introduce her to Stephen Shote, Michael Marsh, and Rene Ricard who, when I turn my back for an instant, is already all over her conversing in French. Joe Dever asks our names for his column. Rene is spilling champagne and placing empty glasses on the floor. Charles Moore asks to take our picture—Andy, Rene, Benedetta, and me huddled together in a mock pose.

October 15, according to my notes, I'm reminded that I'd spoken with Allen Ginsberg earlier in the day—he's nervous about the reading he and Peter Orlovsky are to give at Town Hall. He's reserved four comps for me. Benedetta and I were to pick up Rene and drive uptown, but the plans got turned around. I leave a note for him at the Factory that he should go directly to the box office to pick up his ticket.

Benedetta calls. I tell her to meet me at Max's between 7:00 and 7:30. In honor of Allen I purchase matching white Moroccan robes fashioned with hoods at a shop on St. Mark's Place. Benedetta arrives promptly at 7:30. We have drinks and dinner.

On the way uptown I turn her on to some grade-A j. It takes fifteen minutes to park the car. We put on the robes, walk into the lobby. All eyes are now focused on us. Andy is off to the side. Benedetta walks up behind and kisses him on the back of the head. I introduce Benedetta to Barbara Rubin and Rona Page. The girls get it on. The lights signal that it's time to take our seats. Andy is lost in the crowd. The lights dim. Allen and Peter walk out on stage and take bows and then quickly seat themselves stage center.

The performance opens with two Indian mantras. Peter starts with a Vietnam antiwar poem followed by a series of poems about assholes and vegetables. Allen follows, accompanying himself on the harmonium with a few William Blake songs, some love poems for boys, and concludes the evening with a new poem—a sweeping, panoramic vista called "Wichita Vortex Sutra" with its

> . . . wreathes of naked bodies, thighs and faces,
>   small hairy bun'd vaginas,
>   silver cocks, armpits and breasts
> moistened by tears . . .

> with its . . . houseless brown farmland plains
>   rolling heavenward
>   in every direction . . .[2]

Allen asks, "What if I opened my soul to sing to my absolute self . . ." The audience goes wild. Benedetta folds her hand inside mine and leans her head on my shoulder. This, as I seem to recall, is the first instance of her initiating physical warmth.

After the reading we all meet up in the lobby—Rona, Rene, my secretary, Susan Pile—and on the way down to the Balloon Farm the car fills up with marijuana smoke. The Velvet Underground is performing tonight and I'll be dancing on stage with them. Benedetta watches the show from the balcony, near where Andy and Paul are working the projectors. Tonight I'm dancing from my heart. Allen is now in the audience gazing up at me.

Benedetta and I split immediately after the show for Max's to meet up with friends from her summer in Williamstown. Her enormous appetite

---

[1] Letter dated September 22, 1966.

[2] From Allen Ginsberg's *Collected Poems 1947–1980*, Harper & Row, 1984.

With Benedetta in the photomat, October 1966

consumes her. Finishing her meal she starts in on mine. She claims she has a tapeworm. Rene joins us, making a mockery of everything and everyone around him, turning over ashtrays, and screaming at anyone who dares to walk past our table. Andy walks in, shrewdly avoids Rene for fear of embarrassment, sits at another table.

I'm looking over my "Diaries" now and I see that on October 17 I visited with Edie Sedgwick. "I've never seen her more beautiful. She pulls on red leotards and a tight, red cotton top. I weed out the seeds and twigs and fill one eighth's full Camel with Acapulco Gold. We're high. She tells me her attempt at withdrawing from the media attention, from Andy, the parties. I mention that I've been seeing Benedetta. Edie is very happy for me, comments that 'Benedetta has a good head on her shoulders.'"

I leave Edie falling asleep. Pick up maquettes to be shot for silk screens. Run into Benedetta on Lexington Avenue, near where she lives up the street from Andy's house. Psychic thought providing physical encounter.

On October 18—Benedetta is unable to join me at Timothy Leary's concert, "Turn On. Tune In. Drop Out." She's having dinner with her father, who's in town for one week of conferences with CBS. Says she'll call me at Max's. She doesn't

call but surprises me—showing up a half-hour after me. I order her second meal of the evening. "Where does it all go?" We start joking around. We scribble notes to each other on matchbook covers, like "I missed you when I didn't hear from you Monday night." She replies, "I don't even dare miss you. XXXXXxx."

After dinner we decide to head out for Ondine, a discotheque on the upper East Side. We grab an inconspicuous table off in a corner. During a live set of the Doors, we continue to exchange notes on matchbook covers. Benedetta writes: "Shy in your presence ever since I first met you— Am 'afraid'—can't figure out what it is all about (inside). Am fighting something but would like to know about you—the whys and wheres and hows and things. Do you really talk?" I write out, "I am so shy in your presence and always was from the first time I met you. When I am silent I am really thinking of you." Benedetta writes: "I'm a false person." I cross out the word "false."

Benedetta attempts to relate an incident that occurred several years back—at eighteen she'd been living at the estate of a boyfriend's mother not far from Venice for the summer. She'd walk the dogs in the rock garden, curl up with a book in the candlelit room. Time passed slowly and then at summer's end she realized he was not coming back, the feeling of suddenly being dead inside consumed her. I could picture her words even now. She buries herself among the bedsheets. The boyfriend not in Venice ends in the dream of her cutting her hair-ends. The footsteps that never reach her . . . the long, silent walks in the rock garden all afternoon become a dream, but the feeling of injury leaving her empty is not a dream.

The next day I pick up silk-screen transparencies and drop them off for Andy to look at. I visit Edie in Lenox Hill Hospital. Two days earlier, after leaving her asleep, her apartment caught fire.

"Tonight Benedetta said she loved me" is a line in the "Diaries" for October 23. Did she tell me this over the phone or in person? I can't recall now. The entry also states that she is with her father, visiting Philip Johnson in Connecticut at his "house left out in the rain," as Rene calls it.

On October 24, Rene and I go shopping for a leather jacket, scarf, one dozen red roses for Benedetta. John Wieners is giving a reading at the Ninety-second Street Y, but for one reason or other Benedetta can't make it, so we arrange that she meet me at the Paradox afterwards. "I take a mescaline trip, but am very tense inside and on the way up to the Y we have the taxi stop at least five times so I can get out and vomit, though my stomach is empty."

After the reading we head down to the Paradox. Rona is with me. Benedetta arrives wearing the same dress I remember her in when we first met at Rauschenberg's loft. "My head is on the table. Benedetta lifts my head up and I hand her the roses. She looks at them as a child would, curiously, and looks at me with a smile and concern. She hugs me and kisses me on the head, on the lips. I feel so good inside."

We drive over to the reception Bob Wilson has arranged for John in the West Village, at the home of a friend. Benedetta meets John for the first time. As she unwraps the roses to show John, "all the petals fall to the floor like snowflakes."

October 29 was a very fortuitous day. The *Exploding Plastic Inevitable* is scheduled for a light-and-sound performance at the Boston Institute of Contemporary Art to coincide with a show of Andy's art. I suggest the trip to Benedetta and she's excited to come along.

That morning, Rene and I wait outside Paul's apartment. Benedetta drives up at 10:00 and we head up Third Avenue to Castelli Gallery to pick up a signed Warhol Liz Taylor poster—Benedetta's gift to a friend, a Harvard student.

Leo asks Benedetta if there's room in the car for a French writer from *Réalités* who is doing a story on Andy. Jean Clay would characterize me in his article as a "disheveled poet."[3] I write poems in the front seat the whole way up.

I have arranged with Gordon Baldwin, a close friend, for Benedetta and I to spend the night, so when we arrive in Cambridge to drop off our bags, he has set aside his own bedroom for us.

We drive over to the ICA. The movies, including *Vinyl*, are being projected and two spotlights are aimed directly on the rotating mirror ball, giving the auditorium a luminous revolving glow.

The movies end. The Velvets walk on stage and begin setting up and tuning their instruments. Fifteen minutes into the first number I step out on stage and slowly work my way into a new dance routine—a crucifixion attitudinal pose. Rona stands behind me with two flashlights, aiming their beams, through my outstretched arms, at the audience.

At the show's end, backstage, I notice Benedetta in an unusually upbeat mood. I step outside the dressing room for a moment and Rona follows me. She tells me that Benedetta is having "woman problems." Rona, smiling, tells me "how beautiful Benedetta looks at this moment and how much Benedetta loves me."

We head over to Ed Hood's flat where a small party in our honor is underway. She places her hand over my own on the front seat. Within the hour it's become a Buñuelian nightmare—one can barely move any which way. The room fills with cigarette smoke. Time to skidoo.

We make our way out into the open night air and walk a few doors east on Mount Auburn Avenue to Gordon's flat. While Benedetta is taking a shower I turn off all the lights and take a match to a candle and then light up a joint from its flickering, golden flame.

Focus for remembering it all. Now a mental picture: Small, damp tendrils of hair over neck and ears. Neck curving gracefully into collarbone. The skin is translucent, the face aglow, the head backlit, as if a halo instantly took form and changed also. Candlelight bouncing off wall. Nightgown lifting past shoulders . . . flat-bellied. A Lucas Cranach painting in posture and grace. Her eyes wide open in love, I could see in the darkness. She remembered herself bleeding for the first time in five years, suddenly awakened in her passion—that she could feel alive once again. The evaporation of the long wait on the Venetian estate she'd hinted at became the end of a part of her life now beginning with me. Benedetta is smiling at me; her shy, sorrowful, catlike gaze, her innocence, her guilt and "the last few years of struggling and suffering, from the inside"—as her father once put it in a letter to me—come to an end.

She climbs into bed and we hold onto each other for what seems an eternity. The candlelight flickers . . . goes out. I kiss her gently behind the ear. I press my lips against her temple, the hollow of her cheek. Benedetta looks into my eyes, stares straight into me, and says, "If I get pregnant, we'll have the child anyway."

Sunday morning in Cambridge, Massachusetts. Sunlight cast on the bloodstained white sheet. The night never ending . . .

We pose for Marie Cosindas's large-format Polaroid camera set on tripod in Gordon's kitchen. Marie makes three attempts on getting it right and presents me with the third shot, commemorating this most auspicious occasion of having us pose for

---

[3]Jean Clay, "Andy's Warhorse," *Réalités* (Paris), December 1967.

Malanga as part of Andy Warhol's Exploding Plastic Inevitable, *which featured the Velvet Underground (John Cale on guitar in background), at the Balloon Farm, NYC, 1966*

her. Marie also made a triple portrait with John Wieners, Rene, and me.

"No woman is virtuous / who does not give herself to her lover / —forthwith"—William Carlos Williams, in Book Five of his long poem, *Paterson,* apropos to what's now realized. It's October 31 now. According to "The Secret Diaries," it's my first night back in New York. I'm staying with John Wieners at the Chelsea. I phone Benedetta at 3:00 A.M. She tells me she loves me. November 1—Benedetta calls, tells me she has to meet "someone" at the Plaza and we arrange that I meet her at 10:00 across the way at the Pulitzer Fountain. We walk the entire block circling the fountain, arms around each other's waist, trying to come up with a place to have supper. Head over to Serendipity III. We have cheese omelettes—Benedetta having more than her share, digging into my plate as well—and finish off with a pineapple frost lime, coffee, and icebox cake. I joke about getting Duchamp to sign his name to a shovel for her as a Christmas gift.

It's November 2 now—my last night in New York before I leave for a tour of Ohio and West Virginia with the Velvets. I arrive at the Tucci apartment and Benedetta introduces me to Mrs. Tucci as we're about to head out. We drive to Chinatown for dinner. Afterwards we head over to the Chelsea to pick up John and Rene for drinks at Max's. It would be around midnight that we leave Max's and drive up to her place, because I see now that the time is noted in the "Diaries" as 2:00 A.M., about the time I would have departed and headed home.

We sprawl out on her bed looking at each other's family snapshots and talk about what it was like for us growing up, discovering similar interests, similar dreams, goals, aspirations.

Benedetta telling me it has been five years since her last period. . . . Could this be directly linked to her sense of abandonment a few years earlier on the Venetian estate? I don't ask. The fact that she has even brought it up is relevant to her personal history and the way in which she places trust in me indicates as much—that what we are feeling for each other is not illusion.

I ask Benedetta if she has ever thought about marriage. She asks me to repeat what I just said. "She tells me she loves me," I have typed here, followed by, "I ask her to marry me." She says, "Yes." Looking at her long enough I understand what she has been seeing in my face for some time now.

We take a vow not to call long-distance, not to break the self-imposed silence we've promised each other during the four days that I'll be away. Time will be suspended for us. We will continue as if a break hasn't occurred. I remember what she wrote in one of those matchbooks I've saved—"I don't even dare miss you."

Next day—November 3—before I would meet up with Paul, Nico, and the Velvets at the Factory—Andy would not be coming on this trip—"I phoned my mother," according to the "Diaries," "to tell her the happy news about my marriage with Benedetta." My mother says, "When you come home in a few days the wedding bands will be here waiting as my gift to you and Benedetta."

(It's August now, the second to be exact, 1992. I call my mother long-distance. I want to hear her words about this personal history, these private moments, of someone she's never met. After all, she's eighty-seven and she had a direct part in this too. She says, "No, I don't know who even she is [sic]." Just as I thought.)

Benedetta, at the last minute, thinks to meet up with me in Morgantown, West Virginia—the last stop on the tour—where as plan would have it "we would stop here and there on the way back to New York." For some unknown reason, now that I look back at what I've written, I discourage this plan, simply feeling that to undertake such a trip seems a bit impractical, as we have work waiting for us the start of the week. I foolishly don't consider the romantic implications involved.

On November 3, after arriving in Cincinnati, in what would be the first show of the tour, I send a telegram: "The most beautiful question receives the most beautiful answer. I love you, Gerard." When we reach Columbus—November 5—I wire her flowers.

On November 5, upon arriving at the University of West Virginia—the last leg of the tour—I note that I will be sending Benedetta a wire to reserve a double at the Chelsea. I still maintain our vow with regard, calling her directly.

It's November 7—"the last leg of my journey home—United Flight #146 to Newark. I draw B's on the starless night sky window. I keep thinking she should have received the news of my arrival on such-and-such time."

It's nearly 1:30 A.M. when we arrive in Newark. Close-ups of an empty airport conjure images in an Antonioni movie of the mind. "A few people. Silence. Loudspeaker occasionally announcing an arrival/departure to nowhere. The newsstand bathed in a ghostly blue hue. Faces staring out from magazine covers." I call. No answer. The phone rings four or five times. I ask at the check-in counter, but no message has been left in my name. No use standing around waiting for the probable/improbable. I hitch a ride with Paul, Lou, and Nico. It's 3:00 A.M. when we reach Paul's flat. I try once again. This time Benedetta picks up. She tells me "the four days we were apart from each other felt like one hundred years had passed. I'll phone you tomorrow at 6:00 at the Factory. Goodnight. Ciao."

Benedetta Barzini and Gerard Malanga in Richard Ballarian's photography studio, November 1966

The entry for the night of November 7 is a bit confusing. It's noted that although I missed Benedetta's call, I told Paul Katz that she'd be meeting me at the Paradox after 10:30. So, to kill time, I attend a poetry reading: Louise Bogan and W. S. Merwin at the Ninety-second Street Y, just up the street from where Benedetta lives. It's 9:30 now—the reading over. I head south along Lexington and as I pass the building where Benedetta lives I notice her Dodge Dart parked out front. "I stop. Go back. Walk up the stairs. Meet her in hallway." Long moment of silence as we walk to the car. A few words here and there. I give her the lead. We drive to a small bar on Seventy-third Street, Third Avenue. Wine is brought to the table. "She explains that she cannot love me. I am speechless and in a state of shock" is what I have typed here. It's very cut-and-dry. It all sounds rehearsed, as if she spent double time seeing her analyst. It's as if a bomb went off at the table and I no longer exist, or I'm just plain dreamin', unable to get back through to the other side, as if observing all this at a short distance. My pride prevents me from making an attempt to be persuasive or argumentative. I've lost all sense of speech, but more than that I've lost my magic and power. In a matter of a few minutes the happiest man on earth is reduced to unfathomable unhappiness.

She drives me to Anne Waldman's flat on St. Mark's Place. As I'm stepping out of the car, she leans over and says, "Don't do anything foolish." The Dodge pulls away, turns the corner, and is gone. All else—traffic and honking sounds, cabs whooshing by, crowds of pedestrians, shop-window lights—dissolves slowly into white.

Warhol and What Came After

The year is 1967, September. I am twenty-four. The story has never been accurately told, but my reason for leaving Andy had much to do with the political intrigue pervasive in Andy's circle, encouraged by him to a degree, I would learn later, which was affecting my work. Also, Benedetta was returning to Italy to live. These incidents were coincident with an invitation from the Bergamo Film Festival to submit my film *In Search of the Miraculous* for its "New Director" series.

This would be an opportune time for a much-needed break, to think things out, to re-evaluate my role and function at the Factory. Subconsciously, I was following my former girlfriend back to Italy, not wanting to lose the connection. In this

respect, I much agree with Proust's sense of how we change the whole course of our lives in pursuit of a love that we will have forgotten within a few months.

I reserved a one-way ticket to Milan. That was all I could afford. As the date drew near, Andy (aware of my financial circumstances) assured me that he would send me the return ticket. All I would need to do is call. My fate was sealed.

A couple of weeks after my arrival, a close friend, Flavio Lucchini, founding editor of *Vogue Uomo,* offered me the use of his office phone, where I spent nearly a week calling and sending wires to the Factory. No one was responding. I was in a country where I not only didn't speak the language but was flat broke besides.

An acquaintance from New York, Peter Hartman, composer and poet living in Rome, wired money through a friend for train fare. Suddenly I was being guided by mysterious forces I had no control over. I wasn't returning to New York, I was travelling south to Rome.

*

When Che Guevara died in 1967, his face was plastered over thousands of posters throughout Rome. He took on the aura of a movie idol or religious icon here, so I had no idea what impact his death night have had in New York, or with Andy for that matter.

A relationship had developed between me and a young girl, donna Patrizia Ruspoli. Aware of the work I had done with Warhol, and anxious to have a wall space in her new studio on the via Nargutta filled with a portrait of Che—as it would be the "in" thing—she offered to finance a project for which I would create a silk-screen painting of the Cuban revolutionary. We set out and canvassed nearly all the local printing houses to have a screen made, but no one in the area was familiar with the process. It subsequently dawned on me that the only way a screen could be fabricated was to order one directly from Harry Golden, the silk-screen manufacturer with whom Andy and I had worked in New York.

In the meantime, Patrizia thought of a way in which I might benefit from this project to raise money for my airfare home, by simply financing two paintings and exhibiting the extra one in the gallery of a friend. I foolishly reasoned that since I was applying the skills I had used when working with Andy, I naively assumed that he would

Donna Francesca Patrizia Ruspoli di Poggio Suasa, Rome, 1967

consent to my making this painting—one he could call his own—which would then provide me with the airfare home. Images of Che were in abundance, so in my research I carefully selected one which would be appropriate to Andy's aesthetic, had we been making this painting together.

The image I chose out of an Italian tabloid shows a horizontal shot of Che stretched out on a slab in a morgue, with a Bolivian officer holding a handkerchief to his nose. Coupled with this shot is a cropped close-up of Che's face. The image is highly macabre: although Che's eyes are wide open, he's very dead. I liked the ambiguity.

Patrizia went ahead with the necessary arrangements and the gallery dealer, aware of my association with Warhol and not questioning the painting's provenance, agreed to exhibit it in his space, thus claiming to be the first gallery in Rome to exhibit a Warhol artwork.

Two weeks following the order with Mr. Golden, Patrizia was informed by an airport official that the parcel had arrived. Because the

family name had instant clout, her mother's chauffeur had no problem retrieving the parcel from Customs. I now had all the requisite materials and quickly mapped out the series of steps involved in creating the multiple portrait.

With the gallery's commitment, I then realized I could run off any number of images and came up with the idea to include a series of twenty-six works on paper of a single image, lettered A to Z, signed "Warhol," each in a different color. This meant I would need to clean the screen twenty-six times!

I proceeded to make two paintings, identical in size, approximately 5′ × 6′. The color combination for Patrizia's painting, I recall, consisted of chartreuse on a silver ground. The combination chosen for the exhibition canvas was blue on a field of red. The preparation was painstakingly long. I first had to spray-paint each canvas and let them dry for an entire day. On the following day I traced through the acetate containing the tabloid image onto both canvases, setting up a grid of registration marks to control the application of the multiple images on canvas. This took two days, one for each canvas. The third day I screened twenty-eight sheets of fine drawing paper, reserving two of the sheets as A/Ps (artist's proofs). Each sheet was screened in a different color, ranging from black to white, with the two A/Ps repeating two of the twenty-six selections, red and blue. (A few months later I would present the red one to Charles Henri Ford, which immediately got swallowed up in his archive. The blue one was included in my archive, later deposited with the University of Texas Special Collections. Upon recent research, it turns out the print is nowhere to be found.) Lastly, I prepared a couple of samples on blue oaktag and set one aside to send to Andy.

In drafting the letter to Andy and enclosing one of the samples in a mailing tube, I reminded him of his promise to send me the airfare, but indicated that if I did not hear from him, I should assume he was in agreement with what I proposed; simply that to sell the painting would provide me with the means to purchase a ticket, thus relieving him of any obligation. Not hearing from him in the two weeks that followed, I went ahead with arranging the exhibition. I delivered the painting and twenty-six prints to the gallery about a week prior to the opening.

In the four months I had been living in Rome, Patrizia and I began collaborating on a book. It was agreed that she would photograph many of the persons for whom I had written poems. In turn I made preliminary arrangements with Chris Cerf, then an editor at Random House, to consider the manuscript for publication. On the weekend before the gallery opening, Patrizia and I had a serious blowout regarding the photographs that were to be included with the manuscript sent to New York. She became neurotically possessive, not wanting to let the photos out of her hands. It was a volatile confrontation. There was so much at stake. I quickly packed up the pictures, the screen and acetate, the remaining samples, and stormed out of the studio. An evening rain soaked me to the skin. I stopped by a street-corner wastebasket and decided there and then to destroy the screen. With a quick whack I propelled my boot through the nylon mesh and trashed the frame and then made my way back to Peter's flat, about a mile distant on the Lungetevere delle Armi, visualizing how it might have all played out had it been a scene in an Italian neo realismo movie. Patrizia called an hour later to apologize and came by to stamp the verso of the prints. I would not see her again until the gallery opening, a few days later.

Upon entering the gallery I was taken aback to behold Patrizia's Che painting side by side with the one I'd provided for the exhibit, making it seem a bit odd for a second, almost identical painting to suddenly turn up out of nowhere. Had

there been a hole, surely I would have crawled in. From the corner of my eye I could see the dealer off to one side, a peculiar grin on his face. Had he suspected something, I wondered? Better yet, did he think I was holding out? The gallery started to fill up. The atmosphere was electric. The critics raved. The paparazzi popped. The show was a media and artistic success. The dealer was beside himself. I was the boy of the hour.

Cy Twombly, an artist living in Rome, bought one of the prints and Leo Castelli wired a reserve from New York. All twenty-six prints were sold the day of the opening. I was told someone was interested in purchasing the red-and-blue multiple portrait. The euphoria was not to last, however. About a week into the show Leo wired the dealer again, only this time to state that Andy had not authorized the painting and that nothing could be sold. (I was to find out years later, through David Bourdon, that Andy had attempted to negotiate a deal with the gallery to give him the money from the sale of the painting, which at that point was put on hold.) The dealer urged me to obtain authorization in order for him to proceed with the sale, as his reputation was now on the line and he had to save face. I was obliged to arrive at the gallery promptly at 7:00 each evening for the next three or four nights to call New York to turn things

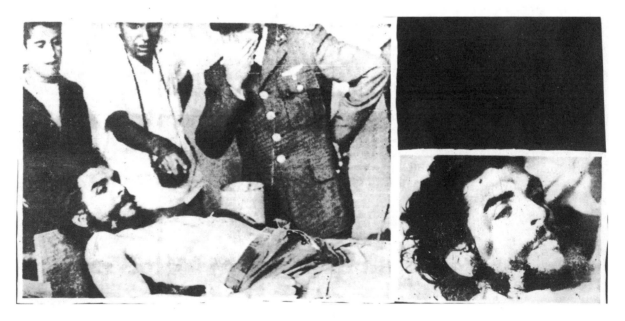

Detail from Che Guevara, Portrait of Death, *by Gerard Malanga,*
silk screen and acrylic on canvas

around. I got through once, only to have Fred Hughes tell me that Andy was in Arizona shooting *Lonesome Cowboys* and couldn't be reached. I stalled for time, reassuring the dealer (who barely understood English) that Andy would be getting back to me soon and that I would check with him later that week.

Then unexpectedly, a few days later, a letter arrived from Bob Wilson of the Phoenix Bookshop with a $600 check as payment for working drafts of my poetry, which he'd sold to Syracuse University. As it would take at least a week for the check to clear through Peter's account with the Italian bank, I went into hiding. I sensed, perhaps correctly, that the dealer was growing more and more impatient. I couldn't predict what he would do next. I couldn't risk anything at this point.

The check finally cleared. I gathered up my baggage at Peter's flat, including a substantial archive, and brought everything over to the Pan Am ticket office on Via Veneto, to be shipped to New York. I would follow on the next day's flight.

Substantive changes were implemented throughout the Warhol operation during my stay in Rome, I would soon learn. The Factory had moved from East Forty-seventh Street in midtown to a loft space overlooking Union Square Park. It was located on the sixth floor of a building with an Italianate facade that included a balcony. Ron and Serene Zimardi picked me up at Kennedy Airport and brought me to their flat on St. Mark's Place, where I quickly settled in. This would be my new home for the next several months.

Chill in the air now, scarf wrapped around face, I walked up Fourth Avenue to Union Square, arriving at the new Factory about twenty minutes ahead of Andy. He stepped out of the elevator and, seeing me seated off to the side, his face turned a beet red, perhaps out of embarrassment or worse—anger. He greeted me in his typical halting tone of astonishment. "Oh, gee, hi . . . how was Rome?" I followed him into a little back room of an office. I started to apologize and then explain, by way of what I thought to be logical reasoning, how and why I came to create the Che portrait, emphasizing that I wouldn't have gone ahead with the project had he informed me otherwise. His response was an abrupt and cold "You should have known better." He then turned his attention to the mail piled high on the desk. Here I recalled, with a smile, Allen Midgette—the person who impersonated Andy on that scandalous college tour a couple of months before my return

to New York—saying to me, "Let's face it, it takes a lot of people to make a Warhol."

It's quite likely Andy felt betrayed that I would just pick up and leave my work with him and equally betrayed and angered at my creating a Warhol artwork without his consent. Can I blame him? No. But I was forced to act on whatever control he thought he had over me. He lacked backbone to stick by me, going back on his word, which I took at face value. We were both to blame for misreading each other's signals. We were bound by different codes of ethics.

*

Henri Cartier-Bresson writes that "We photographers deal in things which are continually vanishing, and when they have vanished, there is no contrivance on earth which can make them come back again. We cannot develop and print a memory." Perhaps it was my perception of Bresson's theory that finally led to the creation of what

The Appalachian Trail, Warner Mountain, Great Barrington, Massachusetts

Gerard Malanga, 1992

I am doing in my own picture taking. The works that were made over the past twenty-five years emerge from my commitment to an essentially private vision: The desire to look and to make a record of that looking.

As an ardent admirer of Duchamp, who believed that aesthetic boundaries exist to be breached, I remain open to all possibilities and alternatives in the creative process. I embrace the mistakes.

"In the city time becomes visible. In the country time is invisible." Lewis Mumford said that. The present tense: Where I now live affords me the opportunity of a retreat in order to look inside myself. When I create a new work—whether it be a poem or photograph—I do not begin with a concept or an image, but rather allow the experience to dictate the direction and focus of the piece. Each experience has its own essence and reality.

Moving to the Berkshires was not an escape but a release. In my capacity to be alone I'm constantly discovering myself. I'm my own best

company. The art of learning has always been an adventure.

BIBLIOGRAPHY

Poetry:

Prelude to International Velvet Debutante, Great Lakes, 1967.

(With Andy Warhol) *Screen Tests: A Diary,* Kulchur Press, 1967.

Three Poems for Benedetta Barzini (with photographs by Stephen Shore), Angel Hair Books, 1967.

The Last Benedetta Poems, Black Sparrow Press, 1969.

The Blue Book, Being a Series of Drafts and Fragments of Poems in the Rough (with photographs by Wren de Antonio), Doctor Generosity Press (New York), 1970.

Christina's World Im(media)cy: Poemworks, Poetry on Films (New York), 1970.

Ten Poems for Ten Poets, Black Sparrow Press, 1970.

Chic Death: Reproductions of the Death Paintings Series by Andy Warhol, Pym-Randall, 1971.

Nine Poems for César Vallejo: The Poetry of Night, Dawn and Dream, Vanishing Rotating Triangle (New York), 1972.

Poetry on Film, Telegraph Books, 1972.

Wheels of Light, White Light (nonprofit) Foundation (Upper Dharmsala, India), 1972.

Light-Licht (bilingual text in English and German), Expanded Media Editions (Gottingen, West Germany), 1973.

(With A. T. Mann) *A Portfolio of Four Duographs,* privately published, 1973.

Seven Poems for Pilar Crespi, Del Sol Press (Kenosha, Wis.), 1973.

Incarnations: Poems 1965–1971, Black Sparrow Press, 1974.

Twenty-two, Black Sparrow Press, 1974.

(With Salvador Dali) *The Explosion of the Swan: Salvador Dali on Federico García-Lorca and Three Poems by Gerard Malanga,* Black Sparrow Press, 1975.

Rosebud (illustrated by Michael McCurdy), Penmaen Press, 1975.

Devotion, Black Sparrow Press, 1976.

Leaping over Gravestones, Four Zoas Press (Hardwicke, Mass.), 1976.

Bringing Up Baby, privately published, 1977.

Ten Years After: The Selected Benedetta Poems, Black Sparrow Press, 1977.

One Hundred Years Have Passed: Prose Poems, Little Caesar Press (Los Angeles), 1978.

Equal Time, Bellevue Press (Binghamton, N.Y.), c. 1979.

Other:

(Editor) *Intransit: The Andy Warhol-Gerard Malanga Monster Issue,* Toad Press (Eugene, Ore.), c. 1968.

(Editor) *The Personal Cinema of Gerard Malanga,* privately published, 1968.

The Rubber Heart: A One-act Soap Opera (produced in Cambridge, Mass., at the Loeb Drama Center, 1968), published in *Art and Literature,* summer, 1966.

Beatle Calendar (with photographs by William Katz), Bouwerie Editions (New York), 1970.

Selbsportrat eines Dichters, Marz, 1970, translation by Ralf-Rainer Rygulla and Rolf Dieter Brinkman published as *Gerard Malanga: A Poet's Self-Portrait,* 1970.

Six Portraits, Nadada Editions (New York), 1975.

This Will Kill That (experimental autobiography), Black Sparrow Press, 1978, enlarged edition, 1983.

Little Caesar #9/ "Unprecedented Information," Little Caesar Press, 1979.

(Editor) *Angus MacLise Checklist, 1959–1979,* Dia Art Foundation, 1981.

The Legacy of Gaile Vazbys, AUšRA, privately published, 1983.

(With Victor Bockris) *Up-tight: The Velvet Underground Story,* Quill/William Morrow, 1983.

Autobiography of a Sex Thief, Lustrum Press, 1984.

(Editor) *Scopophilia: The Love of Looking,* Alfred Van der Marck Editions, 1985.

Andy Warhol (catalogue), Vrej Baghoomian, Inc., 1989.

Gerard Malanga: Thirty-year Survey in the Arts, Archives Malanga, 1991.

Three Diamonds, Black Sparrow Press, 1991.

Contributor:

Poems Now, Kulchur Press, 1966.

Young American Poets, Follett, 1968.

Contemporary American Poets, World, 1969.

New Yorker Book of Poems, Viking Press, 1969.

Contact: Theory, Lustrum Press, 1980.

Portrait: Theory, Lustrum Press, 1981.

Also translator of Giuseppe Ungaretti's *Rivers,* published in *Signal* (New York), fall, 1965, and of poems by Cesar Vallejo. Poetry represented in numerous anthologies, including *Another World, The East Side Scene,* and *The World Anthology.*

Contributor of photographs, poems, and criticism to many periodicals, including *Art and Literature, Camera, Details, Elle Fame, Locus Solus, Lugano Review, New Yorker, Nuovi Argomenti, Paris Review, Partisan Review, Photo, Poetry, Rolling Stone, Tarasque, Transatlantic Review* (autumn, 1975), *Tri-Quarterly* and *Vogue Italia.* Editor of various issues of numerous publications, including *The Ant's Forefoot, Film Culture, Little Caesar,* and *Transatlantic Review.* Co-founder and co-editor, *Interview,* New York City, 1969.

James A. McPherson

1943-

CHANTPLEURE

James A. McPherson, Jr., in Kyoto, Japan, 1989

I

News came recently that my father's half sister, Eva McPherson Clayton, is about to be elected to Congress from the First Congressional District of North Carolina. Along with this information, there came additional news that Vanzetta McPherson, the wife of Thomas McPherson, my father's half brother, has already been confirmed as a Federal District Court Judge in Montgomery, Alabama. While I am naturally very proud of them, the news caused me to think back on the differences in our childhoods. And I

find myself wondering just what my father, their half brother, James A. McPherson, might have accomplished if he had been born at a later time or under a different set of historical circumstances. I think about what he might have achieved with his own native intelligence if he had had better luck. I wonder how far he might have risen if he, like Thomas and Eva, had been wise enough to move to a place where his talents would have been allowed to develop naturally and where he might have prospered.

And I think about my mother, Mable McPherson, who, almost four years ago, was finally released from all her pain. I imagine that she would now be feeling her usual despair, or fear, over the recent accomplishments of Eva McPherson Clayton and Vanzetta McPherson. I can still read in her face the tentative pride fading into her bedrock pessimism over the likely consequences for black people of any display of talent or intelligence or ambition. I can imagine my father arguing with her, and perhaps losing his temper, over what would be his insistence that she should take pride in the triumph of native intelligence over racism. I can also imagine my mother's response, which would be her conventional response to any open display of ambition or intelligence which guaranteed to attract the attention of jealous white people: "You've got to crawl before you can walk." I am sure that this expression of her homespun philosophy must still have had the power to enrage my father.

Mary, my older sister, and I agree that something must have happened to our mother, early in her life, to cause her to become so sad or unconfident that she would want to retreat back

About seven or eight years old

toward slavery. Her life was a constant battle with those around her who wanted to walk. She was not a malicious person. She was universally admired. She was unusually kind and gentle, and she lived the Christian virtues. She possessed great intelligence and humor and had a memory like an elephant. She carried herself with a natural grace. In her youth, according to a picture I once saw, she was also quite attractive. Her African, Creek, and Cherokee ancestries had struck in her a very refined balance. But she also seemed very sad in that picture, as if something deep in her had already been defeated, how many times I do not know. She seemed to have spent the rest of her life thinking back on these defeats. I have seldom seen her as anything other than sad.

I once participated in an experiment in recollecting previous lives. The volunteers were put under hypnosis, lulled to sleep, and prodded with a series of ritual questions. One of the time periods focused on was the times of our births. We were asked to recall the events surrounding our arrivals on this earth. I was asked to remember where I was just before I was actually born. I was in the company of *something* that gave me great peace and a profound feeling of security. I was asked to describe my feelings at the moment of birth. I was extremely frightened, much more frightened than I have ever felt since, except for once, in my life. I was asked to describe how my father looked. He was a very happy-looking young man. He seemed very pleased to have a son and a namesake. I was asked to describe how my mother looked. She was sitting up in bed, holding me, but her face was turned away from me and she looked very sad. She had long black Indian hair. At that particular moment, she should have looked beautiful. But she did not. Her sadness dominated the moment.

I think that one of the best-kept secrets in the world is what event wounded my mother, at such a deep level, early on in her life. My earliest memory of my mother is of her during my first years of school. The children had been taught to make valentines out of carbon paper and to stuff the pockets in them with little candies. I made one for my mother and took it home and gave it to her. She accepted it, but with great sadness. Perhaps I can remember this moment so clearly because it marked the beginning of my resolve to make my mother smile, to make her happy. But she spent a tremendous amount of energy trying to prove that her emotions were beyond cultivation. Her only other resolve was a steadfast dedication to the life after this one. She wanted to be a perfect Christian in this world so as to be assured of a place in the next world. Nothing else seemed to matter to her. Because of this intense focus, she was like the ancient Cathars of eleventh-century France, who identified all aspects of this world with Rex Mundi, the Prince of Darkness, and focused their full energies on avoiding the pitfalls and snares of this transitory earthly life. Our mother always told us, in response to our insistence that we wanted to do what others were doing, "No. I'm raising you all the old-fashioned way." I have learned that, when she was herself a child, she studied the Bible with Pentecostal people. To this day, I do not know whether her "old-fashioned way" had more to do with the Biblical codes than with the consequences of some personal defeat in her spirit. Whatever she kept so closely guarded must, at one time, have given her very great pain. Mary remembers, when she was a child, waking up at night to hear our mother crying and saying to herself, possibly in her sleep, "There just has to be a Judgment Day. There just *has* to be!" My father's favorite song was "Over my head, I hear trouble in the air . . . There must be a God somewhere." Their marriage, it seems, was in its spiritual aspects a union between a belief in hell and a belief in heaven.

Such a fixation in adults on spiritual absolutes, if allowed to influence sensitive children trapped in a material world, often leads the children into a deadly form of romanticism. Not as secure in the same celestial certainties as our parents, my sisters and brother and I learned to impose otherworldly standards on people in this world. That is, because we could not muster the same degree of faith in heaven as our father, or the same fear of Judgment Day as our mother, we tended to put too much faith in other people, to view them from an unrealistic perspective beyond all their faults. This "blindness" helped us to make friends easily, but it also put us at risk because we tended to idealize too much. Each of us has suffered deep betrayals by people to whom we gave all our trust. Our mother never made this mistake because she never trusted the world or its people, and had no ambition in life beyond mere survival. Our father was betrayed many times. Our mother's constant watchword to us was, "You children are just like your daddy. You'll learn one day that you only get a few friends in this life."

Now that my mother is dead, I find myself, sometimes, conjuring up a romantic vision of heaven and of what it is like. I assume that if there is indeed a heaven, my mother is sure to be there. I want her to be with my father again, and I want to see her laugh without pain and circumspection. I want her to take happiness as her God-given right. I want there to be a heaven where people, black people especially, will be free of pain and can laugh and speak honestly and freely and can use their intelligence, even in bold ways, without fear of negative consequences. I want there to be a heaven where my mother will be free of her fear of white people and of her anticipation of their hatred. I want my mother and father to be equally proud of Thomas and Eva. But some deep part of me can still imagine my mother looking down from the heaven I have imagined for her, shaking her head at Thomas and Eva, and saying with her usual sadness, "You've got to crawl before you can walk!"

I live in a small town in Iowa now, and I have survived the worst of my mother's fears. I attended college. I graduated from the Harvard Law School. I have been awarded a Pulitzer Prize and a MacArthur Fellowship. Mostly because of these accomplishments, I was subjected to some very vicious attacks when I taught at the University of Virginia. The life of my daughter, Rachel, was put at risk. In order to keep my bond with her, I would have been obliged to remain in Charlottesville, Virginia, as a kind of slave. It was, those many years ago, the appropriate time for me to follow my mother's advice and crawl. But instead, I walked away, leaving behind my own flesh and blood. I survived what I was not supposed to survive. During the last years of my mother's life, I wanted to tell her, "Do you see? It is still possible to live, and to keep standing, after they have done to you the worse thing they can do to you. Don't you see, they have taken their best shot and I am still alive. Here in Iowa, even in exile from the South, I have been able to start over. I have made new friends. I have touched a great number of students. I have earned the respect and the friendship of many new people, including a great number of Japanese. The world is much larger than the South. We are no longer obliged to crawl." But I never told my mother this. I don't think she would have believed me.

When my mother was dying in a hospital in Atlanta, I used to call her every night to encourage her to eat. She had apparently lost the will to live and refused to follow the advice of her doctor that she should eat her food. My brother, Richard, became her primary caretaker, and did everything humanly possible for her. Since I could not travel

"With my brother, Richard McPherson, after church on Palm Sunday," Savannah, Georgia

to Atlanta to join my brother and sister Josephine at her bedside, I did the next best thing. During the evening hours, I tried my best to become her lifeline. She knew my reasons for choosing a condition of exile, so she never asked me to come to Atlanta to see her during her last days. But she liked me to call her in the hospital and talk with her about inconsequential things. During those evening hours, I pretended to much greater emotional strength than I actually possessed at the time. I tried to make her know that I was standing tall. Now, in retrospect, I want to believe that I actually taught her something during her last days. Mary disclosed to me after our mother's death that several times, during the last year of her life, our mother said that she had always wished, secretly, that she could have used her intelligence in some better way. She talked about her academic record at a normal school in Jacksonville, Florida, when she was a girl, and about how she had always been an outstanding student. She talked about what she might have done with her life if circumstances had not obliged her to enter domestic service for white employers. Soon after this, she lost her will to live, retreated into herself, refused to eat her food, and died.

I hope now that my mother is using all her intelligence. I hope now that she is free from fear, in the Christian heaven I try to imagine for her. My final words to her were certain parts of a Psalm that I thought appropriate. I thought that it, the 139th Psalm, spoke in some very meaningful ways about what had sustained my mother's life:

> O Lord, thou hast searched me and known me,
> Thou knowest my downsitting and mine uprising,
> Thou understandest my thoughts afar off.
> Thou compassest my path and my lying down,
> And art acquainted with all my ways.
> For there is not a word in my tongue but, lo,
> O Lord, thou knowest it altogether.
> Thou hast beset me behind and before,
> And laid thine hand upon me.
> Such knowledge is too wonderful for me;
> It is high. I cannot attain unto it.
> Whither shall I go from thy spirit? Or
> Whither shall I flee from thy presence?
> *If I ascend up into heaven, thou art there.*
> *If I make my bed in hell, behold, thou art there.*
> If I take the wings of the morning,
> And dwell in the uttermost parts of the sea;
> Even there shall thy hand lead me,
> And thy right hand shall hold me.
> If I say, Surely the darkness shall cover me;
> Even the night shall be light about me.
> Yea, the darkness hideth not from thee;
> But the night shineth as the day:
> *The darkness and the light are both alike to*
> *thee . . .*

II

My family background is very complicated, although no more complicated than that of most black Americans. Genetically, my family represents a mixture of African, Creek, Cherokee, Seminole, Scottish, Irish, and Anglo-Saxon influences. Geographically they are rooted in three Southern states: Georgia, South Carolina, and Florida. In terms of names, each generation represents the extension of the past into the present. There are very few new names in my family. We maintain the practice of keeping the names of ancestors alive. Thus my older sister, Mary Alice McPherson, is named for both my mother's mother, Mary Smalls, and my father's mother, Alice Scarborough McPherson. My younger brother, Richard Benjamin McPherson, is named for Richard Allen, who founded the African Methodist Episcopal Church in the late eighteenth century, and also for Benjamin McPherson, one of my grandfather's brothers. My youngest sister, Josephine McPherson, is named for my mother's cousin, Josephine Martin, who was also my grandfather's second wife. My father, James Allen McPherson, was also named for Richard Allen. I was my father's first-born son, and was elected to bear his name and, ultimately, his character and his fate.

The older I become, the more I believe that our lives are not random occurrences. I am tempted sometimes to believe, rather, that they have an authenticity far beyond our everyday understanding. I am led to believe that there exists a standard of values external to everyday human consciousness, and that our lives are played out in response to these metaphysical values much more than they are responses to the "realities" around us. I am tempted to believe that we *choose* our parents precisely for their limitations, and that one of the primary "reasons" for the specific circumstances of our births is the challenge to transcend in our lives the limitations of the parents to whom we are born. This seems to me the fundamental purpose of life, the thing that gives authenticity and meaning to what we call living. Our human duty seems to be accepting the challenge imposed by the limitations of our parents and the making of a major effort toward transcending them. This assumes, of course, an ideal of spiritual progress which contradicts the Western ideal of material progress. It is a much more private matter, one having to do with the progression of, and the growth of, one's own soul. In this broader view, all things having to do with facts are illusions. What really matters, in deepest actuality, is how we complete the challenges assigned to us by the life we *choose*, at birth, to live. In this speculative and metaphysical sense, the fundamental plan of my own life had already been settled at my birth. If I think carefully and coldly about my parents and their flaws, I can see more clearly some that are my own. My only real purpose in this life is to transcend them.

James Allen McPherson, my father, despite his minor flaws, was simply much too large and complex a human being for the time and place in which he tried to live. Born in 1913 in a small village named Green Pond, South Carolina, he moved with his parents, Thomas and Alice McPherson, to Savannah, Georgia, when he was a small boy. Thomas McPherson was an insurance salesman who spent a great deal of time on the road. He and his wife, Alice Scarborough McPher-

"My father, James A. McPherson, Sr., taken at his mother's family home," Hardeeville, South Carolina, 1930s

son, were divorced soon after my father was born. In those days, men had an easier time maintaining custody of their children, so my grandfather kept his son while his former wife remarried. He put my father in a boarding school while he was on the road. I can imagine my father as a very intelligent and curious young man left to himself a great part of the time. I know that he was able to survive, although I don't know just how adequately, by depending on an extended family of his father's relatives and his own friends who lived at all levels of the Savannah community. All his life, my father was most comfortable with an eclectic grouping of friends. At some point in his youth, he developed an interest in electricity. While he was still in his twenties, he became the first, and only, licensed black master electrician in the state of Georgia. He did this without a high school education. He was heading toward a successful and prosperous future even before he met my mother and, when he was nearing thirty, married.

My mother had come to Savannah from Green Cove Springs, Florida. She had come to live with her cousin, Josephine Martin McPherson (called "Mother Dear" by the family), who had just married Thomas McPherson, my father's father. Up until this time, my father had been making periodic trips to Atlanta to see his mother and her new husband. His mother was an alcoholic by this time, and I can only speculate whether the natural sympathy he had for her was transferred to Mable Smalls, the new young woman in his father's house. I know that, when I knew him, my father was always doing things to make my mother happy, to make her smile. It was his deepest nature to "take care" of people in need. He was known to give the shirt off his back to anyone who asked him for it. He was regarded by sensitive people as extremely kind, but was regarded by other people, my mother included, as a fool. One of his stock replies to criticism of his habits was, "My church is in my heart!" In recent years, the field of psychology has coined a new phrase to describe my father's kind of behavior, defined now as a category of neurosis. This new phrase is "co-dependency." Its causes are easy to understand: because my father was the product of a broken home, and because he had an alcoholic mother for whom he cared a great deal, he projected his own desire to be supportive of his wounded parents onto the other significant people in his life. He took great soul-healing pleasure in taking care of them. In this way, so the psychologists tell it, he attempted to assume an equal partnership with God. My father was, in fact, called arrogant. He was also very proud. And he was, up until the time of his death at forty-eight, generous to a fault.

When I was undergoing my own crisis in Charlottesville, I was advised by an expert that this same trait was in me. I was told, "The power structure is not trying to destroy you because of anything wrong that you did. They are after you because, without even knowing it, you were operating as a leader and you threatened established power centers." That I had been perceived as a leader was news to me. So far as I knew, I had only been operating out of the values that had been taught to me by my mother and father. I was simply trying to do for others what I would want them to do for me. But the expert attempted to show me how this approach in life would always put me at risk. He determined that he would attempt to help me "nip the neurosis in the bud" so that I could proceed through life in a much more "normal," much more self-interested and self-protective way. He tried to teach me how to say "No" to people, how to put myself first. I tried this for a while, but kept running into the same old problems: a woman crying for help, a student with some special need, a request from an acquaintance that I just could not deny. I soon found that changing myself was very difficult work. The degree of circumspection required, and the consequent rigidity of behavior, tended to undermine the spontaneity of my daily responses. I soon found myself backsliding into my old habits. And while I got satisfaction out of doing things for people, each time I was thanked, or even noticed, I felt the deep fear that I felt back in Charlottesville in the immediate aftermath of receiving a MacArthur Fellowship. I felt I was about to be attacked again for calling attention to myself, or worse, for presuming to stand in the place of God. At such times, I thought of my father, and about what he might have done that I should avoid doing, about how very limited his options were compared to my own.

Operating openly with this same trait of character just on the outskirts of the structure of white supremacy in the Georgia of the 1940s and 1950s, my father must have posed a threat to a great many people. He wanted to get out, but had a wife and four children who were dependent on him. He must have wanted intimate friends, as always, on all levels of Savannah society. But increasingly, as the obligations and pressures on him took their toll, he could only find comfort and escape among social outcasts, those men and women who had already given up, and in the steady consumption of alcohol. I remember one of the lowest points in his life: the time, when I was not yet in my teens, of his father's death and funeral. My father had been put into Reidsville Prison, for the first of many times, as punishment for not honoring the contracts he had made. The guards from Reidsville Prison, or what was then called "the chain-gang," brought him to his father's funeral in handcuffs. I watched the metal handcuffs sparkling in the winter sunlight while all around me people, in grief and embarrassment, cried. Not too many years after this, my father's spirit was finally broken. He kept walking, worked as an electrician whenever he could, but he was already dead before he died.

These many years later, I still find it impossible to change in myself the things that were derived from him, and these many years later I still live with the fear that they will cause me to end up the way he did.

My mother observed my father's slow decline, and the instruction must have confirmed a deeper lesson, secreted in the safest part of her long memory, of similar destructions stretching back into the days of slavery. Whatever it was that my mother knew, whatever had happened to her, she took in secret with her to the grave. She left it to her four children to speculate about what it was that had wounded her so deeply that it led her to give up on life. She left us only a handful of clues. When I was grieving for my mother, and guilty over the fact that I could not see her during her last days, I went to see her last remaining sister, Suzie Johnson, in Detroit. I wanted to try again to understand my mother by adding to the few facts that I knew about her background those I could get from her sister. My aunt Suzie repeated her family facts with the same mixture of precision about some things and ambiguity about others that my mother practiced. Their father, John Smalls, had been born in Blackshear, Georgia. He had worked as a sharecropper and as a laborer on a number of plantations in Georgia, South Carolina, and Florida. My mother, Mable, the oldest girl, had been born in Blackshear, Georgia, but the other members of the family—Bill, Joe, Mary, Martha, Beulah, and Suzie—were born in various other places. The full family wound up eventually in Green Cove Springs, Florida, where John Smalls apparently prospered very quickly. All five girls attended what was then called "normal school," while the two oldest children, Joe and Bill, became laborers themselves. This was apparently the strategy, or custom, that had been worked out by black people in the South during the very hard years which followed the betrayal of the Reconstruction. Since the structure of white supremacy was most threatened by, and most set against, the rise of black males, the males were encouraged to forego their own ambitions and to support the ambitions of the females, who constituted less of a threat. One result of this practical arrangement was the creation of a matriarchy, a private social structure in which females seemed to enjoy greater social prestige because of greater education and somewhat higher job status. But in terms of practical realities, despite the sociological differences, there was a functional equality between males and females because most maintained as a paramount goal the survival of the family in the face of entrenched and vicious white racism.

All of my mother's sisters, except for her and Suzie, married laboring men. Suzie's husband, Johnny, had been a career cook in the navy and a heavyweight contender who was set to challenge Joe Louis for a title shot when the outbreak of World War II ended his career. The three other sisters, Mary and Martha and Beulah, had many children, some of whom also became laborers. There was only one factual inconsistency between the story my mother had told her children and the story that Suzie Johnson told hers. Suzie claimed for her family descent from a runaway slave named Robert Smalls.

Born to a slave master named Henry McKee and his slave Lydia Smalls in 1839, Robert Smalls was raised in the port city of Beaufort, South Carolina, during the years preceding the outbreak of the Civil War. He was trained by his master to pilot ships in and around Beaufort and Charleston harbors. When the Civil War broke out, Smalls sailed a ship full of slaves and their families, a ship named "The Planter," out of Beaufort Harbor, under the guns of the Confederate blockade, toward freedom. He delivered "The Planter" to the Union forces and was made its captain during the remainder of the war. He had tremendous fame, and often spoke on the same platform with Frederick Douglass. He was elected to the Reconstruction Congress and served five terms. He wrote or sponsored much of the legislation that created a public school system in South Carolina. Toward the end of the Reconstruction period, he was betrayed by white politicians in his home state, accused of accepting bribes, and spent time in jail. He reclaimed his seat in Congress after his name was cleared and led the fight against reclamation of the old Southern order under "Pitchfork" Ben Tillman and his Red Shirts. Through the exclusion of black voters from the voting rolls, he was denied once again his seat in Congress. This time he challenged his exclusion by calling for a hearing and then a vote in the House of Representatives. Among those voting in his favor in the Committee on Elections were Henry Cabot Lodge of Massachusetts and Robert "Fighting Bob" La Follette of Wisconsin. On Robert Small's behalf, La Follette said, "Confused, baffled, discouraged, cheated, the colored vote of the South has quietly and speedily disappeared from the returns. The new election methods of the South have done their perfect work. You say in justification that the Negro is ignorant, inferior, incapable of growth. Secretly, do you not fear the opposite? Is it against the dull and submissive that you direct your hardest blows? Or are they aimed at those who, like Robert Smalls, have shown intellect, courage, and determination to lift their people to a higher level and maintain their rights as free men?''

There were 127 votes for Robert Smalls, but there were also 142 against him. He was the last black participant in the Reconstruction Congress to be forced out.

Suzie Johnson claimed Robert Smalls as an ancestor. My mother had denied any connection. Suzie's children, Otis and Suzetta, had grown up with the belief that one of their ancestors was a great man. My mother had attempted to guide her children into "service." There was, though, one mysterious thread of consistency binding the two branches of my mother's family. This was a song. It was a song my mother used to sing to us at night. I recited what I could recall of its words to my cousin Suzetta. She sang most of the rest of the song back to me:

Mother dear, come bathe my forehead, for I'm
    growing very weak.
Let one drop of water, Mother, fall upon my
    burning cheek.
Tell my loving playmates, Mother, that I never
    more will play.
Will you do this for me, Mother? Put my little
    shoes away.

Santa Claus he brought them for me, with a lot of
    other things,
And I think he brought an angel, with a pair of
    golden wings.
I will be an angel, Mother, but perhaps another
    day.
You will do this, won't you, Mother? Put my little
    shoes away.

Soon the baby will be larger, then they'll fit his
    little feet,
And he'll look so nice and cunning, when he walks
    upon the street.
I am going to leave you, Mother, so remember
    what I say.
Do it, won't you, dearest Mother? Put my little
    shoes away . . .

I found out many months later that this nineteenth-century sentimental song, bathed in morbid self-pity, was once very popular among middle-class people. Even though I could not imagine sharecroppers singing it, the song must have had great emotional significance for my mother's family, since my mother's cousin, Josephine Martin, who married my father's father, was called affectionately "Mother Dear." I am convinced that, whatever the great secret was, it was somehow connected with memories associated with this song.

For a while, after our mother's death, my sister and I tried our best to research the history of our mother's family and the history of Robert Smalls. I wrote to Ms. Dorothy Sterling, an elderly white female historian who had written a biography of Smalls in the 1950s. I talked with my mother's father's relative, a great-aunt named Mary Terrell, who had been collecting materials on Robert Smalls for most of her adult life. She showed me letters that she had written to Dorothy Sterling during the 1950s, letters to which Ms. Sterling never responded. I tracked down, in a South American country, Mr. Okon Edet Uya who, as a young historian from Ghana, had made a study of Robert Smalls and had published it under the title *From Slavery to Public Service* when he was a graduate student at the University of Wisconsin during the 1970s. Both Ms. Sterling and Mr. Uya, who was then his country's ambassador, wrote back to me and promised to provide me with access to their notes and records.

But then my interest in Robert Smalls suddenly cooled. It became of greater interest to me why our mother had taken such pains to disassociate herself, and therefore her children, from a connection with any level of society other than that of a sharecropper. It had always been a mystery to me how her father, my grandfather, could have acquired so much property in Green Cove Springs, Florida. According to my mother, he had been a laborer for most of his life. And yet when I met him, toward the end of his life, he owned a number of homes, a general store, several farms, and even a service station. Also, many of his relatives, mulattoes in Savannah and in parts of South Carolina, owned considerable amounts of property. Sharecroppers are rarely this affluent.

Toward the end of her life my mother had made several mistakes in her personal narrative. She had reached the age when the earliest parts of her life were much clearer in her memory than the immediate past. During one of Mary's stays with her, the clarity and the fullness of our mother's memory disrupted the lifelong lock she had placed on her past. She talked about her father, about how they were always moving from town to town, from plantation to plantation. She talked about how much she would cry, as a little girl, each time they moved and she was forced to leave behind the new friends she had made. She talked about the nine of them, her parents and her five brothers and sisters, having dinner at a railroad depot, in a small town in Georgia, while the train was pulling out. They had to leave their dinner and run to catch it. She said her father was very mad and said, "If I didn't have all these children, I wouldn't have to run to catch trains." Mary said, "Mama, how could a sharecropper afford to take nine people on a train?" The relentless clarity of my mother's memory, at that moment, exposed the additional fact that her father had been a manager of J. C. Penney stores on plantations in Florida.

Mary and I have concluded that something very terrible had happened to our mother, something that froze her spirit in fear at a certain very impressionable time. It was something that she could never get beyond. I do not see how this terrible thing could have happened within her family, since I remember all of them as being very close. I speculate that the thing that wounded her so deeply must have come from the outside world. I speculate that it derived, in large part, from the racism she experienced when she was growing up. She told us stories about her father being threat-

ened by a white man for having a foreman's job. She talked about watching her father sitting in a chair on their front porch all night, with a shotgun resting on his lap, waiting for the white man to come back and act on his threat. She told my brother and me about how, during World War II, the Japanese would hide in trees at night and wait until "the Americans" came under the trees before jumping on them and killing them. My sisters have no memories of these stories, so I assume they were told to my brother and me for a specific purpose. I believe now that she was really talking about incidents she had witnessed in her own life, about what in her day white Southerners did to black men. Perhaps she had heard some of these stories, but it is possible that she witnessed some atrocity herself. It seems likely that some brave or intelligent black man, perhaps someone very close to her, had gotten "out of place" and was destroyed, in some cruel way, as an example to the others. This would have left a deep impression on her child's memory, and it would have severely

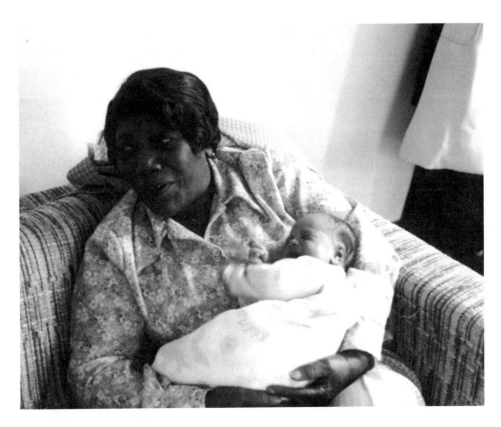

"My mother, Mable Smalls McPherson,
and my daughter, Rachel," New Haven, 1979

tempered her view of intelligence as the source of ambition for black people. Her very practical solution to this problem was to teach my brother Richard and me to take care of our sisters, and to do her best to limit our ambitions, to turn us, gently, back toward slavery. In her own deeply pragmatic way, she must have loved my brother and me very much.

But my mother must have been deeply frightened for, if not of, my father and his family. They were kept on the outskirts of our lives. My father just did not "fit" into the strictly segregated world of Savannah, Georgia, in the 1940s and 1950s. His spirit was much too large. He tended to operate as if there were no caste system, as though the expression of his full range of human traits were possible. He had a number of white friends. He was a closet intellectual. To him, the structure of white supremacy, with its deadly implications for intelligent and "uppity" black men, must have seemed a joke. For a while, he ran circles around it. Then the structure began to close in around him.

If my mother's major flaw was a fear of any worldly use of her intelligence, my father's major flaw was a belief that his own promiscuous kindness toward people would be reciprocated. I think now that his life was a futile but heroic search, within the context of a system that had already decreed that he should not exist, for enough personal space to sustain the way of life he had chosen for himself. He ended up in prison, again and again. His spirit was slowly murdered. My mother must have watched this murder from within the zone of safety provided by her past experience of, and subsequent numbness to, such tragic things. She must have thought hundreds of times before my father finally died, "I told you so!" I think she might have made an object lesson out of his slow destruction, and this new confirmation of the futility of ambition must have added fuel to her desire to guide her sons into what she called "service." I know that, from the time I was eight years old, I worked as a yard boy, as a house servant, as a paperboy, as a baby-sitter, as a janitor, as a grocery clerk. I was never encouraged to excel in school, and when I did I was never congratulated.

III

The major damage caused by a broken-home environment is to the self-esteem of the children, who are deprived of the positive images, or role models, that provide emotion-laden clues to who they are. My sisters and brother and I were moved closer to the center of our mother's family and its carefully elaborated mythology of sharecroppers and laborers and domestic servants. My father's family became abstractions, people whose lives were on the margins of our world. The closest ones were my grandfather and his second wife, Josephine Martin McPherson, perhaps because she was also my mother's cousin. Both Thomas and Eva McPherson were born during this second marriage, and they became like older brother and sister to us. By the time they were born, my father, James McPherson, was old enough to be their father. They called him "Bubba." And there were other people. My grandfather's brother, Uncle Joe McPherson, ran a small restaurant in Savannah with Ora Lee, his wife. He drank a lot, and he always said when he was drunk, "When I die, take me back to Hickory Hill!" We thought that Hickory Hill was his favorite bar in the world. Another of my grandfather's brothers, Uncle Robert McPherson, also lived in Savannah. These people formed a protective, though distant, circle around us. If our family needed food or money or support of any kind, it was always forthcoming from them. But there was very little that we could learn about their lives, about where they had come from. They had no special status in our world. They were simply "there." They moved into and out of our lives, as our basic needs dictated, but we were not allowed to enter too far into theirs. In many respects, we knew the habits of the welfare caseworkers much better than we knew the facts of our father's family. The walls that were constructed between our home and their homes were there, I believe, because of some private necessity of great importance to our mother. We never learned to question any of the restrictions these walls placed on our curiosity.

My experiences over the past twelve years have taught me to better appreciate the nuanced nature of what I used to call lies. I have come to understand that some lies are noble, or at least serve some higher purpose, while others become increasingly mundane as they approach the category that I was trained to call sin. As always, the most basic, and perhaps the most base, is the lie that seeks some immediate advantage over another person. This type of lie is an assertion of a fact which conceals self-serving and cleverly contrived loopholes. A child sometimes practices this manipulation in order to get its way. A higher class of lies is based on the falsification of one's outside appearance, a dissembling, which has as its goal one's basic survival in a hostile environment. Certain forms of animal life practice this counterfeit: blending into the nooks and crannies of their environments in order to pass unnoticed, in order to survive. This kind of lie can be excusable in certain extreme situations, but if practiced in an habitual way it can also become destructive of the self. Once the split between words and feelings become habitual, once the discrepancy between outside and inside, the view and the clue, becomes of no vital importance, there begins to take place an erosion deep within one's spirit, an erosion so thorough that eventually one no longer knows the difference between right and wrong, truth and fiction.

It is at this point that a self-protective lie begins to have very complex implications. Do the same moral sanctions apply if the lie, although it goes against a fundamental sense of self, is for some higher purpose that is worthy of such self-sacrifice? What if the sacrifice of the spirit is not for some personal gain but for the protection of others in a life-threatening situation? And what if the lie is of such fundamental importance in the general scheme of things—say, the protection of one's own children—that it introduces very intricate weights and balances into the ancient, all-sifting scales said to be held in the hands of God? There might be in this a positive, an example of an enforced nobility of practical purpose, that may cause even God to ponder. But there is also a negative. What if the fear, which begets the lie, has itself become an object of worship? What if the sources of the fear have been allowed to assume Godlike importance and omnipotence? Would this not be an expression of idolatry? And if it is, would it not constitute a sin of the first rank?

I want to believe that my mother's fear was justified. But I also believe that her seeking safety from her fear by moving backwards, toward slavery, for herself and for her children, did some violence to God's intention that we move forward in life in full possession of, and in celebration of, all our gifts. The display of them should be to the glory of God. The handling of outside acts of violence against this display, the defenses arrayed against those who would destroy them, should be God's work and not our own. The self-prohibition placed on this display, in anticipation of the negative reactions of others, is in reality the usurpation to ourselves of the place and the power of God. This is the real sin.

It was the great obstacle placed at the center of my mother's life. It was what she, or the fates, set for me to transcend.

IV

During the late 1980s, Mary, my older sister, shifted her attention from research into the history of Robert Smalls to making a connection with my father's family. She knew that my father's roots were in Green Pond, South Carolina, and she knew that the remnants of my father's mother's family could put her in contact with these people. I don't know how Mary was able to make herself known to the core of my father's family in Green Pond, but in about 1989 she was invited to attend a family reunion. This was a reunion of the "McPherson-Campbell" families, and there were, she said, many, many hundreds of them. She told me afterwards, "Do you remember Uncle Joe, when he was drunk, saying 'When I die, take me back to Hickory Hill'? Do you know what Hickory Hill is? It's the McPherson graveyard." The members of the clans, she said, were doctors, lawyers, nurses, officers in the military, teachers, accountants. They came from Florida, Georgia, Maryland, Washington, D.C., New York, Connecticut, and Massachusetts to the family compound in Green Pond, South Carolina. Mary sent me a listing of the family tree made by Flora Campbell. In the late nineteenth-century line, there were nine brothers. My grandfather seemed to have been the eldest. Seven of the eight other lines seemed to have developed wonderfully. But under Thomas McPherson's name there were only the names of Alice Scarborough, his first wife, and their son, James Allen McPherson. All the history and pain that resulted from that union were not part of the family consciousness. The seven intact lines had many levels. There is, in one of them, the name of a young man named McPherson who was once in the news as a rising black American quarterback. I found listed in one of the other lines the name of a jazz musician named Charles McPherson.

The core of the family, those who had remained behind in Green Pond, was Geechee, or Gullah. They are of the private, reclusive Sea Island people who keep apart from outsiders. This tight group used to inhabit all the Sea Islands stretching along the Atlantic seaboard from Georgia to South Carolina and North Carolina. Mary told me that one of the elderly women, Cousin

Susie Middleton, took her and her family to their family church on Sunday morning. She announced to the old people there, "The Lord's been good to us. Now, ya'll remember Tom and his boy James that went over into Savannah? Well, these are Tom's grandchildren and his great-grandchildren and his great-great-grandchildren." Mary told me that the people gathered around her and her daughter and her daughter's children, sharing with them their memories of our grandfather and our father. One old man, Paul McPherson, told her, "James was a good boy. But dere's one t'ing dat still bother me. When Tom died, I went over into Savannah for Tom funeral. I see dem bring James to de funeral in handcuffs. Why dey bring de boy to his daddy funeral in handcuffs?" Another old man, Tom Edwards, who was drunk, laughed and said, "McPhersons like to drink, gamble, and run dey mouths!"

Mary now occupies herself with tracking down, and visiting, my father's relatives in the Northeast. She calls, from time to time, with news of her discoveries: of visiting a cousin who has an elegant home in the Connecticut suburbs; of a cousin named Thelma, who is an accountant and who has "McPherson eyes," from a branch of the family in Harlem; of a distant relative who has dropped out of sight but who might possibly be tracked down by using the genealogical library maintained by the Mormons. Mary has grown fat, and self-confident, with McPherson lore. She is now busily updating the family tree. I think I know the reason for this obsession. My father's family, unfearful of using their native intelligence, has survived and has prospered, while our small branch of the family has had to struggle against the mythology of an origin among sharecroppers. Mary sometimes expresses the wish that she could have introduced our mother to some of these people, as proof that our mother's point of view was not the only one worth considering. She would have done this to help change our mother's mind.

But I suspect that, even in the face of all this proof, our mother's mind would not have been changed. She would have retreated into her old nostalgia for an unthreatened, and unthreatening,

Rachel McPherson (left) with her friends Jarilyn Woodard (middle)
and Yarri Lutz (right)

way of life, a life grounded firmly in "service." She would have insisted still that the truly meaningful goals could only be reached when one was assured of entering heaven. This is why I hope now that— for the sake of all the happiness that was denied to her (or that she denied herself) here on earth— peace is within her possession now. I hope that she has been relieved of all her closely guarded burdens. I hope that she is now under the care of angels, busy with self-confident ambitions.

As for myself, I have survived. I know there are still, and will remain, obstacles and traps for black males who demonstrate intelligence and ambition. But I also know that places like Charlottesville, Virginia, are no longer representative of the evolving South. And I know that the world is a very large place. Because I know these things, I now believe that, in the *authentic* sense, in terms of the real meaning of my own life, it was necessary for me to enter Charlottesville so I could reclaim a deeper understanding of the lives of my mother and father. I also believe that I would not have been given the traits that were limitations in my parents if it had not been the fate assigned to me to transcend them. I have found that public displays of intelligence, even in black males, is not a "sin," as my mother might have thought. I have also found that the forces that conspire to destroy such intelligence are not always successful. The fact that they do exist should not be used to justify what can ultimately become a self-defeating stasis in the self. People do survive. They do proceed in the face of, and in spite of, the worst that can be done to them. I wanted very badly for my mother to know these things, as I had slowly come to understand them, before she died. As for my father, I have come to believe that his trust in people, regardless of race, was not so dangerous a thing. His church *was* in his heart, but he needed a better context for his kindness. When I consider how large and how populated the world is, I am not so sure now that I even want to try to transcend this trait in myself. My experience of other cultures, especially that of Japan, has taught me that kindness is often a universally respected trait. One need only find the right culture, or the right people, as a context for its general expression. Knowing this now, I want to try to be much more kind.

There is one final mystery about my mother, one that seems to contradict everything I claim to remember about her. Several years after her death, my youngest sister, Josephine, felt strong enough to sort through our mother's possessions. She had never had anything of material value, so

the chore became only a final opportunity for a communion, or conversation, with the enigma that was our mother. In the process of going through our mother's closets, Josephine found a very special treasure, part of which she eventually sent to me as a legacy. Because she was by habit a secretive person, one with a very long memory, our mother had kept everything. The packet of papers that I received from Josephine contained a record of my entire life. There was my graduation certificate from the Ada Bolden Kindergarten, dated May 1949. There was one of my father's contracts for work about to be undertaken in January 1950. There was my Certificate of Baptism in the African Methodist Episcopal Church, dated June 19, 1955. I found a Certificate of Membership in the National Junior Honor Society, dated February 1958. There was also, in 1958, a letter my father had written to her on June 24, soon after her father's death. It had been stamped by a censor in Reidsville Prison: "Sorry I could not have been with you . . . I am going to fight to clear my name. It is going to hurt somebody. But it will help you and children *soon.*" She kept a certification that I had passed inspection as a handler of food for beginning work in a supermarket in August 1960. There was a notice that I had received a scholarship from Morris Brown College, in June 1961, totalling $800 for a period of four years, to be paid at a rate of $100 per semester. There were poems I had written to her, and there were many letters. I found my high school diploma, and I found records of most of the grades I earned in college. There was my membership card from entering the Hotel Workers' Union, when I worked as a dining-car waiter during the summers of 1962 through 1965. I have my diploma from the Harvard Law School, and also the diploma from the University of Iowa. There were newspaper clippings about me: spending one year at Morgan State College, in Baltimore, Maryland, as a Visiting Scholar; having been accepted into the Harvard Law School from Morris Brown College. I found the stub of a check for $300, representing First Prize in the *Reader's Digest*–United Negro College Fund jointly sponsored creative writing contest in 1965. She kept a postcard that I sent her from Seattle, when I was working as a waiter on the Great Northern Railway and was able to visit the Seattle World's Fair. There was a letter to my mother from a judge in Savannah, a woman named Phyllis Kravitch, congratulating my mother when I won a Pulitzer Prize in 1978. There were pictures of my mother holding my daughter, Rachel, in our

The Father's Day gift from Rachel

apartment in New Haven in the summer of 1979. My mother is smiling, but in a guarded way.

It seems that I had gone out and accomplished things and sent the records of these things back home to my mother. She had been most especially secretive about her pride in me. She had never let on a word. Perhaps the kindest interpretation to be made of this stoic silence, as well as of the silence that guarded her deepest thoughts for most of her life, was the hold of a certain tradition that used to exist within the black community. Older people learned to expect the worst while secretly hoping for the best. If the worst happens over and over, the spirit suffers total defeat, or else the hope is driven down into the deepest levels of the self, where it survives as a closely held secret. Those who maintain this deeply secret hope, those who have not yet completely given up, learn to guard their last vestiges of optimism through the practice of a public pessimism. They become used to saying "I told you so!" or "It won't do any good" or "You've got to crawl before you can walk!" But, secretly, they want very badly to believe otherwise.

I think that the record of my life kept by my mother was evidence of just how secret her hope was, and it was also a record of how I had fed her hope, kept it alive. I did not know until I saw all those old documents just how long I had functioned as my mother's lifeline. I will never know just how many of her private defeats, her disillusionments, these scraps of paper countered. I know that she kept them all. I would like to believe that, by the time she died, I had already done enough to compensate for much of what had been taken from her, and from her family, during the long, hard years that followed the betrayal of the hope held out by the promise of Reconstruction.

And there is still a deeper irony. The records kept by my mother showed me that she had been right all along: you *do* have to crawl before you can walk. Up until the time I settled into the role of a teacher, I had worked all manner of service jobs, from houseboy to cook to janitor to waiter. Beginning in 1981, when I left Charlottesville for Iowa, I have had to synthesize all these service jobs into one broad pattern, or net, which would enable me to nurture and to see to all the needs of Rachel, my daughter. I have cooked, cleaned, found and cultivated playmates for her. Each month, since June of 1981, I have relied on my old training as a railroad man to coordinate the two flights and one long car trip to move the thousand miles between Iowa City and Charlottesville. Each summer I take care of a houseful of very young girls, and I call upon my old skills as a houseboy and baby-sitter. For this past Father's Day, my daughter gave me a card, illustrated with her own symbolic language, thanking me for my display of some of these old skills. Among the symbols I can see celebrated are my old skills as a cook, as a waiter, and as a person who was trained to take care of children. My mother forced me to learn to crawl so I would be able, under absolutely any hard circumstance, to walk. Because I was made to do this, for the past twelve years, each and every month, I have been able to fly. Because I can fly, I have become Rachel's lifeline, much as I was once my mother's. This feels good, comfortable, and somehow *right.*

These days, I am a teacher, and I seem to have won the respect of most of my colleagues and students. Last year the University of Iowa gave me an award for Excellence in Teaching. I also try my best to be a good father, even though Rachel is not with me most of the time. Despite the great geographic distance between us, I try my best to teach her to be kind and generous, but to her *friends.* I take pleasure in providing her with access to people who have the capacity to return her kindness. I want very badly for her to be, or to remain, a whole human being, to consider all her considerable gifts a treasure entrusted to her by God. I know full well by now that I am only a medium for the transition of my parents' gifts to a much safer, and much more secure and self-assured, possessor. This is what I am doing with the rest of my life.

More than this, I have learned from my Asian friends an ethic I did not understand before. What is of paramount importance in terms of what survives, in their world view, is not the personal will, which is the basic ethic of the West, but the family. In this view of what is of true authenticity, we are only momentary possessors of the talents and the traits lent to our ancestors by God. We must not allow others to defile them. Nor must we defile them with our own fears. Nor should we squander them. Because of who I am, because of the circumstances that produced me, I am guilty of all three sins.

But I am now very conscious of these flaws in myself.

I have no desire now, and no real need, to return to, or even to visit, any part of the South. There is just too much pain invested in that landscape for me to endure. But I am also wise enough not to say "never." So I am determined to be, one of these days, in my father's family home in Green Pond, South Carolina. I am still his name-sake, and I want the people there to know that I managed to stand where my father fell. When I die, following my uncle Joe McPherson, I want them to take me back to Hickory Hill. I want to be with my long line of ancestors there, even though I do not drink that much, am now a very careful gambler, and do not like to run my mouth. As for my mother, Mable Smalls McPherson, whoever and whatever she was, I want her now to *live* the song that encased what was so painful in her memory. After having taught her children to walk, I want her now to be with the angels, put her shoes away, and learn to fly.

BIBLIOGRAPHY

Fiction:

Hue and Cry: Short Stories, Atlantic–Little, Brown, 1969.

Elbow Room: Stories, Atlantic–Little, Brown, 1977.

Editor:

(With Miller Williams) *Railroad: Trains and Train People in American Culture,* Random House, 1976.

Contributor:

J. Hicks, editor, *Cutting Edges,* Holt, 1973.

Nick A. Ford, editor, *Black Insights: Significant Literature by Afro-Americans, 1760 to the Present,* Wiley, 1976.

Llewellyn Howland and Isabelle Storey, editors, *Book for Boston,* Godine, 1980.

Kimberly W. Benson, editor, *Speaking for You,* Howard University Press, 1987.

Alex Harris, *A World Unsuspected,* Chapel Hill, 1987.

Dudley Clendinen, editor, *The Prevailing South,* Longstreet Press, 1988.

Gerald Early, editor, *Lure and Loathing,* forthcoming.

Walt Harrington, *Crossings,* forthcoming.

Also contributor of short stories or articles to *Best American Essays, Best American Short Stories, New Black Voices, O. Henry Awards Short Stories;* and to numerous periodicals, including *Atlanta Constitution, Callaloo, Chiba Review* (Japan), *Esquire, Harvard Advocate, Meiji University Journal of International Studies* (Tokyo), *New York Times Magazine, Playboy, Reader's Digest, Reconstruction, The Rising Generation* (Japan), *Subaru* (Japan), and *Tikkun.* Contributing editor, *Atlantic Monthly,* 1969–; editor of special issue, *Iowa Review,* winter, 1984; *Ploughshares,* 1985, 1990.

Jessica Mitford
1917-

Jessica Mitford at her childhood home, Swinbrook House, England, about 1980

From 1929, when my sister Nancy's first novel was published, throughout the 1930s and 1940s when we younger girls went our separate ways politically, our every move took place in a blaze of newspaper publicity "Whenever I see the words 'Peer's Daughter' in a headline," my mother once commented rather sadly, "I know it's going to be something about one of you children."

Here goes with an effort to summarize events leading up to my late-blooming writing career, which dates from 1956, when I was thirty-eight years old.

In the beginning there were Farve and Muv, drawn to the life as Lord and Lady Alconleigh (or Uncle Matthew and Aunt Sadie) in *The Pursuit of Love,* my sister Nancy's supreme fictional account of our family. In reality they were Lord and Lady Redesdale; the Radlett children were the seven Mitford children, with some variations.

My parents have been described as eccentric, although I did not consider them so, perhaps because it is impossible to imagine one's own parents being any different than they are.

Farve was a man of violent passions and prejudices, the terror of housemaids and governesses—and of us children, on the not infrequent occasions when one of us might be unlucky enough to trigger an unpredictable outburst.

As a Younger Son (his older brother, who would normally have inherited the title, was killed in the First World War) he had received little education, having gone from an obscure public school straight into the usual murky colonial venture—in his case, tea farming in Ceylon—to which Younger Sons were then relegated. Perhaps it was there, shouldering the White Man's Burden, that Farve acquired that extra degree of British jingoism, remarkable even for his class and generation, that has been commented on by Harold Acton and others. "Farve is one of Nature's Fascists!" my two Nazi sisters used to say approvingly, and accurately.

By the time I was growing up, Farve, caricatured by Nancy as General Murgatroyd of her first novel, *Highland Fling,* and later as Uncle Matthew in *The Pursuit of Love,* had more or less resigned himself to the role in which she cast him—had become, in fact, a successful caricature of himself.

My mother was a far more complex person. After her death in 1963, James Lees-Milne wrote in the *Times:*

. . . One of her peculiar charms was a patrician reserve . . . that enigmatical, generous, greatminded matriarchal figure, with her clear china blue eyes and divinely formed, slightly drooping mouth which expressed worlds of humour and tragedy.

This moving description fits my mother as I came to see her towards the end of her life. When I was a small child I loved her, or believed I did. But by the time I was a teenager, I am afraid I actively disliked her. Nancy has written that she was "abnormally detached," giving this example: "On one occasion Unity rushed into the drawing-room where she was at her writing-table, saying 'Muv, Muv, Decca is standing on the roof—she says she's going to commit suicide!' 'Oh, poor duck,' said my mother, 'I hope she won't do anything so terrible,' and went on writing."

To me (the poor duck Decca) she seemed cold, strict, unapproachable, a person to whom one could never open one's heart or confide one's

The Mitford family, about 1922: Muv and Farve, with (in front) Unity,
Decca (the author), Debo; (center) Diana, Pam; (back) Nancy, Tom

dreams. Her "patrician reserve" held no peculiar charms for me.

Home was Swinbrook House, deep in the Cotswolds, a self-contained enclave from which it was unnecessary and undesirable, from my parents' viewpoint, ever to stir forth. It had aspects of a medieval fortress prison, from which quite early on I determined to escape.

In some ways, the seven of us (six girls and a boy) were almost like two families. Nancy, the eldest, was born in 1904, followed in quick succession by Pamela, Tom, and Diana who was born in 1910. After a four-year gap (during which my mother may well have thought her family complete) Unity appeared in 1914, I in 1917, and Deborah in 1920. Thus Nancy, thirteen years older than I, seemed of a different generation. I adored her as a distant star, while fearing her sharp, sarcastic tongue.

Yet the routines of childhood were much the same for all of us sisters. My parents, who grew up in Queen Victoria's reign, were Victorian in outlook, and ordered our upbringing accordingly.

The dream of my childhood was to go to school and to prepare for university. Our only brother, Tom, of course, went to Eton; but my parents were implacably opposed to education for girls.

My mother taught us to read, beginning at the age of five; by the time we were six we were supposed to be able to read out the *Times* editorials without mistake. This did turn out to be useful, but thereafter we graduated to the schoolroom, presided over by a fast-changing series of governesses whose departures were hastened, I regret to report, by our relentless misbehavior towards them. Needless to say, we learned nothing during those seemingly endless schoolroom years. The one advantage, however, was unlimited time to read. The library, Grandfather Redesdale's collection, was for me a heavenly escape from schoolroom boredom. To this day, when confronted by the intimidating word *Education* on the *Who's Who* biographical questionnaire, I perforce write in "Nil. Autodidact."

It never occurred to me to be happy with my lot. Knowing few children of my age with whom to compare notes, I envied the children of literature to whom interesting things were always happening: "Oliver Twist was so *lucky* to live in a fascinating orphanage!"

When I was about twelve I decided that one day I would run away from home, and to this end I opened a Running-Away account in Drummonds, our family bank, into which I deposited most of my weekly allowance plus such extras as birthday presents from uncles and aunts.

The four older Mitfords, who matured in the twenties, bore the stamp of that decade— Nancy, in fact, must have been a potent influence in shaping its distinctive character. In memoirs of the day, and her own novels, we see her darting about in the society of the fashionable and the intellectual like a magnificent dragonfly: "a delicious creature, quite pyrotechnical, my dear, and sometimes even profound, and would you believe it, she's hidden among the cabbages of the Cotswolds," as Brian Howard remarked to Harold Acton.

If the four older Mitfords were twenties products, Unity and I were very much creatures of the thirties (Debo was, and is, unclassifiable). To telescope the events of that decade as they affected our family:

In 1933 Diana divorced Bryan Guinness whom she had married at the age of eighteen, took up with Sir Oswald Mosley, head of the British Union of Fascists, to whom she was secretly married some years later in Germany, with Frau Goebbels, Hitler, and Goering as wedding guests. At the time of the Guinnesses' divorce, Unity, now an eighteen-year-old debutante, was a frequent visitor at Diana's London house. She joined Mosley's Fascist party, then went to Germany, where she lived on and off as a member of Hitler's inner circle until the war broke out.

My parents accompanied Unity to Germany on one or two occasions and became ready converts to the Nazi cause. (After my mother's death I was looking through one of her engagement books, a meticulous record of births of calves and foals, family happenings, Nanny's holiday, dances, dinner parties. Sandwiched between these items was an entry for June 1937: "Tea with Führer.")

Oddly enough, it was I rather than Unity who first became interested in politics. Before her sudden conversion to fascism, Unity's main preoccupations had been literary and artistic. I, on the other hand, was passionately engrossed with the other world that lay beyond Swinbrook, a Depression world in which students were demonstrating against the Officers' Training Corps, in which great hunger marches protested the treatment of the unemployed.

From within the Swinbrook fortress I watched these developments with avid interest and responded, like many another of my generation, by first

*The Mitfords, about 1934: (back row) Nancy, Diana, Tom, Pam, Farve;
(front row) Muv, Unity, Decca, Debo*

becoming a pacifist, then quickly graduating to socialism. I became an ardent reader of the left-wing press, and even grudgingly used up a little of my Running-Away money to send for books and pamphlets explaining socialism.

When Unity became a Fascist, I declared myself a Communist. Thus by the time she was eighteen and I fifteen, we had chosen up opposite sides in the central conflict of our day.

The endless schoolroom talk of "What are we going to do when we grow up?" changed in tone. "I'm going to Germany to meet Hitler," Unity announced. "I'm going to run away and be a Communist," I countered. Debo said that she was going to marry a duke and become a duchess. Perhaps seldom have childhood predictions materialized with greater certainty.

At first my political feud with Unity was something of a joke. At Swinbrook we divided up a disused sitting room at the top of the house and decorated it with our respective insignia: her Nazi pennants, photographs of Hitler, Italian "fasces";

my hammer and sickle, bust of Lenin, file of *Daily Workers*. Sometimes we would barricade with chairs and stage pitched battles, throwing books and records until Nanny came to make us stop the noise.

By the time of the outbreak of the Spanish Civil War in 1936, the joke had turned bitter and my political differences with the family dead serious. I was now officially grown up, having endured the traditional English upper-class puberty rites of a year in Paris and a miserable London "deb" season, consummated by presentation at court.

I had a comfortable balance of fifty pounds in my Running-Away account, yet escape from home seemed as far away as ever. The war in Spain now became my major preoccupation, and my thoughts centered obsessively on ways of getting there to join Loyalist guerrillas.

The opportunity to run, when it did come, was afforded by one of those improbable chance encounters that can in one dazzling flash change the course of one's life. In early 1937 I had gone to stay with an aged relation. There I met for the first time Esmond Romilly, a second cousin of ours whom I had long admired from afar. As a nephew of Winston Churchill, he was constantly in the news from the age of fifteen when he had run away from Wellington, his public school, to publish a magazine, *Out of Bounds,* designed to foment rebellion in *all* the public schools. When we met he had just returned from Spain, where as the youngest volunteer in the International Brigades, aged eighteen, he would shortly return as a correspondent for the *News Chronicle,* a left-wing London daily. I asked him to take me along; to my delight, he immediately agreed. Having concocted a suitable alibi to lull my parents into thinking that I was going to stay with some girlfriends, we departed for Spain the following week.

We lived in Bilbao for some weeks, until my parents discovered my defection from the family. There ensued a mammoth row: the British consul forced us to leave Bilbao, Anthony Eden sent a destroyer to fetch us away, Esmond in a masterly stroke of teenage diplomacy arranged for us to be deposited in Bayonne, rather than returned to England. We stayed in a Basque refugee hotel and were married in Bayonne. Now liberated from all parental control, we were at last free agents, childhood behind us.

That autumn we returned to London, where we lived in a friend's house, in Rotherhithe, an East End district near the river, supporting ourselves in the manner of the untrained and unskilled: Esmond as advertising copywriter and sometime journalist, myself as market research canvasser.

Politics were, as ever, paramount. In 1938, Chamberlain's betrayal of any hope of a united front of the democracies against fascism propelled us into our next move. Having just received an unexpected windfall of a hundred pounds, we decided to go to America for a spell, until the political scene in England should become clearer.

In February 1939 we embarked for New York—steerage class, one-way tickets. To describe the events of the next seventeen years, when I first started writing, would fill a volume—in fact, it has: my autobiography, *A Fine Old Conflict.* For the purpose of this memoir, the briefest of recapitulations:

We lived in New York for some months, then explored the East Coast, earning our keep as we went at a variety of jobs.

In early 1940, when following the "phony war" period Churchill became prime minister and it was clear that the war against fascism had started in earnest, Esmond left for Canada to train in the Royal Canadian Air Force. I stayed in Washington, where our baby, Constancia (nicknamed Dinky), was born in February 1941. In November of that year Esmond's plane was lost over the North Sea.

I worked in the Office of Price Administration, the wartime price and rent control agency, with the depressing job description of "Subeligible Typist"—and this in the days when the personnel shortage was so great that it was said that an applicant was shown a washing machine and a typewriter: if she could identify the typewriter she was hired forthwith.

My typing was, however, so atrocious that I was soon promoted to investigator, which paid twice as much and required no typing. (It now occurs to me that what I learned in this job, which consisted in tracking down wartime price gougers from lumber companies to landlords and black

The author with her first husband, Esmond Romilly, about 1939

market profiteers, was good early training for my future muckraking efforts.)

In 1943 I got a transfer to OPA's San Francisco regional office. Bob Treuhaft, a lawyer in the enforcement division, came out and soon thereafter we were married. We joined the Communist Party—in those days, the only game in town for the likes of us, who not only admired the impressive history of the CP both in the U.S. and Europe, but were convinced that this was the route to true *liberté, égalité, fraternité*—the age-old goals of revolutionaries.

In 1947, we moved to Oakland where I was the executive secretary of the local East Bay chapter of the Civil Rights Congress, high on the Attorney General's list of subversive organizations. Bob was CRC's legal representative. In these capacities, we were often subpoenaed by the House Un-American Activities Committee (HUAC) or its California state senate equivalent. (I put these subpoenas down on the *Who's Who* autobiographical form under *Honors, Awards, and Prizes*.)

The CRC, a forerunner of the militant civil rights movement of the 1960s, consumed every minute of every working day: running our office, campaigning on a dozen fronts from segregated housing to job discrimination to the ever-escalating instances of police brutality and police frame-up.

In 1956 the CRC was disbanded, having been chased out of any useful existence by the dirty tricks of the FBI. The CP was in crisis, following the revelations in the Khrushchev report and the Soviet assault upon Hungary and Czechoslovakia. The Party responded by organizing an intensive discussion period in which sides were soon chosen up: should the CPUSA (Communist Party, U.S.A.) continue to follow the Soviet line, or should it adopt an American agenda, a policy attuned to this country's specific problems?

I was unemployed and unemployable—I still had no marketable skills. While I had become adept at organizing picket lines and writing protest leaflets, these were not the qualifications sought by the average employer.

To fill the empty days I decided to try my hand at writing. *Noblesse Oblige*, a collection of essays by Nancy and others about U and Non-U usage, had just been published. "It is solely by its language that the upper class is clearly marked off from the others," as one contributor observed. An idea flashed into my mind: Was this not also true of the Communist Left? Why not a booklet on L usage, patterned after Nancy's book? The annual *People's World*—the CP newspaper—fund drive

With her daughter, Constancia "Dinky" Romilly, about 1941

was under way; if I wrote the booklet, charged fifty cents a copy, and managed to sell a hundred of them, I would make my quota for the year.

It was tremendous fun writing it. The title (with a bow to Stephen Potter) immediately suggested itself: *Lifeitselfmanship, or How to Become a Precisely-Because Man*. It was actually a very collective piece of work, although in the end I got all the credit—as, after all, Nancy did for *Noblesse Oblige*.

If ever a book wrote itself, as publishers are fond of saying, this one did; the whole thing was ready in a couple of days. In fact, by far the most time-consuming aspect of its production was the assembling, collating, and stapling, which we did on our kitchen table.

Cautiously I sought out a few carefully chosen comrades who I hoped would approve of *Lifeitselfmanship*, to test their reactions. To my absolute delight, they simply shrieked and pronounced it a Contribution to the Struggle against Left-Sectarianism.

Emboldened by this reception, I set about organizing a sales and promotion campaign for

Lifeitselfmanship that became for a while an absorbing, full-time occupation.

The response was nothing short of thrilling. Far from taking a censorious attitude to *Lifeitselfmanship,* as I had feared would be the case, the CP and left-wing press warmly embraced it.

Orders poured in from bookshops, libraries, and individuals all over the United States, from Canada, England, and Australia. Some comrades in London wrote for permission to reprint the booklet for the use of the Movement over there. Before it was over we had sold 2,500 copies, enriching the *PW*'s treasury (since there were no expenses) by the undreamed-of-sum of $1,250.

I basked in the sudden, unexpected fame I had achieved in our circles, in the ineffable feeling of having produced what amounted to a best-seller within the Party, in the delightful mental images I conjured up of the 2,500 buyers and their families sitting around their dinner tables, actually reading something I had written. (I do not know if other writers indulge in these fantasies about their readers; I do, and am kept afloat by them.)

Moreover, I felt I had done something positively useful. *Lifeitselfmanship* seemed to be an idea whose time had come; one could not imagine its smashing reception were it not for the unaccustomed, liberated atmosphere created in the Party by the discussions. Steve Murdock had written in the *People's World:* "The idea that the American Left can laugh at itself appears to be an engaging one," a thought expressed over and over again in the fan letters. The winds of change are blowing, as we L speakers would have put it; for an End to Dogmatism! I congratulated myself that *Lifeitselfmanship* might in its small way help to hasten that end.

After the dust had settled following the Communist Party convention of 1957, all such hopes vanished. The old-line Stalinist leadership once more seized control, followed by yet another spate of resignations. In 1958, Bob and I relinquished our CP membership.

"The Ex's," as they were called in Party parlance, suddenly freed from years of intense pressure and discipline, ran in a thousand directions, like schoolchildren when the dismissal bell rings. Some went back to college to prepare for new careers. Bob, together with some members of the Berkeley Coop, devoted all his spare time to organizing the Bay Area Funeral Society, its objective to arrange cheap funerals—preferably, cremation—for its members. I, unemployable as ever and encouraged by the success of *Lifeitself-*

manship, was slowly getting on with a book I had started writing shortly after the CP convention of 1957.

This book evolved in a curious way. One day when sorting out some papers, I came across a large folder containing all Esmond's letters to me, written in 1941 while he was training for the air force in Canada and later from his air base in England. They were long, fascinating letters written mostly in pencil, indecipherable, I thought, by anybody but me; before long, the writing might fade altogether. To preserve them for Dinky, I spent a week or so making typewritten copies. I showed friends the letters, which they thought gave a wonderfully vivid account of air force life and, as a collection, would make an interesting book. None of us had the faintest idea of how one went about getting a book published; but they did suggest it would be well to write a little foreword which would put the reader in the picture about Esmond and me, how we happened to meet and marry, a few words about our respective childhoods.

I wrote the foreword, nineteen pages long, in one day, hoping they would not think it too discursive; it seemed difficult to condense further. That evening they came over, and together with Bob went over what I had done. "Oh, but you've left out a lot," they all kept saying. "What about the Hons' cupboard? Your mother and the good body? The time you stole five pounds from the Conservative Fête to send to the London *Daily Worker?* You don't at all explain how you and Unity happened to be on such opposite sides."

The next day I started filling in some of that. And the next, and the next, for almost two years. My production soon dropped to three pages on good days, more often less. By the time the book was finished it had metamorphosed entirely; it ended with Esmond's death and his letters were not in it.

Writing is said to be a lonely task; I did not find it so. Perhaps thanks to my Party training, and to the method I had found so useful in writing *Lifeitselfmanship,* I turned it into a thoroughly collective endeavor, enlisting the help of several friends who became known as the Book Committee. They were absolutely invaluable, all enthusiasts, each contributing his or her particular skills.

The beginning writer is frequently warned to put no stock in the praise heaped on his work by friends and family, who are bound to see it through deeply prejudiced eyes and who have no experience or professional yardstick by which to judge it. I do not agree with this advice; had I not been sustained by Bob and the committee, I should soon have abandoned my effort, for the professional opinion of my manuscript, when it eventually began to be heard, was almost unanimously adverse.

There were some devastating moments. After the book was half-finished, the committee urged me to get an agent, but how? None of us had entrée into that rarefied world which seemed to exist only in New York. Finally I got an introduction to Barthold Fles, a New York agent who had represented some of the Hollywood Ten and other blacklisted screenwriters. Fles, a Dutch immigrant, had stuck with these throughout the worst years of repression, selling their books to small left-wing firms—Cameron and Kahn, Monthly Review Press, Liberty Book Club—the only outlets in those days for such authors.

I sent him the manuscript and he told me to call him in three weeks, by which time he would have read it and decided whether or not to

Jessica and husband Bob Treuhaft, 1943

represent me. The weeks dragged interminably. On the appointed day I rang him up to get his verdict. "Eet ees ex-ecrab-lee typed," were his disheartening first words, but he said he would take it on anyway.

Assiduously Bart sent it on the rounds. Between April 1958 and January 1959 it was turned down by Dial Press; Morrow; Dodd, Mead; Atlantic Monthly Press; Doubleday, and several others. Once or twice it got a good report from some assistant editor, only to flounder when it reached the top executives.

I hovered uneasily between two views of the rejections. On the face of it, all those editors had found it to be without merit. Yet I clung to the hope that another factor just might be involved: the aversion of publishers in those days to any book that smacked of radicalism or whose author had been tagged with the subversive label.

My committee loyally adopted the latter view. The publishing industry, they pointed out, no less timorous than the rest of the media, had for the past ten years sedulously avoided books that might incur the displeasure of the various witch-hunting committees. There was every indication that some publishers prudently imposed their own tacit form of censorship, less visible than that of the film industry—which took great pains to proclaim and reiterate publicly its subservience to the witch-hunters—but comparable in its effect.

One last possibility remained. Our passports, confiscated by the State Department at the height of the witch-hunt, were restored by the Supreme Court ruling. Bob and I were going to England in the spring of 1959. I would take the manuscript along, hoping it might have a better reception in that more temperate political clime. If it met with no success there, I would give up the idea of becoming a writer.

A few days after we arrived in London, I asked one of the CP lawyers if he knew of an English literary agent who might consider representing me. He suggested James MacGibbon of Curtis Brown, one of the largest and most eminent English literary agencies. I went round to MacGibbon's office, manuscript in hand. We were chatting about this and that when he asked casually, "By the way, Mrs. Treuhaft, are you a member of the Communist Party in California?" I was floored; in America, this could only be a hostile question, coming as it did from a stranger in the course of a business discussion. It seemed too cruel to have it sprung on me in England of all places. I peered closely at his face; disingenuous, friendly eyes gazed back. "Well, I was," I replied, "but I resigned about a year ago because the Party was becoming so inactive and ineffectual." "Oh, *so* was I," said MacGibbon. "I left for about the same reason." What a superbly un-American conversation, I thought.

Developments now unfolded with incredible rapidity, as in a speeded-up movie. James had said he would read the manuscript within the next few weeks. But the day after our meeting he rang up to say he had read it that evening and his enthusiasm was unbounded—not even a reservation about the typing. Which publisher would I prefer? he asked. I explained it wasn't quite like that, and told him about all the rejections. It was settled that he would offer it to Victor Gollancz (whom I had admired from afar since the Left Book Club days before the war) for publication in England, and for the U.S., to Lovell Thompson of Houghton Mifflin, who happened to be in London at the moment. I should expect to wait about six weeks for a decision, James thought.

Three days later, James rang up—both Gollancz and Houghton Mifflin had taken my book! It was published the following spring, called *Hons and Rebels* in England, *Daughters and Rebels* in America—Lovell Thompson thought *Hons* too obscure for the American public. (Virginia Durr, then living in Montgomery, wrote to say that as a consequence of its title, it was displayed in the Alabama bookshops on the shelves of Civil War books.)

An unforseen by-product of the book was the instant respectability its publication in America seemed to have conferred on me. Suddenly I was in demand for press interviews, radio and television appearances, as speaker at women's clubs and colleges—hardly forums to which I could have aspired formerly.

I soon discovered that as a published author one could get away with almost anything. It was a new and curious sensation and one that I found most enjoyable, to be swimming freely in the "mainstream," to find doors heretofore closed to me magically opening on every side.

Furthermore, magazine editors who had in the past contributed their share to my bulging files of rejections now began to ask me to write for their publications.

Just as *Hons and Rebels* had evolved in its own peculiar way, so did my next book. The unformed embryo of what was to become *The American Way of Death* had its origins many months before *Hons and Rebels* was accepted for publication.

At a time when I was hopelessly mired in the manuscript of my autobiography, with no publisher in sight and no immediate way out of the dread condition known as writer's block, Bob urged me to write an article about the Bay Area Funeral Society. I am sorry to say that I had rather mocked these good folks, an assortment of Unitarians, Quakers, college professors, and other eggheads whose oddly chosen field of endeavor was to fight the high cost of dying by securing inexpensive, simple funerals for the members through contract with an undertaker. I had called them the Necrophilists and teased them about their Layaway Plan. Why pick on the wretched undertakers? I asked Bob. Are we not robbed ten times more by the food industry, the car manufacturers, the landlord? But Bob, whose idea the Funeral Society had been in the first place and who was one of the prime movers in the organization, was absolutely immersed in it.

After I began reading the trade magazines he brought home I could see why. Their very names could hardly fail to invite a closer look: *Casket and Sunnyside, Mortuary Management,* and my favorite of all, *Concept, the Journal of Creative Ideas for Cemeteries.* I was fascinated by the fantasy world revealed in their pages, the world of "Futurama, the casket styled for the future," of burial negligees, street wear, and brunch coats, of Practical Burial Footwear featuring the Fit-a-Fut Oxford, of Natural Expression Formers (an embalmer's aid), and of the True Companion Crypt, "where husband and wife may truly be together forever." Drawing on the trade press for inspiration, I wrote the piece entitled "St. Peter Don't You Call Me," and sent if off to Bart Fles.

Faithful Bart circulated it to numerous magazines and forwarded the rejections that poured in from *Coronet,* the *Nation,* the *Reporter,* the *Atlantic Monthly,* and others. "Eet ees too deestasteful a subject," he told me. But eventually it did find a home, for a fee of forty dollars in *Frontier,* an obscure liberal Democratic magazine in Los Angeles with a circulation of two thousand. Prodded by Bob, the Bay Area Funeral Society ordered ten thousand reprints; once more I enjoyed pleasant daydreams about those thousands of readers.

The high point of my new-found respectability came when Caspar Weinberger, a prominent San Francisco Republican, invited me to participate in a debate on a half-hour television show, "Profile Bay Area," which he was then producing for the educational channel. The debate was on the subject of the Bay Area Funeral Society. On the affirmative side were a Unitarian minister and me; for the negative, two undertakers who proved to be wildly comic adversaries. Terrence O'Flaherty, television columnist for the San Francisco *Chronicle,* reported that the program had generated more mail to his column than any public event since *The Bad Seed* was shown at a local junior high school, which was highly pleasing news.

Shortly after this I had a telephone call from Roul Tunley, a staff writer on the *Saturday Evening Post,* who was passing through San Francisco. He had heard about the debate from a journalist friend, he said; the subject sounded juicy, and he thought it might make a good piece for the *Post.* I invited Tunley over to have a look at Bob's growing collection of funeral trade magazines, and set up some appointments for him with leaders of the Bay Area Funeral Society. Although I was actually sadly inactive in that organization, Tunley depicted me in his article as "an Oakland housewife who is among those leading the shock troops of the rebellion in one of the most bizarre battles in history—a struggle to undermine the funeral directors, or 'bier barons,' and topple the high cost of dying."

The article entitled "Can You Afford to Die?" came out in June 1961. The response to it was absolutely astonishing. The *Post* editor reported that more mail had come in about Tunley's piece than about any other in the magazine's history, and observed that it "seemed to have touched a sensitive nerve."

Bob was extremely gratified that at last his fledgling organization had taken wing, not only in the Bay Area but nationally, as a result of the *Post* article. Surely this spate of letters showed enough public interest in the subject to warrant consideration of a book about it. I wrote to Roul Tunley, urging him to expand his piece into a book; we would furnish him with any amount of research material, send him all our back copies of *Casket and Sunnyside,* put the files of the Funeral Society at his disposal. He replied that he was too busy with other assignments to take it on. "Why don't *you* write it?" he suggested.

Bob and I discussed this possibility. I said I would consider it only if he would help, and work with me on it full-time. We wrote off to James MacGibbon and to Candida Donadio, the young and brilliant literary agent who some months before had agreed to represent me in the U.S., enclosing a brief outline and a copy of "St. Peter

While working for
the Civil Rights Congress, 1951

Don't You Call Me." Candida Donadio replied: "It's a superb idea, so kookie that it is definitely possible." She and James set about drawing up the contracts with Houghton Mifflin and Victor Gollancz, both of whom seemed moderately enthusiastic. With this encouragement, Bob arranged to take a leave of absence from his law firm and we got down to work.

It was the best of times, it was the worst of times. Bob now spent his days in the San Francisco College of Mortuary Science, where with the help of two professors at that academy named Mr. Sly and Mr. Grimm he penetrated the mysteries of embalming techniques. I visited dozens of funeral establishments, among them Forest Lawn Cemetery in Los Angeles (immortalized by Evelyn Waugh in *The Loved One),* posing as a "pre-need" shopper. Together we sorted out the material, plotted and wrote the chapters.

Our toughest problem was how to write the factual description of the embalming process. Since embalming is the ultimate fate of virtually all

Americans, we were determined to describe it in all its revolting details, hoping to lighten it up somewhat by casting it in mortician jargon.

By early 1962 we had finished about a hundred pages, which we sent to the agents and publishers for their opinion. James MacGibbon, Victor Gollancz, and Houghton Mifflin were unanimous: the embalming chapter must go. I wrote to Candida, saying we were not going to jettison the embalming passage on which the book was now foundering both in England and America, that we had decided to go ahead, mimeograph the book and sell it ourselves, as we had done with *Lifeitselfmanship*. (A footnote here: over the years, more than a dozen college textbooks have selected precisely these pages of *The American Way of Death*, with such titles as "Behind the Formaldehyde Curtain," "Mortuary Solaces," etc., as examples of good prose. Is there a moral here for the neophyte writer in his dealing with editors?)

Candida, whose steadfast faith in the book had remained unshaken, replied by telegram: she already had a publisher for it, Bob Gottlieb, an editor at Simon and Schuster, who had offered twice the advance given by Houghton Mifflin.

After this, all was plain sailing. In 1962 we went to New York to meet Gottlieb, who at the age of thirty was something of a prodigy of the publishing world. It was love at first sight. He was entranced with the embalming passages and roared at the jokes (although he now complains that for the first year he knew Bob and me, our only topic of conversation was the relative strengths of embalming fluids and the effectiveness of various brands of trocar, a device used by undertakers to pump out the contents of the deceased's stomach). He proved to be an uncommonly good editor, at once perceptive, amused, tough, adept at ferreting out one's weak spots, yet sympathetic with one's difficulties—in fact, he was like all the members of my Book Committee rolled into one.

Months before *The American Way of Death* was published, the funeral industry became aware that the book was in progress, and it was not long before the trade press rounded upon me in full force. A new menace had loomed on their horizon: the menace of Jessica Mitford. Headlines began to appear in the undertakers' journals: JESSICA MITFORD PLANS ANTI-FUNERAL BOOK! and MITFORD DAY DRAWS CLOSER! When *Mortuary Management* started referring to me as Jessica, I felt I had arrived at that special pinnacle of fame where the first name only is sufficient identification, as with Zsa Zsa, Jackie, or Adlai.

Greedily I gobbled up the denunciations: "The notorious Jessica Mitford"; "shocker"; ". . . stormy petrel."

In October, two months after the book was published, Simon and Schuster sent me on a nationwide book promotion tour accompanied by Dan Green, the publicity director. (While such tours are now a routine part of book promotion, in those days they were far from common; yet another example of Bob Gottlieb's innovative and go-ahead methods.) It was a kaleidoscopic six weeks, enlivened for me by some unforseen responses of the undertakers and by Dan's earnest efforts to guide me through the treacherous shoals of sudden public figuredom.

Dan's real troubles began in Denver, where I was to address the Denver *Post*'s annual book and author dinner. Bob and I had been somewhat puzzled from the outset at the failure of the funeral industry to play what must surely be their trump card, exposure of our Red background; but in the euphoria of the book's reception by press and public, this question had receded into the back of my mind. It was now brought sharply to the fore.

On the day of the dinner a UPI reporter telephoned. "Miss Mitford? Have you heard about the statement of Congressman James B. Utt of Santa Ana, California, in today's *Congressional Record?*" I had not, so he read it out to me. It was a classic of its kind, listing my subpoenas by the House Un-American Activities Committee, my affiliation with numerous organizations on the Attorney General's subversive list, and delivering a scorching indictment of *The American Way of Death:*

> While hiding behind the commercial aspects of the mortician and the cemeteries and mausoleums where our dear departed friends and relatives are commemorated, she is really striking another blow at the Christian religion. Her tirade against morticians is simply the vehicle to carry her anti-Christ attack.

The statement ended with the ringing words: "I would rather place my mortal remains, alive or dead, in the hands of any American mortician than to set foot on the soil of any Communist nation." (Incidentally, in 1970 Mr. Utt exercised that option. His obituary in the *New York Times* records that during his ten terms in Congress, "his most newsworthy action came when he called Jessica Mitford a 'pro-Communist anti-American'").

With her mother on Inch Kenneth (her mother's island in Scotland), about 1960

The UPI man asked for my response. I said that I did not feel obliged to affirm or deny Utt's accusations; that loyalty oaths were repugnant to me, particularly when administered by undertakers and their spokesmen in Congress. The UPI man seemed satisfied—"Good for you!" he said.

None of us was prepared to predict the consequences to the book of the Utt revelations, although I braced myself for a cooling, if not a freezing, of its hitherto ardent public reception, accompanied by wholesale cancellations of my scheduled interviews and multitudinous returns of the book by dealers. It was therefore a delightful surprise when a few days later the *New York Times* ran an editorial on the fracas, captioned "How Not to Read a Book." The *Times* derided Utt's "McCarthyite attack," noted that the book had "evoked high praise from Catholic, Protestant, and Jewish clergymen, as well as from reviewers and other commentators in all parts of the country," and declared that Utt's "credentials as a book and television critic can safely be dismissed as nil." From then on, the tour afforded a unique and fascinating opportunity to observe the paradoxical scene of America on the turn, stirring out of the deep spell cast over it by McCarthyism.

Totting up reactions after the tour, it seemed clear that with few exceptions the media reacted much as the *New York Times* had done; the undertakers seemed to have misread the mood of the country. A few years before, I reflected, their

strategy might have worked very well, they might have succeeded in blasting the book into oblivion. But by 1963, the Red label had lost much of its magic as an attack weapon.

Did *The American Way of Death* actually accomplish anything—have there been any significant changes in the funeral industry? There have been changes, but I should be loath to take credit for these; at most, I opened up a formerly taboo subject that became for a while Topic A in the media. Newspapers across the country published their own in-depth surveys of local funeral costs and practices. CBS made a documentary film based on my book, *The Great American Funeral*, said to have been watched by forty million viewers. Cartoonists mocked the undertakers in cartoons syndicated in hundreds of newspapers. My favorite was a *New Yorker* cartoon showing a funeral director in deepest gloom standing outside his establishment, and a passerby calling out to him: "Read any good books lately?"

Looking back over the three decades since *The American Way of Death* was published, it seems to me that there have been three major breakthroughs. First, a heightening of general public awareness of the dangers of being fleeced at a time when for obvious reasons resistance to the hard sell is apt to be at its lowest. Second, a spectacular rise in cremation—when I was writing my book, nationwide about 3.5 percent were cremated; today, the overall figure is close to 40 percent with regional differences; in California, it rises to 50 to 60 percent. Lastly, the federal government finally intervened to provide a measure of protection for the funeral buyer via a Federal Trade Commission rule that requires funeral directors to conform to normal business practices: they must provide price information over the telephone; they are prohibited from lying, such as saying that embalming is "required by law"; they must produce an itemized price list showing cost of casket, embalming, use of funeral chapel, etc.

So much for my first three efforts, *Lifeitselfmanship, Hons and Rebels,* and *The American Way of Death.* That old bromide—"we learn by doing," beloved by teachers from first grade on—actually has some truth to it; at least I found it so. Thinking back over it all, much of the method I more or less stumbled on in the course of writing these came in very handy when preparing subsequent books. For example, I became fascinated by euphemisms when studying the funeral industry, which actually publishes in the trade journals lists of OK and not-

Jessica Mitford and husband Bob Treuhaft with writer Maya Angelou, about 1980

OK words (casket, not coffin; professional car, not hearse; the loved one, not corpse, etc.) and soon found that these abound in many other less-than-savory enterprises. There are no more prisons in America; they have all become correctional facilities; and prison guards are now correctional officers—never mind that their concept of "correction" hasn't advanced beyond use of club and bullwhip.

In 1976, I taught a workshop on journalism at Yale in which we discussed techniques of the trade. Eventually I summarized these for an introduction to a collection of my articles, *Poison Penmanship: The Gentle Art of Muckraking.* Among the points I stressed, drawing from my own experience over a twenty-year period:

Gathering background information—the goal being to know, if possible, *more* about the subject than the target of the investigation does. To this end, I soak up books and articles on the subject and accumulate a store of knowledge before seeking an interview.

Picking other people's brains—I've found it invaluable to consult a friendly expert in a field with which I am unfamiliar, such as a lawyer to unravel some tricky point of law, an accountant to explain corporate records, a doctor to translate medical jargon.

Interviewing is where the fun really begins. I generally divide up those to be interviewed into Friendly and Unfriendly witnesses—the Friendlies are people likely to be sympathetic to your viewpoint, such as victims of a racket you are investigating; the Unfriendlies, the target of the investigation. For the latter, I list the questions in graduated form from Kind to Cruel. Kind questions are framed so as to lull your quarry into a conversational mood. For a funeral director: "How did you first get interested in funeral directing as a career?" For a prison warden: "Could you suggest any reading material that might help me to understand more about the problems of corrections?" and so on. By the time you get to the Cruel questions—"What is the wholesale cost of your casket retailing for six thousand dollars?" "How

Jessica Mitford, about 1990

do you justify censoring a prisoner's correspondence with his lawyer in violation of the California law?''—your interlocutor will find it hard to duck and may blurt out a quotable nugget.

Having said this much, it would be tedious to relate the specifics book-by-book of how I happened to write them, and how I went about the long and arduous task of preparing the manuscript. Suffice it to say that in each case there were plenty of low points akin to those I have described earlier (in the case of commissioned articles, editorial disagreements sometimes resulting in rejection of the finished product; failure to stimulate any reforms, as in the case of *Kind and Usual Punishment,* my book about prisons which have gone from awful to atrocious in the past many years)—but also, some high points.

The zenith was reached in 1970, when *Time* magazine called me "Queen of the Muckrakers" in a story about the débacle of the Famous Writers School. I cherished that sobriquet—but above all, I loved every minute of researching and writing about the Famous Writers School, and the aftermath of my article.

As background, the FWS was an enormously successful enterprise—listed on the New York Stock Exchange, no less—that flourished throughout the 1960s. Headed by Bennett Cerf, the school's "Guiding Faculty" included a dozen well-known writers of the day, who promised in full-page advertisements in scores of magazines and newspapers throughout America to teach the would-be writers via a correspondence course how to become rich and famous, like them. To take advantage of this rare opportunity, all one had to do was to send in for an aptitude test which would be "graded" (the ads implied) by Bennett Cerf et al. The talented few who qualified would be on their way to literary stardom.

Investigating this patently fraudulent offer was most pleasurable. Predictably, it was almost impossible to flunk the aptitude test. Cost of the course: about nine hundred dollars in 1970, roughly twenty times the cost of extension courses in writing offered by universities. The Famous Faculty had nothing to do with any part of the school's operation—they just lent their names, and raked in huge profits.

I interviewed Bennett Cerf and his Guiding Faculty colleagues; spent a day at the school headquarters in Westport, Connecticut; studied the annual shareholders' reports; talked with numerous dissatisfied students; ploughed through the four hefty volumes of FWS textbooks—which proved to be a worthless miscellany of platitudes. I even induced a neighbor to conjure up a FWS salesman by sending in the aptitude test which, of course, she passed with flying colors. His pitch was all I had hoped for—an elaborate web of outright lies about the great achievements of FWS students, and the role of the Guiding Faculty in their instruction.

At the beginning, my article was beset by publishing problems. It had been commissioned by *McCall's,* which without explanation rejected the finished piece—my suspicion that Bennett Cerf had got to the editor turned out later to be true. It was eventually taken by the *Atlantic Monthly* (July 1970), whose editor, Robert Manning, did a bang-up job of producing it, with the title "Let Us Now Appraise Famous Writers," and a brilliant cover cartoon by Edward Sorel, depicting Famous Writers William Shakespeare, Oscar Wilde, Samuel Johnson, Gertrude Stein, Voltaire, Ernest Hemingway, Mark Twain, Leo Tolstoy, Edgar Allan Poe, and Dylan Thomas gathered to pose for their publicity photograph.

Developments came thick and fast. Both the *Washington Post* and the *Des Moines Register* reprinted the piece in their Sunday editions . . . television shows ranging from "Dick Cavett" to ABC's "Chicago" invited me to discuss the school . . . Congressman Burton of Utah read the whole thing into the Congressional Record as a warning to the public . . . the Attorney General of Iowa enjoined the school from sending its literature into the state, charging use of the mails to defraud . . . the New York State Attorney General announced a crackdown on the school's deceptive practices . . . the school's stock declined precipitately, plunging from 35 to 5.

When the stock started creeping up again, $5\frac{1}{4}$, $5\frac{3}{8}$, $5\frac{1}{2}$, Bob, alarmed at my despair, bought me ten shares as a secret surprise: "That way, you won't mind so much if the stock goes up," he said.

In May 1971 I was in Washington doing research on prisons. I got a telegram from Bob: "SORRY, YOUR FAMOUS WRITERS STOCK WIPED OUT. SUSPENDED FROM TRADING ON THE STOCK EXCHANGE." Early the following year, the school filed for bankruptcy.

At the risk of sounding self-serving, I cannot refrain from quoting what Carl Bernstein said in his afterword to *Poison Penmanship:*

> Jessica Mitford has reminded us again of some of the dormant essentials of our craft: Use common sense. Write well. Make a joyful noise—after all, journalism can be fun. Hallelujah. Her feats seemed all the more impressive because of her amateur status. Armed with a sturdy pair of legs, a winsome manner, an unfailing ear and an instinct for the jugular, she sets on her merry way—looking very much the picture of a slightly dotty English lady struggling with a term paper for a class at her community college.

BIBLIOGRAPHY

Nonfiction:

Lifeitselfmanship, or How to Become a Precisely-Because Man (also see below), privately printed, 1956.

Daughters and Rebels: An Autobiography, Houghton, 1960, published in England as *Hons and Rebels,* Gollancz, 1960.

The American Way of Death, Simon & Schuster, 1963, Hutchinson, 1963.

The Trial of Dr. Spock, the Rev. William Sloane Coffin, Jr., Michael Ferber, Mitchell Goodman, and Marcus Raskin, Knopf, 1969, MacDonald, 1969.

Kind and Usual Punishment: The Prison Business, Knopf, 1973, published in England as *The American Prison Business,* George Allen & Unwin, 1973.

A Fine Old Conflict (autobiography; includes *Lifeitselfmanship* in appendix), Knopf, 1977, Michael Joseph, 1977.

Poison Penmanship: The Gentle Art of Muckraking, Knopf, 1979, published in England as *The Making of a Muckraker,* Michael Joseph, 1979.

Faces of Philip, Knopf, 1984, Heinemann, 1984.

Grace Had an English Heart, Dutton, 1988, Viking (England), 1988.

Sons and Rebels, Transaction Publishers, 1991.

The American Way of Birth, Dutton, 1992, Gollancz, 1992.

Mitford's book *The American Way of Death* was made into a documentary film called *The Great American Funeral,* televised on CBS. Contributor to various magazines and newspapers, including *Atlantic Monthly, Esquire, Harpers, Ladies' Home Journal, Life, Los Angeles Times, McCall's, Nation, New West, New York, New York Review of Books, New York Times Book Review, San Francisco Chronicle,* and *Saturday Evening Post.*

John Frederick Nims

1913-

The first time I became aware that my private name had been shared by others was when I found myself staring at it on a tombstone in Deerfield, Massachusetts. There it was, only too plain: MR. JOHN NIMS. I had not previously associated my name with mortality. Born in Northampton, Massachusetts, in 1679, that John Nims had died, the tombstone read, "A.D. 1762 in the 83rd year of his Age." He was the elder brother of the Nims I am descended from.

The name "Nims" is not common, a fact partially explained by a bloody event in the family's early years in America. A literary friend, recalling Corporal Nym in Shakespeare and the Old English verb "to nim," suggested that it meant "one who steals." An unkind critic associated my name with the Latin "nimis," which means "too much." Both are wrong; the name itself is French. Since there is no other French blood in my veins than that of the original Nims in America, I am now, as an eighth-generation descendant, 1/256th French. The rest is English and Irish.

Reports tell us that the original settler was a young French Huguenot refugee, Godefroi de Nismes, a name Anglicized to Godfrey Nims. Long before, a certain Godefroy des Nismes had taken part in the Crusades, but only a wild-eyed genealogist would claim kinship. An even wilder one might recall that in the eleventh-century *La Chanson de Roland* the Duke Neimes appears as a friend and counsellor of Charlemagne: "Meillor vassal n'aveit en la curt nul." I make no claim beyond Godfrey, to whose historical existence various records and a seven-ton memorial boulder on land originally his, now the grounds of Deerfield Academy, are weighty evidence.

The background of the young man who appeared in New England is mysterious. He is said to have come from Nîmes in southern France, a strongly Huguenot town, many of whose citizens went into exile abroad. Even before the revocation of the Edict of Nantes in 1685, Protestants in Nîmes had been under increasingly heavy pressure; between 1657 and 1663 a number of Hugue-

John Frederick Nims, 1986

nots who had gone to Holland crossed over to America; others came here by way of England.

Godfrey's first appearance in court records is in 1667, when he is named as one of "three young lads of Northampton" who, with "an Indian called Quequelatt," broke into a house and stole some silver and wampum "with the intention to run away to the French"—that is, to French Canada. Could it be that Godfrey, "who it seems hath been a ringleader in their villainies," had memories of a childhood in France that left him unhappy with the more rigid Protestantism he found in Massachusetts? Later records show him as a solid citizen: he is involved in skirmishes with the Indians in defense of the town; he buys several plots of land in Deerfield and in time is a considerable landowner there; he becomes a member of the school committee; is appointed constable and holds other public offices. Except that his son John, whose tombstone I saw, had been captured by Indians and taken to Canada the year before, by February of 1704 it would seem that all was going well with Godfrey and his family. But on the 29th of that month disaster struck. In the predawn hours, 200 French soldiers from Canada and 142 Indians scaled the fourteen-foot snow-drifted stockade, pillaged and burned the town, leaving for dead, of its 285 inhabitants, the 50 who resisted, and forcing over 100, including women and children, through the snowy wilderness back to Quebec. Some, including Godfrey's wife, were killed as they faltered. It seems that Godfrey himself was away the night of the attack; if so, he returned to find his house burned, a son, a married daughter, and a grandchild slaughtered, an eight-year-old daughter and her six-year-old twin sisters burned to death in the house, and his wife, a son, a daughter, and two step-daughters carried off by the attackers. Godfrey himself died within the month, perhaps of grief, perhaps of injuries, if indeed he had been present the night of the attack. Two sons, John and Ebenezer, survived to carry on his name. John escaped and made his way back to Deerfield the following year. Ebenezer, seventeen when captured, figured in a romantic episode during his ten years in captivity. When a French officer fell in love with the Deerfield captive Sarah Hoyt, she refused him and was allowed to marry her fellow captive and childhood friend. It is from this couple that I am descended; my daughter Sally perpetuates the romance of the captives in her own name, Sarah Hoyt.

(A sidelight: Godfrey's daughter Abigail, only three when taken to Canada, was given an Indian name and raised by "a squaw of the mountain." When offered a chance to return with other captives in 1713, she chose to stay with those who had raised her. She and her husband, also a Deerfield captive, had many children and founded the French-speaking branch of Godfrey's descendants.)

The Deerfield story of the attack, the trek to Canada in dead of winter, the romance of the two captives—all of this could make a spectacular movie. There is nothing so cinematic in the story of my other Nims ancestors. Moses and Ariel were soldiers in the Colonial Wars and the Revolution; James was a farmer in Conway, Massachusetts; Dwight became a country doctor in Michigan,

Tombstone of an ancestor, Deerfield, Massachusetts

where my own grandfather Frederick A. Nims was born in 1839. After a couple of years at what is now Albion College, he went on to Hobart College for three years of a classical course. In 1858 he began to read law in a Grand Rapids office, and, while serving also as political editor for a local paper, was admitted to the bar two years later. When the war broke out, he was commissioned second lieutenant, served in several battles before being taken prisoner and held at Winchester, from which he escaped during the confusion of Lee's retreat after Gettysburg. After further battle experience he returned to the practice of law. In 1865 he moved to Muskegon, Michigan, where he became a partner in the leading law firm, was active as an attorney in the development of railroads, was consultant for the "Electric Light Company" and president of the streetcar company. He was also chief advisor to the millionaire lumberman whose many benefactions, estimated to total over $8,000,000 in money of those days, enriched the city—among them the impressive Hackley Public Library, which recently celebrated the centennial of its founding. With a hand in so many businesses in those rich lumbering days, it seems my grandfather might have accumulated a fortune, but apparently that was not among his ambitions. He gave his time rather to such matters as serving on the school board for thirty-six years, fifteen of them as its president, and was described as being "the first to advocate and adopt progressive measures." At a time when the science of psychology was new, he offered a course in "mental physiology" for teachers, meeting with them every other week, and using the text used in a similar course at the University of Michigan.

It was in his home, large and comfortable, handsomely furnished but not luxurious, that I spent the first four or five years of my life, and there that I had an early introduction to the world of books. A cousin who visited him in 1892 wrote home in some amazement that he found there, "besides his law books," a very large library, in which he noticed three sets of encyclopedias and a wide selection of magazines ranging from *Harper's Weekly Bazaar* to *Scientific American.* "Most of the family read," he added, as if that was unusual in his experience. Only a half-dozen books from that library are with me today, but these few give some idea of his wide-ranging interests.

Among them is a two-volume edition of *Poems* by Alfred Tennyson, published by Ticknor and Fields in 1855. Both volumes are signed "Fred A. Nims, Grand Rapids," and must have been purchased soon after they came out. Each has a stamp of his name, in ink now purple, and the library numbers 871 and 872; he had hundreds of books while still a young man. All of the pages have been cut, some a bit hurriedly; quite a few lines and stanzas have been checked in pencil. More elegantly bound, in sculptured leather, is an edition of William Cowper's *Poetical Works,* published also in 1855, with the stamp and number 892. A book of poetry I came to know early was a little leather-bound edition of Longfellow's *Flower-de-Luce,* published by Ticknor and Fields in 1867. It contains about a dozen poems, including the famous *Divina Commedia* sonnets. These did not attract my attention then; the one I loved was "Killed at the Ford," which I knew by heart:

> He is dead, the beautiful youth,
> The heart of honor, the tongue of truth,
> He, the life and light of us all,
> Whose voice was blithe as a bugle-call. . . .

I must have appropriated the little book a few years after leaving there; beneath my grandfather's library stamp is my own childishly printed name. Another book from his library that riveted me as a child was an oversize edition of Cary's translation of the *Inferno,* its leather binding sculptured and gilded, with seventy-five full-page plates by Gustave Doré illustrating the horrors of hell. Even more elaborate was a seven hundred-page tome, which I doubt I could have lifted at the age of five. Translated from the German, nearly every page was lavishly illustrated with drawings of things Egyptian from ancient days to the nineteenth century.

On a brown page just inside the cover of the Cowper volume, I can just make out, in faded ink, the words "Christmas 1859" and the signature of someone whose last name was McReynolds. In 1862, during the war, my grandfather had married Mary McReynolds; on her death ten years later he married her sister Ellen, my grandmother. They were the daughters of Colonel (later Brigadier General) Andrew T. McReynolds, the soldier-lawyer with whom my grandfather had been associated in Grand Rapids. The Colonel, my great-grandfather, was an awesome figure I heard about as a child. Born on Christmas Day, 1806, in Dungannon in County Tyrone, Northern Ireland, of a Scotch-Irish family of prosperous lawyers, he decided, while still a child, that he wanted to come to America, partly because, like many Irish, he admired what he knew of it, and partly because his mother's cousin, Andrew Jackson, was doing well here. When he came into his inheritance, the story goes, he turned the proceeds into gold, packed it into a satchel, and sailed for New York. Jackson, then president, welcomed him to New York. In 1834 McReynolds married Elizabeth Brewster, a direct descendant of Elder William Brewster of the Mayflower. Six years later he was admitted to the bar in Detroit. In 1847 he became a Democratic member of the Michigan senate, where the eloquence of his speeches caught the attention of President Polk, then involved in the Mexican War; Polk offered him a captaincy in the dragoons. There he served so effectively that when the Civil War broke out President Lincoln commissioned him, as colonel, to form the regiment known as the Lincoln Cavalry. In 1864 he was made a brigadier general. After distinguished service in the war he resumed the practice of law, which he carried on with success into his eighties, although, owing to Republican control of the state, he never again held any prominent political post. (Lincoln was the only Republican he ever voted for.) When in 1898 he died at the age of ninety-two, the Grand Rapids evening paper gave him the front-page headline: "HE RESTS! GENERAL A. T. McREYNOLDS' LONG CAREER ENDED," and hailed him as "one of the grandest old men Michigan ever knew, and one whose record has been a part of the best history of the state." The obituary notice also mentions another circumstance of interest to prize-winning authors of our time. "Among other achievements with which he is credited is the starting of Joseph Pulitzer, now proprietor and editor of the *New York World,* upon his journalistic career. General McReynolds became acquainted with Pulitzer in St. Louis and is said to have furnished the financial backing for Pulitzer's first start upon the journalistic sea. Every Christmas and on many occasions in between, the old gentleman has been remembered by the great journalist with fitting and appropriate remembrances." One of the soldiers under General McReynolds had been the teenage Joseph Pulitzer, whose desired military career had been discouraged by the Austrian army, the French Foreign Legion, and the British Indian service. Recruited by Union agents, he had come to America in 1864 and found himself a soldier in McReynolds' Lincoln Cavalry. It is unlikely that the young private, who at first spoke little English, came to the attention of the fifty-eight-year-old general at that time.

Paternal grandmother,
Ellen McReynolds Nims

I have no memory of my grandfather, who lived only long enough to see his new grandson in the cradle. But I remember something of his house in which I spent my first years. Upstairs were the large bedrooms, in one of which I would sit on the floor to do paper cutouts of cars and locomotives and animals and people. Nearby, in a closet with an oval window over the street, a sword was hanging; perhaps it had really seen service, perhaps it was a Masonic ceremonial sword. In another closet was a mysterious being called a "punching bag"; some mischievous elder had cautioned that it would come and get us, my two younger sisters and me, if we were bad. Overlooking the deep backyard was the sleeping porch on which we bedded in fresh air when the weather allowed. Above us, in the great attic with dormers on every side, were many kinds of treasure to be explored; I particularly remember the enormous horn of an early phonograph and the cylindrical records it could play. Downstairs was the library with its vast library table and the slender brass and onyx one, today waist-high in our dining room, but then taller than I, so that it

nearly toppled over on me when I tried to climb it. Downstairs too was the kitchen with its cookies and the pancakes-and-gravy that were my father's regular breakfast before his arduous work day began.

But my most important memory of the house is how I was introduced to poetry there. I must have been only four or so when I first heard my father, in a melancholy surf-booming voice, intoning

> Break, break, break
>   On thy cold gray stones, O sea!
> And I would that my tongue could utter
>   The thoughts that arise in me.
>
> Oh, well for the fisherman's boy
>   That he sings in his boat on the bay . . .

and the melodious rest of it. I suppose I had little sense of what it meant, but I knew what it *felt* like, and that fascinated me. My sister, a year younger than I but with a fresher memory, recalls that my father would also chant Whitman's

> O Captain! My Captain! our fearful trip is done . . .

Those were the days of the "Great War," World War I. "Kaiser Bill" was the enemy; I had dreams of hostile forces, dressed in green and wearing spiked helmets, parading in front of our very house. In France my uncle Leslie was shot through the leg; I learned from that what "puttee" meant, and improvised some of my own. Once we got together with an aunt and some cousins on the porch of their lake cottage and sang

> Somewhere in France is daddy,
> Somewhere in France is he,
> Fighting for home and country,
> Fighting for lib-er-tee . . .

Not that our own father was "over there." Frank McReynolds Nims, born in 1879, was then in his mid-thirties with three children under five. I

Paternal grandfather, Frederick A. Nims

suppose we were what held him at home, where we all "kept the home fires burning." About his early life I know less than I do about the Lieutenant or the General or even the remote Godfrey. He had enlisted in the navy and served long enough during the Spanish-American War to qualify later for a veteran's pension. While drilling on the Guantanamo beach in midsummer he had collapsed with dizziness and with the first of the splitting headaches that were to be a lifelong affliction. The only souvenir we had of his navy days was an oil painting he had done of the head of a rugged sailor. The features were handsomely realistic, but the way the paint was applied surprises me when I recall it now: instead of being conventional flesh color it resembled the pointillist technique of tiny daubings of mauve and orange and other colors. Could he possibly have been aware of what artists in France were doing toward the close of the century?

He was innovative, sometimes in odd ways. When I was very young he owned a little roadster—a Saxon? an Essex?—and once fell for a scheme to substitute for air in the tires some sausage-like cylinders of a material like the art-gum erasers of our childhood. It turned out to be crumbly too, like art-gum. I remember cartons of it in the attic under the horn of the phonograph. Years later, when I was about ten, he got a patent on what he called "Anti-Skid Plus Tire Chains," differing from the conventional ones in that the cross-chains had an X-shaped pattern: XXXXXX. This patent never got beyond the expensive photographs he had made. "In this photograph," he wrote, "note the mark of the chain on the ground, the absence of contact lapses, creating firm smooth-flowing tractive pressure. Note too the balanced variance of the bite." Perhaps he should have been in advertising?

All I know about his life between his navy days and his marriage to my mother in 1913 is that he spent the summer of 1903 in Corning, California, in the Sacramento Valley—but doing what? There he met a 104-year-old Irishman whose liveliness ("he danced a little jig") influenced my father's notions of longevity. Sometime during those early years he made a short-lived marriage I know little about; it was never mentioned in the family.

His five brothers all became successful professional men: engineers, lawyers, political administrators. My father marched to a different drummer. He had spent some time at an agricultural college; he loved the country and visited when he could his forty acres of meadowland with a woods full of crows and a little brook in a dell the bumblebees were fond of. I think he meant to build there—a dream he never managed to achieve. It was probably his love of country ways that attracted him to the job he held through the years we were in Muskegon. Some time after 1903 he became a rural letter carrier, at first with horse and buggy and later with the very tall Model T Ford that had a running board, side curtains with isinglass windows he could buckle on in the rain, and a crank whose crotchety temper once broke his wrist. Pleasant enough in summer, the job can't have been easy work year round. I remember staring one evening through the ice-glazed window until I saw his tall figure wading the snowdrifts, bringing me the present I had asked him to pick up at the Five and Ten, a box of what must have been called "modelling wax" but which was "molding wax" to me.

Everything my father did, he did with a characteristic dignity. He was tall, straight, slim, athletic in his movements, though as an adult he played no games and was uninterested in sports. The only event he ever took me to was a boxing match in the ballpark across the street. He was an excellent swimmer, the few times I saw him in the water. His may have been the archaic cork-handled tennis racquet I never saw him touch.

Reserved and taciturn, he never spoke about himself or his possible early adventures. Reserved, yes—but never cold. He was always gentle and even long-suffering with us and with our mother. I don't remember his criticizing us; he wasn't one to nag with "Do this . . ." or "Do that. . . ." Sometimes our more passionate and impulsive mother would threaten us with a spanking "when daddy gets home," but his gravely administered spanking consisted of a single firm smack, with never a second one.

He would have been in his early thirties when he met the spirited Irish girl, Anna Marie McDonald, whom he married. She was vacationing on his mail route with her parents in their little yellow retirement farmhouse with its big red barn. Those parents, John McDonald and Mary Ann Burke, had come there from Wisconsin, where John had been a railroad stationmaster. I have no stories to tell of their undocumented ancestry; being Irish, of course, meant they were descended from kings. Born in Tremore, County Waterford, he had come to America when seventeen. Mary Ann had been born of Irish parentage in Wisconsin. I saw them only a few times at their hospitable farmhouse. He was handsome and hardworking; she

was mild, smiling, sympathetic; she made sugar cookies with a raisin in the center and raspberry pies with rich juice damsoning the crust.

My mother had several sisters and a brother, a fact that insured us children many gaudily wrapped presents when Christmas came. She had taught for several years in a one-room schoolhouse in Wisconsin, making the ten-mile trip from her home by bicycle or horse and buggy. In winter she had to get there an hour early to get a fire going in the pot-bellied stove. Later she had taught in a Catholic school in Chicago. Her daughters called her, affectionately, their "wild Irish Rosie." Though she shared my father's interest in books, the only poet I remember her quoting was Byron:

> Fare thee well! and if forever
> Then for ever fare thee well:
> Even though unforgiving, never
> 'Gainst thee shall my heart rebel . . .

She seemed fond of "Mad Jack" Byron's romantic son—strange choice for a passionately Catholic Irish girl. She was also fond of romantic songs:

> A Spanish cavalier
> Stood in his retreat,
> And on his guitar played a tune, dear.
> The music so sweet
> Would oft times repeat
> A blessing on my country and you, dear . . .

The grandparents' house where Nims spent several years of his childhood, Muskegon, Michigan

She'd also sing a couple of railroad songs she must have learned from her father. One was about "the little red caboose behind the train." Another began:

> We are two bums, two jolly good chums,
>   We live like royal Turks,
> And if we've luck in bumming for chuck
>   We'll shoot the man that works!

All I know about their courtship, which may have begun as he handed her the mail, is that some time before they were married he wrote a poem "To Anna McDonald," which begins:

> Oh men sang much of such as you
> Before I saw the light of day,
> And men will sing in years to come
> When my heart's still and my tongue's dumb,
>
> Sing fairer songs than I can sing
> Because more apt in song than I,
> But never since the world began
> Lived fairer maid to sing of, Nan.
>
> Your hair so blue-black in its sheen
> Would shame the glossy raven's wing,
> Your clear brown eyes so like the doe's,
> Your lips the bud, your cheek the rose . . .

Maternal grandfather, John McDonald

He signed it "FMN." A graceful rhythm, gracefully handled; he had clearly read more than a little poetry as a young man. This is the only poem of his I know of. But he had what Auden called the first requirement for a poet: a love of words. Reticent as he was, he cared about them and was good with them. When the letter carriers had any kind of formal banquet, he was the one they would ask to make a speech; he seemed happy to oblige them.

Rarely, I've said, was he inclined to talk about himself. But it seems he was leading a richer inner life than any of us, except perhaps my mother, realized: a life revealed only toward the end of it when he began dictating to my mother, who was proud of her penmanship, a book he planned to call *The Benign Art,* by which he meant a kind of "psychotherapy" of the imagination. She wrote out in pencil, in college bluebooks I must have provided her with, five chapters of it, and then in ink a fair copy of a revised first chapter. I knew earlier that my father possessed and read more than once Frederick Myers's *Human Personality and Its Survival of Bodily Death* (1903). But with the smugness of youth, I assumed this was some kind of spiritualistic mumbo-jumbo. Now I find that Myers gets respectful notice in the *Britannica,* and

that his book was admired by William James. But I didn't know that so often in my father's thought were reflections on the human spirit, on the power of the imagination to influence our health and even our longevity, on immortality, and perhaps most of all on what religious writers call "the presence of God." An awareness of "the Omnipotent" seems to have been with him since boyhood. In the manuscript he describes an experience he had while swimming with a group of boys around a pier in a local lake. Trying to outdo the others in underwater distance swimming, he had struggled, holding his breath, to the very limit of his endurance. Abruptly surfacing, he felt his head thump against the underside of a broad flat-bottomed scow used in towing lumber. The air in his lungs exhausted, he thought his end had come; his mind became, he wrote, "a kaleidoscopic phantasy of hopelessness and fear and a longing more truly a prayer than words could be" that the "Infinite One" would help him. Not knowing how, he fought his way out from under the broad scow. The memory was with him forever.

Mother, Anna Marie McDonald

The "Infinite One"? "The Omnipotent, Omniscient, Omnipresent God, so near, so dear, so necessary to mankind . . ."? But what is this? He never talked that way, never in my presence said anything that showed concerns so ardent. Nominally an Episcopalian, he was, like his father, no churchgoer. All this was his secret life, and perhaps as much as anything accounted for a kind of dreaminess that explains what most would think of as his lack of worldly ambition.

When my parents were married in 1913, their families may have had doubts about the wisdom of the match. For my father's family, their son was marrying an Irish Catholic—a foreigner, in their ambience. For her family, their daughter was marrying not only a Protestant but one who had been divorced, although the local Catholic pastor, who knew my father and the circumstances of the divorce, approved of the marriage. Still, she was charming and very pretty; he was clean-cut, intelligent, reliable. The thought has crossed my mind that my mother too may have found herself disappointed: here she had married into this locally

distinguished family and yet seemed destined for a life of modest means as the wife of a simple letter carrier. We always had a snug and loving home, sensible food, decent clothes, good schooling. My father was never without his job until the injury, years later, that forced him into retirement. Though no doubt in as comfortable circumstances as most of the people around us, we would probably have been thought of as "poor," and, except for my Thoreau of a father, were sometimes embarrassingly aware of it, even though there was a Nims Street and a Nims School in our town, and even though we were "Mayflower descendants," a distinction, we may have smugly felt, that the rich factory owners could not claim. Cold comfort. A few years later, it was the beautiful daughter of one of those owners who said to me, "Wasn't that you I saw on the porch of that bungalow on Peck Street as we drove by?" She didn't add "in our limousine," but I thought her tone implied that. I don't know what linguistic sensitivity made the word "bungalow" offensive, unless it was because it would never have been applied to her great white mansion in its square block of shrubbery and a lawn strewn with expensive toys, among them a ten-foot-long play fire engine with a working hose and real ladders.

When we left my grandparents' big house, we moved for a few months into the country. In "The Powers of Heaven and Earth," the only poem I've written about my childhood, I describe the house as

> a musty-colored clapboard in the country;
> Absentee Nooley owned it; it was "Nooley's."
> The front door, from the parlor, opened on
>   nothing:
> No steps; we could hiphop down from it into the
>   milkweed.
> The barn was mostly skeletal; a ladder
> Sagged to its sagging roof. Once, halfway up, I
> Looked downward: dead leaves stirred, then came
>   in focus
> As a rattler coiled. I wrenched myself off sideways,
> Streaked for the kitchen door, stepped on a nail
> —A phrase of some foreboding then: it meant
> Pre-antibiotic festering that lingered
> In the sole of a foot like the Savior's in Mantegna.
>
> In spite of the serpent there, it wasn't Eden.
> The garden was radishes, rachitic carrots,
> Some ruffles of lettuce, potato bugs under the
>   leafage
> Sartorial in their striping; these we picked and
> Consigned to the fumes of kerosene in fruit-jars.

All of these, though—the snake, the gaudy insects,
The nail—I interpret by feelings that came later,
Remember as emblem only. Adumbrations.

In the same poem is a dramatization of my mother, which I quote to balance the account I have given of my father, and to show how her own passionate beliefs affected me in those impressionable years. I wrote, after describing a "morning memory":

> Now the night one,
> And my mother's crooning tune to the *casta diva.*
> A night of thunder and floodlit bursts of lightning,
> Rain dinning the windows' timpani—kind of night
>   she'd
> Get up in a ghostly smock, her lavish curls
> Afloat on her shoulder, wander and unfasten
> The fronds of palm festooning her holy pictures,
> Palms blessed at the altar, Sunday before Easter,
> In memory of those the Lord on His donkey
>   scuffed through.
> Ancestral voices led her? It must have been
>   something
> From cabin thatch and the banshee airs of Eire.
> She'd light the tips of the fronds in a chimney-
>   lamp's
> Blue flame and walk the shuddering house, her
>   fingers
> Flicking the myrrh of ash from leaf ends, till
> It floated in flakes toward rag-rug and linoleum,
> To save the house from lightning. As it did.
> That it didn't burn down the house was another
>   miracle.
> Sometimes, to back up ash, she'd sprinkle water
> Also blessed in the church. That special night
> The thunder—in awe of her leafy hands?—had
>   lessened
> To a cool and pitchdark stillness. Then she took
>   me
> To a window, brushed the curtains back, and
>   *there!*
> From between the jagged horror of two clouds
> Such a flood of moonlight as I've not seen since,
> All the more glamorous for the blackness round it:
> The full moon, mottled with its scarps and craters,
> Afloat magnetic there, a globe so luminous
> The luster reflected in my mother's eyes.
> Then she breathed something eerie, breathed a
>   breathless
> Spell in my ear: to think what heaven must be
> If the merest country moon could pulsate such
> Profusion of treasure! Did she mean, let's move
> From Nooley's into the moon's hallucination?
> Enough of the bugs and rattlers, rusty nails?
> Whatever she meant, some meaning haunts me yet
> —Beglamored young, is one ever at home in the
>   world?

JFN with his sisters, Ellen Mary (left) and Margaret, Muskegon Heights, about 1919

After that summer stay in the country we moved into a recently constructed little house in Muskegon Heights. The lower half of its single story was of white clapboards, the upper half of brown shingles—some contractor's idea of chic. Half a century later, when I drove by, the clapboards and shingles were still there, but the house was tinier than I remembered: I don't see how it could have been partitioned into more than four rooms. There must have been a tiny kitchen too, next to the great pot-bellied stove in the center of the house, its compound isinglass eyes dangerously aglow in winter. The yard had a magnificent oak tree—only a jagged stump when I drove by as an adult. The tree yielded an abundance of chunky acorns, which, with prosthetic toothpicks, could be made into little figures the imagination found as satisfactory as any I could buy. With these I could dramatize, in the landscape of mountains, winding roads, caves and pitfalls I would engineer in our sandy yard, the scenes from movies we walked downtown on Saturdays to see. My early favorite

JFN and his sisters "with the ballpark in the background," about 1921

fling the young Buster around like a sack of flour until he developed his famous acrobatic flexibility.

When I wasn't being creative in the yard with my cast of acorns and toothpicks, I was busy inside the house with the "molding wax." This came in strips of earthen reds and blues and greens, but after many reincarnations as cars and ships, heroes and villains, it merged into a dingy grey. Often my protagonists were accoutred in armor made of "silver paper" from cakes of yeast. Acorns, clay, and the connectable green railway cars from the dime store were my favorite toys, until the Christmas when my grandmother brought me a brightly painted cast-iron hook-and-ladder, drawn by three horses that surged up and down as it moved—the kind of toy one sees today in antique shops priced in hundreds of dollars. I also had a yellow roadster I could pedal in, pretty classy for that neighborhood, sent us by an uncle who had made good in the state capitol. His letter accompanying the gift referred to it as a "conveyance."

Just around the corner from us was a little "variety store" that had, besides its groceries, punchboards and a rack of colorful penny candies, including miniature paraffin bottles out of which we could swig a cherry-colored liqueur. Just a block away was the Oak Grove School (now the Lindbergh School) where I went to kindergarten and perhaps through a grade or two; there was much activity here with scissors, crayons, and watercolors. It may have been then, or a year or two later, that my mother would push me forward in company to "speak a piece," and I would declaim

> Breathes there a man with soul so dead
> Who never to himself hath said:
> This is my own, my native land . . .?

or

> Under the sod and the dew,
>   Awaiting the judgement day—
> Under the laurel, the blue;
>   Under the willow, the grey . . .

or "Sheridan's Ride" or "Columbus" or "Little Boy Blue" or the lugubrious stanzas that included

> Somewhere in a darkened place
>   Where others come to weep,
> Your eyes shall see a weary face
>   Calm in eternal sleep . . .

was *Tarzan of the Apes,* starring Elmo Lincoln as the paunchy posturing Tarzan. More sophisticated was the movie starring Wallace Reid, in leather helmet and goggles, as the race-car driver struggling with adverse weather the length and breadth of the land. Not long after, he was involved in a Hollywood drug scandal, its details beyond me. In the following years came cowboy movies. The rugged-jawed Buck Jones was my *primus inter pares;* Hoot Gibson and others were on his heels. The very favorite movie of my childhood was *Robin Hood* (1922), with Douglas Fairbanks as the acrobatic hero and Wallace Beery as a burly Richard the Lionhearted. Great castles! great armor! as I felt even when it was revived in Chicago sixty years later. Another favorite was the Buster Keaton movie, probably *The Boat* of 1921, about a man who builds a boat in his basement so big he has to knock the walls down to get it out. The Keaton family used to summer near Muskegon; my father had some acquaintance with them and enjoyed telling how the older Keatons would

I was about eight when we moved into a larger house back in Muskegon itself; it was there I spent the rest of my Michigan boyhood. Muskegon (accent on *key*), on the shores of Lake Michigan, had Muskegon Lake as its natural harbor. When its thriving lumbering industry declined toward the end of the century, the city had turned to manufacturing, though the factories, on the outskirts, were never an oppressive presence. In my boyhood it had an old-fashioned small-town air.

Only the corners of the two-block-square section we lived in had a house or two; the rest was thickly wooded. A leafy diagonal through the trees brought us to the farthest corner, where another little variety store had crusty apple turnovers worth walking over for. The owner, if he rummaged long enough among cartons under the counter, could come up with boxes of metal soldiers which relieved my toothpick-and-acorn platoons. In the woods, boys would shoot red-headed woodpeckers with their BB guns. I had scruples about killing the dapper birds, and besides had other uses for my silver-finish Daisy air rifle, which my mother had almost refused to order from the Monkey Ward catalog when she read "including tube of shot." I'd use it to pick off my imperturbable metal soldiers, which I'd then resurrect from their battlefield in the yard.

Beyond the woods, on the street behind us, right by the porch where the twins Wanda and Monda would giggle at us from their swing, was the trolley stop from which I, and a couple of years later my two sisters, went off to school. In the white house next to ours lived Marcella and Jean, my sisters' occasional playmates. Their athletic father, after work, would sometimes persuade me to put on his catcher's mitt and let him warm up with me (he threw *hard!*) along the sidewalk, where the black pinching bugs looked ominous at twilight. On our other side, beyond a vacant lot and the unpaved side street, lived my friend Leo Gilbert, typical American boy of the magazine covers, with his baseball glove and bicycle. His hard-working parents were Seventh Day Adventists, so he was unavailable for play on Saturdays. I couldn't have had more wholesome companionship.

Across the busier Peck Street, which we faced on, were the weathered green wooden stands of the ballpark, with enough open field around so that the kids, and sometimes their fathers, could shag fungoes through spring and summer and in autumn fill the hazy air with pigskin. The ballpark itself had a roofed grandstand reaching from first base around to third, with a stretch of cheaper bleachers beyond that. The rest of the field was fenced, but here and there convenient burrows would develop under it, so that we had no trouble squiggling through, unless the authorities had their occasional crackdown. Pretty good baseball was played there: Muskegon had a team in the old Michigan-Ontario ("Mint") League, representing cities just below the major-league level. Sometimes the long-bearded aggregation from the religious colony called The House of David would come up from Benton Harbor; that was a game to see! My favorite player on the Muskegon team was a hard-hitting outfielder named Steve Cosington. I still have a vivid memory of Steve loping far to his right to spear a long drive with a leaping one-hand grab. One year our catcher made it big; he actually worked for a time with the Chicago White Sox.

All in all, my friends and I had a Norman Rockwell boyhood. As I survey the world today, "idyllic" seems not too strong a word for it, in spite of the embarrassments, frustrations, and compulsions that afflict childhood everywhere. "I remember little of childhood but its pain," wrote Yeats. I can only say that such was not my experience. I remember the pleasures of baseball, of small-boy football, of swimming not in pools but in living water, of skating on gravelly sidewalks or on glistening ice. We had new fielder's gloves we greased with lard until they were compliant; our bat handles were spiraled with black tape, and often the much-used balls, like fat little mummies, were crisscrossed with it. Our new football helmets breathed the randy scent of leather; they squealed like live things when we'd compress and knead them in our palms. Our skis, bought as tall as we could reach with lifted fingertips, were tallowed again and again with candle ends; they had only single straps instead of today's fancy harnesses. To ski we had to trudge the mile or so across frozen Muskegon Lake, between the ice fishermen's shacks, to the hills of North Muskegon. It was on the black ice of the lake that we skated too, clamping the Hans Brinker skates to our regular shoes with the skate keys we were never without.

Sometimes our parents would take us on the streetcar out to Lake Michigan Park, where we could wade into the swirling surf and bob up and down with the whitecaps as they broke nearly over us. Or we could slip and slide our way up the great white sand dunes, especially Pigeon Hill, highest of all, or unpack our picnic baskets on the breezy verandas of the ornate pavilion. Or we could ride and snatch at rings on the merry-go-round, its music gaudy as the lacquer on its circling stallions, lions, swans, and unicorns.

Indoors there were other sources of entertainment. Planning at times to be an architect, I especially liked construction sets out of which I could build daring castles and squatty forts. Then, the Shiva of my universe, I could pelt them with projectiles from across the room: many a kingdom fell before my missiles. One year I found a length of waist-thick old stove pipe in a trash heap; stood on end, it served as a caitiff knight I could unhorse again and again, galloping at it with a tree branch for a lance. Of course I did a good deal of reading. First came fairy tales in their books of many colors, then adventure stories of Boy Scouts camping by Crater Lake or in the Dismal Swamp, and then on to Joseph A. Altsheler's novels about Indian wars on "the dark and bloody ground" or that later war between the blues and the greys. But my favorite books were the Arthurian epics as told and illus-

trated by Howard Pyle in his handsome volumes with the black and red armorial designs on the tawny covers and the theatrical illustrations of knights, armored cap-a-pie, jousting beneath the pennoned castles, or courting fair ladies like Ettard or the dangerous Vivien. We had a big leather chair from my grandfather's, so capacious I'd be fairly ensconced in it as I'd read, a plate of cheese and crackers or of apples sliced and cinnamoned beside me.

Most of the books I read came from the castle-like stone library my grandfather's advice had largely sponsored. With its winding stair, its timbered ceilings, and its windows of stained glass, it was an enchanted place to browse and spend the hours in. When the library celebrated its centennial in 1991 I tried to recall those hours in "The Library," a pair of childish sonnets. The first told how, steel-shod on roller skates, I ventured the long way downtown, "my bookbag swinging like Excalibur." The second told what I experienced there:

Some Merlin's hand dissolved the granite round
  me,
Spread worldwide panoramas, scene by scene:
First, the effects of faërie to astound me,
Prismatic tales in crimson, azure, green.
Soon after, knights came riding two and two
And taught what valor meant, against the odds
—"Odds" meaning churls or dragons, while in
  view
The enchanted princess—waking—stretches,
  nods . . .

More augury than I knew in ladies waking,
In all the early world my browsing found,
In wigwam, igloo, atoll, cavemen flaking
Their flint, Antietam, Shiloh's fertile ground.
I read, rose, left exalted; the great door
Swung on worlds wider than an hour before.

Margaret and Ellen Mary Nims

My sisters and I took the pitching trolley to St. Mary's School, clutching our fare in our hands, our return fare knotted in the corner of a hankie. Of that school I have random memories. I think I skipped second grade or maybe third. One year I had a job as chairman of the eraser committee; I stayed after school to do the dusty work. Regina McCarthy had honey-colored corkscrew curls of the kind that Shirley Temple would make famous. At recess we played marbles with our mibs and glassies or collected glossy horse chestnuts from a schoolyard tree. One year I wrote a poem about Ichabod Crane; I remember none of it. Besides the three R's, we studied geography, civics, Bible history. When I was in sixth grade, my last year there, I was elected class president, an honor of which I felt inordinately proud later on, thinking that at that age justice and candor prevailed, since the young voters were innocent of the sleaze and self-interest likely to influence adults.

Our church, St. Mary's, was next to the school. As an altar boy there I learned the Latin responses, without knowing what most of them meant, though here and there I could guess a phrase. It was my introduction to linguistics: I realized that people had spoken and did speak in other ways than I had learned. In processions in the church I sometimes carried the gold and crimson gonfalon of the Holy Angels Sodality; I took part too in other ceremonies, lavish with candlelight and incense, that required a carnation in the buttonhole of my dark jacket.

If we didn't bring our lunches to school in wax paper, we'd go down a block or two to the main street with its Coney Island hot-dog diner, where the hot dogs, at 5¢ apiece, were the best ever: steamed buns enfolding them, a splash of meat-filled chili ladled over them, mustard, sliced onions—the works. Piccalilli was I think a city sophistication that came later. For a dime we could have the deluxe lunch, a hamburger with a round bun. For dessert we could get a Tango bar for another nickel, or go down to the cool dark drugstore for a Green River or a Ginger Mint Julep. While we are talking gourmet, I must mention the fragrances we came home to after school. My mother's specialties were macaroni with chunks of American cheese crisped and almost blackened studding its creamy top, and pots of baked beans, not richly maroon like the New England kind, but delicately blond, with frills of crispiness flouncing the surface. And her apple pies! Her doughnuts!

In the summer of 1925 we moved to Chicago. My mother had four sisters there—in their younger days they had been called "The Five Irish Roses." She liked the bustle of big cities, having lived in one herself; she also liked the excitement of moving, of not being, as she would say, "a stick in the mud." My father would have preferred his leisurely mail route through the countryside. But he gave that up, gave up his fields and grove and brook, which he sold soon after, to drive a mail truck through the dingy and sometimes dangerous Chicago streets. I don't remember that he ever complained.

The first year in Chicago we lived on Dorchester Avenue, near Sixty-third Street, with its variety of gaudy shops under the El. We were not far from the walks and lawns and tree-shaded lagoons of Jackson Park, not far from the University of Chicago with its grassy Midway, flooded for ice-skating in the winter. After Muskegon, our apartment did seem cramped and gloomy, and to our annoyance turned out to have a bug problem unknown in Muskegon, where unwanted bugs stayed outdoors. To get rid of them now, my mother made valiant use of corrosive sublimate, which the dictionary glosses as mercuric chloride, "a strongly acrid, highly poisonous solid." She used it in solution. I had a windowless bedroom I gave the collegiate look to by hanging up, at a jaunty angle, my father's old tennis racquet and a pennant from Muskegon High. One day a week my mother helped out her more prosperous sister with her household work in distant Rogers Park. When she came home it was likely to be with a wire-handled carton of lamb stew and a silvery pineapple cake from Sixty-third Street.

The move to Chicago took me from Norman Rockwell country to Studs Lonigan turf. Walking six blocks, under the El and through a viaduct, I found myself at St. Cyril's, the grammar school affiliated with the high school across the street that James T. Farrell had attended. Both schools and St. Cyril's church were in charge of the brown-robed Carmelites. I don't remember the classes very well; they must have been uneventful. I was not elected to any office. We had no schoolyard with glossy chestnuts; only concrete to play on. Across the street, a little grocery store made hot dogs with butter on the buns and piccalilli instead of the tangy goo of chili. One gourmet novelty I remember, served at a drugstore soda fountain, was a chocolate sandwich, made by putting a Hershey bar between two pieces of bread and slipping it into the toaster until it was melty. Once was enough. Near our apartment was a comfortable branch library I often visited. Sax Rohmer is an author I remember; I think too I read some mystery stories, a genre which has never appealed to me: why should I care who done it to whom, when all were cut-outs?

For a couple of years I belonged to the Boy Scouts and went on a few camping trips on which we carbonized our meat over smudgy campfires. Though I rose to be Assistant Patrol Leader of the Flying Eagle Patrol (was there a Sitting Eagle Patrol?), my career was not illustrious; I earned no merit badges. But I did learn Morse code, how to wigwag, and how to tie a sheepshank, a knack I have never been called on to use. Mostly I liked the natty uniform and the official knives and compasses in the catalog. The baseball we played was "softball" or "indoor." I grew citified; I even bought some cheap clubs and a few times played golf in the park.

After a year on Dorchester we moved west into the Englewood section of Chicago. Because I was unhappy at the idea of changing schools, my parents let me take the long ride, transferring from streetcar to streetcar, back to St. Cyril's for eighth grade. It was that year, 1927, that I made my literary debut, with a poem saluting Lindbergh for his solitary flight across the Atlantic. The smiling nun liked it so much that she had a colleague *type* it—my first appearance in print. I remember only the beginning, with its reminiscence of "Paul Revere's Ride":

Ladies and gentlemen, listen with care
To the tale of a flyer who conquered the air,

Defying the wild sea's bloodthirsty crave
He steadily flew on, to France or the grave.

For thirty-three hours he flew on through the
      clouds,
While under him flowed the vast sea that
      enshrouds

Nungesser and Coli, the aces of France,
Who struggled and perished on old Neptune's
      lance . . .

If a fellow eighth-grader had been an aspiring critic, he might have noted the metrical variations in the logaoedic third line, the use of the verb "crave" as a noun (the kind of thing E. E. Cummings was doing about the same time), the telling juxtaposition of contemporary allusion and classical mythology in the fourth couplet, and the expressive enjambment after line 6. Much better poetry has been written by thirteen-year-olds, but this won me fame for a day or two in my own classroom and one down the hall. After that triumph, my Muse was modestly quiet for some years.

In the corner house of our block in Englewood lived a boy whose father was rumored to be an associate of "Scarface" Al Capone. The boy was swart and squat and ominously walleyed, but he turned out to be conversable—too conversable, as he'd buttonhole me with his mumbled jokes which I thought were about sex but didn't fully understand. Passing his house, which I did in a hurry,

and making a sharp left through a railroad underpass, I'd be in Hamilton Park, which had a central field broad enough for several baseball diamonds or football fields, all surrounded by walks, lawns, and shrubbery, a fieldhouse with a gym for basketball, rooms for Ping-Pong, and a branch library. But the glory of Hamilton Park was its tennis courts, probably kept in topflight condition because the park director, an Australian, was a tennis fan. The eight clay courts were tended and watched over by Steve, a saturnine Middle-European who guarded them as a dragon does its treasure. Steve and his assistant sprinkled the courts almost daily, shoved and lugged a heavy roller back and forth across them, brought out a little tank-and-brush on wheels and laid on the immaculate white lines. Besides these courts there were about the same number of asphalt ones, generally left to the "dubs" when the clay courts were in order, but usable the year round. It may have been the excellence of the courts that attracted to Hamilton Park probably the best group of players in Chicago. These were the home courts for our city champ, who had even won the national public parks title, had beaten Frank Shields, the Davis Cup star, and been invited to try out for the Davis Cup squad himself. I saw the great George Lott playing on our courts more than once. The Hamilton Park teams, graded A, B, and C, played teams from other parks and private clubs in Chicago and the suburbs, and were always among the best. A few years later, I was proud of the "H" on my sweater.

Anyway, there I was near the best tennis in town, and I took advantage of it. For the next six or seven years tennis, not poetry, was my main interest. Older players were helpful in coaching and giving suggestions; one summer the park hired a pro, when pros were fewer, to instruct us. Giving it as much time as I could, and imitating the players around me, it is no wonder I learned fast; two years after the Lindbergh poem I was awarded a ribboned medal for some kind of boys' park tournament.

Often we'd play all day, going home only as the lamps came on in the evening. Through much of an open winter, the asphalt courts would be clear; sometimes we'd shovel the snow off and play in mittens. One winter an older friend and I had the use of an indoor court in a church gymnasium. There wasn't much room behind the baselines, but it was great practice for our serve-and-volley game. During my last year in high school I was the winner of a junior tournament at the Beverly Hills

Country Club; the following year the same tournament was won by Frank Parker, soon to be internationally famous. None of his greatness rubbed off on me because of this; but somewhere in a dusty attic of the country club is a cup with his name right after mine: vanity of vanities. Going to exhibition matches when I could, I once saw Bill Tilden and Vinnie Richards in spectacular doubles. Soon it was the era of Budge and Vines; their clean flat ground strokes made us consider switching from our generally "western" grips.

Near the indoor court was a secondhand bookstore, in which I once found, for just a couple of dollars, the Cambridge edition of Dryden, bound in red leather. That, with my racquet, went home under my arm with me; I hadn't quite given up literature for the tennis court.

Graduating from St. Cyril's, I had gone on to Leo High School, a mile or so from where we lived. I remember the hatless walks to school in winter, my hair, combed down with water, frozen stiff as a helmet. Leo High was run by the Christian Brothers of Ireland; most of our teachers had come directly from the old sod; they had not lost the rhythmical brogue of their earlier years. All were well trained and hardworking; later, when I was teaching at Notre Dame, I used to see them there, studying for their higher degrees. They were tougher disciplinarians than the nuns, and would sometimes—only sometimes—haul a rowdy pupil from his seat and give him a resounding smack on either cheek. Some of the students, many of them Irish, were streetwise and tough themselves. One stocky apple-cheeked fellow used to threaten others with "I'll DEEFen yuh!" but he generally said it with a grin, and never to my knowledge "deefened" anybody.

I was lucky in getting a really sound high school education from the Irish brothers. What I enjoyed most were the four years of Latin. Our teacher, the last two years, was also the winning basketball coach. He drilled his students as rigorously as his athletes; after the workouts he gave us I had little trouble reading Virgil on my own. Besides Latin, we had two years of Spanish. Our teacher, called "Dusty" because his commendation for a correct answer was "Not so dusty!" had studied in Spain. He taught us the language with a Castilian accent, for which I was grateful years later when we lived in Madrid. Physics and chemistry were fun, since they involved playthings. Mathematics I was not good at; I don't know to this day what trigonometry is all about, except that

it involved complicated tables of decimals we were always looking up. Geometry was better; at least it had shapes and could be "vee-zualized," as one of the teachers would say. Nowadays, when I try to read books on quantum physics, I regret my innumeracy. I did have good English teachers, who tried to tone down a style too exuberant, too literary. Instead of just writing "horse" I was likely to write "solidungulate quadruped," words I had seen while browsing through a dictionary. When I wrote a story that began "Billy Smith had invented a hair tonic," the teacher commented, "That is the best sentence in the story."

I'm not sure what I was reading in high school; it was not, I think, precocious. When one teacher suggested we write a book report on Sigrid Undset, who had won the Nobel Prize a year or so before, I remember thinking, "Who's that?" Most of the writing I did must have been class assignments, in which I was encouraged by my mother's admiring my "command of the English language." But during the last two years at Leo I was writing some verse on my own, probably enough to fill a notebook or two. Some were sonnets; I always found such forms easy and natural to write in. I felt at home with them, as I did with the lines on the tennis court. Technically, the sonnets I wrote were competent, but they show I had not discovered, and not been guided toward, what contemporary poets were doing at the time. One Petrarchan sonnet begins:

You say she has such beauty? Possibly.
You say her velvet skin would shame the snows,
Her lips are fairer than a dew-decked rose?
That she is fresher than the morning lea
When night's soft fragrance lingers yet? That
she . . .

No one had told me what a cliché was. My education, strong in some things, had been weak in others.

I recall also writing and illustrating many pages of a burlesque cowboy story which began with the zeugma, "Bang! Bang! Bang! Three shots split the midnight air and the skull of Mexican Pete!" None of this augured well for my literary future.

For other hobbies during those years, I collected stamps, and then cigar-bands, "scuffing the Chicago curbs," as I wrote later, "head down, an eye out for those crinkled bits of gold and crimson, with their foreign mottoes and tiny portraits of exotic señoritas. Sometimes crouching, almost underfoot, on a busy sidewalk in the December winds to chip a rare specimen out of the frozen gutter, its ice marbled with the ocher veinings of those who preferred to chaw and spurt their tobacco rather than light up." Before I had finished high school both stamp and cigar-band collections had been sold to get money to buy a basketball, which I kept in my locker at school. I played some games on an intramural team, but what I really liked was to get to the almost-empty gym an hour before classes started and shoot baskets, baskets, baskets until they *swished*.

When I graduated from Leo High in 1931, I borrowed my father's middle name and gave my own as John McReynolds Nims for the diploma. Pity I didn't keep it that way; I might have had a different career. I never much liked the mild "Frederick." Just before graduation, the principal called me into his office to say that a one-year scholarship to De Paul University was available, and was mine if I wanted it. The offer couldn't have been more timely; just a few days later my father's mail truck was broadsided by a speeding car; his leg was crushed. Later the doctors said it was only because of his government uniform that the leg had not been amputated immediately. It was saved, but when he was released from the hospital many painful months later he was left with only his retirement and navy pension to live on.

That fall I walked the eight or nine blocks to the El, took the long ride to the North Side, and found myself on the De Paul campus—in those days not so much a campus as a scattering of buildings set among city blocks. There was no Midway, no quads, no trees to lounge or study under. I'd go there, troop to classes, spend time in the library in between them, and then, reinforced by a Milky Way or a Clark Bar, take the long ride home. Though there was not much of the jolly campus fun I had read about in college novels, the classes themselves were rewarding. When asked to choose a course of studies I thought of my grandfather and signed up as a pre-law student, forgetting earlier ambitions to become an architect or a "commercial artist." Pre-law meant I was to take not only Latin but also classical Greek. The Greek I had not planned on; it was pure serendipity. From the beginning I loved the look of the alphabet, loved what we moderns could guess of the way it sounded. After my years of Latin, the syntax seemed easy—more alive and flexible than the rigidly quarried Roman speech. I had good professors. The first of them, sensing my interest in the language, suggested I might go into archeol-

ogy. So for a time I tried, on my own, to learn German, necessary tool of scholarship, but I doubt I got beyond *der Bleistift*. First-year Greek was mostly grammar and then Xenophon, marching his many parasangs toward the sea. We began the second year with Demosthenes; I don't think I've ever so struggled with a sentence as I did with the opening of one of his speeches: it occupied me over the first weekend of the semester. But it soon got easier, and then we had the delight of going on to Homer.

Freshman English was a pleasure too. We had a young professor whose ambition was to be an opera singer; he brightened our sessions with references to the actress Ina Claire and the Russian bass Chaliapin. His opinions were decided and often startling. "If the poets are compared to birds," he once told us, "then Wordsworth is a chicken." Browning he liked and so did I; unfortunately that was as close as we ever came to the contemporary. Our professor the following year was less congenial; he had us read Shakespeare for the statistics: such matters as the ratio of end-stopped to run-on lines in the early plays as compared with the later ones. Perhaps because I looked bored, he called me aside one day to say that while my freshman professor had good things to say about me, he saw no reason to concur in that opinion. In college he had been a football player (a lineman) of some repute; it may be he had my welfare at heart and thought such a challenge was sound coaching strategy. I think it was in a writing class of his in which Walter Kerr, later the celebrated drama critic, sat right behind me; when pupils would exchange papers for "correction" we would write comments on each other's work.

There was a course of European history that I liked, but of all those wars, deals, manoeuvres, shenanigans, all I remember is a single rhythm: after his divorce, our textbook read, Henry VIII "was free to wed some princess, or haply Anne Boleyn." That was catchy, especially if one gave the lady's family name the iambic accent it tends to have in America. Sociology was dull; all I got out of it were three hours of credit and a merry moment or two, as when the professor, no genius, said of Mary Magdalen that she "lifted the jar of alabaster and poured all the alabaster out."

By winning the university tennis tournament that spring I became more involved in extracurricular life. I practiced on the school courts, travelled to local universities for matches there. After being a Greek and Latin grind, it was fun being a minor jock and flaunting, first, the sweater with

JFN (center) as a member of the De Paul University tennis team, 1932

my freshman numerals, and then, in my sophomore year, the royal blue sweater with its scarlet "D."

Most of the writing I did in college consisted of class assignments. As a freshman I turned in one poem the professor liked, but thought the assonance too insistent in "the dew-jeweled moon." I added a few poems to the notebooks I had started in high school. I also did a good deal of reading on my own. In one of the dusty bookstores I frequented I found a set of drably bound Dickens for a few dollars; proudly I had it strapped and lugged it home. A little later there was a set of Scott's novels. I read all of the Dickens; much of the Scott. I also prowled the bookstores for old textbooks of Greek and Latin classics. A little red book I bought and dated "October 1932" was an edition of Catullus with good notes and a long commentary on versification and meaning. My penciled marginalia show that I read the poems with regard for their quantitative meters, the longs and shorts so different from our English accentual rhythms. I think it was that year that I covered the endpapers of the Catullus with poems and fragments of Sappho in tiny neat Greek characters. The following spring I did the first of many verse translations I was to do: a version in heroic couplets of Virgil's first eclogue.

I finished my sophomore year in 1933, the very depths of the Great Depression. Our family did not suffer as many Americans did; we had moved to a pleasant apartment; my father had a modest but assured income. But though my parents generously did all they could, we could not afford to send me back to college. There were no "rides" for tennis players. I was not much help; either I was inept or unresourceful in finding work that would have enabled me to stay in college, or there just was no work for one of my dubious qualifications. I answered an ad for a helper in a college bookstore; that sounded like my kind of thing. But in my enthusiastic letter of application I said that my pleasure in working in a bookstore would be "dithyrambic." Little wonder I got no response. Besides answering ads I haunted an employment agency, paid them a "deposit" it was hard to scrape up and which they refused to return after doing nothing but send me on one wild goose chase after another. No wild geese were to be found. My father tried gallantly but quixotically to help: he had some pencils printed up with RE-MEMBER THE MAINE in gilt letters which he tried selling from door to door. Perhaps he did it only to have something to do. A strange figure he must have cut, this neatly dressed man with a cane, no longer young, dignified in speech and manner. His project was no more successful than the inner-tube sausages or the "Anti-Skid Plus" tire chains.

Use of the tennis courts was free. I'd walk there with my racquet under my arm and in my pocket the red "Little Leather Library" copy, palm-size, of *Fifty Best Poems of England,* from Drayton's "Since there's no help, come let us kiss and part . . ." to Swinburne's "The Garden of Proserpine." Both of these I knew by heart, and quite a few of the poems in between.

But life on the immaculately kept courts was about to betray me. Midway in one strenuous set, I felt a sudden sharp pain—felt, as I melodramatized later—as I'd been stilettoed in the back. It didn't last; I finished the set. But traces of the same pain suggested that a medical opinion was in order. After several tests, the doctors concluded that I had what they called "an enlarged heart," or, a term I preferred, "an athletic heart." There were also periods of arrhythmia, with the regular iambics of normal health lapsing into logaoedics if not quite free verse. After all the time I had devoted to regularities of rhythm, I thought that unfair of nature. Anyway, I was told to "take it easy"; no more tennis, at least for a while. I don't think I stopped all at once, cold turkey, but I did ease up, and by the end of the summer no longer found myself hanging around the courts. Occasional admonitory pangs would remind me of the doctors' advice.

As it turned out, they were only partly right. The heart itself was sound; as I write this I am nearing eighty. But its rhythms had been disturbed by hidden infection: not only tonsils but a couple of teeth whose nerves had been killed by "impact injury" when they collided with the skull of an opponent in a boyhood football game outside the ballpark. The teeth were extracted by a hard-fisted dentist with a blunt chairside manner; at work he wore a little black fez of a cap, like something a blacksmith might wear against the sparks. The sturdy golden bridge he constructed was something that other dentists, half a century later, would still chuckle over.

In a way these cautionary troubles were a blessing; they took me away from the world of games and afforded me leisure for the writing I was doing with deepening interest. That summer I copied out, on the blank front pages of my Catullus, hendecasyllabic translations I had done of a couple of his poems, including the introductory one:

> Whom'll I offer my clever little volume
> Polished recently with abrasive pumice . . .?

In October I bought Harrington's *The Roman Elegiac Poets* with its generously annotated Latin texts. From it I did verse translations of more Catullus and of the first elegy of Tibullus; I read Propertius and Ovid. All of the poems in Harrington were in elegiac couplets, a rhythm that fascinated me and that I was later to use in English.

I was also writing "my own" verses and discovering the intoxication of seeing them in print—real print, this time, and not just typescript. Early efforts appeared in our neighborhood paper, the *Southtown Economist,* which some years before had presented me with a dozen Wright and Ditson tennis balls, each shrink-wrapped in red cellophane, because I had done well in a boys' tennis tournament they sponsored. The paper had a column of wit and wisdom called "The Passing Show." In September it presented my first published poem, "Sonnet to the Sky," which opened sonorously with

> Mirror of mighty moods! Immensity
> Of varying portent binding pole to pole . . .

I had not then read Robinson Jeffers, or it might be suspected I had in mind his

> *Flammantia moenia mundi,* Lucretius wrote,
> Alliterating like a Saxon—all those M's mean
>   majesty . . .

But I daresay I was attempting a similar effect. When I sauntered by the courts a day or so later, Rosemary and Marie, our prettiest tennis players, chanted my lines back to me with I thought unnecessary satiric vigor. A few days after this debut I made a city-wide one in the *Chicago Daily News,* which, on its automobile page, had a column called "Motor Sparks." My verse, called "Song of the Tires," began "Sweeter than symphonies heard in the twilight. . . ." *This* is what I learned from reading Propertius?

But I was off and running. That month I had eight other pieces published in the two newspapers. Success—though unpaid—went to my head; in the next dozen weeks I published with a frequency that fortunately I have never equalled. Clearly I scorned Horace's admonition that one should hold a poem for nine years before daring to offer it to the public. *Nescit vox missa reverti:* the once published cannot be recalled.

Many of these fledgling poems were lugubrious:

> But one day your feet will grow still on the hillside,
> And silent your song that is beautiful yet,
> And all will forget but the rose by the headstone,
> And after a little the rose will forget . . .

It was not because, after scary sessions with the doctor, I felt the shadow of mortality hovering over me—in fact, I rarely felt ill at all. It seems to have been the natural gloom of youth. Almost a year before, my health unimpugned, I had written such lines as "Song of the Cynic," which began

> The bright wine thy pale fingers proffer,
>   Louisa, lorn mistress of mirth!
> Has lost all allure for a scoffer
>   Dismayed by ironical earth . . .

In December I wrote a "Dedication to Poetry," eight pages of consecration to the art, in Spenserian stanzas:

> Friends of my youth! if any art I own
> That holds dominion in the world of
>   dream . . .

It seems the world weighed heavily upon me.

In these incursions into musecraft, I had a companion, a red-headed tennis-playing friend named Chuck Norris—Charles W. Norris to our newspaper public. I think we discovered each other's interest when he saw my *Economist* stanzas and confided that he too had been writing verse. We had both read and imitated the same poets; Keats had both of us in thrall and had waved us on to Spenser and his "sea-shouldering whales." We had both read, lovingly, *The Faerie Queene;* indeed, I was halfway through it a second time. (Years later, when I gave a reading at the YMHA in New York, Kimon Friar approached me with the comment, "I see you've been reading Spenser." I had, much earlier, but I didn't know it was showing.)

Sometimes Chuck and I would get together for an evening of collaboration or rivalry. We'd write sonnets, villanelles, triolets, Spenserian stanzas, or whatever other forms we knew of, as often as not burlesquing them. That was the only time I have been a social writer and not a solitary one. Even then we did our serious work alone. Our English teachers had done nothing to bring us up to date. I doubt we knew about Pound, Eliot, Stevens, Marianne Moore. Even Frost escaped our attention. Yeats we might have known as a name. But we had much of Housman and Millay by heart. We could have done worse, as we could have done worse than continue our calisthenic exercises with forms and rhythms. My friend had as genuine a talent and as honest a love for poetry as any of the many students I later had in workshops; only circumstance has thwarted that talent and that love. After high school he had been lucky enough—or unlucky enough?—to get a job in some kind of advertising. Once on a salary, he stayed with it. After six or seven years, during which we rarely saw each other, I was engrossed in poets like Donne and Webster at the University of Chicago; he was still writing graceful and accomplished stanzas in the manner of the early favorites he had never had the opportunity to outgrow.

With me, circumstance had been more indulgent. What some might call chance and others providence had interposed by favoring me with the financial and physical limitations that let me enjoy that leisurely autumn devoted to writing.

The same chance or providence interposed again when I found myself—exactly how I can't recall—in social chat with a bluff no-nonsense missionary from Notre Dame who was giving a retreat at St. Bernard's, then our parish church.

When he happened to quote Shakespeare, I was emboldened to mention my own interest in poetry, and so on to Greek and Latin and the elegiac couplet, which he hadn't come across in his own reading. I illustrated its curtailed second line by quoting, from my recently read Tibullus,

Abstineas avidas, Mors precor atra, manus . . .

With that he seemed to eye me with interest: was I, a young man who seemed adrift but knew some Greek and Latin, a prospect for his own line of work? The thought took me by surprise; this had not been among my ambitions, even though, with my childhood memory of my mother's longing for "brave translunary things," a sense of the otherworldly had never left me. I had no wish to be his kind of preacher, but he did represent a university, where there might well be a place for a professor of Greek or Latin, or even of English. That sounded poetically feasible. Did I imagine myself going, like Milton's thoughtful man

> To walk the studious cloister's pale,
> And love the high embowèd roof,
> With antique pillars massy proof,
> And storied windows richly dight,
> Casting a dim religious light . . .?

My experience with the employment bureau and its sleazy operative, with the tacky anterooms where I had squirmed on wooden seats waiting for a pointless interview, had left me disillusioned with the world of business, which seemed to have no place for me. The life the retreat master suggested seemed a possibility worth checking out. He thought so too. In the weeks that followed, some letters were exchanged about university credits; since I looked healthy, nothing was said about medical records. So one blustery January day I found myself trudging through deep snow on the Notre Dame campus to a snug and pleasant haven beside the frozen lake.

I wasn't destined ever to walk among the black-robed seminarians with their downcast eyes—young men who looked so different accoutered for hardball in the springtime or hockey on the lake in winter. But I considered that life, and was considered. What I found there was congenial and fulfilling: the Greek and Latin classes, the light housework in dormitory or kitchen, Ping-Pong in the recreation room with agreeable if competitive companions, the gorgeous Gregorian music from centuries ago. Even the hours of services and meditation in the homey chapel had a solemn pleasure of their own, opening as they did into infinite vistas of space and time. I was not troubled, there or elsewhere, by the rigid, guilt-ridden experience of religion that Joyce describes in his *Portrait of the Artist as a Young Man*. For me it was more a matter of love than of fear, a love whose earthly richness and variety were to be subsumed in the excitement of a life beyond space and time—an eternity with none of the psalm-singing silliness and vacuous adoration some religious people seem to envisage, and which I later described as the "grosser whimsy" of

> Cherubs a-larrupin' the lyre,
> Rumps roly-poly overhead . . .

It was the kind of love I was to find later in the works of San Juan de la Cruz, or in St. Augustine with his "Dilige Deum et fac quod vis." Perhaps I was just lucky in never running into the kind of religious gestapo that Joyce knew. Or perhaps providence decided I was too simpleminded to be worth testing with the agonies of Job, or even those of Gerard Manley Hopkins, whose work I was to discover a few years later.

Though I probably shouldn't have done so, I did join in the rough-and-tumble basketball games in the old barn of a gym, sprinting up and down from basket to basket. For a couple of hours afterward I could feel my heart still slogging on heavily; actual pangs were only occasional.

Busy with classes, I did little writing; all I had to show for those first months was a translation of Horace's "Integer vitae" ode. When I went back to Chicago for the summer, I again prowled the bookstores. There I chanced on a little bilingual *Inferno;* I found I could puzzle out the Italian with the help of the Latin I knew. In another bookstore I stumbled on a real treasure: several volumes of the classics, bound in honey-colored leather, scuffed and cracking, with the bookplate of Racine College—whatever that was—on a flyleaf. Nobody wanted them; I could have them cheap. So I bought four or five, including a Statius I wish I had today. I still have the two-volume *P. Vergilii Maronis Opera Omnia . . . in Usum Delphini. . . .* At the top of each yellowing page, beautifully printed, would be a few lines, sometimes only two or three, of Virgil's text. Around and beneath it was explanatory matter, first a paraphrase, in simpler, more literal Latin. Under that, in small roman type, were the textual suggestions of generations of scholars. Lower still were the *Notae*

proper, identifying names, explaining allusions, etc. I don't believe I read these books immediately, but my dated pencilings of four years later can be traced through most of the *Aeneid*.

That summer I also got back to the busywork of my own verse. "Lancelot," a new piece in blank verse, began:

> Blind to the climbing branches, arch on arch,
> The sable glossy leaves, the lofty gloom,
> Contorted roots, dull-tapestried with moss,
> Through woods whose shadow was a soft despair
> Rode Lancelot . . .

This project, like others of the time, was left unfinished, but Lancelot did ride on for some twenty-four pages. That summer I published nothing; perhaps I was walking "the studious cloister's pale"?

Somehow the question of health had come up; authorities at Notre Dame asked me to come down for an examination by the university physician. The team doctor, when I found him, seemed a bit too sober as he listened to my pulse. He must have turned in a negative report and referred me back to doctors in Chicago. However it happened, it was decided by all concerned—all except me—that a period of "rest" would be a good idea. "Better not climb stairs," one doctor advised. Inwardly I laughed at him. Romping on the basketball floor was one thing—but *climbing stairs?* Stairs or not, I was to drop out of the university for the fall semester.

Perhaps for economic reasons, perhaps for the country quiet, my parents had moved to the little town of Montague, north of Muskegon. It and its sister city, Whitehall, were on White Lake, where as a child I had several times stayed at my cousins' summer cottage. No question the town was restful; so, through the colorful autumn and half of a Christmas-card winter, I "rested." I walked a lot through the woods and into town, made up games with a broomstick and a tennis ball, in which my right arm would swat the teed-up ball as far as it could in one direction, then the left arm would swat it back from where it lay.

Early each morning I'd trudge to the little church presided over by young Father Passeno, who was cared for in the rectory by his French-Canadian parents. It turned out that he read recent poetry; it was he who introduced me to such poets as Ruth Pitter and Paul Engle, who had just made a spectacular appearance at Oxford. At night school in Chicago I had studied French; that fall I read *Maria Chapdelaine,* my first novel in that language, a very appropriate one for winter reading amid the snows. Evenings I'd tune in to the French-speaking Canadian radio stations and try to imitate the accent. On Saturdays my mother and I would listen to the Notre Dame football games; she understood nothing of what was happening, but was sure that God was coaching from above. My father read and read, went for walks with his cane, smiled at our follies. The lady down the road sold us crusty new-baked bread, delicious, when fresh and warm, with country honey. One evening I did something I thought poetic: the full moon was so bright that I read "Ode to a Nightingale" by the pale silvery light that filtered between the curtains of my bedroom window. I worked at verse. In November I wrote, no doubt with Milton in mind, a sonnet "For My Twenty-first Birthday":

> The riddling years their fatal seed have cast
> Across what slope my lotted acres lie . . .

In midwinter I took the Greyhound bus down to Notre Dame for the new semester. There, except for brief vacations, I spent that entire year and the following spring. I can sum up that period by saying that I studied, played this and that game, found happiness in the duties and meditations of that life. Much of the happiness was physical, but the gratitude I felt for it was not. Spring meant meanderings around the lake, real baseball for the proficient, softball for the likes of me. In the summer there was swimming; in the fall touch football. One winter we made a ski run through the trees down onto the ice of the lake. One boy broke his leg.

On my own I read a good deal of Greek poetry. It was probably Shelley who directed me to Bion and Moschus; somehow I came on the catchy rhythms of Anacreon. I read my first Greek plays: the *Prometheus Bound,* the *Alcestis,* and more than once the gorgeous *Agamemnon,* appropriately bound in blood-red cloth. I had no reason to be unhappy with my classes. A close reading of Juvenal with a worldly-wise professor-priest was especially rewarding. I had several French classes with an elegant French-Canadian who liked to show off his uvular *r* by prolonging it. We had one course in such writers as Bloy and Péguy; both were a little too evangelical for me. But it was in that class that I did a verse translation of Péguy's poem to Our Lady of Chartres, and it must have been then that I turned a sonnet of Shakespeare into a French version that began

> Souvent j'ai vu venir l'aube couleur de rose
> Flattante les montaignes d'un oeil royal et
>   clair . . .

This is the only translation I have ever done *out* of English.

In science, I had a math-free course in astronomy, which I took for the poetry of it. There was a stiff required course in plant and animal biology (echinoderms! cotyledons!); the professor prided himself on a scientific rigor that showed itself in aloofness toward his students. He quoted with approval the saying of a botanist as austere as he: "Whenever I remember the name of a student, I forget the name of a plant." I learned more about science from a professor in the residence hall who had time for us and let me toy with a real microscope: there I saw for the first time the terrifying wonders that swim in a drop of swamp water. The literature we studied was mostly "from *Beowulf* to Thomas Hardy," but not beyond. One rugged Tennyson expert, gaunt and rough-looking as Tennyson himself, conceded, "I like some modern poetry; I like Walt Whitman." He did discuss free verse in cursory fashion: "It's like doing carpentry without using a hammer and nails; good trick if you can do it."

That spring, trying to keep the metrical quantities correct, I wrote my only poem in Latin, a couple of dozen lines in the elegiac meter I was fond of. It began,

> En ego nil solitus iam carminibusque alienus
>   Ausoniis, Musae, carmina prima cano . . .

But it was verse in English that kept me busy. Home on vacation, I submitted a poem to a classier newspaper column than I had previously patronized—or been patronized by. It was called "A Line O' Type or Two" in the *Chicago Tribune;* every year the editor would reprint what he thought the best poems in a brightly produced little booklet for the newsstands. Over the next year I had probably a dozen poems printed in the "Line," some of them reprinted in the annual. The following spring, before leaving Notre Dame, I also had several poems in the student literary magazine, one of them a long dramatic monologue in which Penelope bemoans her treatment at the hands of Ulysses.

When I left Notre Dame after the spring semester, it was decided that the career proposed for me there was not to be. The main reason, as I recall it, was the lurking uncertainty about my health: electrocardiograms were still a bit iffy. It is possible too, though I don't remember any statement made about this, that the poetry I had been publishing indicated a diversion toward worldly interests. I had been cautioned by a friendly superior—and all were generous with their friendship—that I would need permission for such publication in the future. We parted on the best of terms, with gratitude on my part and encouragement on theirs. It was agreed that in return for the schooling I had received I would teach during the following school year for just my keep and pin money at the prep school attached to the University of Portland, which the Notre Dame fathers were in charge of.

I spent the summer of 1936 in Montague, where my parents had rented a pleasant little house surrounded by clumps of white and purple lilacs. Hummingbirds hovered outside the open windows; at evening I would see the nighthawks diving with their cries; as it grew darker we would hear whippoorwills from the fields around. The "Line" in Chicago printed half a dozen or so new poems, including a translation of Menander.

Setting out for the Far West in September, I boarded "The Portland Rose" in Chicago for the trip across the prairies and through the mountains. The train stopped for a while in Cheyenne at night; walking beside it, I was thrilled to think that it was western air I was breathing, those were western stars in the sky above.

Columbia Prep in Portland was on high bluffs over the Willamette River; below us we could see the ocean freighters shipping—so everyone said—scrap iron to Japan. I loved that part of the country, which to my midwestern eye seemed primitive, pristine, with its soaring evergreens, its mountains and cataracts, its soft continuous rain we called the "Oregon mist."

A medical check-up advised a second tonsillectomy to supplement the first one; I spent a drowsily sedated evening by a hospital window with great vistas of evergreen forest and the distant mountains. When I asked about playing tennis again, the doctor shrugged, "Why not?" After a few games with the other teachers it was decided that I was the new tennis coach; I was happy to find, after the four-year layoff, that I could hold my own with the high school stars. For other exercise I used to jog up and down the hills along the river, or I'd throw a heavy stone back and forth, shot-put fashion. The priests and brothers who taught there were companionable, sympa-

thetic when called on, witty and ironic dinner companions. I taught a class in English composition and one in Virgil, which I tried to make like the class I had so enjoyed in high school. I read books of poetry from the Portland library and kept writing away on my own.

In the spring, at the end of the school year, instead of taking the direct route home I planned a touristy train trip, with stopovers in California and the Grand Canyon. Unfortunately I have never kept a journal; much that I'd wish to relive in memory has been lost forever. I have vague impressions of a hotel in Los Angeles, from which I took a bus or trolley out to Santa Monica. There I was so taken by the beach, the ocean surf, and the seedy beachcomber air of the place that I moved into a sandy-floored rooming house right on the water for a week or so. Also in the house there happened to be staying a divorcée with her eighteen-year-old daughter Miriam, in my eyes the typical California girl who had no trouble finding work as an extra in Hollywood. The fly in the ointment was her pest of a little brother, who was like those bratty kids in the TV sitcoms who interfere with their romantic elder siblings. All three were about to drive back to northern Michigan for the summer. Boarders in the house agreed with mother and daughter that it would be good "to have a man along" on the lengthy and perhaps lonely transcontinental drive. I was invited. It didn't take long to decide to cash in my railroad tickets and join them. Actually I was little or no help; I didn't drive then, and was only a conversational resource next to the suntanned princess at the wheel.

I was a happy camper. Besides the companionship, I enjoyed the changing panoramas, the rustic motels of those days, the roadside picnic lunches, the lazy evenings. We drove north along the ocean and then cut over to Sacramento. Once, driving by night near San Luis Obispo, we thrilled to the cry of some wild creature in the woods. Another night we stopped near Salt Lake City; sitting on the wooden steps of the motel we breathed in the redolence of a campfire and heard a cowboy keening about burial out on the lone prairie. Looking at a map now I see that we must have taken Interstate 80 all the way from California to Illinois.

It was probably the night after our Salt Lake City stop that our car was blindsided in Laramie by a carful of soldiers on furlough. Some years later, in a poem called "Wreck," I told how, after the crash,

From the other car men stumbled, all their eyes
Bright with the secret wisdom of the drunk,
Goggled and swore, and slowly blanched to sober.
Hands lifted our knees from a glass-and-oil mosaic.
And when they had ferried, darling, with rough
　care
Your gold and crimson pity to ethered sheets,
I blundered dazed to a bleak hotel and hired
A somber mound of a mattress, hospital-sweet,
Where grief all night on alien linen lay
Face-upward, eyes unfocused, drowned in shock,
As the blood in its frantic alley tossed and cried
Like fugitives rocked in a raided town by night.

I was honest about the behavior of those in the other car; the rest was more true to my feelings than to the facts. No one was hurt; there was no pitiful blood-stained blonde in need of ether—if indeed ether would have been called for in such an emergency. I did have a nervously sleepless night, but I was not as ravaged as the lines would have it. Poetry is not journalism.

The car was banged up; we had to spend several days in Laramie while it was repaired. I remember the town only as a main street on which half of the doors seemed to lead into bars, into none of which we, in our innocence, ventured. There was a little park that had a weedy tennis court with sagging net and overhanging trees; when Miriam got racquets out of the luggage, it was a weird setting for our games there—somehow, in that place, at that time, and with her, it was unreal as playing on the moon.

Since, after the wreck, her mother thought that my sitting beside Miriam interfered with her vigilance, for the rest of the drive I was banished to the backseat with little brother, whose idea of fun was pinching people amid spasms of giggling. My companions had relatives to see in Kankakee; there our ways diverged. Had I known Goethe's poetry then, I would mournfully have agreed with him that "Scheiden ist der Tot."

Waiting for the night train to Chicago, I sat glumly on a riverside bench near the station. Soon an aging unfortunate shuffled up, cap pulled low, collar upturned, features blurred with stubble, wreathed in fumes of alcohol. He settled near me, wanted to talk. "I s'pose evvybody," he hinted, eyeing me with bleary speculation, "would like a little messin' now and then?" Abruptly I was jostled off my operatic clouds onto a sadder world than I had yet experienced. Mumbling some excuse, I rose and moved into the station. The train soon came. When I glanced back, the bench was empty.

Miriam and I exchanged a few letters that fall. Since she was a fan of Nelson Eddy and Jeanette McDonald, I sent her a glossy photograph of both which a South Bend theater handed out at an Eddy-McDonald festival. Our mini-romance dwindled into some theatrical lines written a year or so later. When I found them, still unpublished after half a century, I added a reflective stanza.

A Song for Miriam

1938

Tonight I found your letters here,
And felt your presence over me
In wind that whipped the blood to storm
And swept my moorless soul a-sea.

I shall not brag my coffin holds
Your shade to ease that crawling time
When neither sun nor star—Oh damn
The weary rhetoric of rhyme!

But I can say: this vaulted brain's
Tableau'd by Michelangelo;
Along its stoa Sophocles
Beholds the sheeted figures go;

Beethoven in the darkened room
Is brooding and unquiet still.
And by what virtue do you claim
The court that such retainers fill?

But look what worthies stir for you,
O far away and never seen!
What plumes and mantles sweep aside
Before the coming of the queen!

1992

Tonight, some fifty years gone by,
I read these lines of long ago,
Mistrusting, but with jealous eye,
Such fervors! Were they really so?

Back at Notre Dame in September, I discovered that with the addition of a couple of summer courses I could graduate in August as a Latin major. I registered and set about writing a thesis on the odes of Horace. It was a summer of leisurely reading and of lounging in the sun by the tree-pillared lake. Nor was it bad on cloudy days: I remember the shivery pleasure of clinging to an underwater pier support to marvel at what seemed the worldwide rustle of rain on the watery roof above me.

The head of the English department then was Father Leo L. Ward, called "Literary" Ward to distinguish him from Father Leo R. ("Rational") Ward of the philosophy department. He had studied at Oxford, published poems in *Poetry* and short stories in the literary journals. Father Ward, dignified, kindly, with a mischievous sense of humor, was regarded with an affection close to awe by those lucky enough to know him. So that I could work on my master's degree while doing some teaching, he now offered me an assistantship. This was the beginning of my quarter-century teaching affiliation with Notre Dame, although during five of those years I was away as a visiting professor in Toronto or with teaching fellowships in Italy and in Spain.

My master's thesis was on the concept of civil authority in the prose of John Milton, but I was more interested in classes which introduced me to such poets as Hopkins, Pound, and Eliot. During the next two years I had at least a dozen poems published in *Script,* the student literary magazine, under such names as Harry Mullen, John C. Kleiner, and Conrad Paine, the last pseudonym perhaps in tribute to Conrad Aiken, an admired influence at the time. My work was also beginning to turn up in such poetry journals as *Spirit, Voices,* and *Wings,* and in such magazines of more general interest as the *Christian Century.* I felt quite set up when "Revere This Land" was reprinted, from *Wings,* in half a dozen newspapers from which I got press clippings, and who knows how many others. In the *New York Herald Tribune* it was in a column called "A Week of Verse," right next to a poem from *The New Yorker* by Dorothy Parker. There it was again, glory by contiguity: first Frankie Parker and now Dorothy. My sonnet began:

> There is no room for darkness underground,
> So thick the bright and lovely dead are
> lying . . .

Dorothy Parker would have sniffed at that, and a couple of years later I would have sniffed with her at the hollowness of the sentiment. What did I know about a decomposing corpse? (But when Rilke poeticized the death of a young person, one of his best expositors objected, "Had Rilke ever seen a child die?") Anyway, to such pretentious work I should have preferred simpler verse like "Silver Penny a Year Ago," from *Spirit:*

> Remember the sunlit maple trees
> and the queer little pool called Silver Penny?
> Here three of us walked that afternoon,
> and one of us thought it was one too many.
>
> An enemy thought so too. That's why
> my eyes are wet for all their winking.

> I am sick with the jealous thought I had.
> But how could I know what death was
> thinking?

By the summer of 1938 my parents had moved to Grand Haven, as far south of Muskegon as Montague had been north of it. It seems my mother was edging back to Chicago. The house they had rented there was close enough to Lake Michigan so that, books and beach towel under my arm, I could walk to it every afternoon, balancing much of the way on one rail of the spur track that led toward the beach. One of the books I cherished that summer was Jebb's edition of *Oedipus at Colonus,* which came into my possession, as I penciled on a flyleaf, "Grand Haven, Aug., '38." By early September I had finished it. Much later, recalling those hours of reading in bathing trunks on the warm sand, I wanted to begin some reminiscent verses with "Siliceous lollings of my youth!" But in "Time's Arrow," written decades later, they began:

> The seaside lollings of our youth! One summer,
> Gold as that sunflecked bevy in the dunes,
> I read, between my viewings, much of
> Homer . . .

The winter before, I had skidded to a fall on some icy steps and wrenched my left shoulder. From then on, it would gratingly dislocate if I carelessly threw the raised arm forward, as one does in swimming. I could have coddled it with a less flashy sidestroke, but never did; swimming and diving became things of the past. But lolling by the surf and trampolining up and down with the billows did not.

Afterwards I'd drop in at the cool pharmacy with its old-fashioned soda fountain. Betty Jean, a girl I'd observed among the "sunflecked bevy," worked there; we'd joke with each other as she brought me a Cherry Coke or a chocolate soda. Once we went for a long walk. Tall and slender, she was the classic American model of the Coca-Cola ads. If I say, as I do, that she was Botticellian, I am not being hazily poetic; her features were those of the blue-eyed flower-bedecked Flora, just to the right (in the picture) of the central figure in the *Primavera,* the young woman whose fey smile suggests that she stepped into the painting from an eldritch world of her own. Betty Jean gave me themes for two or three poems that summer, though I would not have told her so. Poetry was not the kind of thing she talked about. My closest and most electrifying moment with her came when the ballet-like gesture of setting a Coke down in front of me brought her lips close to my ear, the Botticellian curls brushing my cheek as she did so.

"Listen," the fey lips breathed, "when we gonna go out and get plastered?"

That was probably stronger stuff than I wanted from Sandro's lady. A poet describing the incident today would likely enough have done so bluntly, supplying only end-stops to what I have said above. But I called on the help of literature and mythology in some verses with the title "Remembering Catullus."

> When she above the fountain leaning
> Said the aloe word she said
> —Hot bright word whose ambushed meaning
> Missed that young and shining head—
>
> Then cool and mocking to the eye
> Gleamed olive Sirmio, half the sea's;
> And clearly on Kitoros high
> I heard the talking in the trees.
>
> I saw the words in water blaze,
> The flower beneath the sickle's kiss . . .
> And did she know what nights and days
> Could follow on a word like this?

In "fountain" I suspect I had the drugstore in mind, though no doubt I hoped that readers would be carried off into ancient Greece. "Aloe?" Probably I got that word from Juvenal, who uses it as a contrast to the sweetness of honey. Other allusions are to passages, bittersweet and bitter, in the poetry of Catullus.

Next to the September date I noted on finishing the Jebb, I had penciled her name. That fall, when I got back to Notre Dame, my mother sent me a package from Grand Haven. The inner wrappings were pages from her local newspaper; on one was a photo of my friend with the caption "CHOSEN MISS GRAND HAVEN." I sent her a note of congratulation. Botticelli would have been pleased.

During those years I was attempting poems of divine as well as of human love. In "Dedication," a longish work of a couple of years later, embedding quotations from Euripides, Virgil, and Villon, I listed some of the earthly pleasures of that time, concluding

> More than seven times, abruptly I have turned
>   from you,
> Yet always found you actual in the new place,
> Tavern or grove: "I am this too, and all things."

But Miriam, and the soda-fountain naiad, and a year later Elaine, were also serviceable Muses. Elaine, out of sequence here, was even more lithe than Miriam; she had been the nightclub dancer I described in my earthly pleasures poem:

> And a dancer one. In caverns of kleig
> Among dim tables where the shirt-fronts gleam
> She had swayed, her waterfall hair aglow.
> Her eyes were the color of sea waist-deep, with
>   grey sand under.
> We raced on the beach, her long hair free. One
>   midnight
> On a ledge at the looming wave, by foam and
>   starfire lanterned,
> My cheek on her hair, we shared the dark. Streets
>   echoed
> Vacant and long, when we came home.

She was a Southern Cal student I met in a poetry class at the University of Chicago summer session. In those days the Southern Cal–Notre Dame game was a big one; we had some good-natured bantering about it and made a bet or two. Added to her personal glamour was the fact that she was a California friend of Robinson Jeffers and his sons. Was it for her I wrote such lines as

> Briefly the beautiful lotus of your favor
> Rested upon my troubled waters then . . .?

Or was it someone else? Quite a few poems of those days profess a longing for someone who lived by a remote ocean—poems of an *amor de lonh* like that of the Provençal poets I had not yet read. When I was getting a book of poems ready a few years later, none of these ardent verses seemed worth including.

Back at Notre Dame after the Arcadian summer by the lake in Grand Haven, I resumed work on my master's degree. In those years many American campuses were enlivened by distinguished refugees from Europe. Notre Dame had its share of these; they were sometimes referred to by the less well paid locals as "the broken English department." One of them was the philosopher Yves Simon from Paris. Besides his graduate course in philosophy, he gave one whose purpose was simply to help the students read French. I sat in on the Descartes readings. His comment on my pronunciation, delivered in a rich accent of his own, was Delphic: my accent, he said, was perfect, but no Frenchman would understand me. An even more distinguished guest was Charles Du Bos, to whom, I see now, an admiring paragraph in my *Concise Oxford Dictionary of French Literature* is devoted. He was born, it says, in 1882, and so was in his fifties at Notre Dame; in my memory he is in his seventies or beyond. I wrote a long essay for a class of his on what I called "literature of the shadow," by which I meant literature which, by its very godlessness, reveals something about the sun of truth which it occludes. His written comment on my paper was to the effect that he had been meditating on this problem for thirty years; now for the first time it was clarified for him. From anyone else, such a comment would have been ironic or effusive. But not from him: he was showing sympathy toward the stupid gropings of a student. The very sympathy and courtliness of the dignified older man with the handlebar mustaches and the morning coat made him a figure of fun for the more irreverent students. They guffawed when he offered a course in "Robert and Elizabeth Browning: The Plenitude of Human Love." They snickered when, objections having been made to Shelley's morality, Du Bos defended the poet by saying that certain traits of Shelley, in an ordinary human being, would indeed have been faults. But not so in Shelley: "Shelley was an angel."

On receiving my M.A. in June 1939, I enrolled in the summer session at the University of Chicago for the Ph.D. studies which would occupy me for the next six years. Through the regular school year I had courses from individual professors with whom I'd confer by taking almost weekly railroad trips to Chicago, in that way managing to complete my Ph.D. work while teaching a full schedule at Notre Dame.

I was lucky with my graduate studies; they afforded a maximum of pleasure with a minimum of drudgery. My field was comparative literature: the history and theory of tragedy in Greek, Latin, French, and English. The first summer was given over chiefly to classes in Greek tragedy with Gertrude Smith, then head of her department. I had already read several Greek plays on my own, but now we went into the grammatical and prosodic intricacies of the text as well as questions about the development and staging of drama in ancient Athens. I still have and refer to the five volumes of the Oxford Classical Texts editions of Aeschylus, Sophocles, and Euripides, as well as quite a few editions of individual plays, all scrawled with my early annotations. That summer and in classes with Professor Smith over the next year or so we read twenty-five of the thirty-odd extant tragedies. That first summer I also had a course in Shake-

speare with Professor Tucker Brooke, a courtly Southerner from Yale. The following summer I went on to the sensational Latin tragedies of Seneca with a professor in the Latin department, and began courses in the pre-Shakespearean and Elizabethan drama with Gerald Bentley, about to publish his two-volume *The Jacobean and Caroline Stage*, which continued the history of English drama begun by E. K. Chambers. That summer I also managed to crowd in the aforementioned course in twentieth-century poetry given by George Dillon, then editor of *Poetry*. I continued my studies with Bentley through the year, and came in to Chicago for two rigorous semesters of criticism with the formidable Ronald Crane. My third summer I studied the plays of Ben Jonson with a distinguished lady who lectured under a large floral hat; I began courses in French tragedy with William Nitze. My Bibliothèque de la Pléiade editions show that we read, then or later, over a dozen plays by Corneille (*devoir!*) and nine by Racine (*amour!*). I had further lectures, this time in French, on classical French tragedy from a flamboyant visitor from France, known only by his last name. Drama could not have been presented more dramatically than it was by the wildly gesticulating Étiemble, later to be *professeur de littérature comparée* at the Sorbonne. Besides the courses in tragedy, I was given a list of a couple of dozen dramatists mentioned in Lanson's *Esquisse d'une histoire de la tragédie française* whose works I was supposed to know. Today, *hélas!* I remember nothing of the plays and barely the alluring names of their authors: Jodelle, Garnier, Montcrétien, Rotrou, Tristan, Lagrange-Chancelle.

One of these summers I also had a crash course in German to prepare me for my reading exam. After passing it, I read some early Rilke for pleasure, and then no more German until I came back to Rilke and went on to Goethe nearly two decades later.

Much of the last three years at Chicago was spent on my thesis, a critical edition of James Shirley's *Love's Cruelty*, published in 1640, at the end of the great age of English tragedy. I chose this partly because it was to be directed by Professor Bentley, partly because it seemed a cut-and-dried thesis subject, unlike the grander projects in which I had seen other Ph.D. candidates embog themselves for years and years. The thesis was a formality I wanted to despatch.

Though that subject did involve a good deal of work, much of it was fun—like the trivial pleasure of doing crossword puzzles. To establish as sound a text as possible I first collated, not just word by word but letter by letter, comma by comma, photostats of eleven copies of the first edition from rare book rooms here and abroad. The established text I then typed out, with all variants. It was preceded by a sixty-page introduction which investigated date of composition, evidences of revision, possible sources in French, Italian, and earlier English literature, the nature and date of the original quarto, and the relation of this play to other plays by Shirley. At the end of the text were appended eighty pages of notes on questions raised by it, ranging from printers' ornaments used at the time and the genealogy of Endymion Porter, father of the dedicatees, to the explication of mythological allusions and the meaning of obsolete words. A bibliography listed over a hundred books I had consulted in the process. There was much plodding here for two or three years, but the bogs were never more than knee-deep.

Thirty-five years after the thesis was typed and accepted, an unexpected phone call from Garland Publishing in New York asked if I was the editor of *Love's Cruelty,* and if they could republish it in their Renaissance Drama Series. In 1980 they did publish a handsome little book that reproduced, on a smaller page, my typescript. I wrote a preface for the Garland edition which began: "I don't seem to recognize the young man who edited *Love's Cruelty.* The young man with his head full of variants and analogues, prompt-books and squarish fonts, swash *I* 's, misattributions. . . ." I concluded with the suggestion that, in an age rife with sex and violence, the play could, "without many changes . . . focus into a sultry television drama—speaking, as it does, a language closer to the soaps than most of Shakespeare."

Busy as I was with teaching and with studies in Chicago, I still found time for writing. When the university announced its annual poetry prize, I got together a group of ten new poems and submitted them. All were in accentual lines of varying length; none, surprisingly, in the iambic pentameter I had used so often. Perhaps I thought of these as experiments; only one seemed worth republishing in later collections. In June of 1940 my group, announced as a co-winner of the prize, was published in a trim little booklet. The following September "Parting: 1940" made its appearance in the "Poets on War" issue of *Poetry,* my first acceptance by a magazine I was to be associated with over the years. Between that appearance and

the completion of my Ph.D. in 1945 I had nearly thirty poems in the magazine and had received three of its annual awards. During these years I also published in *Accent* and elsewhere; Étiemble looked on me with more forbearance after noticing a couple of my poems in *Partisan Review.*

George Dillon, whose own poetry had received a Pulitzer Prize some years before, was the editor who accepted the first dozen or so of my poems. When he was called into the army in 1942, Peter De Vries and Marion Strobel took over as editors. In the habit of dropping in at the office when in town, I soon felt at home there. When they needed a first reader, I was the one on hand and available. Every week a satchel packed with manuscripts went back to South Bend with me to be read there. My name first appeared on the masthead as associate editor in December of 1945, but I had been doing the first readings for most of that year. The following year the masthead listed six of us, including George, Peter, and Marion, as editors; after a couple of shifts of personnel, in 1947 it became George, Marion, and I.

Of the thirty poems I had published there, "Parting: 1940" had been suggested by the wartime atmosphere. So had several others, especially the four-part "Apocalypse," later reprinted in the *1967 Peace Calendar.* "Mozart," addressed to the composer whose music has been a lifelong delight, is set against the background of that war:

> Because you have come between us and a time
> When solid kingdoms tumble like Niagara,
> When treason lands accoutered in the garden,
> And even the holy sky is raining arsenals . . .

Several are poems of earthly love; "Prayer" expresses a more spiritual longing. "Race Riot" is an expression of social protest, as, in a way, is "Pigskin Abbey," later, out of deference toward the university at which I taught, more blandly titled "Football Game." Three or four might be called meditations, or maybe maunderings, on life, love, and death, among them "The Blonde Sonata," which appeared in Spanish translation as "La Sonata Rubia" in a Mexico City journal not long after its presentation in *Poetry.* Some ten poems of 1943, all in the same "Venus and Adonis stanza" (except that lines 1 and 3 are generally unrhymed), evoked and pondered details of the city landscape: "Poolroom," "Magazine Stand," "Penny Arcade," and others. These may well have been suggested by such poems as "Hospital," and "Pharmacy," which Karl Shapiro had published in *Poetry* a year or two before. In German, I learned later, such pieces are known as *Dinggedichte* or "thing-poems." I don't believe I was then familiar with Rilke's own famous *Dinggedichte*.

In 1944 a selection of my work was published as the third of New Directions' "Five Young American Poets" series, earlier volumes of which had introduced Jarrell, Berryman, and Shapiro. In the same collection as my own were poems by the then unknown but soon celebrated Tennessee Williams, who, the publisher J. Laughlin had assured me, was despite his name "no hillbilly." Indeed he was not: that very year "The Glass Menagerie" was presented, to great acclaim, in Chicago. I came in for a performance. J. Laughlin and Williams were both present; since he had seen the production, Laughlin gave me his ticket and I had the privilege of watching the play with the playwright. Afterwards we went backstage and met Laurette Taylor and the rest of that memorable cast. A day or so later, after I had a scotch or two with Williams, he brought out his volume of Hart Crane and began reading several of his favorite poems. He might have read on, but I was drawn, as Hamlet says, by "metal more attractive": on the far South Side an English major just out of Bennington was waiting for me, with much to say about Kenneth Burke and especially Roethke, just beginning his theatrical classes in Vermont. We had some pleasant times together that fall and winter, sometimes by the fire in her grandfather's cozy library. Once I picked up there a large leather-bound copy of *The Faerie Queene,* and was startled to find it was the first folio edition of 1609.

Back at Notre Dame, Father Ward and other professors had organized a poetry group which met at St. Mary's College, the women's college just beyond the lake and across the fields from Notre Dame. To the meetings, which some of the St. Mary's nuns also attended, we brought unsigned copies of our poems for criticism. A devil's advocate, appointed each time, saw to it that the criticism was unsparing. After the discussions in the formal parlor, some of the men would prolong the evening in Pete's, the neighborhood beer joint.

Most noons, between classes, I'd go to the gym to work out or shoot baskets, sometimes with lanky Ed O'Connor, later well known for his novel, *The Last Hurrah.* Another friend, in the gym and elsewhere, was Bob Schorsch, who had come to Notre Dame to develop his promise as a halfback. Becoming an English major after a year on the freshman team, he confined his athletics to the gym and the annual boxing tournament. After

Bonnie Larkin at a St. Mary's College horse show

graduation he began working for his Ph.D. in philosophy, with a thesis on the aesthetics of play, along the lines of Huizinga's *Homo Ludens.* For all of his athleticism, Bob, physically the Aryan ideal, was given to cogitations of Teutonic earnestness. From someone who admitted he had once gone to bars in the hope of provoking a brawl, he had turned into a sober philosopher. Most of the time he lived in a state of marmoreal calm; the only time I saw him edgy was when, once after summer school, we drove to Cape Cod. He let me share the driving, though I had just received my driver's license and, through ignorance, took chances I did not know were chances. That was the year of my first appearance in *Poetry;* I carried the letter of acceptance proudly with me and could hardly keep myself from showing it to Joan, the college girl who, when not buried in Proust or Mann, tended bar at a wharfside tavern. I was never quite blatant enough to show it to her; it was Bob she talked to.

He finished his Ph.D. early in the war. Since he did not quite have the keenness of vision to qualify for pilot training, he did the next best thing: became a paratrooper. On a visit to Notre Dame while in training, he invited me to dinner with a friend, a witty and attractive senior from beyond the lake, whom he teasingly introduced as "the St. Mary's Prom Queen." As indeed she had been. She had also been class president for three of her four years, having been wangled out of it one year, according to her amusing account, by a scheming cabal of rivals. At dinner she entertained us with another tale of her political adventuring: during the Roosevelt-Landon campaign she had made the front page of all the newspapers in Kansas as the innocent-looking young girl who had passed out Democratic flyers at a Republican rally. She was Bonnie Larkin, born in Kansas but raised partly in California; hers is a name likely to occur as frequently as my own in these reminiscences. We had a few dates in South Bend in the spring of her graduation, and were to see each other later in Chicago.

Robert Schorsch, 1944

When Bob was commissioned a lieutenant and shipped to Europe, he entrusted me with entertaining Donna, the girl he had just married. (We used the Shakespearean "girl" in those innocent and insensitive days, and would have been regarded as prissy if we had used such terms as "young woman" or, worse, "young lady.") Bob gave me enough money to take Donna to dinner now and then and to buy gifts for her. It was not a difficult assignment; Donna, a drama student, had been turned down in Hollywood, the story was, because she was a look-alike for Anne Rutherford. I had just about spent all of the money when one noon, at a high-spirited faculty lunch in the Notre Dame cafeteria, I was approached by the alumni director, more somber than usual. He leaned close and told me softly that our friend Bob had been killed in Europe. When I think of it, I think of lines from a chorus of Aeschylus I was reading:

> Whom he sent forth, each knew, but
> what came home, of that flesh and blood?
> Nothing but urns and ashes.

The only memento I have of Bob is his copy of Jacques Maritain's *Art and Scholasticism,* with his name, in a neat schoolboy hand, on the title page. Tucked inside is a slip of paper with a note in his handwriting: "On the analogy between Fine Arts, Wisdom, and Games, cf. p. 34."

My dislocating shoulder excused me from the war. It seemed I might get into an army program for training meteorologists (does one need two free-swinging arms to forecast weather?), but I was turned down for that. Thinking it might be of some practical help, I took a night course in electronics, but was discouraged to find that electricity was a dangerously embodied form of mathematics.

The closest I came to firearms had been just before the war, when one of my students introduced me to pistol shooting—I think he wanted to sell me his K-22. I did buy it, and later acquired a Colt Woodsman and a .38 Super, which looked, and was, fearsomely like the army's .45. A knowledgeable friend tells me it was much used by officers of South American military regimes. We employed these handguns against tin cans and such in a wooded hollow near St. Mary's. Today, with our big city gun-control problem, I might well have scruples about that kind of recreation. But then it seemed guilt-free; in 1943 I published "Colt Automatic" in *Poetry.* For a couple of years I carried on my keychain a quarter with the embedded .22 bullet I had plugged it with. A few years later, when married, I traded in my small pistol collection for a really good set of golf clubs, as earlier I had traded in the stamps and cigar-bands for a basketball.

Though I had many good friends at Notre Dame, during my years at *Poetry* much of my social life was in Chicago. Often I'd be there for the Saturday lunches the staff and their guests would have at Mike Fish's Restaurant on the corner. These were convivial affairs, with serious talk about the magazine often lost amid spontaneous merriment. Sometimes we would be joined by poets who happened to be in town, or by celebrities who might be doing a benefit for the magazine. Once James Thurber was with us. His sight, we knew, was not good; at lunch I saw him stub out a cigarette. With great care—but in the sugar bowl.

Generally Augustine Bowe and his wife Julia would come. Gus, a lawyer who in later years was to be chief justice of the Municipal Court of Chicago, had a knowledgeable interest in music, painting, and especially poetry. Later president of the Modern Poetry Society, he deserves as much credit as anyone for the survival of *Poetry* in difficult times. Gus had traveled in France every summer for years; his wife, Julia, shared his cultural interests: she spoke French, Spanish, and Italian, and studied Russian and Arabic; toward the end of her life she was beginning Hebrew in the hope of reading the Old Testament.

Often I stayed with the Bowes in their apartment on the lake, just a short walk from the offices of *Poetry.* Sometimes, after a date, I would let myself in late at night to find Gus in his favorite chair in a corner of the living room—the book-lined room in which he had entertained Gogarty more than once, and to which I had brought Allen Tate and his violin, ready for duets with Julia at the piano. When I came in Gus would stop me for a midnight brandy and water and would talk for a time, wisely but ironically, about what he had been reading, Surtees perhaps, or Toynbee, or Benavente. Or, sitting under the single lamp with the drapes fluttering about him in wind from the lake, he might pick up and read from one of the yellow legal pads which, on many an evening, he would fill with his surprising and curious poems, aphoristic as those of Emily Dickinson, whose stanzas his own resembled. When he died in 1966—his body found in the snowbank he had collapsed into on one of his long walks, winter and summer, along

the lake—I edited a selection of the poems and wrote an introduction. It was published by Macmillan the following year as *No Gods Are False,* with a portrait drawing of Gus by young Claes Oldenburg, a family friend.

Other evenings I might spend with Marion Strobel and her family: Dr. James Herbert Mitchell, the dermatologist, their daughters Sally, just finishing at Sarah Lawrence, and Joan, then a champion figure skater but beginning to be known for the paintings that before too many years would bring her celebrity among the Abstract Expressionists in New York and Paris. One diversion we enjoyed was the writing of limericks. Dr. Mitchell could draw on much colorful detail from his practice; some of the results may have embarrassed the worldly but less earthy Marion. Sometimes in the afternoon I drove with Sally or Joan to the Saddle and Cycle Club for a couple of hours of easygoing tennis—although with Joan everything was competitive.

Upon her graduation from St. Mary's in 1943, Bonnie Larkin found employment with a Chicago advertising agency and took an apartment on North Wabash. After a day with poetry manuscripts or in the rare book room of the Newberry Library, I'd drop by for a refreshing change from the world of first readings and bibliography. Other tenants in her building tended toward the outré. There was Bill Battleson, who had as elaborate a filing system of three-by-five-inch cards on batting averages, pitchers' records, and assorted stats as any scholar I knew had on his own specialty. Bill made not a bad living by betting on baseball games. There was Rita the G-string designer, a former chorus girl who ten years before had danced the carioca in the movie *Flying Down to Rio.* On their way across country young men from the military would drop by. Witty and literate friends from the agency might be there, or sleek young women from the world of modeling associated with it. Quite a heady ambience for an academic! I remember how Bonnie and I left one of her own parties just as a squad car drove up in response to a call from a niggling no-fun neighbor. "The noise seems to be on the second floor," we advised the officers as we brushed by them in the lobby.

Soon it was 1945, and I had my Ph.D. I spent the summer with my parents, then in Evanston. That August my father fell suddenly ill; within a week or so, strangely and peacefully, he died. "I have never seen anyone," the hospital chaplain wonderingly admitted, "so eager to see God." His death was another revelation of that inner life we saw the reflection of in his behavior, but never, by so much as a word, in his speech.

That fall I had been invited to be a visiting faculty member at St. Michael's College of the University of Toronto. My sister Margaret, though offered four college scholarships when she finished high school, had become a nun in the order that taught there. Having done graduate work at the University of Chicago in Chaucer and his predecessors, she became a specialist in medieval rhetoric and the author of a book on the thirteenth-century *Poetria Nova* of Geoffrey of Vinsauf. Meanwhile Ellen Mary, my other sister, had graduated with honors in architectural sculpture from the Art Institute of Chicago, had studied with Meštrović, and done further work in the Department of Art and Archaeology at the University of Edinburgh. For many years she gave college workshops in art.

Toronto in 1945 was not the handsome modern city whose team, in 1992, won the World Series. Derided as "Toronto the Good" by residents of less prosperous localities, it was burdened by a number of blue laws. Beer was available only at certain times of the day, one of them, I seem to remember, from 10:00 to 12:00 in the morning. As the closing time approached, patrons would snatch an extra glass or two from the tipsily loaded trays the waitresses passed by with. Everything except churches seemed to close on Sundays; something like winter gloom settled over the city.

But my year there was by no means a gloomy one. I had a room and took my meals, unless invited out, in a residence hall with the Basilian priests of St. Michael's College and its famous Medieval Institute. All were distinguished scholars; they were also amused and amusing companions, tolerant of their young colleague from the south. Just down the hall from my room lived the historian-priest who had been a hockey star in his younger days; it was he who introduced me to the sport in which plays developed with an intricacy too speedy for me to follow. Later my hockey advisor became the red-robed cardinal of a western province.

In Toronto I made a number of literary friends: E. J. Pratt, dean of Canadian poets, the novelist Morley Callaghan, and young professor Norrie Fry, who one day outlined for me the body of critical work he had in mind. Among others who sometimes joined me for dinner or a beer or in my explorations of wintry Toronto was Margaret Avison, later twice awarded the Governor General's medal for her books of poetry.

For some reason I experimented there with an unusual schedule I have never followed elsewhere. Many nights I would go to bed soon after an early dinner. Setting my alarm for midnight, I would then wake up and work for three or four quiet hours in the dead of night, catch a couple more hours of sleep, and be up for breakfast. Classes in the novel and poetry kept me too busy to do much writing. Some verses did have a Toronto setting; one, about to be published for the first time only now, was suggested by a mouse I surprised on my desk when entering my room one night. At least once I flew back to Chicago; Bonnie Larkin came up once for a weekend and an introduction to life and letters Toronto-style. During that year I remained on the staff of *Poetry;* bundles of manuscripts were periodically mailed to me for my opinion.

Next spring as the school year drew to its early close I was offered the chance of remaining at St. Michael's, but after some soul-searching returned to the Midwest. By late spring I was back in Chicago. Joan Mitchell had found me a summer rental, an old store on Eugenie Street, its wide front windows made opaque with swirls of Bon Ami. A painter from the Art Institute had turned it into his studio; it consisted of one large room, its bare splintery floor the size of half a tennis court. There was little in the way of furnishing except for the shelving, some art students' canvases of geometric nudes or cubist sailboats, and many *objets* the painter had collected in his travels: foreign wall hangings, clay animal figurines from Mexico or Peru that whistled tunefully when blown through, and a human skull. In the cabinets under the shelving there were regiments of dead soldiers: empty bottles that had once held rye or bourbon. The dusty vacancy was dominated by a frameless spring and mattress against one wall in the middle of the room; on the shelf beside it was an up-to-date telephone, except for the pictures the only concession to modernity in the room. There was electricity, cold running water I learned to shave with, and a double hot plate for cooking. In the wall opposite the bed was a door admitting to the little bathroom that must have protruded, like an outdoor privy, into the parlor of the Mexican family who shared the building with me.

In that studio I set up housekeeping for the first time. There was a real icebox which a real iceman, in response to my sign in the back window, would resupply with real ice every few days, great chunks of iceberg his oversize tongs would wedge into the box of corrugated metal, a box so dingy that Bonnie said she would not keep her garbage in it. Friends loaned me pots and pans and an egg-poacher. I discovered frozen food. Instead of taking a date out to dinner, I'd sometimes invite her to share the chores of eating in. The studio was a good place for parties; housewarmings continued into the summer. Most days I'd go to the office of *Poetry* for a few hours; at other times I'd walk the few blocks to Lincoln Park to row on the tree-shaded lagoons for an hour or so.

Early in my stay there I wrote a poem whose origin I can date with more precision than any other's. The first few lines were scribbled on the face of an envelope from Commonwealth Edison, enclosing my electric bill and postmarked May 28, 1946. The lines were much revised and added to before "Love Poem" was published in *Poetry* the following February. For some reason its combination of good-humored chaffing and heartfelt devotion struck a chord with more readers than anything else I have written. Though composed with Bonnie in mind, other women have seen themselves in it; several have requested that it be read at their wedding. Years later a friend of mine, travelling in England, where it had been published in *The Penguin Book of Modern American Verse,* came across a magazine article by an English actress who told how, when once in the depths of depression and on the verge of suicide, she had happened to see a poem by "an American poet" which restored her perspective and her spirits. The poem she quoted a few lines from was my own. When a volume of my *Selected Poems* came out in 1982, I reprinted it as the dedicatory poem.

That fall I was working toward what was to be *the* event, for me, of the school year, the appearance in the spring of 1947 of *The Iron Pastoral,* my first book of poems. It came about as it did because a year or two earlier I had given a joint reading with Robert Penn Warren at the YMHA in New York. At the reading I met Helen Stewart, another Bennington graduate, friend of E. E. Cummings, and assistant to William Sloane, an editor at Henry Holt. When I thought I had a book ready, Bill and Helen were willing to publish it—provided it could be brought out not by Holt but by William Sloane Associates, the new publishing house Bill was leaving Holt to establish. Bill and Helen remained my publishers there and later at Rutgers University Press until Bill's death in the 1970s.

The title, *The Iron Pastoral,* referred to the group of city thing-poems. The drawing on the jacket illustrated their theme: behind an iron

girder, like those of the El tracks in Chicago, was a view of a steel bridge spanning a busy river that flowed under what looked like the New York skyline. Many of the poems did have a background of then-contemporary urban America. When, in fact, the book was offered to Faber and Faber for an English edition, the response—could it have come from T. S. Eliot himself?—was that the poems were "too American."

That summer Bonnie Larkin abandoned Chicago for a long stay in Colorado; I was glad to sublet her apartment. While there I fulfilled a long-standing ambition: I rented a piano and, as an adult, took my first music lessons. In the two summer months I covered what were described as Year I and Year II of piano instruction. When Bonnie returned we went up to Gus and Julia Bowe's summer cottage at Saugatuck on Lake Michigan. We enjoyed lake and sun and Gus's magical after-swim martinis; on the way back we made plans for our wedding. I claimed I had sacrificed a promising musical career for love.

In Chicago we had a simple ceremony with Gus Bowe as best man and just a few friends. Instead of splurging on pomp and circumstance we bought a house in the country near Niles, Michigan, and bought the car, my first, we would now have need of. I liked the idea of living in a different state from the one I was teaching in. The house, though big enough to have a study, was a perky little place painted white with red trim; it reminded me of those Swiss weather indicators from which toy figures alternately swing out to predict rain or shine. We had the fun of scouting furniture stores and the cheaper antique shops to furnish it. Around it was a sprawling unfenced yard; fortunately the seller had left us his rusty power mower. Edging the yard were some spindly evergreens; across the unpaved gravel road were woods in which we could wander through the fall and winter—our first seasons in the country.

We acquired two whiskey-colored Irish setters we named Bushmill and Jameson and a glossy black cat we named Melaina, the Greek feminine adjective for "black." A miniature of the black leopard she thought she was, she lorded it over house and yard and much of the surrounding countryside, particularly disdaining the tykish dogs with their gawky pawing. "That," Bonnie would muse admiringly, "is one hell of a cat."

There were no other houses in sight, but we had congenial neighbors within cocktail distance. Behind us, on the steep wooded banks of the St. Joe River, lived a couple who had gone to the

University of Chicago. Just down the gravel road lived Bob and his wife Wanda; Bob became our obstetrician; Wanda too had a medical background. With them we celebrated the holidays and often in between; many evenings Wanda and I would take on Bob and Bonnie at canasta—the only months of our lives we had time to spend at the card table. The setting was suburban rather than rural; we were even induced to join the Niles Town and Country Dancing Club, whose parties O'Hara or Cheever would have observed with interest. As a householder, I developed a new range of concerns: I learned about sump pumps and the coal-fed furnace; visited nurseries to look at saplings and shrubbery, priced flagstone for a terrace we did not really need. Autumn, winter, and spring I drove the ten miles to Notre Dame along a six-lane interstate known as "Homicide Highway." Bonnie learned to make pies and bake bread, talents that she soon let lapse.

When our first son was born the following June we were persuaded by Bonnie's father to move into town—not into South Bend itself, but into the little town of Niles, a couple of miles further from the university. There we had a new "ranch-type" brick house on a large corner lot: more work for me. There was a new lawn mower, hand-pushed this time, visits to nurseries to get a couple of Norway maples, a blue spruce that was really blue for the front yard, and a hedge of tall spiraea to put between us and the too-close neighbors on the side. I drudged for two weeks putting in a rustic post-and-rail fence along the two streets; the clayey soil was resistant even to the heavy post-hole digger I had borrowed. I did a good deal of lawn work, learned about plant food and weed killers. In the vacant fields across the side street I had my eye on an eight-foot hawthorn tree; when I saw it was about to be trashed for a road-widening project, I schemed to rescue it. Not sure of the legality of my rescue, on a particularly dark and rainy night I went over with flashlight and shovel and began to trench around it. I was dismayed at how tough the roots were and how far they extended—this was a wilding, no tame nursery tree. It was a couple of hours' labor in a heavy rain that turned the earth to ankle-deep mud before I could amputate enough of the roots to tug the tree loose and drag it, in its heavy ball of earth, across the street and into our yard, where I dug another deep hole and embedded the roots. When I drove by the house twenty and more years later, my tree was still flourishing, twice as high as on the night of the abduction.

"Bonnie and I at a wedding party given to us by the Mitchells, in Chicago. Directly behind Bonnie is Henry Rago, later editor of Poetry,*" 1947*

During the summer of 1948 I went to my first writers' conference, held at the University of Kansas in a season of spectacular thunderstorms. I shared the poetry sessions with Allen Tate. His wife Caroline Gordon was there, as was Katherine Anne Porter—exciting company to be in. One evening Katherine Anne and I listened to the broadcast of a heavyweight championship fight; obviously participating, she would hunch forward, her hands shadowboxing with the radio. With Caroline I wandered the campus and the neighboring groves for mushrooms. Every now and then she would tug one free from its nest of dirt and rootlets and, brandishing it, alarm me with "This one we eat tonight!" Perhaps some mycologist could explain what she meant by inscribing a book to me "with fond memories of the day we ate the alligator."

Later that summer I went to a second conference, this time at Indiana University. More exciting company: Lillian Hellman, Jessamyn West, Stephen Spender, and others. With Jessamyn I

Bonnie with firstborn, Jackie, 1948

drove around the picturesquely named places that are the background of her *The Friendly Persuasion:* Bean Blossom, Gnaw Bone, Stony Lonesome. Years later, visiting Jessamyn in California, I was to meet Gary Cooper, Dorothy McGuire, and Tony Perkins on the set where the movie was being made. After the conference, Jessamyn and I drove up to Niles, stopping on the way to pick a bouquet of wayside flowers for Bonnie. Jessamyn stayed with us for a couple of days and then I drove her to the South Bend airport.

It was while I was at the Kansas conference that our first son, Jackie, was born. Amid the happiness we all felt, I tried to celebrate the event in "The Child," with such lines as

How the greenest of wheat rang gold at his birth!
How oaks hung a pomp in the sky!
When the tiptoeing hospital's pillowy arms
Godsped him in suns of July.

Then dizziest poplars, like green and white tops,
Spun spinning in strings of the wind,
As that child in his wicker
With two great safeties pinned

Slept twenty-two hours with a Buddha-fine face
(His hands were palm-up like a dancer's).
Or his tragic mask's sudden pink-rubbery woe
Sent us thumbing four books for the
    answers . . .

Friends admired the baby, cards of congratulation came from those unable to admire in person. Katherine Anne sent us a set of little homemade stuffed animals from a country fair.

But all was not well with the upturned palms, the "Buddha-fine face." Marion Strobel, a doctor's wife, told us later of her uneasiness on seeing the child. Our good friend the obstetrician seemed somewhat constrained. Several months of uncertainty went by before it was confirmed that our child was a victim of Down's syndrome, a prognosis that seemed worse then than it does nearly half a century later. Bonnie was then under treatment for a thyroid condition; when she was about to go into the hospital for an operation late the next winter, Jackie was placed for a while in a nursing home. Then Bonnie's middle-aged aunt and her husband, well-off but childless, made a home for the child, who became the central interest in their life until his death years later. Our second son, Frank, was born the following August; his brother George in the summer of 1952. Many months after Jackie left us, *Poetry* published my "The Masque of Blackness" (the title that of a Ben Jonson masque), a series of sonnets about what we saw as the loss of a son.

Partly as a distraction at the time, I went in for carpentry. First, with advice and help from a fellow professor whose hobby was woodworking, I paneled a basement room as combination playroom and study. When it seemed somewhat confined and better adapted for other basement uses, I made more ambitious plans. Behind the house was a double brick garage, the roof pitched from four sides. We would never have two cars; Bonnie, not always on the best of terms with machinery, does not drive. This time doing the work myself, I converted half of the garage into what I thought an elegant study—doing little or no studying during the two months or so I labored on a place to study in. Through a friend who designed furniture, we bought, from a dealer in the South, some tongue-and-groove walnut paneling. Unfinished, it had a delicate violet cast. I partitioned the garage with a framing of studs, covered the garage side with Sheetrock, packed insulation between the studs. The overhead door on the study side was fastened down and a large window set in it, studs put all around the room, and the walnut paneling nailed over them. The concrete floor I first waterproofed, laid two-by-fours as joists, and then nailed in the handsome hickory flooring, so hard I couldn't drive an unbent nail through without drilling first. The ceiling, pitched three ways after the partitioning, I covered with a heavily textured paint that looked like stucco. I had an electric heater installed in one wall, brought out my desk and armchair and an old piano on which I could now play, badly but to my solitary satisfaction, a few such pieces as "Down in the Valley," "Careless Love," "The Red River Valley," and several of the twelve days of Christmas. One day I bought myself the music of Mozart's piano sonata in C Major (K. 545), which Mozart had described as *eine kleine Klavier Sonate für Anfänger*—"for beginners"! Surely that meant me. I learned to tinkle the first three or four bars of it. When I heard Glenn Gould perform it later, I thought his bustling tempo less faithful to Mozart's *für Anfänger* than my pensive hesitancy had been. Perhaps Gould did not read German.

Sometimes I regretted the books I could have read and the writing I could have done in the time it took to build the study. But perhaps all of the work with measuring and sawing and nailing, the work with steely tools and the rigidity of lumber, confirmed the sense I already had of formal structure. Is there any free-form carpentry?

Our Irish setters were too fond of ranging to be happy in town; we gave them to a relative of Father Ward who had an Indiana farm. Before we left the country Melaina had taken to the woods. In place of our rural pets we bought a collie puppy who grew into a handsome tricolor. Imperial as he looked, he turned out to be weirdly neurotic. Was it our fault in naming him Apple? Could the foolish name have warped his fragile dog-psyche? If I walked into a room with a hat on, he'd bark at me as if I were an intruder. If anyone dropped a Kleenex, he'd scoot from the room in nervous dread. If we moved his dog dish a few feet from its place, he wouldn't eat till we moved it back. Once we saw him confront a rabbit that had hopped into our backyard; the two were crouched facing each other about ten feet apart, each aquiver and afraid to make the first move. But with us he was affectionate, and certainly beautiful to look at. Was that aristocratic nose achieved at the expense of brain space?

Probably because of my experience at the two writers' conferences, the Notre Dame English department decided to sponsor one of its own in the summer of 1949. From our faculty we had Richard Sullivan, novelist and short-story writer, and John T. Frederick, founder and editor of *The Midland* and conductor of a CBS radio literary program. Our invited staff members were Jessamyn West and the literary agent Henry Volkening

of the New York agency of Russell and Volkening. Henry represented both Jessamyn and Dick Sullivan; theoretically he was my agent too, although, despite some efforts, I never had anything of commercial interest. We were all friends; it was a congenial staff, with much off-campus and after-hours conviviality. When the conference ended, Bonnie and I drove Jessamyn down to Bloomington just as the Indiana conference was getting under way. There we saw Spender again and other friends of the summer before; there we met the Tennessee novelist Andrew Lytle, a racy raconteur then and just as lively forty years later, when I saw him, then eighty-eight, at Sewanee. When the conference ended, we drove around southern Indiana with Jessamyn, this time going as far as Madison on the Ohio River. Just for the feeling of being for the first time in what I thought of as a southern state, I crossed the river one day and lounged for a while in a pleasant small-town park in Carrollton. It had an old-fashioned fountain of faded green metal with naiads and dolphins in the spray. This experience became a poem in irregular strophes called "A Fountain in Kentucky" and gave the title to my second book, published in 1950, in which the poem is dedicated to Jessamyn. Besides that poem and "The Masque of Blackness," the verse in it had reminiscences of summers in Chicago, of lakeside Saugatuck, of the country near Niles, of my own readings about such civilizations as that of Crete. There were two Horace translations in stanza forms suggestive of his own.

While we lived in Niles, literary friends who happened to be traveling by would drop in on us. The most memorable visit was by Dylan Thomas in 1950. Having arranged for him to give a reading at Notre Dame while on his first American tour, I had tried to prepare the students by giving a talk or two on his poetry—in one comparing his "Fern Hill" with certain aspects of Wordsworth's immortality ode. He was to give his reading on March 17, St. Patrick's Day, at 8:00. I was to pick him up when he arrived at Niles on an afternoon train; we would take him to dinner, then drive the ten miles or more to Notre Dame. I met the train; no sign of Dylan Thomas. I met the next; not on that either. Finally he did arrive, about 6:30, on the late "Shoppers' Special." His University of Chicago hosts, with whom he had spent the day, had not sent him to us in good condition. When he lurched off the Pullman, I saw him press a wad of bills, about the size of a tennis ball, into

Bonnie with second son, Frankie, 1949

the surprised porter's palm. I hoped they were only dollar bills, loosely packed. We hurried him off to Rocco's, our favorite Italian place in town, for a quick dinner. Rocco, who had spent some time with the army in England, felt grateful to that country and wanted to welcome the "famous poet" we told him would be there. Dylan was grumpy, half asleep, and indifferent to the best spaghetti around. His eye brightened, however, when a waitress went by balancing schooners of beer on a tray. "That's what I want," he demanded, pointing to—the beer? Or the waitress? The beer. Sipping at it, and then at a second one, he tortured us with mutterings about how we'd get no reading from him that night. Finally, as the crowd was already gathering for his reading ten miles away, we cajoled him into the car. First we had to go by our house so he could change into his "lecture suit." He slumped between us, under the impression that Bonnie was the young woman we had provided for his evening pleasure. When she asked him to be careful with the cigarette he was brandishing like a

sparkler, he glowered at her, more drunkenly than disagreeably, "I loathe you!"

We parked by the garage in back of the house. As we went in through the kitchen door, Dylan tripped over the slim aluminum edging and fell spread-eagled across the linoleum, terrifying Apple, who tried to flatten himself against the opposite wall. Dylan sized up the dog, then reached out and stroked the trembling fur. "As long as there's someone worse off than you are," he told the animal, "you're all right." And Apple was worse off than he was—just a little.

He got to his feet, unsteady, but in a better mood. While he was doing his Pullman-porter imitations for Bonnie, I made, from another room, a discreet call to Notre Dame to say we'd be late. Very late. Then I called Bob, our doctor friend, to ask if there was any quick way to sober up a very drunk famous poet. Bob said he'd come by and take a look, tactfully leaving his satchel outside the door. Meanwhile Dylan, discovering he had no wearable shirt, had borrowed a pink one of mine that didn't quite close at the collar. When Bonnie asked if she could press and freshen up the "lecture suit," which he had hauled out of what looked like a knapsack, he waved her off with a "Don't bother. It's just covered with old vomit."

Bob dropped in for a few minutes, trying to look casual. As he left, picking up his case in the backyard, he said, "I could give him a shot. It would either sober him up or knock him out. I don't think I should. But I'll tell you one thing," he grinned, "that man is in no shape to get up on a stage and read *anything!*"

When I came back in, Bonnie nodded toward the bathroom. "He's shaving."

"You loaned him a razor? He could cut his throat."

"So he could." She shrugged.

When somehow we did get him to the auditorium, the packed crowd had been waiting an hour and a half. I handed Dylan over to the old priest who was backstage custodian. As they passed a water fountain, Dylan leaned over it; the jet of water shot up and hit him in the eye. "Jesus Christ!" he rumbled, "they're shootin' at me!"

With what I thought a pertinent witticism or two, I introduced the Welshman on St. Patrick's Day. When I finished, I made an introductory gesture toward the stage curtains behind which he was waiting, but all I saw was a great billowing as he tried to thresh his way through them. When he did welter out and grasp at the lectern, there occurred that miracle I am told other audiences have witnessed: he began to read, in that richly sonorous voice of his, never stumbling, never missing a word, so eloquently that I wondered briefly if the drunkenness had been an act.

After the reading the usual faculty party took an unusual turn. Faculty wives and members of the clergy prudently withdrew as Dylan herded the men into another room and launched into a routine of bawdy tales. But all went well enough. On the drive home he fell asleep, slumping now against me, now against Bonnie.

The next morning he slept so late that we became concerned. "Maybe he's dead?" I speculated.

"We should be so lucky!" said Bonnie. But a few hours later she relented, "Maybe I should offer him some coffee?" She peeked into the darkened guest room, where a form was huddled under the blankets.

"Like some coffee, Mr. Thomas?" The blankets shuddered.

"Like a hot cup of tea?" A disgusted grunt.

"O.K.," she sighed. "How about a nice cold beer?"

Dylan, pajamaless, threw back the covers with a ringing, "I adore you!"

That was the beginning of a pleasant and sober weekend. He made friends with Apple, chatted about his family, asked how to get a tuition check to Wales, complained about the "lion tamer" who had arranged his tour. We drove about the country, dropped in on a couple of friends, including Bob, who was surprised to see Dylan on his feet. Since Dylan had lamented the scarcity of food in post-wartime England and said he had been longing for some good pork, we took him for a late lunch to a truckers' stop, famous for the generosity of its portions. They did have pork. But when his plate, heaped and steaming, was laid before him, Dylan could only stare at it helplessly. "I can't do it. I just can't get it down."

We had invited a group of friends in for the evening. After a long nap, Dylan peered out in some surprise. "Is this what you do every Saturday night?" he wondered. "Fill your house with people?" Fastening his trousers up with a necktie instead of the belt he couldn't find, he joined the group in the living room. He was good company all evening, had a beer or two, complied when asked to read some poems.

Sunday was blessedly uneventful. We lounged, talked, drove a little, went back to Rocco's for a couple of schooners and a leisurely dinner, with Rocco himself in his chef's apron beaming down on us.

Early Monday we put him on the train for Urbana. After he left, I called Kerker Quinn at the University of Illinois with the suggestion that if he wanted a manageable guest he would do well to offer only beer and spare the "Let's-get-Dylan-drunk" routine. I later heard that the Urbana visit was a success and that Kerker had relayed my message on to Iowa City. I don't believe it carried far.

In July we received a letter from Dylan in Laugharne. It began, "Remember me? Round, red, robustly raddled, a bulging Apple among poets . . ." In a richly illustrated book about him that came out years later there is a photo of him in a New York bar, with the caption under it from the sentence I have quoted above: "a bulging Apple among poets . . ." Only a few of us know what the "Apple" refers to. His letter said he hoped that he and Caitlin could visit us in Niles "for some days" on his next trip to America. But that didn't work out. Anyway by the time his letter reached us, our guest room was being turned into a nursery for our second son, Frank, born in August. This time our happiness was undimmed by the kind of shadow that hovered over Jackie's birth.

It was about this time that I received an odd invitation from a Chicago firm of industrial designers, Atwood and Goldberg—the Bertrand Goldberg who was later to plan Marina Towers and other well-known buildings in Chicago. They had designed a freight car made chiefly of plastic. Crashed against steel cars, it proved the sturdier. Proud of their product, the designers called in the Muses to celebrate it. In 1950 Richard Florsheim did a series of lithographs depicting the history of the railroad up to the triumph of Unicel, the plastic car. The next year I was asked to do some poems to accompany the lithographs. That was enjoyable; for a while I read up on the history of railroads, and then wrote nine sonnets hailing their achievements, including Unicel. Lithographs and poems were published in a handsome portfolio, two feet high and three feet wide, its lustrous brass-hinged cover tied with ribbons, in an edition of fourteen copies. Also in December 1951, a fourteen-copy edition of the poems alone was produced, using a silk-screen technique that, to indicate progress, showed the nine sonnets brightening from black to lively blue. Thirty years later Bud Goldberg reprinted the poems in an edition of one hundred copies. Meanwhile, I had concentrated and reworked the 126 lines of the sonnets into a 44-line poem called "The Caveman on the Train" for my 1960 volume. When in 1989 the *Gettysburg Review* announced a railroad issue, I reworked that poem for them, this time turning it into "Freight, 1–8," eight sonnets differing from those of three decades before. Besides researching railroads, around this time I was also reading about Africa, and especially Egypt. A longish Egyptian poem, "Parallax at Djebel-Muta," was one result. I had plans to do a poem on Africa, in which the typography was to have the shape of that continent on the page. Nothing came of this project except the shape itself, worked out in nonsense letters.

For several months in 1950–51 I was distracted from poetry by ventures into prose fiction. I embarked on what I planned as a novel, which, on the evidence of a hundred or more extant pages, was to be about a young advertising man and three women he knew: his irresponsibility was to lead to tragedy for at least one of them. Some of the characters were based on those I had known or

imagined from the world of advertising, fashion, and society in Chicago settings or on the lake in Michigan. Both satiric and romantic, it was, as I described it on one of the many pages of notes outlining characters, structure, and plot, to be "a novel in which aesthetic perception is more highly developed than moral responsibility." Four or five long sections were written, but then either my interest dwindled or more pressing ones took over.

But it was for fiction that I applied for a summer residency at Yaddo for 1951. Going there at least once, I must have felt, is what writers do. While there I worked at half a dozen short stories, which I shipped off to Henry Volkening in New York; he passed them on from editor to editor with no success. The closest I came was a near acceptance from *Harper's Bazaar,* whose fiction editor did want to publish one of the stories. But the chief editor came back from Paris just in time to overrule her; she found the story too downbeat. That may have been the acme of my career as fiction writer—though the story was exhumed five years later and published in *Accent.* The flaw in my fiction was that it had too many poetic details and too little action: it seems that "aesthetic perception" had indeed prevailed.

In many ways the weeks at Yaddo were rewardingly rich and strange. I had a large sunny room in the mansion, my several windows overlooking vistas of woods and meadows stretching off to the Green Mountains in Vermont. But for me there was something unsettling about the place. Although no ghosts floated through the corridors or up the stairs, it is no wonder that many a ghost story did. The baronial mansion itself was spectacular in a spooky way; stage set led to stage set. Both it and the wooded lands of the estate seemed strangely haunted, somehow out of a world in which real people lived. It was a relief to escape into town and admire the wide porches and corridors of the old Grand Union Hotel, which Henry James had described. A few of us went to the colorful races at Saratoga's famous track; there we devised a surefire strategy for placing our bets. It had only one flaw: it lost money. The last story I wrote had the racetrack for its setting.

After dinner some of the writers, artists, and composers would gather in the chapel where, brow buried in their palms, they would listen to Berlioz. The frivolous would play croquet or Ping-Pong. Though Yaddo was an idyllic place to work and every provision was made to insure the privacy of the guests, and though I had many quiet hours to be grateful for and new friends I did not forget, still I found the atmosphere was a little heavy with the religiosity of art. I heard that Kenneth Fearing had come and left the next day; I sympathized with him. A couple of weeks before my stay was up, I arose very early one morning, left notes of apology for my friend Polly and two or three others, and drove off for Niles, happy never again to try my inept hand at fiction.

On my return, Bonnie and I drove up to northern Michigan, stopping on the way to visit the Bentleys at their summer home in the dunes near Pentwater. One of the topics that came up in conversation was the Fulbright program. I had never been to Europe; this seemed a possible way of experiencing something of its life and culture. Gerald Bentley, who was familiar with the program, said that he thought fellowships to some countries were not difficult to get. Queried further, he mentioned Finland. I decided to apply. When the application forms reached me that fall, I noticed that I was free to suggest a second choice. Why not Italy? I had learned enough Italian to read Dante and some Mozart libretti, and had indeed taught a course or two in the *Divine Comedy*. I had other interests too in Italian literature and culture. With these interests, Bonnie suggested, the judges might think it perverse of me to prefer Finland to Italy. So at the last moment I switched: Italy first, Finland second.

About the time I sent in the application, I had made a discovery that was to hold my interest for the rest of my life. In a bookstore, I happened to pick up and open Campbell's translation of the poems of St. John of the Cross (his real name, San Juan de la Cruz, is not so pallid). Opposite the English version was the Spanish original. I remembered enough Spanish from my high school days to follow much of it. I knew something about San Juan as a mystic from my reading of T. S. Eliot and others, but I had not realized that in Spanish opinion, including that of García Lorca, he was regarded as one of the very greatest of their poets. The first line of the first poem caught my attention: "En una noche oscura . . ." Ah, here was the famous "dark night of the soul." Campbell rendered it "Upon a gloomy night . . ." This, I felt, was wrong; however dark San Juan's night was, it did not have the connotations "gloomy" has in English. I took the book home and was immediately fascinated by the music and imagery of the Spanish. I read all of San Juan's not so many poems, and read what I could find about him. I bought his three-volume complete works, with his own line-by-line explication of what he meant by

Bonnie, 1952

his poems. It was clear that Campbell had not read the prose; it would have saved him from some embarrassing blunders in his translation. I also felt that his English did not have the qualities of colloquial directness and simplicity which Spanish critics find in their poet's style. I began to meditate, then and for years thereafter, on the problem of translating poetry, which, as Robert Frost had said, is what is "lost in translation."

So what could I do but try to translate the poems myself? The first result was a version of the forty-stanza "The Spiritual Canticle," which Karl Shapiro, editor of *Poetry* since 1950, published in June of 1952. In the same issue I reviewed Campbell's translation, thanking him for calling our attention to the poetry, but pointing out shortcomings which had prompted me to try a translation along rather different lines. Soon realizing that my own version was unsatisfactory, I set about revising it for the book I would publish several years later. This and other translations of his poetry were to be reworked many times over the next thirty and more years.

In April, with another child about to join us, we decided to move to a larger house in South Bend itself. We found what seemed to us the perfect place, a large square-build older house of two stories, originally constructed for a nephew of Frank Lloyd Wright, who (it was said) was consulted about the plans. The roomy attic, with dormers on the four sides, was like that of my childhood. The house was on one of the few hills in South

Bend, its wide screened porch looking into the treetops of that hill. About seventy concrete steps wound up through the trees from the street to our front porch, steps never used except by the unwary or the adventurous. Instead one entered through a little back alley called Maple Lane that dead-ended just beyond our garage. Back beyond the alley, through a wide bushy hollow, ran the rusted tracks on which a lazy freight would draw its two or three cars maybe once a day. On one side of the house was a wooded vacant lot, on the other a sort of ravine between us and the next house, which was the last on Maple Lane. We had almost as much privacy as in the country. In the large yard was a well-built playhouse for the children. A former owner had put in a flagpole; we did not fly a flag, but our waggish friends did refer to the place as Fort Nims. The hill would have been not easy to scale; I spent a good deal of time slipping and sliding on it, either putting new myrtle clumps in the bald spots or using Q-tips to touch with weed killer the poison ivy along the steps.

It was just what we wanted; we put down earnest money toward the purchase. The catch was that we'd have to sell our Niles home—and my laboriously built study!—to get funds to complete the deal. As time dragged by with no purchaser in sight, we became jittery. But our artist friend George had an idea.

"There's this guy down in that god-forsaken country somewhere who's up for sainthood," he explained. "He needs a miracle or two in his dossier. Ask him to help." George was devoutly religious, but, in his Mediterranean way, often irreverent. "But he's a laborer, low-class. You don't ask him; you *tell* him—that's what he's used to. You say, 'Listen, man, I want you to sell this piece of real estate. I mean pronto. Get movin'!'"

We did call the future saint's attention to the matter, but I also took practical steps. I had a handsome **FOR SALE** sign printed in colors that matched the house. I took it out in front and was sledging the stake deep in the clay turf when a car drew up at the curb. A man got out, briefly

JFN

surveyed the house, then called to me, "This the house that's for sale?"

Almost then and there, he bought it. Without his wife even seeing it. It turned out he was a new executive in town who needed a house, as the saint might say, pronto. He even bought our draperies. I hope his wife liked them.

The same month that we moved into the new house I learned that I had been given a Fulbright Fellowship to lecture on American literature in Milan. That spring and summer I began to prepare for the trip. In my room I put up a large map of Italy. I subscribed to the *Corriere della Sera* to help modernize a vocabulary I got mostly from Dante and Da Ponte. I read through Dante again, this time listing places he mentions, with the intention of seeing as many as I could.

I no longer had to go into Chicago for *Poetry,* but we sometimes went in to see friends. On one notable occasion I saw Dylan and Caitlin, who were staying with Marion Mitchell. We had a chance to reminisce until Dylan was picked up for his reading at Northwestern. Caitlin did not go with him. My assignment was to see that she was entertained for the evening. We went to one north side bar, and then I think another. The memories become fuzzy.

On July 20, amid the excitement of planning the trip, our third son, George, was born. He would be not two months old when I was scheduled to leave for the Fulbright orientation program at Perugia, not quite ready for some of the shots he should have. So it was decided I would go alone to Perugia and meet Bonnie and the children at Genoa in early November. In mid-September I left for New York. Jessamyn happened to be in town then to see Henry Volkening. When I phoned her hotel that evening she was having drinks in her room with Eudora Welty and Jean Stafford. "Come on up," she said. "Join the party." Feeling I had lucked into a sort of *bon voyage* celebration, I was glad to do so. A good omen. Such an evening should have been rich in memorable moments and memorable talk, but it seems I was too lost in shipboard anticipations to be able to retrieve any of it.

At noon the next day, September 15, I found myself waving to other friends from the railing of the USS *Constitution,* my mind *allegro vivace* with imaginings of a year—one blessed year!—in Europe. But it was not to be one year; for nearly half of the next ten my family and I would be living on the Ligurian coast, in Rome, in Florence, in Madrid. Could I have foreseen those years, which would bring with them the birth of our two

daughters, the death of our three-year-old son, it would have been with a deeper bourdon of emotion.

BIBLIOGRAPHY

Poetry:

(With others) *Five Young American Poets: Third Series,* New Directions, 1944.

The Iron Pastoral, Sloane, 1947.

A Fountain in Kentucky and Other Poems, Sloane, 1950.

Knowledge of the Evening, Rutgers University Press, 1960.

Of Flesh and Bone, Rutgers University Press, 1967.

The Kiss: A Jambalaya, Houghton Mifflin, 1982.

Selected Poems, University of Chicago Press, 1982.

The Six-Cornered Snowflake, New Directions, 1990.

Zany in Denim, University of Arkansas Press, 1990.

Criticism:

Western Wind: An Introduction to Poetry, Random House, 1974, revised edition, McGraw-Hill, 1992.

A Local Habitation: Essays on Poetry, University of Michigan Press, 1985.

Editor:

(Also contributor) *The Poem Itself,* Holt, 1960.

Ovid's Metamorphoses: The Arthur Golding Translation, Macmillan, 1965.

Augustine Bowe, *No Gods Are False,* Macmillan, 1968.

James Shirley's Love's Cruelty, Garland, 1980.

The Harper Anthology of Poetry, Harper, 1981.

Translator:

Andromache, in *Four Tragedies,* by Euripides, University of Chicago Press, 1958.

The Poems of St. John of the Cross, Grove Press, 1959, revised edition, University of Chicago Press, 1979.

Andromache, in *Euripides III* of *The Complete Greek Tragedies,* University of Chicago Press, 1959.

Sappho to Valéry: Poems in Translation, Rutgers University Press, 1971, revised and enlarged edition, University of Arkansas Press, 1990.

Also member of editorial board *Poetry*, 1945–48, visiting editor, 1960–61, editor, 1978–84. Contributor to periodicals, including *Accent, American Scholar, Atlantic, Georgia Review, Grand Street, Harper's, Kenyon Review, Mademoiselle, New Republic, Partisan Review, Poetry, Saturday Review,* and *Sewanee Review.*

Al Purdy

1918-

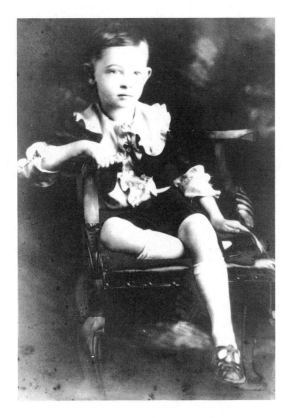

Al Purdy, age three, "first memory"

When my father died and we moved from the farm near Wooller into the redbrick house in Trenton in 1921, the house was already more than a hundred years old. The floors sagged upstairs and down, as if the house was tired from that century of years and couldn't stand properly upright any longer. Some of the doors wouldn't open or close without a struggle. At night when I was a small boy awake and listening, noises came to me from everywhere: old floor joists creaking, boards and square-headed nails talking together.

*

My mother was raised on a farm north of Trenton; her maiden name was Ross. But I think her Scots blood never thrilled to the sound of bagpipes. Eleanor Louisa Purdy was forty when I was born in 1918; my father, Alfred Wellington, was fifty-eight, and died of cancer two years later. I know so little about either of them that I am ashamed.

Among the few scraps I am sure of, my father's ancestors were United Empire Loyalists (traitors to patriotic Americans), who came to Canada from New York State after the American Revolution. He was an educated farmer, attending Guelph Agricultural College during his early years. Eleanor Louisa was a farm girl, not especially beautiful. She married late, became very religious, and spent the Trenton years raising her only son.

These statistics are painful to me; they awaken so few memories.

*

McLean's pumpworks stood just across the street from our house. The rusty tin-covered building was too small to be called a factory, but too large for a workshop. Old McLean, sandy-haired, sour-faced, and bad-tempered, made wooden pumps for farmers' wells. His pumpworks hummed with belts and pulleys, whirring lathes in pine-scented gloom, shavings piled deep on the

When electricity came to our street in Trenton, Ontario, around 1921 or '22, I was three or four years old. In late evening when lights flashed on for the first time, people rushed outside to see what the streetlights looked like, each with an aureole of moths and flying insects.

Some people left their house lights burning all night, just for the novelty, and being so pleased at not having to use messy oil lamps and candles any longer. And the birds on our street kept on singing, probably thinking this new kind of daylight would never end, no doubt feeling hoarse and exasperated.

I was, of course, too young to remember all this, only a little; my mother told me the rest.

Father, 1919

floor, small boys crowding the doorway, deeply interested in yellow-bearded McLean and the small men he made from wood.

That's what they looked like, small men. When chisels and lathes had done their work, and black metal bands encircled the four-foot bodies to prevent splitting, with an iron mouth and long wooden pump handle attached, then by an act of magic a small man was born. Other people might be doctors and lawyers and storekeepers, but the small men old McLean brought to life spent their days lifting water into daylight and sunlight. It was cold and sweet. It tasted of deep springs and wells and rivers under the earth.

*

The child is still me as I remain still him. We are sitting on a pile of fresh lumber behind Redick's Sash and Door Factory near the river, watching red willow roots like drowned girls' hair waving underwater with the waves' motion.

Overhead a bird goes *Wow-ee! Wow-ee!* among willow leaves that gleam and flash, having trapped the sun a million times on three-inch strips of green. Then another bird, who sounds like a medieval musical instrument which I have never seen or heard, joins the first bird's singing.

Later, days later or maybe only hours, lying on my back in deep grass, watching clouds drifting toward the world's edge. Adjust their shapes slightly with my mind, and they are altered into fat faces, thin faces, and have the body of someone I know. My grandfather springs into life.

He was called "Ol Rid" by his friends. "Old Nick," my mother would probably have called him, since he came to live with us shortly after we moved to town from the farm. Grandfather Ridley Neville chewed tobacco, drank whiskey, used a few cusswords at strategic moments, and played cards for money with other ancients (he was about eighty in 1920) at a "floating" poker game in downtown Trenton.

Grandfather's unregenerate character and my mother's religious one forced him out of our house shortly after his arrival. He rented a long narrow room, resembling a bowling alley, over a downtown dry-goods store, where poker was king and chewing tobacco decorated the greasy hardwood floors whenever it missed the spittoons.

I visited him there as often as I could, with the feeling of being slightly wicked. My mother permitted these visits, but I'm sure she felt suspicious that he was somehow corrupting me. (She may even have been right.) And I listened to his stories when he wanted to tell them, which wasn't very often, for he was a taciturn old man with cold, watery blue eyes and a look of calm ferocity.

Grandfather was slightly over six feet tall. He weighed 260 pounds. His nose was a parrot's beak; his face still had the remains of youth—not of happy and carefree childish days, but the bull-moose time of being a lumberjack and backwoods wrestler, barnraiser and don't-give-a-damn-about-anything stud and hellraiser. He was.

Grandfather tolerated me. And all the time something smoldered and burned inside him, which I felt too—something out of the far-distant past. He was eighty years back of me in time, and seemed less a relative than a queer aging animal from the forests, where other animals wisely avoided him. My parents had been old when I was born, and my own connection with these people seemed many generations distant. All the world was old, this very world that was closest to me.

My grandfather's ferocity, that smoldering and burning self, concealed or half-concealed in rotting flesh! His talk about wrestling the woods bully; and no doubt he was a bully himself, although that thought never occurred to me then. Barn raisings and booze, and "I wanted to get into her pants." Nothing softened or euphemized for me; he said what he thought and felt. Death became, "I'll turn up my toes." About life: "You don't dast stop," or everything would fall down.

*

I learned to read when I was five or six. From that time onward I devoured a book a day and as many as a dozen a week from the town library. Words capered into my head like a swarm of articulate wasps. *The Wizard of Oz, Doctor Dolittle, Peter Rabbit, Tom Swift,* and Horatio Alger. *A Princess of Mars, The Warlord of Mars* by Edgar Rice Burroughs, when I was older. The big red "Chums" books with their school stories from England. Books by Zane Grey, Frank Packard; heroic tales of Bulldog Drummond, and Raffles, the gentleman crook. Pulp magazines, *Black Mask, Argosy, The Shadow, Doc Savage* (the "Man of Bronze"), the whole Street and Smith pantheon of pulps, sport, adventure, western, science fiction, and love. I didn't care for the love stuff much, but I read them too when there was nothing else.

The pulps were fascinating reading, much more exciting than the town library could provide. One Sunday, sneaking into Merker's junkyard from the river side because I knew I wasn't supposed to, I noticed that among the newspapers compressed into huge wirebound bundles by the screw press were many copies of my favourite reading matter. The pulps.

After that discovery, on Sundays and holidays when no one was working there, I'd slip into the junkyard from the unfenced river side. It was necessary to climb over wrecked auto bodies with battered fenders twisting into dangerous mountains of steel and iron.

The magazines were not easy to either locate or extract from their compressed six-foot bales. But I'd worry and work away at them, twist back and forth patiently until the bright covers of *Doc Savage* and *The Shadow* were freed from bondage. Always nervous that I might be caught. And one day I was.

Mr. Merker must have noticed that his newspaper bales were looking a little anemic from my magazine extractions, and perhaps some of the bundles would even fall apart. If they did, it must have meant a great deal of extra work, pressing and baling them all over again. Therefore he patrolled the junkyard on foot at unexpected times. And I was caught red-handed, or "Doc Savage"–handed.

Mr. Merker's face was terrible, skull-like and black with anger. He was Isaiah the Prophet, he was Jeremiah about to pronounce doom. My head shrank down into my shoulders when he grabbed me by the ear and collar, frog-marching me toward the yard's front entrance.

But that was all. Surprisingly he didn't tell my mother. And I wasn't thrown into jail to languish for days on bread and water, as I had feared. I was free, but much too scared ever to return to Merker's junkyard. Reading can be dangerous.

*

Around this time our neighbours, the Shaws, moved away from their house behind ours. Before leaving, Mrs. Shaw presented me with a parting gift of a hundred or so copies of paperbound "Frank Merriwell" books by Burt L. Standish. I knew there was no possibility of having time to read that many books and still keep up with my schoolwork. The problem was baffling. How would Doc Savage, the Man of Bronze, have solved it? What bold stratagem could he have devised in order to deceive my mother's watchful eye?

I became suddenly ill. My stomach was upset, my legs ached. My mother quickly realized the seriousness of this illness. She put me to bed—with stacks of "Frank Merriwell" books piled high on chairs and tables around the bed. And perhaps ice cream would be good for what ailed me? Presto, the ice cream materialized. Comfort me with oranges and apples? The chest of drawers blazed with multicoloured fruit. But still I languished.

And read Frank Merriwell. He went to Yale University, Frank did, in New Haven, wherever that was. His loyal girlfriend was Inza Burriage. She was very beautiful, of course. And Frank Merriwell played games, baseball, hockey, football, basketball, track and field, everything. He was very good at games, scoring the winning run or goal or basket, generally at the last moment when the outcome of the contest seemed still in doubt.

It was borne upon me fairly soon that Frank Merriwell was an American, and that Americans always won, whatever the issue might be. While a band, hidden somewhere in the bleachers, played "The Star-Spangled Banner." Or if the American Frank Merriwell did not win, then skullduggery was near afoot and close at hand.

However, justice did generally prevail, given enough pages for the blind goddess to see her way clear and glimpse *what evil lurks in the hearts of men*

("The Shadow"). It was also impressed upon me that winning was very important, while I nursed some doubts that I would ever personally achieve such invariable triumphs. I was lousy at games—in fact it was hard to find anything at which I really excelled; perhaps a rather good disappearing act when work or bedtime was mentioned.

Doctor Johnson called at our house. He examined me carefully, with stethoscope and finger thumpings of my anatomy, questioned my mother about diet and bowel movements. After lucubration, cogitation, and colloquy with her, Doctor Johnson agreed that the illness was serious. But he had difficulty with his diagnosis. And it was decided that I should remain in bed somewhat longer.

My mother continued the ice-cream treatment. I finished reading all the "Frank Merriwell" books, rose from my bed of pain after a month or so and went back to school. The kid from next door, Jack Clegg, said to me, "Where were you?" And I said, "Catching up on my reading." And he said, "Yah, I just bet."

High school. Looking back, there seems little transition from the time of being a small child on whom adults doted and smirked over and then becoming a pimpled lout of a teenager, reading books concealed in textbook covers in class and playing football. And always being a little scared when I stopped to think, which my teachers said wasn't very often.

I was writing poems during the early 1930s, and getting them published in the school magazine, called *The Spotlight.* They were pretty bad poems, but I didn't know that, and thought them wonderful. The school magazine paid a dollar each for poems published. Enthralled with Bliss Carman's stuff (he was once well-known), I began to write at a furious rate, filling notebooks with endless doggerel. Copying the poems on a neighbour's typewriter, I bound them into little leather-covered, stapled books. These homemade books contained some fairly long effusions, an iambic epic on Robin Hood, another on the Norse myths, Thor, Odin, etc.

Our neighbour Harry Moore, was editor of the local newspaper, *The Courier Advocate.* He printed several of my verses in his paper, along with a short article about me. This was a kind of schoolboy triumph. But I failed to pass from Grade 9 to Grade 10, despite my mother's exhortations. I remained in school to play football, to which I had become addicted as well as poetry (I was a big kid,

about 180 pounds). However, life for me had become completely aimless; in every sense I was at a dead end.

*

In 1936 I rode the freight trains west to Vancouver, B.C. The object of this expedition was to get a job on West Coast fishing boats. It was Year Seven of the Great Depression, called "The Hungry Thirties" in a later era. The poor were poorer; farmers traded eggs for groceries; the mood of nearly everyone was bleak and discouraged. Jobless Canadians by the thousands were also riding the freights from town to town, searching desperately for work.

At first I hitchhiked: west to Toronto, north to Sudbury where I slept in a used-car lot, raped by passionate mosquitoes. Then west again on the Trans-Canada Highway to Searchmont, a few miles north of Sault Ste. Marie. And had to stop there. No more highway. It hadn't been built yet. For western transport there was only two shining rails plunging into the green wilderness.

The freight train arrived at Searchmont water tower at midnight, hissing steam and accompanied by the flashing lanterns of brakies. It groaned painfully and drank like an animal, great sloshing gulps of water. I clambered into what seemed to be half a boxcar with the upper part removed, a gondola that had once held coal. Wearing a waterproof canvas jacket, clutching a bag containing an extra pair of shoes, shaving cream and razor, a large hunting knife, I was equipped for adventure.

Hours passed and it began to rain. I huddled into one corner of the gondola, sheltering from wind. Dozing and sleeping alternately in acute discomfort, I awoke into an abnormal stillness. In half-light and half-rain I stirred, desperate to escape that dirty coal car and water that trickled down my neck in cold discomfort.

Scrambling down the gondola's steel ladder I searched for shelter, with lines of brick-coloured boxcars shouldering endlessly on either side. In early-morning light I ripped the strip of metal seal from a boxcar door with my hunting knife, then tried to haul open the heavy door. The thing wouldn't budge. Feeling dull acceptance I went back to that miserable coal car, lost in wet misery.

A black-slickered railway cop materialized in the rain. He climbed into the gondola, regarding me with distaste. "You broke the seal on a car," he accused. I admitted the charge meekly, knowing he wouldn't believe a denial anyway. "You could get two years for this," he said.

The cop locked me up in a railway caboose car with bars on windows and a padlocked door. At noon I was escorted to his house for lunch with his wife and daughter. They looked at me with commiseration. And I discovered that the little railway town I had landed in was called Hawk Junction, 165 miles northwest of Sault Ste. Marie. Then I was incarcerated again, sitting in misery all afternoon: what will my mother think? Two years.

I examined the prison car's interior more carefully. The windows were all broken, presumably by desperate criminals attempting escape. The steel bars of those windows were firmly embedded in their frame, and moved not at all when I tried to shake them loose. The door was wood, opening inward, secured with a padlock and metal hasp on the outside. Apparently no one had escaped, despite being probably older and stronger than me.

Mother, about sixty years old

Still, they might have overlooked something. The window bars were obviously much too formidable. That left only the door. It was heavy, with the hinge keys outside so they couldn't be tampered with from inside. I tried the doorknob, releasing the latch enough to allow the door to move inward a quarter inch or so; and ran my fingers along the narrow springy opening between the upper part of the door and its sill. My heart was beating heavily and I felt breathless. The door was flexible enough at the top to permit my fingers to work around its edge and clasp the outside.

I was tall—six feet, three inches. That helped a great deal. I swung myself off the floor, body supported by finger grip between upper sill and door, feet jammed against the sill opposite my hands. And pulled. Yanked inward as if I were about to fall off a cliff and my fingers were holding onto life itself.

I hung high in the air for at least a minute, like a giant clothespin. It seemed the door was too much for me. And yet it was a kind of triumph to make this all-out effort to escape, muscles straining, bones cracking in their sockets. But stalemate: I just hung there, blood pounding in my ears.

Then a sound like ripping cloth. The door pulled inward, screws yanked from outside hasp. The boy, who was not exactly me, plunged to the floor on his back, almost too scared to realize what had happened. Lying there, listening to a strange sound, my own labouring breath. Then peering outside, into an early Sunday afternoon. Into freedom.

Nothing was visible beside my prison caboose except long lines of boxcars ahead and behind. I dropped quietly onto the cinders between cars, and started to walk toward Sault Ste. Marie. Travelling farther west by this route seemed out of the question. I felt too nervous to even think about it.

Walking the tracks south I crossed a bridge over a river, then decided that a desperate criminal like me was liable to be pursued. I went into the woods about thirty feet, just far enough I thought so that no one could see me from the tracks, which I meant to follow from that distance away. A few minutes later I'd wandered into the woods much too far, tried to reverse my steps and couldn't.

Those first few minutes of being lost left me terror-stricken. Never in my life have I been able to distinguish north from south or east from west. I have to ask the telephone operator how to get out of a phone booth. In the bush that long-ago day, I started to run. Abandoning all my outdoor gear and equipment, I ran; and kept on running. Uphill and down, across angry little creeks and spongy bottomland. Blood pounded in my veins; I could feel my face grow hot and red, rational thought simply vanished. Probably there has been no succeeding time in my life when I've been so afraid.

Two days and two nights I spent in the Algoma bush country. Stumbling on an old rotting hunting camp, I circled around unknowing, then found myself at the same place again, just as stories of people lost in the woods have previously described. Fortunately the weather was fairly mild. I slept curled fetally around a tree on a hillside, and awoke hungry.

The second day passed as the first one had, except that it rained. I drank water from woodland creeks, listening to trains shunting back and forth at Hawk Junction, but unable to walk consistently in that direction, mind confused and disoriented. Old logging roads criss-crossed the forest floor, petering out in green nowhere. Thankfully there were few bugs; once I thought I saw a bear, probably an illusion.

I like to think my escape from those woods in 1937 was the result of rational thought and calm, considered cerebration. Today I am not so sure. But it entered my mind that after escaping my prison caboose I had crossed a bridge over a river: and therefore the river and railway tracks formed two sides of a triangle. If I could just walk in a fairly straight line for an hour or two, either the river or railway tracks ought to be easy to find.

Even when it stopped raining the sun was obscured by dark clouds, only a vague brightness showing in the sky from time to time. Climbing trees and sighting ahead to other trees, I made slow progress in what I hoped was just one direction. Thankfully it was: bursting through thick undergrowth, I nearly fell headlong into that blessed river. And followed it back to the railway, and thence south again to Sault Ste. Marie.

Several times in that long-ago Algoma forest I had prayed to a possibly nonexistent deity. Since then, as a professed agnostic, I have taken full credit for my own escape from the woods, allotting none to a possible God. David Williams, a prof in the English department at the University of Manitoba, gave me some food for thought when I was Writer-in-Residence there in 1975–76. He said, "The railway was presumably man-made; the river God-made. Too bad you didn't find the railway tracks first." So much for my rational self. Or maybe I was just lucky.

*

After some adventures and misadventures with railway cops and Mounties, I finally achieved Vancouver. And didn't like the place much. I went to a Dorothy Lamour movie, using money I'd stashed away inside the rubber ankleband on my running shoes. Then caught a freight train east from the downtown level crossing that same evening.

For the next two summers I rode the freight trains west, wandering from town to town, sleeping in empty boxcars and hobo jungles, begging handouts from housewives, writing poems when there was a quiet moment. Then in 1939 came World War II.

In mid-summer of that year I joined the Royal Canadian Air Force, although I was not officially inducted until January 1940. The air force motto is *Per Ardua Ad Astra,* "Through difficulties to the stars." I never achieved the stars, but did make corporal, then sergeant. But my tenure at the latter rank was fairly brief. I was the Non-Commissioned Officer placed in charge of some two hundred air crew, mostly Americans, at Picton, Ontario. These boys were waiting for space to open up for them at the appropriate training school. I appointed several of the bright American kids as temporary NCOs, and went on the town.

Predictably, I was shipped back to the Trenton military base for gross dereliction of duty or something. There I am in 1940, flanked by an armed guard, hatless, marching into the CO's office, awaiting my condign punishment.

NCO in charge of guard detail: "Prisoner and escort, HAW! Raight—taw-awn!" (I think he had a mouthful of rusty razor blades.)

The GOLD BRAID slowly raised its head: "Do you accept my punishment?"

ACTING SERGEANT PURDY (whimpering): "Yessir."

GOLD BRAID: "Reduced in rank to acting corporal."

Lo and behold it was so.

I acquired a girlfriend that same year and, next in order of importance, an automobile. (I bought a 1927 Whippet in Toronto, learned to operate it by driving the hundred or so miles back to Trenton on a forty-eight-hour pass.) My girlfriend, one Eurithe Mary Jane Parkhurst, lived in Belleville. She got a job as a waitress in Niagara

Falls, some two hundred miles away. When she returned to her home in Belleville one weekend, I was on duty as corporal of the guard and couldn't get away to see her.

I brooded about that, lonesome for female company. And just one word (or two) from Eurithe would have eased this inner yearning, which, ridiculous as I knew it was, couldn't be sublimated by anything except the female gender.

After the midnight guard shift was escorted to their posts, I brooded some more. Then drove the guard truck to Belleville, wearing the full regalia of webbing and sidearms. Nobody stopped me at the gate or said: "Nay, Corporal Purdy, thou mayest not desert thine assigned post—though even now at this fateful moment sixteen German saboteurs are crawling under the fence at Trenton Air Base's outer periphery." Nobody said that.

NCO in charge of guard (it *was* getting a little monotonous): "Prisoner and escort, HAW! Raight—taw-awn."

This time my rank went still lower. And successive demotions make it impossible to imagine what depths I might have achieved if the war hadn't ended first. Several weeks after crime and punishment, I was finally allowed outside the military base and onto the streets of Trenton town. There I encountered a very drunk civilian. He regarded me sneeringly. In his heart of hearts he despised me as he despised all uniforms. I saluted him smartly.

In 1941 I got married, and was posted west to Vancouver in the spring of '43. Eurithe followed me there a couple of months later. From the RCAF base at Kitsilano I was dispatched north to Woodcock, a whistlestop on the Canadian National Railway nested in high mountains, some one hundred and thirty miles from Prince Rupert. The air force construction arm (#9 CMU) was building a landing field there, the Japanese being expected to invade northern Canada almost momentarily. (As things turned out, they had better sense.)

I was not pleased with my wifeless condition at Woodcock. I kept firing requests back to Eurithe

In RCAF uniform at age twenty-one, with his wife, Eurithe

attitude I was able to maintain for two minutes at most.

*

In 1943–45 the *Vancouver Sun* had a poetry page on weekends. They paid a dollar for each poem published: therefore, I was never short of a buck on weekends. The morning *News-Herald* handed out prizes of two tickets to the downtown Vogue Theatre, for completing verse limericks with suitable advertising come-ons. Eurithe and I, therefore, saw enough bad movies to account for my present good taste.

In 1944 I published my first book of poems, *The Enchanted Echo.* I paid two hundred dollars to have five hundred copies printed at Clarke and Stuart, Vancouver. Perhaps seventy-five or one hundred of them were sold or given away. The poems were atrociously bad. I went back to the publisher years later when the book's price was rising because of subsequent books: they had thrown them all out.

Still, that less-than-mediocre book resulted in some friendships that are well-remembered. Joan Buckley, editor of the *Sun* book page, for her I have warm feelings. And Sammy, a nurse in the RCAF hospital with a turned-up nose: dear Sammy. And that orderly room flight sergeant at Kits whose name I've forgotten, whose face I remember.

In 1945 the Hitler war ended, and my son Jim was born. Eurithe and I went back east, and I was discharged at Toronto Manning Pool. My military memories include extreme dislike of uniforms and discipline in which I am involved, and also one marching tune. During my first years at Trenton I'd wake up early in the morning hearing it: DAH-DAH—DAH—DAH—DAH, "Colonel Bogey." DAH-DAH, winter is over and spring arrived in the blood forever. R.52768 A.C. 2 Purdy, I can hear it still.

For three years, immediately after the war, I was in the taxi business with my father-in-law, Jim Parkhurst. All I can say about that partnership is to warn others against similar deals. This one involved all the money I'd gotten together over the previous five years, as against none contributed by my partner. Instead of money, he was supposed to throw his labour and know-how into the pot, to the point where our separate contributions matched each other in value.

Well—they never did.

Eurithe, about 1960

in Vancouver, asking her to apply for a travel warrant, which would enable her to join me without cost in the northern wilderness eight hundred miles away. At the same time, I wrote a letter to the flight sergeant in charge of the Kitsilano base orderly room, requesting a transfer back to Vancouver on compassionate grounds, mentioning my newly married state.

Both of those two things happened at nearly the same time: Eurithe got her travel warrant, and started north to Woodcock; and I was posted back to Vancouver. We passed each other on trains going in the opposite direction, without either of us knowing what happened. I figured the crossing point to be near a small town called Smithers, my soul yearning with romantic love and sexual fantasies.

While at Woodcock, Eurithe took a liking to the place and wouldn't come back to me. She got a job as a waitress in the airman's mess, while I raged with jealousy in Vancouver, writing countless fruitless pleading letters. When she finally did return, I received her stiffly and formally, an

To top things off, Eurithe and I were running into increasing marriage difficulties. We separated for a couple of years, each going our own way. The cause? Who knows? She had been only sixteen when we married; I was perhaps a little older mentally. But looking backwards provides no answers.

*

When the taxi business went bankrupt, and after two more years of odd jobs and failure, Eurithe, Jimmy, and I went west again in 1950. It was meant to be a new beginning to everything. You know—the sunset land, where everyone is three hours younger than back in the grey east, and love may blossom again under a warmer sky, if it doesn't rain. Who knows, maybe that isn't all bullshit.

After a few months of nearly desperate poverty in Vancouver, we climbed back on our collective financial feet. I got a job at Sigurdson's Lumber Company, then a more permanent one at Vancouver Bedding, where I became an apprentice mattress-maker.

Perhaps almost as important as the job, I got to know a lot of people. Curt Lang, a fifteen-year-old whiz kid at a science fiction fan club meeting (one of those articulate kids who can talk the pants off any theologian under the grade of cardinal). And Alex LaFortune, a good young poet who died a year later. Steve McIntyre, a bookseller whose other friends regarded him as a combination of Socrates and Nostradamus, with also maybe a dash of Herodotus.

McIntyre's comment on my unlettered state: "Purdy, you ain't read nothin'."

So I plodded through Tolstoy, Thomas Mann, Proust, Virginia Woolf (etc.), and they certainly were just as boring as I'd expected. Well—no, maybe not: but they certainly didn't resemble Elmore Leonard or Mickey Spillane.

When a young ex-seaman named Doug Kaye came to work at Vancouver Bedding, a triumvirate was formed, which included Doug, Curt Lang, and myself. Our pastimes included beer, music, and long discussions about nearly everything. Curt's ex-French teacher, name of Downie Kirk, had translated a drunken beachcomber's novel from English into French, critics of both languages nearly unanimous in declaring the novel genius. The guy's name was Malcolm Lowry; his opus, *Under the Volcano.*

The three of us, Downie Kirk, Curt Lang, and myself, visited the great novelist at his shack on the wooded shores of Deep Cove, some twenty miles from Vancouver. Bearing gifts of booze and feeling apprehensive (Lowry was said to be very bad-tempered), we knocked on his door. And that afternoon was one of the most enjoyable I've ever experienced.

Lowry was a genial and good-tempered man—at least on this occasion. Barrel-chested, red-faced, and short of stature, he was also a drinker of Olympian magnitude. When we ran short of booze early on, Lowry and I drove to the Vancouver Main and Hastings store to renew our supply. He bought six bottles of Bols Gin, and figured that ought to last the weekend. I was speechless, a rare condition.

"There's a church with beautiful windows near here," Lowry said. So we headed for the church.

A wedding was in progress at the waterfront church. And a priest was on guard at the doors, moving to meet wedding guests as their cars drew up at the curb. He wouldn't let us in. I spoke to the man of God requesting entry, figuring that I was a little less sloshed than Lowry, but the degree was minuscule. At that moment another car arrived, and the priest went to greet the new arrivals. I turned to where Lowry had been standing, "Now's our chance." But he was already inside.

Lowry was kneeling on the floor between pews in the rainbow-coloured light, praying to some god or other—with six bottles of Bols Gin in a brown grocery bag on the seat behind him. I thought of Coleridge's "Ancient Mariner." And Lowry was transported back to that time in my mind: dressed in strange medieval seaman's garb instead of his frowsy sweater and dirty corduroys. Hung around his neck, instead of a dead albatross, six bottles of Bols Gin.

Then, while I watched in fascination, Lowry grabbed a wedding guest on the curb outside, whisking the man away from that officious priest. "Listen," he would say to the wedding guest, "Once in a Mexican town called Quauhnahuac, there was a consul . . ."

*

Doug Kaye, before he became a fellow worker at Vancouver Bedding, had been responsible for planting a labour union in Restmore Mattress Factory. Lacking seniority at his new place of employment, Doug began agitating with me to introduce the upholsterer's union into our own factory. I was to be the "front man" because of my seniority—in less polite words, "a patsy."

However, I took the bait: we signed up everybody for the union. The end result of that was a nickel raise, which hardly seemed worth it at the time. I had to sit in the boss's office with the union negotiator, and was very ill at ease. Then I got stuck with the job of shop steward, to whom everyone came with their complaints. In addition. I took on the job of recording secretary for the union, feeling quite puffed-up and self-important. That didn't last long. Realization suddenly overwhelmed me that what all these extra duties amounted to was WORK. I resigned from everything.

My writing models at this time were Bliss Carman, G. K. Chesterton, W. J. Turner, and the like. But as a result of McIntyre's unflattering opinions about me, I was adding T. S. Eliot and Dylan Thomas to my repertoire—this on the interurban tram going to work in early-morning light.

My first small book, other than the self-published *The Enchanted Echo,* came out with Ryerson Press in Toronto, *Pressed on Sand.* And I was writing a verse play, *A Gathering of Days,* a bad imitation of Thomas's *Under Milk Wood.* The play was produced by John Reeves and the CBC in 1954.

As might be expected, I had become somewhat unpopular with management at Vancouver Bedding because of my union activities. I quit my job, just on the verge of being fired anyway, and went to Europe.

*

During my last days as a mattress-maker, I'd been writing admiring letters to Irving Layton in Montreal. Before catching the liner *Ascania* to France, I slept on Layton's studio couch three or four nights; and his kids begged me for nickels and dimes by daylight. And two friends joined me for the European jaunt, the aforementioned Curt Lang and Jim Polson.

I regard this 1955 trip as pivotal in my life—throwing up a safe but poorly paid monotonous job, and taking a chance on my own nearly minuscule abilities with which to make a living. I really had no idea how I would live from then on, except that writing would be involved. Meeting

About 1962

Layton, Louis Dudek, and Frank Scott in Montreal had contributed some friendly glamour to the writing life. But all three of these people were profs, occupying lucrative niches at universities. Their examples provided no hints whatever as to how I might make a living.

In Paris, Curt, Polson, and I speculated about the uses of French bidets; visited an expatriate Canadian painter living in a ruined tenth-century church that was also used for wine storage, in central France; and I visited the Scotch Hebrides alone—after ducking the artist in a subway entrance the last time he tried to borrow money. Returning to Vancouver, Eurithe hardly recognized me because of my suave and courtly continental manners. But she took a chance, and we moved back east.

In Montreal, Eurithe got a job as secretary with the Canadian Pacific Railway. I started out to make a living writing radio and television plays for the CBC. It's not a course I'd recommend for any beginning writer: I did sell four or five scripts that first year, and perhaps seven or eight more in the course of time. However, I had to write a dozen plays to make one sale with the hard-boiled producers in Toronto. This 1 in 12 ratio of acceptance so annoyed my wife that she quit her job, having decided that if I could get away without working for a living she could too.

Milton Acorn was my closest friend in Montreal. Irving Layton sent him hot-foot to my apartment by telling him I could provide some tips on writing plays. Acorn was heavily built, red-faced as a fire hydrant, ugly in a rather attractive way, and scarcely ever took a bath. His home province was Prince Edward Island. He was a carpenter and poet.

My first thought on reading his stuff was that he was a very bad poet. Then I had to change my opinion, realizing later that he was a much better poet than me, which felt quite hurtful. His work had the quality of teaching you both how to write and how not to write at the same time. The paradox was quite puzzling.

At that time my own writing had come full circle from its beginnings. I was reading voraciously, including Tolstoy and Virginia Woolf, more in spite of McIntyre than because of him. But my first precept then and now remains: take no one else's word re the best writing: make up your own mind, and do not be swerved easily from those opinions.

Nevertheless, my admirations did include the conventional figures: Yeats (nobody overlooks Yeats); D. H. Lawrence, both poems and prose, especially his ideas on prosody, and *Birds, Beasts, and Flowers;* Dylan Thomas, though my feeling for him has faded since; Robinson Jeffers for his romantic nihilism, a necessary ingredient, as it is with Housman; add the early Bukowski; Olson and the beats who are anathema to me, but whom nevertheless I learned from; and a host of minor figures, with whom I rank myself.

e. e. cummings, despite that lowercase affectation; Kipling, not least because of Eliot's stuffed-shirt strictures. But there are really too many "influences" to make an adequate listing. In fact I can make a reverse listing instead.

While admitting Whitman's style and methods have been seminal, to think of old Walt tramping down the highway clapping everyone on the back and greeting them with "Comrade, Hail fellow American," makes me think of Frank Merriwell, and I want to throw up. I expect the reverse of Whitman is Philip Larkin, who is on my "like" list. And I don't care for Frost much, while acknowledging his abilities. (I always remember Shapiro saying Frost had no "passions.") Add Emily Dickinson to my loves, although my eyes blur after a dozen of her poems. I don't care for Robert Lowell's own poetry, but think he's a marvelous translator, or should I say "imitator"? And that's enough.

*

So there I am in Montreal, going broke with my wife: "indigent poet" and crummy playwright. What a way to spend your life! It reminds me of Melbourne's injunction that you have to realize you're a fool before you can be a human being. I was a fool, and probably still am. But Eurithe and I were wise enough to get the hell out of Montreal, back to the Belleville-Trenton area where we were both raised.

One reason for going there was my mother: nearly eighty years old, she was getting a little mixed up as to which day was Sunday and attending church on weekdays. We had to take care of her.

My feelings about myself at the time were a mixture, a sense of failure, but as well the almost-knowledge of an impending literary rebirth. And more personally, everything about me was changing, a new thing that I couldn't quite grasp or even properly describe.

Eurithe and I made the down payment on a lot beside Roblin Lake near Ameliasburgh in Prince Edward County. And bought a pile of used building materials from some government buildings being torn down in nearby Belleville. We found some plans for an A-frame house in a magazine, adapted them to our own needs, and started out to build the house ourselves.

I was, of course, writing poems and getting published in magazines. Another Ryerson chapbook was on the verge of appearing; also a skimpy selection was published by Fiddlehead Press at the University of New Brunswick, via the good agencies of Fred Cogswell in the English department.

Was I on my way? No, but at least I had a better view of the highway. Writing is never easy, no matter what fools say about it. Your own ego will give you the best of it almost always, the flattering opinion that means nothing at all. When that silly ego pops up, you hafta say, "Down boy!"—the time is not yet for you to speak your piece and may never be.

So we built the house ourselves, quarreling bitterly over how to pound nails and lay concrete blocks. For a man and woman to build a house together, the necessity of gagging one or the other becomes at all times foremost. I do not advise it. However, any advice I might give to my wife is habitually ignored. Building that house on Roblin Lake, Eurithe and I would both have gone mad and attacked each other physically, except for the occasional presence of other people plus my own basically phlegmatic temperament.

We did all the rural things together: raised garden vegetables, worked at a nearby cannery together, our son attending the village school. I wrote poems about old Owen Roblin and his gristmill. Roblin was an early pioneer of our area. I worked at whatever pick-up jobs I could find; and made gallons and gallons of wild grape wine. And we went broke, absolutely poverty-stricken.

I made plans to hitchhike the two hundred and fifty miles or so back to Montreal, on a very cold winter Sunday. It had become obvious that a job for me was a clear necessity. I had no gloves, and standing beside the road my hands felt like red-hot horseshoes. Reaching Gananoque some seventy miles east of my starting point, I could go no farther; motorists would not stop for the self-pitying ragged scarecrow almost too ashamed to stick up his thumb. (Well, I couldn't entirely blame them.)

I was stuck beside the highway at Gananoque for at least an hour, stamping my feet up and down to keep warm in the sub-zero weather. Completely discouraged, I reversed myself, walked to the other side of the road, sticking up my thumb to plead for a ride westward. And it worked too. I walked the last six or seven miles homeward to Roblin Lake. That was one of my low points; although I'm bound to over-dramatize.

Entering the house: "How do you feel about being married to such a failure?"

"How would you like some hot soup, dear?"

*

1959: back in Montreal, Eurithe and I both got jobs. My first play was again produced on CBC radio, and I blessed public broadcasting for putting meat on the table. A half-hour television play of mine, *Point of Transfer*, was produced on Montreal's "Shoestring Theatre." (A couple of years later under the title *Just Ask for Sammy*, it became a stage play at Theatre in the Dell, Toronto.) Milton Acorn slept on our floor when he was short of money, quite often. Annette and Henry Ballon were friends: Henry worked in a drugstore which supplied the malt ingredients when the three of us brewed homemade beer.

Purdy (in foreground), in Peru, about 1970

Social life in Montreal involved knowing nearly all the writers: Louis Dudek, Irving Layton, Frank Scott, Ron Everson, and many others. My own writing was changing and changing. Inversions, monotonous rhyme, and metre were either dropped or being unrecognizably altered. My tastes in literature were, I think, catholic and individual. But definitions in literature are a quicksand in which I don't want to get stuck.

*

My mother had died in 1958, when Eurithe and I were in the midst of house-building at Roblin Lake. Her will was not probated until 1964, leaving our own financial situation in continual doubt. Returning again to the unfinished house from Montreal in 1960, I worked at whatever jobs were available. Among these were picking apples, and selling them door to door on expeditions north to Bancroft; gathering scrap iron for sale at Belleville junkyards; doing nearly anything that brought in money. Occasional play sales and this "casual labour" brought in so little remuneration that we were sometimes on the verge of actual hunger.

In 1962 my small book *The Blur in Between* was published in an edition of three hundred copies by Emblem Books. I'd received a small Canada Council grant in 1960, and this was one result. I regard the book with some fondness, since it's the best-looking of any book of mine. Contact Press published *Poems for All the Annettes,* also in 1962. That last one is/was a transitional book for me, and marks the point at which my writing style had changed completely, in which there were still some crudities but few traces of other writers—at least I hope that's true.

During this period, from 1960 to 1965, perhaps a dozen of my radio plays were produced. Alice Frick and Doris Hedges of the CBC script department in Toronto were responsible for any small success I had writing plays. They sent me scripts for adjudication as well; and to read bad plays and contrast them with good ones is a way of improving your own writing. And I had so far to go I couldn't help improve.

I've said that *Poems for All the Annettes* was a watershed in my own development. But "development" sounds like a pole vaulter or sprinter prepping for a big athletic meet. However, I do admit to being almost fully aware of the changes taking place in my own mental equipment, changes

In Mexico, about 1975

that were partly the result of discontent with nearly everything about myself.

And some interesting questions might be raised here: how and why does a person change, whether a writer or anyone else? Of course writing was part of the reason for my own small movements from what I was to what I am. And the journey never ends, except with death. One might say a poem researches an adjacent universe for truth and beauty. But those last two words sound ridiculous in this day and age.

My own idea is that writing poems is a mental discipline that stretches the mind to a degree beyond any other activity. "Inspiration" is a word I dislike: but I do think there is a mind-cloistered condition in which the outside world is extinguished like a match, and thoughts float free like small clouds inside infinite space of the human skull. Which sounds very romantic.

In 1964 I went to Cuba, one of eleven Canadians on that trip. They were guests of the Cuban

With friend Ron Everson, 1980

government, and our arrival was part of a public relations exercise in response to U.S. hostility.

My own role in this expedition was more or less accidental. I'd read poems at Ross Dowson's Trotsky bookstore in Toronto some months previously. And since my own politics are New Democratic Party–leftist, Dowson asked me if I'd be interested in going to Cuba. I was. In fact I felt ecstatic about the trip. Visions of new poems flashed in my head—maybe even a prose narrative about Cuba?

A Toronto photographer, Michel Lambeth, was one of the eleven Canadians invited. It occurred to me that his photographs and my prose might go well together in a book. But Lambeth, a few days before departure, decided the expedition was not for him. He was afraid of being blacklisted as a Communist. He mentioned to me that the McCarthy witch-hunting days in Washington were fairly recent, only ten years before.

Travelling from Canada to Cuba couldn't be managed in a straight line, south in the U.S. to Miami, say, and south again to Cuba. American hostility to Cuba precluded such a simple travel itinerary. One had to fly much farther south to Mexico City first, then wait for a scheduled Cubana Airlines flight to Havana. And you needed a visa.

Among the Canadian visitors was a Montreal lawyer, a man of about forty. He was lean-faced, of average height and balding, athletically built, his manner self-possessed and confident. I was very impressed by this man: his name was Pierre Trudeau.

The future Prime Minister of Canada caused me to be very careful of what I said within his hearing. I had the feeling anything stupid would be immediately noticed. On one occasion the Canadians were sitting in a country school room, listening to a Communist official explain the *modus operandi* of things since the revolution. When questions were called for I raised my hand like a small boy in kindergarten, asking if they arrived at decisions by majority vote.

There was a little stir behind me, and Pierre Trudeau's voice said, "Don't be naive, Al." I nearly blushed.

One highlight of this trip for me: sitting in a huge concrete stadium on May Day, listening to Fidel Castro speak for about three hours, and not understanding anything he said. Before the speech, I had become aware of a man moving like a small brown cloud among the foreign visitors in the rows of seats below ours. Then he stepped up to the group of Canadians: a short and stockily built man, wearing olive-drab fatigues and black beret.

"Who is it?" I whispered to Pierre Trudeau. "Che Guevara."

There were other memorable times: visiting Playa Giron, site of the American-sponsored invasion at the "Bay of Pigs." Visiting a ballet performance, featuring a prima ballerina named Alicia Alonzo, Trudeau and I were bored, and walked back across the city together to our hotel, stopping to drink cider and admire Havana architecture by moonlight.

Another incident: travelling through mountains in our nearly wornout 1958 Cadillac late at night. Encountering an army convoy. Moonlight on camouflaged troop carriers; big guns trundling behind trucks; tropical palms overhead. Reaching Havana, anti-aircraft guns were lined up near the waterfront, their snouts like open mouths. In daylight an American warship, the *Oxford,* could be seen vaguely just outside the then twelve-mile limit, its spy apparatus focused on the Communist island. Cubans were not pleased about that warship.

All this remains in memory as part of a nightmare world.

*

The Cariboo Horses, 1965, was published with McClelland and Stewart, Toronto, who became my principal publishers since that year. It received the Governor General's Award, given for the best book of poems to be published in Canada that year. One of its poems, "The Country North of Belleville," had previously received the President's Medal (of the University of Western Ontario) as the best poem of its year of magazine publication. I guess you could say my cup runneth over—at least it was close to the rim. *Horses* was certainly my best book to that date, the one in which I think "influences" were pretty much invisible, form and style merging with subject matter.

In 1964 my mother's will was finally settled, thus relieving some of our financial near-despera-tion. For six years we had expected this to happen daily, weekly, or monthly, and those expectations had resulted in a curious stasis in our lives. In some sense our very existence was held in suspense, waiting for the word GO from the probate courts.

Finally I had despaired of the inefficient hack lawyer I'd retained for more than five years, and asked Frank Scott in Montreal for the name of a good attorney. This was Andrew Brewin in Toronto; but Brewin ran for an NDP seat in the House of Commons and was elected. He deputized a young lawyer in his office, Ian Scott, to act on my behalf.

Years later, when I received the Order of Ontario in 1987, Scott was Attorney General in the Ontario Liberal government. When I ran into him in the Toronto legislative buildings after the ceremony, he said, "Do you remember me?" "Sure," I said, "you saved my life in 1964." We laughed and it was funny, but serious as well.

One result of *The Cariboo Horses* was that monetary grants became much more accessible to me than before. Over the next twenty years I travelled across the world, to Mexico, Japan, South Africa, the Soviet Union, Peru, England, and the

Lecturing, 1986

Galapagos Islands. Several books came out because of my travels, travels financed in large part by the Canada Council. I suppose you'd say that grants from the Canadian Council are similar to the American Guggenheims, except that the CC is an independent body funded by the Canadian government. I believe it deserves much of the credit for the healthy condition of the arts north of the border.

*

Most of the summer of 1965 was spent on Baffin Island in the Canadian arctic. I flew from Montreal to Frobisher Bay by Nordair DC-4. From Frobisher I went with a mining company charter to Pangnirtung near the Arctic Circle, taking along a full set of arctic clothing and a forty-ounce bottle of booze in case of snakebite. Times might have changed since Robert Service.

In Pang I stayed at the hostel for Inuit schoolchildren, wandering all over the settlement of some two hundred Inuit and whites by day, and sat up half the night writing. But after a few weeks I began to think I hadn't really arrived at the last frontier after all. Wayne Morrison, the government regional administrator, arranged for me to accompany an Inuit family and live with them on the Kikastan Islands in Cumberland Sound.

At the time of starting out with Jonesee and his family in their canoe, I had no idea where the Kikastan Islands might be or how far. The outboard motor racketed along for several hours. We passed rocky islands, with dogs running beside the shore barking at us hysterically (I found out later that some hunters leave their dogs on these islands in the summer when there's no sled work for them).

In mid-afternoon we stopped at an island like the peak of a small mountain. On the beach there I inherited the job of hoisting a blind husky bitch with white milky eyes over the boat's gunwales when we landed. I was given charge of her pups as well, being obviously useless for anything else. Jonesee and the other hunters climbed to the island's summit, firing their rifles at seals in the water below. I could see canoes scoot out from the garbage-littered beach to pick up the furry bodies.

We stopped on that island of slaughter my first night away from Pangnirtung. None of the hunters knew any English, and I didn't know their language: I couldn't ask them where we might be. In my sleeping bag atop the stone island, I listened to Old Squaw Ducks calling mournfully among the

ice floes: "and the RUNNER IN THE SKIES / I invented / as symbol of the human spirit / crashes like a housefly / and I think to the other side of that sound . . ." In the poem, I think to the other side of bad things, to where there's human laughter and human warmth. In life as apart from poems I try to do that as well.

The book that came out of those weeks spent on Baffin was called *North of Summer*, 1967. And from that time on books appeared every two or three years.

*

In 1982 I became an Officer of the Order of Canada. There's probably an equivalent to this in the U.S., but I don't know what it is. In 1987 I received the Governor General's Award a second time, for my *Collected Poems*, published the previous year. This book also got the Canadian Author's Association Award. Also the aforementioned Order of Ontario. For that last one I had to wear a dress suit, and bought a pair of black shoes at a thrift shop. They hurt my feet, and I left them under the banquet table at the King Edward Hotel where I was staying that night.

Over a fairly long lifetime, Friends. Many of them have gone in different directions from me, and I can't remember some of their names. That doesn't mean they weren't important to me: they were and are. How could I forget the guy with whom I rode the freight trains in 1936, and tramped with through the Okanagan Valley, and stole apples with and went hungry with . . . ? Especially the room we rented for fifty cents a night above a Chinese greasy spoon in Calgary. Then spent the rest of the afternoon in a downtown park, picking bedbugs off our clothes and bodies.

Harold Wannamaker, ex-football hero and RCAF officer. After the war he became a civilian flying instructor, crashed his plane at Oshawa and killed himself. Curt Lang, of course, the kid who could out-talk every theologian he never met. That flight sergeant who got me posted back to Vancouver from Woodcock, B.C.—on "compassionate grounds." Sammy, the nurse's assistant who used to give me alcohol stomach rubs at Kitsilano base hospital, causing multiple erections. It's like remembering the wind, those names, or those faces with names I can't remember.

Rolf Harvey, who defected from poetry to become a set designer in the movies, which paid much better. Milton Acorn, the first socialist poet I ever met, and much the best. Janet Lunn, who writes children's books, and is much more beautiful, younger, and smarter than I will ever be. Dennis Lee, to whom I owe much, for his analytic criticism and for his erroneous belief that my stuff will outlast the century. George Galt, editor and novelist, whose own name will certainly outlast his father's name, not to mention this century. Tom Marshall and David Helwig, both poets and both novelists. Sam Solecki, professor, editor, author, intellectual, and over—not in that order. And Alex Widen, who will read this looking for his own name.

I owe them, and love them all.

*

I've written plays, reviews, short stories, magazine and newspaper articles, as well as poems. I made up my mind early that I must try my hand at everything, since I'd be lucky if I was good at anything. In 1990 the novel *A Splinter in the Heart* was published. Strongly autobiographical, it's a rites-of-passage story of a sixteen-year-old boy achieving some understanding of himself one summer at the end of the First World War.

In 1993, letters to and from Margaret Laurence will be brought out by McClelland and Stewart, Toronto. And I am myself, with Alex Widen, also becoming a publisher. My essay about Roderick Haig-Brown, British Columbia magistrate, fisherman, and conservationist, will appear in a limited edition, which will include letters between us. The title: *Cougar Hunter.*

*

It's doubtful if very many people in the U.S., where this short autobio is to be published, have ever heard my name or seen any of my writings. In the very nature of writing poems, the poems themselves are autobiography, my own more than most. And when I read book reviews of poetry, my eye flies first to the excerpts the reviewer has chosen to demonstrate his/her point of view re literature. Therefore, I regard the following excerpts as better and more accurate indices to my life and character than any mere record of events.

Al Purdy and his wife, Eurithe, at home, 1989

"Old Alex" is about the death of a man who cheated everyone he could, known locally for the nastiness of his character:

> . . . I search desperately
> for good qualities, and end up crawling
> inside that decaying head and wattled throat
> to scream obscenities like papal blessings,
> knowing now and again I'm at least God.
> Well, who remembers a small purple and yellow
>   bruise long?
> But when he was here he was a sunset!

And this passage, about the complete defenselessness of lovers in a poem called "Postscript":

> The snail has lost its shell and toothless lion
> grumbles alone in dangerous country—
> The rhino's horns have fallen along a trail
> deep in dark woods and crowded with big game
>   hunters—
> The eagle has left its claws in the blood-red sky
> the antelopes have all gone lame and
> the lover has no luck at all—

From "Roblin's Mill 2," a poem about the end of the nineteenth century, when gristmills became relics of the past, and sailing ships were supplanted by steam:

> The wheels stopped
> and the murmur of voices
> behind the flume's tremble
> stopped
>   and the wind-high ships
> that sailed from Rednersville
> to the sunrise ports of Europe
> are delayed somewhere
> in a toddling breeze

From "About Being a Member of Our Armed Forces," concerning my military career, which was long but inglorious:

> I wasn't exactly a soldier tho
> only a humble airman
> who kept getting demoted
>   and demoted
>   and demoted
> to the point where I finally saluted civilians
> And when they trustingly gave me a Sten Gun
> Vancouver should have trembled in its sleep
> for after I fired a whole clip of bullets
> at some wild ducks under Burrard Bridge
> (on guard duty at midnight)
> they didn't fly away for five minutes
> trying to decide if there was any danger

From "Elegy for a Grandfather":

> And earth takes him as it takes more beautiful
>   things:
> populations of whole countries
> museums and works of art,
> and women with such a glow
> it makes their background vanish . . .

From "My Grandfather's Country":

> —there are deserts like great yellow beds of
>   flowers
> where a man can walk and walk into identical
>   distance
> like an arrow lost in its own target
> and a woman scream and a grain of sand will fall
> on the other side of the yellow bowl a thousand
>   miles away
> and all day long like a wedge of obstinate silver
> the moon is tempered and forged in yellow fire
> it hangs beside a yellow sun and will not go down

From "For Robert Kennedy":

> There are public men
> become large as mountains or the endless forests
> in the love men bear them
> and when they die it is as if a great emptiness
>   became
> solid things turn misty and hard to hold onto
> and the stunned heart clutches at dear
>   remembrance
> retraces its steps back somewhere in the past
> when nothing changed and the high sun hangs
>   motionless
> friends remain fixed there and dogs bite gently
> it is always morning it is always evening
>   it is always noon

From "Quetzal Birds," about the three-and-a-half-foot-long tail of the quetzal:

> Only chiefs might wear those tail feathers
> not dukes duchesses belted earls
>   just Kings
> —in another life on the hot dry plains of Anahuac
> I have seen thousands waiting—the commoners
> Aztec Mixtec Toltec Mayan unemotional
> unquestioning yearning they-know-not-what
> faces like scabbards of swords

It's the conjunction of cliché and sword image here that tickles me.
    End of anthology.

*

The conclusion of even this brief autobio calls for some assessment of the way you've spent your time on earth, which I intend to avoid. However, reasons for writing at all: to make a discovery, of yourself and something outside yourself. Something that will stand up to your own most rigorous scrutiny, which means something—even if it disappears in an evanescent flash. Doors opening in your mind, other doors closing, beyond all distances and barriers on the edge of things.

The Woman on the Shore, my last book of poems, was published in 1990. I hope and expect there will be more poems. But the gift that was once given is now slowly being taken away, although not yet lost to view. Much of my life has been living for the "exaltations," the high moments; as against what Edwin Muir called "the desolations." The feeling of something marching in the blood, near the end of your life—so much like triumph it sounds like an overture.

That blind husky bitch I lifted in and out of the canoe on Baffin Island, I think of that dog now. The feelings in her head at that moment, to allow a complete stranger to hoist her onto land and later back onto trembling water.

The arctic itself provided some high moments for me: landing on an island whose name I didn't know, with a man whose language I couldn't speak—I was scared and exhausted and alive. It's a condition I recommend to all dead men.

Arctic Places

—they are mileposts of old passage
echoes of our hinterlands
plunging name sounds
of things we felt or dreamed or imagined
this farthest earth
summers beyond our lives
with nothing of ourselves wasted
we used what there was
our bones flow onward
blood breaks and stops

BIBLIOGRAPHY

Poetry:

The Enchanted Echo, Clarke & Stuart, 1944.

Pressed on Sand, Ryerson, 1955.

Emu, Remember!, Fiddlehead Poetry Books, 1956.

The Crafte So Long to Lerne, Ryerson, 1959.

The Blur in Between: Poems 1960–61, Emblem Books, 1962.

Poems for All the Annettes, Contact, 1962, enlarged edition, Anansi, 1968, enlarged edition, 1973.

The Cariboo Horses, McClelland & Stewart, 1965.

North of Summer: Poems from Baffin Island, McClelland & Stewart, 1967.

Wild Grape Wine, McClelland & Stewart, 1968.

Love in a Burning Building, McClelland & Stewart, 1970.

The Quest for Ouzo, M. Kerrigan Almey, 1971.

Hiroshima Poems, Crossing, 1972.

Selected Poems, McClelland & Stewart, 1972.

On the Bearpaw Sea, Blackfish, 1973.

Sex and Death, McClelland & Stewart, 1973.

In Search of Owen Roblin, McClelland & Stewart, 1974.

The Poems of Al Purdy: A New Canadian Library Selection, McClelland & Stewart, 1976.

Sundance at Dusk, McClelland & Stewart, 1976.

A Handful of Earth, Black Moss, 1977.

At Marsport Drugstore, Paget, 1977.

Moths in the Iron Curtain, Black Rabbit, 1977.

No Second Spring, Black Moss, 1977.

Being Alive: Poems 1958–78, McClelland & Stewart, 1978.

The Stone Bird, McClelland & Stewart, 1981.

Birdwatching at the Equator: The Galapagos Islands, Paget, 1982.

Bursting into Song: An Al Purdy Omnibus, Black Moss, 1982.

Piling Blood, McClelland & Stewart, 1984.

The Collected Poems of Al Purdy, edited by Russell Brown, McClelland & Stewart, 1986.

The Woman on the Shore, McClelland & Stewart, 1990.

Editor:

The New Romans: Candid Canadian Opinions of the U.S., Hurtig, 1968.

Fifteen Winds: A Selection of Modern Canadian Poems, Ryerson, 1969.

Milton Acorn, *I've Tasted My Blood: Poems of 1956–1968,* Ryerson, 1969.

Storm Warning: The New Canadian Poets, McClelland & Stewart, 1971.

Storm Warning 2: The New Canadian Poets, McClelland & Stewart, 1976.

Wood Mountain Poems, Macmillan (Toronto), 1976.

Other:

No Other Country (prose), McClelland & Stewart, 1977.

(With Charles Bukowski) *The Bukowski/Purdy Letters 1964–1974: A Decade of Dialogue,* edited by Seamus Cooney, Paget, 1983.

Morning and It's Summer: A Memoir, Quadrant Editions, 1983.

The George Woodcock–Al Purdy Letters, edited by George Galt, ECW, 1987.

A Splinter in the Heart (novel), McClelland & Stewart, 1990.

Cougar Hunter (essay about Roderick Haig-Brown), Phoenix Press, 1993.

The Margaret Laurence–Al Purdy Letters, McClelland & Stewart, 1993.

Contributor of radio and television plays to Canadian Broadcasting Corporation, including *A Gathering of Days,* produced by CBC-Radio, 1954; *Point of Transfer,* produced on CBC-TV's "Shoestring Theatre," Montreal, renamed *Just Ask for Sammy,* produced as a stage play at Theatre in the Dell, Toronto; *Poems for Voices,* 1970.

Work represented in anthologies, including *Five Modern Canadian Poets,* edited by Eli Mandel, Holt, 1970; *The Norton Anthology of Modern Poetry,* edited by Richard Ellman and Robert O'Clair, Norton, 1973; *Twentieth Century Poetry and Poetics,* edited by Gary Geddes, Oxford University Press, 1973; *Canadian Poetry: The Modern Era,* edited by John Newlove, McClelland & Stewart, 1977.

Contributor of poems, reviews, articles, and essays to numerous publications, including *Canadian Forum, Canadian Literature, Fiddlehead, Maclean's Magazine,* and *Saturday Night.* Selected poems have been translated in the Russian language.

Nahid Rachlin

MY AUNT—MY MOTHER

Nahid Rachlin, "from the balcony of our apartment in Manhattan," 1991

As I sit in a room in my apartment in Manhattan I see myself clearly coming back from high school in Ahvaz, a town in southern Iran. I am looking for my older sister Pari, so that I can read to her a story I had written during history class, instead of listening to the lecture. "I wrote a story today," I would say as soon as I found her in one of the many rooms in our large, outlandish house. I would sit next to her on the rug and read to her, about the rigidities at school, or some shocking scene I had encountered on the street. (Walking by the lettuce fields one early morning I saw a half-naked woman lying among the bushes, her blouse torn, blood flowing out of her face which was so badly beaten that it was barely recognizable, and then police appearing on the scene.)

Pari always responded not to the story itself but to the anguish that the story expressed. She listened not so much to my story as to me. I remember the intensity of my desire to express my feelings and reactions to what went on around me, and equally matched eagerness to hear her reassuring voice. I was also an avid reader. I would read some of the passages to her and she would say, "You could do that."

She loved movies and the two of us would go to see whatever was shown in the two movie houses in town, mostly American and European movies dubbed into Farsi. She had vague aspirations to one day become an actress. We would stop on the main street at a shop that carried photographs of actors and actresses and she would buy a few—of Jennifer Jones, Gregory Peck—to add to an album she kept. If I close my eyes I can still vividly see her standing on the stage of our high school's auditorium (a school for girls only—a similar high school for boys stood in another part of the town), wearing striped pajamas, a mustache, and dancing and singing along with other girls dressed similarly, doing an imitation of an American musical. I would watch her and dream about writing something myself that one day would be put on a stage, with her acting in it.

I can hear my father's voice saying to her scornfully, "Don't you have any sense? An actress is a whore." (About my writing he would say, more respectfully, "You're just a dreamer.") In those days I wrote about my immediate experiences; now, as an adult, I find myself mostly writing obsessively about the faraway past, people, cities I knew growing up. It is as if that period of struggle has much more meaning for me than what is

occurring at the present. How could my stable, predictable married life (I have been married to the same man for thirty years and we have one daughter who is now a lawyer and has a clear vision of her own goals) compete with the turmoil of those days? Though I have been writing various versions of the same events, so many times, I still have not managed to diminish the feelings raging behind them. . . .

When I was nine months old my grandmother took me away from my mother, who already had six children before me (two had died), to be raised by my aunt, my mother's older sister. My aunt had been unable to have children herself even though she had been trying for years. My mother had promised her, before I was born, that the next child would go to her. This was in response to my aunt repeatedly begging my mother to let her raise one of her children. "God has enabled you to have so many of them, so easily," she had kept saying to my mother. So early one morning my grandmother bundled me up, and carrying a bottle of my

"Mother and father, oldest brother, Pari, Manijeh, and younger brother," in Abadan

mother's milk with us she took the ferry from Abadan (where my father was a judge) and then the old sooty train to my aunt's house in Teheran. My aunt had been married to a man twice her age who had died not long before I was taken to her.

My grandmother described to me so many times how she took me to my aunt that it is like my own memory. "As I was about to leave, your mother was upset, hesitant. I just grabbed you out of her arms and practically ran away." (In an old, faded photograph my mother is holding me, an infant then, on her lap. She is wearing a long, surprisingly fashionable dress, her hair is cut to the nape of her neck; I am wrapped in a thin, lacy blanket and have a cotton hat on my head. She is looking at my face while my eyes are focused on the camera. I am waving my clenched hands in the air—my face, posture reflecting, what is it, fright?)

The train ride to Teheran was long and bumpy and I cried a great deal. After the milk from my mother's breast ran out, my grandmother bought milk for me at the little stations where we stopped at various intervals. Other families in the compartment asked her questions about me, were amazed at the task she had taken on herself. I would stop crying for periods of time and gaze at the faces of the other women with curiosity—who were they, where was I going? The women tried to help my grandmother, holding me so that she could sleep a little. We arrived at my aunt's house at dawn. She was sitting outside the door of her house at the end of a narrow lane, her *chador* wrapped around her, waiting for us. It was a mild spring day with a mellow breeze blowing through the sycamore trees lining the lane. "Here, I brought you the baby," my grandmother said, putting me in my aunt's arms. My aunt began to cry as she held me tightly. "Oh, I'm so happy, God has finally fulfilled my wishes," she said over and over.

She had a wooden cradle set up for me in a large room, where she slept herself. Before putting me to bed she gave me a bottle of milk she had warmed up for me. I stared at her but did not protest. "I held you to myself so tightly, loved you so much, that you didn't miss your mother," my aunt told me when I was older. "Do you know how much you've added to my life?" My grandmother left a few days later to go back to Ahvaz to help my mother with her other children.

My aunt lived in a house connected to two other houses, all of which she had inherited from her husband. She rented the row of rooms on the other side of the courtyard of the house she lived in to two widowed women and the other two houses to families with children. For days neighbors and relatives dropped in to my aunt's house to bring baby presents, to congratulate her.

The other two women living in my aunt's house—soft-spoken, gentle women—helped my aunt to take care of me. They watched me grow, shared impressions of me, talked about every one of my movements and gestures, childhood pains and illnesses. When I was sleepless because of a tooth coming out, when I had gotten fever and kept talking all night deliriously, my aunt lay on a mattress next to my crib, getting up periodically to check on me. I would open my eyes and, in the dim glimmer of an oil lamp set on the mantel, could see her bending over me, her eyes rivetted on my face, concerned.

She took me everywhere with her, to the public baths, to the market to shop, to visit a neighbor. On hot summer nights we slept on the roof under mosquito nettings and she told me stories about the stars, the moon, old kings, and mythical figures. We ate breakfast in the courtyard, where a breeze blew through the pomegranate and plum trees, and rose bushes gave out a steady fragrance. She would heat milk for me the way I liked it and serve me my favorite bread, thick with sesame seeds on it. She was indulgent with me. I went to bed when I wanted, threw my toys around, roamed through the courtyards freely. She took me to the pastry store on Ghanat Abad Avenue running perpendicular to the alley and let me choose what I wanted, took me to the little bazaar at the end of the alley and bought a piece of jewelry for me, to the tailor to have a dress made for me. I had many rag dolls which I had arranged against a wall in my room. On the mantel I had put brightly painted clay animals and marbles. I had covered one wall with collages I made from cuttings in a magazine I bought on the newsstand as soon as it came out. The house we lived in was the biggest of the three with four flower beds, a large, shallow pool at its center. A porch extended from the rooms my aunt and I shared and protruded into the courtyard. There were columns on the porch with friezes at the top, with the same animal and floral patterns on them that decorated the fireplace in the living room. I particularly remember stained glass on several of the windows of the living room, all the colorful light cast on everything.

In the spring the fruit trees were filled with flocks of birds that whistled and sang continuously, flew out of the branches together. Butterflies flitted around the four red and pink rose bushes and fish always tumbled in the pool. I sat on the porch, completely immersed in all that joyous activity. Sometimes vendors would shout in the street, "Come and buy the best and sweetest white strawberries anywhere," and, "I have the most fragrant pears and reddest pomegranates." If my aunt was busy washing dishes or sweeping the ground, she would send me to the door to buy some. The vendor would lower the wooden tray from his head for me to choose the fruit.

Still I would ask my aunt over and over, "Do you love me, do you want me here?"

"Of course I do. What would I do without you?"

Once a year, my mother came to Teheran to visit her relatives, all my uncles and aunts, and stayed with us part of the time. She usually left her children with my grandmother. Sometimes she held me on her lap, kissed me, but there was no particular bond between us. I called my aunt Mother and my own mother Aunt Mohtaram or nothing at all. On one visit my mother brought my sisters Manijeh and Pari with her. Pari took a special interest in me. "Oh, look at those large alert eyes," she said. She picked a rose and put it in my hair. "You ought to come and live with us. Do you want to?" she asked. "No," I said. Another time my mother came with the whole family, including my brothers and father. My father and brothers, though, did not stay with my aunt. After a brief visit they left to stay with my father's bachelor brother. That was the extent to which I saw my own family. My mother always cried as she was about to leave. "You're so lucky to be together like this," she would say to the aunts and uncles. "I feel like an exile."

"We'll come and visit," they promised, though they rarely ever did. The trip to Ahvaz (where my parents had moved for my father to set up a private practice as a lawyer) was long and arduous and, the truth was, they all agreed, it made more sense for my mother to visit—when she came to Teheran she saw everybody at once. The fact that she was my biological mother did not have much relevance for me, did not register anything significant.

Once I asked one of my cousins, "Which one of your aunts do you love the most?"

"Aunt Mohtaram," she said, naming my mother.

"Not Aunt Maryam?" I asked, astounded, hurt.

"Myself in Iran (Teheran) on a recent visit in my aunt's neighborhood (the scarf is required by law now)"

"No, Aunt Mohtaram has all those children."

"But Aunt Maryam is prettier," I said, trying to find something to say in her favor. "That beautiful wavy hair."

My cousin shrugged casually, not aware of my feelings.

My other two aunts and my two uncles lived nearby and their children came over all the time and the pack of us would carry on, playing loud games, going on a spree through the neighborhood, telling horror stories to each other. Aroused by the stories, we would begin to run, holding hands for protection, through the back, narrow, cobble-stoned streets, lined with ancient houses in different conditions, some half-dilapidated. We would come out into the small bazaar, where each store carried a different kind of merchandise, from dairy to produce to clothing and jewelry, pause by our uncle's shop (the one married to our oldest aunt) and be served ice cream by him, then enter Ghanat Abad, a wide avenue full of banks, carpet shops, stationery stores, more expensive jewelry stores and then go home through another set of streets. It was as if the group of us were enchanted by something beyond our understanding. After supper we slept on mattresses spread on the floor or inside mosquito nettings and talked late into the night.

In the month of Ramadan my aunts and uncles and their children all living nearby spent a lot of time in Aunt Maryam's house for the adults to fast together. I would wake at midnight to the bustle of their activities, cooking food in large pots on gas stoves in the courtyard for them to break their fasts. One by one we children would wander into the courtyard. Karim, a male cousin who was my own age, and I would go into the room adjacent to mine opening into the entrance hallway and walk out quietly into the street, lit now by moonlight and stars, the water in the *joob* running more clear and without obstructions. Through the half-open doors of other houses we would see flames of food being cooked and hear the hum of conversation. Ghanat Abad Avenue at this hour had a different feel to it, with no cars going by and the storefronts shut. The ancient caravansary and mosque standing next to each other in the middle of the avenue, glowing with dim lights inside, had a mysterious aura at that hour. Then we would walk back and slip into the house, into the room, triumphant that our absence had not been noticed.

I was seven years old when Rahbar appeared in my aunt's life. I remember vividly the first time I met him. One afternoon, coming home from school, I found a man with her in the living room. She was wearing her *chador* and sitting on a chair, something she rarely ever did, and he was sitting on another chair across from her, drinking tea.

She blushed when I came into the room. Then she introduced us to each other. He seemed to be about my aunt's age, thirty-five or so. He was wearing a blue suit and a red bow tie. He had ruddy skin, light brown hair neatly combed and parted, and large blue eyes, very unusual. I smiled and then went into the adjacent room.

In a few moments I heard him saying good-bye. Then my aunt came over to me and said, softly, shyly, "He was sent here by a matchmaker. Why would someone like him want me?"

Clear changes came over her. She became more conscious of her appearance. She started wearing well-fitting dresses in bright prints. She splashed rosewater on herself. Her hips swung as she walked and her black wavy hair swayed over the fabric of her clothes. She made improvements in the house too. She restored the chipping friezes of animals and fruit on the porch columns and above the fireplace, put blue tiles on the bathroom floor, replacing the old brown ones. She filled the flower beds around the pool with bright asters, morning glory vines, black-eyed susans.

Within three months she was married to Rahbar. It was a quiet wedding, amounting to an *aghound* coming over and performing the ceremony in the living room. Only her two sisters and brothers and some of us children were present at the ceremony.

I liked Rahbar. He worked in an import-export company and brought me unusual presents, an onyx box he said he had bought in one of his travels in which I could keep my pens and pencils, a music box with a dancing girl coming out of it when opened. He took me to the rose garden at the edge of Teheran. Another time we climbed the hills in Shemiran together. It was a hot, dusty walk but when we got on the top of the hills we had the view of a huge expanse of the city. We stood there until stars came out one by one and lights went on in houses underneath. He told me about his own growing up with his mother and three sisters in Mashad, about all his travelling. He had worked for a while on a ship going from the Caspian Sea to many other countries. He made everything he had done sound adventurous and exciting. I had a feeling that evening that he could see right through my thoughts as if they were transparent, an odd sensation that there were no barriers between us. He asked me to call him Rahbar rather than Uncle.

He had his bad moods when he became withdrawn, looking lonely, as if he were totally on his own, not blending in with anything or anyone around him, even my aunt or myself. He mumbled when my aunt asked him questions and seemed intolerant of my presence. My aunt would say to me then, "It's time for you to go to bed now, you have school in the morning."

Then for several nights Rahbar did not come home. Every night my aunt stayed up late waiting for him. She would sweep the floors, dust everything, bake bread to pass time, her face looking cloudy and preoccupied. Loneliness emanated from her even when I was by her side. When he returned he said an old friend of his was in a fatal car accident and he had gone there to help. A few weeks later he stayed away again and when he returned he said he had been sent out of town by his company to meet a customer. Looking downward he said, "I don't know if I'm going to last at the company. They don't like my ideas." A strange grimace hovered on his face.

His bad moods took over more frequently and I was no longer at ease in his company.

"He isn't going to stay with me much longer," my aunt told me. "I know it."

He continued with that pattern of disappearing and then returning. Once he came home late at night with a young boy and they stayed in a room together. He said the boy was a nephew visiting him from his village. The same thing happened again on another night. I saw my aunt standing outside of the door behind which Rahbar and his companion had vanished. I joined her and held her hand. It was shaking with a faint tremor.

The next day I heard her whispering to my other aunts, "He likes boys."

"You must get a divorce from him," my older aunt said.

"Yes, it's a sin for you to live with him," my younger aunt said. "And neighbors are going to begin to talk."

Tears streamed from my aunt's eyes. "I can't just divorce him."

She kept pushing aside the idea. She always looked despondent now. And Rahbar's coming and going became even more erratic, with him spending many more nights away.

Then my own life changed suddenly. I remember that day vividly. It was an autumn day with a pale, cool sunlight shining on everything. I was playing with a friend in the yard of our elementary school when I saw a man standing on the steps of a hallway, looking for someone. I recognized my own father, a thin, short man, with a pockmarked face and a brush mustache but giving the impression somehow of being strong, powerful. My heart gave a lurch. What was he doing there?

"Let's go home," he said as he approached me.

I looked at him for an explanation. He was so alien, I hardly knew him.

He picked me up and held me against him. "I'll tell you on the way." He kissed me and then put me down.

I said good-bye to my friend and followed my father outside.

"I have already spoken to your teachers, you aren't coming back here anymore."

"What?"

He held my hand in his and said, "I'm taking you back to live with us. You're reaching an age that you need me to look after you. Your aunt's house isn't right for you anymore."

I did not reply. A knot had formed in my throat, preventing me from speaking. I was on the verge of crying. But it was not until I saw my aunt, her *chador* wrapped around her, her face wet with tears, that the reality of what was happening hit me full force.

She went to the adjacent room to get my suitcase and I followed her. I clung to her, "I don't want to go," I said.

"I don't want you to go," she whispered to me, "But what can I do if your father insists on taking you back?" I could see, from her tears and the hunched way she stood, that she was feeling helpless. Her soft, fleshy body seemed without strength. I suddenly understood the meaning of her actions in the last few days. She had become exceptionally attentive to me, taking me to the bazaar to buy a new pair of earrings for me, in general always hovering around me and touching me a lot. Once she said, "You know how much I care for you, don't you? You mean much more to me than Rahbar. If he leaves one day, I'll manage to survive it, but you . . ." She pulled me to herself and kissed me hard on my forehead, cheeks.

"Why didn't you tell me?" I said through constricted throat.

"I was still hoping he wouldn't come, that my prayers would be answered. How else could I stop him?" she whispered. (What she was telling me was true, she had no legal right to me. But I have often wondered if she had not been so afraid of men or so passive, whether she would have been able to persuade my father to let her keep me.)

"We have to go," my father called to us. "The plane will be leaving in less than two hours."

As we were leaving he said, "Your aunt will visit you all the time." He turned to her. "Won't you?"

She nodded.

"I haven't said good-bye to anyone," I said, a wave of pain shaking me.

"You can write to them," my father commanded.

My aunt saw us to the door and stood there in the alley until we disappeared into Ghanat Abad Avenue—I took a glance at her then, before we turned.

It was all so quick—we took a taxi to the airport and then were on the plane. On the plane my father told me again, "At your age you need me to look after you."

I lay my head back.

Was this really happening? The stewardess brought trays of food and put them in front of us. I picked up a fork and played with the pieces of rice and stew on my plate, taking bites reluctantly. Nausea rose from my stomach in waves. I mustn't get sick, I said to myself. "I have to go to the bathroom," I told my father timidly.

"Go ahead."

A stewardess standing near us came over to me. "The toilet is in the back," she said, smiling at my father. He smiled at her in a flirtatious way.

I tried to hold it until I got to the toilet but my stomach tightened sharply and I began to throw up in the aisle.

"Look what you did," my father said, taking out a bag and handing it to me. "Do it in this." Then he began to caress my back. "Poor child, you're upset, I understand. It will be fine when we get home, your own real home. Your mother, sisters, and brothers are all waiting for you."

I held the bag in front of me and walked with it to the bathroom. I threw up more in the toilet. Then I washed my face, aware of intense shame.

When I got back the stewardess had cleaned up the aisle. "How do you feel?" she asked me. "Better?" She had an angular face with sharp, small features. I looked at her and nodded with hatred as if she had been the cause of my nausea.

After that I fell asleep and when I woke we were in the airport in Ahvaz. I was transported from my home with my aunt within a few hours, with no previous warning.

I was groggy and disoriented as we got out of the airport and then rode in a taxi to my parents' house. Fine brown dust covered everything, the leaves, the top of the horsecarts, the ground. We went through several wide, crowded, noisy streets and squares and then the taxi came to a stop in front of a two-story house. The house had a brown-ash color like everything else in the town. A long, narrow balcony surrounded the house. A group of boys had drawn rectangular shapes on the asphalt of the sidewalk and were playing hopscotch. I had an urge to run away. My father took my hand and led me into the house. "You'll like it here," he said.

We went into a hallway and then entered an arid-looking courtyard. My mother was sitting at the edge of the round pool, talking to the servant,

"Oldest brother, Pari, younger brother, myself (far left), mother, father, and Manijeh," in Ahvaz

Ali, a small, shrunken man, his eyes red, almost without lashes.

"Here, I brought her back," my father said in a bouncy tone.

"I see," my mother said with a vague, dreamy smile. She got up and came over to me. She embraced and kissed me in a tentative, hesitant way (I missed my aunt's strong arms around me). Then she stepped back. She was wearing red lipstick and her hair was set in a permanent. I missed my aunt's face free from makeup, her long, naturally wavy hair.

"That dress you're wearing is too big on you, and it has too much orange in it," my mother said. "I'll have to get you some new clothes."

"I picked it out myself," I said, shyly. My aunt and I had bought it in the bazaar. My mother turned to Ali. "Is her room ready?"

"Yes, it's all ready. I spent the whole day on it." Then he came over and kissed my hand. I blushed but I felt a warmth toward him that I could not for my parents.

I remained in my spot, waiting for something to happen. Someone was coming down the steep stairway from the second floor.

"Come with me, I'll take you to your room." It was my sister Pari. On the few occasions I had met my family I had always felt the most connected to Pari though there was a five-year gap between us.

"Go ahead," my father said to me.

"Your room is next to mine, I asked them to put you in that one. I'll show you the whole house," Pari said.

I followed her through the house in a daze. Many of the doors had holes, eaten by termites, and the windows were covered with dust. Grasshoppers and pigeons rested on the railway of the balcony. The house had more than a dozen rooms, set on two floors. All the children had their rooms upstairs, but there was nothing about the rooms to indicate that they belonged to children or teenagers—no toys, no posters on the walls, no color in the furniture. It was as if we were not allowed to be young, indulge in whimsical or frivolous activities or tastes.

"Mother is absorbed in too many things," she said, attempting to comfort me against my mother's cool greeting. Then we sat in her room and she told me about the movie house across the street we could go to, the park we could walk around in, and the schools we would be going to. (School started a month later in Ahvaz than in Teheran because of the heat, so I had not missed any of it.) From her intense focus on me, it seemed she had been lonely in the middle of her own family.

I ate with my mother and two sisters that night, while my father and brothers stayed out late. My older brother was already working in an oil refinery company and waiting for his papers so that he could go to the United States to study engineering. My younger brother was finishing up high school and also planned to go to the United States. After supper, my mother just said, "You know where your room is," and then she vanished somewhere in the house.

I lay in bed listening to the sounds from the outside, cars going by, stray dogs barking, someone whistling a tune. I missed my aunt. So many evenings I had sat by her and watched her work, black strands of her hair hanging over her forehead. I missed Karim—doing homework together, having lunch together, walking together, and that spark between us that kept flaring up and subsiding—and my other cousins and aunts and friends,

as if I had been away from them for a long time. I missed the three houses, the mourning doves cooing softly in the afternoon in the courtyards, the alley cat mewing by the pool as it stared at the fish. I missed the streets, my school, the objects belonging to my aunt—the red velveteen trunk she kept her good clothes in, the black and white cloth she spread on the floor to pray on, her white *chador* with green leaves scattered on it, smelling of rosewater. The picture of my room in my aunt's house stood in front of my eyes—a sunny, corner room with gauzy curtains on its windows blowing with a breeze. Everything was so bright and shiny there from this distance. I could almost see my aunt coming to the porch and saying, "How about some lunch now?" Tears began to seep out of my eyes. I got out of the bed and, from my suitcase which I had not completely unpacked yet, took out the green scarf with gold leaf designs on it that my aunt had brought back for me from a trip to Qom. I carried it to bed with me. I kept rubbing my face against it. I could smell the rosewater my aunt had dabbed on it . . .

I woke at dawn, disoriented, not knowing for a moment where I was. Then I remembered. I got out of the bed and looked out of the window at the busy Pahlavi Avenue. The shops were just opening and horse carriages and taxis transported people to their destinations. Rows of women were carrying milk in large pots on their heads. Stalls selling cooked beets and milk products were already busy with customers. But there seemed to be a slow motion to everything. The air was already hot and damp, very different from the cool, crisp, autumn mornings in Teheran, and it smelled of oil from the oil fields. The sights and sounds were so different from what I was used to in my aunt's house, neighborhood. Loneliness hit me again so intensely that I thought I would faint. Then there was a knock on the door and my sister Pari walked in. It was always she who came to my aid.

After breakfast my mother handed me a gray uniform with a white collar on it and said, "Here wear this for now until we get you your own. It's Manijeh's from last year."

I tried it on. It fit well enough but I was aware of a rebellion inside me. "I don't want to wear this."

"You have to, it's the schools' rule here in Ahvaz." Then she walked away, clearly not wanting any arguments.

My father took me to school. I walked with him through the streets, this time smaller back streets. The river, mud-colored, with rowboats gliding on it, was visible in the distance.

"Don't be upset with your mother, she works so hard, sacrifices so much for all of you," my father said suddenly. "It's hard enough to have carried each one of you for nine months in her womb and then the difficult labor, and the responsibilities following. She had a very difficult pregnancy with you. You kicked hard, she had sickness all day long. She was in labor for more than twenty-four hours. When you were finally born you sucked at her breasts so hard they almost bled. But then there was that promise. Your grandmother insisted it should be carried out. I was never happy with it; neither was your mother really. I want you to start calling her Mother. She is your real mother, she always has been."

We were practically at the school when he said, "One day you'll be able to understand all this." He patted my arm. "I couldn't bear anymore to hear about how you were being raised in that household. I had to take you back."

I was silent, with a strange feeling of shame.

"There was no one to be a father to you. That man Rahbar sounds very shifty." I was shocked that he had kept track of what was going on in my aunt's household. "Anyway the whole neighborhood where she lives breeds ignorance."

We were approaching the school. Other young girls in gray uniforms swarmed through the street, some walking, some dropped off by cars. They greeted each other and went in bouncily, heedlessly. I was full of dread.

We went through the cement-covered courtyard of the school toward the principal's office. "I have given them large donations, they should be nice to you," my father told me.

He knocked on the office door and we went in. The principal, a tall, hefty woman with her hair tied in a knot at the back of her head, greeted my father and then turned to me. "This is your daughter, how nice."

"Yes." Then as if I were not there, he said, "She's a little shy right now, but she'll do fine."

"I'm sure she will. I'll see to it myself."

"I'm leaving her to you then," my father said and started to leave the office. By the door he asked me, "You know the way back now, don't you?"

I nodded.

"Follow me," the principal said, after my father was out of the door.

I followed her to the classrooms on the other side of the courtyard. "This is the fourth grade," she said, pointing to a room with a cluster of girls standing by it.

"I want you to show her around, our new student, Nahid, make her welcome," the principal told the students who were now staring at me.

"We sure will," one of them said. A soon as the principal left they went back talking among themselves, ignoring me.

A man walked over to the large bell hanging from the ceiling of the porch and banged it with a brass pole a few times. Students began to line up in front of classes. I joined the line in front of the fourth grade. The bell rang again and everyone began to sing the national anthem. "Iran, oh, land full of jewels." After we finished singing that, we were inspected by a truant officer, a middle-aged woman with a saturnine, bitter face, to make sure our nails were not too long and our uniforms were properly buttoned up and had our white collars on them. I stood there stiffly, giving in to the inspection. Then we all went inside. I was among the shortest in the class and I sat close to the front, staring at the board. A young, stern-looking man, the teacher, walked in and after calling everyone's names and checking them off in a notebook he began to write some numbers on the blackboard. The numbers, everything, swam before my eyes. Why did this have to happen to me, given away and then taken back? It isn't fair, I thought, in utter misery.

At the lunch recess I immediately left the school. As soon as I got outside I saw Pari standing by the steps. "Oh, here you are," she said. "I thought I would walk you home." Her presence made me feel a little lighter.

"Let's go to the ice-cream parlor," she said.

We stopped in a park and sat in a cafe under trees and ordered ice cream. Scrawny, dusty palm trees with dates hanging on them in clusters and wilted-looking flowers filled the park. We talked again like we had the day before.

The first time my aunt visited after a year of separation, I skipped school all day to be with her. She had come with my grandmother, who was now living with her at her house. She had finally gotten a divorce from Rahbar to which he had readily conceded. I stayed close to my aunt, basking in the warmth of her presence. I could see clearly how upset she was. She would sit in dark corners, her hands clenched on her lap, her head lowered, and would say, "My life has no meaning." I would say, "Take me back with you." "How can I?" At night we slept in the same room and I would keep her up

Pari, as a teenager

and ask her question after question, or ask her to tell me stories like she used to do. Legends, fairy tales, and the true stories of our neighbor's lives were all told to me by my aunt in the same slow, formal way with beginnings—climaxes and morals at the end. And all were equally rivetting, equally believable.

So I had to adjust to a new set of parents with very different values from my aunt's. My parents, having lived in Ahvaz and Abadan, cities filled with foreigners employed by the oil refineries, were in some ways Westernized, did not practice any religion, whereas my aunt was old-fashioned and staunchly religious. I had to learn to live with siblings, all the rivalry. I can see us sitting at the dining table in the kitchen. It is eight o'clock in the morning but harsh sunlight is streaming into the dining room as we sit around the long wooden table to eat breakfast. I sit between Manijeh and Pari, my mother and father at the two ends of the table, my two brothers on each side of my father. I am feeling vulnerable, cut off, neglected. My

mother has not looked at me or addressed me once since we sat down. Everyone is eating quickly, ravenously. Ali comes in and refills our cups with more tea.

My mother's face lights up as she turns to Manijeh. "How did you end up looking like an angel? How did you get those beautiful hazel-green eyes, those waves in your hair?" Manijeh smiles and rubs her head against my mother's arm.

Pari's loneliness mingles with my own. I stare at her, assessing her looks. She is very pretty, though in a different way from Manijeh. She is robust with distinctive though not quite so delicate and well-proportioned features as Manijeh's. Where do I stand compared to them, I wonder?

My mother adds more food to Manijeh's plate. "You need to eat more." Then addressing no one in particular, as if to excuse the extra attention she is paying to this one child, she says, "She's weak, she needs more nourishment."

"Mohtaram, I'm full," Manijeh says. She is the only one among us sisters and brothers who calls our mother by her name.

"Eat just a little more," my mother says to her.

My father gets up and pulls the shades over the windows to cut out the light pouring in mercilessly, making the ceiling fan going around slowly seem lame, useless. When he sits down again he looks very serious as if about to give a lecture. At any rate a hush falls over the table. There is something forbidding about his aura—from his expression you never know what he is about to say or do. The fear that has silenced everyone, that clutches at me, passes as he says, "We have to change a lot of things in this house after we're finished with all you children's expenses, after you're all settled down in your own lives."

"Some families don't care about their children's futures as your father and I do," my mother says.

After we finish eating, my father rises. "I have to get ready, I had to schedule a client early."

The early morning havoc follows—with all the children flitting around the house, looking for something or the other, a misplaced shoe, an iron to press the collar of a school uniform. My mother tends singularly to Manijeh—"Here take this orange with you" or "Let me braid your hair for you today." After I get into my gray school uniform, I stand by the old mirror hanging on the wall of my room and examine my face. Would I look better if I had a different hairstyle, shorter to the nape of my neck? I press one finger into my cheek and remove it quickly to see the dimple formed. I wish I had dimples. I wish my breasts would begin to grow like Pari and Manijeh's. Manijeh is only two years older and her breasts are already full.

My mother was always trying to indoctrinate everyone to see how wonderful Manijeh was. I once heard her say to a friend of hers while they were having tea, "My Manijeh is so sweet to me, none of my other children are like her." The woman said, "She's like an angel, in looks and personality." And how many times had I seen my mother give in to her whims at the expense of Pari and me? For instance, close to the time we were leaving to go and see a movie together, Manijeh said, "I'm not feeling good, I don't want to go." Pari suggested, "Well you rest, we'll go." But my mother said, "Let's wait and go tomorrow night, when she's feeling better." Pari complained to me, "Is she a princess?"

My mother scolded Ali if he did not answer to Manijeh's requests quickly. If Pari and I spent a long time in her room, my mother would knock on

Manijeh, teen years

the door, "Why can't you include your other sister? What do you have against her?" Then she would push open the door and prod Manijeh, who clung to her, to come in. We would fall into a hushed silence in Manijeh's presence, excluding her further. (Awareness of our cruelty to Manijeh eluded us at the time).

One afternoon I came home and found Pari sitting in her room, dressed up in a silk blue dress and gold jewelry.

"Are you going somewhere?" I asked.

"A suitor is here with his mother. They are in the living room with Mom and Dad. Do you want to see what he looks like?"

I nodded. The two of us walked softly, slowly, to the living room.

"Look in through the keyhole," Pari whispered.

I leaned over and put my eyes to the hole. Our parents were sitting with a man and a woman on the maroon, velvet-covered sofa and the two matching armchairs and having tea. The suitor was thin and tall and had a desiccated, humorless face. He was only a few years younger than our father, it seemed. I pulled back, then Pari looked through the hole.

We walked back to Pari's room. She giggled. "Did you see his ears? They were sticking out."

In a moment our father came to the door of the room. "Come in now. His mother wants to talk to you." Then he left the doorway.

Pari got up in a reluctant way and followed him.

An hour or so later from my room I heard an argument going on from the porch. The suitor and his mother must have left.

"I don't want to marry him," Pari was saying. "He's old and ugly."

"Have some sense. He has a very good income and he's well educated and kind," my mother said.

"When you have your own children you'll be happy to have a husband who can provide well for them," my father said.

I heard my younger brother's voice. "She could go to the university."

"Give up a good prospect like him?" my mother said.

"Anyway when has she ever showed interest in school?" my father said.

"He's willing to give a huge *mehrieh*," my mother said. "You can't throw that away."

"You're trying to sell me."

"Pari, don't talk nonsense."

Gradually their voices subsided and the argument seemed to dissolve with no resolution.

Later that day Pari complained to me, "They want to marry me off at the end of the year."

I remember thinking then: how much lonelier it is going to be for me here when Pari gets married and leaves the house.

Not long after that she got married to the man. A few months before the wedding, my parents started to get things ready. My mother and Pari prepared a dowry and searched for a wedding dress. The groom's parents came over several times to bring jewelry for Pari and talk about the practical matters of the wedding. Ali dried up vegetables, crushed pods to make spices. Invitation cards were made. The day before the wedding Ali and two other women hired for the occasion started cooking stews, rice, cakes, cookies, and other food. They hung lanterns in the tree branches, set up chairs and tables in the salon and the large terrace extending out from it. On the day of the wedding platters of fruit, nuts, *sharbat* were set on the tables. My mother took Pari to a beauty parlor to have her hair set.

Many people were invited to the wedding. Even the elementary school principal came. Musicians and a belly dancer performed all evening, late into the night. I fell asleep on the couch at some point and when I woke the next day Pari was already gone with her husband to his family's house, where they would live for a year before setting up their own household.

Nahid, high school years

By the time I was in the middle of my high school years I began to focus entirely on studying and reading whatever I could get hold of, mainly novels and short stories through which I could find myself in other worlds, other people's lives, connect to emotions expressed in a person. I consumed any dark, pessimistic books I could find in the Setareh Bookshop. One called *Claws* was about a brother and sister who were caught in such a narrow world that they end up in a double suicide-murder pact. Another, *The Abyss,* was about a young girl trying to escape the confinement of her village and then ending up as a prostitute. I also read translations of whatever books I could find—novels and short-story collections by American and European writers—Hemingway, Dostoyevsky, Balzac. I read books, wrote sketches and stories, and dreamt of escape. My father, although not as mocking of my writing as he was of my sister's aspirations to act, was suspicious and afraid of what the written word could do. He occasionally would eavesdrop on me as I sat at my desk writing or reading. He took away from me a novel by Maxim Gorky called *The Mother* and tore it into pieces. "Where did you get that communistic filth? I could lose my license if my daughter were caught reading a book like that." In fact I had bought it from a bookstore which occasionally would smuggle a book in against censorship. Communism was considered the enemy of the country at the time. One female teacher in my high school who I admired was arrested on the charge that she was spreading "communistic" ideas in the school, the word also being catchall for anything even remotely progressive or liberal.

I made one close friend at school. We stood separate from the more carefree, lighthearted girls who laughed freely, who wore makeup and pretended it was their natural coloring, who cheated on tests. The two of us would walk around the school yard, wearing our gray uniforms, fear of the teachers in our hearts, and talk obsessively about our plans for escape from the narrow confinement of that town, the life prescribed for us: graduating from high school, marrying someone selected by our parents, having a lot of children.

"I want to become a writer," I said.

"I want to become a ballet dancer," she said.

Once a famous Iranian writer, whose fiction she and I read avidly, was coming to town and I found out, to my excited amazement, that he would be visiting my father one afternoon to discuss a legal matter. My father, after looking through some of his books, promised to let me and Nazan meet him. Nazan and I started to plan for his visit. We each bought a new dress to wear and a copy of his latest novel to ask him to autograph. The novel was about a young girl going to college in France, falling in love with her professor, a man much older than herself, who treats her as if she were a child, not taking her attraction to him seriously. I read the book twice, and some of the passages several times. How could he make these characters so real? When the afternoon finally arrived, Nazan and I waited in my room for my father to call us in. As we entered the room where the writer was sitting, I felt as if I were going into a magnetic field. We sat across from him and he asked us questions about ourselves, smiling at us in a patronizing way, like the professor's attitude toward the young girl in the novel. Then we gave him the books to autograph. As soon as we left the room, Nazan and I opened the books to see what he had written for each of us. (I have no memory of what he actually wrote but recently I wove a story around it, how his two autographs, one more complimentary than the other, break up the friendship between the two girls. I called it "A Poet's Visit," and it became the first story I published in a commercial magazine.)

Not long after that visit I kept asking my mother and father to let me join my brothers in the United States. To break their resistance I wrote my brothers, asking them for help. It was a long battle but my parents finally gave in to it. My father came into my room and said, "I'm letting you go because I see how hard you work at school. You're my only daughter who likes to read. And I see all the friction between you and your mother. It makes me sad."

I think my mother also wanted me apart from Manijeh who was doing worse and worse at school, practically flunking. Once she frightened me by telling me in a threatening tone, "You are doing better at school than Manijeh, and she's older than you." What did she expect me to do?

It was also made easier since my brothers managed to get a generous scholarship for me, paying tuition and room and board, at a small, Southern women's college.

Pari, now settled in her marriage, pregnant and unhappy, said to me, "I wish I had had your determination to study harder, try to go abroad. This is no life. This is prison." (Several years later she managed to get a divorce at a high price: giving up her son—the custody of the child automatically went to the husband even when, as in my sister's case, the grounds for divorce were his cruelty to her—"He put a lit cigarette to my skin," she told me.)

The closeness Pari and I had, sustained itself throughout the years I was at my parents' house, lasted during my early years in college in the United States; at that time she had remarried. She married the second husband, she confided to me, mainly to get out of the grip of my parents who never stopped blaming her for the divorce—my father had screamed at her almost daily, "You're ruining your own life and bringing disgrace to your family," and my mother repeatedly scolded her for being "foolish" and "impractical" to give up all that wealth. (To get a divorce she also had to give up all claim to her husband's money.) Our closeness was ruptured by a tragedy that remains painfully in the background of my life: her beginning to have manic-depressive episodes, making communication with her nearly impossible at times. The illness led to a second divorce and has landed her in a mental hospital in Teheran, where she will probably spend at least part of every year, maybe for the rest of her life. In the last conversation I had with her, long distance from New York to Teheran, when she was in a period of relative calm and lucidity, she asked me, "Are you still writing? Will you send me the last thing you wrote?"

In college I withdrew for periods of time every day and wrote. Occasionally I would mail a piece to Pari and wait eagerly for her response. But I did not think I would make writing my profession. I was eager to be independent and refused to plunge into an occupation that entails no guarantees of publication or financial support. So I studied psychology. I met my American husband right after college (now he teaches psychology at a university). Only when home with a baby was I able to justify spending some time every day writing fiction.

I began to take writing courses. In one taught by Richard Humphreys in Columbia University's general studies, I wrote three one-page sketches which became my first publication in a small literary magazine. One was a story I heard from my aunt about a woman who abandoned her blind child in the desert because she was afraid a man she had met would not marry her otherwise; another was about Ali, the live-in servant at my parents' house, an illiterate man from the villages who asked me daily to read over and over again from an adventure book he had; the third one was about an insane woman tied by her family to a porch railing in their house—I had seen her myself from the roof of my aunt's house.

My first visit home after twelve years of absence, the feelings brought out in me, in addition to my psychological search for a mother, was the inspiration for my first published novel, *Foreigner*, which I wrote on a Stegner Fellowship at Stanford University. The crumbling marriage of my second sister (Manijeh's life did not turn out to be easy. She never went to college and like Pari she married twice, the first one ending in a stormy divorce), combined with my own adolescent dreams, constituted the core of my second novel, *Married to a Stranger*.

There is another reason I am drawn to writing about my past: it has to do with a desire to bring into the present a reality which is no longer represented in my present life. The differences between the Iranian and American cultures are so vast that in order for me to have adjusted to the American way of life I have had to, without always

With husband, Howard, and daughter, Leila, in Boston, 1968

being conscious of it, suppress much of my own childhood and upbringing. Sometimes I wake in the middle of the night with a nightmare that my past has vanished altogether and I am floating unanchored. I get out of the bed and begin to write. Then it is all with me again. I can see Pari's face radiant, wearing a tight red dress, drawing the eyes of the passersby to herself, the pretty daughter of a well-known lawyer in town; and myself, intense, shy, wearing a white cotton dress with butterfly designs on it, holding on to her arm as we walk across the Square. I can see her following a man into a room of a film studio and myself waiting for her in the reception area, she coming out, her face all flushed, and telling me, as we get to the street, "He wanted me to take my clothes off." I am sitting with her at the edge of the pool in the middle of the courtyard of our house, frogs jumping in and out of the water, bats darting back and forth under a canopy on the other side, telling her about something that happened at school. I can see her in a wedding gown, sitting next to her dark-suited husband among the guests, her face reflecting a vague dreaminess and discontent.

I am lying next to my aunt and she is telling me stories. I keep demanding, as she is about to fall asleep, "Tell me another one."

I am coming home from school with other girls, all of us in uniforms, passing through a bazaar full of food shops, clusters of smoked fish, fresh dates, bananas hanging on their doors; through streets lined by palm trees and occasionally by boys from the other high school who would come close and furtively brush their arms against us or sneak a letter into our hands, expressing a desire to meet us secretly somewhere. Coming home and being hit by loneliness if Pari is not there. My mother, remote and agitated, going from room to room, trying to put everything in order, or sweating over her cooking in the kitchen, my father talking in mysterious tones with a client behind the shut doors of the large upstairs room he uses as his office. Standing on the balcony with Pari and talking and laughing about the boys passing by whom we know by sight and have classified as, "The handsome but conceited one," "The one trying to imitate Alan Delon," "The one with the tiny eyes and funny-looking head." Reaching over to the tall palm tree on the street and picking golden fresh dates and eating them. . . . All that becomes a part of me again, though the scene before me is of Manhattan high rises, some of their windows still lit at late hours of the night.

Nahid Rachlin "with Aunt Maryam on a visit, meeting in a Turkish Hotel," 1985

In addition to writing fiction I also teach fiction at various universities. There is one piece of advice that I am always confident to give to the students: write about subjects that you are obsessed or fascinated by, that matter deeply to yourself.

Will I myself ever run out of material writing about my past? It seems to me I could write indefinitely drawing from that period—about my mother who married at the age of twelve and had ten children (she had three more girls after me, one of them died of malaria), whose oldest son is only fifteen years younger than herself; about my aunt's suffering with the two husbands, her yearnings for a child in a culture where a woman's life is meaningless without children; about various aspects of my sisters' and brothers' lives; about all the young girls I grew up with, some of them becoming trapped in bad marriages arranged for them, some of them with enough determination to get away to freer worlds. Then I could go back and expand some of those early brief sketches and short stories and bring to them new perspectives I have gained through writing and living longer myself.

There seems to be no end to the material I can draw from. But one question is always with me, haunts me. Would I have become a writer without

Pari's encouragement? The question is always followed by a sadness that I have not been able to give her anything as sustaining in return. She, like myself, was always looking for escape from the circumscribed roles set for her as a woman in a culture that discriminates so grossly against women. In what way do her flights into mental illness correspond to my flights into the fantasy world of fiction? For though I draw from experience, much of what I write still has to be imagined, fabricated, distorted. When Pari looks at her hand and says, "It's turning black from the lotion you sent to me," or when she burns any money she gets hold of, saying, "I can always make more of them," is she trying to say something else?

This essay was expanded from a piece titled "Would I Have Become a Writer without My Sister?" published in the anthology The Confidence Woman, *edited by Eve Shelnutt, Longstreet Press, 1991.*

BIBLIOGRAPHY

Fiction:

Foreigner (novel), Norton, 1978.

Married to a Stranger, Dutton, 1983.

Veils: Short Stories, City Lights, 1992.

Contributor:

Jack Carpenter, editor, *Elements of Fiction,* W. M. C. Brown, 1979.

A Writer's Workbook, St. Martin's, 1987.

The Uncommon Touch, Stanford UP, 1989.

Stories from the American Mosaic, Graywolf, 1990.

Eve Shelnutt, editor, *The Confidence Woman,* Longstreet Press, 1991.

Lovers, Crossing Press, 1992.

Fabric of Desire, Crossing Press, forthcoming.

Author of numerous short stories, including "Shadow Play," "Office Song," "Journey of Love," "Blizzard in Istanbul," "Fatemah," and "Full Circle," which have appeared in popular and literary journals, including *Ararat, Columbia, Confrontation, Crazyquilt, Crosscurrents, Fiction, Four Quarters, Minnesota Review, New Laurel Review, Prism International, Redbook,* and *Shenandoah.* Her stories have been translated into the Iranian language Farsi.

James Still
1906-

A portrait of James Still, 1987. Painting by Sam McKinney.

I

Most people carry in their hearts a picture of the land of their childhood, and while other impressions fade, this picture grows stronger and stronger.

—Thorkild Hanser

Who we are, where we came from, what our ancestors did before us, and where we lived and how we lived has much to do with what we might compose in verse and story.

Of English and Scotch-Irish stock, my ancestors settled in Virginia during pioneer days, the Lindseys at Berryville, the Stills near Cumberland Gap. A roadside marker at Jonesville denotes the birthplace of Alfred Taylor Still (1828–1917), who conceived the medical system of osteopathy. One of our "set." On my mother's side my great-grandmother was a Georgia Lanier. Tradition has it both ancestors fought in the American Revolution and wilderness land was allotted them as reward, the Lindseys first settling in north Georgia, the Stills in Alabama. In my mother's childhood the kitchen floor was beaten earth. Grandpa Lindsey mined enough gold on his land to fill his teeth. (The gold rush in Dahlonega, Georgia, predated Sutter's Mill by twenty years.) The move to Alabama when my mother was sixteen was occasioned by the destruction of the home by a cyclone. An often-heard account was of Uncle Joe surviving burial under the rocks of the chimney.

When my parents married in 1893 they homesteaded in Texas and two of my sisters were born there. Papa's farm is now a part of the Fort Hood reservation. On moving back to Alabama he ran a drugstore for a time and boarded the schoolmaster in order to be taught the requisite Latin. Papa always trusted to return to Texas although it never came about, for a sister died of scarlet fever and Mama would never agree to leave her. He generally dressed "western," boots and hat, and we ate sourdough bread. I recall bits and pieces of Texas lore passed on to us and I've always thought of Texas as a distant home. My collection of Texas writings reflects this nostalgia. I soldiered at San Antonio during World War II.

Papa undertook his life's profession as a "horse doctor," a veterinarian with little formal training, along with farming and horse trading. "Short courses" at what is now Auburn University fitted him for a license to practice veterinary medicine. He once told me, "I've never cheated anybody in my life except in a horse trade. That doesn't count. It's a game." Papa appeared to know every equine in the county by their dubbing, having been present at their procreation, or birth, or having ministered to them. In passing he always spoke to them and sometimes raised his hat. Papa was fair of countenance, redheaded, and never lost a hair to his dying day, eyes blue as a wren's egg. I recollect an aunt informing me, "Too bad you're not good-looking like your daddy."

I appeared in this world July 16, 1906, on Double Branch Farm near LaFayette in Chambers County, Alabama. After five girls I was the first boy. Eventually the count ran to five girls and five boys. Our black wet nurse was "Aunt Fanny" who helped Mama care for us. She diapered us, comforted us, shielded us. We loved her with all our hearts. When my legs were long enough I would run away to her house and she would let me sop syrup out of a bucket lid. When they came hunting for me she would make out to hide me under the bed. Her unmarried companion was named Porter and uncommonly white for his race. He had been struck by lightning twice and survived and that we thought was the reason.

Sometimes I tell folk I was born in a cotton patch as one of my first memories is of running about with a small sack Mama had sewed up for me, picking a boll here and there, and of urging my sisters to pick faster as Papa had promised I could go to the cotton gin with him if we finished

out a bale that day. And of the wagon trip atop two thousand pounds of cotton and of losing my cap up the suction tube. A memorable happening for a boy of four.

After Grandma Still's death we moved in with Grandpa and Aunt Enore, a maiden aunt, on the farm between Pigeon Roost and Hootlocka creeks, near Marcoot. I was five and a brother had long since kicked me out of the cradle—almost before I could walk. I believe that was a deciding factor in my development. About then I fell and stuck a rusty nail in my stomach and had to learn to walk a second time. In our family, once you learned to stand alone, you were treated as an adult. Though a quiet child, I'm told, I was independent. One who wouldn't allow my aunts or my kissing cousins to "smack" me. I began to think for myself early. Yet my father once told me, "You had a long childhood." He meant my youth was spent in a schoolroom instead of in the fields. Of his own schooling Papa said he got as far as "baker" in the *Blueback Speller.*

Grandpa Still's homestead was antebellum with all the attributes associated with pre-Civil War architecture. Gray, with sand mixed in the paint. Large rooms, high ceilings. The kitchen and dining room were set back from the living quarters as a precaution against fire. An attic with a full measure of artifacts of the past. Clear in memory are the boxwoods crowding the front steps and the paths among Grandma's flower beds. And the buckets of water thrown on the cape jasmines on summer nights to enliven the fragrance.

I was six when we moved to the Carlisle Place two miles from LaFayette on the Buffalo road. Within a year we were living in our own newly built and mortgaged home. Standing today in Chambers County are many dwellings of the same pattern—roomy, hall down the middle, veranda halfway round, a frosted pane distinguishing the front door. From a rise on our forty-acre farm a body could see the Talledega Mountains like a train of smoke to the north. To the south, out of sight, were the Buckelew Mountains where Joe Barrow Lewis, the boxer, was born in 1914.

Chambers County has several historical connections. Woodrow Wilson's grandfather taught school weekdays in the old Presbyterian church and Stonewall Jackson's father-in-law was pastor for a time. Here the "Mark Twain" in my nature won't let me skip a pleasantry. One Papa told me. Passing through LaFayette on a Sunday he heard the Baptist congregation singing "Will There Be Any Stars in My Crown?" and the Methodist simultaneously, "No, Not One." Papa liked a good joke—such as when Grandpa Lindsey accused Papa's bull in an adjoining pasture of "demoralizing" his cows. When Papa and my uncles laughed they could be heard a half mile.

At the Carlisle Place in summer we children worked in the fields, Papa with us when not on call, Mama alongside when she could spare the time from cooking, sewing, laundry, preserving fruits and vegetables, and varied household tasks. To ward off suntan and freckles my sisters greased their faces and necks with cream, wore stockings on their hands and arms, and covered their heads with wide-brim straw hats. My sisters would never work in sight of the road. While our main crop was cotton, we raised sugarcane, sorghum, soybeans, and corn. The sun was hot, the days were long, and the rows of cotton seemed to stretch to the horizon.

One day, hoeing cotton on a row next to my sister, Inez, she began to tell a story, and as I thought a true one. It continued for hours as our hoes chopped and pushed and covered and rang against stones. Then I learned it was a fabrication. She had created it as she spoke. From that moment my horizon expanded into the imaginary. I could make my own tales and did. Oral ones.

The boll weevil made an appearance in the South and we walked the rows with a cup of kerosene and picked them off. We picked potato bugs as well and rooted out nut grass. An established colony of nut grass was considered the death of a farm. Also known as chufas and their bulbs good to eat. The taste of coconut. When we located a plant we ate the enemy.

At seven I started in school, walking the two miles to the "college" in LaFayette with my three sisters, bearing a lunch of two biscuits and slices of bacon. The first teacher, Miss Porterfield, wrote my name on the desk with chalk and handed me an ear of corn. My duty was to outline my name with the grains. A hands-on beginning. By day's end I knew its shape and could write it myself. Small for my age, I was the only pupil needing to stand on a box to reach the blackboard. On Class Day I stood in chapel and recited Stevenson's "Birdie with a yellow bill . . ." and brought down the house. My knee pants were unbuttoned. We acted out "Hiawatha" and I was Adjidamus, the squirrel. Hiawatha's thanks linger:

> Oh, my friend, the squirrel
> Bravely have you toiled to help me,
> Take the thanks of Hiawatha.

On Field Day I participated in the sack race. Inez won the fifty-yard dash and the reward of a box of chocolates. When a second layer emerged it was like the discovery of gold on California's American River. Some thirty years later Miss Porterfield was to tell me, "I can still call the name of every child in your class, but I never thought *you* would be the one."

The two events which figure largely in my youth were the American Civil War and the Great Depression. My grandfather Still had served in the Confederate Army and had a finger severed by a Yankee bullet. My maternal grandmother's first husband lost his life in north Georgia attempting to head off Sherman's march to the sea. Many veterans were alive and sometimes sat on Grandpa Still's veranda and reminisced. I recall vividly the account of the tunnel the Yanks dug under the Confederate trenches at Petersburg and the aftermath of the explosion. On Confederate Day we students were given small "bonny blue flags" and marched to the cemetery to decorate the graves of veterans. Although we harbored little knowledge of the cause of the struggle, we were certain it would be fought again and next time won. In later years I visited the major battlefields and the sites of many of the smaller engagements. Appomattox brought tears. I was readying myself to write a novel based on the prison at Andersonville, Georgia, only to be thwarted by MacKinlay Kantor publishing his own.

Aside from the Holy Bible, we had three books at home: *The Anatomy of the Horse, The Palaces of Sin, or the Devil in Society,* and a hefty volume with a missing back, *Cyclopedia of Universal Knowledge.* I learned from *Palaces* the sin of drinking gin and playing at cards. The author, one Colonel Dick Maple, who "spent his fortune with lavish hand, but awoke from his hypnotic debauch at Society's shame," the scene of action Washington, D.C. A full-page drawing depicts "Jenny Manley of Alabama rebuking guests at table for drinking wine." The *Anatomy* was beyond my comprehension.

The *Cyclopedia* was my introduction to a wider world. Subjects covered were eclectic—philosophy, physics, rhetoric, as well as such topics as the pruning of fruit trees, rules for games, social and business correspondence, the language of flowers, and capsule histories of nations. A miscellany of subjects. There was a selection of poems, including Shakespeare, Byron, Shelley, and Keats. I memorized the haunting "Ozymandias" and Cleopatra's swan song, "I am dying, Egypt dying." The

Cyclopedia was my first stab at a liberal education. During those years I saw my first motion pictures, *Damon and Pythias,* and *The Kaiser, the Beast of Berlin.* With a ticket provided by a teacher I attended Chautauqua—a classical guitar performance and a lecture which I choose to believe was the famed "Acres of Diamonds." Jean Webster read from *Daddy Long Legs* at the school. William Jennings Bryan came to town. The warden of Sing Sing Prison lectured. Papa pulled me through a crowd to have me shake hands with Governor Comer. A circus came to town and our class learned to spell *elephant, lion,* and *tiger.*

I remember the day World War I ended. A truck loaded with celebrants passed, shouting, "The war is over! The war is over!" One morning we hurried to LaFayette early to attend a hanging. We stood in the road before the jailhouse while this gruesome rite took place. On that day I became the foe of capital punishment, and in my teens, witnessing a Ku Klux Klan initiation involving the burning of a cross with citizens in bed sheets taking the oath, my liberal instincts rose and remained.

At school there was "Old Black Joe," the janitor who befriended a generation of children, and such was his respect in the community he was one of the two blacks allowed to vote. The other to share the privilege was the barber Green Appleby, who served only whites. Appleby's advertisement in the *LaFayette Sun* listed him as a "Tonsorial Artist . . . Neat shop . . . Sharp razors." Another black held in esteem was "Puss" Irwin, the wiry courthouse janitor, who dutifully held us youngsters up to the fountain for a drink of ice water. His assistant was Joe Barrow, the father of Joe (Barrow) Lewis. I recollect him usually dozing on the courtroom steps.

I was grown and in graduate school before I became acquainted with the writings of Johnson Jones Hooper, author of *Some Adventures of Simon Suggs, Late of the Talapossa Volunteers*—antebellum humor of the Old Southwest. Born in North Carolina he came to Alabama and founded the *LaFayette East Alabamian* in 1842, a newspaper with the motto: "It's good to be shifty in a new country," and later, while practicing law, edited the *Chambers-County Tribune.* In my first encounter with Hooper's works I was put off by the rash of dialect. A briar patch of contractions, elisions, and apostrophes. Not aware that I had lived in the same geographical spot, critics have more than once suggested that Simon Suggs is the father of my character Uncle Jolly in both my novels *River of*

Earth and *Sporty Creek.* Uncle Jolly was my great-grandpa, with some of the attributes of a cousin, as near as I've come to using actual persons in my fiction. When I came to be writing about Kentucky, dialect was both a problem and a challenge. Edward Weeks, editor of the *Atlantic,* warned me early on, "Dialect is out of fashion." My intentions are to evoke speech. Dialect too strictly adhered to makes a character appear ignorant when he is only unlettered. Yet *Simon Suggs* overcomes all obstacles, and has lasted, and is a pleasure when read aloud by an apt interpreter.

We moved to LaFayette for a couple of years—something to do with the mortgage—and into the Judge Norman house, a dwelling of many rooms, spacious grounds, flaming crepe myrtles, giant magnolias. The air was scented with cottonseed oil being processed in a nearby plant, a match for frying smoked ham. Within earshot of the back fence lived "darkies," as they were referred to in those days. We heard their laughter and singing and cheerful banter and mistakenly judged them as being without the cares which plagued white society. Our neighbor was "Cotton Tom" Heflin, U.S. congressman or senator for decades. The Heflins were rarely at home. The straw mat on our hall floor was a gift of Mrs. Heflin. His son once fired a shotgun in our direction, raining pellets on our roof. The Norman house has long since been demolished, the white-pillared mansion of the Honorary J. Tom Heflin still stands.

The "college" which I was to attend through the fifth grade had actually been one in times past and was in need of major repairs. A proposed three-mill tax was put on the ballot and defeated in the election. In talking to the editor of the *LaFayette Sun* next day my father said, "The building will have to fall down for the voters to wake up." The roof of the auditorium collapsed that night.

At war's end the price of cotton fell. We had moved back to the Carlisle Place for two or three years when our long-carried mortgage on the farm was foreclosed. We moved to Shawmut, a textile town in the Chattahoochee Valley. Although we lived on "Boss Row" (Lanier Avenue), my father was not employed in the factory. Many townsmen kept a cow in the backyard, some a horse. The company wanted a veterinarian handy. On Christmas Eves we children hung our stockings by the chimney and were rewarded with an orange, an apple, peppermint sticks, and a handful of nuts. Once, a toy pistol. The first Christmas at Shawmut the factory gifted every child with a paper bag brimming with a variety of fruits and nuts and candy and a toy.

Up to then the only fiction of value I had read was *Treasure Island*. Not even *Tom Sawyer* or *The Last of the Mohicans* or *Robinson Crusoe*. There was to be much catching up in the years to come. Against the librarian's suggestion, I borrowed Balzac's *Father Goriot*. It was a revelation. I can still smell the boardinghouse depicted in the early chapters. And I began to write my first novel, of boats and sailors and whales. I had never beheld a boat larger than a bateau, known a sailor, or viewed the ocean. I have no further memory of this venture.

I got caught up in the game of basketball. Often played from school's end until dark. Our team was invited to the state tournament at Birmingham. Only one member of the team was taken along, the other players being "ringers" recruited from the factory. They attended classes a half-day to qualify. We were joyful when they were roundly defeated their first game, probably by another team of ringers. Such affairs are better ordered nowadays. I won second prize in a *Birmingham News* essay contest on the subject of insect control in gardens. First prize went for chemical treatment. I plumped for birds.

I was in the ninth grade when we moved farther down the valley to Jarrett Station. I attended Fairfax High School in another factory town which was within walking distance. Joined the Boy Scouts of America, earned twenty-three merit badges and achieved the status of Eagle Scout, and published my first poem in *Boys' Life* titled "A Burned Tree Speaks."

During my senior year I happened upon a catalog of Lincoln Memorial University located near Cumberland Gap, Tennessee. A college established after the Civil War by General O. O. Howard due to the loyalty of the area to the Union cause. Flourishing to this day and in a natural setting probably unequaled in America. The ability to work my way was the draw. In the fall I set off with sixty dollars earned as an office boy at the factory and door-to-door delivery of the *Atlanta Constitution* for this school of some eight hundred students drawn mainly from the mountain areas of the three adjoining states. I had made a genealogical circle. Up the road in Virginia was the site of the Stills' pioneer home.

Most students worked for their tuition and keep at Lincoln Memorial, on the farm, at the hatchery, dairy, rock quarry, and upkeep of the campus. I was assigned to the quarry where I pried limestone croppings out of a pasture and sometimes operated a rock crusher. One Christmas vacation, lacking a ticket home, a nickel in my pocket, I spent shoveling gravel onto roads and crosswalks. I spent the nickel on chewing gum. Once, I put a hand in my pocket and found a silver dollar. An "angel" had put it there. My grades suffered the freshman year as I was too fatigued to study. They picked up the other terms after a change of chores—raking leaves, mixing concrete, roof mending, house painting, janitor at the library. I attended classes mornings and worked afternoons. As janitor I took over the library at 9 P.M.

A majority of the students had no money to buy extra food. My overriding memory of those years was of being hungry. We ate everything off of the tables. Walnut trees were plentiful on the hills of Harrogate and we cracked bushels. We raked our hands through snow under apple trees for overlooked fruit. The president of Lincoln Memorial spirited me into his house to try on a suit he could spare. It fitted perfectly. I broke into tears when he presented it to me. Not from joy, as reported, from humiliation. I never wore it.

The third and fourth year I kept the job of janitor at the library. At nine o'clock I locked the door, emptied the wastebaskets, swept the floor, and rubbed up the tables, and until daylight it was my private domain. Many nights I became too sleepy to make it to the dormitory and slept in the stack room, a book for a pillow. I hardly knew what to take up first, what book, what periodical. Discovering the scholarly journal *American Speech*, I wrote two articles which they published and which H. L. Mencken was to quote in the *American Language*. I particularly noted the *Atlantic* and it became the future target for my poems and short stories. The library became the recipient of many years of this journal and I was bid to check the files for missing issues and dump the rest into the furnace. That summer I freighted virtually a ten-year collection of issues home and with the Great Depression in full swing and work unattainable, I read every story, poem, and essay. During the next quarter century they were to publish three poems and ten short stories of mine.

At Lincoln the provider of the "work" scholarships was an elderly gentleman by the name of Guy Loomis, heir to a sash-and-blind fortune, and who was providing assistance to students in several institutions in the southern mountains. I managed to learn his address and wrote in my senior year to thank him and to invite him to the graduation exercises. He actually came, driving down from Brooklyn in a chauffeured Cadillac, remained several days, and attended class exercises. After I won the Rush Strong Medal and prizes in four other essay contests, he offered to sponsor me for a year in graduate school, provided it was in the South. In extending the scholarship he said, "I'll make it possible, not easy." His warning proved correct. I chose Vanderbilt University and was off to Nashville in the fall.

II

January 20, 1985

Dear Professor Stoneback,

Vanderbilt was long ago and to answer your questions about my graduate year there will require a bit of head scratching. I had my noggin inside one book or another the whole year. Edwin Mims picked the courses for me, which did not

The author, taken his senior year of college, 1928

include one of his own. He was the spit image of my Grandpa Lindsey down in Buffalo Wallow, Alabama. I attended his lectures on the subject of evolution, the "monkey trial" at Dayton, Tennessee, being a sizzling issue of the day. At term's end I presented my thesis for his approval and signature and he said he would sign it after Dr. Curry and Professor Ransom affixed theirs. He did, without riffling a page. In a lecture at Alumni Hall he introduced me to the poetry of T. S. Eliot, a newcomer on the literary horizon. His recently published *The Advancing South* was held in considerable disregard by some faculty members. They would shortly offset it with a publication of their own.

The "Fugitives" of Vanderbilt University were on the verge of publishing *I'll Take My Stand,* a manifesto on Jeffersonian agrarianism as well as presenting a sardonic view of industrial society, and which over the past sixty years has built up a literature of its own. Those present read their chapters to us. Robert Penn Warren, who later recanted his part, was at Oxford University, Andrew Lytle at nearby Sewanee University. Lytle read a play to us, not his contribution. John Crowe Ransom with his book *The New Criticism* inaugurated a method of close reading of poetic texts which caught hold in English departments here and abroad. One of the great teachers, according to the *American Scholar.* Quiet, kindly, a Southern gentleman of the old school, he stretched our imaginations beyond the subject at hand, "The English Novel."

During the first week in the American Literature class, Dr. John Donald Wade tested our familiarity with the authors of merit from the Civil War forward. I made a perfect score. Nobody else managed a passing grade. Dr. Wade called me to his office next day, told me he was now my advisor, and said, "You don't have to bother with my class. Just drop in once in a while and learn what we're up to." Or some such statement. I took him at his word and skipped every other class. I was being sorely pressed by Chaucer. My contribution to the *History of American Literature* the class composed was the chapters on Cotton and Increase Mather. Some twenty years later when Katherine Ann Porter told me she was writing about the Mathers I was prepared to discuss the subject.

The Chaucer class under Dr. Walter Clyde Curry, as we would say here, was "a horse." Attended by me with fear and trembling as I suspect did others, and yet it was the most rewarding of all. I once calculated that I spent seventeen hours in preparation for each of the two classes per week. And I chose to write my thesis under his direction: "The Function of Dreams and Visions in the Middle English Romances." Why, given a choice, did I opt to do a thesis under this strictest of professors, unrelenting, a perfectionist, some said cruel? Or select a subject which required learning practically overnight to read Middle English and to wade through more than one hundred volumes of the Early English Text Society? Dr. Curry read each section of the thesis as I presented them during the year, gave no suggestions, never the slightest hint I was doing acceptable work. At school's end he remarked to me in class, "From where you started you have made more progress than anybody in the course." But how far did I get? I was never called for orals or to defend my thesis. Probably an oversight. The professor's wife wrote to me at a later date after reading a story of mine and added the comment, "I understand that while you were at Vanderbilt you did not have a course under my husband."

I spent a weekend at Wilder, Tennessee, where a strike had been in progress for more than a year. I had gone to this benighted mine camp along with two other Vanderbilt students to deliver a truckload of food and clothing collected in Nashville for the strikers. I was to ride in the truck with the driver, Barney Green, who was to lose his life in the cause later. Barney thought it an unnecessary risk as he was subject to being hijacked.

We found the people drawn and pale from malnourishment, although their resolve was strong and unshaken. They were held together by their common misery. The town was divided, the scabs living in the camp houses on one side, the strikers on the other. There was a "dead line" and one crossed it at his peril. On the strikers' side, the water and electricity were cut off. It was my first inkling that folk could starve to death in the United States of America in plain view of a largely indifferent populace. At that time the Red Cross had not yet allowed their flour to be distributed to these people.

I lodged in the home of Jim Crownover, president of the union that year, and caught "thrush," an infection of the mouth, from which his children were suffering. We attended a gathering at one of the homes after dark, blowing out the light before leaving, thus not to provide a ready target for a sharpshooter. Arriving men deposited pistols, rifles, and shotguns on a bed. The conversation was as gloomy as the light shed by a coal-oil lamp. When the meeting was over a banjo picker provided music for a bit of square dancing.

Until spring, when my benefactor increased my stipend a bit, my two meals a day consisted of a ten-cent bowl of cereal in the morning and a thirty-five-cent supper at a boardinghouse. I lived in the home of a widow at 1913 Broad Street, the only roomer in a house of heavy mahogany furniture and drawn curtains and silence. The widow considered it an aberration that I insisted on a hot bath every day. I blew the speckles of soot from the railroad yards off my pillow at night. The widow's children were adults, rarely encountered. The son operated a nightclub on the river; the daughter, probably in her late twenties, had some sort of night work, presumably at the club. The few times I passed the daughter in the hall she was swathed in mink and her "Night in Paris" perfume lingered after. She never spoke. The nightclub burned in March, the son in it. I never set eyes on the widow again. I pushed the rent money under her door when due.

In December, en route to Florida, Mr. Loomis stopped by Nashville and had me to lunch. It was raining and he inquired, "Have you no raincoat?" Instead of saying no, I skirted the question with, "You said you would make it possible, not easy." Though he didn't provide the coat—I believe he forgot about it as we talked—he seemed impressed enough with my progress to mention staking me to another year in school. To learn something practical, with earning possibilities. He would choose this time. The library school of the University of Illinois at Urbana-Champaign. I had never considered being a librarian, yet the Depression was still with us and it was something to do. A force-put, as we say.

After a year at Illinois I had earned three diplomas; I had graduated three times in the same pair of shoes. And I had no prospects for employment. First, I applied to the Library of Congress for their reference division. They waited three years to suggest an interview. I was ashamed to go home. I tried the CCC—Civilian Conservation Corps. I attempted selling Bibles for Nashville's Southwestern Publishers in Lee County, Mississippi. I picked cotton in Texas. I recollect a hungry night atop a lumber pile in Shreveport, Louisiana. I walked, thumbed, rode the rails. An open freight car I jumped into as it departed a station bore a contingent of World War I veterans on the way to join the Bonus Army in Washington, D.C. I tried Sears, Roebuck, in Atlanta. Signed up with an employment agency. When I tackled the boss of a stove foundry in Rome, Georgia, for a job he burst into laughter. Nothing worked.

In Nashville I looked up Don West, a former classmate, at that time preparing for the ministry. He informed me he and his wife would be conducting vacation Bible schools in Knott County, Kentucky, during July and August. He invited me to join his son-in-law, Jack Adams, in organizing a recreational program at three sites, three Boy Scout troops and three baseball teams. As a volunteer. So it came to be. We camped and played ball all summer and I became enamored with the forested mountains, the valleys and hollows of this backwoods country, and with the independent and forthright folk. I was toying with the notion of moving into an abandoned log house and trying my hand at writing when the Hindman Settlement School at the forks of Troublesome Creek offered the job of librarian, again as a volunteer—room, board, and laundry furnished. At that period the school was in severe financial straits.

Don West departed and I was not to see him again for many years. He went on to found Highlander Folk School with a partner near Chattanooga, Tennessee, where they trained blacks and whites in social awareness and union organization. Martin Luther King and Rosa Parks were among his students. He headed the National Miners Union in Harlan County, Kentucky, during the "mine wars" and suffered every indignity—jail, beatings, maiming, and visits from the Ku Klux Klan. When the Freedom of Information Act was passed and he had access to FBI files, his record covered more than four hundred pages. J. Edgar Hoover had stayed on his trail. Jack Adams joined the Abraham Lincoln Battalion and died in a trench in Spain.

Founded in 1901 by two Kentucky women, graduates of Wellesley College, the Hindman Settlement School evolved from a summer session in a pitched tent to eventually eight buildings at Hindman, the county seat. The instructors were mostly Wellesley graduates. Men on the staff usually locals. The students were drawn from adjoining counties and rigidly selected. At most this boarding school could accommodate one hundred and there was no tuition. It was not church-related. Students worked in the vegetable garden, dairy, or upkeep of grounds and buildings. Outstanding graduates sometimes achieved scholarships at Wellesley and Harvard though most continued their education at Berea College. A

At the Hindman Settlement, 1932

member of the first graduating class obtained a doctorate at the Sorbonne.

Hindman was a village of some two hundred souls with a single blacktop road leading from Hazard in Perry County and terminating abruptly in midtown at the creek bank where a bridge had washed out. Until another bridge was in place, a body had to walk a plank during low-water or resort to a jumping-pole when there was a "tide." You could cash a check at 4:00 A.M., the cashier an early riser, and call for mail at midnight, the postmaster an insomniac. I was assigned Box 13. Nobody else would have it. I had come to the "jumping off place." The first week I witnessed a fatal shooting and admitted the fact whereas several bystanders would not. There followed warnings to stay out of town, a court trial, an embarrassment to the school, and a sense of being in the "doghouse."

I remained at the Hindman Settlement School for six years. The library was excellent, the students eager, the staff highly motivated. Aware that the many one-room schools of the county were without access to a library, I began spending one day a week—my own undertaking—walking from school to school with a carton of children's books on my shoulder, and changing the collection every two weeks. I could serve only four schools in this manner. Often as I approached I would hear the cry, "Here comes the book boy." The first three years at the Hindman Settlement I received no salary. The Depression slackening they paid me a few dollars the next three. Averaging it out I had worked six years for six cents a day. One of the summers I served as social worker for the Federal Emergency Relief Administration (FERA) and this experience sparked my novel *River of Earth*. And the murderer my testimony had helped to send to the penitentiary was pardoned and came to see me. An encounter too complicated to relate here. He lost his life shortly after in a shoot-out.

I started creative writing rather suddenly. I can almost point to the day. I was twenty-six. First were poems which appeared in the *Atlantic*, the *Yale Review*, the *Nation*, the *Virginia Quarterly Review*, and other journals. The few dollars earned kept me in razor blades, socks, and other human necessities. The Viking Press published a collection of poems in 1937. I took up the short story and my first appeared in the *Atlantic*. Several were chosen for the *O. Henry Memorial Prize Stories*, one winning an award, and in *Best American Short Stories* in the years following. Martha Foley, editor of the latter, commented: "A delight to read are James Still's warm-hearted stories of his Kentucky neighbors whom he depicts in an English language as unspoiled as when Chaucer and the Elizabethan first made it into glorious literature." A heady encomium for a novice.

I recall distinctly the Saturday morning I began writing a novel in the storeroom of the high school. Here I always retreated for my one hour off during the school day, and on Saturdays when my duties allowed. The principal was to remark, "He goes in, bolts the door, and only God knows what he does in there."

I began *River of Earth:*

> The mines on Little Carr closed in March. Winter had been mild, the snows scant and frost-thin upon the ground. Robins stayed the season through, and sapsuckers came early to drill the black birch beside our house. Though Father had worked in the mines, we did not live in the camps. He owned the scrap of land our house stood upon, a garden patch, and the black birch that was the only tree on all the

barren slope above Blackjack. There were three of us children running barefoot over the puncheon floors, and since the year's beginning Mother carried a fourth balanced on one hip as she worked over the rusty stove in the shedroom. There were eight in the family to cook for. Two of Father's cousins, Harl and Tibb Logan, came with the closing of the mines and did not go away . . .

It was time to move on.

Yours truly,
James Still

III

On a day in June I moved nine miles over a wagon road and two miles up a creek bed to a two-story log house in an area of the Cumberlands known in pioneer days as the Big Brush. Erected in 1837 by immigrants from the Black Forest of Germany, it is the birthplace of the noted dulcimer maker, Jethro Amburgey, whose instruments nowadays are sought by collectors. A mile above once lived Edward Thomas whose dulcimers are rarer yet. The dwelling faces east, fair to the sun, bounded on one side by Dead Mare Branch and on the other by Wolfpen Creek, facing toward Little Carr. Wooded mountains rise before and aft. Mine was to be a domain of thirty-one acres, most of it standing on end, once a farm, now long lain fallow. I had found a home.

I marked the day by an observation in a Notebook:

> A pair of black and white warblers teetered along the banks of Dead Mare and minnows riffled the glassy pools. Partridges called in the water meadow and from a cove sounded an occasional *e-olee* of a woodthrush. A rabbit flashed a tail in the wild flax.

A hedge behind the house reached from Dead Mare to Wolfpen, a distance of some one hundred fifty yards. By count, thirty-seven varieties of shrubs and vines erected a wall dominated by sumac, blackberry, and sawbriar, crowned by wild cherry, hawthorn, and a crab apple. Anchoring the row an aged oak at whose foot during the first warm days of spring I was to gather an edible fungus (morels), locally known as dry-land fish. Along the creek banks flourished wild mint and bluing weed. The high ground before the house was to become my yard, garden, and farm. It gave onto a marsh where frogs bellowed in spring and red-winged blackbirds frequented in summer. Swamp violets reached up through the sedge on foot-long stems. Partridges nested along the dryer reaches and sometimes exploded from cover like a shotgun blast.

Save for three broken chairs and a small table the house was bereft of furniture. The back door was painted green to ward off witches. I slept on an army cot, cooked on a two-burner coal-oil stove until I could gather other furnishings. My work-table was two stacked steamer trunks supporting a portable typewriter. A neighbor when asked who had moved into the old log house had replied, "We don't know yet. A man person. We call him the 'Man in the Bushes.'" I was reported to be ancient with a two-foot beard. A hermit shunning human contact.

Of the Wild Man

It will take a little while to find him.
He may be in some unlikely place
Lying beneath a haw, lost in leafy sleep,
Or atop a high field digging his keep.
He is somewhere around. Go and look.

It will take a little while to find him
For hunger drives no wild man home.
Dark bays no hasting to a will like his.
He may dine on berries, abide where he is.
He is somewhere around. Go and look.

The second week in June was late to start a garden and plant a field of corn, moreover the signs of the zodiac were being ignored. I planted nevertheless and as hard frosts held off until middle October I had vegetables aplenty, both to eat and store for winter. Four apple trees furnished fruit for eating, canning, and drying. Following local custom, in the fall I heaped cabbages, turnips, parsnips, and potatoes in mounds and covered them with layers of leaves and dirt. They were unearthed as needed. For those without "warm houses" (cellars) this was the alternative. And come March, when cornstalks were ritually burned at the break of winter, I had my own stack to set afire and greet the spring.

I acquired two stands of bees. I never left home overnight without "telling the bees." Folk wisdom had it they would swarm and depart otherwise. Common superstitions often have psychological reasons. This one, I believe—never leave home without checking the hives. I acquired a cat, sawed a hole in a door so it could come and

The log house at Wolfpen Creek, Kentucky, home of James Still since 1939

go at will. Snakes don't linger where felines are. One day I rescued a ground squirrel despite having been told never to take anything away from a cat. If you do, they will bring you a snake. She brought me four snakes in due course. A dulcimer hanging from a nail began to play in the night, however faintly. A struck match revealed a grand-daddy spider walking the strings.

Toward the end of March there came a warm spell. The meadow greened and buckeye buds swelled. A wren began a nest under an eave and frogs bellowed in the swamp. I heard a whippoor-will and mentioned the fact in print. Promptly came a letter inquiring into this unlikely event. Overnight frost nipped the buds and silenced the frogs.

Early Whippoorwill

I have a letter from Oklahoma—
A professor of logic, part-time ornithologist,
Doubts that Kentucky has had the chance to hear
A whippoorwill's song the third month of the year
When the Sooner State must wait till April at least.

I'd heard a whippoorwill's stout-hearted call
And printed the fact and thought it within reason
For bird or man to sing in or out of season
As any might err, might sound a note quite new,
Deny the systems and set the graphs askew.

I hold this state is not alone in being lucky
It has a whippoorwill uncommonly plucky;
I believe I'm not indulging in idle misnomer
By calling all fortunate, including Oklahoma,
When bird or thought makes lists and manuals
    vain.
O earliest whippoorwill, come again!

Before World War I, I called for my mail once a week at Bern Smith's store at the foot of Little Carr. After the war the mail arrived on horseback from Bath, named for the oldest Roman town in England. I became the unappointed "Mayor" of Bath in that both postmasters added to my mail any addressed to His Honor. When I went for necessities—coffee, sugar, salt—to Mal Gibson's store he informed me, "If you're going to start hanging out at my place of business you're going to have to learn two things, to chew tobacco and tell lies." Mal was a trickster. He had a joke on every customer, or was working on one. A daughter went North to attend a modeling school and married a Broadway producer. We saw pictures of her at Lake Arrowwood, the Claridge in London, the George V in Paris. More entries in my Notebooks involve Mal than any other person, I had begun to record anything unique to the region, of a community that hardly exists today. Folk living in the nineteenth century with the twentieth threatening.

It was said of me that I had quit a good job and gone to the backside of Nowhere and sat down. I did sit down and finish *River of Earth* and compose in leisurely fashion an occasional poem and short story. If you are digging your living out of the ground, there is little time for sitting. Along with farming and gardening, I began experiments with the wild strawberry and the wild violet, an attempt by natural selection to discover superior plants. I began a study of the leaf miner, an insect needing a bit of magnification and living a varied and fascinating existence. There are some two thousand known varieties. My evenings were spent reading by lamplight and the library of the Virginia Polytechnic Institute supplied by mail any book I wished to borrow. After selling a short story to the *Saturday Evening Post*, I began to buy books: I commonly subscribe to periodicals I hope to

appear in. There was the Sunday *New York Times* to cope with.

River of Earth was published February 5, 1940. *Time* called it "a work of art." I was standing by a potbelly stove in a railroad station in Jackson that frozen morning waiting for a train going north to connect with one heading south. The train was late. In walked a deputy sheriff, warmed his hands a moment, and responded to a call from the door, "They need you across the road." I followed out of curiosity. The sheriff entered a building where commodities were being distributed and was shot dead in my face.

The train came. I boarded and wrote a letter to *Time* to thank them for the kind words and briefly stated what I had witnessed on this long-awaited occasion. Two weeks later I entered a barber shop in Florida and was handed a copy of *Time* to peruse while I waited. Leading the "Letter" section was my message bearing the heading, "Bloody Breathitt." A touchy designation then as now. Breathitt County is the only one in the Commonwealth where nobody was drafted during World War I. Volunteers filled their quota. Stop-

Still's worktable, Wolfpen Creek.
Photo by Dean Cadle.

ping by Jackson on the way home to access the damage, I learned citizens in high office were enraged and it would be wise to cool my heels elsewhere. My guilt was I had given a local matter national attention.

IV

*On Being Drafted into the U.S. Army
from My Log Home in March 1942*

Weather and time, time and weather
Shriveled the wall, crumbled the chinking,
Raised the top log, the lower sinking,
Opening a space between upper and nether,
Making a crack for inside to look out
And outside to peer wonderingly in;
Peer wonderingly in where I am sleeping,
Trouble the dark, harry and flout
Slumberer from sleep, cricket from neeping.
But who on an evening at a quarter past seven
Stared from dusk and weight of heaven?
Mars hung bright in the Wolfpen sky
And glared and met me eye to eye.
Mars looked in and routed me out.

Three years went by and a great deal was happening out in the world but nothing was happening to us. World War II was declared and I was drafted among the first in the county. My age would have been a factor elsewhere. They were getting rid of the jailbirds, the riffraff, and those without families to protest. I belonged to the latter. A recent operation to remove a branchial cleft cyst would have given me an "out" had I chosen to exercise it. The average age of the men in my squadron was to be twenty-two. I was thirty-six and subject to the same physical demands, no quarter granted.

Off to Fort Thomas where my rating on the AGCT test allowed me to choose the Army Air Force. Shipped out to San Antonio, baked in the Texas sun for six months, staged at Fort Dix, and I was off for the invasion of North Africa via New York, Rio de Janeiro, and Cape Town. My ninety-nine percent Texas-born outfit, the 8th Air Depot Group, loaded onto barges on the Jersey shore at night and headed for the SS *Aquitania* somewhere beyond. As we pushed off, the men began to sing a bawdy song, a not uncommon practice. Running without lights we entered New York harbor. The

The back door of Still's house

Sergeant James Still (mounted, far right), in Cairo, Egypt, 1944

towers of Manhattan were lost in mist. Suddenly the mist parted and there bathed in moonlight stood the Statue of Liberty, the base hidden, floating in air as it were. The singing stopped and only the breathing of hundreds of men and the slapping of waves against the hull could be heard. It was a solemn moment. With hand in air Miss Liberty seemed to be waving farewell. For some it was the last view of America forever. The singing began again, and the song was "Shall We Gather at the River."

There were some ten thousand of us on the *Aquitania* which had served in World War I at Gallipoli and had been slated to be broken up when war erupted. Before us a journey of twenty-six days to Cape Town on the first leg of the trip. We poked along, changing directions every six minutes to thwart submarines, putting into Rio for a week, going in circles for days as we neared Cape Town until destroyers were sent to lead us in. The harbormaster at Cape Town turned out to be a German spy which accounted for the sinkings of numerous merchant vessels in the area. What a prize we would have made, ten thousand putrid men who hadn't bathed for nearly a month, some

never removing their shoes. Good for an iron cross.

We transhipped to the Antenor after a spell at Palls Moor, joined a fleet of ships north, and made a landing at Freetown, Sierra Leone. Every soldier aboard will remember the hour we awaited the signal to board the landing craft, each of us a walking arsenal. The order rang out, "Let's go men!" We were excited but I think not afraid. We went. We hit the beach and nobody was there. We'd half-expected the Vichy French. We had no inkling of the vast movement of men investing the horn of Africa that day. I subsequently learned we liberated Graham Greene the novelist serving with British intelligence and in hiding in Freetown.

My outfit settled down at Accra, Gold Coast Colony (now Ghana), our base for the more than two years overseas. I traveled to Egypt, Palestine (Israel), and to Eritrea where I picked up a dysentery I was long in overcoming. Survived a crash landing in the Anglo-Egyptian Sedan. Endured two cases of blackwater fever, an often fatal form of malaria. In the Ashanti kingdom I enlarged a collection of pre-Columbian counter-gold-weights made of hand-smelted ore and shaped by the "lost wax" method.

It is said that every soldier is glad to come home but he comes home angry. I came back disoriented. For months I sat in the door of my log house and could not arouse interest in things I had done before. Gradually I adjusted and again joined the staff of the Hindman Settlement School, with a modest salary. Next I taught ten years at a state university, resigned and returned to Wolfpen Creek. Since 1970 I've spent fourteen winters in part in Central America pursuing an interest in Mayan civilization, and five trips to Europe to visit World War I battlefields, Passchendaele to Verdun. I have an irremovable reputation of being a hermit.

Yesterday in Belize

Yesterday in Belize
A dog barked, a rooster crowed,
Laughter rocked across the tidal river
And the sun rang its clarion chimes
Through pellucid air.

Yesterday at Altun Ha
The chachalaca hooted from a palm,
A coach-whip wove its eight-foot length
Amid the custard trees,
A tinamou whistled the half-hour.

Yesterday at Xunatunich
My severed heart was offered to Chac,

Tikal, Guatemala, 1973

And the rains came,
And the Mayan gods smiled
And poked out their tongues.

V

Wolfpen Creek
Sunday

Dear William,
Butterfly weather though it is a bit cool for them this early in the morning. My neighbor across the creek is already up and busy with his saw and hammer, despite it being Sunday, despite his having worked in the mines all the other six days of the week, often in water shoe-mouth deep, as he tells me, and in spite of there not being a plank requiring sawing or a nail needing driven. He must be doing something, creating something, just as I, propped up here by pillows on my four-post walnut bed, itself a creation of Jethro Amburgey, the dulcimer maker. I find I've written seven pages in a notebook—extraneous matter, hardly any page belonging in subject to any other, pages looking toward books or manuscripts partially written, or only projected to a number I could not possibly complete given my age and biological life span.

The lady who once asked me, "Do you do your own writing?" and to whom I replied, "No, I have seven dwarves," has lately inquired, "Where do you get your ideas?" For me ideas are hanging from limbs like pears, from fences like gourds. They rise up like birds from cover. They spring out of reports in the *Troublesome Creek Times,* from a remark in a country store, a happening. The first summer I moved here was a dry one and the creek dried up to a series of potholes crowded with minnows. Every day I drew water from my well and replenished the holes to little avail. Few survived until the next rainfall. Thus:

Leap Minnows, Leap

The minnows leap in drying pools,
In islands of water along the creekbed sands
They spring on drying tails, white bellies to the
  sun,
Gills spread, gills fevered and gasping.
The creek is sun and sand, and fish throats
  rasping.

One pool has a peck of minnows. One living pool
Is knuckle deep with dying, a shrinking yard
Of glittering bellies. A thousand eyes look, look,
A thousand gills strain, strain the water air.

There is plenty of water above the dam, locked
and deep,
Plenty, plenty and held. It is not here.
It is not where the minnows spring with lidless
fear.
They die as men die. Leap minnows, leap.

Log houses are not as warm as reputed. Not
mine at least. My first winter here was "a horse."
A February blizzard dipped many degrees below
zero. I pushed my bed as close to the fire as dared;
I heated a rock, wrapped it in a towel, put it at my
feet. I wondered how my neighbors fared, many of
them in less sheltered quarters. Spring came and
there they were, without complaint.

Spring on Little Carr

Not all of us were warm, not all of us.
We are winter-lean, our faces are sharp with cold
And there is the smell of wood smoke in our
clothes;
Not all of us were warm, though we hugged the
fire
Through the long chilled nights.

We have come out
Into the sun again, we have untied our knot
Of flesh: We are no thinner than a hound or mare,
Or an unleaved poplar. We have come through
To the grass, to the cows calving in the lot.

As Coleridge composed "Kubla Khan" in a
dream, a dream disturbed, one of my poems came
unbidden after an imagined telephone ring in the
night.

In My Dreaming

Last night the telephone rang in my head, in
my sleep, in my dreaming.
You had passed from all reckoning of our days
without number,
From our knowledge and practice of love,
From terrestrial sleep to infinite slumber;
The coils which bound us snapped in two,
The bowl was broken at the well,
Our sky of crystal cracked and fell,
The seeds of surfeit sprouted and grew,
In my head, in my sleep, in my dreaming.
And it was true.
And it was true.

There was a period in Africa during World
War II when I had little assurance of ever returning to my home in Kentucky. Thus this verse of
remembrance.

*Brothers and sisters: William Comer, Elloree, Inez,
and James Still, 1976*

Wolfpen Creek

How it was in that place, how light hung in a
bright pool
Of air like water, in an eddy of cloud and sky,
I will long remember. I will long recall
The maples blossoming wings, the oaks proud with
rule,
The spiders deep in silk, the squirrels fat on
mast,
The fields and draws and coves where quail and
peewees call.
Earth loved more than any earth, stand firm,
hold fast;
Trees burdened with leaf and bird, root deep,
grow tall.

As you are aware, from childhood I've been a
reader, when there was anything to read, and I
suppose I've read an average of three hours a day
for half a century. Reading jaunts with mountain
climbers in the Himalayas, the South Pacific, the
American Civil War, World War I, the mysteries
of Mayan civilization to name a few tangents, and
the entire corpus of many an author. Curiosity like
an itch that needs scratching.

Madly to Learn

Madly to learn,
To fathom, to discern,
To master the Gobi, the ruins at Petri,
Climb K-2 and Nanga Parbat,
Swim the Strait of Malacca,
Be Ahab aboard the Peaquod,
Milton in his agony,
Shakespeare treading the boards;
To unravel, to grasp, to speak
Freud's Theory of Seduction,
The mathematical beauty of irregular surfaces,
The Quantum theory, the leap genes,
The invisible morghognetic fields
Transmitted across space and time—
Bridges to infinity—
And why Tennyson's "Flower in a Crannied Wall"
May not tell us all and all and all.
Madly to learn.

The question is often asked: "Who influenced you to write?" Certainly it wasn't handed down in the family, and I can't think of an author I wish to emulate although I have admired the works of many. I was already scribbling before the great books came to hand. As an English observer of Appalachian folk in Harlan County, Kentucky, said, "Not knowing the *right* way to do things they did things *their* way." I did encounter the novels of Thomas Hardy during college days and the fact that I've always written about the common man may have been sparked by him. The only class I ever cut was when I was deep in *Far From the Madding Crowd* and could not put the book down. The most memorable book read in college, and in French, was Alphonse Daudet's *Le Petit Chose.* I must grant some credit to a decade of issues of the *Atlantic* I came upon during the late 1920s. Otto Jespersen's *The Philosophy of Grammar* directed me toward "living language" as opposed to the formal.

It took time, my own time, to figure out the King of England is a myth, and all that implies— the myths we live by, county lines, state lines, imaginary acts made actual by acceptance. I learned an apple is a modified leaf. My self-education proceeded from such facts. I am more an autodidact than a classroom scholar.

"How did you escape the stereotype 'hillbilly' writing?"—a frequent question. That is, the stereotypical mountaineer and his dialectical speech as rendered by several authors of fiction in the past. I was hardly aware of them, didn't have access to their books. My experience was with the folk themselves. As for handling dialect in my fictions and Notebooks, the way folk actually talk, well, now, dialect of any sort on a printed page always bothered me. Peculiar spellings can't account for the tone of voice, body language, the intent behind the statement. My aim is to invoke speech. To expect the true sound of it to happen in the reader's head. Aberrant spelling rarely accomplishes it. I trust to preserve the "voice" of the speaker.

I answered a set of down-to-earth questions at Carmus Combs' store the other day. A fellow inquired, "How many years have you lived amongst us?"

"This year makes forty-six."

"You're the last 'possum up the tree. Everybody your age when you come here are dead. Hain't that so?"

"I thought they'd live forever."

"What's your notion about dying?"

"Death is as natural as sleep," I said, quoting Benjamin Franklin. "We will arise refreshed in the morning."

My neighbor is still hammering and sawing. He has apparently decided on something to build—a doghouse, a chicken coop, perhaps a

Representative of Kentucky legislature reading citation to the author (center) on the fiftieth anniversary of River of Earth, *James Still Room, Morehead State University, 1990*

James Still, at home, Wolfpen Creek, 1988

playpen for his children. He will not halt until it is accomplished. It is his act of creation.

Your brother,
Jim

BIBLIOGRAPHY

Poetry:

Hounds on the Mountain, Viking, 1937.

River of Earth: A Poem and Other Poems, King Library Press, 1983.

The Wolfpen Poems, Berea College Press, 1986.

Fiction:

River of Earth, Viking, 1940, University Press of Kentucky, 1978.

On Troublesome Creek (short stories), Viking, 1941.

Pattern of a Man (short stories), Gnomon Press, 1976.

Sporty Creek: A Novel about an Appalachian Boyhood, Putnam, 1977.

The Run for the Elbertas (short stories), University Press of Kentucky, 1980.

Nonfiction:

The Wolfpen Notebooks: A Record of Appalachian Life, University Press of Kentucky, 1991.

The Man in the Bushes: The Notebooks of James Still, 1935–1987, University Press of Kentucky, forthcoming.

Contributor:

O. Henry Memorial Prize Stories, Doubleday, 1937, 1938, 1939, 1941.

Wilbur Cross and Helen MacAfee, editors, *The Yale Review Anthology*, Yale University Press, 1942.

Martha Foley, editor, *The Best American Short Stories*, Houghton, 1946, 1950, 1952.

Barbara Howes, editor, *Twenty-three Modern Stories*, Random House, 1963.

C. B. Levitas, editor, *The World of Psychoanalysis*, Braziller, 1966.

Helen White and Redding S. Sugg, Jr., *From the Mountain*, Memphis State University Press, 1972.

For children:

Way Down Yonder on Troublesome Creek: Appalachian Riddles and Rusties (illustrated by Janet McCaffrey; also see below), Putnam, 1974.

The Wolfpen Rusties: Appalachian Riddles and Gee-Haw Whimmy-Diddles (illustrated by J. McCaffrey; also see below), Putnam, 1975.

Jack and the Wonder Beans (illustrated by Margot Tomes), Putnam, 1977.

Rusties, Riddles, and Gee-Haw Whimmy-Diddles (contains *Way Down Yonder on Troublesome Creek: Appalachian Riddles and Rusties* and *The Wolfpen Rusties: Appalachian Riddles and Gee-Haw Whimmy-Diddles;* illustrated by J. McCaffrey), University Press of Kentucky, 1989.

Other:

(With Robert Penn Warren) *Promise and More Than Promise* (video), Appalshop Films, Inc. (Whitesburg, Kentucky), 1975.

James Still at Home (video), Kentucky Educational TV, 1987.

River of Earth in Song and Story (cassette), Appalshop
    Films, Inc., 1992.

Contributor of stories and poems to popular maga-
zines and literary journals, including *Atlantic, Esquire,
Nation, New Republic, Poetry, Saturday Evening Post,
Sewanee Review, Virginia Quarterly Review,* and *Yale
Review.* Manuscript collection located in the James
Still Room at Morehead State University.

Tomas Tranströmer

1931-

(Translated from the Swedish by Robin Fulton)

AUTOBIOGRAPHICAL CHAPTERS

Memories

"My life." Thinking these words, I see before me a streak of light. On closer inspection it has the form of a comet, with head and tail. The brightest end, the head, is childhood and growing up. The nucleus, the densest part, is infancy, that first period, in which the most important features of our life are determined. I try to remember, I try to penetrate there. But it is difficult to move in these concentrated regions, it is dangerous, it feels as if I am coming close to death itself. Further back, the comet thins out—that's the longer part, the tail. It becomes more and more sparse, but also broader. I am now far out in the comet's tail, I am sixty as I write this.

Our earliest experiences are for the most part inaccessible. Retellings, memories of memories, reconstructions based on moods that suddenly flare into life.

My earliest datable memory is a feeling. A feeling of pride. I have just turned three and it has been declared that this is very significant, that I am now big. I'm in bed in a bright room, then clamber down to the floor stunningly aware of the fact that I am becoming a grown-up. I have a doll to whom I gave the most beautiful name I could think of: Karin Spinna. I don't treat her in a motherly fashion. She is more like a comrade or someone I am in love with.

We live in Stockholm, in the Söder area, at Swedenborgsgatan 33 (now called Grindsgatan). Father is still part of the family but is soon to leave. Our ways are quite "modern"—right from the start I use the familiar "du" form to my parents. My mother's parents are close by, just round the corner, in Blekingegatan.

My maternal grandfather, Carl Helmer Westerberg, was born in 1860. He was a ship's pilot and a very good friend of mine, seventy-one years

Tomas Tranströmer

older than myself. Oddly enough, there was the same difference in age between him and his own maternal grandfather, who was born in 1789: the storming of the Bastille, the Anjala mutiny, Mozart writing his clarinet quintet. Two equal steps back in time, two long steps, yet not really so very long. We can touch history.

Grandfather's way of speech belonged to the nineteenth century. Many of his expressions would today seem surprisingly old-fashioned. But in his mouth, and to my ear, they felt altogether natural.

*Tomas and his mother, Helmy,
at Swedenborgsgatan 33, in 1932*

There was a trickle of comers and goers who didn't belong there. The occasional drunk would slowly return to his wits on the stairway. Several times a week beggars would ring. They would stand there in the porch mumbling. Mother made sandwiches for them—she gave them slices of bread rather than money.

We lived on the fifth floor. At the top, that is. There were four doors, plus the entry to the attic. On one of them was the name Orke, press photographer. In a way it seemed grand to live beside a press photographer.

Our immediate neighbour, the one we heard through the wall, was a bachelor, well into middle age, yellowish complexion. He worked at home, running some sort of broker's business by phone. In the course of his calls he often gave vent to hilarious guffaws that burst through the walls into our flat. Another recurring sound was the pop of corks. Beer bottles did not have metal caps then. Those Dionysiac sounds, the guffaws of laughter and the popping of corks, seemed hardly to belong to the spectrally pale old fellow sometimes met in the lift. As the years passed he became suspicious and the bouts of laughter diminished in frequency.

Once there was an outbreak of violence. I was quite small. A neighbour had been shut out by his wife; he was drunk and furious and she had barricaded herself in. He tried to break down the door and bawled out various threats. What I remember is that he screamed the peculiar sentence: "I don't give a damn if I go to Kungsholmen!" I asked mother what he meant, about Kungsholmen. She explained that the police headquarters was there. And that part of town then acquired a sense of something fearful. (That was a feeling intensified when I visited St. Erik's Hospital and saw the war-wounded from Finland who were cared for there in the winter of 1939–40.)

Mother left for work early in the morning. She didn't take a tram or bus—throughout her entire adult life she walked to and fro between Söder and Östermalm—she worked in the Hedvig Leonora School and was in charge of the third and fourth classes year after year. She was a devoted teacher and greatly involved with the children. One might imagine it would be hard for her to accept retirement. But it wasn't—she felt greatly relieved.

Since mother worked we had a home-help, a "maid" as she was called, though "child-minder" would have been nearer the truth. She slept in a minimal room which was really part of the kitchen

He was a fairly short man, with a white moustache and a prominent and rather crooked nose—"like a Turk's," as he said. His temperament was lively and he could flare up. His occasional outbursts were never taken too seriously and they were over as soon as they had begun. He was quite without aggression of the insistent kind. Indeed he was so conciliatory that he risked being labelled as soft. He wanted to keep on the best side even of people who might be criticized—in their absence—in the course of ordinary conversation. "But surely you must agree that X is a crook!" "Well, well—that's something I don't really know about . . ."

After the divorce, mother and I moved to Folkungagatan 57, a lower-middle-class tenement. A motley crowd lived there in close proximity to each other. My memories of life there arrange themselves like scenes from a film of the thirties or the forties, with the appropriate list of characters. The lovable concierge, her strong laconic husband whom I admired because, among other things, he had been poisoned by gas and that suggested a heroic closeness to dangerous machines.

and which was not included in the official flat-with-two-rooms-and-kitchen designation of our home.

When I was five or six, our maid was called Anna-Lisa and she came from Eslöv, in Skåne in the south of Sweden. I thought she was very attractive: blond frizzy hair, a turned-up nose, a mild Skåne accent. She was a lovely person and I still feel something special when I pass Eslöv station. But I have never actually stepped off the train at that magic place.

She was particularly talented at drawing. Disney figures were her specialty. I myself drew almost uninterruptedly throughout those years, in the late 1930s. Grandfather brought home rolls of brown paper of the sort then used in all the grocery shops, and I filled the sheets with illustrated stories. I had, to be sure, taught myself to write at the age of five. But it was too slow a process. My imagination needed some speedier means of expression. I didn't even have enough patience to draw properly. I developed a kind of shorthand sketching method with figures in violent movement, breakneck drama yet no details. Cartoon strips consumed only by myself.

One day in the mid-1930s I disappeared in the middle of Stockholm. Mother and I had been to a school concert. In the crush by the exit I lost my grasp of her hand. I was carried helplessly away by the human current and since I was so small I could not be discovered. Darkness was falling over Hötorget. I stood there, robbed of all sense of security. There were people around me but they were intent on their own business. There was nothing to hold on to. It was my first experience of death.

After an initial period of panic I began to think. It should be possible to walk home. It was absolutely possible. We had come by bus. I had knelt on the seat as I usually did and looked out of the bus window. Drottninggatan had flowed past. What I had to do now, simply, was to walk back the same way, bus stop by bus stop.

I went in the right direction. Of that long walk I have a clear memory of only one part—of reaching Norrbro and seeing the water under the bridge. The traffic here was heavy and I didn't dare set off across the street. I turned to a man who was standing beside me and said: "There's a lot of traffic here." He took me by the hand and led me across.

But then he let go of me. I don't know why this man and all the other unknown adults thought it was quite in order for a little boy to wander by himself through Stockholm on a dark evening. But

that's how it was. The remainder of the journey—through Gamla Stan, the old town, over Slussen and into Söder—must have been complicated. Perhaps I homed in on my destination with the help of the same mysterious compass that dogs and carrier pigeons have in them—no matter where they are released they always find the way home. I remember nothing of that part. Well, yes, I do—I remember how my self-confidence grew and grew so that when I did at last arrive home I was quite euphoric. Grandfather met me. My devastated mother was sitting in the police station following the progress of the search for me. Grandfather's firm nerves didn't fail him; he received me quite naturally. He was glad of course, but didn't make a fuss. It all felt secure and natural.

Museums

As a child I was attracted to museums. First, the Natural History Museum. What a building! Gigantic, Babylonian, inexhaustible! On the ground floor, hall after hall where stuffed mammals and birds thronged in the dust. And the arches, smelling of bones, where the whales hung from the roof. Then one floor up: the fossils, the invertebrates . . .

I was taken to the Natural History Museum when I was only about five years old. At the entrance, two elephant skeletons met the visitor. They were the two guardians at the gateway to the miraculous. They made an overwhelming impression on me and I drew them in a big sketchbook.

After a time those visits to the Natural History Museum stopped. I was going through a phase when I was quite terrified of skeletons. The worst was the bony figure depicted at the end of the article on "Man" in the Nordic Family Lexicon. But my fear was aroused by skeletons in general, including the elephant skeletons at the entrance to the museum. I became frightened even of my own drawing of them and couldn't bring myself to open the sketchbook.

My interest now turned to the Railway Museum. Nowadays it occupies spacious premises just outside the town of Gävle but then the entire museum was squeezed into a part of the district of Klara right in the centre of Stockholm. Twice a week grandfather and I made our way down from Söder and visited the museum. Grandfather must himself have been enthralled by the model trains, otherwise he would hardly have endured so many visits. When we decided to make a day of it we would finish up in Stockholm Central Station, which was nearby, and watch the trains come steaming in, full-sized.

The museum staff noticed the zeal of the young boy and on one occasion I was taken into the museum office and allowed to write my name (with a back-to-front *S*) in a visitors' book. I wanted to be a railway engineer. I was, however, more interested in steam engines than in electric ones. In other words, I was more romantic than technical.

Some time later, as a schoolboy, I returned to the Natural History Museum. I was now an amateur zoologist, solemn, like a little professor. I sat bent over the books about insects and fish.

I had started my own collections. They were kept at home in a cupboard. But inside my skull there grew up an immense museum and a kind of interplay developed between this imaginary one and the very real one which I visited.

I went out to the Natural History Museum more or less every second Sunday. I took the tram to Roslagstull and walked the rest. The road was always a little longer than I had imagined. I remember those foot marches very clearly: it was always windy, my nose ran, my eyes filled with tears. I don't remember the journeys in the opposite direction. It's as if I never went home, only out to the museum, a sniffling, tearful, hopeful expedition towards a giant Babylonian building.

Finally arriving, I would be greeted by the elephant skeletons. I often went directly to the "old" part, with animals which had been stuffed away back in the eighteenth century, some of them rather clumsily prepared, with swollen heads. Yet there was a special magic there. Big artificial landscapes with elegantly designed and positioned animal models failed to catch my interest—they were make-believe, something for children. No, it had to be quite clear that this was not a matter of living animals. They were stuffed, they stood there in the service of science. The scientific method I was closest to was the Linnean: discover, collect, examine.

*Tomas (left) with Grandfather, Mother, Cousin Margit, and Father Gösta,
at Runmarö, 1933*

I would work through the museum. Long pauses among the whales and in the paleontology rooms. And then the part which detained me most of all: the invertebrates.

I never had any contact with other visitors. In fact, I don't remember there being other visitors at all. Other museums which I occasionally visited—the National Maritime Museum, the National Museum of Ethnography, the Museum of Technology—were always crowded. But the Natural History Museum seemed to stay open only for me.

One day I did encounter someone—no, not a visitor, he was a professor or something like that—working in the museum. We met among the invertebrates—he suddenly materialized between the showcases, and was almost as small in stature as I was. He spoke half to himself. At once we were involved in a discussion of mollusks. He was so absent-minded or so unprejudiced that he treated me like an adult. One of those guardian angels who appeared now and then in my childhood and touched me with its wings.

Our conversation resulted in my being allowed into a section of the museum that was not open to the public. I was given much good advice on the preparation of small animals, and was equipped with little glass tubes which seemed to me truly professional.

I collected insects, above all beetles, from the age of eleven until I had turned fifteen. Then other, competing, interests, mostly artistic, forced their attentions on me. How melancholy it felt, that entomology must give way! I convinced myself that this was only a temporary adjustment. In fifty years or so I would resume my collecting.

The activity began in the spring and then flourished of course in the summer, out on the island of Runmarö. In the summerhouse, where we had little enough space to move around in, there stood jam jars with dead insects and a display board for butterflies. And lingering everywhere: the smell of ethyl acetate, a smell I carried with me since I always had a tin of the insect killer in my pocket.

It would no doubt have been more daring to use potassium cyanide as the handbook recommended. Fortunately that substance was not within my reach and so I never had to test my courage by choosing whether or not to use it.

Many were involved in the insect hunt. The neighbourhood children learnt to sound the alarm when they saw some insect that could be of interest. "Here's one!!" echoed among the houses,

"*My maternal grandparents, Carl Helmer and Maria Westerberg*"

and I would come rushing along with the butterfly net.

I was out on endless expeditions. A life in the open air without the slightest thought of thereby improving my health. I had no aesthetic opinions on my booty, of course—this was, after all, Science—but I absorbed unawares many experiences of natural beauty. I moved in the great mystery. I learnt that the ground was alive, that there was an infinite world of creeping and flying things living their own rich life without paying the least regard to us.

I caught a fraction of a fraction of that world and pinned it down in my boxes, which I still have. A hidden mini-museum of which I am seldom conscious. But they're sitting there, those insects. As if they were biding their time.

Primary School

I began in Katarina Norra Primary School and my teacher was Miss R, a tidy spinster who changed her clothes every day. As school ended each Saturday, each child was given a caramel, but otherwise she was often strict. She was generous when it came to pulling hair and delivering blows,

With Anna-Lisa at Runmarö, in 1936

although she never hit me. I was the son of a teacher.

My chief task that first term was to sit still at my desk. I could already write and count. I was allowed to sit and cut out shapes in coloured paper, but what the shapes were I can't remember.

I have a feeling that the atmosphere was fairly good throughout my first year there but that it chilled somewhat as time passed. Any disturbance to good order, any hitches or snags, made Miss R lose her temper. We were not allowed to be restless or loud-voiced. We were not to whine. We were not to experience unexpected difficulties in learning something. Above all, we were not to do *anything* unexpected. Any little child who wet himself or herself in shame and fear could hope for no mercy.

As I said, being the son of a teacher saved me from blows. But I could feel the oppressive atmosphere generated by all those threats and reproaches. In the background there was always the head teacher, a hawk-nosed dangerous character. The very worst prospect was to be sent to a

reform school, something which would be mentioned on special occasions. I never felt this as a threat to me personally but the very idea gave a disagreeable sensation.

I could well imagine what a reformatory was like, the more so since I'd heard the name of one—"Skrubba" ("Scrub"), a name suggesting rasps and planes. I took it as self-evident that the inmates were subjected to daily torture. The world view which I had acquired allowed for the existence of special institutions where adults tortured children—perhaps to death—for having been noisy. That was dreadful, but so must it be. If we were noisy, then . . .

When a boy from our school was taken to a reformatory and then returned after a year there, I regarded him as someone who had risen from the dead.

A more realistic threat was evacuation. During the first years of the war, plans were made for the evacuation of all schoolchildren from the bigger cities. Mother wrote the name TRANSTRÖMER with marking ink on our sheets and so on. The question was whether I would be evacuated with mother and her school class or with my own class from Katarina Norra, i.e., deported with Miss R. I suspected the latter.

I escaped evacuation. Life at school went on. I spent all my time in school longing for the day to come to an end so that I could throw myself into what really interested me: Africa, the underwater world, the Middle Ages, etc. The only thing which really caught my attention in school was the wall charts. I was a devotee of wall charts. My greatest happiness was to accompany teacher to the storeroom to fetch some worn cardboard chart. While doing so I could peep at the other ones hanging there. I tried to make some at home, as best I could.

One important difference between my life and that of my classmates was that I could not produce any father. The majority of my class came from working-class families where divorce was clearly something very rare. I would never admit that there was anything peculiar about my domestic situation. Not even to myself. No, of course I had a father, even if I met him only once a year (usually on Christmas Eve), and I kept track of him—at one point during the war he was, for example, on a torpedo boat and he sent me an amusing letter. I would have liked to have shown this letter in class but the right chance never came.

I remember a moment of panic. I had been absent for a couple of days and when I came back a classmate told me that the teacher—not Miss R but a substitute—had said to the class that they must not tease me on account of the fact that I had no father. In other words, they were sorry for me. I panicked, hearing that. I was obviously abnormal. I tried to talk it all away, my face bright red.

I was acutely aware of the danger of being regarded as an outsider because at heart I suspected I was one. I was absorbed in interests which no normal boy would have. I joined a drawing class, voluntarily, and sketched underwater scenes: fish, sea urchins, crabs, shells. Teacher remarked out loud that my drawings were very "special" and my panic returned. There was a kind of insensitive adult who always wanted to point me out as somehow odd. My classmates were really more tolerant. I was neither popular nor bullied.

Hasse, a big darkish boy who was five times stronger than I was, had a habit of wrestling with me every break during our first year at school. At first I resisted violently but that got me nowhere for he just put me to the ground anyway and triumphed over me. At last I thought up a way of disappointing him: total relaxation. When he approached me I pretended that my Real Self had flown away leaving only a corpse behind, a lifeless rag which he could press to the ground as he wished. He soon grew tired of that.

I wonder what this method of turning myself into a lifeless rag can have meant for me further on in life. The art of being ridden roughshod over while yet maintaining one's self-respect. Have I resorted to the trick too often? Sometimes it works, sometimes not.

The War

It was the spring of 1940. I was a skinny nine-year-old stooped over the newspaper, intent on the war map where black arrows indicated the advance of the German tank divisions. Those arrows penetrated France and for us, Hitler's enemies, they lived as parasites in our bodies. I really counted myself as one of Hitler's enemies. My political engagement has never been so whole-hearted!

"I am second from the left, second row, in primary school," 1939

To write of the political engagement of a nine-year-old no doubt invites derision, but this was hardly a question of politics in the proper sense of the word. It meant simply that I took part in the war. I hadn't the slightest conception of matters such as social problems, classes, trade unions, the economy, the distribution of resources, the rival claims of socialism and capitalism. A "Communist" was someone who supported Russia. "Right-wing" was a shady term because some of those at that end of the political spectrum had German leanings. My further understanding of "Right-wing" was that one voted in that direction if one were rich. Yet what did it really mean to be rich? On a few occasions we were invited for a meal with a family who were described as rich. They lived in Äppelviken and the master of the house was a wholesale dealer. A large villa, servants in black and white. I noticed that the boy in the family—he was my age—had an incredibly big toy car, a fire engine, highly desirable. How did one get hold of such a thing? I had a momentary glimpse of the idea that the family belonged to a different social class, one in which people could afford unusually large toy cars. That is still an isolated and not very important memory.

Another memory: during a visit home with a classmate it surprised me that there was no WC, only a dry closet out in the backyard, like the kind we had in the country. We would pee into a discarded saucepan which my friend's mother would swill down the kitchen sink. It was picturesque detail. On the whole it didn't occur to me that the family lacked this or that. And the villa in Äppelvik did not strike me as remarkable. I was far short of the capacity which many seem to have acquired even in their early years of grasping the class status and economic level of a given environment merely at a glance. Many children seemed able to do so, not I.

My "political" instincts were directed entirely at the war and Nazism. I believed one was either a Nazi or an anti-Nazi. I had no understanding of that lukewarm attitude, that opportunistic wait-and-see stance which was widespread in Sweden. I interpreted that either as support for the Allies or as covert Nazism. When I realized that some person I liked was really "pro-German," I immediately felt a terrible tightening over my breast. Everything was ruined. There could never be any kind of fellow feeling between us.

From those close to me I expected unequivocal support. One evening when we were on a visit to Uncle Elof and Aunt Agda, the news inspired my generally taciturn uncle to comment that "the English are successfully retreating . . ." He said this almost with regret yet it struck me there was an ironic undertone (on the whole irony was foreign to him) and I suddenly felt that tightening. The Allied version of history was never questioned. I stared grimly up at the roof light. There was consolation to be found there. It had the shape of a British steel helmet: like a soup plate.

On Sundays we often had dinner in Enskede with my other uncle and aunt on Mother's side; they provided a sort of support family for Mother after the divorce. It was part of the ritual there to turn on the BBC's Swedish broadcast on the radio. I shall never forget the programme's opening flourish: first the victory signal and then the signature tune, which was alleged to be "Purcell's Trumpet Voluntary" but which in fact was a rather puffed-up arrangement of a harpsichord piece by Jeremiah Clarke. The announcer's calm voice, with a shade of accent, spoke directly to me from a world of friendly heroes who saw to it that it was business as usual even if bombs were raining down.

When we were on the suburban train on the way to Enskede I always wanted Mother—who hated attracting attention—to unfold the propaganda paper *News from Great Britain,* and thus silently make public our stance. She did nearly everything for me, including that.

I seldom met Father during the war. But one day he popped up and took me off to a party with his journalist friends. The glasses were standing ready, there were voices and laughter and the cigarette smoke was dense. I went round being introduced and answering questions. There was a relaxed and tolerant atmosphere and I could do what I wanted. I withdrew by myself and sidled along the bookshelves of this strange house.

I came across a newly published book called *The Martyrdom of Poland.* Documentary. I settled on the floor and read it just about cover to cover while the voices filled the air. That terrible book—which I have never seen again—contained what I feared, or perhaps what I hoped for. The Nazis were as inhuman as I had imagined, no, they were worse! I read fascinated and disturbed and at the same time a feeling of triumph emerged: I'd been right! It was all in the book, the proof was there. Just wait! One day this will be revealed, one day all of you who have doubted will have the truth thrown in your faces. Just wait! And that in the event is what happened.

Libraries

"M edborgarhuset" (*lit.* "The Citizens' House") was built around 1940. A big four-square block in the middle of Söder, but also a bright and promising edifice, modern, "functional." It was only five minutes from where we lived.

In it there were, among other things, a public swimming pool and a branch of the city library. The children's section was, by obvious natural necessity, my allotted sphere, and to begin with it did have books enough for my consumption. The most important was Brehm's *Lives of the Animals.*

I slipped into the library nearly every day. But this was not an entirely trouble-free process. It sometimes happened that I tried to borrow books which the library ladies did not consider suitable for my age. One was Knut Holmboe's violent documentary *The Desert Is Burning.*

"Who is to have this book?"

"I am . . ."

"Oh no . . ."

"I . . ."

"You can tell your dad he can come and borrow it himself."

It was even worse when I tried to get into the adult section. I needed a book which was definitely not to be found in the children's section. I was stopped at the entrance.

"How old are you?"

"Eleven."

"You can't borrow books here. You can come back in a few years."

"Yes, but the book I want is only in here."

"What book?"

"*The Animals of Scandinavia: A History of Their Migration.*" And I added "by Ekman," in hollow tones, feeling the game was lost. It was. Out of the question. I blushed, I was furious. I would never forgive her!

In the meantime my uncle of few words—Uncle Elof—intervened. He gave me his card to the adult section and we maintained the fiction that I was collecting books for him. I could now get in where I wanted.

The adult section shared a wall with the pool. At the entry one felt the fumes from within, the chlorine smell came through the ventilation system and the echoing voices could be heard as from a distance. Swimming pools and suchlike always have strange acoustics. The temple of health and the temple of books were neighbours, a good idea. I was a faithful visitor to the Medborgarhus branch

of the city library for many years. I regarded it as clearly superior to the central library up on Sveavägen—where the atmosphere was heavier and the air was still, no fumes of chlorine, no echoing voices. The books themselves had a different smell there; it gave me headaches.

Once given a free run of the library I devoted my attention mostly to nonfiction. I left literature to its fate. Likewise the shelves marked Economics and Social Problems. History, though, was interesting. Medicine scared me.

But it was Geography that was my favourite corner. I was a special devotee of the Africa shelf, which was extensive. I can recall titles like *Mount Elgon, A Market-Boy in Africa, Desert Sketches* . . . I wonder if any of the books which then filled the shelf are still there.

Someone called Albert Schweitzer had written a book enticingly called *Between Water and Primeval Forest.* It consisted mostly of speculations about life. But Schweitzer himself stayed put in his mission and didn't move, he wasn't a proper explorer. Not like, for instance, Gösta Moberg, who covered endless miles (why?) in alluring, unknown regions, such as Niger or Chad, lands about which there was scant information in the library. Kenya and "Tanganyika" however were favoured on account of their Swedish settlements. Tourists who sailed up the Nile to the Sudd area and then turned north again—they wrote books. But none of those who ventured into the arid zones of the Sudan, none of those who made their way into Kordofan or Dar Fur. The Portuguese colonies of Angola and Mozambique, that looked so big on the map, were also unknown and neglected areas on the Africa shelf—and that made them even more attractive.

I read a lot of books standing there in the library—I didn't want to take home too many books of the same kind, or the same book several times in succession. I felt I would be criticized by one or other of the library staff and that was something to be avoided at all costs.

One summer—I don't remember which one—I lived through an elaborate and persistent daydream about Africa. That was out on the island of Runmarö, a long way from the library. I withdrew into a fantasy—I was leading an expedition right through central Africa. I trudged on through the woods of Runmarö and kept track of roughly how far I'd gone with a dotted line on a big map of Africa, a map of the whole of Africa which I had drawn. If I worked out, for instance, that in the course of a week I had walked 120

A drawing from his African period

kilometers on Runmarö, I marked in 120 kilometers on the map. It wasn't much.

At first I'd thought of starting the expedition on the east coast, more or less where Stanley had begun. But that would have left much too great a distance to traverse before I could reach the most interesting parts. I changed my mind and imagined that I travelled as far as Albert Nyansa by car. And that was where the expedition proper started, on foot. I would then have at least a reasonable chance of putting most of the Ituri Forest behind me before summer ended.

It was a nineteenth-century expedition, with bearers, etc. I was half aware, though, that this was now an obsolete way of travelling. Africa had changed. There was war in British Somaliland; it was in the news. Tanks were in action. It was indeed the first area where the Allies could claim an advance—I took due note of that, of course—and Abyssinia was the first country to be liberated from the Axis powers.

When my Africa dream returned several years later, it had been modernized and was now almost realistic. I was thinking of becoming an entomologist and collecting insects in Africa, discovering new species instead of new deserts.

Grammar School

Only a couple of my classmates from primary school progressed to secondary school ("real-skola"). And no one apart from myself applied to Södra Latin Grammar School.

There was an entrance exam I had to sit. My sole memory of that is that I spelled the word "särskilt" ("especially") wrongly, I gave it two *l*'s. From then on the word had a disturbing effect on me which persisted far into the 1960s.

I have a distinct memory of my first day at Södra Latin in the autumn of 1942. It is as follows. I find myself surrounded by a number of unknown eleven-year-old boys. I have butterflies in my stomach, I'm uncertain and alone. But some of the others seem to know each other well—those are the pupils from Maria Preparatory. I look and look for a face from Katarina Norra. My mood consists of about equal parts of gloomy unease and hopeful expectation.

Our names are called out and we are divided into three classes. I am assigned to Class 15B and told to follow Dr. Mohlin, who is to be our class teacher. One of the oldest teachers. His subject is German. He is small, with a sort of catlike authority. He moves swiftly and quietly, he has bristly, reluctantly greying hair, and a bald wedge above each temple. From someone nearby who seems to know him, I catch an assessment of him: Målle—as he is called—is "strict but fair." Ominous.

From the first moment it was clear that grammar school was something quite different from primary school. Södra Latin was throughout masculine, the school was as single-sexed as a monastery or barracks. It was not until several years later that a couple of women were smuggled into the staff.

Each morning we all assembled in the school hall, sang hymns, and listened to a sermon delivered by one of the religious studies teachers. Then we marched off to our respective classrooms. The collective atmosphere of Södra Latin was immortalized by Ingmar Bergman in his film *Hets*.[1] (It was shot in the school and those of us who were pupils then appear as extras in several parts of the film.)

We were all supplied with a school manual which included, among other items, "Directives as

---

[1]*Hets* —in Britain the film was called *Frenzy* and in the USA *Torment*.

to order and discipline, in accordance with the school's statutes'':

> The pupils shall attend instruction at the determined times, neatly and decently attired and in possession of the necessary textbooks. They shall observe good order and proper conduct and shall follow the instruction with due attention. The pupils shall likewise attend morning devotions and there deport themselves quietly and attentively . . .

> Pupils shall give due respect and obedience to the staff of the institution and shall accept with compliance their commands, corrections, and chastisements . . .

Södra Latin occupied the highest site on Söder, and its playground formed a plateau above most of the district's rooftops. The bricks of the school building could be seen from far away. The route to this castle of sighs was one I generally completed at a half-run. I hurried along by the long piles of wood—a sign of the crisis years—in front of "Björns Trädgrd," made my way up Götgatan—past Hansson and Bruce's bookshop—swung to the left into Höbergsgatan and there, every winter morning, stood a horse chewing straw in a nosebag. It was a brewery horse, a big steaming Ardenne. For a moment I found myself in its reeking shadow and the memory of that patient beast and of its smell in the cold and damp is still vivid. A smell that was at once suffocating and comforting.

I would rush into the playground just as the bells began to summon us to morning service. I was hardly ever late, for everything between the hours of eight and nine in the morning was well-timed. The spring was firm and tense as the school day began.

The end of the day at school was of course more relaxed, less regulated. Sometimes I went home with Palle. He was my closest friend in my first year at Södra Latin. We had quite a lot in common: his father, a sailor, was absent for long periods, and he was the only child of a good-natured mother who seemed pleased to see me. Palle had developed many of the characteristics of a single child, as I had, and he lived for his interests. He was above all a collector. Of what? Anything. Beer labels, matchboxes, swords, flint axes, stamps, postcards, shells, ethnographic oddments, and bones.

In his home, which was crammed full of his booty, we would duel with the swords. Together we carried out excavations at a secret spot on Riddarholmen and managed to retrieve bits of skeleton which my dentist identified as "parts of a human being."

Having Palle as a friend was an enriching experience but gradually we drifted apart. Further on in school Palle came to be absent for long periods because of illness. When he was transferred to another class we lost touch. My old friend was very far away. In fact he was marked by death. He appeared at school now only occasionally, pale and serious, with one leg amputated. When he died I found it impossible to accept. I developed a bad conscience but refused to recognize it. It felt as if I ought to suppress the memory of all the fun we'd had.

I feel I'm the same age as Palle, who died forty-five years ago without having grown up. But my old teachers, the "oldies" as they were collectively termed, remain old in my memory in spite of the fact that the older among them were about the same age as I am now as I write this. We always feel younger than we are. I carry inside myself my earlier faces, as a tree contains its rings. The sum of them is "me." The mirror sees only my latest face, while I know all my previous ones.

The teachers who stand out in my memory are of course those who generated tension or excitement, those who were vivid, colourful, original. They were not in the majority but there was a fair number of them. There was something tragic about some of them, which we were able to sense. A critical situation which could be described thus: "I know I can't be loved by those enviable turnip-heads in front of me. I know I can't be loved but at least I can make sure I won't be forgotten!"

The classroom was a theatre. The leading player, the teacher, performed on the stage, subjected to merciless scrutiny. The pupils were the audience and sometimes—one at a time—they would act a part as well.

We had to be on our guard, unfailingly. I had to get used to the recurring outbursts of aggression. Miss R had laid a good foundation—she had been strict and heavy-handed. Yet not really theatrical. At home there was nothing for me to learn in that direction. There were virtually no scenes at home, no rows, no bellowing father figure. Mother was spontaneous but undramatic. Giving vent to anger was childish. I had often been furious as a child but now I was a reasonably balanced youngster. My ideals were English—a stiff upper lip and so on. Outbursts of rage belonged to the Axis Powers.

At school there were choleric prima donnas who could devote most of a lesson to building up a tower of hysterical indignation, with the sole purpose of then emptying their vessels of wrath.

My class teacher Målle was hardly a prima donna. But he was the victim of a periodical and irresistible fury. Målle was really a charming person and a good teacher in his more harmonious periods. But, unhappily, what I remember best is that fury. Possibly the more violent outbursts did not come more often than three or four times a month. But it was upon those occasions that his great authority undoubtedly rested.

In the course of such lessons the thunder rolled to and fro across the landscape. That lightning would strike was clear to everyone, but no one could predict where. Målle did not victimize certain pupils. He was "strict but fair." Anyone might be struck by the lightning.

One day the lightning struck me. We were told to open our German grammars. I couldn't find mine. Was it in my schoolbag? Forgotten at home? I was lost. I couldn't find it.

"Stand up!"

I saw Målle dancing down from his desk and closing in on me. It was like being out in a field watching a bull approach.

The cuffs rained on me. I staggered this way and that. The next moment Målle was back sitting at his desk, frothing with rage, writing out a note for home. It was worded rather vaguely, accusing me of having been "careless during a lesson" or something like that.

Many of the teachers hoped that those written notes home would lead to interrogations and the infliction of further punishments at the hands of parents.

Not so with us. Mother listened to my story, took the note and signed it. She noticed then that I had blue marks on my face, caused by the ringed hand of the pedagogue. Her reaction was unexpectedly strong. She said she would contact the school, perhaps ring the headmaster.

To which I protested. She couldn't do that! Everything had turned out OK. But now "scandal" threatened. I would be called a mummy's boy and

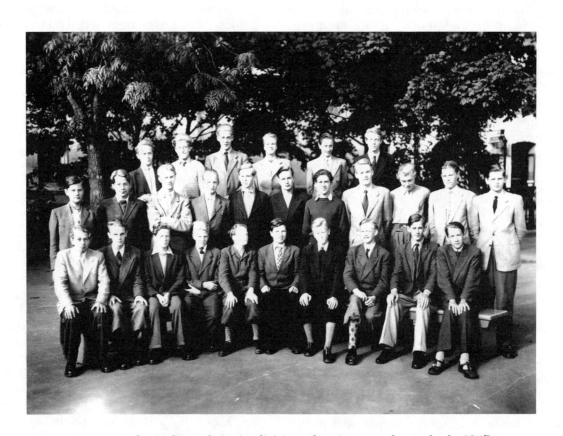

First row, far right, with Latin division of senior secondary school, 1947

then persecuted forever, not just by Målle but by the entire staff.

She dropped the idea of course. And throughout my school days I made a point of keeping the two worlds—of school and of home—apart. If the two worlds were to seep into each other, then home would feel polluted. I would no longer have any proper refuge. Even today I find something disagreeable in the phrase "cooperation between home and school." I can see also that this holding apart of the separate worlds which I practiced gave rise in due course to a more deliberately maintained distinction between private life and society. (This has nothing to do with political inclinations, whether to the left or to the right.) What we live through in school is projected as an image of society. My total experience of school was mixed, with more darkness than light. Just as my image of society has become. (Although we could well ask what we mean by "society.")

Contact between teacher and pupil was intensely personal and important personal characteristics were magnified in the classroom atmosphere as the result of the many tense situations. Personal, yes, but not in the slightest private. We knew virtually nothing about the private lives of our teachers although most of them lived in the streets around the school. There were, naturally, rumours—e.g., that Målle had been a light-weight boxer in his youth—but they were feebly supported by proper evidence and we scarcely gave them credit. We had trustworthy information about two of the most discreet younger teachers, men who never inspired any drama. One of them, allegedly, was poor and eked out his salary by playing the piano in a restaurant in the evenings. He had been seen. The other, allegedly, was a chess champion. That had been in the newspaper.

One day in the autumn Målle came into a lesson with a *Russula aerugina* in his hand. He set the mushroom on his desk. It was both liberating and shocking to have caught a glimpse of his private life! We knew now that Målle gathered mushrooms.

None of the teachers expressed political opinions. But at that time there were of course unprecedented tensions in the staff room. The Second World War was being fought out there too. Many of the teachers were convinced Nazis. As late as 1944 one of them, it was said, exclaimed in the staff room, "If Hitler falls then *I* shall fall!" He didn't fall, however. I had him in German later. He recovered so well that he was able to welcome Hesse's Nobel Prize in 1946 with triumphant bellowing.

I was a worthy pupil but not one of the best. Biology ought to have been my favourite subject, but for most of my secondary schooling I had a biology teacher who really was too odd. At some point in the past he had blotted his copybook hopelessly, he had been warned and was now like a quenched volcano. My best subjects were geography and history. There I had an assistant teacher called Brännman, ruddy, energetic, a youngish man whose straight blond hair had a tendency to stand on end when he got angry, which happened quite often. He had plenty of goodwill and I liked him. The essays I wrote were always on geographical or historical subjects. They were long. On that point I heard a story much later from another Södra Latin pupil, Bo Grandien.[2] Bo became a close friend of mine in the later years of school but what he told me related to an earlier year when we didn't know each other.

He said that the first time he heard me mentioned was as he passed some of my classmates in one of the breaks. They had just been given back their essays and were dissatisfied with their grades. Bo heard the indignant remark: "We can't ALL write AS FAST as Tranan, can we?"[3]

Bo decided that "Tranan" was a detestable character who ought to be avoided. To me, this story is in a way comforting. Nowadays well known for deficient productivity, I was then clearly noted as a prolific scribbler, someone who sinned through excessive productivity, a literal Stakhanov.

Exorcism

During the winter when I was fifteen I was afflicted by a severe form of anxiety. I was trapped by a searchlight which radiated not light but darkness. I was caught each afternoon as twilight fell and not released from that terrible grip until next day dawned. I slept very little, I sat up in bed, usually with a thick book before me. I read several thick books in that period but I can't say I really read them for they left no trace in my memory. The books were a pretext for leaving the light on.

---

[2]Poet and journalist (b. 1932).
[3]"Tranan": the crane (the bird).

"With Cousin Margit and my Södra Latin Grammar School friend, Bo Grandien,"
1949

It began in late autumn. One evening I'd gone to the cinema and seen *Squandered Days,* a film about an alcoholic. He finishes in a state of delirium—a harrowing sequence which today I would perhaps find rather childish. But not then.

As I lay down to sleep I reran the film in my mind's eye, as one does after being at the cinema.

Suddenly the atmosphere in the room was tense with dread. Something took total possession of me. Suddenly my body started shaking, especially my legs. I was a clockwork toy which had been wound up and now rattled and jumped helplessly. The cramps were quite beyond the control of my will, I had never experienced anything like this. I screamed for help and Mother came through. Gradually the cramps ebbed out. And did not return. But my dread intensified and from dusk to dawn would not leave me alone. The feeling that dominated my nights was the terror which Fritz Lang came near to catching in certain scenes of *Dr. Mabuse's Testament* especially the opening scene—a print works where someone hides while the ma-

chines and everything else vibrate. I recognized myself in this immediately, although my nights were quieter.

The most important element in my existence was *Illness.* The world was a vast hospital. I saw before me human beings deformed in body and in soul. The light burned and tried to hold off the terrible faces but sometimes I would doze off, my eyelids would close, and the terrible faces would suddenly be closing in on me.

It all happened in silence, yet within the silence voices were endlessly busy. The wallpaper pattern made faces. Now and then the silence would be broken by a ticking in the walls. Produced by what? By whom? By me? The walls crackled because my sick thoughts wanted them to. So much the worse. . . . Was I insane? Almost.

I was afraid of drifting into madness but in general I did not feel threatened by any kind of illness—it was scarcely a case of hypochondria—but it was rather the total power of illness that aroused terror. As in a film where an innocuous apartment interior changes its character entirely when ominous music is heard, I now experienced the outer world quite differently because it included my awareness of that domination wielded by sickness. A few years previously I had wanted to be an explorer. Now I had pushed my way into an unknown country where I had never wanted to be. I had discovered an evil power. Or rather, the evil power had discovered me.

I read recently about some teenagers who lost all their joy in living because they became obsessed with the idea that AIDS had taken over the world. They would have understood me.

Mother had witnessed the cramps I suffered that evening in late autumn as my crisis began. But after that she had to be held outside it all. Everyone had to be excluded, what was going on was just too terrible to be talked about. I was surrounded by ghosts. I myself was a ghost. A ghost that walked to school every morning and sat through the lessons without revealing its secret. School had become a breathing space, my dread wasn't the same there. It was my private life that was haunted. Everything was upside down.

At that time I was skeptical towards all forms of religion and I certainly said no prayers. If the crisis had arisen a few years later I would have been able to experience it as a revelation, something that would rouse me, like Siddhartha's four encounters (with an old person, with a sick person, with a corpse, and with a begging monk). I would have managed to feel a little more sympathy for and a little less dread of the deformed and the sick who invaded my nocturnal consciousness. But then, caught in my dread, religiously coloured explanations were not available to me. No prayers, but attempts at exorcism by way of music. It was during that period I began to hammer at the piano in earnest.

And all the time I was growing. At the beginning of that autumn term I was one of the smallest in the class, but by its end I was one of the tallest. As if the dread I lived in were a kind of fertilizer helping the plant to shoot up.

Winter moved towards its end and the days lengthened. Now, miraculously, the darkness in my own life withdrew. It happened gradually and I was slow in realizing fully what was happening. One spring evening I discovered that all my terrors were now marginal. I sat with some friends philosophizing and smoking cigars. It was time to walk home through the pale spring night and I had no feeling at all of terrors waiting for me at home.

Still, it is something I have taken part in. Possibly my most important experience. But it came to an end. I thought it was Inferno but it was Purgatory.

Latin

In the autumn of 1946 I entered the Latin division of senior secondary school (upper high school). This meant new teachers: instead of Målle, Satan, Slöman (*slö* = dull) and Company came characters like Fjalar, Fido, Lillan ("the littl'un"), Moster ("Auntie") and Bocken ("The Buck"). The last of these was the most important because he was my class teacher and came to influence me more than I would have been willing to admit then as our personalities clashed.

A few years previously we had had a moment or two of dramatic contact, before he became my teacher, that is. I was late one day and came running along one of the school corridors. Another boy came hurtling in the opposite direction towards me. This was G., who belonged to a parallel class and was well known as a bully. We screeched to a halt, face to face, without managing quite to avoid a collision. This sudden braking generated a lot of aggression and we were alone in the corridor. G. took the chance offered—his right fist slammed into my midriff. My sight blackened and I fell to the floor, moaning like a ma'm'selle in a nineteenth-century novel. G. vanished.

As the darkness cleared I found myself staring up at a figure stooping over me. A drawn out, whining, singing voice kept repeating as if in despair, "What's the matter? What's the matter?" I saw a pink face and very neatly trimmed chalk-white beard. The expression on the face was worried.

That voice, that face, belonged to the Latin and Greek teacher Per Venström, alias Pelle Vänster (*vänster* = left), alias Bocken.

Fortunately he refrained from any kind of interrogation as to why I was lying in a clutter on the floor, and he seemed satisfied when he saw I could walk away unaided. Since he showed himself to be worried and almost helpful, I formed the impression that Bocken was at heart a well-meaning person. Something of that impression persisted later as well, even when we had our conflicts.

Bocken's appearance was stylish, quite theatrical indeed. He usually accompanied his white beard with a dark wide-brimmed hat and a short cloak. A minimum of outdoor clothes in winter.

An obvious touch of Dracula. At a distance he was superior and decorative, close up his face often had something helpless about it.

The half singing intonation which characterized him was a personal elaboration of the Gotland dialect.

Bocken suffered from a chronic arthritic condition and had an emphatic limp, yet he managed to move swiftly. He always made a dramatic entry into the classroom, throwing his briefcase onto his desk; then, after a few seconds, we knew without doubt whether his mood was favourable or stormy. The state of the weather evidently affected his mood. On cool days his lessons could be downright jovial. When an area of low pressure hovered over us and the skies were cloudy, his lessons crawled along in a dull and fretful atmosphere punctuated by those inescapable outbursts of rage.

He belonged to the category of human being which it was quite impossible to imagine in a role other than that of schoolteacher. It could be said

The author about 1952

indeed that it was hard to envisage him as anything other than a Latin teacher.

In the course of my penultimate year at school, my own brand of modernistic poetry was in production. At the same time I was drawn to older poetry, and when our Latin lessons moved forward from the historical texts on wars, senators, and consuls to verses by Catullus and Horace, I was carried quite willingly into the poetic world presided over by Bocken.

Plodding through verses was educative. It went like this. The pupils first had to read out a stanza, from Horace perhaps:

> Aequam memento rebus in arduis
> servare mentem, non secus in bonis
>   ab insolenti temperatam
>   laetitia, morituri Delli

Bocken would cry out: "Translate!" And the pupil would oblige:

> With an even temper . . . aah . . . Remember that in an even temper . . . no . . . with equanimity . . . to maintain an even temper in difficult conditions, and not otherwise . . . aah . . . and like in fav- . . . favourable conditions . . . aah . . . abstain from excessive . . . aah . . . vivacious joy O mortal Dellius . . .

By now the luminous Roman text had really been brought down to earth. But in the next moment, in the next stanza, Horace came back in Latin with the miraculous precision of his verse. This alternation between the trivial and decrepit on the one hand and the buoyant and sublime on the other taught me a lot. It had to do with the conditions of poetry and of life. It was through form that something could be raised to another level. The caterpillar feet were gone, the wings unfolded. One should never lose hope!

Alas, Bocken never realized how captivated I was by those classical stanzas. To him I was a quietly provocative schoolboy whose incomprehensible nineteen-fortyish poems appeared in the school magazine—that was in the autumn of 1948. When he saw my efforts, with their consistent avoidance of capitals and punctuation marks, he reacted with indignation. I was to be identified as part of the advancing tide of barbarism. Such a person must be utterly immune to Horace.

His image of me was tarnished further after a lesson in which we were going through a medieval Latin text dealing with life in the thirteenth century. It was an overcast day; Bocken was in pain, and some kind of rage was just waiting to explode. Suddenly he tossed out the question—who was Erik the Lame Lisper? Erik had been referred to in our text. I replied that he was the founder of Grönköping.[4] This was a reflex action on my part coming from my wish to lighten the oppressive atmosphere. But Bocken was angry, not simply there and then but even at the end of term when I was given a "warning." This was a brief written message home to the effect that the pupil had been negligent in the subject, in this case Latin. Since my grades for written work were all high, this "warning" presumably had to be seen with reference to life in general rather than to my performance in Latin.

In my last year at school our relationship was better. By the time I took my exams it was quite cordial.

Round about then two Horatian stanza forms, the sapphic and the alcaic, began to find their way into my own writing. In the summer after matriculation I wrote two poems in sapphic stanzas. The one was "Ode to Thoreau," later pruned down to "Five Stanzas to Thoreau," the more juvenile parts having been erased. The other was "Storm," in the sequence "Autumnal Archipelago." But I don't know if Bocken ever acquainted himself with these. Classical meters—how did I come to use them? The idea simply turned up. For I regarded Horace as a contemporary. He was like René Char, Loerke, or Einar Malm. It was so naive that it became sophisticated.

BIBLIOGRAPHY

Poetry:

17 dikter (title means "Seventeen poems"), Bonnier, 1954.

Hemligheter på vägen (title means "Secrets on the way"), Bonnier, 1958.

Den halvfärdiga himlen (title means "The Half-finished heaven"), Bonnier, 1962.

Klanger och spår (title means "Echoes and traces"), Bonnier, 1966.

---

[4]The archetypal smalltown. According to the satirical weekly *Grönköpings Veckoblad* the town was founded by King Erik Eriksson (1216-1250), known as Erik the Lame Lisper.

Kvartett (contains *17 dikter, Hemligheter på vägen, Den halvfärdiga himlen,* and *Klanger och spår*), Svalans Lyrikklubb, 1967.

Twenty Poems, translated by Robert Bly, Seventies Press, 1970.

Mörkerseende, Seelig, 1970, translation by Bly published as *Night Vision*, Lillabulero Press, 1971.

Windows and Stones: Selected Poems, translated by May Swenson and Leif Sjoeberg, University of Pittsburgh Press, 1972.

(With Bly and Janos Pilinszky; and translator) *Stigar* (title means "Paths"; includes translations of works by Bly and Pilinszky), Författarförlaget, 1973.

Elegy: Some October Notes, translated by Bly, Sceptre Press, 1973.

Citoyens, translated by Robin Fulton, Sceptre Press, 1974.

(With Paavo Kaavikko) *Selected Poetry of Paavo Haavikko and Tomas Tranströmer* (translations and introduction for Haavikko's works by Hollo; translations and introduction for Tranströmer's works by Fulton), Penguin, 1974.

Östersjöar: En dikt, Bonnier, 1974, translation by Samuel Charters published as *Baltics*, Oyez, 1975.

(With Harry Martinson and Gunnar Ekeloef) *Friends, You Drank Some Darkness: Three Swedish Poets*, translated by Bly, Beacon Press, 1975.

Sanningsbarriären, Bonnier, 1978, translation by Bly published as *Truth Barriers: Poems by Tomas Tranströmer*, Sierra Books, 1980.

Dikter: 1954-1978 (title means "Poems: 1954-1978"), Bonnier, 1979.

How the Late Autumn Night Novel Begins, Sceptre Press, 1980.

Tomas Tranströmer: Selected Poems, translated by Fulton, Ardis, 1982.

Det vilda torget: Dikter, Bonnier, 1983, translation by John F. Dean published as *The Wild Marketplace*, Dedalus, 1985.

Selected Poems of Tomas Tranströmer: 1954-1986, translated by Bly, edited by Robert Haas, Ecco Press, 1987.

Collected Poems, translated by Fulton, Bloodaxe Books, 1987, Dufour, 1988.

For levande och doda: Dikter (title means "For living and dead"), Bonnier, 1989, appears in *Four Swedish Poets: Tranströmer, Ström, Sjögren, Espmark*, translated by Fulton, White Pine, 1990.

Anne Waldman

1945-

I was conceived on the Fourth of July 1945 shortly before my father was shipped overseas from Fort Bragg army base, North Carolina, to Europe. After "Tennessee Maneuvers," his unit was conveyed secretly to Hoboken where they joined the General Gordon Troopship headed for Marseilles. My mother had been living in a rented room on Macdougal Street, Greenwich Village, in a house full of women, some single, others with husbands away "at war." When her child was due, no relatives close by, she went to the town of Millville in southern New Jersey where my father's family lived. My grandfather John worked at Whitehall Tatum as a principle glassblower. His father, Frederick, who had immigrated from Hesse, a small town near Bremen, Germany, in the 1850s had also been a glassblower. John was a taciturn man, sober, serious. Dona Hand, his wife, my grandmother, had a sharp tongue. She was of Black-Irish English extraction. Her father had been a sea captain, lost between Cape May and Liverpool, delivering the New Jersey oak and pine they craved abroad.

My mother's parents, Frederick LeFevre and Alice Baker LeFevre, had lived in York, Pennsylvania. A devout Christian Scientist, Alice had hoped to be a missionary in Africa but due to delicate health couldn't. She lived as a semi-invalid, rarely travelling anywhere. Her husband played violin and was descended from the Huguenot LeFevres who escaped persecution at the hands of the Catholics from northern France. He died when my mother was five years old. I remember visiting York at an early age and seeing in a museum the family Bible that a devout LeFevre had hidden in a loaf of bread as they escaped. How could this enormous tome have ever fit inside a loaf of bread?

My father was a musician, playing the piano with accomplishment. After high school he worked as a piano player at various local movie theaters. He took up the peripatetic musician's life for a number of years, playing swing jazz with various bands around the East Coast, and accompanying modern dance artists such as the experimental Tamiris.

Anne Waldman and her son, Ambrose Bye, in Bali, 1989

John and Frances met in New York City at a party at the home of Isamu Noguchi in 1940. My mother had been an early "dropout," sailing off to Greece upon marrying Glaucos, the son of the celebrated Greek poet Angelos Sikelianos, having one child, Mark, and living abroad for a decade. My father by this time had had an early marriage as well—to the daughter of labor journalist Mary Heaton Vorse.

Committed to a new marriage, having abandoned the uncertain vocation of musician and the wild lifestyle it implied, as well as sobered by the war, my father went back to school on the GI Bill, eventually receiving a doctorate from Columbia

Parents John and Frances Waldman, married August 8, 1943, in Millville, New Jersey

University. During this time he took on many "hack" writing jobs, later wrote articles and books on reading and education, including the popular *Rapid Reading Made Simple.* He began working at Pace University in downtown New York, was director of the reading laboratory there, served as chair of the English department (hosting guests Marianne Moore and Allen Ginsberg, among others), and also as secretary of the university.

I remember the marvelous sobering smell and presence of my father's writing accoutrements in the cramped apartment at the top of Macdougal Street: yellow foolscap, messy typewriter ribbons, wheel eraser with its pert green whisk-skirt, and the obligatory cup of coffee and cigarettes close by. I was anxious to replicate these exotic environs, which carried associations of solitude, daydreaming (one looked off as though in trance when thinking "what to say"), and sacred daily ritual. There was the clatter and peck—a noisy rhythm— of the fingers at keys, a sound both soulful and playful. A mind at work, quite simply that, making

something out of nothing that appeared in code on an unassuming sheet of paper. And then you had a few typed pages, the "work," to peruse, edit, read out loud. To show the wife who was keen on getting into it. She was the grammatical perfectionist, wrote her own "stuff" furtively in clandestine notebooks. Why did this practice of writing seem heroic, attractive to me? What could be humbler yet more romantic? Professional as well. Who wanted to go work for somebody else every day, sit in a dull office 9 to 5? Little checks might eventually arrive in the mail. You might see your name in print.

But more importantly, I was a voluble reader as a child and wanted, too, to have power as a writer to make people's hearts beat faster, change a pulse with the energy of language. Make others as exhilarated as I felt myself become reading those terrible books, books that changed your life, carried you into mad and exciting particulars of experience. And were subtle as well, nestling you in a sweet and sharp language, mysterious language, more powerful even than music. Was it that the characters came alive, and you could actually in many instances *become* them, that there was conflicted plot to follow, denouement, surprise, reconciliation at end? Of course I loved novels: *Jane Eyre, Lorna Doone, Wuthering Heights,* and *Silas Marner.* Yet more complex as experience was what poetry offered, raising its lyric jolt to the ear. Different, poetry, in that it was something I might join as well. Had a bent for, liked reading aloud. The muse, that energy demon sent out a call. Being musical I would study piano, but resist, never be a musician except in the vocalizations of my own text, later. To make something exquisite come alive in words and be shocking in a beautiful way was the vow. And later the vow included others in a like-minded community that took its stand as poets. To imagine another world or hear words a particular way and communicate this to others. And poetry did need characters. Your persona, energy, your consciousness was the heroine of the song.

Thus through my childhood, my father was professional, cranking out articles, for example, on the perils of smoking for popular magazines; he was a college student, then educator: Dr. Waldman. He was an avid reader of prose. My mother was the poet and translator (French of Cesar Moro and Greek of Sikelianos) but her practices, as said, were covert. She was hard on herself and others. Intellectual, artistic, an autodidact, never satisfied. In love with poetry. Poetry was, in her view, the highest art. These two persons with their particular bents and turns and passions certainly helped form mine.

Yet this was not an easy household, it harbored certain contradictions—there was something rigorously protestant in my upbringing—an expectation on the one hand to succeed, excel, to fit in, to have people's respect. An upbringing which, for example, emphasized education (not the exclusive province of schools either). A smart person was never satisfied, was always hungry for more knowledge, devoured books, asked questions, kept "at it." Rarely idle. On the other hand, both parents carried much of their earlier bohemianism and tolerance and permissiveness into this new marriage. My mother was a terrible housekeeper, scorned Mother's Day, resented and was critical of anything "phoney." She threatened to leave when—I must have been thirteen or fourteen—my father and younger brother, Carl, arrived home one day with a TV set in tow, bought on an "installment plan." "It's either me or the TV. I swear I will leave if that abomination crosses the threshold." They beat a quick retreat back to Macy's. We were "atheists"—"agnostics" my parents would more accurately say. They had both flirted with the Communist party, like many

Mother, Frances, holding Anne, and brother Mark Sikelianos, 1945

liberal-minded people of their generation, but this was before they had met, before the war. Later, they attended services at the Church of the Ascension in lower Manhattan which had an excellent organist and choir. My mother started going there, she said, "for the music." My older half-brother, Mark Sikelianos, lived with us some of that time. He was a gifted music student at the high school of music and art. An avid fan of folk, classical music, and jazz who would later work at Broadcast Music Inc., major music publishers in New York City.

The tiny apartment was cramped. We were "strapped" or "broke" much of the time. I loved listening to the Saturday morning radio shows. And afternoon opera, broadcast live from the Metropolitan Opera House. We ate out once or twice a year in Chinatown. We all read a lot.

I joined the Childrens' Theater at Greenwich House at the age of six, a community arts center on Barrow Street near Seventh Avenue, and also participated in "rhythm classes." Director Helen Murphy was the guiding inspiration for the highly unusual and creative productions. One show, "Americana," told the history of the States through song, including work songs, Negro spirituals, lullabies, Appalachian tunes, and lyrics from various other folk traditions. I remember one of my lines in the voice of a would-be prospector: "There's gold in Californy and rangin' land in Texas!" Largely a gaggle of girls, all ages, we dressed in simple green silk tunics and suede "rhythm sandals" á la Isadora Duncan. Christmas season found us singing carols at local banks and hospitals. At age twelve I played Alice in *Alice in Wonderland*, loving the wit and magic of those scenes.

The Childrens' Theater was a complement to the literary and theatrical activities at Public School 8 grammar school which I also enjoyed tremendously—writing contests (a best poem about a tree for Arbor Day), the magazines, participation in school plays, playing a character named "Tomboy Joe" in one production, and Puck in *A Midsummer Night's Dream*. Reading aloud, mouthing syllables, dramatizing the sense of the words all came naturally. Although I was never good at memorization (too impatient), I had a flair for the stage.

PS 8 was directly around the corner from Macdougal on King Street. A modest public school, later a Six Hundred School for Wayward Girls, now a semifashionable condominium, at the edge of SoHo. The school had a working-class

As Alice (left) in Alice in Wonderland, *Greenwich House Childrens' Theatre, New York City, 1957*

atmosphere as well as an ethnic, racial, artistic mix. James Agee's children attended school there a time and we became friends. Another close friend was Portuguese. Many Italian immigrants had settled in this neighborhood aptly dubbed "Little Italy" and attended the neighborhood school or the parochial school close by. A group of us, inspired by an infectious religiosity, one day saw the devil in the girls' room at school. "I swear, Mrs. Mulhere, I did, I did see the devil and he had little red horns and a barbed tail!" My best girlfriend was Randa Haines (currently one of a handful of female movie directors now working in Hollywood), dark, pensive for one so young. I saw my first television programs in the small apartment on Bleecker Street she shared with her eccentric mother. I remember now, she the same perhaps, thinking how compelling television was. My mother in her disdain for television seemed old-fashioned. These were exciting times, faster times. We lived in a new electric universe swift with communication of infinite form. One could effect changes, could

infiltrate a more penetrating truth through a vast network of powerful media, could actually be a kind of conduit or example for "higher practice." At the same time, being a poet one was free of accoutrement, ornament, technology. Poet, the role of, linked one back to a simpler past. It didn't matter what version of the world you lived in, you were there as witness, you had your sensitive ears, vigilant eyes. The eye altering alters all, said Blake. You could transform reality without a lot of props. But was poetry a "higher practice"? A spiritual path? Poetry, what mind or game was that? What was I getting into? Escape? I resorted to words to imagine a parallel universe. I could express the emotional subtext of all my experience in a kind of secret code. I was in many ways living a life through the eye of romantic watcher. I could skip around, be elliptical, condense a day, a year, tell the exhilarating or horrific images of a dream. So poetry was a weave which could encompass all data, all heartbreak and vision, and could sound the world back at itself. Quote the seed syllables of others and honor the masters, men and women, of the past. Some of this inspiration came in stronger waves later, but by the seventh grade I felt myself to carry the identity of poet.

I grew into the neighborhood, most definitively a parallel universe. "Little Italy" had the pageantry and high ecclesiastical tone of the Catholic religion as well as peasant superstition, exotic cafes, and aromatic restaurants, another language to consort in, street life, the Mafia, annual street fairs or "festas"—on the whole a highly distinctive flavor and rich cultural identity. Other layers to the Village included bohemian bars, folk music gatherings at Washington Square Park, jazz clubs, off-off Broadway arenas. It was also within the larger cosmopolitan environment of New York. My mother was eager to have me *taste it all*. She scrimped to send me to art classes at the Museum of Modern Art. We had tickets regularly to ballet, modern dance, and classical music concerts.

Could one be as great a writer as Henry James, Wallace Stevens, Yeats, Shakespeare, Sappho? I wondered, reading voraciously. Not likely, presumptuous in fact, but the connection, thrill of heart to their text was immediate, electric, so that you might vow to put yourself next to that work and be the constant reader, a votary in the service of. And scribble a bit on the side:

Tell me your secrets o success
It is said your fruits are desired by ambitious men
Tell me, if I were to taste the sweetness of these fruits
Would I be able to remain unhaunted by dreams of
  more?

I was an ambitious child, age eleven or so this poem, a fool, romantic, "just a girl." Yet fighting the cultural conditioning of being "girl," aided by supportive parents who were sufficiently original. With a brother, Carl, two years my junior, who would also be a professional writer. Frances wanted the best, of course, for her attractive, precocious children. And by seventh grade she had saved enough (and I had partial scholarship as well) and both my brother and I started going to Grace Church School, which was, I later realized, directly across Fourth Avenue from where poet Frank O'Hara lived. Had our paths intersected? Grace had a solid academic reputation, was a "Village" school, Episcopalian backdrop. Neo-Gothic spires. I liked leading the short, ecumenical religious services in the chantry. Always had a religious "messianic" streak, wanted to guide others

to . . . what? I was involved with the school's literary activities and some of us started meeting after school as well, at 54 Fifth Avenue in the large rambling apartment of the Hourwich twins, two brothers, whose parents had known the painter Norma Millay, Edna St. Vincent's sister, and had quite a few of her paintings on the walls. This was my first official "salon." We read plays by Shakespeare and Molière (in translation) aloud, argued politics with Hourwich, Sr., who was, in spite of his bohemianism, an archconservative Wall Street broker. Gladys, the mother of my schoolmates, was from the West Indies, a beautiful dusky woman who smoked incessantly and wove gorgeous fabrics on several large looms.

From Grace Church I went to Friends Seminary, a Quaker school on Rutherford Place, and continued with literary activities, editing the school newspaper the *Oblivion* ("for what is a newspaper but a rag for oblivion?") and contributed to the *Stove* literary magazine. My best friend in high school was Jonathan Cott, the journalist, critic, and poet, who was loyal literary cohort, comrade-in-arms. We showed each other poetry, traded books. He turned me on to Rilke and *The Dream of the Red Chamber*. I was subscribing to the *Evergreen Review* by then, dutifully reading the *Village Voice* and even sending out my poetry for rejection by the *New Yorker* and other notable magazines. I remember the pleasure, the private pleasure—kind of erotic activity?—of secretly writing romantic love poems, sending them off unbeknownst to parents, friends, and then the thrill of the return envelope, although it presaged no great success. Jon and I considered ourselves "existentialists," discussed Camus, Gide among others. He was two years ahead of me at school. He and my mother became close. And Frances was by now actively reading contemporary poetry, in particular the New American Poets. We three had an obsession with poetry. Another link to poetry at this time was Jon Beck Shank, provocative high school English teacher, erudite, Wallace Stevens scholar, who read Stevens aloud with gusto and passion. His "performance" of "An Idea of Order at Key West" sent tremors through my body and mind. I would never be the same.

And the spiritual side was nurtured at Friends by teacher Dr. Earle Hunter, a Quaker, who taught an excellent course in comparative religion, touching on fundamentals of Oriental traditions. The praxis and notions behind Taoism, Hinduism, and Buddhism were fire in my brain. And I appreciated, too, the regular Quaker "silent meetings" in which we'd spend an hour in meditation then speak out our secret observations, doubts, delight. These were surprisingly secular occasions. Awareness practice with simplicity and rigor. No hierarchy, no priests. Closer, as I was discovering, to the Asian traditions I was attracted to. And a political edge. As we took cover in the bomb shelters in the school basement, Quakers would be outside leafletting on behalf of "banning the bomb." This was 1961.

During these high school years I had a wide circle of friends, many of them artistically pitched. Close companion was Kathy Emmett, daughter of Kim Hunter, the actress. I lived with her family in Stratford, Connecticut, working backstage, age sixteen, while Kim acted in *As You Like It* and *Macbeth*. Jessica Tandy, Pat Hingle, Philip Bosco, Morris Carnovsky, also in residence, were impressive actors, articulate persons, and attentive to my youthful questions. I thought I would write a novel one day using Stratford as backdrop. The summer season ended on a tragic and dramatic suicide: one of the walk-on sword-bearers stabbed himself to death during a performance of *Macbeth*. On the train home alone to New York, I remember staring out the window, stunned by the empty horror of death, and the ironic mix of stage and life. Was one inspired to write out of these moments of irony, death, pain?

Years thirteen to seventeen were spent in the glorious labyrinthian playground of New York City. And the particular playground of the Village with its attendant glamour, anarchy, experimentation, derangement of the senses through drugs and alcohol, intensity of relationships. Toward the end of this high school period I was spending more time with neighborhood friends—creative types, musicians, artists, "dropouts." Kids from both the neighborhood—working class, bohemian—and sons and daughters of the affluent, liberal, and artistic literati. Martin Hersey, John Hersey's son, carried a well-thumbed copy of *Naked Lunch* around with him in an old, battered guitar case. John Hammond, Jr., was already becoming a serious musician. I called myself a "writer." We were weird. All the kids were getting weird. The times were weird, contradictory. If you didn't have a focus or path you could even get twisted. Reflecting on this period now I appreciate how rich and unique it was as an early ground for a developing sense of alternative community. Realities of racism, anti-abortion, economic social inequities, other poisons permeated the urban atmosphere.

"Vow to poetry," about 1960

Bennington College, then almost completely a women's college, was in many ways a continuation of some of these developing threads for my life, although it carried an onus of exclusivity and one wondered about the label "dilettantism" applied to the place. Nonetheless it was a true harbor from the city, and the faculty expected a maturity, self-discipline, and rigor from its students. I submitted poetry with my application, having been impressed by the accord given to poets on the Bennington faculty. Highly strung, sensitive, creative, and gifted students were the norm. Howard Nemerov was mentor to me, a quirky teacher—particularly of William Blake and Yeats. He often showed up in class rumpled and exhausted after a night with the "muse," pulling a fragile piece of foolscap from his pocket—the latest poem. He was accessible, human, "troubled," but could always turn an embarrassingly delicate or grievous moment around with his caustic wit. Sympathetically inclined, I think he sensed my vow to poetry as a practice and way of life. We would argue about John Ashbery, Frank O'Hara, the Beats—particularly Allen Ginsberg—as he favored a traditional poetry and poetics. I realized then how certain lines might be drawn between the so-called academic world of poetry—exemplified by a kind of white male heterosexual angst ("Tamed by *Miltown* we lie on Mother's bed" is a quintessential line by Robert Lowell) and what I've come to call the "outrider" tradition, characterized by wild mind, spontaneity, a less secure life-style, political opposition, experimentation of form, and other unspeakable acts and digressions.

Poets I was drawn to were not products or proprietors of English departments. And as a woman I was increasingly interested in a breakdown of semantics, grammar, derangement, or deconstruction of solid narrative mind-sets and tight-jawed preconceptions about writing. These issues seemed close to my own concerns, my own mental grammar and experience. Gertrude Stein's work was smart, amusing, playful, pushed boundaries. I enjoyed the way *Tender Buttons* moved in time, and the odd juxtaposition, auditory associations Stein pulled off, all with an exceedingly simple, ordinary vocabulary. The vernacular of William Carlos Williams was rich and startling. When I suggested Stein and Ezra Pound be taught seriously at Bennington I was distressed by what I saw as an inexplicable prejudice. Not only dismissed as "silly," this formidable grande dame with the Picassos, Matisses, and lively salon was the butt of unkind jokes. Pound was an anti-Semite and thereby beyond the pale. It was in some respects a lonely battle. But Bernard Malamud encouraged my curiosities and explorations in modernism and contemporary poetry and my own work as well. The private seminar allowed for an intense give-and-take, critical feedback on creative work. Apprentice formats were extremely rare in other universities and colleges at the time. Thus I felt myself fortunate to come up against real writers, who practiced their art with fury and ambition. Opinionated, egocentric, solipsistic "masters." Teaching was often a passion but secondary to the true practice—the work. Also it was fascinating to witness firsthand another alternative, albeit somewhat academic and exclusive, community. And to be part of it as well. Stanley Edgar Hyman, married to the eccentric and brilliant Shirley Jackson who dwelled in a kind of dark study on the margins of the campus mandala, taught an exciting "Myth, Ritual, and Literature" class, exposing us to the Dionysian delights of classical Greek drama, dark mysteries of Childe's ballads, and the tender delicacies of youth Parsifal

in search of the goblet that would unlock the secrets of life. Hyman challenged my own preconceptions about origins of language and *why we make poetry.* He brought text down to a primal, psychological level. He himself looked the part of a satyr, heavily bearded, wild gleam in an already mischievous eye. I wondered where to place myself as female. What were my rites of passage, rituals? Envying the freedom of the male protagonist, the male poet, I was still a daughter yet carried a lot of male energy. Was it necessary to inebriate my father and subsequent fathers to steal their secrets? Coax them, seduce them? Or would I be virginal Athena, sprung forth from and forever indebted to Zeus's mind? It was hard to be "girl." I was competitive with men. I wanted their freedom. Yet Emily Dickinson, Stein, Laura Riding, Hilda Doolittle were writers to study, emulate. And I wanted to know more about their lives. How they had loved. How they had made their art. I was starting to feel the torments of intense relationships, and the conflict between so-called life and so-called art. It seemed a struggle to assert the work.

My poetic confidence welled up in spurts. I trusted my ear. Some deeper rhythm in the nervous system demanded attention. Images from dreams demanded attention. And I was in love with poetry. This was my vulnerability, my soft spot. This was where the struggle would occur. In my own head with my own imagination and emotions. Was that the battleground? Outsiders (including the so-called "canon") were demons, distractions from the work I had to do. If you listened to the men, and stayed in love with the classics, you were intimidated, crippled, but if you could hold them at a distance, steal their secrets, look them in the eye you were safe. Could I love a man on equal terms? My reading was inspiring my writing. I was inept but ambitious. I was the best of students without having to really set foot in the classroom, metaphorically speaking. But as I wanted to do this work with other like-minded practitioners of the glorious art, have cohorts who felt as passionately as I did, I formed important alliances with the "guys," many of whom were closer to where I positioned myself. This was particularly true during my last year of college where I had developed and cultivated some correspondence with poets of my own generation and had already travelled out to Berkeley. And where were the women? There were several fine aspiring writers at Bennington and in New York City. Who would be there to hear us? I was sure a time would arrive.

Bennington was famous and attractive for its out-of-residency work-period and I returned to New York City the first year, taking a number of odd jobs—several in the theater, working at the newly developing Theater Genesis. I worked at the Shakespeare Festival in Stratford the following summer again, and then the subsequent winter landed a volunteer job with the American School of Classical Studies in Athens working with one of the leading experts on amphora handles, Dr. Virginia Grace. Dr. Grace was a rarity, classically trained, a devotee of the antique world, a spinster with a club foot. There was something mythological in her situation. She was the lame votary, chained to the temple of Apollo, or was it Athena? Eschewing a normal life, an oddity, yet close to the women I'd been reading about—often daughters of the educated American class who became exiles abroad because they were misfits at home. Driven, not wanting to settle for a married existence, often sexually disinclined towards men, early rebels. Her profile, to my eye, bore a striking resemblance to photographs I'd seen of the seminal writer H. D. She took me under her wing. I sat for hours in the icy cold Stoa of Attalos, surrounded by tiny electric heaters, reading and cataloguing the numerous amphoras that had been found during a recent dig around the Stoa. They bore attractive, often mystical-looking seals which located their places of origin and helped determine ancient trade routes. The lovely amphoras, shapely vessels, carried wine to and from the islands and further off—to Africa, Asia? And what remained but the phallic handles, shards of cold runic clay in the hand.

I took a side trip to Egypt by boat, felt my life charged, changed. Poet identity empowered. Why? I was witness, got outside myself and a restricted sense of my own impoverished culture (or so I thought it then) yet wanted to internalize those external experiences through rhythmic language. Wanted to be able to both condense and move around these intense experiences with grace and ease. Wanted to make sense, or poetry, of what I saw. How else to hold it, even briefly, as it flashed by? I would feed off the adventures inside that vivid country—which was but a part of a much larger continent, Africa!—for many years. Never forget kissing the ground as we embarked in Alexandria (I'd been reading *The Alexandrian Quartet* with some fervor). Never forget the night waylaid by the Ali brothers in a rickshaw, who wanted to take off my clothes and see a real American girl! Never forget camping at the edge of and diving—knife in my thick rubber belt—for fish in the Red Sea whose water was a beautiful rich blue. And how forget the kindness of the elegant Copt and his family who worked at the Benaki Museum and took me to dinner on the Omar Khayyam houseboat restaurant with sumptuous courses of exotic food, skilled belly dancer? I remember being extremely embarrassed by a drunken American at a table close by. And the Coptic children in Old Cairo throwing stones at me . . . I never understood why. Ugly American? Riding a camel at Giza and crawling on all fours through the narrow passageways of Cheops, imagining suffocation by sand. And the questions everywhere from young Arabs about the murder of President Kennedy. It must have been Lyndon Johnson! I had some questions, too. Never forget trying to sleep out in the desert near Luxor under stark, crystalline moon, yet on alert, terrified, for ubiquitous deadly scorpions. Ambushed by a violent stranger as I tried to board the boat heading back up the Nile from the temple at Abu Simbel. I wrenched free. The temple was slated to be moved further inland to avoid flooding caused by the ambitious but ill-conceived Aswan Dam and I watched it disappear from view from the stern of the boat, a magnificent tribute to a megalomaniacal state of mind. Ramses wanted immortality at all costs. These sacred sites—the pyramids, Thebes, Denderah, Abu Simbel—resonated in my imagination. They were power spots. I felt curious vibrations. I kept a journal. I wrote a long poem that has since disappeared. Swallowed by the sands of time. . . . This, surely, was what a writer was meant to do: travel around the world collecting images, stories, sleeping in temples, feeling the power of sacral architecture, conjuring alien gods, commenting on the folly of kings. "The lone and level sands stretch far away." Anubis, Horus, Setekh were guardian presences. Already an inveterate romantic, this auspicious Egyptian voyage was a heady taste of trips to come and confirmed and legitimized an early propensity for travel and adventure. Travel, wanderlust, was in the marrow, *de riguer* for the poet. And my curiosity about reincarnation was sparked further. I read *The Egyptian Book of the Dead* and imagined the royal barge crossing the great divide to the other side. Or saw the setting sun as a ball of dung being pushed across the sky by an invisible beetle. Everyone was an Egyptian princess in a past life. Why be an exception?

In the summer of 1963 while working with an arts group in the inner city of Philadelphia, I was taken by some friends from Harvard to meet a Mongolian Buddhist lama, Geshe Wangyal, who had come to America on a Tolstoy Foundation grant and was residing in the small town of Freewood Acres, New Jersey, in a pink suburban house. I was nervous, knowing little about the protocol for meeting such a formidable personage, and had worn a dress and put on lipstick as was my wont. My close friend commented on the impropriety of the makeup but I held my ground, sensing the conflict that might arise if one became sycophantically inclined, always trying to please, impress the teacher. Come as you are seemed the better motto. I had been reading some of the odd and stilted translations of prayers and texts emanating from the work with Geshe Rinpoche, mimeographed on a bright goldenrod-colored mimeo paper, but didn't quite understand the student/teacher relationship and who the prayers were to. Buddha? This was unfamiliar territory. I remember my friends asking a lot of questions about LSD and the nature of consciousness and "cessation." I remember feeling that when I looked into the lama's face he reflected back my own projections of himself and my own projections of him looking at me. They were simply nonexistent, the projections. He was sweet to me. I was intrigued by the colorful shrine with seemingly garish and exaggerated iconographies, vivid textures, silks, offerings, pungent incense, the musky, slightly rancid odor of Tibetan tea. Peeking in the dining room, I was a bit startled seeing a flock of young monks in their maroon robes gnawing on chicken bones. Weren't Buddhists supposed to be vegetarians? I seemed to be one of the few women on the premises. I visited the lama on several occasions. What was the nature of this early connection to a living lineage-holder of a centuries-ancient, continuous unbroken lineage? Was this simply curiosity on my part? Tempting as exotic and resource material? Grist for the poem mill? A karma link to a spiritual past and path of some kind? The enduring impression was one of being at ease and comfortable with this "tradition," whatever it proved to be.

During the summer of 1965, I travelled across country with my younger brother, Carl, and a school friend who had a job lined up in Hollywood. Yet Berkeley—then the mecca of creative and political scholarship and action, where an important poetry conference was just about to begin— was the tangible destination. Little did I realize how this trip would affect the entire direction of my life. In retrospect it seems miraculous that being in a particular place at a particular time should activate or propel one's life in such a purposeful way. I was perhaps already primed. I was a novice, naive young votary who'd read the now historic Donald Allen anthology, *The New American Poetry.* I was curious to hear some of the live voices of these persons I was privately emulating. Robert Duncan, Charles Olson, Ed Dorn, Ted Berrigan (Jon Cott had been sending Ted and Ron Padgett's *C* magazine to me at school), Ed Sanders, Lenore Kandel were a refreshing contrast to the poets I'd been hearing at Bennington: May Swenson, Richard Eberhardt, Stanley Kunitz. They were less predictable, far ranging, their field was much more open, expansive. So-called subject matter was sexually explicit, tender. The poems were political, spiritual. Lines were shocking, dissonant, powerful, beautiful, lyrical, strange. The audience stayed with these poets all the way. Responsive to the point of shouting out commentary. These were not entertainments. The poet was not a politician or salesman pitching a product. There was a tribal feel to these events. An exchange of energy taking place. I took a further vow to poetry at the Charles Olson marathon event, for he spoke and raged and wept more than he technically "read." But Olson was powerful that night, vulnerable, arrogant, bombastic, poignant, embarrassing. He was the poet coming apart before our eyes, scapegoat, shaman, doing it for us, enacting some kind of atavistic ritual. His friends were dismayed. But I could feel the power of his troubled presence, the groping for . . . what was it? More light? More glimmers that were poems? *Outside* poems? The sense that one had a personal dance or motion in the world, a "job" to do, seemed to sustain this huge bear of a man whose feet lifted off the ground as he read, arms supporting his massive frame on the podium. And Robert Duncan's arms had waved and danced in the air as he read, gestures into the ether. This was a body poetics. And these poets had put their whole beings on the line. Was I being too romantic? And I made a vow, too, to the larger community that sustained this poet and would sustain others, a vow that I would spend my life developing and maintaining such a community. I envisioned a compassionate human cadre of like-minded illuminati and practitioners of the art who could really "hear" the new music in their nervous systems. And who were outspoken rebels as well, challenging the status quo. And would "take the whole ride." Psychedelia expanded the consciousness, as did the possibilities for a liberated sexuality. Women could be empowered, more in touch with their bodies as landscapes for writing, not imprisoned by hope and fear of being desirable, feminine. Language could stretch to these new parameters. Other cultures—ancient cultures—were being rediscovered. We could see newly, freshly, through prehistoric eyes. Sappho's fragments were suddenly modernist poems. Ethnopoetics was as relevant—more relevant in fact—as it studied the songs and rhythms of the indigenous people of this continent—than the European canon. "Make it new," Ezra Pound harangued. "Projective verse." "No ideas but in things." "Exploratory poetics." "Form is no more than an extension of content." "Duende." "Personism." "Continuous present." Although I never eschewed commas, Gertrude Stein said they were only good for hanging your hat on. Of course!

The night of the Robert Duncan reading I was introduced to a young writer-poet and novelist

Anne Waldman, Lewis Warsh, and Kate Berrigan, Bustin's Island, Maine, 1967

from New York, Lewis Warsh. Lewis had been travelling to San Francisco regularly during the summers, to sit at the feet of Jack Spicer, Robert Duncan, Robin Blaser, others. He was obsessed with poetry and the French "nouvelle vague," highly disciplined as a writer, having written several novels in high school. We were to become fast friends, romantic comrades hitchhiking to Mexico at the end of the poetry conference, hitching back to New York City, founding *Angel Hair* magazine and books, living together (even marrying in 1967 at St. Mark's Church in a gala wedding studded with poet friends) until 1970, feeding and pushing on each other's writing, working together at the St. Mark's Poetry Project, running a round-the-clock salon at 33 St. Mark's Place which had regular weekly parties after the poetry events at the church. The ubiquitous cops were frequently roused by disgruntled neighbors to quiet down the scene. Energetic "cultural workers," tireless poetry fiends, a close friend called us the "A" students. You could always spend a night on our sofa, have a meal, a milkshake, an audience for your poem, a new Angel Hair or Poetry Project publication thrust into your hands.

The following spring after the Berkeley Poetry Conference I met Frank O'Hara, introduced to him by Bill Berkson who was teaching at the New School. Frances, my mother, was in Bill's class and Bill was having a party at his bachelor's pad on posh 57th Street for his students—which included Bernadette Mayer, Hannah Weiner, Michael Brownstein, Peter Schjeldahl, others—and various accomplished New York School literati. Frank walked in—waltzed in?—with the painter Larry Rivers. They seemed metabolic brothers, led by an air of curiosity, grace, speed, high talk. Gossip? Frank was kind to me, insisting that upon graduating from Bennington I come work at the Museum of Modern Art—as a volunteer, of course, I'd learn lots. And *he'd* started at the bottom. Bill also introduced me to poet and dance critic Edwin Denby, who was to become a close friend, mentor. Edwin tried to teach me, if anyone could, to stand before things, to simply stop and stand and look, and trust what came to mind. An "off detail," odd gesture, obscure angle, the marginal detail, the awkwardness between objects, buildings, people were what caught his uncanny eye and ear. He was one of the most attentive listeners and observers of the various poetic activities on the downtown scene, as well as being a fixture at the New York City Ballet to which I frequently accompanied him. He encouraged my love of Dante, telling me to read it every day in the original even if I knew only little Italian. The sound would carry, he assured me, would lift my spirit!

I'd moved into the St. Mark's Place apartment upon graduating from Bennington and after interviewing with the folks who were doing the hiring (including the dynamic and liberal rector Michael Allen) for the newly conceived St. Mark's Church In-the-Bowery arts projects, theater and film as well as poetry and I was selected as a poetry assistant to Joel Oppenheimer, who was to direct the poetry program.

I was writing nightly, completely charged by the constant activity—artistic, political—of the Lower East Side environment. I was also free of school, of a certain kind of useful yet, from another point of view, pernicious influence. I was interested in my own energy patternings, conversations and dialogues in my own mind, not in conceptualizing "the poem." The voices in my brain wouldn't sleep. And when I did sleep I'd awake with the tail end of a dream demanding to be writ, heard, remembered—startling language figment, image of another world, time, place. Use it! An immediacy and urgency took hold to write all waking and sleeping details down quickly—as witness, as eyeballer of phenomena—and accept whatever shape they took. I surprised myself. *Logopoeia, melopoeia, phanopoeia:* Pound's three muses were entering from all directions. I worked with tape recorders. I recorded phrases off the radio, the telephone, the street, overheard conversations, stole lines from other poetries. I'd look out my window on St. Mark's Place and there was a "revolution" going on and I was part of it. We were angry about the war in Vietnam, about police brutality, strict drug penalties, racism, social injustice everywhere. I felt like an antennae, receiver, conduit for "my time." I was reeling—like so many of us in the sixties—from the intensity of a passionate vision of a better world and from all the sweet and painful informations that sang in my ear. Drug induced? Not entirely. More appropriately, poetry induced. Poets had always been oppositional, liberated, angry about the right things or at least tuned in to where the energy, power was. Witnesses drawn to the flames. Witty, too. Were poets dangerous? The FBI thought so. And yet as an artist I never felt lost in the version of that particular time. Poetic lineage went further back. In retrospect I think as activists we were politically naive. As poets we were working hard to save the world. "The DeCarlo Lots," haunted pubescent poem drawing on memory from earlier junior high

school summers (Union Lake, New Jersey, near Millville where my father's family was from), seemed an important piece. It was looser than other pieces I'd written yet organized with recurrent tangibles—details—in a collage-like structure. This was written before the Poetry Project had even begun. Having not entirely disowned my Bennington manuscript, which included pieces like "College Under Water" and "The Blue That Reminds Me of the Boat When She Left," I still wanted to break free of a lugubrious "poetical" tone I felt those poems carried. I wanted to start all over again, needing to forget the boring rules of prosody. Metaphor, simile, objective correlative. I wanted the person I was (liberated young woman in love with her own thinking and with poetry) to shine through. Persona was the clearer notion. I wanted an unbound line, physical freedom. And I wanted my passion, a kind of natural exuberance, to be in back of every line, syllable, consonant. "The DeCarlo Lots" poem seemed to bode well for subsequent pieces. It had a nostalgic tenderness rooted in specificity.

Of course the New American Poets had explored so much terrain already—explicitly, thoroughly. The poem was a field, the landscape was scary, rugged. These terrific beacon poets—like boddhisattvas pointing the way with generosity, offering to be vehicles, bridges, sources—had already by 1965 left an important legacy. And they were still around, alive, active. They were a tremendous inspiration as elders. Community was significant, necessary. The contact provided by correspondence, literary magazines, and small-press work, as well as readings and workshops, was considerable. And what was to develop over the years was a major poetic network, unparalleled. The Poetry Project existed to preserve a legacy and to continue to "make it new." This was its command. I saw the peripatetic community as tribal, connected by invisible poetic gossamers, mind to mind glints and gleamings. I felt the tremendous "mission" of the work, sense of purpose to make the world safe for poetry.

Frank O'Hara's tragic death in 1966 at age forty stunned the New York artists and poets community. He was young, dynamic, generous, a stimulating reference point to so many poets and friends. Although I'd only just met him, I'd felt his "transmission," an energy charge, which somehow gave permission to having direct experience in and with poetry.

With Edwin Denby, "a mentor," celebrated dance critic and poet, Gotham Book Mart, NYC, about 1973

How to appropriately honor and describe the countless events, readings, performances, first encounters with some of the most controversial and outrageous thinkers and writers of any time, New Year marathons, memorial readings, collaborations, benefits, all-night planning sessions, fundraisers, magazine collations that were to take place under the protective wing of St. Mark's Church? How to record the imprint in heart and mindstream of language, sheer sound and beauty of vocables as they resounded ear to ear? How to tell here the sweetness of Charles Reznikoff, the trajectory of his work, unique, modest, tough? How to capture the hilarity of Gregory Corso streaking at a Michael McClure reading? The symbolic "assassination" of Kenneth Koch with unloaded pistol during the period of Columbia University insurrection where he was viewed as "establishment" hierarchy, by poetic anarchists who stormed up the aisle in Marxist raincoats? Denise Levertov's sharp political concern during the Vietnam War, yearning and impassioned rage

in her voice clear as a bell. Ken Kesey making the audience stand and "really breathe," the rafters shaking with hyperventilation? John Wieners's fragile and dreamy movie-star reading, one pant leg rolled up, gold lamé scarf around his head? Burroughs's "comeback" to America, with gravelly, demonic, prophetic voice from even darker side of *samsara?* Yoko Ono's minute of white silence during the annual New Year's benefit reading. Barbara Guest, elegant, brave, and lucid after a serious concussion. Light streaming in the church's stained-glass windows the morning we began the all-day all-night Gertrude Stein marathon. Some of the story will never be told, held in magical interstices in secret mind-computer chambers, deeper in heart's tender spaces. How many times could you have your heart broken, reading after reading, event after event? I bow under the task of this description. Suffice it to say it was and continues as of this writing to be a holy place for poetry. And continues to be a project in the sense of an outward projecting: "to direct one's voice to be heard clearly at a distance."

Angel Hair magazine and books, along with *The World* magazine kept us additionally occupied. We used an inexpensive printer, Ronnie Ballou, in Vermont, whom I'd gotten to know editing *Silo* magazine at Bennington. When we couldn't afford printing or offset, we'd use the mimeo machine. Early issues of the magazine were honored with poems by Robert Duncan, Denise Levertov, James Schuyler. We published lovely mimeo books by Frank O'Hara, John Wieners, many others. Terrific covers by generous artists: Jim Rosenquist, Jim Dine, Philip Guston, Donna Dennis. We continued the press from both coasts even after Lewis moved for several years to California. We published many writers of our own generation: Bernadette Mayer, Jim Brodey, Larry Fagin, Alice Notley.

My own writing: what was going on then? I was editing the first *World Anthology* to be published in 1969. Two books, *Giant Night* and *Baby Breakdown*, were published almost simultaneously in 1970. Lita Hornick's Kulchur Foundation brought out *No Hassles* in 1971. I was writing to talk to myself, writing notes to myself and to my friends. Telling, spilling out the fast takes in my head. These early poems have energy, naivete, are guileless. Intimate. Dailiness is the measure. Quick, sometimes "stoned" associations. Tangibles from my domestic world are present. Love poems. Always honoring the "lyric."

During the wee hours of the morning of January 2, after the marathon New Year's event of 1970 when we were starting to vacuum the church rugs (a monumental task), an English fellow named Nik Douglas showed up with a film under his arm and asked to show it on the screen we hadn't yet dismantled. It was entitled *Tantra* and as it unfolded its vivid documentation of various Hindu and Buddhist tantric rites, I was mesmerized, riveted. I remember in particular scrawny jackals in a charnel ground, in a place where holy rites were being performed. Eating leftovers? Or were they gnawing on bodies? What I'd heard of India and images I'd seen were vivid like this charnel ground. Places of life and death, ritual initiation. I wanted to witness the burning ghats. I'd been studying Indian singing with Lamonte Young, who was a student of Pandit Pran Nath. I listened to recordings of Indian music, heard Ravi Shankar play, had seen various other singers and dancers from India. Satyajit Ray's *Apu Trilogy* were haunting films. How to get to India or make a deeper connection with some kind of study, practice. I wasn't attract-

ed to the Hindu guru "scene," as I perceived it, but was extremely interested in the culture or cultures of India. The philosophy of Buddhism and my earlier encounter with the lama had suggested a different atmosphere or tone in terms of a spiritual pursuit. Many Tibetan Buddhist teachers were living as refugees in India, having escaped persecution in Tibet under the Chinese Communists during the 1950s. That would be another reason to go there. Zen Buddhism was decidedly austere. Perhaps too austere for women? I was reading Evans-Wentz, D. T. Suzuki, Alan Watts. Poets and artists I admired—John Cage, Gary Snyder—had made a connection to Buddhism. Jack Kerouac was rich with Buddhist notions, crazy notions! What was "empty." Empty of what? Ego? I thought you needed a "healthy ego," as my mother called it, to be an artist. I'd already had an initial transmission from Geshe Wangyal and I understood the non-theism of Buddhism. No savior, no salvation, no soul. Sentient beings were just bundles or conglomerations of tendencies. Did you have to travel across the planet to find someone to explain this to you? Did you need to sit at the feet of someone who spoke in a language you couldn't begin to comprehend it seemed so alien to your ear? Would muttering mantras help anyone? Was personal "suffering," a revulsion with the "business" of the world, propelling me toward dharma? Or was it some other kind of inspiration? I think the ideas I was grasping from readings into dharma were consistent with ideas I already had. I was finding descriptions and words for what I already had an inkling of, propensity for. And the notion of *sangha* or community was familiar. Weren't the poets a kind of sangha? Didn't we too honor sacred text, practice the sacred and ancient art of poetry? Weren't some of the greatest poets in the Japanese and Chinese tradition Buddhists?

A party shortly thereafter at the loft of artist Wyn Chamberlain brought yet another messenger, another Englishman. He carried the Tibetan name Kunga Dawa and spoke enthusiastically about a Buddhist lama named Chogyam Trungpa who was coming to America to a small center in Vermont with the charming name Tail of the Tiger.

That summer poet Michael Brownstein and I, after visiting poet Kenward Elmslie and artist Joe Brainard in Calais, Vermont, found our way to the small Buddhist community in Barnet. I'd been invited by political activist friends Nancy and Jerry Rubin in New York on an artists' mission to Cuba. I'd only have to find my way to St. John's, Canada, where presumably there would be a boat waiting. The trip never panned out, financing fell apart, but I was poised to go in any case, and Tail of the Tiger was a step along the way. As we drove up to Tail, we saw a modest group of long-haired folks— college kids, dropouts, some elders. We were asked, please, since we seemed to have a functioning car (handsome white Volvo) if we'd go pick up "Rinpoche" (literally "precious one" or "precious teacher") at the airport who was just returning from Disneyland in California. A provocative request. We drove with one of the Rinpoche's students to St. Johnsbury (Brattleboro?). Chogyam Trungpa emerged from the plane inebriated, full of amused talk about the hologram of Casper the Friendly Ghost he'd seen in Disneyland. This was in retrospect a first interesting taste of this particular teacher's mind, his passion and delight in *our* crazy culture. And he'd come to America curious about the poets. Where were the poets?

Michael and I stayed two weeks, particularly for the Milarepa teachings. Milarepa was Tibet's great cotton-clad poet-yogin who lived on nettle leaves and composed on the tongue beautiful songs of realization, songs of devotion. I remember before leaving asking Trungpa what he thought about the direction "things were headed," meaning political. What about the end of the world? Many friends were getting "back to the land." He suggested I stay in New York City and work even harder since it was a "holy city" and required a superhuman energy and tolerance. But of course the City had always been a challenge.

Back in New York I did work even harder, as if that were possible. My life already was subsumed by the Poetry Project and all the duty that enormous undertaking required. Ron Padgett, Joan Simon, and I had started Full Court Press. And there were magazine publications, books in the offing, more demands for my own work. And I was starting to give readings and invited to participate in performance events. And writing with new confidence.

"Performance" interested me in that it expanded text off the page. I think of myself as a kinetic writer, thinker: amazed at the places writing originates from. Not just a conceptual place. Is it "voices" in the head? Emanating from all sense perceptions in concert? Is it innate psychophysical-personal rhythm? My own sound? The gestures and sounds of the phenomenal world? Do I write the way I think—ungrammatically? Do I write the way I move? Found language? I'd felt, from my

first reading at St. Mark's Church, where I sat, head bowed to page, that the voice coming out of me was only partial, and that I had a bigger sound to exhibit and explore. A sound that I would literally "have to grow into." But I was nervous. Next time, I stood positioned to honor the poem, to let it guide me. I saw how the text demanded a particular rendering, and it was often close to how I heard it, how words sounded in my ear. A particular kind of resonance increased after chanting mantra, I noticed as well. And since I'd had some early experience with theater, I appreciated the way voice could carry, inflect, conjure up various psychological and emotional states. How the words carried very particular and expressive energy pulses in its minutest forms—phones, phonemes. And although I couldn't pinpoint the effects of such experience of poetry, I knew I felt something "awakening" in my body, even when I was to read other poets in books. This was a kind of performance, a ritualized event in time. I wanted to be able to bring poems of my own alive. To have them sing or rage through my body, transmit them through vocal intention. And this worked best in a group context. *Parformir:* to enact a ritual or feat in front of an audience.

Fast Speaking Woman, long chant poem—inspired in part by the texts and recording of the shaman Maria Sabina, who intones chants, and speaks through an all-night hallucinogenic mushroom rite of passage and begun during a trip to South America—was a particularly seminal piece for me. Allen Ginsberg after hearing me read had suggested I "write long." Kenneth Koch had praised my "vibrato like an opera singer's." I was already extending my performance pieces into longer time frames. The poem was every woman's song in a sense and hung on the very simple structure "I'm a this woman, I'm a that woman," allowing, too, for improvisation. Upon hearing me read the poem on stage in San Francisco, Lawrence Ferlinghetti rushed backstage afterwards to ask to see it, saying he wanted to publish the poem in a City Lights Pocket Poets edition. Childhood fantasy come true! I'd been enamored of those compact and handsome editions for years. This was the maverick publisher of Ginsberg, Mayakovsky, Gregory Corso, Diane DiPrima. Ten poems appeared in the edition, which sported a glamorous photo that had been taken during "The Palm Casino Revue," an off-off Broadway show which featured transvestite Jackie Curtis, Candy Darling, others, and the exceptional musical poet and librettist Kenward Elmslie, a close friend. There

Anne Waldman with Bernadette Mayer—"beloved poet friend," 1974

was the sense of it being a "live" or "oral" book. A kind of performance. In retrospect, its publication in 1975 put my work and the performance of it into a wider cultural context. And I was busier from then on managing an even more active public career. Is "managing" the word? I never felt I managed myself well, a tendency to drive myself beyond certain physical boundaries, get too pressured, speedy. An over-achiever, workaholic. There were not only the various projects to attend to, but this more demanding travel/work schedule. And I was always up late writing after everything else had been put to bed. I snatched those precious bands of open dark time from the night. I was beginning to work in a focused way with dream and travel journals.

From 1971–1973 I'd done some earnest travelling. To the West Indies, in particular the unique black-sand island of Dominica, about two hundred years behind the other islands in exploitation and development. To Colombia, Ecuador, and Peru, a trip which taught me something about that extraordinarily violent history, but also about the contemporary American subculture, particularly the drug culture which spanned the Americas. These were the dread Nixon years. It was interesting to perceive our "influence" everywhere, the crass materialism—infectious, insidious, and wickedly irresistible. Meeting renegades, desperadoes, smugglers, dealers, thieves. I was writing little travel stories based on these vivid folk. Reading, too, "magical realism," *One Hundred Years of Solitude,* which affected how I experienced Colombia, in particular. Also spent many days at extraordinary ruins and museums, musing on the origins of the unique cultures I was studying. Who made the Nazca lines? Why did those Mochica figures look as if they were meditating, as if they were in Buddhist *samadhi?* Finally in 1973, with poet companions Michael Brownstein and John Giorno, I made the long-awaited pilgrimage to India. I was supposed to attend a Buddhist seminary in the States that fall, but all the omens (including very inexpensive tickets—only $250 to Delhi) were propitious to going.

How complex, contradictory the sense, senses of India. One experiences every possible state of mind. Emotion, as well. Feels the endless grind and turning of the immense wheel of life, as phenomena plays out its flickering show—witnesses the wheel of birth, old age, sickness, and death. I saw burning ghats by the holy Ganges, watched the construction of yet another funeral pyre, stuck my head in the Ganges, visited rat temples, listened to ecstatic chants of sadhus and Bauls, contemplated the strange mix of myriad luminous details. Benares: one of the oldest cities in the world, Biblical. People were doing things as they'd done them thousands of years ago. And yet there was a harsh modern edge at every turn. Which causes a kind of schizophrenic chaos. India is never sentimental. We travelled north to Darjeeling, and spent over a month taking teachings from the Tibetan lamas resident there, nestled under the splendid Kanchenjunga mountain range.

Did this visit change my life? It certainly enhanced it. It gave me an alternative vision, or version, of reality. India carried its old thrust into the present. Stubborn, adamantine, titillating. At the same time savagely scarred. Ennobled through suffering? Hardly, but it existed as a repository for all levels of human and inhuman expression. Women seemed so beaten down, stoical, long-suffering. Children both cursed and blessed from birth. The caste system was horrific to my mind, but had its own unflinching logic. How could I, logical liberal Westerner, ever understand the web, the Indra's net of this vast and complicated landscape with all its strange yearnings and wraith-like beings? Wrathful Hindu goddess Kali seemed the totemic deity of the place: she chews up and spits out the "stuff" of life, the material, over and over again. Gives life, takes it back. Strong connections were made with Buddhist teachers, particularly with lama Chatral Rinpoche, a yogin who had spent many years wandering and living in caves and whose own teacher had been a woman he'd begun studying with at the age of thirteen. He was rugged, earthy, direct, and had a distinctly "no nonsense" aura about him. After I "took refuge" in a ceremony which required the aspiration to give up one's personal history as neurosis and limitation, and to enter a larger vision or path where you cut your own ego or trips and begin to serve others, I was afraid he'd set me out to pasture tending cows with the Belgian nun, another student, who'd just done the same ceremony. I was expecting a more rigorous command. But he was lenient, encouraging me to continue my practice and studies back in the States. It can be done anywhere, he said. Achieve a certain level of practice, and I will teach you everything your mind desires.

In 1974 I was invited along with Allen Ginsberg and Diane DiPrima to Boulder, Colorado, for the first summer program of the Naropa Institute, founded by Trungpa and some of his senior students. I'd spent time during several summers at Allen Ginsberg's farm in Cherry Valley, New York, approximately four hours from the city. Many friends, poets, artists, distinguished guests, Zen teachers, others would pass through. Allen was for the most part busy elsewhere but his longtime companion Peter Orlovsky was in residence during most of the two summers I spent time there, tending a large and energetic vegetable garden. The summer of 1974 poet Bernadette Mayer and some other friends joined me at the farm—she and I had just completed a reading/performance in Art Park near Niagara Falls—which started me thinking how best to take some of the poetic energy out of New York and generate an alternative place where poets could gather. Some way to live off the Lower East Side a spell. We should be able to schedule writing or contemplative retreats, write epic poems under the influence of a gibbous moon, sing to our vegetable garden. But the invitation had arrived to visit Naropa, the newly gathering experimental Buddhist school on the spine of the Rocky Mountain continent, an auspicious journey which altered the direction of my life.

At a meeting, which included John Cage, Gregory Bateson, poet Jackson Mac Low, Allen Ginsberg, Diane DiPrima, myself, and others, Trungpa said the Naropa Institute would be a "hundred year project at least." It sounds trite to say a chill went up my spine, but the experience was something like that. I felt a "charge" that seemed to shoot beyond my own boundaries. I could feel the surge of this larger "command." It was amazing to think of something that might conceivably continue—if it had worth—beyond our own lifetimes. John Cage was asked to speak to how Black Mountain, the experimental college in North Carolina, had "worked," to which he replied, "It all came together at lunch." Allen and I were asked to design a poetics department in which poets could learn about meditation and meditators could learn about poetry. Fired up with the assignment we went back to the apartment (we were roommates that summer) and started making lists of all the people we'd want to invite, all the chairs we'd create to honor poets. The Emily Dickinson Chair of Silent Scribbling. The Frank O'Hara Chair of Deep Gossip. We founded the Jack Kerouac School of Disembodied Poetics that same night, delighted we had a title, a moniker we both agreed upon and giddy with the imagination of what this school could be. Kerouac, because he had realized the first Buddhist Noble Truth, the truth of Suffering, and had written the spontaneous *Mexico City Blues,* an ecstatic series of choruses inspired by Buddhist thinking ("first thought, best thought"), be-bop, and his own lively poet-mind. Also a writer both generations of peers—my own and Allen's—might agree upon, acknowledging Kerouac's original praxis (nonstop spontaneity), tenderness of heart in the actual language, prodigious accomplishment in both prose and poetry. As well as being an influence on Ginsberg himself, a goad to William Burroughs, Gregory Corso, and

others, he had influenced writers such as Clark Coolidge and Ted Berrigan who were closer to my poetic generation. In addition, Kerouac had been not simply writer but culture hero, taking personal risks, epitomizing in his own "search" the yearning of the North American "soul" for higher consciousness or "satori"—a poetic realization of the tenderness and emptiness and interconnectedness of all beings on the planet. He represented for me the genius-witness to both the decline of our Western civilization—its *cri de coeur*—as well as its outrageous wisdom and delight. I threw the term "disembodied" into our school's banner to augment the notion that we were honoring a lineage, elders that had tread the path before us, such as Sappho, Blake, Whitman, H. D., Stein, Pound, W. C. Williams, Lorine Niedecker, Frank O'Hara. Our faculty was to be for the most part "at large," peripatetic. It was a bow, too, to the tantric Buddhist backdrop—the word "disembodied" sounded provocative, otherworldly?—of the Naropa Institute.

The Jack Kerouac School had its first full summer in 1975 with an impressive roster of faculty, including William Burroughs, John Ashbery, Diane DiPrima, Gregory Corso, and Joanne Kyger. I decided to make a commitment to help develop the Naropa Institute as a year-round school and moved into an inexpensive apartment at the Hotel Boulderado, a turn-of-the-century mining hotel in downtown Boulder, in the fall of 1975, keeping the apartment on St. Mark's Place as well for my trips back there, since I continued to work part of the time with the Poetry Project. Longer collage pieces and serial poems such as *Sun the Blond Out* were coming out of me. Sometimes I felt like a "channel" in the dream work, a conduit for disassociative phrases that intersected at odd junctures. Late nights found me in the tiny hotel apartment gathering together and editing a lot of the dream and travel and journal work for a book Stonehill wanted to publish, entitled *Journals and Dreams,* which was released in 1976. This seemed a more mature selection that any of my other books to date and investigated my own psychology—linguistically—as a woman.

More opportunities were arising for travel to a number of universities and other venues to present my own work. That fall I was also invited to accompany Allen Ginsberg on Bob Dylan's "Rolling Thunder Revue" tour as a "poet in residence" and to help work on the movie *Renaldo and Clara,* travelling through much of New England and Canada as the show made surprise stops in various towns and cities. Like a nomadic caravan wending its way across cool desert, we'd often travel by night in the exotic buses—except our fancy vehicles came complete with showers, bar, buckets of ice, handy curtained cots, intense conversation, and live music through the night. Many musicians joined in for performances along the way: Joni Mitchell, Eric Anderson, Joe Cocker. Old friend, playwright Sam Shepard from Theater Genesis days at St. Mark's Church was also present, writing dialogue for the film. The shows were phenomenal: energetic, various, unpredictable. Dylan wore white face and had turkey feathers sticking out of his felt hat. He looked, at times, like a Kachina doll. . . . The poem-journal I kept (entitled *Shaman*) during the tour was published about a year-and-a-half later by a little press in Boston entitled White Raven, then afterwards in a German bilingual edition translated by Jurgen Schmidt and published by Apartment Editions. I had a few salient ideas for the film—one was to show Joan Baez meeting with the Shakers in Maine to ex-

change songs and sing "Tis the Gift to Be Simple," but the advance team sent ahead to make the contact which I had initiated thought the Shakers "too old." The idea for the brothel scene filmed at the Chateau Frontenac in Quebec City was mine also, after one look at the chateau's garish red wallpaper and heavy red velvet drapes. I was also filmed in Native American costume reading from *Fast Speaking Woman* in front of Niagara Falls, a ridiculous scene mercifully cut from the movie, although two minutes of the audio survived as sound track. I had a close look at the rock 'n' roll world and as compelling and glamorous as it was, I felt starved for the conversation of poets and spent much spare time on the telephone "home." When the tour came to Fort Collins, Colorado, I joined in to "design" head gear (I was myself sporting a turban headdress which everyone else wanted to imitate) for the performance which was videotaped and marketed as *Hard Rain.* I also pressured Bob Dylan to finally let Allen Ginsberg get up on stage to read a poem, which Allen did during the break.

With William Burroughs in a classroom at the Naropa Institute, Boulder, Colorado,
1975

Allen Ginsberg and Anne Waldman, New Year's Eve, NYC, 1979

He read "On Neal's Ashes," a tribute to desperado Neal Cassady, the legendary inspiration for Kerouac's hero Dean Moriarity in *On the Road*. I came away appreciating the opportunity to have travelled with an artistic community, to have been supported for the work I did, and the serendipitous nature of the voyage. We never knew exactly where we were going to be next and the public only had twenty-four-hour advance notice. Crowds were delighted by the sudden intrusion. It was a generous occasion. I romanticized the possibility of a similar, scaled-down poetry caravan for years.

The idea of living outside Boulder in the rugged and rocky terrain with views of magnificent snow mountains close by was attractive to one cooped up so long in New York City. Rentals were relatively cheap and I lived in four different mountain dwellings over the subsequent five years. It was difficult commuting to Naropa, especially when the snows came, but poet companion Reed Bye and I braved the Boulder Canyon (heralded as the most dangerous road in the West!) many a

wintry night, chains on Reed's old, red, International Ford truck. William Burroughs had lent us his apartment in town when he was away, convenient for days I was teaching. And I found I enjoyed teaching. Interesting, challenging students were arriving because of the "alternative" quality of education at Naropa. I found teaching pushed my writing to new places. I followed my own assignments. Collaborative work with students ensued, also publishing students' work was a priority. The women in particular seemed strong, independent, and much of their writing felt "riskier" than that of the men to me—more provocative, exploratory.

I had met Reed Bye at a poetry event in Boulder which local poet Jack Collom, old friend Lewis MacAdams, and I had organized to mix the Naropa scene with the local scene. Reed had been a student at the university, dropped out to join the Merchant Marines, and had settled back to Boulder modestly writing poems, doing "tree work" and roofing for a living. We immediately felt a powerful and passionate bond, an attraction of opposites. Reed was an introvert, conservative by nature, domestic, private, and was to become a serious Buddhist practitioner. We felt we could live and work together and did for a number of years (until 1991) on our magazine and press and then through various projects at Naropa where he was also at times teaching poetry and poetics. We married in 1980 and I gave birth to our son whom we named Edwin Ambrose on October 21, 1980. I had had dreams for many nights about a boy who would be named "our man," who would travel to me "through mountains and snows." I felt his nose pushing against my spine during excruciating labor. Every woman will tell how much pain and ecstasy is involved in childbirth. How as a woman you reenact the primordial birth of the "first being," and how you finally recognize your body's secret agenda. Ambrose was a miracle, a blessing—I hadn't necessarily expected to have a child, being driven by a sense of career and not settled enough in a relationship which could accommodate "family." This was an inspiring turning point. I experienced unconditional love for the first time and in many ways a deeper political commitment to the survival of the planet, the species. My child became my teacher.

My best poems—and by that I mean those poems free of the stain of ego, ownership—were written during the pregnancy and shortly after the birth of Ambrose, and then appeared in the book *First Baby Poems.* We were living in a small cabin in the mountains with an adjoining smaller cabin which I used for a work space when I could wrench free from attending the baby. But of course once I'd be "out of the house" all I could think of was the baby and so all the writing was of, and around, and about and inside baby. Wanting to make a poem for the baby's father as a gift at Christmastime I once again tackled the pantoum, a form I'd been struggling with for a number of years. This wonderful form ("pantun") first appeared in Malayan literature in the fifteenth century although it is most likely based on an earlier oral form from India. Its structure is simple: four line stanzas in which the second and fourth lines return as the first and third lines in subsequent stanzas and the opening lines from the first stanza return in the poem's very last stanza. Suddenly I found myself writing—late at night—in the voice of the baby. The lines flowed out effortlessly. Because I was the baby speaking I couldn't get fancy in my vocabulary. I didn't strain to make the repeating lines coalesce. I found the repetitive structure of the pantoum conducive to expressing the baby's

thought processes. The baby's mind would observe things in a series of unconnected glimpses and realizations. Because each line has to be repeated in another context, it's difficult not to have every line be a single phrase or statement. In an older person that might get artificial or coy. Here, single thoughts in the blue don't refer back to a self-conscious body of knowledge. So the pantoum became the primary observations of an empty mind, a new arrival. A few lines:

> Unusual I don't sleep really
>   unless it's dark night everyone in bed
> Other sound are creak of chair and floor, water
> dripping on heater from laundry, cat licking itself
>   and occasional peck on typewriter, peck on my
>   cheek
>
> Unless it's dark night everyone in bed
>   I'm wide awake hungry wet lonely thinking
> occasional peck on typewriter, peck on my cheek
>   My brain cells grow, I get bigger
>
> I'm wide awake wet lonely hungry thinking
>   Then Mamma pulls out breast, says "Milky?"
> My brain cells grow, I get bigger
>   This is my first Christmas in the world

Reed Bye and I had started Rocky Ledge magazine and Rocky Ledge Cottage Editions on a secondhand mimeo press that we picked up for thirty-eight dollars in Denver. We published some lively issues of the magazine which included interviews with Diane DiPrima, Peter Orlovsky, a transcript of conversations with Edwin Denby, of a class with Gregory Corso. I was writing: "Cabin," "Dialogue at 9,000 Feet," many of the meditative poems that appeared in the book *Makeup on Empty Space.* Handsome black-and-white covers were generously commissioned from Alex Katz, Glen Baxter, Jane Freilicher, others.

We'd travelled abroad in 1978, starting in Germany on a reading trip which took us "singing for our supper" to Venice. The political intrigues, terrorist threats were everywhere. We were stopped near King Ludwig's castle outside Munich as police searched cars for members of the Baader Meinhof gang. Aldo Moro had been kidnapped in Italy. We boarded the Orient Express and headed for Turkey, travelled through Iran which seemed on the edge of revolution. Enormous portraits of the Shah and his family greeted us at the border. How long would they remain in place? Rebellion was afoot. In Teheran I boarded a train for India and Reed elected to continue on through Afghanistan by bus. This was just before the Russian occupation there. The borders were closed shortly

Ron Padgett, Anne Waldman, Pat Padgett holding Ambrose, Reed Bye, "Poet's Corner,"
Calais, Vermont, 1981

after he got to India. We finally reunited in Kathmandu. Some of this journey is reflected in the piece *Blue Mosque,* which was written in New Delhi. We spent time in Nepal with Tibetan friends, disaffected "Ingies," spiritual seekers from all continents. We made pilgrimages to Buddhist gompas and other sacred Hindu and Jain and Newari sites. One lama spoke to me about an ancient prophecy which predicted that a third of the planet would be destroyed in our lifetime.

I returned to Boulder that summer for the Writing Program and Reed stayed in New York to work as a consultant on the new roof at St. Mark's Church In-the-Bowery as part of the Preservation Youth Project which gave work to neighborhood youth to renovate the historic building. July 27: I will never forget being called out of the pool at the Varsity Town House complex where I was taking a swim with Robert Duncan, one of our Naropa faculty that summer, to the telephone to hear news of the devastating fire at St. Mark's Church which had completely gutted the main sanctuary. Most

probably started by an oxyacetylene torch employed to weld new copper downspout sleeves from the gutter, the fire destroyed the entire roof, second story of the church, historic beams, old wood floor. The bell had fallen down from the base of the steeple and cracked. I felt a part of the poetry world, this Lower East Side holy spot, this artistic landmark which went beyond my own "scene," my own world, coming apart. . . . Luckily no one was hurt. I stood there soaking wet feeling like a fool. Why wasn't I in New York to help out? I wrote a poem that night in the voice of the church. It would take many years to rebuild its ravaged "self."

We had moved back to New York City in 1981, taking a leave from Naropa, to the apartment on St. Mark's Place in order to be closer to both our families. I had a job teaching several semesters at the Stevens Institute of Technology in Hoboken. These students were so different from their Naropa counterparts, engineers for the most part, who groaned when I announced as distinguished visiting guest professor I'd be teaching poetry. "Poetry? No!" I made them take a vow not to sell their books upon graduating. "Keep them on the shelf," I implored, "they might come in handy. You might need the appropriate quotation from Gertrude Stein, Djuna Barnes, Hilda Doolittle, one day." Three female students sat in the front row, the males at the back, decorously sipping their illegal beer. It was a night class.

My mother's illness and long bout with diabetes complications kept us on tenterhooks most of the year. I cared for her, took notes by her bedside of her strange verbal effusions and ramblings. She had utopian visions that included elaborate ceremonial events from many traditions—Christian weddings, Jewish seders, Native American dancing, participation of the grandchildren of William Carlos Williams and other famous poets, and last funeral rites. Grateful to be with her the moment she died—one of the most "real" moments I'd ever experienced as I felt the life leave her body, take flight like a bird—I remember chanting, "Let go let go let go" over and over again inside my own body until I made myself dizzy. Don't cling, the Buddhists recommend. We had a memorial service for her in the St. Mark's parish hall, she being well-loved and appreciated by so many of the younger poets she had befriended and encouraged, as well as "elders" of the tribe.

Back in Boulder that summer of 1982 for the Jack Kerouac Conference at Naropa, then by fall in San Francisco for a stint at the New College of California, more readings and travels, and then a return to New York by Christmas. My son Ambrose's serious asthma and consequent hospitalizations (three major episodes) took us to Boulder to settle into a permanent domestic situation, deemed sensible for his health. It had been an emotionally difficult, painful year, lying under the boy's crib at Bellevue hospital all night fighting off cockroaches, haunted by his labored breathing and panic, still grieving my mother's death, never sleeping, writing chaotic monologues and tirades such as the piece "Drugs." Worried about everyone's mortality and suffering. Inspired by the ongoing work and activities at Naropa and the Poetry Project (I'd already begun editing a new mammoth anthology of work selected from issues of the Project's *The World* magazine) but worried too about their survival during the Reagan years, and the continued marginalization of artists in the culture. Friend and former student turned music producer Lynn Lynn produced a 45-rpm single of

Ambrose, 1988

my song "Uh-Oh Plutonium!" with the flip side in French, as an anti-nuclear warhead proliferation "statement." I worked with a band performing this and other songs on several occasions around the city. Utilizing exaggerated sound, intense instrumentation, I was performing/singing from the gut, now. Ted Berrigan's advice was "Be like Mayakovsky." Reed Bye and I also collaborated with dancer Douglas Dunn, a very close friend and brilliant choreographer, on writing a text for, and appearing in an ambitious dance-video production commissioned by Boston's WGBH television station, entitled "The Secret of the Waterfall." As poets, we look very strange and "lost" wandering around the various "sets" in Martha's Vineyard amongst confident and energetic dancers. Who are we? Tourists? This piece is a kind of reverie inspired by the odd and beautiful gestures of the dancers.

The death of Ted Berrigan on July 4 followed by Edwin Denby's suicide several days later plunged the poetry community into grief and despair. Ted's death was in many ways the result of poverty, poor health care. He was only forty-eight years old. Edwin did not want to be a burden to anyone as his health declined. He was eighty-three. Could we even take care of each other properly? Did most poets die tragically: botched health, unsung, obscure, soon forgotten?

A relief to return to Boulder as Ambrose's asthma condition lessened. The boy blossomed in the cleaner Colorado air. He could run around outside. Beautiful, bright, highly verbal, curious. His speech was entering my writing in an energetic way. I renewed my commitment to the Naropa poetics vision. In the semesters away from the school, Allen Ginsberg had "spelled" me and I hadn't missed any of the summer sessions. The summer program, which brought students from around the country and abroad, students from other schools, scholars with varying credentials and a creative writing faculty of the highest caliber, was obviously the centerpiece of the entire poetics plan. It became the nexus for the master of fine arts degree. Naropa was now a fully accredited Institute, and ready to enter a larger educational arena. It needed to declare itself as a contemplative college, a stronger alternative to more traditional and academic programs. I was getting more work around the country and abroad and found myself not only manifesting as poet, performer, lecturer but as ambassador for a viable alternative community vision. In addition to the Poetry Project anthology, I had already started gathering work for a Ted Berrigan homage, *Nice to See You.* My own book *Skin Meat Bones* was released in 1985. I commuted to the Institute of American Indian Arts in Santa Fe to teach for a semester that spring, intrigued by the writing of these highly gifted Native American students who seemed outside the mainstream of white materialist culture. Their lives seemed naturally more integrated with their art. It was important to continue to work with these exceptional students—they were from many tribes throughout the States—and a relationship began with Naropa for scholarship possibilities, particularly during the summer programs.

The opportunity arose to return to India as a guest of the Indian government to act as a consultant for the Festival of India, helping organize the visits of Indian poets to the States. My work took me to Bhopal, just a year after the heinous Union Carbide disaster, where I saw firsthand some of the devastation and results of chemical leaks. Listened to stories of residents, survivors. How to bring the perpetrators, those

responsible, to their knees? It would take years. The open-air festival in Bhopal, with participants from all over India, representing various poetic traditions, was convened to determine what poetries might be best exported to the States. Vedic masters, trained since childhood, Baul singers and dancers, poets of different tongues—Assamese, Marathi, Hindi, Tamil—Khond tribal dancers enacting ritual human sacrifice, all took part. It would be a difficult decision. As an exchange, I read my poem *Skin Meat Bones,* where the three words repeat as notes in varying registers, to a startled audience. It's a lively performance with extensive vocal flourishes. "Do all American women poets do this sort of thing?"

The following winter I travelled to Nicaragua as a guest of the Sandanistas for the annual Ruben Dario festival which hosted poets from the States, staying with Nicaraguan poet Christian Santos, activist, mother of five, passionately in love with her country. A woman whose grandfather had been hacked to death by Samosa, whose parents had also been tried and suffered, a religious woman in many ways who had been radicalized through difficult experience. She was stronger, more active than her husband, from whom she was estranged. The women seemed generally more vocal, "empowered," the stronger writers, had taken up arms, and many were estranged from husbands and lovers who expected them to "stay at home." Her beautiful young son was just that day bravely "off to the front," in well-pressed uniform, hair combed, A-K rifle slung over handsome shoulder. We shared a light bulb which moved from kitchen to bathroom to tiny sleeping quarters. We went without water at least two days a week. She was exceedingly generous. Her old Russian car kept breaking down. The kind of tires it required might never arrive. Everyone seemed a poet or else could recite the poetry of others by heart. Ernesto Cardinal, Catholic priest, then Minister of Culture, was highly visible, an inspiring moral presence, uncompromising. I had met him some years before at a festival in Berlin where we rode together down the Wannsee. These were difficult times, how many young people had been killed by the Contra? How many missing? How many Contra dead? Families divided? The brilliant assistant to the minister of culture—also a poet— had a husband on the other side, fighting for the Contra. It was insane to see the United States pitting itself against a country with only two elevators! Insane to realize how few Americans had any picture of the tangible reality. Nicaragua: one main street, dirt roads, no toilet paper, how rare a decent cup of coffee. Encouraging, heartening to spend time with these artist-revolutionaries, articulate, tender. Daunting to think how they'd come out from under thumb of dictatorship only to find themselves pitted against the most militarily powerful country in the world, a country they admired for many artistic and cultural reasons, and yet experienced as enemy, as obstacle to economic stability, peace. I met many people there, not one of them cynical. Modest apartments with extensive libraries of American literature, posters of Marilyn Monroe, Jack Kerouac, Malcolm X, Roberto Clemente on crowded walls. Important to have emotional solidarity with people who were fighting for a better system, regardless of how you felt about the terms of that war. And they wanted to hear poems, and news from us, the norteaméricanos.

Writing began on the long poem somewhere in here, the long ongoing weave in and around and about and beyond male energy. The poem was later to be named *Iovis,* subtitled *All Is Full of Jove:* Iovis being the generative of Jove. All is full of Jove, his sperm presumably to people space. Not simply an attack on the patriarch but a celebration of male energy and experience in all its myriad forms. So I would need other languages, voices, descriptions, and words from the other: the male. I began research, I travelled to "get" the work, I let everything speak to me of this theme. Gathered many threads, random strands together. Worked extensively with autobiographical material, memory, journals, with letters, particularly those of my grandfather Waldman, who lived in a different time zone, as I perceived it, between two devastating wars. Drew on descriptions of my father's from World War II, Germany, severed limbs sticking out of the sand at the Maginot line. Travelled to Bali—a country where they have no word for "art" it is so integrated into daily practices—to

The immediate and extended family, after an AIDS benefit performance reading, Albany, New York, 1991: (from left, back row) John Waldman, Anne Waldman, Chris Sikelianos, Carl Waldman, Mark Sikelianos, Louise Sikelianos, Gina Sikelianos, and T'Chaka Sikelianos; (clockwise, from front center) Devin (in striped shirt), Nick, Alix Braun, Molly Braun Waldman, Chloe Waldman, and Alisha

study religion and gamelan with Ambrose and returned with more luminous details, phrases that caught the ear, some in Indonesian. Seized notion there studying music, of cyclical time, how different cycles intersect at various pitches, points of intensity and karmic fruition. Bits of Mayan, German, French, eight-year-olds in conversation in the backyard flitted through. Poem developed into an architectonic puzzle filled with chromosomal clusters, charms, spells, incantations. A poem written for the end of the millennium, end of the world? Scribed words of others as I travelled further: an old man on a train in northern Germany who had been intrigued by Nazi uniforms, their shiny gold buttons, a brilliant European transsexual who became an intimate friend. Remembered a camel-driver speaking at Cheops, how many moons ago? I worked my studies in Buddhist Mādhyamika philosophy, a process of thinking which deconstructs apparent reality, into a long section of the poem. Dreams of Hegel, Wittgenstein, Allen Ginsberg entered its pages. I honored Robert Creeley and John Cage. Fathers, teachers, brothers, husbands, lovers, friends. As he chanted the various ways to cover up plutonium on a long car ride and I noted them down, my son became the ultimate guide for the poem. This is the most extended piece I've ever written and attempts to catch the vibration, or patterned energy, of one woman on this planet as she collides with all apparent and non-apparent phenomena.

Allen Ginsberg and I travelled to Czechoslovakia right after the Velvet Revolution, read to thousands of liberated young people, lectured on American poetry and poetics, met with President Vaclav Havel, and visited Temorin, the enormous and problematic nuclear power plant. Allen—crowned King of May twenty-five years previously—handed over his crown to a young anarchist artist in enormous festive ceremony in the main square. We listened to stories everywhere—narrations of suffering to stop the mind. Elderly woman who had "seen it all"—a child in World War I, translator of Marx and Lenin into Czech, later harassed, husband imprisoned in last decades, and now beyond the conditions of the world. Her face glowed with a strange weathered beauty. She seemed unattached, but tremendously engaged at the same time. Stories from people my age, of unbelievable repression, staggering oppression, petty little oppressions, backbiting, spying, double-dealing, of stunted educations, careers. We were shown hiding places for samizdat publications—much-fingered copies of Allen's *Howl* in typescript

for example. People told how they started every time the doorbell rang, sure they were to be arrested for reading the wrong book. Merriment in the streets now, to be followed by chaos, instability, need for retribution? Havel is a visionary who wants to govern with absolute compassion. You feel this acutely in his presence, in his writings. He sported a bright red heart decal on his windshield.

My selected poems, 1966–1988, entitled *Helping the Dreamer,* was published in 1990. *Out of This World* and *Nice to See You* were published in 1991. The first book of *Iovis* in 1993. Other recent projects include *Disembodied Poetics: Annals of the Jack Kerouac School,* a collection of lectures, talks, interviews, and political documents from the poetics program at Naropa, co-edited with Andrew Schelling.

Andrew Schelling, poet, essayist, little-magazine editor, Sanskritist, translator, had been a guest teacher during several summers when the opening as assistant to the program arose in 1990. Instance of auspicious coincidence perhaps, certainly from my point of view in that I desperately needed someone who could not only share the ever-increasing and demanding administrative workload but someone who passionately believed and supported what we were trying to do. Who was kin to the "outrider" notions, carried in his own lifestream the "crazy wisdom" tradition of poets, mystics, saints, and boddhisattvas. Who was schooled at Berkeley and Santa Cruz, bastions of subtle gnosis, who left academia to follow more interesting pathways of creative thinking and practice. Who came of age as poet in the challenging Bay Area arena of polemic, rivalry, politics, and poetry wars. Who was Zen Buddhist practitioner, and translated delicate and tough Sanskrit poetries (many by women), as well as inspired teacher who would be generous with students. Who saw beyond his own immediate finite circumstance, willing to put his energy into these marginal, original, outrageous ventures that would benefit countless poet misfits to come. I loved his attention, dedication, his own work, his sympathy for others. I fell in love with him.

Also aboard, aiding and abetting the great plan of the Jack Kerouac School of Disembodied Poetics are core faculty Bobbie Louise Hawkins, overseeing the prose track; Anselm Hollo, enlisted to develop translation as an ongoing practice; and adjunct faculty Jack Collom, whose specialty is ecological poetics. The department has been con-

Andrew Schelling and Anne Waldman at Naropa Institute, 1992

siderably strengthened and expanded and now attracts a wide range of talented writing students from all over the world. Several scholarships are available for minority students, thanks to the efforts of the student organization SUEI (Student Union for Ethnic Inclusion). An outreach track is developing as well, where students work teaching writing workshops in prisons, in grade schools, with the homeless, in attention homes, among the elderly. More small presses and publications are being spawned around the poetics department. Celebrated guests from many dimensions of the poetics spectrum join core faculty during the summer session for a month of intense colloquia, panels, reading, workshops, lectures, performances. We cover many fronts in our discussions: political, ecological, activist, feminist, dharmic, literary, hermetic, ethno-poetic, translation, mythological. I spoke at a recent panel under the "big top"—the large tent where the poetics community gathers daily during the summer session—out on the Naropa lawn:

"Should we as artists become actively disinterested instead of complaining about politics? This was something John Cage said recently, seeing how drained we get by pain of politics, how hopeless it seems. And it's interesting that here, we, in our temporary shelter, have become so focussed on what we are making, doing, that somehow those events out there—like the Republican National Presidential convention—seem mere figments, irritations but not threats to what we really do, are engaged in, how we live, and put our lives on the line. That's not to say we forget about the endangered species, the fallout from the war in Iraq—all those maimed children—because as you hear here, all those realities come into our awareness as poets, as writers. I dreamed at first we were a "words-only" school, but then we started to dance. I dreamed that we had to travel all over the world to collect what it was that was precious to us, all those teachings in dusty tomes and illuminated manuscripts, all those stories whispered late at night over fires in far exotic corners of the fragile globe that we had to commit to memory, all those gestures of compassion that were obscured in a rush to avoid dying, all the last gasps of animals, humans, hungry ghosts. That we had to "catch" them up and gather them and take them and ourselves underground. That this was the cure for a sick planet. And that some would come later and unlock the codes, the runes, and feel the best poetry in their blood, their marrow, their genetic streams. Maybe it could someday, later, be a safer world. That we needed to do this because "they" were burning books again. Lore, instead of "school." Mystery instead of "materia." And this was a choiceless task and we would go about it cheerfully. What are you, students, doing in this tent? Did you merely pay to get here? We need to start our own mental country, our own universe, our own temporary autonomous zone that exists in opposition to our own worst barbarism, cruelty, and ignorance. We need to write luminous invisible texts that change the world in the glow of true exile. How hard the human consciousness has worked to get us where we could be. You want to let that go? I bow to all our honorary guests, fellow-travellers, witnesses here today, and to their unflinching commitment and purpose. And I bow to the aspiration of the students. May you live and practice the alchemist's worthy art a longtime."

BIBLIOGRAPHY

Poetry:

On the Wing, Boke, 1968.

O My Life!, Angel Hair, 1969.

Baby Breakdown, Bobbs-Merrill, 1970.

Giant Night: Selected Poems, Corinth Books, 1970.

Up Through the Years, Angel Hair, 1970.

Goodies from Anne Waldman, Strange Faeces Press, 1971.

Holy City, privately printed, 1971.

Icy Rose, Angel Hair, 1971.

(With Ted Berrigan) *Memorial Day,* Poetry Project, 1971.

No Hassles, Kulchur Foundation, 1971.

Light and Shadow, privately printed, 1972.

Spin Off, Big Sky, 1972.

The West Indies Poems, Adventures in Poetry, 1972.

Life Notes: Selected Poems, Bobbs-Merrill, 1973.

(With Joe Brainard) *Self Portrait,* Siamese Banana Press, 1973.

The Contemplative Life, Alternative Press, n.d.

Fast Speaking Woman, Red Hanrahan Press, 1974.

Fast Speaking Woman and Other Chants, City Lights, 1975, revised edition, 1978.

Sun the Blond Out, Arif, 1975.

Hotel Room, Songbird, 1976.

Journals and Dreams, Stonehill, 1976.

Shaman, White Raven, 1977, bilingual edition in German and English, Apartment Editions, 1990.

(With Reed Bye) *Four Travels,* Sayonara, 1979.

(With Eileen Myles) *Polar Ode,* Dead Duke, 1979.

To a Young Poet, White Raven, 1979.

Countries, Toothpaste Press, 1980.

Cabin, Z Press, 1981.

First Baby Poems, Rocky Ledge, 1982, augmented edition, Hyacinth Girls, 1983.

Makeup on Empty Space, Toothpaste Press, 1984.

Invention (with drawings by Susan Hall), Kulchur Foundation, 1985.

Skin Meat Bones, Coffee House Press, 1985.

Blue Mosque, United Artists, 1987.

The Romance Thing, Bamberger Books, 1987.

Helping the Dreamer: New and Selected Poems, 1966–1988, Coffee House Press, 1989.

Not a Male Pseudonym, Tender Buttons Books, 1990.

Lokapala, Rocky Ledge, 1991.

Fait Accompli, Last Generation Press, 1992.

Iovis: All Is Full of Jove, Coffee House Press, 1993.

Troubairitz, Fifth Planet Press, 1993.

Also author (with Denyse duRoi) of *Sphinxeries,* 1979; and *Tell Me about It: Poems for Painters,* Bloody Twin.

Editor:

The World Anthology: Poems from the St. Mark's Poetry Project, Bobbs-Merrill, 1969.

Another World, Bobbs-Merrill, 1971.

(With Marilyn Webb) *Talking Poetics from Naropa Institute: Annals of the Jack Kerouac School of Disembodied Poetics,* Shambhala, 2 vols., 1978.

Nice to See You: Homage to Ted Berrigan, Coffee House Press, 1991.

Out of This World: The Poetry Project at the St. Mark's Church In-the-Bowery, an Anthology 1966–1991, Crown Publishing Group, 1991.

(With Andrew Schelling) *Disembodied Poetics: Annals of the Jack Kerouac School,* University of New Mexico Press, 1993.

Sound recordings:

(With Allen Ginsberg) *Beauty and the Beast,* Naropa Institute, 1976.

John Giorno and Anne Waldman, Giorno Poetry Systems Records, 1977.

Fast Speaking Woman, "S" Press Tapes (Munich), n.d.

Uh-Oh Plutonium!, Hyacinth Girls Music (NYC), 1982.

Crack in the World, Sounds True (Boulder), 1986.

Made Up in Texas, Paris Records (Dallas), 1986.

Assorted Singles, Phoebus Productions, 1990.

Live in Amsterdam, Soyo Productions, 1992.

Other recordings include *The Dial-a-Poem Poets, Disconnected* and *The Nova Convention, Big Ego,* Giorno Poetry Systems; and *The World Record.*

Films and videos:

Uh-Oh Plutonium!, Out There Productions (NYC).

Eyes in All Heads, Phoebus Productions, 1989.

Battle of the Bards, Metropolitan Pictures (Los Angeles), 1990.

Live at Naropa, Phoebus Productions, 1990.

Also performed in Bob Dylan's film *Renaldo and Clara* and her recording of *Fast Speaking Woman* is included in the sound track. Featured with Allen Ginsberg, William Burroughs, and Meredith Monk in the documentary film *Cooked Diamonds, Fried Shoes.* Appeared in *Poetry in Motion,* directed by Ron Mann, Sphinx Productions (Toronto).

Other:

(With Bernadette Mayer) *The Basketball Article,* Angel Hair, 1975.

(Contributor) *Five/I/'77,* Archer Press, 1977.

Co-editor, *Angel Hair* magazine and books, 1965—. Editor, *The World* magazine, 1966–78. Co-editor, with Ron Padgett and Joan Simon, Full Court Press. Co-editor, Rocky Ledge Cottage Editions.

Contributor of poetry to numerous anthologies, including *The Young American Poets,* Follett; *Earth Air Fire and Water,* Coward-McCann; *Silver Screen, Acid,* Marz Verlag (Germany); *Rising Tides,* Simon & Schuster; *Shaman Woman, Mainline Lady,* William Morrow; *Technicians of the Sacred,* University of California Press; *Deep Down,* Faber & Faber; *The Stiffest of the Corpse,* City Lights; and *The Postmoderns,* Grove Press.

Contributor of poetry to several journals, including *American Poetry Review, Bombay Gin, City Lights Review, Conjunctions, Intent, Iowa Review, Lucy and Jimmy's House of "K," Mademoiselle, New Directions, Notus, "O" Press Anthology, Oink! Acts, Paris Review, Partisan Review, Poetry* (Chicago), *Poetry Review* (London), *Rolling Stone, Scarlet, Transatlantic Review, Tyuonyi, Unmuzzled Ox, Village Voice,* and *Yale Literary Magazine.*

Collaborator with visual artists, including Elizabeth Murray, *Her Story* (boxed limited edition of lithographs), Universal Limited Art Editions, Inc., 1989; Yvonne Jacquette, *Night Wing* (poem and drawing), 1989; and Red Grooms, *Triptych: Madonnas and Sons,* 1990.

Anne Waldman's poems have been translated into many languages, including Czechoslovakian, French, German, Italian, Norwegian, Spanish, Swiss, Turkish, and Yugoslavian.

Cumulative Index

CUMULATIVE INDEX

The names of essayists who appear in the series are in boldface type. Subject references are followed by volume and page number(s). When a subject reference appears in more than one essay, names of the essayists are also provided.

"A" **2**:138, 142, 146
A for Anything **10**:203, 216, 217, 219-20
A la Carte **1**:38
A la recherche du temps perdu **8**:153
A la Rencontre du Plaisir **5**:195
Aarhus University **1**:156
ABC of Reading
  McCord **9**:180
  Pinsky **4**:244
ABC of Relativity **5**:314
Abel, Sherry **2**:398, 399
Abelard-Schuman (publishers)
  Gunn **2**:249
  Williams **3**:424
Aberdeen Express **5**:125
Abigail **2**:127
Abish, Walter
  Katz **14**:176
  Klinkowitz **9**:116
Abortion **10**:22
Abortionist, The **16**:14
"About Being a Member of Our Armed Forces" **17**:212
About My Table **2**:156
Abraham's Knife **7**:14
Abrahamsen, David **1**:376
Abse, Dannie 1:17-32
  Rosenthal **6**:283
  Silkin **5**:262
Abse, Joan **6**:283
Abse, Wilfred **1**:317
Absence of Unicorns, Presence of Lions **7**:132
Academic Festival Overtures **15**:221
Academy Award
  Corcoran **2**:119
  Nichols **2**:335
Academy of American Poets
  Dillard **7**:12
  Meredith **14**:230
  Wagoner **3**:410
Academy of American Poets Awards
  Allen **11**:13
  Rosenblum **11**:347
Accent **2**:438
Accord **14**:273-74
ACE **11**:305
Ace Books
  Brunner **8**:9, 13
  Hoffman **10**:173
  Knight **10**:225
  Niven **12**:218
  Pohl **1**:294-95
  St. Clair **8**:273

  Silverberg **3**:276
  Williams **3**:424
Achebe, Chinua **3**:426, 427, 428
Ackerman, Diane **7**:280-81, 282
Ackerman, Forrest **2**:27
Ackerman, Jack **3**:216
Ackley, Gardner **3**:244
Acorn, Milton **17**:205, 206
Acquired immune deficiency syndrome
  Andre **13**:25
  Hansen **17**:72
  Mathews **6**:239, 250
  Picano **13**:232, 234
Across a Billion Years **3**:281
Across the Bitter Sea **3**:64
Across the Lagoon **11**:96, 99
Act of the Imagination, An **9**:255
Actes retrouvés, Les (Recovered acts) **13**:186
Actors and acting
  Jennings **5**:108-09
  Madden **3**:192-93
  Mano **6**:208, 209
  Nolan **16**:214
  Peters **8**:249-50
  Thayer **11**:362-63
Acts of Love: An American Novel **10**:9, 10, 13
Acts of Mercy **4**:213
Acuario **15**:10
Ada **10**:318
Adam and Eve and the Devil **9**:279, 282
Adam International Review **7**:127, 128
Adamic, Louis **1**:167, 168
Adams, Ansel **12**:339-40
Adams, Hazard **7**:299
Adams, Henry
  Stegner **9**:270
  Whittemore **8**:299, 310
Adams, Kay **1**:169-72
Adams, Léonie
  Belitt **4**:62, 65
  Federman **8**:76
  Root **11**:321
Adams, Phoebe Lou **3**:415
Adams, Stephen D. **1**:303
Adelphi Community, Langham, England
  Ashby **6**:36-37
  Woodcock **6**:320
Aden-Arabie **8**:179
Adler, Jacob **2**:125
Adoption **7**:69

Adventure on Wheels: The Autobiography of a Road Racing Champion **16**:213, 214
Adventures in the Skin Trade **5**:272-73
Adventures of Robina by Herself, The **9**:294
Adventures of the Letter I **4**:295-96
Adversary in the House **3**:370
Advertisements **13**:288, 289
Aeneid **10**:315-16
Aeschylus **6**:89, 98, 100
Affinities of Orpheus, The **8**:118
Africa
  Awoonor **13**:29-54
  Bourjaily **1**:76
  Caute **4**:109
  Crews **14**:114, 115, 117-18
  Hahn **11**:112, 116, 118-19
  Killens **2**:298-303
  Lessing **14**:187-203
  Turner **10**:311-13
African-Americans **16**:105-19
  See also Blacks
African Methodist Episcopal Church **13**:238, 248
African Methodist Episcopal Zion Church **3**:418
Afrikaners **8**:48-49, 50, 51, 54, 58
Afro-American **6**:264
After Every Green Thing **1**:21, 24, 25
After Such Ignorance **9**:218
After the First Death, There Is No Other **12**:247
After the Lost Generation **1**:70
Afternoons in Mid-America **1**:155
Against the Circle **10**:136
Age of Defeat, The **5**:324
Age of Fiction: The French Novel from Gide to Camus, An **15**:136
Age of Magnificence, The **4**:231
Agee, James
  Madden **3**:198
  Malzberg **4**:215
  Markfield **3**:222, 224
  Slavitt **3**:318
Agency for International Development (U.S.) **3**:244, 245
Agent of the Unknown **8**:273
Agony and the Ecstasy, The **3**:372
Agony of Christianity, The **11**:213
Agrarian movement **11**:176
Aguilera-Malta, Demetrio **9**:204
Agusta, Leon **9**:147

Agyu, the Ilianon Epic of Mindanao
    9:164
Ahern, Maureen Maurer   **6**:138-39
Ai   13:1-12
AID See Agency for International
    Development (U.S.)
AIDS See Acquired immune
    deficiency syndrome
Aiken, Conrad   **3**:88, 90, 92
Air Freight   **7**:125
Air Training Corps See Great Britain,
    Royal Air Force, Air Training
    Corps
Airmail Postcards   **13**:68
Airs and Tributes   **14**:57, 60
Akalaitis, JoAnn   **14**:176
Akgulian, Avak   **2**:271
Akhmatova, Anna   **11**:377
Akpalu, Vinoko   **13**:44-45
A.L. Rowse's Cornwall   **8**:255
Alashka   **16**:282
Alaska
    Matthews   **15**:260-61
    McCord   **9**:186
Albany, N.Y.   **13**:333
Albany State College   **13**:248
Albee, Edward
    Purdy   **1**:302, 304
    Saroyan   **5**:217-18
Albert Camus: A Biography   **12**:207-08
Albrecht, William   **5**:348
Albright, Larry   **11**:284
Albuquerque Journal   **3**:128
Albuquerque, N.M.
    Anaya   **4**:19
    Creeley   **10**:68-69
"Alcestis"   **15**:233
Alcheringa   **13**:47
Alcoholics Anonymous
    Kerrigan   **11**:218
    Ray   **7**:147
Alcoholism
    Bradley   **10**:21
    Kerrigan   **11**:214-18
    Knebel   **3**:174-175
Alderson, Dan   **12**:220, 221
Alderton, John   **9**:253, 254
Aldington, Richard   **14**:126
Aldiss, Brian W.   2:15-32
    Pohl   **1**:295, 296
    Wolfe   **9**:308
Aldridge, John W.
    Bourjaily   **1**:70, 71
    Garrett   **5**:77
Alegría, Ciro   **12**:100
Alegría, Claribel   15:1-15
Aleixandre, Vicente   **15**:69, 93
Alexander, Herbert
    Bourjaily   **1**:70
    Killens   **2**:303
Alexander Technique   **1**:314
Alexander the Great   **1**:195
Alfred the Great   **4**:153
Alfred University   **14**:39-41
Algeria   **15**:134-35
Algerian War   **4**:227-29, 230

Algren, Nelson
    Bourjaily   **1**:76
    Malzberg   **4**:209
    Ray   **7**:142
Alice at Eighty   **3**:322-23, 324
Alice Fay Di Castagnola Award
    8:249
Alice Fell   **9**:293
Alice in Wonderland   **3**:322
All Her Children   **7**:199
All-Night Visitors   **6**:184, 185, 186
All Souls and Appeasement   **8**:257
All the Brave Promises   **1**:318, 322
All the Little Heroes   **3**:221
All the Little Live Things   **9**:269
"All Things Considered" (radio
    program)   **3**:82
All This Every Day   **16**:201
Alleluia Affair, The   **11**:55-56
Allen, Betty   **1**:304
Allen, Dick   11:1-23
    Allman   **15**:23
    Feirstein   **11**:84
    Shelnutt   **14**:297, 298
Allen, Donald A.
    Koller   **5**:163, 164
    Kyger   **16**:190, 196
    Rechy   **4**:260
Allen, Richard Sanders   **11**:2, 3
Allen, Walter   6:15-28
Allen, W.H. (publishers)   **2**:385
Allender, Nina   **1**:100, 104-05, 120
"Alley Oop"   **2**:37
Alley Theatre, Houston, Tex.   **5**:79
Alligator Bride, The   **7**:65
Alligator Report, The   **7**:107
Allin, John   **7**:243
Allingham, Margery
    Gilbert   **15**:188
    Keating   **8**:169
Allman, John   15:17-32
Allston, Washington   **6**:210
Almanac for Twilight, An   **15**:261
Almighty Has His Own Purposes, The
    7:95
Almighty Me   **14**:29-31
Almighty, The   **1**:399
Along the Arno   **9**:22, 23-24, 25
Alpaugh, Lloyd
    Kennedy   **9**:78, 79
    Wilson   **5**:349
Alpert, Richard   **13**:293
*Alphabet: the iconography of the
    imagination*   **15**:307
Alsace-Lorraine   **11**:123, 127
*Alternate Worlds: The Illustrated History
    of Science Fiction*   **2**:257
Altmann, Stuart   **16**:301
Altoon, John   **10**:69
Altshuler, Harry   **2**:252, 254, 255
Alumni Magazine (University of
    Kansas)   **2**:252
Alvarez, A.
    Rosenthal   **6**:283
    West   **7**:276
Am I Running with You, God?   **11**:56

Amalgamated Press   **5**:177, 178
Amateur radio   **14**:36-37
Amazing Stories
    Anderson   **2**:37
    Knight   **10**:202, 205
    Silverberg   **3**:271
    Williamson   **8**:316-17
*Ambidextrous: The Secret Lives of
    Children*   **13**:219-20, 233
America   **9**:38
America Hurrah   **2**:407, 414-16, 417
American Academy and Institute of
    Arts and Letters
    Meredith   **14**:230
    Taylor   **7**:187
    West   **7**:285
American Academy, Rome, Italy
    Kazin   **7**:95
    Simpson   **4**:294
    Stegner   **9**:267
    Williams   **3**:414
American Association for the
    Advancement of Science   **1**:285
American Atheists   **7**:100
American Book Awards   **2**:214
American Book Review   **8**:293
American Broadcasting Corp.   **2**:254,
    255
American Child Supreme, An   **2**:332
American Citizen   **1**:118
American Committee on Africa
    3:424
*American Dreams, American
    Nightmares*   **3**:194
American Folkways Series, The   **1**:150
American Friends Service
    Committee   **3**:137
American Heritage (publishers)
    1:313, 317
American High School, Paris   **2**:218,
    222
American Jazz Music   **10**:91-92
American Jewish Committee   **3**:218,
    220
"American Literary Establishment,
    The"   **2**:399-400
American Mercury
    Brossard   **2**:67
    Stone   **3**:370
American Museum of Natural History,
    New York City   **3**:271
American Negro Theatre   **6**:267-68
American Novel and Its Tradition, The
    6:210, 211
*American 1960s: Imaginative Acts in a
    Decade of Change, The*   **9**:116-17
American Philosophical Society   **9**:215
*American Playwrights: A Critical
    Survey*   **2**:365
American poetry   **2**:59
American Poetry Review
    Ai   **13**:10
    Bell   **14**:49
    Smith   **7**:165
American Repertory Theater   **2**:418

American Review See *New American Review*
American Rocket Society **1**:285
American Romance, An **10**:10
American Society of Aesthetics **15**:361-62
American Students Union **2**:207
American University
    Bausch **14**:30
    Grumbach **2**:210-11, 212, 213
    Taylor **7**:185
American Victorians: Explorations in Emotional History **9**:219
American Way of Death, The **17**:145-48
American Writers against the Vietnam War **7**:143
American Youth for Democracy **3**:209
Amherst College
    Guerard **2**:223
    Kazin **7**:95
    Kirkup **4**:189-90
    Root **11**:325
    Symons **3**:393
Amichai, Yehuda **2**:387
Amis, Kingsley
    Aldiss **2**:23, 27
    Jennings **5**:109, 110
    West **7**:276
Amistad 1 **3**:431
Amistad 2 **3**:431
Amnesia **4**:149, 157, 158
Amnesia **13**:280, 281, 290-91
Amnesty International **7**:134
Among the Beasts **8**:78
Among the Cinders
    Becker **1**:44
    Shadbolt **3**:251
Amor de Cosmos: Journalist and Reformer **6**:323-24
Amsterdam, Netherlands **3**:427, 430
Amsterdam News **6**:264
Amulet (Carl Rakosi) **5**:199
Amulet, The (Isaac Rosenberg) **5**:263
Amussen, Bob **10**:9
Anaeus Africanus **5**:84
Anagogic and Paideumic Review **6**:180
Analog See also *Astounding Science-Fiction*
Analysis of Poetic Thinking **9**:45
Anand, Mulk Raj **6**:319
Anarchism
    Beltrametti **13**:56
    Jerome **8**:132
    Kostelanetz **8**:191
    Woodcock **6**:319, 320, 322, 323
Anarchism: A History of Libertarian Ideas and Movements **6**:322
Anarchist Prince: A Biographical Study of Peter Kropotkin, The **6**:321
Anatomy of Proserpine, The **14**:112
Anavrita Academy **15**:74, 81
Anaya, Rudolfo A. 4:15-28
And Keep Your Powder Dry **8**:181

And Then We Heard the Thunder **2**:286, 295, 297, 304-05
And Then We Moved to Rossenarra **1**:197
Anderson, Donald **1**:164, 165
Anderson, Lindsay **7**:240
Anderson, Margaret **1**:99
Anderson, Poul 2:33-46
Anderson, Sherwood **6**:47-48
Anderson, Wendell B. **14**:109, 111, 112, 113
Andersson, Claes **10**:71
Andover Academy
    Slavitt **3**:313-14, 317
    Whittemore **8**:298, 300
André Gide **2**:221, 223, 226
Andre, Michael 13:13-27
Andreas, Osborn **1**:300, 301, 302
Andrew and Tobias **3**:356-57
Andrews, Clarence **7**:103
Andrews, Jim **1**:253
Andreyev, Leonid
    Solotaroff **2**:392
    Wallace **1**:391
Angel Hair **17**:276, 279
Angels and Earthly Creatures **8**:227
Angier, Bradford **2**:126
Angle of Repose
    Coppel **9**:4
    Stegner **9**:269
Angleton, James **8**:306
Anglo-Welsh movement **4**:306, 310
Angry Black, The **3**:427
Angry Ones, The **3**:424
Angry Young Men (literary movement)
    Sinclair **5**:270
    Wilson **5**:321, 323
Angulo, Ximena de **3**:140, 142
Anillo de Silencio **15**:2, 6
Animal Farm **9**:21
Animal rights **15**:239
Animism **3**:406
Anlo-Ewe dirge **13**:44
Ann Arbor, Mich. **1**:273
Annette **1**:155
Annie Wobbler **7**:243, 244-45, 260, 261-62
Anon and Various Time Machine Poems **11**:15
Another Country **3**:425
Another Time **6**:39
Anouilh, Jean
    Brossard **2**:69
    Van Itallie **2**:411
Anpao **7**:78, 81, 82
Anrig, George **1**:192
Ant, Howard **1**:364
Antaeus **1**:93
Anthologist (Rutgers University) **4**:244
Anthology of Concrete Poetry **8**:89
Anthony, Peter **1**:19
Anthony, Piers **12**:217
Anthropology
    Manuel **9**:156-57, 163-65
    Tarn **16**:274-75, 278, 282-83

Anthropos-Specter-Beast, The **9**:125
Anti-Defamation League of B'nai B'rith **3**:217, 227
Anti-Semitism
    Epstein **12**:64
    Glanville **9**:18
    Hamburger **4**:170
    Hentoff **6**:165-66, 167
    Kazin **7**:87
    Kumin **8**:208, 213
    Lifshin **10**:237
    Lind **4**:196-97, 198, 199-200
    Nichols **2**:310
    Piercy **1**:268
    Rimmer **10**:296
    Roditi **14**:253-54
    Rosenthal **6**:273
    Schevill **12**:275, 277-78
    Silkin **5**:243, 248-49, 251, 254, 256, 260, 261
    Solotaroff **2**:391
    Wallace **1**:391
    See also Jews
Antigone **16**:128-29
Antioch College
    Block **11**:27-29, 30-31, 38
    Hamburger **4**:171
    Jerome **8**:132-34, 136, 138
Antitheses **8**:190-91
Antivivisectionism **4**:90
Antiwar movement
    Allen **11**:21
    Dennison **6**:117
    Eshleman **6**:140-41
    Heyen **9**:42
    Highwater **7**:79
    Livesay **8**:232-34
    Nichols **2**:332
    Olson **11**:256
    Settle **1**:319
    Sukenick **8**:290
    Turner **10**:318
Anton, Robert **2**:417, 422
Antoninus, Brother See Everson, William
Ants **16**:291-308
Ants, The **16**:305, 306
Anything Can Happen **8**:293
Anzilotti, Rolando **6**:283
Apartheid
    Awoonor **13**:47
    Brutus **14**:54-6
    Cassity **8**:51, 52, 53-54
    Wright **5**:370
Apes of God, The **3**:385
Apollinaire, Guillaume **9**:82
Apostolidis, Penny **16**:245-70
Appalachian region **15**:273-9
Appeasement: A Study in Political Decline, 1933–1939 **8**:257
Apple Butter **15**:306, 307
Appleton-Century (publishers) **1**:196
Applewhite, Cynthia **7**:107
Arab-Israeli conflict
    Hassan **12**:156
    Megged **13**:148, 151-52

Wiesel **4**:359
Arab Women Solidarity Association
  11:70-71
Arafat, Yasser **11**:71
Ararat **2**:273, 274
Arbor House Publishing Co. **3**:285
"Archaeology, Elegy, Architecture: A
  Poet's Program for Lyric"
  16:286
Archer, David **5**:368, 370
Architectural Forum **2**:208
Architecture **13**:58, 59, 61
Arctic Desert, The **9**:184
"Arctic Places" **17**:213
Arden, John 4:29-47
Are You Running with Me, Jesus?
  11:48, 49-50, 51, 55, 57, 59
Arendt, Hannah
  Epstein **12**:71-72
  Weiss **2**:438, 450
Argosy
  Brown **6**:47
  Knight **10**:209
Arguedas, José María **12**:101
Argyros, Alex **10**:321
Ariadne's Thread **10**:257
Ariel **11**:35-36
Arizona State University **3**:129-30,
  131
Arkansas State Teachers College
  6:51
Armadillo in the Grass **11**:165-66,
  167
Armenian-Americans **2**:273-74
Armstrong, John **10**:314
Armstrong Junior College **10**:169-70
Armstrong, Lil Hardin **6**:181
Arnold, Bob **5**:169
Arnold, Danny **9**:244
Arnow, Harriette Simpson **15**:283,
  287, 289
Aron, Edith **2**:138
Around about America **1**:153
Arrivistes, The **4**:293
Arrondissements **15**:228
Arrow in the Blue **7**:196
Arrowsmith, William
  Raffel **9**:217
  Taylor **7**:187
Art
  Atkins **16**:4-5, 10
  Bell **14**:39-40
  Hine **15**:228
  Ouellette **13**:179
Art criticism
  Andre **13**:15, 21
  Kerrigan **11**:208-09
Art in America **2**:197
Art of Being Ruled, The **3**:385
"Art of Biography, The" (lecture)
  3:393
"Art Poétique" **6**:281
Art, Pre-Columbian **3**:371
Art Students' League, New York City
  Disch **4**:155-56
  Gray **2**:190

Artaud, Antonin
  O'Faolain **2**:347
  Van Itallie **2**:412
Articulate Energy
  Davie **3**:37, 38, 40
  Pinsky **4**:247
Artists-in-the-Schools program **13**:314
ARTnews **13**:14
Arts **6**:113
Arts Council of Ireland **3**:64-65
Arts Council Prize **5**:110
Arvon Foundation
  Booth **2**:58
  Wright **5**:369
As a Man Grows Older **3**:218
As for Love: Poems and Translations
  6:280
*As I Live and Breathe: Stages of an
  Autobiography* **11**:50, 51
As Wolves Love Lambs **2**:223-24
As You Like It **6**:290
Asahel **13**:154-55, 158
Asbury, Herbert **11**:108, 111
Ascensions **3**:96, 98
Ascent into Hell **7**:41
Ashbery, John
  Baumbach **5**:27
  Hall **7**:63
  Mathews **6**:235-36, 237, 245
  Rodgers **13**:250
Ashby, Cliff 6:29-44
  Sisson **3**:302
Ashes of Izalco **15**:3
Ashman, Richard **3**:335
Asia Foundation **9**:212
Asian Minor, An **13**:233
"Asian Shore, The" **4**:152
Asiatic Romance, An **3**:301
*Ask for Love and You Get Rice
  Pudding* **2**:126
Asking Myself/Answering Myself **2**:144
Aspects of Alice **13**:205
Aspen, Colorado **11**:166
Aspen School of Art **11**:253
Aspen Writers' Workshop **11**:253,
  255, 257
Assault with Intent **1**:242
Assembling **8**:191-93, 194
Assistant, The **8**:285
Associated Negro Press **3**:421, 424
Associated Press
  Higgins **5**:98-99
  Wallace **1**:376
Associated Writing Programs **1**:173,
  174
Association of Literary Magazines of
  America **8**:307, 308
Astounding Science-Fiction
  Anderson **2**:37, 39, 40, 41
  Brunner **8**:5
  Budrys **14**:66
  Gunn **2**:244, 247
  Kennedy **9**:78
  Knight **10**:202, 203, 204
  Malzberg **4**:207
  Silverberg **3**:271

Astounding Stories See *Astounding
  Science-Fiction*
Astronauts, The **1**:259
At Fever Pitch **4**:103-04, 105
At Freddie's **10**:108-09
At the End of the Open Road **4**:294
At the Front Door of the Atlantic
  11:205
"At the Lake" **3**:24
At the Western Gates **16**:286
Atheism
  Caute **4**:96
  Kinsella **7**:100, 109
  Rabassa **9**:192
  Wilhelm **5**:303
Athens, Greece
  Corman **2**:138
  Samarakis **16**:245-5, 257-66
Athill, Diana
  Caute **4**:103
  Mott **7**:127
Atitlán/Alashka **16**:282
Atkins, Russell 16:1-19
Atlanta Constitution **1**:142
Atlanta, Ga.
  Cassity **8**:56, 60
  Mott **7**:130-31, 132
Atlanta Journal **1**:146, 147
Atlantic Awards in Literature **5**:359
Atlantic City, N.J.
  Boyle **1**:108-11
  Kumin **8**:203-04
Atlantic Flyway **13**:98
Atlantic Monthly
  Cassill **1**:167
  Davison **4**:135, 137, 138, 139,
    141
  Higgins **5**:97
  Still **17**:235
  Wakefield **7**:197-98
  Williams **3**:415
Atlantic Monthly Press **4**:135-36,
  137, 139, 141
Atlantis **14**:139-40
Atomic Age **13**:324-25, 327
Attic of Ideals, An **13**:308, 313
Atwood, Margaret **15**:158
Auburn University **11**:180-81
Auden, W.H.
  Allen **6**:18, 24
  Ashby **6**:36, 39
  Bowles **1**:86
  Broughton **12**:45
  Burroway **6**:90
  Fuller **10**:120, 123
  Hazo **11**:148, 150
  Hine **15**:230-32
  Howes **3**:143
  Jennings **5**:110
  Jones **5**:121
  Kizer **5**:146
  Major **6**:185-86
  Malanga **17**:97, 100
  Meredith **14**:224-25, 229-30
  Roditi **14**:279
  Rosenthal **6**:282

Shapiro **6**:307-08
Simpson **4**:291
Sinclair **5**:272
Symons **3**:383, 385
Wain **4**:327
Audiotape **8**:187
Auer, Jane **1**:84, 85-94
Auerbach, Walter **6**:235, 236
Augusta Chronicle **1**:142
Augustana College **9**:264
Augustine, St. **7**:7
Ault, Nelson **9**:182
Aurora: New Canadian Writing 1978
    7:103, 104
Austin Community College **2**:127
Austin, J.C. **7**:26
Australia **13**:118-20
Australian National University **3**:242
Austria
    Garrett **5**:72, 81, 86, 89
    Van Brunt **15**:377
Austro-Hungarian Empire **7**:208,
    209
Author and Journalist **8**:272
Authors Guild **1**:295
Authors League of America
    Corcoran **2**:117
    Wallace **1**:402
Autobiographical Stanzas **5**:249, 257
Autobiographies (Richard Kostelanetz)
    8:179, 183, 184
Autobiography: A Novel **4**:265
Autobiography of Bertrand Russell
    5:42
Autobiography of My Mother, The
    10:42-43
Autobiography (William Butler Yeats)
    3:142-43
Automobile racing
    Nolan **16**:207, 213-14
    Thayler **11**:359-60, 363
Auxiliary Territorial Service, Great
    Britain **8**:23-24
Avakumovic, Ivan **6**:323
Avant-garde
    Beltrametti **13**:65
    Kostelanetz **8**:184-85
Avedon, Richard **5**:212
Avery, Milton **5**:221-22
Aviation
    Cartland **8**:23
    Ciardi **2**:90
    Clement **16**:89-91, 92-94
    Connell **2**:102-06
    Gunn **2**:243-44
    Kerrigan **11**:207-08
    Roditi **14**:239-40
    Voinovich **12**:312
Awoonor, Kofi Nyidevu **13**:29-54
    Major **6**:196
Axe-Time, Sword-Time **2**:118
Axelrod, George **1**:196
Axes **3**:95
Axmann-Rezzori, Hanna **10**:160
Aydy, Catherine (pseudonym of
    Emma Tennant) **9**:291

Babbitt, Irving **7**:220
Babble **5**:26-27
Babel, Isaac
    Blaise **3**:19
    Silkin **5**:260
Babes-Bolyai University **5**:353
Babi-Yar (monument) **4**:360
Baby, Come On Inside **3**:408
Baby-Sitters, The **4**:108
Bacall, Lauren **5**:56-57
Bach, Johann Sebastian **3**:95
Bach, Julian **12**:207
Bachelor, Joseph M. **3**:169
Back Door **7**:163
Back River **5**:169
Backtrack **17**:71
Bad for Each Other **1**:383
Bad Sister, The **9**:291, 292
Bad Streak, A **9**:27
Baedeker guidebooks **2**:383
Baez, Joan **11**:288
Bailey, Charles W., II **3**:174, 179,
    180, 181
Bailey, Margery **12**:45
Baird, Newton **3**:335
Baker, Elizabeth **5**:165
Baker, Josephine **7**:28
Balakian, Nona **2**:363
Balboni, Loredana **6**:240, 242
Baldwin, James
    Clarke **16**:84
    Corman **2**:139
    Hinojosa-Smith **16**:145
    Killens **2**:306
    Major **6**:195
    Petry **6**:256, 266
    Williams **3**:425
Balfour, Arthur **4**:196
Ball, David **11**:300, 301, 302
"Ballade of Good Counsel" **3**:144
Ballades and Rondeaus, Chants Royal,
    Sestinas, Villanelles, Etc. **3**:144
Ballantine, Betty **3**:278
Ballantine, David **10**:10
Ballantine, Ian **1**:291-92, 294
Ballantine (publishers)
    Pohl **1**:292
    Silverberg **3**:281
Ballard, J.G.
    Aldiss **2**:25, 28
    Disch **4**:151
    Moorcock **5**:187
    Tennant **9**:291
Ballet Rambert **5**:366
Ballou, George **15**:57, 59-60, 67
Ballou, Jenny **15**:59
Baloian, James **2**:272
Baltimore Catechism **4**:145
Baltimore, Md. **1**:280
Balzac, Honoré de **2**:385
Bamberger, Bill **14**:179
Bamboo Bed, The **1**:212
Banciulescu, Victor **9**:26
Band Has Won, The **1**:344
Bankrupts, The **9**:25-26

Banks, Russell **15**:33-45
    Baumbach **5**:29
Bantam Books
    Cassill **1**:173
    Knebel **3**:180
    Pohl **1**:295
    Rimmer **10**:299
Baptist Church
    Bennett **13**:73-74, 76-78, 82, 87
    Dillard **7**:7
Baraka, Amiri
    Clarke **16**:85, 86
    Crews **14**:117
    Forbes **16**:112
    Killens **2**:298
    Major **6**:180, 188, 193
Baraka, Imamu *See* Baraka, Amiri
Barbados **16**:71-76
Barbary Shore **1**:72
Barbusse, Henri **5**:320
Barcelona, Spain
    Charyn **1**:181
    Connell **2**:108-09
Bard College
    Menashe **11**:228-29
    Settle **1**:317, 318, 319, 321
    Weiss **2**:436-39, 441-47, 449
Barker, Arthur (publishers) **1**:389
Barker, George
    Ashby **6**:42-43
    Wright **5**:359, 367, 368, 369,
        370, 371
Barker, Kit **5**:368, 369
Barker, Margaret **1**:304
Barker, Richard **10**:2, 5
Barlow, Gillian **8**:157
Barlow, Wilfred **1**:314
Barn, The (artists' colony) **15**:381
Barnard, Allen **1**:295
Barnard College
    Brown **10**:38
    Burroway **6**:87, 89-90
    Gray **2**:192, 194
    Swenson **13**:311-12
Barnes, Clive
    Gray **3**:114
    Slade **9**:248, 250
Barnes, Djuna **15**:243
Barnes, Joe **1**:38
Barnes, Peter **12**:1-16
Barnes, Steven **12**:212-13, 221
Barnet, Sylvan **9**:85
Barney, Dave **7**:179-80
Barney Oldfield: The Life and Times of
    America's Legendary Speed King
    16:214
Barnstone, Aliki **15**:94, 103, 105,
    107
Barnstone, Helle **15**:59-103
Barnstone, Tony **15**:65, 92, 94, 103,
    105, 107
Barnstone, Willis **15**:47-108
Barnum, Phineas T. **1**:387-88
Baro, Gene **5**:264
Baron, Richard **1**:74, 75
Barr, Richard **2**:414

Barr, Roger **2**:108-09
Barr, Stringfellow **12**:23-24, 26, 27, 28, 39
Barracini, Angela (pseudonym of Barbara Corcoran) **2**:117
Barrell, John **11**:308
Barrett, Waller **1**:157
Barrio, Raymond 15:109-26
Barry, Geoffrey **5**:113
Barth, John
    Klinkowitz **9**:111, 113, 120
    Sukenick **8**:290
Barthelme, Donald
    Klinkowitz **9**:108, 112, 115, 117
    Sukenick **8**:291
Barthes, Roland **9**:114, 116, 118, 119
Bartlett: The Great Canadian Explorer **15**:251, 252
Barzini, Luigi **4**:232
Barzun, Jacques
    Dillon **3**:59
    West **7**:277
Basak, Subimal **14**:90, 91, 92, 93, 98
Baseball
    Bowering **16**:24, 26
    Brown **6**:48-49
    Bullins **16**:64-65
    Hood **17**:78, 81-82
    Kinsella **7**:98, 99, 103, 108, 110
    Klinkowitz **9**:107, 118-20
Basketball **9**:38
Basler National Zeitung **11**:130-32
Bass Saxophone, The **1**:348, 350
Bastin, Cliff **9**:20
Bates, Alan **3**:114
Bates College
    Ciardi **2**:88
    Rimmer **10**:285, 286-87
Bates, Harry **8**:318
Bates Student **10**:286
Bateson, F.W. **7**:275-76
Bathory, Elizabeth **8**:246, 248-50
Bator, Paul **6**:234
Bats Fly Up for Inspector Ghote **8**:173-74
Baudelaire, Charles **6**:289, 304
Baum, Cliff **6**:234
Baumbach, Jonathan 5:15-30
    Sukenick **8**:293
Bausch, Richard 14:1-16
    Bausch, Robert **14**:17-23, 25, 26, 27, 28, 29, 30-31
Bausch, Robert 14:17-31
    Bausch, Richard **14**:1-5, 7, 12
Bax, Martin **13**:287-88
Baxandall, Rosalyn **3**:78
Baxter, James K. **3**:259
Bay Area Funeral Society **17**:145-46
Bay of Arrows **16**:241, 242
Bayes, Ronald **9**:146
Baylor University **14**:108, 109, 110
Baynes, Cary F. **3**:142
BBC See British Broadcasting Corp.
Beach, Sylvia

Corman **2**:139
    Lottman **12**:206
"Beasts, The" **5**:209
Beat Generation
    Brossard **2**:72
    Broughton **12**:57
    Enslin **3**:92-93
    Kherdian **2**:268-69
    Kyger **16**:189-200
    Lifshin **10**:255
    Pinsky **4**:244
    Saroyan **5**:214, 218
    Wright **7**:293-94
Beatles, The
    Kerrigan **11**:197-98
    Moorcock **5**:176
    Raffel **9**:216
Beattie, Ann **16**:237
Beaumont, Charles **16**:212, 213, 214, 215
Beaumont, Vivian **2**:418
Beautiful Contradictions, The **16**:280
Beautiful Greed, The **3**:188
Beauty Operators, The **6**:96, 99
Beauvoir, Simone de **1**:272
Beaux Arts Trio, The **2**:162
Bechet, Sidney **6**:166
Beck, Julian **6**:116
Becker, Stephen 1:33-46
    Shadbolt **3**:264
    Wiesel **4**:353
Beckett, Samuel
    Federman **8**:77
    Lottman **12**:199
    Sukenick **8**:290
    Van Itallie **2**:412
    West **7**:284
Beclch **2**:361, 363
Bed, The **12**:53
Bedford Reader, The **9**:85
Beerbohm, Max **1**:191, 198
Before the Dawn **3**:271
Before Winter Comes **5**:272, 273
"Beggar Maid, The" **7**:240
Beggar of Jerusalem, The **4**:359
Beginner's Luck **11**:115
Beginning of Spring, The **10**:109
"Beginnings of Charity, The" **17**:50, 52, 53-54
Behold the Man **5**:180
Being Geniuses Together **1**:98, 114, 115
Belafonte, Harry **2**:289
Belgrade, Yugoslavia **4**:267-71, 273, 274
Belitt, Ben 4:49-68
Bell, Charles G. 12:17-40
Bell Jar, The **4**:134, 137
Bell, Marvin 14:33-51
    Katz **14**:179
    Major **6**:181
    Wright **7**:297
Bellah, James Warner **6**:54
Bellarosa Connection, The **11**:190, 197
Belle Bête, La **4**:72-73
Belleau, André **13**:183, 184, 187

Bellevue Hospital **13**:23-24
Belloc, Hilaire
    Greeley **7**:51
    Morris **13**:166
Bellow, Saul
    Honig **8**:115
    Kazin **7**:93
    Kerrigan **11**:190, 194, 197, 210, 213-14, 219
    Lem **1**:258
    Solotaroff **2**:398
    Weiss **2**:439, 441
Beloit Poetry Journal **17**:27
Beloved Enemy **2**:127
Belshazzar's Feast **6**:210
Beltrametti, Franco 13:55-72
    Raworth **11**:310
Bemelmans, Ludwig **12**:81
Ben Ali, Robert **17**:63-65, 72
Ben-Gurion, David **1**:28
Benét, James Walker **12**:47
Benét, Stephen Vincent **1**:164
Benét, William Rose **12**:47
Benjamin, David (pseudonym of David Slavitt) **3**:322
Bennett, Arnold **6**:17, 22, 27
Bennett, Hal 13:73-88
Bennett, Lerone **2**:298
Bennett, Paul **3**:22, 24
Bennington College
    Becker **1**:39
    Belitt **4**:53, 62-64, 65-66
    Busch **1**:133
    Delbanco **2**:159
    Elman **3**:74-75
    Howes **3**:136-37
    Mathews **6**:223, 249
    Vivante **12**:301, 302
    Waldman **17**:272-74, 275, 277
Bennington Writing Workshops **2**:157, 159
Benny, Jack **1**:383
Benson, Graham **2**:386
Benton, Jessie See Fremont, Jessie Benton
Benveniste, Asa **11**:302, 303
Beowulf
    Raffel **9**:214
    Wright **5**:370, 373
Berdyayev, Nikolai **2**:191-92
Berea College **15**:280-81, 282, 283-84, 285
Berenson, Bernard
    Howes **3**:142
    Stone **3**:373-74
Beresford, Anne **4**:165, 166
Berg, Alban **3**:95
Bergé, Carol 10:1-17
    Choudhury **14**:93
    McCord **9**:186, 187
Berger, Art **6**:186
Bergman, Ingmar **7**:13, 17
Bergonzi, Bernard **5**:262
Bergstrom, Louise **10**:174
Berhama Account, The **3**:432
Berkeley, George (Bishop of Cloyne)

Davie **3**:38
  Wilson **5**:313
Berkley (publishers) **10**:222
Berkson, Bill **17**:276
Berlin Cemetery films (Richard
    Kostelanetz) **8**:189-90
Berlin Festival **2**:364
Berlin, Germany
  Bowles **1**:83
  Easton **14**:152
Berlin, Irving **1**:395
Berlin Lost, A **8**:190
Berlitz School of Languages
  Andre **13**:14, 17
  Hassan **12**:154
Bernal, Olga **8**:79
Bernanos, Georges **4**:72
Bernardin, Joseph **7**:46, 48-49, 51
Bernardo, Gabriel A. **9**:159, 162,
    168
Berneri, Marie Louise **6**:320, 321,
    326
Bernhardt, Sarah **1**:401
"Bernie Rhodenbarr" series **11**:37-
    38
Bernstein, Leonard **2**:415
Berrigan, Daniel 1:47-62
  Andre **13**:15, 19, 20, 21, 24
Berrigan, Philip **2**:198
Berrigan, Ted
  Saroyan **5**:215
  Waldman **17**:288-89
Berry, Michael, Lord Hartwell **5**:371
Berry, Wendell
  Creeley **10**:67
  Root **11**:324
Berryman, John
  Allen **11**:13
  Davison **4**:138
  Honig **8**:115, 116, 118, 121
  Kerrigan **11**:216
  Weiss **2**:446-47
Bertocci, Peter **10**:287
Bertolucci, Attilio **10**:141
Bessie, Mike **1**:35, 38
Bessinger, Jess **9**:214
Best American Short Stories **17**:239
Best Father Ever Invented **3**:127
Best Hour of the Night, The **4**:296
Best of Barry N. Malzberg, The **4**:215
Best of Margaret St. Clair, The **8**:278,
    281
Bester, Alfred **1**:290
Bestsellers **1**:395
Beta Sigma Phi Award **15**:247
Betjeman, John
  Roditi **14**:247
  Thomas **4**:309
*Better Half: The Emancipation of the
    American Woman, The* **5**:271
Between the Lines **7**:202
Between the Thunder and the Sun **9**:5
Beulah Quintet, The **1**:308, 316,
    317, 319, 321, 322
Bevan, Aneurin **5**:123-24
Bevin, Ernest **8**:258

"Bewitched" **9**:244
Bewitched, The **12**:11, 13
Beyer, H. Otley **9**:156-57, 159, 162,
    163, 165, 168
Beyond **2**:258
Beyond Apollo **4**:213
"Beyond Mars" **8**:324
Beyond the Angry Black **3**:429
Beyond the Blue Mountains **6**:326
Beyond the Hundredth Meridian
    9:268, 269
Beyond the Outsider **5**:324
*Beyond the Road: Portraits and Visions
    of Newfoundlanders* **15**:251
Bhagavad Gita
  Sillitoe **2**:380
  Wilson **5**:317
Bhatia, Vishnu **9**:182
Bialik Prize **13**:157
Bible
  Becker **1**:43
  Brewster **15**:151
  Cassity **8**:29
  Jones **11**:172-73
  Katz **9**:51, 65-66
  Kizer **5**:145
  Menashe **11**:234
  Shreve **5**:230
Bible, Jewish
  Josipovici **8**:147
  Silkin **5**:251
Bible, King James Version
  Anderson **2**:46
  Brown **6**:73
  Nichols **2**:317
  Sillitoe **2**:372, 379
Bible Story **5**:179
Bibliophily **15**:269-70
Bickel, Shlomo **2**:398-99
Bidart, Frank **4**:248-49, 250
Bidstrup, Darell **5**:170
Bienek, Horst **13**:134, 136
Big Diaphanous Wild Man, A **2**:332,
    335
Big Kill, The **7**:6
Big Rock Candy Mountain, The **9**:259,
    260, 265, 266
Big Shot, The **5**:56
Big Table **6**:181
Bigger Light, The **16**:80
Biggle, Lloyd, Jr. **10**:224-25
Bijou **3**:192, 195, 199
Billion Year Spree **2**:29
Binder, Judith Perlzweig **2**:138
Biodiversity **16**:306
Biography
  Sinclair **5**:274-75
  Whittemore **8**:310-11
Biology and Values **1**:263
Biophilia **16**:306
Bird, Bill **1**:119
*Bird of Paper: Poems of Vicente
    Aleixandre, A* **15**:69
Birmingham, Ala. **17**:26
Birmingham, England **10**:81, 87, 88
Birstein, Ann **7**:94-95

Birtwistle, Harrison **8**:147, 158
Bischoff, Herman **10**:215
Bisexuality **10**:23-24, 25
Bishop, Elizabeth
  Gregor **10**:148
  Pinsky **4**:248-49
  Stevenson **9**:283-84
Bishop, Jim **1**:248
Bishop, John Peale **10**:133
Bishop's Progress **6**:209, 210
Biton, Lucien **16**:275
Bitter Fame **9**:287
Bitter Glass, The **3**:59, 61, 64
Bitterroot **9**:66, 67
Black Alice **4**:151
Black, Alta **7**:76-77
Black and White Keys **17**:83
Black Boy **6**:185
"Black Flag of Anarchism, The"
    8:191
Black Grate Poems **9**:287
Black, Hugo **1**:181, 182
Black Like Me **7**:132
Black Man's Burden **2**:295, 305
Black Marina **9**:293-94
*Black Marsden: A Tabula Rasa
    Comedy* **16**:135
Black Mountain College
  Bell **12**:31
  Creeley **10**:68
  Gray **2**:194
  Kazin **7**:93
Black Mountain Review **14**:333
Black Panthers **5**:273
Black Sparrow Press **1**:368
Black Tide **14**:159
Blackbird Dust **12**:352
Blackburn Junior College **12**:28
Blackburn, Paul
  Bergé **10**:6
  Corman **2**:137, 138
  Eshleman **6**:132, 134, 135, 138,
    140
  Koller **5**:165
  Olson **11**:255-56, 257, 259
  Rosenblum **11**:345, 352
  Souster **14**:314
  Thayler **11**:363-65
Blackburn, Sara **9**:203
Blackburn, Thomas **5**:261
Blackburn, William **4**:114-15, 116,
    117, 120
Blackheath, England **10**:111-27
Blackheath Poisonings, The **3**:390
Blacklock, Jack **9**:240-41
Blackmur, Alan **8**:300
Blacks
  Ai **13**:10-11
  Bennett **13**:73-74, 79, 81, 83, 84-
    85
  Bullins **16**:62-65, 67-68
  Clarke **16**:75-76, 77-80, 82-86
  Easton **14**:154-55, 156
  Forrest **7**:31-32
  Garrett **5**:86
  Giovanni **6**:152, 160-61

Petry **6**:257, 265-66
Rodgers **13**:244, 245, 246, 250
Simpson **4**:286
Stafford **3**:332
Still **17**:234, 238
Williams **3**:414, 415, 416
Blackwell, Betsy Talbot **6**:87
Blackwell, Earl **2**:119
Blair, Kathryn **11**:97, 104
Blais, Achille **3**:17
Blais, Corinne **3**:17
Blais, Gervaise (Boucher) **3**:17
Blais, Leo Romeo **3**:17-18, 20-21, 22, 24
Blais, Marie-Claire 4:69-80
Blais, Olivier **3**:17
Blaise, Clark 3:15-30
Blake, William
    Broughton **12**:47
    Eshleman **6**:136
    Lifshin **10**:241
    Menashe **11**:234
    Nichols **2**:328
Blakemore, James **2**:409
Blasco Ibáñez, Vicente **9**:1, 2
Blériot, Louis **14**:239-40
Bless Me, Ultima **4**:23, 24, 26
Blessing, Dick **2**:326
Blind Cross, The **7**:130
Blind Harry **8**:19
Blish, James
    Knight **10**:208, 209, 211, 212, 213, 214, 217, 220, 221, 222
    Niven **12**:216-17
Bliven, Bruce **7**:92
Bloch, Robert **2**:27
Block, Lawrence 11:25-41
Blood and Money **14**:159
Blood Countess, The **8**:246, 247, 248, 249-50
Blood Tie **1**:320, 322
Bloodworth Orphans, The **7**:30-31, 33
Bloody Murder **3**:390
Bloomfield, Morton **9**:211, 212, 213
Bloomsbury Group **3**:36
Blown Away **8**:294
Bloy, Léon **13**:181, 183
Blücher, Heinrich **2**:438, 450
Blue Book **6**:47, 48
Blue Boy on Skates **6**:279
Blue-Eyed Shan, The **1**:42
Blue Girls **3**:117
Blue Hammer, The **3**:204
Blue Monday **16**:106-07, 109, 110, 112, 113-14, 116
Blue Mosque **17**:287
Blues
    Forrest **7**:26, 30, 32-33
    Rosenblum **11**:338, 340-41
Blues People **16**:86
Bluest Eye, The **3**:431
Bluhdorn, Charles **1**:196
Blunden, Edmund
    Booth **2**:50-51, 59
    Corman **2**:140

Woodcock **6**:319
Blur in Between, The **17**:207
Bly, Robert
    Allen **11**:15
    Booth **2**:55, 58
    Hall **7**:62, 63, 64
    Kennedy **9**:86
    Ray **7**:143, 144
    Root **11**:321
    Taylor **7**:179
BMT Theater **16**:67
Boatman's Tenure, The **6**:200
Boatwright, James **3**:23
Bobbs-Merrill Co. (publishers) **4**:293, 294
Bobrowski, Johannes **13**:125-40
Boccaccio, Giovanni **8**:281
Bochet, André du **2**:139, 144
Bocock, Maclin **2**:215, 229, 230
Bodies and Souls **4**:264-65
Body in the Billiard Room, The **8**:177
Body Rags **8**:246
Body Servant, The **4**:190
Boelhower, William **6**:200-01
Boer War
    Stewart **3**:345
    Wright **5**:360
Bogan, Louise
    Belitt **4**:62
    Burroway **6**:90
    Cassity **8**:54
Bohannon's Country: Five Mysteries **17**:71, 73
Bohr, Niels **4**:65
Boisvert, Gaston **13**:180
Bokhari, Ahmed Shah **9**:225
Bold Cavaliers, The **6**:57
Bold John Henebry **3**:62, 64
Bold Saboteurs, The **2**:66, 67
Bolinas, Calif. **16**:200-02
Bollingen Foundation **4**:166
Bolshoi Ballet **4**:148
Bolts of Melody **10**:185
Bombers B-52 **1**:383
Bond, Nelson S. **7**:14
Bonfiglioli, Kyril **2**:24-25
Bongé, Lyle **12**:347
Bonnard, Pierre **8**:158-59
Bonner, Anthony **6**:234-35
Bontemps, Arna **16**:12
Book of Cats, The **2**:58
Book of Changes, The **7**:13, 16-17
Book of Common Prayer **6**:33
Book of Lists, The **1**:378, 379, 384, 400
Book of Predictions, The **1**:400-401
Book of Skulls, The **3**:282
Book-of-the-Month Club
    Becker **1**:38
    Condon **1**:196
    Wallace **1**:395, 400
Book of Urizen **6**:136
Book of Women Poets from Antiquity to Now, A **15**:107
Book Week **2**:400-01, 402

Booker McConnel Prize
    Fitzgerald **10**:101, 107
    O'Faolain **2**:352
Booker, Stephen Todd **9**:67-68
Books in Canada Award for First Novels **7**:110
Bookshop, The **10**:106-07
Boon, Alan **11**:97, 100, 101, 103-04
Boone, Daniel **13**:168
Booth, Curtis **7**:10
Booth, Martin 2:47-61
Booth, Philip **13**:203
Booth, Richard **9**:286
Booth, Wayne C. 5:31-51
    Whittemore **8**:307
Borchardt, George **15**:144
Bordes, François **2**:44
Bordesley College **10**:99
Borejsza, Jerzy **9**:123
Borestone Mountain Poetry Award
    Heyen **9**:41
    Simpson **4**:293
"Borges: A Non-Meeting" **11**:212
Borges, Jorge Luis
    Barnstone **15**:47, 60-61, 65, 67, 91, 97, 100, 106, 107
    Cruz **17**:4
    Kerrigan **11**:209-13
    Lem **1**:263
    Turner **10**:318
Borges: Una vita di poesia **11**:210
Borgese, Giuseppe Antonio **12**:33
Born Indian **7**:105
"Born with the Dead" **3**:283
Bornhauser, Fred **7**:179
Boroff, David **3**:425
Borowski, Tadeusz **2**:72, 74
Borregaard, Ebbe **16**:191, 192
Bosence, Wilfred **5**:120
Bosquet, Alain **14**:273-74
Bossert, William H. **16**:300
Boston Boy **6**:173
Boston Center for Adult Education **8**:216
Boston College
    Galvin **13**:90-91
    Higgins **5**:97, 99
Boston Evening Transcript **2**:397
Boston Globe/Horn Book Honor Award **7**:82
Boston, Mass.
    Ciardi **2**:79-80
    Corman **2**:129, 135, 145
    Hentoff **6**:165
    Piercy **1**:276
Boston Post **3**:179
Boston University
    Clement **16**:98
    Peters **8**:240
    Petesch **12**:245
Boswell, James
    Harris **3**:119, 129, 131
    Morgan **4**:234
Botkin, Ben **6**:53
Botteghe Oscure **2**:383
Bottom Line, The **3**:182

Bottomley, Gordon **5**:255
Bottomley, Horatio **3**:391
Boucher, Anthony
    Anderson **2**:41, 42, 46
    St. Clair **8**:273
    Williamson **8**:321
Boulanger, Nadia **3**:86, 87
Boulder, Colo. **14**:178
Boulez, Pierre **8**:158
Bourgeois Poet, The **6**:305
Bourjaily, Monte Ferris, Sr. **1**:63,
    64, 65, 66, 70
Bourjaily, Vance 1:63-79
    Mahapatra **9**:147
    Stevenson **9**:277
Bourke-White, Margaret **1**:148-50,
    151
Bovie, S. Palmer **6**:89, 90
Bowdoin College
    Barnstone **15**:54-55, 60, 62, 63,
        64
    Bourjaily **1**:67, 69, 70
Bowe, Augustine **17**:182
Bowen, Elizabeth **7**:24-25
Bower, Warren **10**:2-3
Bowering, George 16:21-38
Bowers, Fredson **7**:12
Bowles, Paul 1:81-95
    Morgan **4**:232
    Purdy **1**:302
    Roditi **14**:251-52, 281, 286
Bowley, Victor **2**:387
Bowling Green State University
    McCord **9**:184
    Mott **7**:133
    Raworth **11**:303-04
    Thayler **11**:365
Box Is Empty, The **2**:412
"Box Social, The" (James Crerar
    Reaney) **15**:304
"Box Socials" (W.P. Kinsella) **7**:102,
    110
Boxing **17**:39, 43, 49, 53-54
Boy Scouts of America **2**:88
Boyars, Marion **1**:133
Boyce, Jack
    Koller **5**:164, 165-66, 167, 168
    Kyger **16**:198-99
Boyd, Malcolm 11:43-60
Boyd, Martin **4**:338
Boyer, Harold **2**:19
Boyers, Margaret Anne **13**:314
Boyers, Robert **13**:314
Boyle, Kay 1:97-125
Boynton, Peter **12**:158-59
Brackett, Leigh **8**:322
Bradbury, Malcolm **9**:114-15
Bradbury, Ray
    Nolan **16**:211, 212, 215, 224
    Silverberg **3**:274
    Williamson **8**:321
Bradbury, Walter I. **3**:180, 181
Bradley, Marion Zimmer 10:19-28
Brady, Diamond Jim **4**:237
Brahms, Johannes **14**:127
Braided Lives **1**:272, 280

*Brainard and Washington Street
    Poems* **5**:162
Brakhage, Stan **2**:443
Bramson, Naomi, Trust **4**:91
Brancusi, Constantin **1**:99, 114
Brand, Max See Faust, Frederick
Brandeis University
    Clarke **16**:84
    Lifshin **10**:250
    Petesch **12**:245, 246
    Sukenick **8**:289
Brandt & Brandt (literary agents)
    3:428
Brandt, Carl, Jr. **3**:426, 430
Brautigan, Richard
    Kherdian **2**:269
    Kinsella **7**:107
    Kyger **16**:196-97
    Plymell **11**:289, 292-93
    Sukenick **8**:291
Brave Little Toaster, The **4**:157
Brave New World **4**:146
Braybrooke, Neville **4**:84
Bread and Puppet Theater **6**:118
Bread Loaf School of English,
    Middlebury, Vt.
    Forbes **16**:109
    Sward **13**:282
Bread Loaf Writers Conference,
    Middlebury, Vt.
    Allen **11**:19
    Ciardi **2**:90
    Hall **7**:60, 62
    Jerome **8**:137
    Kumin **8**:215
    Lifshin **10**:250
    Meredith **14**:220-21, 222, 223,
        229, 230
    Stegner **9**:265-66
    Sward **13**:287
    Williams **3**:424
Breadfruit Lotteries, The **3**:81
Breaking Camp
    Elman **3**:77
    Piercy **1**:267
Breaking of Bumbo, The **5**:269, 270,
    271, 274
Breaking of the Day, The **4**:137, 138
"Breaking Point" **2**:248, 249, 256
"Breakthrough" series **3**:411
Breast of the Earth, The **13**:41
Brecht & Co. **4**:107
Brecht, Bertolt
    Mott **7**:127
    Roditi **14**:254-55, 269
Bredvold, Louis I. **2**:134
Brée, Germaine 15:127-48
Brejchová, Jana **1**:344
Breman, Paul **6**:185
Brenendik shtetl **9**:59
Brennan, John Michael **9**:85
Breslin, Jimmy **4**:208
Bretnor, Reginald **2**:42
Breton, André
    Higgins **8**:84
    Roditi **14**:256, 257, 265-66

Brewer, George **2**:116
Brewing: Twenty Milwaukee Poets
    11:348
Brewster, Earl Henry **10**:131
Brewster, Elizabeth 15:149-63
Brides of Reason **3**:40
Brideshead Revisited **7**:235
Bridge at Arta, The **3**:356
Bridge, The **6**:210
Brier, His Book **15**:290
Brigham, Besmilr **5**:347, 349
Brigham, Roy **5**:347, 349
Brigham Young University **5**:40, 43
Brightfount Diaries, The **2**:22
Briley, Dorothy **7**:81
Brill among the Ruins **1**:76-77
Brilliant, Alan **8**:248
Brimstone **2**:174
British Book Centre **1**:361
British Broadcasting Corp.
    Allen **6**:18, 21, 23, 25
    Booth **2**:58, 60
    Caute **4**:100
    Fitzgerald **10**:104-05
    Glanville **9**:26
    Gray **3**:110, 111
    Killens **2**:299
    Saroyan **5**:216
    White **4**:340-42
British Broadcasting Corporation,
    Third Programme **1**:27
British Columbia: A Celebration **6**:324
British Copyright Council **4**:86
British Crime Writers Association
    3:390
British in the Far East, The **6**:325
British International Films **14**:258
British Museum
    Settle **1**:313
    Wilson **5**:319
British School, Bari, Italy **2**:139
British Virgin Islands **1**:42
Brittain, Vera **5**:141
Britton, Burt **6**:189
Bro, Harlan **11**:10
Broadway theatre
    Fuchs **5**:64-66
    Grumbach **2**:206-07
*Brockport, New York: Beginning with
    "And"* **9**:46-47
Brodeur, Arthur **9**:213
Brodie, Fawn M. **1**:376
Brodkey, Harold **6**:217-18
Broken Sword, The **2**:40
Bronc People, The **1**:212
Bronk, William **3**:79, 80, 81
Bronowski, Jacob **4**:65
Bronston, Sam **4**:346
Bronston, Samuel, Co. **4**:345, 346
Brontë, Emily **1**:313
Brookhiser, Richard **9**:98
Brooklyn College
    Baumbach **5**:19-20, 24, 27
    Major **6**:191
    Markfield **3**:209-13
    Raffel **9**:209-10

Brooklyn Museum 1:286
Brooklyn, N.Y.
  Fuchs 5:61-63
  Piercy 1:273, 274
  Pohl 1:286
Brooklyn Public Library
  Pohl 1:284
  Wakoski 1:365
Brooks, Cleanth
  Jerome 8:133
  Olson 12:233
  Slavitt 3:315
  White 4:348
Brooks, Gwendolyn
  Killens 2:298
  Rodgers 13:244-45, 246, 248
Brooks, Robert A. 7:187
Brooks, Van Wyck 7:92
Broom 1:115
Broonzy, "Big" Bill 7:22
Brophy, Brigid 4:81-94
Brossard, Chandler 2:63-78
Brossard, Nicole 16:39-57
Brothers, I Loved You All 6:118-19
Brothers Karamazov, The 2:190
Broughton, James 12:41-58
  Kyger 16:190
  Settle 1:314
Brower, David 9:268
Brown, Alec 10:123-24
Brown, Andreas 1:302
Brown, Bill 5:165, 170
Brown, Charles 9:103
Brown, Claude 3:430
Brown, Curtis (literary agents) 2:331
Brown, David 1:385
Brown, Dee 6:45-59
Brown, Douglas 3:35
Brown, Frank London 6:181
Brown, George Mackay 6:61-76
Brown, Helen Gurley 1:385
Brown, J. Harold 16:13
Brown, Joe 2:449
Brown, John 2:430
Brown, Leonard S. 3:421
Brown, Merle
  Bell 14:48
  Silkin 5:262, 263
Brown, Norman O. 12:152, 157, 160
Brown, Rosellen 10:29-43
Brown, Spencer Curtis 15:192-93
Brown, Sterling 2:295
Brown University
  Allen 11:11, 12-14
  Cassill 1:172-73, 174
  Honig 8:115-16, 117-18
  Kostelanetz 8:180
Brown, William L. 16:294, 296
Brown, William Slater 10:67-68
Browning, Robert 6:230
Brownjohn, Alan
  Booth 2:52, 54
  Silkin 5:262
Broyard, Anatole 3:80
Bruin, John See Brutus, Dennis

Brunel University 4:105
Brunner, John 8:1-17
  Disch 4:151
  Hoffman 10:172
Bruno, Giordano 8:92
Brussels, Belgium 2:405-06, 409
Brutus, Dennis 14:53-64
Bryant, Joseph 4:116
Bryant, William Cullen 9:210
Bryn Mawr College
  Brée 15:133-34, 136, 143
  Gray 2:194
  Weiss 12:331
Buck, Pearl S. 1:390
Buck, Tom 15:246
Budapest, Hungary
  Corcoran 2:124
  Rakosi 5:194-95
Buddhism
  Simpson 4:296
  Van Itallie 2:416-17, 418, 419, 420, 421, 422
  Waldman 17:275, 279, 282
Budrys, Algis 14:65-79
  Knight 10:220, 221
  Silverberg 3:274
Buel, Walker S. 3:177, 178
Bufera, La 7:297
Buffalo Country 2:170
Buffington, Robert 9:146
Bukoski, Anthony 7:103
Bukowski, Charles
  Major 6:180
  Peters 8:244
Bullins, Ed 16:59-70
Bulmershe College 9:285
Bumpus, Jerry 1:74
Bunker, Chang 1:400
Bunker, Eng 1:400
Bunting, Basil
  Fisher 10:94
  Turnbull 14:326, 336
  Williams 12:344-45
Burago, Alla 9:217
Burbank, Harold H. 3:236, 237, 238
Burch, Robert 9:83
Burden, Jean 13:315
Burdick, Bud 9:267
Bureau Creek 5:168
Burgess, Jim 2:136
Burgess, Thornton W. 9:195
Burgum, Edwin Berry 5:120-21
Burhoe, Leslie 5:169-71
Buried Land, A 11:182
Burke, Edmund
  Kirk 9:95, 96
  Stafford 3:338
Burke, Kenneth
  Belitt 4:62, 65
  Olson 12:233
Burlingame, Roger 1:119
Burma
  Aldiss 2:19-20
  McCord 9:180, 182-83
Burnett, Virgil 15:228, 229-30

Burnett, Whit
  Ghiselin 10:133
  Whittemore 8:307
Burnham, James 12:204
Burning Hills, The 1:383
Burning Sky, The 2:172
Burning Village 9:52-53, 59, 63, 66
Burning Water 16:27, 28
Burns, Milo 1:179, 180
Burnt-out Case, A 8:170
Burroughs, Edgar Rice 9:2
Burroughs, Mitchell 2:257
Burroughs, William
  Bowles 1:91, 92
  Creeley 10:72
  Katz 14:176-77
  Major 6:193
  Morgan 4:235
  Plymell 11:289, 291, 293, 294, 295
  Raworth 11:301
  Sukenick 8:290
  Waldman 17:278, 284
Burroway, Janet 6:77-103
Burstyn, Ellen 9:246
Burton, Naomi
  Kennedy 9:84
  Wakoski 1:365
Bury My Heart at Wounded Knee 6:57
Busch, Frederick 1:127-37
Busch, Phyllis 1:127, 128, 133
Businessman: A Tale of Terror, The 4:156, 157
But for the Grace of God 5:328
Butler, Michael 10:94
Butley 3:113, 114
Butor, Michel
  Brossard 2:67
  Lem 1:263
Butterick, George 10:10
Buzzards, The 6:98, 99, 100
By Lingual Wholes 17:14-15
Bye, Reed 17:285-88
Byrd, Harry 7:4
Byrd, Robert
  Olson 11:255, 256
  Wilson 5:349
Byrdwhistle Option, The 10:296, 299, 300, 302-03, 304
Byrne, Stu 2:41
Byron Caldwell Smith Prize 2:255
Byron Exhumed 8:248
Bystander, The 2:218, 219, 228, 231
Byzantium Endures 5:183

Cabala 9:49, 51, 55, 64
Cabeza de Vaca, Alvar Nuñez 15:121
Cabin Fever 13:106, 110-11, 117
Cabot, Frank 6:233
Cabot Wright Begins 1:303
Caetani, Marguerite
  Broughton 12:56-57
  Jennings 5:112
Cafe Cino, New York City 2:413

Cafe La Mama, New York City
　　2:413, 414, 418, 421
Cafe Mimosa　**11**:100
Cage, John
　　Bergé　**10**:7
　　Gray　**2**:194
　　Hassan　**12**:152, 160
　　Higgins　**8**:86, 89, 90
　　Waldman　**17**:283
Cahill, Dan　**9**:113-14
Cain, James M.　**3**:192, 194, 203
Caine, Michael　**9**:250-51
Cairnie, Gordon
　　Enslin　**3**:89-90
　　Hall　**7**:62
Calas, Nicolas　**14**:258
Calder, Alexander　**1**:156
Calder, John　**1**:133
Calderón and the Seizures of Honor
　　8:117
Calderón de la Barca, Pedro　**8**:117
Calderón, Felipe G.　**9**:159
Caldwell, Erskine　1:139-59
Caldwell, Virginia　**1**:151, 153-54,
　　155-56, 157
Calendar of Love, A　**6**:71
Calgary Creative Reading Series
　　7:103
"Caliban"　**3**:282
California
　　Davie　**3**:45
　　Higgins　**8**:89
　　Houston　**16**:155-60
　　Rodgers　**13**:252
　　St. Clair　**8**:274-75
　　Silverberg　**3**:283
　　Sukenick　**8**:289
　　Williams　**3**:423
California Institute of Technology
　　Niven　**12**:212
　　Wakoski　**1**:368
California Institute of the Arts
　　Eshleman　**6**:143
　　Higgins　**8**:89
California Poems　**5**:165, 166, 167
California State University,
　　Northridge　**9**:184
*Californians: Searching for the Golden
　　State*　**16**:157
Calisher, Hortense
　　Bourjaily　**1**:72
　　Burroway　**6**:90
Calisto and Melibea　**8**:117
Call It Sleep
　　Belitt　**4**:60
　　Williams　**3**:429
Callahan, Harry　**12**:339
Callanwolde Poetry Series　**7**:131
Callimachus　**3**:90
Callow, Philip　**11**:377
Cambridge, Godfrey　**2**:293
Cambridge Poetry Festival　**5**:169
Cambridge University
　　Burroway　**6**:91, 93
　　Davie　**3**:35, 39, 40
　　Davison　**4**:133

Gray　**3**:103
　　Mano　**6**:208-09
　　Sinclair　**5**:270, 276
　　Skelton　**5**:281
　　Tarn　**16**:274
　　White　**4**:337, 340, 341, 342
Cambridge University, Churchill
　　College　**5**:271
Cambridge University, Newnham
　　College　**1**:219-20
Cambridge University Press　**1**:223
Cambridge University, Trinity College
　　Gray　**3**:108-09, 110, 111
　　Sinclair　**5**:269-70
Camera Always Lies, The　**17**:89
Cameron, Angus　**2**:303
Camp Concentration　**4**:151
Camp, James　**9**:83, 84
Campaign Capers　**1**:246
Campbell, Bruce　**4**:250
Campbell, John W., Jr.
　　Anderson　**2**:39, 41, 42, 46
　　Budrys　**14**:66, 67, 70
　　Clement　**16**:97, 98
　　Gunn　**2**:247, 249
　　Knight　**10**:203, 204, 205, 209,
　　　218
　　Pohl　**1**:292
　　Williamson　**8**:318, 322
Campbell, Roy　**5**:367, 368
Campbell, Walter　**2**:170
Camus, Albert
　　Boyle　**1**:117
　　Bré　**15**:135, 140, 141, 143
　　Lottman　**12**:200-01, 206, 207
　　Mathews　**6**:245
　　Sillitoe　**2**:385
Canada
　　Andre　**13**:16-17, 18
　　Blaise　**3**:20-21, 28
　　Brewster　**15**:161-62
　　Clarke　**16**:76-77, 81, 87
　　Davie　**3**:44-45
　　Singh　**9**:230
　　Slade　**9**:244
　　Sward　**13**:292-93, 299
Canada and the Canadians　**6**:323
Canada Arts Council
　　Blais　**4**:73
　　Brewster　**15**:159
　　Horwood　**15**:248
Canada Council Explorations Grant
　　Hine　**15**:226, 228
　　Sward　**13**:297
Canada Foundation See Canada
　　Council Explorations Grant
Canada, Royal Air Force
　　Purdy　**17**:200-02
　　Souster　**14**:309-12
Canadian Authors Association　**7**:110
Canadian Booksellers Association
　　7:110
Canadian Broadcasting Corp.
　　Purdy　**17**:204-05, 206, 207
　　Slade　**9**:243
Canadian literature　**2**:367

Canadian Literature　**6**:323, 324
Canadian Philosophical Association
　　15:360
Canadian Poetry　**8**:220
Canadians　**3**:110
Canadians, The　**6**:323
Candidates 1960　**3**:179
Cane　**7**:32
Canetti, Elias　**1**:24
Canfield, Curtis　**6**:93
Cannes Film Festival
　　Broughton　**12**:55
　　Caldwell　**1**:155
Canterbury Tales　**5**:374
Canticle for Innocent Comedians, A
　　4:63
Cantos (Ezra Pound)
　　Allen　**6**:18
　　Enslin　**3**:90
Caoine Airt Uí Laoire ("The Lament for
　　Arthur O'Leary")　**3**:62-63
Cape Breton, Nova Scotia　**14**:176
Cape-Goliard Press　**16**:280
Cape, Jonathan (publishers)
　　Jones　**5**:122, 128
　　Tarn　**16**:278-80
Capital punishment　**15**:248
Capital See *Kapital, Das*
Capitalism
　　Barrio　**15**:112, 124-26
　　Caute　**4**:102
　　Rakosi　**5**:208
Caponegro, Mary　**6**:147
Capote, Truman　**1**:88
Capouya, Emile　**6**:285
Capra, Frank　**1**:380, 383
Caprice　**16**:26, 28
Captain Blackman　**3**:420, 431
Capuchins　**13**:179-80
Caravan　**10**:172, 173
Carcanet Press　**3**:47
Cardboard Garage, A　**15**:357
Cardiff, Wales
　　Abse　**1**:17, 18
　　White　**4**:333-34
Cardinal Sins, The　**7**:51
Cargill, Oscar　**6**:277
Cariboo Horses, The　**17**:209
Carleton College　**8**:305-06, 307
Carleton Miscellany
　　Whittemore　**8**:307
　　Wright　**7**:298
Carleton University　**15**:156
Carlson, John Roy　**6**:165
Carmina　**3**:98
Carnal and the Crane, The　**15**:224
Carnal Island, The　**10**:116
Carnell, E.J.
　　Aldiss　**2**:25, 29
　　Moorcock　**5**:177, 179
Carnell, Ted See Carnell, E.J.
Carnival Trilogy　**16**:124, 130, 131-32
Carnivore, The　**3**:319
Carolina Quarterly　**3**:23
Caron, Richard　**2**:365, 366
Carr, John Dickson　**15**:194, 195

INDEX

Carr, Terry
 Hoffman **10**:173, 174
 Knight **10**:225
Carrambo, Cristobal **2**:421
Carrigan, Andrew **11**:303
Carroll, Diahann **2**:296
Carroll, Donald **13**:132
Carroll, Lewis
 Keating **8**:166
 Slavitt **3**:322
Carroll, Paul **6**:181
Carruth, Hayden
 Corman **2**:136
 Dennison **6**:118-19
 Gregor **10**:150
Cars **7**:158-59
Carson, Herbert L. **7**:29-31
Carter, Jimmy **1**:157
Cartier-Bresson, Henri **7**:85
Cartland, Barbara 8:19-35
 Green **11**:104
Carver, Catharine **3**:405
Carver, Raymond **3**:20, 23, 26
Carver, Wayne **8**:307
Cary, Joyce
 Glanville **9**:21
 Sinclair **5**:272
Casa de los Americas Prize **16**:151
Case of Walter Bagehot, The **3**:304
Casper, Leonard **8**:240
Cassady, Neal **11**:280, 281, 286,
 287-88, 289, 290
Cassandra Singing **3**:187-88, 189,
 195-96, 200
Cassill, Ronald Verlin 1:161-75
 Blaise **3**:25
Cassity, Turner 8:37-62
 Mott **7**:131
Castaneda, Carlos **2**:272, 273, 274
*Caste and Ecology in the Social
 Insects* **16**:304
Castex, Mariano **9**:149
Castiglione, Robert L. **12**:323-37
Castle, Irene **2**:170-71
Castle Keep **1**:206, 211
Castle Tzingal **4**:124
Castro, Fidel **11**:215
Catacomb, The **9**:28
Catch, The **2**:436
Catch Trap, The **10**:25-26
Catcher in the Rye, The **6**:87
Cater, H.S. **6**:20
Caterpillar **6**:140, 142, 144
Cather, Willa
 Grumbach **2**:213, 214
 Harris **3**:132
 Kazin **7**:94
Catholic Church
 Anaya **4**:17
 Blais **4**:70-71, 72
 Brossard **16**:40
 Caute **4**:96
 Ciardi **2**:85-86, 88
 Condon **1**:188-89
 Gray **2**:198
 Greeley **7**:37-51

 Hentoff **6**:173
 Kerrigan **11**:195-96
 Kienzle **1**:237, 239-53
 Nolan **16**:209-10
 O'Faolain **2**:342-43, 349-50, 352-
 53
 Rodgers **13**:243-44
 Shapiro **6**:298
Catholic University of America
 12:332
Catholicism
 Anaya **4**:17
 Brown **6**:73
 Dacey **17**:20-22
 Forrest **7**:24, 26
 Greeley **7**:39, 49-50
 Inez **10**:180
 Jennings **5**:104, 106, 107, 108,
 112
 Kennedy **9**:79, 87
 McCord **9**:181
 Nichols **2**:308
 Rabassa **9**:192-93
 Rechy **4**:258
 Turner **10**:314-15, 316
Caton, R.A. **6**:320
Catonsville Trial, The **1**:55
Cats **16**:221
Cats' Opera, The **3**:63
Catullus, Gaius Valerius
 Dudek **14**:131
 Katz **9**:62
 Sisson **3**:303
 Williams **12**:341-42
 Wright **7**:295
Causley, Charles **11**:377
Caute, David 4:95-111
Cautionary Tales **13**:166
Cavalier **3**:74
*Cave of Trophonius and Other Poems,
 The* **15**:358
Cave paintings **6**:146
Cazenovia College **15**:24
CBC See Canadian Broadcasting
 Corp.
CBS-TV See Columbia Broadcasting
 System
CCLM See Coordinating Council of
 Literary Magazines
Ceccardi, Ceccardo Roccatagliata
 14:125, 126
Cecil, David **5**:108
Cedar Rock **8**:141
Cela, Camilo José 10:45-60
 Kerrigan **11**:200, 205, 206, 210
Celan, Paul
 Corman **2**:138, 144
 Hamburger **4**:170
 Roditi **14**:274-75
Celebration **1**:322
Celebrity Service **2**:119
Céline, Louis-Ferdinand
 Konwicki **9**:129
 Roditi **14**:256
Cenizas **15**:12
Censorship

 El Saadawi **11**:70
 Giovanni **6**:153, 155-56
 Hentoff **6**:172-73
 Jones **5**:127-28
 Kerrigan **11**:205
 Van Itallie **2**:416
Centaur Press **12**:53
CENTER Magazine **10**:10, 11, 16
Central Connecticut State
 University **13**:90, 101
Central Intelligence Agency
 Coppel **9**:6-7
 Kerrigan **11**:207
Centro Escolar University **9**:167
Centro Mexicano de Escritores **13**:84
Century of Innovation, A **2**:366
Century of Science Fiction, A **10**:222
Cerberus **14**:128, 132
Čerepková, Vladimíra **1**:346
Ceretta, Florindo **7**:297
Cerf, Bennett
 Eastlake **1**:201
 Hahn **11**:115
 Mitford **17**:150
Cernuda, Luis **15**:59
Certainty of Love, A **9**:5
Cervantes, Miguel de **1**:299
Ces anges de sang (These angels of
 blood) **13**:181
Césaire, Aimé
 Becker **1**:42
 Eshleman **6**:147
*César Vallejo: The Complete Posthumous
 Poetry* **6**:144
Ceylon **3**:239, 240
 See also Sri Lanka
Cézanne, Paul **7**:301
Chacksfield, Merle **11**:103
Chaikin, Joseph **2**:412, 413, 414,
 416, 418, 419, 420, 422
Chaikin, Shami **2**:418, 420, 421
Chair for Elijah, A **9**:66
Chaix, Marie **6**:223, 240, 242-43,
 245, 248, 251
Challenge Press **10**:297-98
Challenge, The **1**:381, 382
Chalmers, Gordon **9**:98
Chalupecký, Jindřich **1**:336, 338
Chamber Music **2**:212, 213
Chamberlain, Edward **3**:236
Chamberlain, Neville **2**:310
Chambers, Ernest **6**:182
Chambers, Everett **2**:254
Chambers, The **10**:6
Champlain College **13**:336
Chance **7**:222
Chandler, A. Bertram **1**:290
Chandler, Raymond **15**:196-97
Chaneles, Sol **6**:183
Change **8**:136
Change the Sky **8**:275, 281
Channing, William Ellery **5**:36
Chaplin, Oona **5**:221, 222
Chapman, Chandler **2**:441
Chapman Report, The **1**:384, 388-89,
 396

Chapman, Robert **2**:411
Chappell, Fred 4:113-26
    Miller **15**:287, 288, 289, 291
    Root **11**:322
    Shelnutt **14**:298, 299-300, 301
Chapter One of a Work in Progress See "Box Socials"
Charisma Campaigns, The **15**:266, 269
Charles, Mat **9**:211
Charles Olson Journal **10**:10
Charles University
    Hrabal **12**:193
    Škvorecký **1**:333, 347
Charlie and the Chocolate Factory **6**:155
Charlotte Observer **1**:146
Charterhouse **9**:16-17, 18-19
Charteris, Leslie **9**:17
Charyn, Jerome 1:177-84
Chase, Richard **6**:210, 211
Chattanooga News **3**:170
Chatto & Windus (publishers) **5**:112-14
Chaucer, Geoffrey
    Brown **6**:73
    Wain **4**:328
    Whittemore **8**:311
Chavez, Angelico **4**:17
Chavez, Carlos **2**:117
Chayefsky, Paddy **9**:242
Cheever, John
    Becker **1**:36
    Brown **6**:53
    Kerrigan **11**:213
Chekhov, Anton
    Abse **1**:30-31
    Boyle **1**:108, 117
    Samarakis **16**:270
    Van Itallie **2**:417-18
    Wallace **1**:391
Cherry, Kelly
    Dillard **7**:14-15, 17
    Taylor **7**:179
Cherry Lane Theater **2**:419
Cherry Orchard, The **2**:418
Cherry Valley Editions **11**:294
Chesterton, G.K.
    Jennings **5**:106
    Wain **4**:328
    Wilson **5**:314
Chestnut Rain, The **9**:37
Cheuse, Alan **4**:244
Chevalier, Haakon **14**:261-62, 266, 271, 275, 276
Cheyenne River Wild Track **14**:175
Chez Charlotte and Emily **5**:28
Chicago Daily Maroon **13**:14
Chicago Defender **3**:421
Chicago Herald Tribune **2**:400
Chicago, Ill.
    Andre **13**:18
    Greeley **7**:37, 44
    Piercy **1**:271-72
    Pinsky **4**:248
    Raworth **11**:305

    Rodgers **13**:238-40
    Simic **4**:280-81
    Solotaroff **2**:396
    Sward **13**:284-85, 286
Chicago State University **13**:251, 252
Chicago Sun-Times
    Becker **1**:43
    Simic **4**:283
    Solotaroff **2**:400
    Wallace **1**:376
Chicago World's Fair See World's Fair, Chicago, Ill.
Chicano **15**:167-79
Chicano in China, A **4**:27
Chicano movement
    Anaya **4**:23, 24-26, 27
    Barrio **15**:120
Chicano: Twenty-five Pieces of a Chicano Mind **15**:176
Chicken Soup with Barley **7**:243, 245-46, 247, 249
Chico's Organic Gardening and Natural Living **1**:378
Chihuly, Dale **7**:301
Child of the Jago, A **2**:384
Child of the Morning **2**:125
Children of Herakles, The **7**:186
Children of the Ghetto **7**:236
Children of the Holocaust: Conversations with Sons and Daughters of Survivors **9**:33-34
Children on the Shore **2**:412
Children's Encyclopedia, The **2**:311
Children's Revolt, The **11**:83
Child's Garden of Verses for the Revolution, A **1**:211
Chile **15**:9-10
Chimera **3**:139-40
Chimney Sweep Comes Clean, A **2**:71
China
    Becker **1**:34-35
    Hahn **11**:113-15
    Honig **8**:123-24
    Killens **2**:304
    Rosenthal **6**:285
    Salisbury **15**:324-26
China to Me: A Partial Autobiography **11**:113, 115
China Trace **7**:295
Chinese Agent, The **5**:187-88
Chinese Elements in the Tagalog Language **9**:162, 165
Chinese poetry **6**:285
"Chip Harrison" series **11**:35
Chomsky, Noam
    Hall **7**:64
    Parini **16**:230-31, 242
Chorale **4**:219
Choudhury, Malay Roy 14:81-99
Choynowski, Mieczyslaw **1**:259
Chrétien de Troyes **9**:219
Christ and Celebrity Gods **11**:47
Christensen, Charles **9**:85
Christian **11**:56
Christian Brothers **4**:146

Christian Science **12**:226
Christian Science Monitor **8**:216
Christianity
    Awoonor **13**:37-38, 40-41, 53
    Bennett **13**:73-74
    Bradley **10**:22-23
    Dillard **7**:7-8
    Fisher **10**:95
    Garrett **5**:75
    Grumbach **2**:214
    Hamburger **4**:170
    Mano **6**:206, 207-08, 209-10, 212-15
    Rodgers **13**:253
    Silkin **5**:251, 253
    Thomas **4**:310-11
    Wain **4**:326, 328
Christie, Agatha **15**:197
Christine/Annette **2**:215
Christmas Tale, A **2**:225
Christopher Ewart-Biggs Prize **2**:352
Christopher Homm **3**:301, 302
Chucky's Hunch **2**:361, 366
Church and the Suburbs, The **7**:46
Church Divinity School of the Pacific **11**:47
Church in Wales, Anglican **4**:304, 305, 310
Church of England **4**:170
Church of Jesus Christ of Latter-Day Saints See Mormonism
Church World Service (relief agency)
    Markfield **3**:213
    Stafford **3**:334
Churchill: Young Man in a Hurry **4**:234
CIA See Central Intelligence Agency
Ciardi, John 2:79-96
    Allen **11**:19
    Corman **2**:133-34, 135
    Jerome **8**:137
    Kennedy **9**:84
    Kumin **8**:215
    Meredith **14**:220-21
    Stevenson **9**:278
Ciel de Nuit **2**:66
Cigarettes **6**:248, 249
"Cimetière marin" **4**:248
Cincinnati, Ohio **1**:111-14
Cincinnati Symphony Orchestra **1**:111
Circle for the Science of Science **1**:259
Circle, The **1**:223
Circles, as in the Eye **10**:6
Citadel (publishers) **2**:288
Cities and Stones **2**:27
Citizen Hearst **13**:259, 268
Citizens' Advice Bureau (Great Britain) **4**:44
City **10**:98
City College of New York
    Federman **8**:74
    Kazin **7**:95
    Swenson **13**:313
    Weiss **12**:326-28

Williams **3**:431
City Life **11**:84
City Lights Bookstore, San Francisco, Calif. **5**:349
City of Night **4**:258, 260, 261, 263, 265
City of Words **1**:303
City Parables, The **9**:33
City University of New York
  Epstein **12**:72-73
  Hauser **11**:137-38
  Kostelanetz **8**:182
  Major **6**:186
  Markfield **3**:225
  Rabassa **9**:199, 204
City with All the Angles **8**:92
CIV/n, A Literary Magazine of the 50's (book) **14**:133
CIV/n (magazine) **14**:132
Civil Rights Congress **17**:142, 146
Civil rights movement
  Boyd **11**:48-49, 50, 51
  Dennison **6**:116
  Gunn **2**:253
  Hamill **15**:209
  Jones **11**:182-83
  Killens **2**:296-98
  Mott **7**:131
  Petesch **12**:248
  Picano **13**:221
  Wakefield **7**:197
  Williams **3**:427
  See also Segregation
Civil War, American
  Corcoran **2**:113, 114
  Dillard **7**:3
  Hall **12**:108
  Jones **11**:172
  Morgan **3**:231
  Morris **13**:167
  Nichols **2**:323
  Wakefield **7**:193
  White **4**:350
  Wright **7**:287-88
Civil Wars **10**:41
Clair, René **5**:274
Clam Shell, The **1**:311, 318, 319
Clancy, Patrick **10**:172
Clare, John
  Abse **1**:25
  Wright **5**:363
Clarence Darrow for the Defense **3**:370
Clarendon Press **3**:354
Clarion Writers' Workshop
  Knight **10**:225-26
  Wolfe **9**:306-07
Clark, Harry Hayden **9**:111, 113
Clark, Jack **10**:124
Clark, Joanna Rostropwicz **9**:123
Clark, Leonard **2**:59
Clark, Sonia Tomara **1**:120
Clark, Walter Van Tilburg
  Connell **2**:109-10
  Corcoran **2**:119
  Stafford **3**:334
Clark, William **1**:120, 122

Clarke, Arthur C.
  Bergé **10**:9
  Niven **12**:217
Clarke, Austin C.   16:71-88
  Rosenthal **6**:285
Clarke, Dean **14**:127
Clarke, Gillian **9**:286
Clarke, John Henrik
  Clarke **16**:83
  Killens **2**:298
classic plays **8**:92
Classical music
  Jolley **13**:109-10, 111-12
  Olson **12**:227-28, 229
  Rabassa **9**:198
  Rosenblum **11**:342
  West **7**:270-71, 285
"Classics of Modern Science Fiction" series **2**:258
Claudel, Paul **4**:72
Claxton, Patricia **16**:53
Clean Kill, A **15**:197
Cleaver, Eldridge
  Clarke **16**:84
  Sinclair **5**:273
Cleland, John **1**:396
Clem Anderson **1**:170, 171
Clement, Hal   16:89-104
Cleveland Institute of Music **16**:10
Cleveland, Ohio **5**:301, 303
Cleveland Plain Dealer **3**:177
!Click Song **3**:421, 424, 432
Clio's Children **15**:30
Clock of Moss, The **14**:114, 116
"Close Dancing" **17**:47
Close Quarters **15**:189, 192-93
Close the Sky, Ten by Ten **9**:145
Closely Watched Trains **1**:338
Closing of the American Mind **14**:131
Closing the Gap **2**:71-72
Cloutier, David **8**:119
Clown, The **2**:124
Clunies-Ross, Pamela **5**:246
Clute, John **4**:152, 154, 156
Cnot Dialogues, The **2**:57
Coach House Press **13**:296-97
Coakley, Andy **9**:197
Coast Magazine **14**:146
Coastlines **1**:359
Coat for the Tsar, A **3**:74
Coates, Robert **6**:301
Cock of Heaven, The **12**:230, 231
Cocktails at Somoza's **3**:81
Cocteau, Jean
  Highwater **7**:69
  Markfield **3**:214
  West **7**:279
Codron, Michael **3**:112-13
Cody, John **7**:46, 47
Coe College **6**:25
Coercion Review **6**:179, 180
Coffee House Press **7**:107
Coffin, Hal T. **2**:135, 142
Coffman, George R. **2**:434, 435
Cogan's Trade **5**:92
Coghill, Nevill **12**:25, 26, 33

Cogswell, Fred
  Brewster **15**:154
  Purdy **17**:205
Cogswell, Theodore **2**:258
Cohan, George M. **1**:395
Cohen, Arthur **14**:173-74
Cohen, Bob **2**:304
Cohen, Chester **10**:206, 208, 210, 211, 215
Cohen, Isidore **2**:162
Cohen, Morris R. **12**:327
Cohen, Robert **8**:249
Coils **6**:144
Coindreau, Maurice-Edgar **4**:117
Coins and Coffins **1**:364
Colbert, Nancy **7**:105, 110
Colby College **15**:333
Cold Comfort **3**:322
Cold War
  Davie **3**:42
  Guerard **2**:225, 226
Coldspring Journal **11**:294
Coleman, Elliott **11**:292, 293, 294
Coleman, R.V. **6**:56
Coleridge, Samuel Taylor
  Belitt **4**:64
  Jennings **5**:106
Colgate University
  Busch **1**:132, 133
  Sukenick **8**:287-88
  West **7**:280
Colie, Rosalie **6**:89
Colladay Award **11**:83
Collected Greeds, Parts I-XIII, The **1**:368, 371
Collected Plays (Peter Barnes) **12**:14
Collected Poems and Epigrams (George Rostrevor Hamilton) **10**:119
Collected Poems (C.H. Sisson) **3**:300, 307
Collected Poems (Elder Olson) **12**:235
Collected Poems (George Woodcock) **6**:326
Collected Poems of Al Purdy, The **17**:210
Collected Poems, 1956–1976 (David Wagoner) **3**:409, 410
Collected Poems, 1948–1976 (Dannie Abse) **1**:31
Collected Poems, 1968 (Roy Fisher) **10**:98-99
Collected Poems (Sylvia Plath) **4**:134
Collected Poetry (Louis Dudek) **14**:133
Collected Works of J.M. Synge **5**:285
Collectivism **12**:309
College of Saint Rose, Albany, N.Y. **2**:209, 210
College of the Virgin Islands **8**:135-36
College Street Messiah, The **14**:92
Collège Technique, France **3**:107
Collier's Encyclopedia **1**:169
Collier's Magazine **1**:192
Collier's Year Book **9**:99
Collins, Aileen **14**:133-34
Collins, Bob **7**:195

Collins, Wilkie **6**:254
Collins, William, Sons & Co.
　　(publishers) **8**:176
Collisions **4**:104
Colloquialisms
　　Brossard **2**:73-74
　　Mano **6**:216-17
Colmain **3**:109
Colombo, John Robert **13**:299
"Colonel Pyat" series **5**:183
Colonialism **3**:246
Colonnade Club **1**:320
Color of Darkness **1**:302
Color Purple, The **16**:84
Colorado College **13**:321
Colorado State University **11**:48
Colorni, Ausonio **10**:142
Colour of Murder, The **3**:390
Colour of Rain, The **9**:291
Colours in the Dark **15**:307
Coltelli, Laura **6**:283
Colton, James See Hansen, Joseph
Columbia Broadcasting System
　　Caldwell **1**:149
　　Corcoran **2**:120
　　Elman **3**:74
　　Gunn **2**:259
　　Hailey **1**:231
　　Sinclair **5**:273
　　Van Itallie **2**:412
Columbia College, Chicago, Ill.
　　13:248, 253
Columbia Pictures
　　Condon **1**:194
　　Eastlake **1**:211
　　Sinclair **5**:273
　　Slade **9**:244
Columbia University
　　Ai **13**:5-6
　　Baumbach **5**:21-22
　　Block **11**:30
　　Busch **1**:130, 131, 133
　　Cassill **1**:169
　　Charyn **1**:179
　　Connell **2**:107
　　Delbanco **2**:158, 159
　　Dennison **6**:110, 113
　　Dudek **14**:129, 130
　　Elman **3**:76, 78
　　Federman **8**:76-77
　　Hailey **1**:229
　　Higgins **8**:86
　　Highwater **7**:80
　　Inez **10**:191
　　Kennedy **9**:80
　　Killens **2**:286, 287, 288
　　Kostelanetz **8**:180
　　Lottman **12**:198, 205
　　Mano **6**:207, 208, 217
　　Markfield **3**:225
　　Mathews **6**:223
　　Morgan **4**:227
　　Petry **6**:264
　　Rabassa **9**:201-04
　　Rechy **4**:259
　　Silverberg **3**:272

Simpson **4**:291-92, 293, 294
Sinclair **5**:271
Slavitt **3**:316-17
Wakefield **7**:195, 196
Weiss **2**:431-33
West **7**:277
Columbia University Forum **12**:206
Come Hither **5**:146
Come Live My Life **10**:300, 301
Come Out with Your Hands Up **2**:71
Comeback for Stark, A **3**:111
"Comedy of Eros" **17**:49
Comet Press Books **3**:423
Comic Art in America **1**:37, 38
Comic strips
　　Moorcock **5**:177-78
　　Nolan **16**:210
　　Williamson **8**:324
Comic, The **9**:27, 28
Coming Home **5**:131-32
"Coming Out of Mother" **4**:246
Commander of the Order of the
　　Academic Palms **15**:144
Commentary
　　Dennison **6**:121
　　Solotaroff **2**:398-400, 401
Common Sense **9**:177
Commonweal
　　Elman **3**:74
　　Greeley **7**:47
Communes **8**:137-40
Communism
　　Beltrametti **13**:56
　　Guerard **2**:226
　　Kazin **7**:89
　　Kerrigan **11**:201-05
　　Kizer **5**:150
　　Lessing **14**:199-203
　　Lind **4**:196, 197, 200-01
　　Mitford **17**:140-43
　　Mrozek **10**:268-70
　　Roditi **14**:256, 276
　　Simic **4**:271
　　Škvorecký **1**:333-48
　　Voinovich **12**:317
　　Wain **4**:321
　　Wiesel **4**:360
　　Zinoviev **10**:325, 326, 329-30,
　　　　332-33
*Communism and the French
　　Intellectuals* **4**:105
Communism See also Marxism
Communist Manifesto, The **1**:285, 286
Communist party
　　Bowles **1**:85
　　Davie **3**:42
　　Kizer **5**:150
　　Mitford **17**:142-43, 144-45
　　Voinovich **12**:306-07
Communists
　　Samarakis **16**:249
　　Shadbolt **3**:254, 256
Companions of the Day and Night
　　16:135
Company She Kept, The **2**:213
Company We Keep, The **5**:43, 48, 51

*Comparative Culturology of Humanoid
　　Civilizations* **1**:263
"Composed upon Westminster
　　Bridge" **5**:106
Comrade Jacob **4**:105
Conad See French First Army,
　　Continental Advance Section
Concept of Criticism, The **15**:360
Concordia University, Montreal,
　　Canada **3**:27
Condon, Richard 1:185-99
Condon, Wendy **1**:194, 197, 198
Condry, Penny **4**:308
Condry, William **4**:309
*Confederation Betrayed: The Case
　　against Trudeau's Canada* **6**:323
Confessional Poets, The **13**:207
*Confessions of a Bohemian Tory:
　　Episodes and Reflections of a
　　Vagrant Career* **9**:101
Confessions of a Justified Sinner, The
　　9:290, 292
Confessions of a Spent Youth **1**:64, 66,
　　67, 73-74, 77
*Confessions of an English Opium Eater,
　　The* **2**:383
Confusions about X **3**:386
Congo **4**:230
Congo (film) **1**:87
*Congo Solo: Misadventures Two Degrees
　　North* **11**:112, 113
Congregationalism **2**:308
Connecticut College
　　Meredith **14**:222, 225, 227, 234
　　Sward **13**:287
Connecticut College of Pharmacy
　　6:263
*Connections: In the English Lake
　　District* **8**:244, 248
Connell, Evan S. 2:97-112
Conner, Bruce **11**:283, 285
Connolly, Cyril
　　Ashby **6**:43
　　Glanville **9**:21
　　Sinclair **5**:269
　　Wilson **5**:321, 322, 326
Conquerors, The **1**:40
Conquest, Robert
　　Abse **1**:27
　　Davie **3**:31, 38
Conrad, Joseph
　　Brown **6**:48
　　Keating **8**:167
　　Roditi **14**:242-43
　　Škvorecký **1**:349
　　Wellek **7**:222
　　Whittemore **8**:303-04
Conrad the Novelist **2**:221, 228
Conroy, Jack **6**:53
Conscientious objectors
　　Kirkup **4**:183
　　Stafford **3**:332, 333, 334, 337,
　　　　339
Conservatism
　　Kirk **9**:98-99
　　Mano **6**:208, 209

Conservative Mind, The **9**:97-99
Conspiracy of Knaves, A **6**:58
Constructivism **8**:186
Constructivist Fictions **8**:189
Constructs **2**:368
Contact **14**:132
Contact Press **14**:132
Contemporary British and North American Verse **2**:59
Contemporary Center, San Francisco, Calif. **7**:80
Contemporary Poetry Series **3**:410
Contemporary Shakespeare, The **8**:263-64
Conti, Italia **10**:108-09
Continental Drift **16**:160
Continuation **14**:140-41
Contre-Jour **8**:158
Convention **3**:181
Conversations in Another Room **8**:145
Conversions, The **6**:235, 236, 237, 239, 241, 246
Cook, Eliza **2**:356
Cool World, The **1**:345-46
Cool Zebras of Light **8**:246
Cooney, Ray **9**:253
Cooper, Clarence L., Jr. **6**:193
Cooper, James Fenimore **7**:6
Cooper, John R. **3**:173-74
Cooper Union **4**:148
Cooperstein, Nancy **2**:418
Coordinating Council of Literary Magazines
    Anaya **4**:26
    Grumbach **2**:214
    Hamill **15**:212
    McCord **9**:184
    Sukenick **8**:293
    Whittemore **8**:307
    Wilson **5**:353
Coover, Robert
    Baumbach **5**:28
    Dillard **7**:13
    Weiss **2**:447-48
Copeland, Carleton **12**:303-22
Copenhagen University **1**:156
Copland, Aaron **1**:83
Coppel, Alfred **9**:1-11
Copper Beach Press **8**:119-20
Copperhead Cane **15**:283
Coppola, Francis Ford **3**:410-11
Cops and Robbers **13**:342
Copyright **4**:86
Cora Fry **10**:41-42
Corbett, Jim **2**:50, 60
Corcoran, Barbara **2**:113-28
Corday **7**:134
Cordelier, Jeanne **6**:248
Core, George **9**:146, 147
Corman, Cid **2**:129-47
    Beltrametti **13**:61, 62
    Enslin **3**:87, 90-92, 93, 98
    Eshleman **6**:135, 136
    Fisher **10**:96, 97
    Kennedy **9**:82
    Kyger **16**:196

    Rakosi **5**:208
    Rosenblum **11**:348
    Thayler **11**:363
    Turnbull **14**:335
    Wilson **5**:349-50
Cornell College, Mt. Vernon, Iowa **2**:102
Cornell College of Agriculture **14**:164-65
Cornell University
    Grumbach **2**:207
    Katz **14**:165-66, 173-74
    Ray **7**:143
    Sukenick **8**:288-89
    West **7**:280
    Williams **3**:431
Corner of Rife and Pacific, The **15**:336, 338, 339, 341
Cornford, John **1**:18, 25
Cornis-Pop, Marcel **8**:64
Cornish Anthology, A **8**:255
Cornish Childhood, A **8**:254
Cornishman Abroad, A **8**:260
Cornishman at Oxford, A **8**:260
Corno Emplumado, El **3**:94
Cornwall, England
    Corcoran **2**:124-25, 126
    Rowse **8**:253, 258
    Thomas **11**:369-70
Coronis **2**:56
Corpse, The **16**:13, 14, 16
Correspondences: A Family History in Letters **9**:284-85
Corriere dello Sport **9**:20, 22, 24
Corrigan, Robert **10**:321
Corso, Gregory
    Bowles **1**:92
    Weiss **2**:444-45
Cortázar, Julio **9**:191, 203
Cortés, Hernando **4**:348
Corwin, Norman **16**:217-18, 219
Cosmopolitan **1**:385
Cosmos **7**:283
Cost of Living, The **7**:126-27
Cotillion, The **2**:295, 304
Cott, Jonathan **17**:271
Cottey College **7**:164
Cottle, Tom **7**:201
Cotton Club: New Poems, The **6**:185
Cottrell, W.F. **3**:169
Couch, William T.
    Cassill **1**:169
    Kirk **9**:99
Couchman, Gordon **3**:421
Couchman, Jeff **3**:421
Cougar Hunter **17**:211
Council of Economic Advisors **3**:243
Council of Jewish Federations and Welfare Funds **3**:216
Council on Interracial Books for Children **6**:154-56
Count of Monte Cristo, The **2**:373
Counter/Measures: A Magazine of Rime, Meter, & Song **9**:86
Counterparts **10**:127
Counting My Steps **4**:202

Counting the Grasses **7**:132
Country Matters **1**:77
Country of the Minotaur **10**:140
Country of the Pointed Firs, The **6**:254
Country Place **6**:266
Couple Called Moebius, A **10**:9
Cousin Jacks: The Cornish in America, The **8**:253, 263
Couturier, Maurice **6**:194, 196
Covenant with Death, A **1**:38, 39
Cowards, The **1**:328, 338, 340, 341-45, 346
Cowden, Roy W.
    Ciardi **2**:89
    Corman **2**:134
Cowell, Henry **8**:86, 89
Cowles Publication Bureau **3**:179
Cowley, Malcolm
    Katz **14**:173
    Kazin **7**:88-89
    Wagoner **3**:404, 405
Cowley, Rob **4**:233
Cowper, William
    Abse **1**:25
    Nichols **2**:311
Cox, Brian **3**:46
Cox, C.B. **9**:141
Cox, Palmer **5**:299
Coxey, Jacob Sechler **3**:398
Coyote, Peter **5**:168, 169
Coyote's Journal **5**:164
Crabbe, George **15**:155
Crack in the Universe, A **12**:235
Crack, The **9**:291-92
Cracks **1**:304
Craig, Gordon **2**:412
Crane, Hart
    Belitt **4**:63
    Honig **8**:107, 121
    Roditi **14**:248
Crane, Ronald S. **12**:230, 231, 233-34
Creamy and Delicious **14**:167, 175
Creative Choices: A Spectrum of Quality and Technique in Fiction **3**:197
Creative Person: Henry Roth, The (film) **3**:430
Creative Process, The **10**:130, 134, 137
Creature of the Twilight, A **9**:103
Creed, Robert P. **9**:214
Creek Mary's Blood **6**:58
Creeley, Robert **10**:61-77
    Andre **13**:13, 14, 15-16
    Corman **2**:135, 136, 137, 138
    Crews **14**:112-13, 114
    Enslin **3**:90, 91
    Hall **7**:62
    Koller **5**:169, 170
    Major **6**:193
    Mott **7**:131
    Olson **11**:254, 255
    Peters **8**:244
    Saroyan **5**:213, 215
    Souster **14**:315

Thayler **11**:363
Wilson **5**:349, 350
Crespi-Green, Valerie **11**:102-03, 105
Cret, Paul **15**:141
Cretin Military High School **4**:146, 147
Crevel, René **14**:256
Crews, Harry **8**:215
Crews, Judson 14:101-19
Crichlow, Ernest **2**:295
Crime and Detection **3**:391
Crime and Punishment **2**:190
Crime fiction
　Freeling **12**:84-89
　Gilbert **15**:188-89, 193-94
Criminal Comedy of the Contented Couple, The **3**:390
Criminal Tendencies **11**:207
Crisis in Communication **11**:47
Crisis (James Gunn) **2**:259
Crisis (NAACP) **6**:264
Criterion
　Davie **3**:46
　Rowse **8**:258, 259
Critical Observations **3**:386
Critical Quarterly **9**:141
Critics and Criticism: Ancient and Modern **12**:233-34
Crock of Gold, The **7**:78
Crompton, Richmal
　Glanville **9**:17
　Nichols **2**:310
Cromwell, Oliver **1**:319
Cronin, Anthony **5**:370
Cross, Edward Makin **5**:145
Cross of Fire, The **4**:219
Crosscurrents
　Allen **11**:22
　Feirstein **11**:84
Crosse, Gordon **8**:155, 156-57, 158
Crossing in Berlin **3**:182
Crossing Over **3**:83
Crossing to Safety **9**:264, 269-70
Crow **11**:235
Crowell-Collier Publishing Co. **2**:264-65
Crowell, Thomas Y. (publishers) **3**:273
Crowninshield, Frank **1**:114
Crowns of Apollo, The **8**:241, 245
Crozier, Andrew
　Peters **8**:244-45
　Rakosi **5**:209
Crucifix in a Deathhand **8**:244
Cruelty **13**:10, 11
Crumb, Robert **11**:289, 293
Crunching Gravel **8**:238, 250
Crutch of Memory, The **8**:10
Cruz, Victor Hernández 17:1-17
Cry of Absence, A **11**:183-84
Crying Embers, The **2**:54
Crystal, Billy **4**:240
Crystal Palace, St. Louis, Mo. **2**:69
Crystal Spirit: A Study of George Orwell, The **6**:325-26

Cuba
　Alegría **15**:11
　Kerrigan **11**:192-94
　Sinclair **5**:273
Cuba, N.M. **1**:210
Cuba, Yes? **4**:107
Cuban Missile Crisis **4**:73-74
Cubans **11**:193-94
Cue **2**:116
Culbert, Elizabeth **10**:189-90
Culross, Michael **13**:289-90
Culture out of Anarchy: The Reconstruction of American Higher Learning **8**:133, 137
Cumberland Poetry Review **3**:47
Cumberland Station **7**:163, 164, 165
Cumming, Primrose **8**:210
Cummings, E.E.
　Howes **3**:137
　Katz **9**:68
　Whittemore **8**:306
Cummings, Ray **10**:211
Cummington School of the Arts **10**:38-39
Cunningham, J.V.
　Jerome **8**:131
　Petesch **12**:245, 246
　Sukenick **8**:289
Cuomo, Mario **10**:71
Cure for Cancer, A **5**:181
Curley, Daniel
　Elman **3**:73
　Williams **3**:421
Curley, James Michael **6**:167
Curtin University of Technology **13**:114
Curtis, Dan **16**:218, 225
Curtis, Edwina **2**:138
Curve Away from Stillness **15**:19-20
Curwood, James Oliver **1**:327
Cuscaden, Rob **13**:288-89
Cut Pages, The **10**:99
Cutting Stone **6**:102
Cyberiad, The **1**:264
Cyprus **16**:266-67
Czech language **7**:209-10
Czech literature **7**:213
Czytelnik (publishers) **9**:123

Da Silva da Silva's Cultivated Wilderness **16**:134
Dacey, Philip 17:19-36
Dadaism **8**:186
Daglarca, Fazil Husnu **6**:192
Dagon **4**:117, 119-20, 121
d'Agostino, Giovanni **11**:310
Dahlberg, Edward
　Kazin **7**:90
　Kerrigan **11**:210, 216
　Williams **12**:345
Daiches, David **6**:91, 95
Daigh, Ralph **11**:31
Daily Express (London) **5**:323
Daily Forward (New York City) **3**:155
Daily Mirror (London) **5**:322

Daily Mirror (New York City) **4**:148
Daily News (New York City) **4**:213
Daily Spectator (Columbia University) **7**:195
Daily Times (Harrison, Ark.) **6**:50-51
Dakyns, Henry Graham **8**:250
Dakyns, Janine **8**:250
Dalai Lama **6**:324
D'Alfonso, Antonio **13**:177-92
Dalhousie University
　Allen **6**:27
　Gray **3**:106-07, 108, 109
Dalí, Salvador
　Atkins **16**:8
　Bowles **1**:86
Dallas Morning News **1**:227, 228, 229
Dallas, Tex. **1**:226, 229
Damon, S. Foster
　Allen **11**:13
　Kostelanetz **8**:180
Dana, Robert **14**:48
Dance
　Belitt **4**:63
　Highwater **7**:80
Dance Me Outside **7**:102, 103, 107, 108
Dance the Eagle to Sleep **1**:273
Dance to Still Music, A **2**:114, 122-23
Dancer from the Dance, The **6**:95, 96
Dancers in the Scalp House **1**:212
Dancers of Noyo, The **8**:275
Dancing on the Shore: A Celebration of Life at Annapolis Basin **15**:252-53
Dandridge, Dorothy **2**:291
Danger Signal **16**:260
Danger Within, The See *Death in Captivity*
Danger Zone **3**:265
Daniels, Bob **8**:130
Danner, Margaret **2**:298
d'Annunzio, Gabriele **1**:391
Dans le sombre (In the dark) **13**:185
Dante Alighieri
　Anaya **4**:17
　Brown **6**:73
　Ciardi **2**:80, 90
　Katz **9**:58
　Niven **12**:222
　Wain **4**:328
Darantière, Maurice **15**:229-30
D'Arcy, Margaretta **4**:29-31, 46
D'Arcy, Martin **5**:108
Dardis, Thomas A. **10**:222, 224
"Daring Young Man on the Flying Trapeze, The" **7**:90
Dark Conceit: The Making of Allegory **8**:112, 115
Dark December **9**:5
Dark Dominion **11**:133
Dark Encounters **16**:223
Dark Horse **3**:181-82
Dark Houses (Peter Davison) **4**:138, 139
Dark Houses, The (Donald Hall) **7**:65

Dark Night of Resistance, The **1**:59
Darker Than You Think **8**:321
"Darkover" series **10**:25
Dartmouth College
  Caldwell **1**:154
  Connell **2**:101-02
  Parini **16**:235-37
  Rabassa **9**:197-99
Darwin, Charles **3**:377-78
Das Lot **14**:274
Dashiell Hammett: A Casebook **16**:217
Datlow, Ellen **9**:308
Daughters and Rebels: An
  Autobiography **17**:145
Daughters of Passion **2**:345, 352
"Dave Brandstetter" mystery series
  17:68, 70, 71, 72
Dave Sulkin Cares **3**:182
Davenport, Louis **5**:142
David Copperfield **4**:52-53
David Sterne **4**:76
Davidson, Avram **4**:150
Davidson College **7**:293
Davidson, Donald **11**:176-77
Davidson, Lionel **1**:43
Davie, Donald 3:31-48
  Abse **1**:18
  Menashe **11**:233-34, 236
  Pinsky **4**:247
Davies, Hugh Sykes **4**:337
Davies, Peter Maxwell
  Brown **6**:73
  Josipovici **8**:157, 158
d'Avignon, Sue **13**:78
Davis, Bette **1**:383
Davis, Dale **12**:353
Davis, George **1**:314
Davis, John **2**:296
Davis, Madeline Pugh **7**:194
Davis, Ossie **13**:251
Davis, William **2**:335
Davison, Jane Truslow **6**:87
Davison, Peter 4:127-42
  Stevenson **9**:287
Davison, Peter, Books **4**:141
Dawn and the Darkest Hour: A Study of
  Aldous Huxley **6**:325-26
Dawson, Mitchell **11**:110, 111
Day After, The **4**:360
"Day and Night" **8**:220, 233
Day, Dorothy **1**:58
Day I Stopped Dreaming about Barbara
  Steele, The **7**:16
Day Lewis, C.
  Allen **6**:18
  Fuller **10**:117, 122-24, 126
  Jennings **5**:113
  Silkin **5**:261, 263
Day the Bookies Wept, The **5**:54-55,
  67
Day They Came to Arrest the Book,
  The **6**:174
Dayton, Ohio **3**:165
DC Books **14**:133-34
de Angulo, Jaime **14**:108-09, 110
de Beauvoir, Simone **14**:116

de Bosis, Adolfo **12**:284-85
de Burgos, Julia **17**:12-13
de Chardin, Pierre Tielhard **15**:243
De Chepén a La Habana (From
  Chepén to Havana) **12**:103
De Chroustchoff, Boris **4**:338
De Cuevas, Marquis **1**:86
de Gaulle, Charles **12**:87
De Hartog, Jan **1**:40
de Kooning, Willem **6**:112-13
de la Iglesia, Maria Elena **6**:92
de La Mare, Walter **5**:146
de Laguna, Grace **12**:331
De l'Homosexualité **14**:281
de Man, Paul **2**:442
De Paul University **17**:168-69
De Putti, Lya **2**:215, 218-20
De Quincey, Thomas **2**:383
De Saxe, Maurice **4**:341
De Valera, Eamon **9**:231
De Wet, Christian **3**:345
Dead Man over All **6**:24
"Dead Man, The" **9**:304
Dead on Time **8**:177
Deadly Honeymoon **11**:34, 38
Deafness **5**:359, 364, 373
Dear Rafe See *Mi querido Rafa*
Dear Shadows **4**:319
Dearden, John F., Cardinal **1**:246,
  248
Death and Life of Harry Goth, The
  6:210
Death and the Visiting Firemen
  8:168-69
Death at the President's Lodging
  3:353, 354
Death Claims **17**:70
Death in April **7**:50
Death in Captivity **15**:194
Death in the Afternoon **1**:212
Death in the Quadrangle **3**:59
Death Is for Losers **16**:216
Death of a Fat God **8**:168, 171
Death of a Salesman **9**:244
"Death of a Teddy Bear" **3**:111
"Death of Seneca, The" **15**:233
Death of the Fox **5**:76, 80
Death of the Novel and Other Stories,
  The
  Klinkowitz **9**:113
  Sukenick **8**:291
Death of William Posters, The **2**:386
Death on the Ice **15**:250
Death Pulls a Doublecross **11**:32
DeBolt, Joseph Wayne **8**:1
Debs, Eugene V. **3**:370
Decadence **7**:236
Decadence and Renewal in the Higher
  Learning **9**:99, 102
Decameron **8**:281
Decker, Bill **1**:77
Decker, Clarence R. **2**:90, 93
Decline of the West, The **4**:105-06
Dee, Ruby
  Killens **2**:295
  Rodgers **13**:251

Deemer, Bill **5**:164
Deer and the Dachshund **14**:112
Deerfield Academy **2**:410
Defoe, Daniel
  Allen **6**:15
  Wallace **1**:395
Deformity Lover and Other Poems
  13:228
Deguy, Michel **6**:145, 147
del Rey, Judy-Lynn Benjamin **12**:220
del Rey, Lester
  Knight **10**:212-13, 215, 216, 217
  Malzberg **4**:209
  Niven **12**:217
  Pohl **1**:285
Delacorte, George T. **13**:263-64,
  267, 274
Delaney, Beauford **2**:139
Delany, Samuel R. **1**:295
Delbanco, Nicholas 2:149-64
  Becker **1**:40, 43
  Elman **3**:74, 81
  Mathews **6**:249
Delgado, Abelardo B. 15:165-79
Delights of Turkey, The **14**:281
Delineator **7**:91
Dell Publishing Co.
  Gunn **2**:248
  Swanberg **13**:263-64, 274
  Williams **3**:415
Delos **8**:311
Delta **14**:132-33
Delta Canada **14**:133
Delta Return **12**:20, 21, 25-26, 33-
  34, 36
DeMenil, Dominique **16**:83
DeMenil, John **16**:83
Dementations on Shank's Mare **12**:355
Demetrio, Francisco **9**:167
deMille, Cecil B. **4**:146
Deming, Barbara **4**:74-76, 78
Democratic party **1**:291
Demoiselles d'Avignon **11**:194
Demonstration, The **4**:98, 100
Dempsey, Jerry **2**:412
Dempwolff, Otto **9**:162
Denby, Edwin **17**:276-77, 278, 288-
  89
Deng Xao-Ping **2**:28
Denison University **3**:22-23, 24
Denmark **2**:35-36
Dennison, George 6:105-22
  Enslin **3**:97
Denton Welch **13**:207
Deora, Sharad **14**:92
DePauw University **3**:403, 404
Depression, 1894 **3**:398
Depression, 1924 **4**:334
Depression, The
  Banks **15**:35
  Barrio **15**:111
  Belitt **4**:60
  Booth **5**:37
  Bourjaily **1**:65
  Brewster **15**:149
  Brown **6**:52

Bullins **16**:61-62
Caldwell **1**:148
Cassill **1**:163
Ciardi **2**:87
Corcoran **2**:116
Corman **2**:130
Dennison **6**:105, 108-09
Elman **3**:70
Fisher **10**:79
Fuchs **5**:64
Ghiselin **10**:131
Giovanni **6**:160
Greeley **7**:39
Grumbach **2**:204
Gunn **2**:234, 240
Hahn **11**:112-13
Hall, Donald **7**:56
Hall, James B. **12**:111-12, 115
Harris **3**:125
Heyen **9**:34
Higgins **5**:94
Honig **8**:107
Howes **3**:139
Ignatow **3**:154-57
Katz **9**:55-62
Kazin **7**:88, 91
Kennedy **9**:73
Kinsella **7**:98
Kirk **9**:94
Kizer **5**:150
Knebel **3**:169-70, 177
Livesay **8**:220, 232-34
Morgan **3**:231, 234, 235, 236
Nichols **2**:308-09
Olson **12**:229
Petesch **12**:239, 241, 242, 249
Piercy **1**:267
Plymell **11**:276
Pohl **1**:285
Rakosi **5**:207, 208
Rechy **4**:254, 256
Rimmer **10**:284
Roditi **14**:249-50
Rosenthal **6**:276, 278
St. Clair **8**:272
Salisbury **15**:321
Schevill **12**:267
Settle **1**:308, 309
Sisson **3**:297
Solotaroff **2**:391
Sparshott **15**:349
Stafford **3**:330-31
Stegner **9**:263-64
Stone **3**:369
Swanberg **13**:261-64
Sward **13**:282
Vivante **12**:281
Wallace **1**:374
Weiss **2**:428
Westlake **13**:333
Whittemore **8**:299, 301
Wilhelm **5**:304
Williams **3**:418, 422
Wilson **5**:339
Wright **5**:362
Depth of Field **9**:40, 42

Depths of Glory **3**:379
Depuis Novalis (From Novalis)
   13:187-88, 190
Der Nister (pseudonym of Pinchas
   Kahanovitch) **4**:360
Dérobade, La **6**:248
Derstine, Clayton **2**:138, 139
Desai, Morarji **9**:233
Descend Again **6**:80, 92, 95
Deschamps, Eustache **9**:62-63
Deschanel, Caleb **3**:410
Desert Country **1**:150
Desert Legion **1**:383
Désert Mauve, Le See *Mauve Desert*
Deserters, The **2**:381
Detection Club
   Gilbert **15**:194-95
   Symons **3**:391
*Detective Fiction: Crime and
   Compromise* **11**:19
Detours from the Grand Tour **12**:207
Detroit, Mich.
   Federman **8**:72-74
   Piercy **1**:267, 270
Deutsch, André (publishers) **4**:103
Deutsch, Babette
   Abse **1**:25
   Federman **8**:76
Deutsch-jüdischer Parnass **7**:81
Deux Megots, Les, New York City
   10:6
*Development of Modern Indonesian
   Poetry, The* **9**:215
"Devil Catchers, The" **16**:67
Devil in a Forest, The **9**:311
Devil in the Flesh **1**:116
Devil's Picture Book, The **15**:226
Devils' Wine **2**:59
Devine, George **4**:30
DeVoto, Bernard **9**:265, 266, 267,
   268, 269
Dewey, John **2**:135
Dexter, John **3**:113
Deyá, Mallorca **1**:368
D.H. Lawrence Creative Writing
   Fellowship
   McCord **9**:184
   Wilson **5**:351
Dhalgren **1**:295
Dhara, Haradhon See Roy, Debi
Diabetes
   Kinsella **7**:106
   Smith **7**:164
Dial Press
   Bourjaily **1**:72, 74, 75, 76, 77,
   78, 79
   Brossard **2**:68, 73
   Disch **4**:157-58
*Dialectic of Centuries: Notes Towards a
   Theory of the New Arts, A* **8**:91
Dialogue with a Dead Man **15**:284
Dialogues on Art **14**:280
Dialogues (Stanislaw Lem) **1**:263
Diamant, Ruth Witt **1**:360
Diamond **9**:25-26
Diaries and journals

Booth **5**:33-35, 38-39, 40, 42, 48-
   50
Kazin **7**:86, 94
Lifshin **10**:243, 244-45, 257
Mott **7**:120
Diary of a Good Neighbour, The **5**:122
Diary of My Travels in America **1**:40
Diary (Virginia Woolf) **10**:114, 115
Díaz, Porfirio **4**:255
Dibner, Martin **9**:83
Dick and Jane **7**:5
Dick, Kay **4**:84
Dick, Philip K.
   Malzberg **4**:210
   Silverberg **3**:276
Dickens, Charles
   Belitt **4**:52-54
   Busch **1**:134, 135
   Charyn **1**:179
   Gray **3**:104
   Guerard **2**:221
   Higgins **5**:91
   Keating **8**:167
   Rakosi **5**:201
   Stewart **3**:350
   Symons **3**:384, 391, 392
   Van Itallie **2**:409
   Wain **4**:323
   Weiss **12**:334
   White **4**:336
Dickey, James
   Bourjaily **1**:77
   Heyen **9**:40
   Peters **8**:244, 248-49
   Taylor **7**:179
   Weiss **2**:444
Dickinson, Emily
   Inez **10**:185
   Kazin **7**:88
   Kirkup **4**:189
   Livesay **8**:223-24
   Sinclair **5**:276
Dickson, Gordon R.
   Anderson **2**:39, 40
   Knight **10**:213
   Niven **12**:217
*Dicky Bird Was Singing: Men, Women,
   and Black Gold, The* **2**:170
Dictionary of Afro-American Slang
   6:185
Dictionary of Philippine Biography
   9:161, 163-64, 168
Did Christ Make Love? **2**:70, 71
Didion, Joan **6**:87
Diebenkorn, Richard **11**:361
Diebold, John **1**:293
Dies Committee **2**:91
Dietrich, Marlene **1**:38
Diggers **5**:165
Digging In **15**:157
Dike, Donald
   Allen **11**:11
   Elman **3**:73
   Phillips **13**:199
Dilemma **3**:73
Dillard, Annie **4**:123

Dillard, R.H.W.   **7**:1-20
  Garrett   **5**:80
  Taylor   **7**:179, 181-82, 183, 185
Dillon, Eilís   **3**:49-67
Dine, Jim   **14**:173
Ding, Zuxin   **9**:219
DiPrima, Diane
  Wakoski   **1**:364
  Waldman   **17**:282-83
Dirty Books for Little Folks   **2**:71
Dirty Hands   **2**:411
Disch, Thomas M.   **4**:143-58
discovery   **1**:70, 71, 72, 73
Discrimination   **16**:179, 181
*Disembodied Poetics: Annals of the Jack
    Kerouac School*   **17**:291
*Dismemberment of Orpheus: Toward a
    Postmodern Literature, The*
  Hassan   **12**:152
  Klinkowitz   **9**:120
Disney, Roy   **1**:192, 193
Disney, Walt   **1**:192, 193
Disney, Walt, Productions
  Condon   **1**:192
  Disch   **4**:157
Disraeli, Benjamin   **3**:324
Divan and Other Writings   **8**:119
Diversion of Angels   **4**:63
Diversity of Life, The   **16**:306
Divided Voice, A   **15**:356-57, 360
Divine Comedy
  Anaya   **4**:17
  Jones   **5**:118
  Niven   **12**:222
Divine Disobedience   **2**:198
Dixon, Paige (pseudonym of Barbara
    Corcoran)   **2**:121
Dixon, Roland   **9**:157
Dixon, Stephen   **9**:120
Dk: Some Letters of Ezra Pound
    14:130
Do, Lord, Remember Me   **5**:80
Dobie, J. Frank   **2**:170
Dobrée, Bonamy   **10**:113-19
Dobrée, Valentine   **10**:113-17
"Doby's Gone"   **6**:256
"Doctor Christian" (radio program)
    2:118, 119
Doctor Cobb's Game   **1**:173
"Doctor Dolittle" series   **2**:310
Doctor Faustus
  Fisher   **10**:93
  Menashe   **11**:227
  Rimmer   **10**:285-86
  Turner   **10**:318
Doctor Giovanni   **12**:300
Doctor Zhivago   **11**:376
Doctorow, E.L.
  Bourjaily   **1**:75, 77
  Nolan   **16**:216
  Sukenick   **8**:294
  Williams   **3**:427
Doctors   **10**:253
Dodds, John   **6**:57
Dodge, Abigail   **2**:122

*Does This School Have Capital
    Punishment?*   **6**:170
Dog It Was That Died, The   **8**:171
Dog Tags   **1**:40
Dogs and Other Dark Woods, The
    5:163
Doherty, Neil   **10**:296-97
Doherty, Tom   **12**:218-19
Dollfuss, Engelbert   **4**:195
Dollmaker, The   **15**:283, 287
Doll's House, The   **4**:75
Dolphins of Altair, The   **8**:274, 275
Domínguez Cuevas, Martha   **13**:84
Dominican-American Institute   **1**:157
Dominican Republic   **2**:227
Don Giovanni   **10**:158
*Don Juan: A Yaqui Way of
    Knowledge*   **2**:272
"Don Lane Show, The"   **2**:175
Donadio, Candida
  Baumbach   **5**:26
  Cassill   **1**:171
  Markfield   **3**:219-20, 221, 222,
      223, 225, 226
  Raffel   **9**:213, 214
Donald, Roger   **6**:92
Donen, Stanley   **1**:196
Donham, Wallace Brett   **10**:287
Donne, John
  Forbes   **16**:108-09
  Forrest   **7**:23
  Mano   **6**:213
Donnellys, The   **15**:307
Donoso, José   **3**:428
Donovan, Hedley   **13**:270-72
Don't Be Forlorn   **2**:327
Don't Call Me by My Right Name
    1:300
"Door Swings Wide, The"   **4**:59
Doria, Charles   **8**:92
Dorn, Edward
  Creeley   **10**:69
  Raworth   **11**:299, 300, 302, 306
  Wakoski   **1**:364
  Wilson   **5**:349
Dorotea, La   **8**:119
Dorr, Frederick   **7**:77-78
Dorr, Virginia   **7**:77-78
Dorsey, Thomas A.   **7**:26
Dorson, Richard M.   **9**:166, 168
Dorůžka, P.L.   **1**:339
Dos Passos, John
  Brown   **6**:48
  Whittemore   **8**:310
Dostoevsky, Feodor
  Disch   **4**:148
  Guerard   **2**:221
  Ouellette   **13**:181
  Symons   **3**:389
Double or Nothing   **8**:71, 79-80
Double Shadow, A   **10**:318
"Double-Timer, The"   **4**:149, 151
Double View, The   **2**:68-69, 70
Doubleday & Co. (publishers)
  Bowles   **1**:88
  Grumbach   **2**:210

Knebel   **3**:181, 182
Silverberg   **3**:279
Slavitt   **3**:322-23, 324
Wakoski   **1**:365
Wallace   **1**:389
Douglas, Ellen   **12**:38
Douglas, Norman   **12**:341
Douglass, Frederick   **2**:291, 297
Doukhobors, The   **6**:323
Dowling College of Long Island
    1:368
Down and In   **8**:294
*Down at the Santa Fe Depot: Twenty
    Fresno Poets*   **2**:272
Down Beat   **6**:168
Down from the Hill   **2**:387-88
Down Here in the Dream Quarter
    4:215
Down in My Heart   **3**:333
Downes, Juanita Mae   **8**:212
Downward to the Earth   **3**:281, 283
Doyle, Arthur Conan
  Keating   **8**:164
  Symons   **3**:392
Doyle Dane Bernbach   **4**:150
"Dr. Geechee and the Blood
    Junkies"   **16**:67
Drabble, Margaret   **1**:43
Dragons at the Gate   **2**:173
Dragon's Island   **8**:324
Drake, St. Clair   **7**:29
Dream and Reality   **2**:192
Dream Flights   **7**:164
Dream of Love, A   **3**:85
Dreambook of Our Time, A   **9**:129
Dreamers, The   **2**:258
Dreaming of Heroes   **5**:233
Drei shwester   **9**:57
Dreiser, Theodore
  Eastlake   **1**:201
  Kazin   **7**:91
  Kherdian   **2**:265
  Swanberg   **13**:259-60
Dresner, Hal   **11**:32-33
Dresser, Paul   **14**:127
Drew, Maurice   **1**:309
Drowned Man to the Fish, The   **8**:247
Druce, Robert   **2**:51-52, 54
Drug use
  Brunner   **8**:13-14
  Knebel   **3**:173
  Plymell   **11**:280, 282-83, 284-85,
      287
  St. Clair   **8**:279
  Van Itallie   **2**:417, 420
  Williams   **3**:414
Dry Sun, Dry Wind   **3**:404
Du Bois, W.E.B.   **2**:297, 300, 302
Du Bos, Charles   **17**:177
Dublin, Ireland   **12**:79-80
Dublin Magazine   **4**:305
Dubliners
  Dillard   **7**:14
  Solotaroff   **2**:394
Ducasse, Isidore Lucien See
    Lautréamont, Le Comte de

Duchamp, Marcel **1**:99, 114, 120
Dudek, Louis 14:121-42
  Souster **14**:310, 312, 313, 314-15
Dudow, Zlatan **14**:254-55
Duff Cooper Memorial Prize **10**:122
Duffus, R.L. **3**:370
Duffy, Charles J. **5**:203
Dugan, Alan **3**:414
Duhamel, Marcel **1**:156
Duino Elegies **13**:181
Duke University
  Chappell **4**:113-18
  Clarke **16**:84
  Kirk **9**:95
  Rimmer **10**:290
Dumas, Alexandre **2**:373
Dumas, Henry **4**:243, 244
Dunbar, Paul Laurence **2**:284
Duncan, Raymond **5**:317-18
Duncan, Robert
  Broughton **12**:49, 52
  Creeley **10**:69
  Kyger **16**:190
  Rakosi **5**:208
  Saroyan **5**:216
  Turnbull **14**:336
  Waldman **17**:275
  Weiss **2**:442-43
  Williams **12**:349
  Wilson **5**:349
Duncan, Robert L. 2:165-78
Duncan, Wanda Scott **2**:169, 170,
  171, 173, 174, 175-77
Dundee University **9**:285
Dundy, Elaine **4**:30
Dunford, Judith **7**:95
Dunn, Joe **16**:190-91
Dupee, Fred **2**:447
DuPont Fellowship **7**:11
Duquesne University **11**:144-46
Durant, Will **9**:80
Durczak, Jerzy **6**:200, 201-02
Durham University **4**:183
Dutchman **16**:85
Dutton, G.F. **9**:285
Dvořák, Antonín **1**:350
Dye, Alan **10**:8-9
Dying Inside **3**:282
Dykeman, Wilma **15**:285
Dylan, Bob
  Booth **2**:51, 53
  Kyger **16**:197-98
  Waldman **17**:283-84
Dyslexia
  Bergé **10**:10, 14
  Horwood **15**:251
Dystel, Oscar **1**:295

Eagle on the Coin, The **1**:167
Ear of the Dragon, An **3**:265
Earlham College **5**:44, 45
"Early Whippoorwill" **17**:240-41
East & West **6**:181
East Coast **15**:155
East End My Cradle **7**:236
East Side Review, The **1**:365

East-West **13**:315
Eastern Michigan University **6**:147
Eastern New Mexico University
  8:325, 326
Eastlake, William 1:201-14
Eastman, Arthur **9**:82
Eastman, Max **2**:159
Eastman, Richard **5**:162
Easton, Jane Faust **14**:143-60
Easton, Robert 14:143-60
"Eaten Heart, The" **14**:126
Eberhart, Richard
  Major **6**:190
  Malanga **17**:97, 98
  Weiss **2**:445
Ebony **13**:237
Ecco Press **4**:250
"Echo and Narcissus" **4**:150
Echo Round His Bones **4**:151
*Economic Development: Concept and
  Strategy* **3**:246
Economic Development of Kenya, The
  3:243
*Economic Interdependence in Southeast
  Asia* **3**:245
Economic Report of the President
  3:243
Economics **3**:235, 236-39, 241, 245-
  46
Economou, George
  Owens **2**:362-63, 366, 368
  Wakoski **1**:364
Écrire en notre temps (To write in our
  time) **13**:189
Edel, Leon **3**:414
Edelman, Lou **1**:383
Eden **1**:260, 264
Eden, Vivian **13**:141-59
Edgar Allan Poe Special Award
  16:217
Edinburgh Academy
  Caute **4**:96
  Stewart **3**:347-50
Edinburgh University **6**:70-71
Editions de Minuit (publishers) **4**:357
Editions du Sagittaire **14**:254, 256
Edsel **6**:305-07
Education in Blood, An **3**:75, 76, 83
Education of Henry Adams, The **8**:299
Edward Waters College **2**:282
Edwards, Harry Stillwell **5**:84
Edwards, James Keith **5**:335-36
Edwards, Oliver **3**:41
Eggan, Fred **9**:165, 166, 168
Egypt
  El Saadawi **11**:61-71
  Hassan **12**:136, 138, 139-40
  Josipovici **8**:149-54
  Waldman **17**:274
Eight Million Ways to Die **11**:38
Eight Modern Writers **3**:355
Eight Oxford Poets **5**:365
*Eighteen Texts: Writings by
  Contemporary Greek Authors*
  15:75, 94
Eigner, Larry **2**:136

Einstein, Albert
  Bell **12**:29, 30
  Booth **5**:45
  Dillard **7**:7
  Lem **1**:264
  Wallace **1**:391, 401
  Wilson **5**:314
Eisenhard, John **2**:429, 431-32
Eisenhower, Dwight
  Brée **15**:141
  Connell **2**:107
  Kennedy **9**:80
  Swanberg **13**:269-70
E.J. Pratt Award **15**:155
Ekwensi, Cyprian **3**:427, 428
El Crepusculo **14**:111
El Saadawi, Nawal 11:61-72
El Salvador **15**:1-3, 12
Elbert, Joyce **10**:8-9
Electronic Arts (publishers) **4**:157,
  158
"Elegy for a Grandfather" **17**:212
Eliot, George **5**:42
Eliot, T.S.
  Abse **1**:21, 27, 29
  Allen **6**:17, 20
  Bell **12**:33
  Brown **6**:74
  Davie **3**:46
  Fuller **10**:113, 118
  Gregor **10**:148, 149
  Hamburger **4**:160, 167, 168
  Higgins **5**:92
  Jennings **5**:113
  Jerome **8**:130, 131
  Mathews **6**:230, 231
  Nichols **2**:318
  Raffel **9**:219
  Roditi **14**:246, 253
  Rowse **8**:258-59, 260-61
  Shapiro **6**:303
  Simpson **4**:291
  Sisson **3**:301
  Symons **3**:385
  Weiss **2**:440
  Whittemore **8**:303, 308
  Wilson **5**:315, 319
Elizabeth Janeway Prize **6**:90
Elle **2**:194
Elledge, Liane **8**:306
Elledge, Scott **8**:306
"Ellen West" **4**:248
Ellenbogen, Jesse **3**:210
Ellenborough, Jane **1**:397
Ellington, Edward Duke **6**:168
Elliott, George P. **10**:38
Ellison, Harlan
  Disch **4**:150
  Malzberg **4**:209
  Niven **12**:217
  Pohl **1**:285
  Wolfe **9**:305, 308
Ellison, Ralph
  Bennett **13**:84
  Bourjaily **1**:76
  Forrest **7**:23, 31-32, 33

Major **6:**186
  Weiss **2:**441-42
  Williams **3:**414
Elman, Richard 3:69-84
Elmer Gantry **5:**49
"Elric" series **5:**177, 179
Elson, James **11:**10
Eluard, Paul
  Barnstone **15:**69
  Jones **5:**120
*Elves', Gnomes', and Little Men's
    Science Fiction, Chowder, and
    Marching Society* **2:**42
Elvin, Lionel **9:**273-74, 281
Elvin, Mark **9:**281, 282, 283, 284-85
Embassy **3:**29
Emergency Exit **6:**193
Emerson College **16:**116
Emerson, Ralph Waldo
  Allen **11:**7
  Broughton **12:**50
  Heyen **9:**46
Emery, Louise **6:**115
Emigration and emigré life
  Mrozek **10:**272-77
  Pellegrini **11:**262-63, 264-65, 272-
    74
  Zinoviev **10:**335-38
Emma Instigated Me **2:**358, 365
Emmerich, Albert **12:**273, 276
Emöke **1:**345
Emory and Henry College **15:**288
Emory University
  Cassity **8:**56, 59-60
  Mott **7:**130, 131, 132
Empanada Brotherhood, The **2:**329
Emperor of Midnight **14:**282
Empire State College **2:**211
Empires in the Dust **3:**277
Empirical Argument for God, The
    10:287
Empson, William
  West **7:**276
  Woodcock **6:**319
Empty Mirror **5:**213
Emshwiller, Carol **10:**213, 223
En la nuit, la mer (In the night, the
    sea) **13:**189
En México **14:**138
Enchanted Echo, The **17:**202
Encounter **7:**180
Encounter at Shaky Bridge **7:**148
Encyclopaedia Britannica **2:**358
End of an Epoch, The **8:**257
End of Intelligent Writing, The **8:**184,
    185
End of My Life, The **1:**69, 70, 73
End of the Dreams, The **2:**258
End of the Nylon Age, The **1:**342
Endless Race **8:**103
Endless Short Story, The **8:**294
*Enemies of the Permanent Things:
    Observations of Abnormity in
    Literature and Politics* **9:**102
Enemy, The **3:**385
Enfer, L' **5:**320

Engelson, Joyce **2:**68
Engineer of Human Souls, An **1:**333,
    349
Engines of the Night, The **4:**215
England
  Aldiss **2:**21
  Cassity **8:**40, 55
  Hine **15:**226-27
  Houston **16:**181-84
  Kirkup **4:**175-77
  Moorcock **5:**187
  Morgan **3:**228, 239-40
  Sinclair **5:**271
  Singh **9:**226-27, 230
  Turner **10:**321
  Wellek **7:**215, 223-24
  White **4:**347
"England" (Donald Davie) **3:**44, 45
Engle, Huah Ling
  Corman **2:**145
  Mahapatra **9:**147
Engle, Paul
  Blaise **3:**26
  Bourjaily **1:**72, 74
  Cassill **1:**164, 167, 172
  Hall **12:**131-32
  Mahapatra **9:**146, 147
  Stafford **3:**334
English, Isobel **4:**84
English Novel, The **6:**24
English Poetry, 1900–1950 **3:**304
Enough of Green **9:**285
*Enquiry into Goodness and Related
    Concepts, An* **15:**359-60
Enslin, Theodore 3:85-99
  Dennison **6:**119
  Koller **5:**168
  McCord **9:**186, 187
  Rosenblum **11:**348
  Thayer **11:**364
  Wilson **5:**350
Entertaining Angels **15:**161
Environmentalism **9:**268-69
Epiphanies **8:**188-89, 194
Episcopal Church
  Boyd **11:**45-46, 47-48, 49, 51, 54,
    59
  Mano **6:**214
Episcopalianism **5:**145-46
Epitaph for Kings **4:**231
Epoch **7:**142-43
Epstein, Helen **9:**33-34
Epstein, Jason **6:**119
Epstein, Julius J. **12:**60, 61, 67, 68,
    72, 75
Epstein, Leslie 12:59-76
Epstein, Philip G. **12:**60, 61, 62, 67,
    75
Eray, Nazli **9:**147
Erhard, Werner **6:**249
Erhardt, Warren **9:**242
Erika: Poems of the Holocaust **9:**34,
    43-44
Ernst, Max **1:**363
Ernst, Morris **1:**389
Errand into the Maze **4:**63

Erskine, Chester **1:**383
Erskine College **1:**143, 145
Escape Artist, The **3:**410-11
Escape into You, The **14:**50
Escurial **2:**411
Eshleman, Clayton 6:123-50
  Corman **2:**144
  Owens **2:**363
Espionage of the Saints, The **4:**109
Espiritu Santo, New Hebrides **1:**165-
    66
Espousal in August **11:**218
Esquire
  Condon **1:**191
  Mano **6:**215
  Solotaroff **2:**399-400
  Wakefield **7:**197
Essai **1:**208
"Essay on Psychiatrists" **4:**246
Essay on Rime **6:**298-99
Essays (Montaigne) **3:**353
Essential Horace, The **9:**219
Essential Writings of Karl Marx **4:**105
Essex Poems **3:**43, 44
Esslin, Martin **4:**31
Estampas del valle y otras obras
    16:141, 143, 151
E.T. **1:**292
Ethics **5:**99-100
Ethics and Language **9:**277
"Ethics of Our Fathers" **9:**69
Ethier-Blais, Jean **4:**74
Ethiopia
  Samarakis **16:**267-68
  Williams **3:**426
Ethnic discrimination **4:**257
Eton **5:**268, 269
Eugene, Oreg. **14:**169-70
Eugene Saxton Fellowship **2:**108
Euripides
  Highwater **7:**80
  Taylor **7:**186
Europe
  Brossard **2:**72-73, 74
  Kherdian **2:**266-67
  Nichols **2:**327
  Shreve **5:**235
Europe (Louis Dudek) **14:**137, 138
Eustace Chisholm and the Works **1:**303
Euthanasia **6:**170-71
"Evan Tanner" series **11:**34
Evans, Luther **9:**231, 232
Evening Performance, An **5:**80
Evening Standard **11:**115-16
Evening with Saroyan, An **2:**270
Evening's Frost, An **7:**65
Events and Wisdoms **3:**40
Everglades, Fla. **11:**316
Evergreen Review **4:**260
Everleigh, Aida **1:**395
Everleigh, Mina **1:**395
Everson, Ron **17:**208
Everson, William
  Broughton **12:**52
  Kherdian **2:**269, 272
Every Changing Shape **5:**113, 114

Everyman for Himself **3**:408

everyone has sher favorite (his and hers) **8**:92

Ewbank, Thomas **4**:334

Exagggerations of Peter Prince, The **14**:173-74

Exchange Rate Policy **3**:245

Exécution, L' **4**:77

Exhaustive Parallel Intervals **8**:187

Exhibitionist, The **3**:320-21

Exile, An **11**:182

Exiles and Marriages **7**:64

Exiles, The **2**:227, 228

Existentialism
    Mott **7**:119
    Rodgers **13**:253

Expansive Poetry: Essays on the New Narrative and the New Formalism **11**:84

Expansive Poetry movement
    Allen **11**:22
    Feirstein **11**:83, 84

Experiments in Modern Art **15**:118

Explanation of America, An **4**:249

Explorations: A Series of Talks and Articles, 1966–1981 **16**:127-28

Exploring Poetry **6**:280

Extending the Territory **5**:114

Extending upon the Kingdom **2**:57

Extension **2**:117

Eybers, Elisabeth **8**:54

Eyes
    Burroway **6**:95, 96
    Picano **13**:225-26

Eysselinck, Walter **6**:93-94, 95, 96, 99

Ezekiel, Nissim **9**:145

fabelhafte Geträume von Taifun-Willi, Die **8**:92

Faber & Faber (publishers)
    Aldiss **2**:22
    Burroway **6**:92
    Gray **3**:110
    Sinclair **5**:270

Fable **2**:419

Fables for Robots **1**:264

Fabulous Originals, The **1**:386

Fabulous Showman, The **1**:384, 387-88

Facchin, Bruno **2**:139

Faces of India: A Travel Narrative **6**:321

Facts in the Case of E.A. Poe, The **5**:275

Fadeout **17**:68, 69

Fairfax, John **5**:368-69, 370, 371

Faiz, Faiz Ahmed
    Kizer **5**:155
    Singh **9**:225

Fall of the House of Usher, The (Gregory Sandow) **4**:155

Fall of the Imam, The **11**:71

Falling Astronauts **4**:213

Falling Torch, The **14**:70

Fallout **4**:98-99

False Night **14**:69

Faludy, George **5**:292

Families of Eden: Communes and the New Anarchism **8**:137-38

Family Circle, The **11**:82

Family History **11**:74-75, 83-84

Famous Writers School **17**:150-51

Fan Club, The **1**:384, 398

Fantastic **4**:149

Fantasy Level, The **6**:96

Fantasy Press Poets series **5**:110

Fantasy Worlds of Peter Stone and Other Fables, The **11**:54

Far Out **10**:222

Farewell to Manzanar: A True Story of Japanese American Experience during and after the World War II Internment
    Houston, James D. **16**:165
    Houston, Jeanne Wakatsuki **16**:175, 181, 185

Farley, Michael **9**:285-86

Farming
    Ashby **6**:35, 38, 39, 40
    Jones **11**:175
    Katz **14**:164-65
    Morgan **3**:229-31

Farrar, Straus (publishers)
    Brossard **2**:67
    Busch **1**:134
    Williams **3**:414-15

Farrell, George **12**:245

Farrell, James T.
    Kazin **7**:89-90
    Malzberg **4**:210
    Phillips **13**:205, 213

Farrell, J.G. **1**:43

Farrer, David **9**:21, 23-24

Farrow, Mia **9**:251

Farwell, Joan **6**:304

Fascism
    Brée **15**:135-36
    Davie **3**:42
    Lind **4**:203-04
    Roditi **14**:255-56
    Vivante **12**:281, 282-84, 285, 291, 295

Fast Speaking Woman **17**:280, 284

Fatal Attraction **9**:253, 254

Fathering
    Delbanco **2**:156
    Feirstein **11**:83

Fauchereau, Serge **6**:285

Faulkner, Virginia **9**:214

Faulkner, William
    Becker **1**:35, 43
    Blaise **3**:19, 25
    Brown **6**:48
    Busch **1**:128, 132, 137
    Charyn **1**:179
    Dillard **7**:11, 14
    Eastlake **1**:212
    Forrest **7**:23
    Garrett **5**:72
    Guerard **2**:221
    Higgins **5**:91

Kennedy **9**:82
Kerrigan **11**:217
Stewart **3**:357
Sukenick **8**:290
Wright **7**:289, 292

Faust
    Kazin **7**:88
    Wilson **5**:315

Faust, Frederick
    Easton **14**:147
    Nolan **16**:210, 221

FBI See Federal Bureau of Investigation

Fear and Trembling **2**:192

Fearing, Kenneth
    Rakosi **5**:203
    Rosenthal **6**:279

Feast of Icarus, The **11**:153

February Plan, The **2**:172, 174

Federal Art Project **10**:132

Federal Bureau of Investigation
    Anderson **2**:43
    Kerrigan **11**:203-04
    Roditi **14**:262, 263, 269, 275-77, 287

Federal Music Project
    Bowles **1**:85
    Cassity **8**:41

Federal Writers Project
    Brown **6**:53
    Honig **8**:109
    Ignatow **3**:156-57, 160
    Kerrigan **11**:202-03
    Rosenthal **6**:276

Federation of Jewish Philanthropies **3**:216

Federman, Raymond 8:63-81
    Klinkowitz **9**:112, 115, 116
    Sukenick **8**:291, 294

Feel Free **3**:320

Feiffer, Jules **2**:418

Feigl, Herbert **2**:38

Feinstein, Elaine 1:215-24

Feirstein, Frederick 11:73-86
    Allen **11**:22

Felipe G. Calderón **9**:159

Fellini, Federico **7**:9

Fellow-Travellers, The **4**:107

Fellowship of Reconciliation **3**:333

Female Man, The **1**:295

Feminism **16**:48-50

Feminist Writers Guild **1**:276

Fencepost Chronicles, The **7**:107, 110

Fencing **12**:144

Feng Shui **12**:348

Fenton, Charles **3**:314

Ferber, Herbert **6**:113

Ferencz, Benjamin **1**:121, 122

Ferguson, Otis **7**:88, 89

Fergusson, Francis **4**:244-45

Ferlinghetti, Lawrence
    Kherdian **2**:269
    Plymell **11**:286, 287, 288, 289

"Fern Hill" **17**:23

Ferrer, José **9**:245

Ferry, David **4**:244, 248

Festival d'Avignon 2:364
Feynman, Richard P.
  Sukenick 8:288
  Wallace 1:393
Ficciones 10:318
Fiction 10:221
Fiction Collective (publishers)
  Baumbach 5:26-27, 28, 29
  Major 6:191, 193, 194, 198
  Sukenick 8:293
Fiction-Makers, The 9:282, 287
Fiddlehead 15:154
Fiedler, Leslie
  Federman 8:79, 80
  Hassan 12:149, 157, 160
  Kerrigan 11:210
Field 3:339
Field, Shirley Anne 2:385
Fields, W.C. 1:381
*Fierce Metronome: The One-Page
    Novels* 10:13, 14
15 x 13 1:169
Fifth Form at St. Dominic's, The 6:66
Fifth Head of Cerberus, The 9:305,
    307, 311
Fifty Stories (Kay Boyle) 1:115
Fight Night on a Sweet Saturday
    1:317, 321
Fighting Indians of the West 6:55-57
Fighting Terms 1:364
Film
  Fuchs 5:54-58
  Kostelanetz 8:189, 195
Filmi, Filmi, Inspector Ghote 8:174-75
Filmmaking
  Broughton 12:54-56
  Malanga 17:104-06
  Mrozek 10:275-76
  Shadbolt 3:258-59
  Skelton 5:288-89
Final Orders 2:421
Final Programme, The 5:180
"Finding is the first Act . . . "
    5:276
Fine, Donald I.
  Block 11:36, 38
  Knight 10:214
  Silverberg 3:285-86
Fine, Michael 5:168
Fine Old Conflict, A 17:141
Finer, Stephen 8:157, 158
Finished Man, The 7:14
Finland
  Corcoran 2:123
  Creeley 10:74
  Nichols 2:314
Finley, Pearl 1:377
Finnegans Wake
  Jones 5:121
  Pohl 1:285
Finnish Academy of Sciences 10:330
Fire and Ice 9:265, 266
Fire Next Time, The 16:84
Firebrand, The 10:27
*Fireman's Wife, and Other Stories,
    The* 14:15-16

Firestorm 2:174
First and Last Words 4:125
First Baby Poems 17:286
First Blood 13:268
First Freedom, The 6:167, 173
First Light 3:410, 411
First Love 11:376
First Man on the Sun, The 7:7, 17
First Men in the Moon, The 3:271
First Person in Literature, The 14:135
First Statement 14:127-28
First Street School, New York City
    6:116, 119
Fischer, Otokar 7:212-13
Fisher, Alfred Young 10:132
Fisher, Roy 10:79-100
  Turnbull 14:335
Fisher, Vardis
  Allen 6:20
  Brown 6:53
  Ghiselin 10:139, 140
Fisherman's Whore, The 7:162, 163,
    168
Fishermen with Ploughs 6:68
Fisk University
  Giovanni 6:159
  Killens 2:296-98
Fitch, John 16:213
Fitts, Dudley 3:313, 316-17
Fitzgerald, Edward 9:177
Fitzgerald, F. Scott
  Bausch 14:5
  Bourjaily 1:68, 69, 72
  Dennison 6:110
  Glanville 9:21
  Higgins 5:91
FitzGerald, Garret 2:342
Fitzgerald, Penelope 10:101-09
Fitzgerald, Robert
  Hassan 12:149
  Whittemore 8:311
Five Chambered Heart 12:18, 19, 38
Five New Brunswick Poets 15:151,
    157
Five Poems 15:224
Flair 1:314
Flakoll, Darwin J. 15:1-15
Flame of Life, The 2:386
Flanagan, Robert 17:37-58
Flanner, Janet 1:119, 120, 121
Flaubert: A Biography 12:199
Flaubert, Gustave 12:207, 208-09
Flaw, The 16:261, 262-63
Flecker, James Elroy 2:56
Fleming, Ian 1:393
Fletcher, John 2:294
Flight and Pursuit 11:22
Flighty Horse, The 2:317
Fling! 9:245
"Floating Panzer, The" 4:151
Floating Republic, The 10:113
Florence, Italy
  Corman 2:139
  O'Faolain 2:351
  Stone 3:373
Flores, Angel 9:214, 215

Florida 12:201-02
Florida State University 6:101, 102
Florio, John 3:353
Florry of Washington Heights 14:179,
    180
Flow 8:158
Flowering of New England, The 7:92
Fluxus (artistic movement)
  Bergé 10:7-8
  Higgins 8:87-89, 91, 92
Fly Away Home 1:280
Flying a Red Kite 17:79, 88-89
*Flying Camel and the Golden Hump,
    The* 13:155
Flynn, Robert Lopez 16:149-50
foew&ombwhnw 8:92, 93
Fogwill, Irving 15:243
*Foibles and Fables of an Abstract Man,
    The* 8:118
Foiglman 13:158
Folger, Joe 9:198
Folio 6:131-32
Folk music 10:172
Folklore 4:27
*Folklore in English and Scottish
    Ballads* 8:274
Folksay Theater 11:362
Follies 2:419
Fonteyn, Margot 4:148
Foot, Michael 5:123
Foote, Shelby 5:72
Footfall 12:219, 220, 222
*For a Bitter Season: New and Selected
    Poems* 7:181
"For Birds" 17:57
For Love 8:244
For Luck: Poems 1962–1977 15:379
"For Robert Kennedy" 17:212
Forbes, Calvin 16:105-20
Forbidden Tower 10:25
Ford, Cathy 7:110
Ford, Charles Henri 17:95, 97, 104,
    116
Ford Fellowship
  Bell 12:33
  Booth 5:44
  Ghiselin 10:138
  Wagoner 3:407
Ford, Ford Madox
  Davie 3:38
  Ghiselin 10:133
Ford Foundation
  Lottman 12:207
  Morgan 3:242
  Purdy 1:302
  Raffel 9:210
Ford, Jesse Hill 5:75
Foreigner 17:228
Foreshortenings and Other Stories
    8:186
Forest of the Night 11:181-82
Forester, C.S. 4:100
Forests of Lithuania, The 3:39-40
Forever and Ever and a Wednesday
    9:66
Forked Tongue, The 9:214

Form of Woman, A **5**:213
Forman, Miloš **1**:344
Forms (Theodore Enslin) **3**:90, 93-94
Forrest, Leon 7:21-35
Forsaken Garden, The **5**:369
Forster, E.M.
    Burroway **6**:91
    Tarn **16**:279
Fort Knox Dependent Schools
    15:281-82
Fort Ord **1**:202
Fortune Press
    White **4**:338
    Woodcock **6**:320
Fortunes of a Fool **13**:154
Foster-Harris, William **2**:170
Foster, Henrietta **8**:159
Foster homes **7**:138
Foster, Joanna **8**:215
Foucault, Michel **8**:79
Foundation for the Arts and the
    Sciences **2**:439
Foundation News **9**:214, 215
Fountain in Kentucky and Other Poems,
    A **17**:187
Four Banks of the River of Space,
    The **16**:121-22
Four Portraits **7**:249, 252-53
Four Seasons, The **7**:249, 251-52
Four Springs **8**:116-17, 125
$4000 **1**:78
Four Young Lady Poets
    Bergé **10**:6
    Owens **2**:361
    Wakoski **1**:364
Fourth Angel, The **4**:263
Fourth World, The **4**:106-07
Fourth Yearbook of Short Plays, The
    1:386
Fowlie, Wallace **4**:63
Fox, George **9**:78, 79
Fox, Hugh
    Lifshin **10**:242-43, 258
    Plymell **11**:292
Foxes of Beachy Cove, The **15**:247,
    251
Foxybaby **13**:108
F.P. **3**:98
F.R. Scott Award for Poetry in
    Translation **5**:292
Fracture **6**:146
Fragmented Life of Don Jacobo Lerner,
    The **12**:91-94, 103-04
France
    Barnstone **15**:65-72
    Becker **1**:35
    Boyle **1**:115-17, 118, 119, 120
    Brossard **2**:67-68
    Federman **8**:64-71
    Josipovici **8**:146, 148
    Livesay **8**:228, 230-32
    Mathews **6**:223
    Mott **7**:119
    Sukenick **8**:290
    Wright **5**:369
France, Anatole **2**:218

France and England in North
    America **3**:44
Frances Steloff Fiction Prize **9**:213
Franchon, Jacques See Highwater,
    Jamake
Francis, Robert **11**:11
Francisco, Juan R. **9**:167
Franco, Francisco **1**:380
Frank, Glenn **8**:240
Frank Luther Mott Award **13**:268
Frank, Peter **8**:89
Frankel, Cyril **5**:366
Frankel, Gene **11**:81
Frankenheimer, John **1**:196
Frankenstein (Gregory Sandow) **4**:155
Frankenstein Meets the Space Monster
    Dillard **7**:15
    Garrett **5**:80
Frantz Fanon **4**:105
Fraser, J.T. **10**:318
Frazier, E. Franklin **2**:282-83
Freckman, Bernard **15**:70
Fredi & Shirl & The Kids **3**:70, 76,
    77, 78, 82, 83
Free Lance **16**:10, 11-13, 14, 15, 16,
    18
Free Speech Movement **4**:246
"Free Throw" **7**:178-79
Free to Live, Free to Die **11**:50-51
Freedom **6**:320
Freedom Press **6**:320
Freeling, Nicolas 12:77-89
Freeman, Gillian **4**:92
Fremantle Arts Centre **13**:114
"Fremont and Jessie" **3**:370
Fremont, Jessie Benton **3**:370
Fremont, John Charles **3**:370
Fremont-Smith, Eliot **2**:331
French First Army, Continental
    Advance Section **15**:139-43
French Kiss: Etreinte/exploration
    16:42
French literature **1**:43
French Security Police **14**:276-80
French, The **4**:232-33
Freud, Lucian **2**:348
Freud, Sigmund
    Glanville **9**:24
    Jones **5**:118, 119
    Stone **3**:367, 376
    Wallace **1**:392, 401
Friar, Kimon **15**:94
Fried, Al **3**:78
Fried, Erich **1**:24
Friedkin, William **16**:216
Friedlander, Lee **14**:175
Friedman & Son **3**:121
Friedman, B.H.
    Katz **14**:173
    Sukenick **8**:293
Friedman, Melvin **12**:162, 164
Friends Seminary School, New York
    City **11**:258
Friends, Society of
    Booth **5**:40, 45
    Ray **7**:146, 149

    Taylor **7**:178, 187
Friends, The **7**:233
Froebe, Olga **3**:141-42
From a Soft Angle: Poems About
    Women **10**:9
From Here to Eternity **7**:141
"From the Academy" **9**:100
From the Book of Shine **16**:112, 117,
    119
From the Drawn Sword **2**:118
From the Land and Back **9**:93
From the Rivers **13**:126, 136
From the Vietnamese **9**:215, 216
From This White Island **15**:85, 95,
    106
Fromm, Erika **7**:50
Frost, David **6**:92
Frost in May **2**:345
Frost, Nemi **16**:190
Frost, Robert
    Davison **4**:131, 132, 137, 138,
        139
    Galvin **13**:90-91
    Hall **7**:62, 65
    Howes **3**:143
    Ignatow **3**:154
    Kennedy **9**:83
    Lifshin **10**:233-34, 248
    Meredith **14**:222, 230
    Phillips **13**:201
    Stegner **9**:259, 265, 266, 267,
        269
    Van Brunt **15**:374
Frye, Northrop **15**:226
Fuchs, Daniel 5:53-69
Fuck Mother **8**:245-46
Fuentes, Carlos **3**:175
Fugitive Masks **3**:192
Fugitive Pigeon, The **13**:342
Fulbright Fellowship
    Anderson **2**:41
    Bell **12**:37
    Burroway **6**:94
    Cassill **1**:168
    Corman **2**:137
    Epstein **12**:73
    Federman **8**:69
    Forbes **16**:117
    Hassan **12**:160
    Kostelanetz **8**:180
    Lottman **12**:198
    McCord **9**:182-83
    Nims **17**:193
    Rabassa **9**:203
    Stegner **9**:267
    Sukenick **8**:289
    Tarn **16**:276
    Vivante **12**:296
    Wilson **5**:353
    Wright **7**:298, 300
Fuller, Buckminster **12**:160
Fuller, Hoyt **13**:246, 247, 248
Fuller, Jean Overton **2**:52, 54
Fuller, John **10**:113, 126
Fuller, Roy 10:111-28
    Symons **3**:385, 386, 387

Fulton, Robin **17**:249-65
Funaro, Jim **12**:216
Function of the Orgasm **6**:142
Funny Side Up **2**:248
Funston, Keith **3**:316
Furbank, Nicholas **3**:35
Furioso **8**:306-07
Furnace, A **10**:99
*Further Adventures of Slugger McBatt,
   The* **7**:110
Fussell, Paul **4**:243
Futurian Society **10**:203, 206-08,
   211, 212
Futurians, The **1**:284-85
Futz **2**:361-62, 364, 366, 368
Futz and What Came After **2**:362,
   363

Gable, Clark **1**:401
Gabo, Naum **8**:187
*Gabriel Dumont: The Métis Chief and
   His Lost World* **6**:323-24
Gaddis, William **4**:205, 207, 213,
   217
Gadjah Mada University, Jogjakarta,
   Indonesia **3**:242
Gaia **2**:31
Galapagos Islands **3**:378
Galaxy
   Budrys **14**:67, 68, 77-78
   Knight **10**:217-18, 221
   Pohl **1**:290, 291, 292, 294
   Silverberg **3**:277
Galin, Saul **9**:203
Gall, Sally **6**:280
Gallimard, Editions (publishers) **2**:66,
   67, 73
Gallipoli, Turkey **3**:255
Galvanized Yankees, The **6**:57
Galvin, Brendan 13:89-104
   Garrett **5**:75
Game Men Play, A **1**:79
Gamma **16**:215
Gandhi, Indira
   Blaise **3**:26
   Singh **9**:233, 234
Gandhi, Mohandas
   Shapiro **6**:290
   Woodcock **6**:325
García Lorca (Edwin Honig) **8**:109,
   110
García Lorca, Federico
   Abse **1**:21
   Belitt **4**:60, 64
   Corman **2**:135
   Cruz **17**:3, 7, 8
   Eshleman **6**:131
   Honig **8**:107, 109, 110, 118-19
   Roditi **14**:248
García Márquez, Gabriel
   Rabassa **9**:203-04
   Škvorecký **1**:341
Garcia, Nasario **15**:122
Garden City Junior College, Garden
   City, Kan. **3**:331
Garden, Mary **1**:99, 103

Garden Party **6**:90
Garden Spot, U.S.A. **5**:79
Garden, The **10**:318
Gardner Arts Centre, Sussex
   University **6**:96, 99
Gardner, Gerald **8**:274
Gardner, Helen **10**:316-17
Gardner, Isabella **13**:212, 213
Gardner, John
   Delbanco **2**:159
   Klinkowitz **9**:117
Garen, Leo **14**:175
Garioch, Robert **14**:335
Garland, Judy **1**:178
Garland, Patrick **9**:16
Garneau, Saint-Denys **13**:183
Garner, Lee **5**:349
Garrett, George Palmer, Jr. 5:71-90
   Chappell **4**:117, 122
   Dillard **7**:14-15
   Galvin **13**:99, 103
   Kizer **5**:145
   Settle **1**:317, 321
   Taylor **7**:180, 181, 183
Garrett, Helen **5**:84
Garrett, John **10**:123
Garrett, Oliver **5**:83-84
Garrett, Randall **3**:274
Gascoyne, David
   Weiss **2**:446
   Wright **5**:366, 368
Gasperik, Frank **12**:219
Gass, William
   Hinojosa-Smith **16**:143, 144
   Klinkowitz **9**:112
   Sukenick **8**:291
Gassner, John **6**:93
Gate of Hell, The **9**:5
Gates, Richard **1**:164, 167
Gateway **1**:294
Gathering of Days, A **17**:204
Gathering of Zion, The **9**:269
Gatsos, Nikos **15**:80
Gaudy Place, The **4**:121
Gaudy, The **3**:343
Gauggel, Herman **14**:179
Gauguin's Chair: Selected Poems **8**:248
Gauss Seminars in Criticism **2**:448
Gauvreau, Claude **16**:47
Gawsworth, John **5**:281
Gay liberation **13**:227-28
Gay Presses of New York **13**:233
Gay Priest: An Inner Journey **11**:58
Geis, Bernard
   Cassill **1**:173
   Greeley **7**:50-51
   Rimmer **10**:299-300
   Slavitt **3**:319, 320, 322
Gem
   Ashby **6**:34
   Brown **6**:66
General Electric Award **2**:214
General, The **2**:385
Generation without Farewell **1**:123
Genes, Mind, and Culture **16**:304
Genesis **10**:321

*Genesis Angels: The Saga of Lew Welch
   and the Beat Generation* **5**:217,
   218, 219
Genet, Jean
   Barnstone **15**:70
   Dennison **6**:121
   Sukenick **8**:290
Genêt (pseudonym of Janet
   Flanner) **1**:120
Geneva, Switzerland
   Barnstone **15**:65-66
   Condon **1**:197
Gennadius Library, Athens, Greece
   3:377
Genocides, The **4**:150
Genovese, Kitty **3**:138
Gentle Tamers, The **6**:57
Gentlemen, I Address You Privately
   1:115
GEO **3**:80
Geographical Magazine **7**:130
Geography III **4**:249
George, David Lloyd **4**:40
*George Herbert's Pattern Poems: In
   Their Tradition* **8**:91
George Mason University
   Bausch, Richard **14**:8, 9, 11-12
   Bausch, Robert **14**:25-26, 27, 29,
      30
   Shreve **5**:238
George VI **4**:37
George Washington Carver Institute's
   Supreme Award of Merit
   1:393, 395
George Washington University
   Alegría **15**:6
   Brown **6**:52
Georgia Boy **1**:150
Georgia Institute of Technology
   3:317
German Democratic Republic
   13:125, 131-32, 134-36
German language
   Higgins **8**:85
   Lind **4**:201
German-Russian War **1**:149
Germans
   Caute **4**:97-99
   Salisbury **15**:318
Germany
   Caute **4**:97-99
   Hall **12**:129-31
   Hamburger **4**:161-62
   Hauser **11**:128-29
   Lind **4**:199-200
   Phillips **13**:205-07
   Salisbury **15**:320
   Schevill **12**:276-78
   Sisson **3**:297-98
Gernsback, Hugo
   Pohl **1**:292
   Williamson **8**:316, 318
Gerrold, David **12**:220, 221
Gervais, Marty **15**:357-58
Gestalt Therapy **6**:115
Get Out Early **6**:27

Ghana **4**:103
Ghana Revolution, The **13**:51-52
Ghelderode, Michel de **2**:411
Ghiselin, Brewster 10:129-45
  Taylor **7**:184-85
Ghiselin, Michael **10**:133, 136, 137, 138, 140
Ghose, Zulfikar **6**:92
Ghosh, Sudhir **9**:230
Ghost in the Music, A **2**:335
Ghote, Ghanesh **8**:165, 167, 171-72, 173, 175, 176
GI Bill
  Anderson **2**:39
  Easton **14**:155
  Federman **8**:76, 77
  Hazo **11**:144, 146
  Jerome **8**:130
  Kennedy **9**:79, 82
  McCord **9**:180-81
  Menashe **11**:226
  Peters **8**:239-40
Giant Jam Sandwich, The **6**:99
Gibson, Walker **6**:90
Gide, André
  Guerard **2**:229, 230
  Wallace **1**:391, 393
Gielgud, John **5**:108
Gift to Be Simple, The **8**:247, 248
Gig **16**:168
Gilbert, Bernard **15**:182-83, 184-85
Gilbert, H. **3**:135
Gilbert, Michael 15:181-99
Gilbert, Vedder **2**:122, 123
Gilgamesh the King **3**:285
Giligia Press **2**:271, 272
Gilman, Coby **11**:133
Gilmour, Sally **5**:366, 367
Gimbel, Wendy **2**:420, 421
"Gimlet Eye, The" **6**:214, 218
Ginsberg, Allen
  Allman **15**:24
  Bowles **1**:91, 92
  Choudhury **14**:91, 92
  Creeley **10**:72-73
  Cruz **17**:7-8, 10, 16
  Enslin **3**:93
  Eshleman **6**:128, 131-32, 135, 147
  Heyen **9**:46
  Klinkowitz **9**:114
  Kyger **16**:190, 195, 196
  Major **6**:193
  Malanga **17**:109, 110
  Morgan **4**:236
  Plymell **11**:280, 285, 286-87, 288, 289-90, 294, 295
  Saroyan **5**:213
  Škvorecký **1**:346-47
  Waldman **17**:268, 273, 280, 282-83, 284-85, 289, 291
  Weiss **2**:445
Ginsberg, Thomas **2**:70
Gioia, Dana **11**:84
Giotto di Bondone **3**:355
Giovanni, Nikki 6:151-64
Giraudoux, Jean **2**:69

Giri, Varahagiri Venkata **9**:234
Girl in the Black Raincoat, The **7**:180
Girodias, Maurice
  Malzberg **4**:218
  Wallace **1**:396
Giroux, Robert **1**:322
Gist of Origin, The **2**:135, 136, 137, 138, 140, 141, 142, 144
Gitlin, Paul **1**:401
Giuranna, Bruno **2**:162
"Give My Regards to Broadway" **4**:238
Give the Dog a Bone **5**:171
Gladiator-at-Law **1**:293
Glanville, Brian 9:13-29
Glanville, Stephen **4**:341
Glasgow, Ellen **7**:11-12, 17
Glass Face in the Rain, A **3**:335
Glass Menagerie, The **7**:23-24
Glass, Philip **14**:176
Glassgold, Peter **15**:19-20
Gleason, Madeline **12**:52
Gleason, Robert **12**:219, 220
Glock, William **8**:157, 158
Glück, Louise **4**:250
Glynn, Tom **9**:117
Go in Beauty **1**:209, 212
Go-potty Rex **9**:83
Go to the Widow-Maker **7**:141
Go West, Inspector Ghote **8**:176
God
  Anaya **4**:22
  Arden **4**:31
  Bennett **13**:74, 82
  Booth **5**:32, 33, 35, 40, 43, 45, 51
  Ciardi **2**:85
  Greeley **7**:49
  Kherdian **2**:261
  Ouellette **13**:181
  Simic **4**:271
  Thomas **4**:311, 312
  Van Itallie **2**:410
  Weiss **12**:333-34
  Wiesel **4**:355
God We Seek, The **12**:334
Godard, Barbara **16**:53
Godded and Codded **2**:351
Godfrey, Dave **7**:301
Godfrey, Derek **12**:12
Godine, David R. (publishers) **1**:134
God's Little Acre **1**:151, 152
God's Trombones **7**:23
Godwin, Gail **6**:100
Goebbels, Josef
  Lind **4**:198
  Škvorecký **1**:330
Goedicke, Patricia **9**:41
Goering, Hermann **14**:272
Goethe, Johann Wolfgang von
  Kazin **7**:88
  Ray **7**:144
Gog **5**:271, 272, 273-74
Gogarty, Oliver St. John **12**:198
Going All the Way **7**:199
Going Down Fast **1**:273

Gold at the Starbow's End, The **1**:294
Gold, Herbert
  Cassill **1**:169
  Dudek **14**:130
Gold, Horace
  Gunn **2**:248, 249
  Knight **10**:216, 217-18
  Pohl **1**:290, 292
Gold, Zachary **1**:386
Goldemberg, Isaac 12:91-106
Golden Dream, The **3**:278
Golden Positions, The **12**:53
Golden Scroll Award **16**:219
Golden State **4**:248
Goldenhar, Didi **2**:421
Golding, William
  Sinclair **5**:273
  Tennant **9**:293
Goldman, Willie **7**:236
Goldsmith, Cele **4**:149
Goldstein, Moritz **7**:81
Goldwyn, Samuel, Jr. **5**:79
Goliard Press **11**:301, 302
Gollancz, Victor
  Freeling **12**:85-86
  Keating **8**:169, 170
  Menashe **11**:233
  Wilson **5**:320
Gollancz, Victor (publishers)
  Keating **8**:169
  Purdy **1**:300, 301
  Stewart **3**:354
  Symons **3**:389
  Wagoner **3**:406
  Wilson **5**:322
Gomberg, M. Robert **5**:207
Gone with the Wind **1**:311
Gooch, Velma **7**:101
"Good News from the Vatican" **3**:282
Good News of Death and Other Poems **4**:293
"Good Woman, A" **1**:300
Goodbody, Buzz **4**:106-07
Goodly Babe, A **12**:300
Goodman, Mitchell **2**:137
Goodman, Paul
  Dennison **6**:114-15
  Kostelanetz **8**:191
  Roditi **14**:260, 266, 286
  Settle **1**:322
Goodwin, Clive **3**:111, 112, 113
Gorbachev, Mikhail **10**:332, 338
Gorczynski, Renata **4**:250
Gordimer, Nadine **8**:54
Gordon, Ambrose, Jr. **8**:306
Gordon, Caroline **2**:252
Gordon, Charles **2**:307
Gordon, Giles **4**:86
Gordon, Robert S. **10**:3
Gore, Walter **5**:366, 367
Gorki, A.M., Institute of World Literature, Moscow **2**:386
Gorki, Maxim
  Rakosi **5**:201
  Wallace **1**:391

Wesker **7**:236
Gorky, Arshile **7**:174
Gornick, Vivian **10**:13
Goshawk, Antelope **7**:164
Gospel music **7**:26, 30
Gotham Book Mart **9**:80
Gottlieb, Morton **9**:246, 247, 248, 249, 250, 251, 252
Gottlieb, Robert
    Mano **6**:212
    Markfield **3**:223, 225
Goulianos, Joan **2**:368
Government College **9**:225
Governor-General's Award for Literature
    Bowering **16**:37
    Woodcock **6**:326
Governor-General's Award for Poetry
    Purdy **17**:209, 210
    Souster **14**:316
Governor's Bridge Is Closed: Twelve Essays on the Canadian Scene, The **17**:89
Goya, Francisco de **11**:208
Goyen, William **13**:208, 212, 213
Gozzano, Guido **2**:319
GPNY See Gay Presses of New York
Grace, Princess of Monaco **11**:149-50, 153
Graham, Alastair **5**:178
Graham, Archibald "Moonlight" **7**:104, 105
Graham, Donald **2**:298
Graham, Martha **2**:431, 445
Graham, W.S.
    Weiss **2**:446
    Wright **5**:367, 368
Grahame, Kenneth **1**:101
Grainger, Percy **5**:142
Grand Rapids Press **7**:196
Grand Valley State College **3**:174
Grandbois, Alain
    Brossard **16**:46-47
    Ouellette **13**:183
Grandmother Sea **9**:295
Grann, Phyllis **3**:322
Grant, Ulysses **1**:383
Granta **6**:91, 92
Graphis series **8**:92-94
Grass Is Singing, The **5**:122
Grasse 3/23/66 **2**:156, 159
Grassel, Jack **11**:348
"Grassland" **14**:175
Grave of the Right Hand, The **7**:295
Graves Registry **5**:342, 344, 345, 351, 355
Graves, Robert
    Allen **6**:17
    Allman **15**:23
    Arden **4**:29, 30
    Hamburger **4**:171
    Jennings **5**:110
    Kerrigan **11**:210
    Mathews **6**:235, 246
    Menashe **11**:231
    St. Clair **8**:274

Shadbolt **3**:249
Skelton **5**:291
Sward **13**:302
Gravy Planet **1**:291
Gray, Cleve **2**:196-98, 199, 200
Gray, Francine du Plessix 2:179-201
Gray, Kenneth **2**:39, 42
Gray, Simon 3:101-15
Gray Soldiers **7**:166
Great American Funeral, The (film) **17**:148
Great American Poetry Bake-offs **8**:248
Great Black Russian: The Life and Times of Alexander Pushkin **2**:305-06
Great Britain, Royal Air Force
    Abse **1**:23-24
    Brunner **8**:7
    Moorcock **5**:176
    Sillitoe **2**:374-80
    Skelton **5**:281-82
    West **7**:278-80
    Wilson **5**:316-17
Great Britain, Royal Air Force, Women's Auxiliary Air Force **1**:312
Great Britain, Royal Army
    Aldiss **2**:19
    Bourjaily **1**:67
    Gilbert **15**:188, 189-92
    Hamburger **4**:163-64, 169
    Mott **7**:120, 121, 122
    Silkin **5**:256, 257-58, 259
    Sinclair **5**:269
    Sparshott **15**:352, 353, 354, 357, 359
Great Britain, Royal Navy
    Davie **3**:32
    Davison **4**:129
    Sillitoe **2**:375
    White **4**:338-39
Great Fear, The **4**:107
Great Gatsby, The **6**:110
Great Lakes Colleges Association National First Book Award **10**:191
Great Steamboat Race, The **8**:14
Great Things Are Happening **5**:170
Greatest Show on Earth, The **4**:146
Greco, Juliette **7**:119
Greece
    Barnstone **15**:73-106
    Davie **3**:39
    Delbanco **2**:155-56
    Jones **5**:125
    Piercy **1**:272
    Stone **3**:376-77
    Van Brunt **15**:376
    Wright **7**:296
Greed **1**:368
Greek Anthology, The **5**:286
Greek, classical
    Matthews **15**:262-63
    St. Clair **8**:271-72

Greek National Resistance Movement **16**:252-57
Greek Treasure, The **3**:377
Greeley, Andrew 7:37-53
Green, Henry
    Allen **6**:18
    Tennant **9**:291
Green, Joe **2**:44
Green, Kay 11:87-106
Green, Paul **2**:434
Greene, David **12**:199
Greene, Gael **6**:87
Greene, Graham
    Allen **6**:20
    Caute **4**:102, 105, 108
    Hine **15**:226
    Jones **5**:125
    Keating **8**:169-70
    Slavitt **3**:320
    Wilson **5**:325
Greenfield, George **9**:20
Greenspan, Yosl **9**:55-56, 61-62
Greenvoe **6**:72
Greenwald, Ted **11**:302, 303
Greenwich Village, New York City
    Block **11**:28, 37
    Busch **1**:131-32
    Kirkup **4**:190
    Owens **2**:359
    Pohl **1**:289
Greenwood, Robert **3**:335
Greer, Germaine **11**:68
Gregor, Arthur 10:147-62
Gregory, Dick **6**:159
Gregory, Horace
    Owens **2**:358
    Rosenthal **6**:279
Grendel **9**:117
Greybeard **2**:23
Gridiron Club, Washington, D.C. **3**:177, 178, 179
Grief Observed, A **8**:280
Grierson's Raid **6**:57
Griffin, John Howard **7**:132
Grigsby, Frances **7**:77-78
Grigson, Geoffrey **3**:385
Grimond, Jo **5**:179
Grindea, Miron **7**:127, 128
Grist **11**:289, 291, 292
Grito, El **4**:24
Grodin, Charles **9**:246, 247
Groffsky, Maxine **6**:240, 241-42, 246, 247
Grolier Book Shop, Cambridge, Mass. **3**:89
Gross, Ben **12**:203
Gross, Jerry **3**:424
Group Portrait: Conrad, Crane, Ford, James, and Wells **2**:156, 159
Grove City College **9**:59
Grove Press **4**:260
Grove Press Award **9**:231, 232
Growing Up Stupid Under the Union Jack **16**:75, 76
Grumbach, Doris 2:203-14
Gryphon **5**:283

Guadaloupe, French West Indies
  2:215
Guardians, The **3**:355
Guatemala **2**:329-30, 331
Guatemalan-American Institute **1**:157
Guccione, Bob **6**:153-54
Guerard, Albert J. **2**:215-32
  Pinsky **4**:245
Guerard, Albert Leon **2**:215, 216,
  217, 221, 223
Guerard, Wilhelmina **2**:216, 221,
  222
Guevara, Che **17**:115, 117
Guggenheim Fellowship
  Baumbach **5**:28
  Becker **1**:35
  Bowles **1**:86
  Boyle **1**:117
  Cassill **1**:172
  Eshleman **6**:147
  Federman **8**:79
  Feirstein **11**:83
  Galvin **13**:102
  Hassan **12**:160
  Hearon **11**:169
  Honig **8**:112, 115
  Jones **11**:184
  Markfield **3**:220
  Mott **7**:133
  Owens **2**:357
  Peters **8**:244, 249
  Rabassa **9**:204
  Root **11**:325
  Settle **1**:317
  Stegner **9**:267
  Wagoner **3**:406-07
  Wakoski **1**:368
  West **7**:280
Guggenheim Foundation
  Ai **13**:11
  Blais **4**:73, 74
  Purdy **1**:302
  Simpson **4**:295
Guggenheim, Peggy **1**:89, 90
Guidacci, Margherita **10**:141
Guide to Public Lending Right, A **4**:84
Guillén, Jorge **15**:59
Guinness, Alec **3**:113, 114
Guinness Award **2**:56
*Guinness Book of Poetry, 1957/58,
  The* **7**:127
Guiton, Margaret **15**:136
Gullah **17**:131-32
Gun Fury **1**:383
Gundolf, Friedrich (pseudonym of
  Friedrich Gundelfinger) **7**:213
Gunn, Benjamin Jesse **2**:234, 235,
  238, 241
Gunn, James **2**:233-60
  Williamson **8**:322, 324, 325
Gunn, John **6**:64
Gunn, Thom **1**:360, 364
Guns and shooting
  McCord **9**:172, 173, 177, 178,
    180, 181
  Rosenblum **11**:346, 350, 352

Guns of Rio Presto, The **1**:342
Gunsight **2**:436, 437
Guravich, Donald **16**:201, 202
Guss, Jack **1**:208
Guthrie, Ramon **9**:198, 200
Gutwillig, Robert **2**:400, 401
Guyana Quartet, The **16**:134
Guyana, South America **16**:121-22,
  123-28, 132
Gypsies
  Cartland **8**:25, 26
  Simic **4**:269

Hades in Manganese **6**:146
Hadjidakis, Manos **15**:77, 78-80
Hadley, Drummond **5**:349, 353
Hadley, W.W. **5**:367, 368
Haganah
  Megged **13**:146
  Wiesel **4**:355-56
Hagen, Joel **12**:213, 214, 216
Hager, Henry **9**:279
Haggard, H. Rider
  Anderson **2**:37
  Cassity **8**:39
  Thomas **11**:374
Hahn, Emily **11**:107-21
Haifa University **9**:216
Haiku **4**:183, 186, 187
Hailey, Elizabeth Forsythe **1**:225-35
Hailey, Oliver **1**:229-34
Hair of the Dog **3**:189
Haiti **3**:145
Halas, František **1**:335-36
Halberstam, David **1**:40
Haldeman, Joe **12**:212
Haldeman, Marcet **2**:248
Hale, Allen **7**:12
Hales, Steven **4**:250
*Half a Life's History, Poems: New and
  Selected, 1957–1983* **13**:304
Half Gods, The **12**:24, 26, 29-30, 34,
  36, 38
Half Laughing/Half Crying **11**:51, 58
Half Remembered: A Personal History
  4:129, 138
Halflife **7**:298
Halifax, Nova Scotia **3**:106, 107,
  109
Hall, Barry **11**:301-02, 304, 305,
  307
Hall, Donald **7**:55-67
  Burroway **6**:90
  Jennings **5**:110
  Kennedy **9**:83, 84
  Stevenson **9**:282-83
Hall, Elizabeth Cushman **12**:119,
  120, 128, 130, 131, 132, 133
Hall, Graham **5**:184
Hall, James B. **12**:107-34
  Cassill **1**:169
Hall, Peter **3**:114
Hallmark Cards **16**:211
Halman, Talat S. **6**:192
Halpern, Daniel
  Bowles **1**:93

Pinsky **4**:250
Halpern, Stach **2**:138
Halsey, William Frederick **2**:104
Halward, Leslie **6**:20
Hamady, Walter **11**:256
Hamburg, Germany
  Caute **4**:98-99
  Delbanco **2**:160
Hamburger, Leopold **4**:161
Hamburger, Michael **4**:159-73
  Jennings **5**:110
  Mead **13**:130-31, 133, 136, 138
Hamburger, Richard **4**:160, 161,
  162-63, 165, 170
Hamill, Sam **15**:201-16
Hamilton College **2**:326-28, 332
Hamilton, Gail (pseudonym of
  Barbara Corcoran) **2**:121, 122
Hamilton, George Rostrevor **10**:119-
  22, 126
Hamilton, Mark **2**:58
Hamilton Stark **15**:44
Hamilton, William D. **16**:301-02
Hamlet
  Gray **2**:189
  Jennings **5**:108
Hammett: A Life at the Edge **16**:221
Hammett, Dashiell
  Brossard **2**:69
  Symons **3**:391, 392
Hammond Times (Indiana) **3**:404
Hampson, John **6**:18-19, 20, 22
Hanagid, Samuel **8**:145
Hancock, Herbie **6**:179
Hand-Reared Boy, The **2**:29
Handke, Peter
  Blaise **3**:19
  Klinkowitz **9**:116, 118, 119
Handlin, Oscar **5**:271
Handy, Lowney **7**:140-42
Hanger Stout, Awake!
  Heyen **9**:42
  Matthews **15**:268
Hanging Garden, The **3**:410
Hanging Gardens of Etobicoke, The
  15:359
Hankla, Cathy **7**:19
Hanley, James **4**:309
Hano, Arnold **10**:219
Hansen, Al **8**:86-87
Hansen, Alvin **3**:236-37
Hansen, Joseph **17**:59-74
*Happening Worlds of John Brunner,
  The* **8**:1
Happy Man, The **14**:154
Harbor Review **6**:268
Harcourt, Brace (publishers)
  Davison **4**:133, 134, 135
  Wagoner **3**:405
Hard Way, The **5**:57
Hardin-Simmons University **10**:22,
  23, 24
Harding, Gunnar **11**:303, 309
Hardwicke, Paul **12**:12
Hardy, Joseph
  Slade **9**:251

Wakefield 7:200
Hardy, Thomas
Creeley 10:67-68
Guerard 2:221, 230
Kizer 5:141
Wain 4:328
Harford, Thomas 2:24
Harkness Fellowship 5:271
Harlem Art Center, New York City
6:267-68
Harlem Writers Guild 2:286, 287-88
Harlequin's Stick, Charlie's Cane
3:192
Harley-Davidson, Inc. 11:333, 351-
52
Harmon, William 12:345-46
Harold [and] *Sondra* 11:81-82
Harper & Row, Publishers
Disch 4:156, 157
Knebel 3:179, 180, 181
Solotaroff 2:403
Harper, Carol Ely 16:11, 12
Harper's Bazaar
Hauser 11:134, 136
Settle 1:313
Harper's Magazine 1:117, 120
Harrad Experiment, The 10:281, 286,
287, 291, 295, 296, 298-99,
300, 301, 305
Harrad Letters, The 10:305
*Harriet Tubman: Conductor on the
Underground Railroad* 6:253
Harris, Charles 3:274
Harris, Charles F. 3:431
Harris, Frank 1:97
Harris, Jed 5:64-66
Harris, Josephine Horen 3:117-27,
128, 129, 130, 131, 132
Harris, Mark 3:117-32
Greeley 7:38
Harris, Mary Emma 8:179
Harris, Wilson 16:121-37
Harrison College 16:71, 75-76
Harrison, Gilbert
Grumbach 2:211-12
Whittemore 8:310
Harrison, Harry
Aldiss 2:26-27, 28, 29
Gunn 2:258
Knight 10:216, 220
Pohl 1:295, 296
Harry, Bill 5:176
Harry the Magician 2:69
Harry's Fragments 16:28
Hart, Al 7:81
"Hart Crane" 3:386
Hart-Davis, Rupert 4:309, 310
Hart, Jeffrey 6:208
Hart, Moss 1:395
Harteis, Richard 14:219-36
Hartford, Conn. 12:347
Hartley, Anthony 5:284
Hartley, George 3:39
Hartmann, William K. 12:213, 214,
215
Hartshorne, Charles 12:329-30

Hartung, Hans 12:87
Hartwell, David 9:311, 312
Harvard Advocate 7:62, 63
Harvard Glee Club 4:132
Harvard University
Becker 1:33-34
Blaise 3:23, 24
Caute 4:104, 105
Ciardi 2:93
Clement 16:91, 98
Corcoran 2:116
Corman 2:138
Creeley 10:62, 66-67
Davison 4:131-33
Delbanco 2:156, 158
Easton 14:144, 157
Federman 8:77
Guerard 2:223, 226, 227, 228,
230-31
Hall 7:59, 62-63, 64-65
Hentoff 6:166-67
Honig 8:113-15
Kazin 7:95
Kumin 8:213
Mathews 6:223, 232
McPherson 17:123, 133
Morgan 3:232, 236-37, 238, 239
Mrozek 10:271
Rimmer 10:287-88
Sinclair 5:271
Stegner 9:266
Van Itallie 2:410-11, 418
Wakefield 7:197
Weiss 12:327-28
Wellek 7:218
Wilson 16:294-307
Harvard University Press 4:134
Harvey, Anthony 5:126
Harwood, Lee 4:152
Hašek, Jaroslav 1:341
Haselwood, Dave 11:283, 284, 285,
289
Hass, Robert 4:244, 246, 249-50
Hassan, Ihab 12:135-66
Klinkowitz 9:120
Hassan, Sally 12:152, 161, 162, 165
Hatch, Robert 6:279
Hatfield, England 1:320
Hathaway, Baxter
Katz 14:165
Ray 7:142-43
Hauková, Jiřina 1:338
Hauser, Marianne 11:123-38
Hausman, Gerald 2:271
Havighurst, Walter
Hall 12:119, 131
Knebel 3:169
Hawaii
Corcoran 2:125-26
Forbes 16:113, 114-15
Houston, James D. 16:166-67,
168-69
Houston, Jeanne Wakatsuki
16:180-81
Knebel 3:175, 176, 182-83
Morgan 3:234, 238

*Hawaii: A Century of Economic Change,
1778–1876* 3:238
Hawaii: The Sugar-Coated Fortress
2:199
Hawk in the Rain, The 6:90
Hawker 8:248, 249, 250
Hawker, Robert Stephen 8:248
Hawkes, John
Guerard 2:229-30
Van Itallie 2:411
Hawkins, Eric 1:313
Hawkins, John 2:176
Hawk's Well Press 1:364
"Hawksbill Station" 3:279
Hawley, Robert 2:269
Hawthorne, Nathaniel
Jones 11:184
Mano 6:210
Mathews 6:245
Miller 15:282-83
Hayakawa, S.I. 8:132
Hayden, Jeff 2:289
Haydn, Hiram 4:115, 116, 120, 121
Haydon 8:248
Haydon, Benjamin Robert 8:248
Hayes, Harold 7:197
Hays, H.R. 1:392
Hays, Marvin 7:12
Hayter, Alethea 2:55
Hayward, Jack 9:149
Hayward, Mary Sulley 7:10
Hayward, Max 11:216
Hazard of Hearts, A 8:22
Hazard, the Painter 14:234, 235
Hazlett, Theodore L., Jr. 11:148-49,
150
Hazlitt, William 7:232-33
Hazo, Robert G. 11:144, 155
Hazo, Samuel 11:139-55
He Wants Shih! 2:363, 365, 366
Head, Lois McAllister 1:377
Head of the Family, The 3:59
Health care 8:26
Heaney, Seamus
Brown 6:71
Gray 3:110
Parini 16:233, 237
Heap, Jane 5:203
Hear That Lonesome Whistle Blow
6:58
Hearing dysfunctions 5:362-63, 366
Hearne, G.R.M. 8:169
Hearon, Shelby 11:157-70
Hearst, William Randolph 13:259
Heart as Ever Green, The 13:250-51
Heart disease 7:283-85
Heart Is a Lonely Hunter, The 7:93
Heart of Aztlán 4:25, 26
Heath, A.M. (literary agent) 2:58
Heath, Edward 3:46
Heath-Stubbs, John
Kennedy 9:82-83
Wain 4:329
Heaved from the Earth 5:349
Hébert, Jacques 4:76

Hebrew Orphan Asylum, New York City **4**:55-56, 59
Hebrides Islands **4**:305
Hedin, Sven **1**:390-91
Hedva and I **13**:153, 154
Heggen, Thomas **9**:258-59, 267
Heilman, Robert B. **3**:408
Heinemann, William (publishers) **8**:172
Heinlein, Robert
  Gunn **2**:248
  Knight **10**:206
  Niven **12**:222
  Williamson **8**:321-22
Heinz, His Son, and the Evil Spirit **13**:154
Heisenberg, Werner Karl **4**:65
Helen Bullis Award **15**:30
Heliczer, Piero
  Raworth **11**:300-01
  Van Itallie **2**:411
Heller, Michael **6**:140
Heller, Ursula **13**:297
"Helliconia" series **2**:28, 31
Hellman, Lillian **2**:69
Hell's Cartographers **4**:207
Hell's Pavement **10**:203, 219
Helltracks **16**:221
Helmet and Wasps **7**:130
Helps, Robert **1**:304
Hemingway, Ernest
  Blaise **3**:19
  Bourjaily **1**:68, 69, 72
  Busch **1**:130, 131, 132, 133, 137
  Dillard **7**:11
  Eastlake **1**:212
  Guerard **2**:222
  Higgins **5**:96
  Katz **9**:60
  Kerrigan **11**:217
  Klinkowitz **9**:118
  Lottman **12**:198, 206
  Mano **6**:217
  Salisbury **15**:312-13
  Shreve **5**:228
  Solotaroff **2**:394
  Wakefield **7**:195, 196
Hemley, Cecil **3**:415
Hemmings, David **5**:273
Henderson, David **6**:195
Hendrych, Jiří **1**:347
Henley, W.E. **3**:144
Henn, Tom
  Davie **3**:41
  White **4**:341
Hennings, Thomas **1**:122
Henri, Adrian **2**:52
Henri, Robert **1**:104
Henry IV (king of France) **4**:223-24
Henry IV, Part I **5**:108
Henry Sows the Wind **9**:23, 24
Hentoff, Nat 6:165-74
  Corman **2**:135
Heny, Michael **12**:353-55
Herald, Leon **5**:202, 203, 208
Heraud, Javier **6**:138

Herbert, David **4**:232
Herbert, Frank **2**:43, 45
Herbert Read: The Stream and the Source **6**:325-26
Herd, Dale **11**:307
Here I Am, There You Are, Where Were We? **4**:157
Heredia, José Maria de **2**:158
Hereford College of Education **11**:368, 372-73, 377
Hereford, Frank **1**:157
Heritage of Hastur, The **10**:25
Herlihy, James Leo **7**:78
Herman, Jan **8**:90
Hernandez, Miguel **1**:18, 25
Hero Driver **9**:4
Heroes and Heroines **8**:305
Heroics: Five Poems **15**:230
"Heroine, The" **4**:138
Herovit's World **4**:210
Hersey, John **13**:269
Heschel, Abraham Joshua **4**:359
Hesiod **15**:110
Heures, Les (The hours) **13**:186, 190
"Hey!" and "Boo!" and "Bang!" **2**:329
Heydrich, Reinhard **1**:331
Heyen, William 9:31-48
  Booth **2**:58
Hicks, Edward **5**:261
Hicks, Granville **2**:290
Higgins, Aidan **11**:214
Higgins, Brian
  Sisson **3**:302
  Wright **5**:371
Higgins, Dick 8:83-96
Higgins, George V. 5:91-101
Higgins, Marguerite **4**:229
High Castle, The **1**:255, 257, 258
High Cost of Living, The **1**:272, 278
"High John da Conqueror" **16**:67
Higher Education **2**:397
Highlands, N.C. **12**:355-56
Highwater, Jamake 7:69-83
Hill, Abram **6**:267
Hill, Geoffrey **9**:85
Hill, Hugh Creighton **14**:335
Hillel, Ben **1**:209
Hillerman, Tony **16**:146, 150
Hilliard, Richard **5**:80
Hillman, Alex **10**:215-16
Hilton, James **1**:381
Himes, Chester
  Major **6**:186
  Williams **3**:424-25, 429
Hindenburg, Paul von **1**:326
Hindman Settlement School **17**:238-39, 244
Hinduism **14**:81, 86, 95
Hindustan Times **9**:234
Hine, Daryl 15:217-36
  Brewster **15**:156
  Mahapatra **9**:146, 147
Hinnant, Bill **4**:211
Hinojosa-Smith, Rolando 16:139-53
Hirsch, Judd **2**:418

Hirschman, Jack **6**:131, 132, 133, 137
His First, Best Country **15**:289
Hispanic-Americans
  Anaya **4**:15-27
  Hinojosa-Smith **16**:139-53
History Day by Day **2**:373
History of Barry **4**:334
History of English Literature, A **6**:36
History of My Heart **4**:250
Hitchcock, George 12:167-82
  McCord **9**:183
Hitler, Adolf
  Cassity **8**:61
  Eastlake **1**:207
  Kazin **7**:89
  Kizer **5**:150
  Lind **4**:198-99, 200, 202
  Sinclair **5**:267-68
  Sisson **3**:297
  Škvorecký **1**:326
Hoagland, Edward **1**:41
Hoare, Penelope **4**:84
Hobana, Ion **8**:13
Hobart and William Smith Colleges **7**:280
Hobart, Peter **7**:295, 296
Hobsbaum, Philip **9**:284, 285
Hobson, Wilder **10**:91-92
Hocking, William Ernest **5**:35, 44, 48
Hoddinott Veiling **6**:99
Hoffman, Arthur **11**:10
Hoffman, Frederick J. **8**:243
Hoffman, Heinrich **8**:167
Hoffman, Lee 10:163-77
Hofmann, Berenice **6**:241
Hofstadter, Richard **5**:271
Hofstra University **11**:38
Hogg, James
  Simpson **4**:294
  Tennant **9**:290, 292
Hoggart, Richard **10**:115, 116
Hogrogian, Nonny See Kherdian, Nonny Hogrogian
Hōjōki **11**:204
Holden, Ursula 8:97-104
Holden, William **3**:314
Hölderlin, Johann
  Hamburger **4**:163, 167, 169
  Nichols **2**:319
Holding On **5**:128, 129
Holiday
  Bowles **1**:90
  Williams **3**:425-26, 427, 428, 429, 430
Holiday Guide to Rome, The **5**:80
Holland See Netherlands
Hollander, Anne **6**:240-41
Hölldobler, Bert **16**:305
Holleran, Andrew **13**:230
Holliday, Joyce **10**:97, 99
Hollins College
  Dillard **7**:15-16, 18
  Hailey **1**:227, 228
  Taylor **7**:179, 180, 182

Hollins Critic **7**:16
Hollins Writing Conference
  Chappell **4**:122
  Garrett **5**:75
  Taylor **7**:180, 183
Hollo, Anselm **11**:299, 301, 303, 309
Hollywood, Calif.
  Duncan **2**:171-73
  Epstein **12**:60, 63, 67, 72, 75
  Fuchs **5**:55-58
  Wallace **1**:376
Holman, Libby **1**:88-89, 90, 91
Holmes, James Henry **2**:170
Holmes, John
  Ciardi **2**:88, 89, 90
  Corman **2**:133, 136
  Kumin **8**:216
  Weiss **2**:436, 447
Holmes, Sherlock
  Anderson **2**:41, 43
  Keating **8**:164
Holocaust, The
  Federman **8**:64-71
  Grumbach **2**:209
  Heyen **9**:33-34, 43-44
  Josipovici **8**:146
  Katz **9**:62
  Kumin **8**:212
  Lem **1**:256
  Lind **4**:199-203
  Megged **13**:142-43
  Roditi **14**:270
  Wiesel **4**:353-54, 357, 360-61
Holography **8**:190-91
Holt, John **6**:121
Holt, Rinehart & Winston (publishers)
  Boyd **11**:49-50
  Brown **6**:57, 58
Holy Cow: Parable Poems **8**:242
Holy Grail, The **1**:383
Holy Ranger: Harley-Davidson Poems, The **11**:333, 351-52, 353
Holy Sonnets **6**:213
Homage to Adana **2**:271, 272
Homage to Blenholt **5**:64, 65
Homage to Fats Navarro **3**:83
Hombre de paso/Just Passing Through **12**:104
Home **11**:345
Homer
  Dudek **14**:123-24
  Forrest **7**:21
  Harris **16**:123
Homeric Hymns and the Battle of the Frogs and the Mice, The **15**:235
Homo **2**:363
Homosexuality
  Blais **4**:77
  Boyd **11**:43, 46, 47, 51, 54, 57, 58-59
  Bradley **10**:25-26
  Brossard **16**:47-48, 51
  Livesay **8**:226-27, 228
  Peters **8**:245-47
  Picano **13**:222, 226-34

Roditi **14**:244, 248, 251-52, 281
Van Itallie **2**:412
Hong Kong **2**:48-49, 50, 51
Honig, Edwin 8:105-25
  Blaise **3**:20
Honolulu Advertiser **12**:125
Honolulu, Hawaii **12**:123-24
Hons and Rebels See *Daughters and Rebels: An Autobiography*
Hood, Hugh 17:75-94
Hooks, Robert **6**:186
Hoover, Herbert **9**:94
Hope, Donald **9**:83, 84
Hopkins, Gerard Manley
  Brown **6**:71
  Dacey **17**:29, 32
  Ghiselin **10**:133, 135
  Honig **8**:112
Hopkins, Joe **6**:56
Hopkins, Sam "Lightnin'" **7**:33
Hopkinson, Charles **4**:135
Hopscotch **9**:203
Hopwood Award
  Ciardi **2**:89-90
  Kennedy **9**:82, 84
  Piercy **1**:271
  Solotaroff **2**:394, 395
  Stevenson **9**:279
Hora, Josef **1**:341
Horace
  Dudek **14**:123-24
  Tranströmer **17**:264-65
Horáková, Milada **1**:336
Horgbortom Stringbottom, I Am Yours, You Are History **13**:281
Horizons: The Poetics and Theory of the Intermedia **8**:91
Hormel, Al **9**:199, 200, 201
Horn **6**:210, 214, 215
Horn, Edward **14**:263
"Hornblower" series **4**:100
Horne, Hal **1**:192, 193
Horney, Karen **7**:46
Horovitz, Frances **9**:286-87
Horowitz, Vladimir **12**:352
Horse and Jockey **1**:381
Horse Eats Hat **1**:84
"Horse Laugh, The" **1**:381
Horse Show at Midnight, The **7**:181, 182
Horses
  Hoffman **10**:165, 166-67, 169, 170-72
  Jones **11**:177
  Taylor **7**:171-72, 174-77
Horton, Andrew **16**:245-70
Horwood, Harold 15:237-53
Hospital of Transfiguration, The **1**:259
Hot Rock, The **13**:342-43
Hot Rod **7**:158-59
Hotel de Dream **9**:291-92
Hotspur **6**:65, 66
Houghton Mifflin Co. (publishers)
  Davison **4**:141
  Kinsella **7**:104, 105-06
  Mott **7**:132-33

Stegner **9**:267
Wakefield **7**:198
Houghton Mifflin Literary Fellowship
  Kinsella **7**:105, 110
  Petry **6**:264, 265
Hound and Horn **5**:209
Hound of Earth, The **1**:71, 72, 73
Hour before Midnight, The **4**:108
House by the Sea, The **13**:47, 52
House Full of Women, A **15**:160
House of Hospitalities, The **9**:294
House of Leaves, The **16**:281
House of the Seven Gables, The **6**:210
House of the Solitary Maggot, The **1**:303
Housman, A.E. **4**:245
Houston, James D. 16:155-70
  Houston, Jeanne Wakatsuki **16**:175, 180-86
Houston, Jeanne Wakatsuki 16:171-86
  Houston, James D. **16**:157, 163, 164-65, 168-69
Houston, Tex.
  Cassity **8**:57
  Guerard **2**:217
  Shreve **5**:238
How Cities Are Saved **12**:207
How I Blew Up the World **13**:15, 27
How I Escaped from the Labyrinth and Other Poems **17**:27
How I Got Ovah: New and Selected Poems **13**:250
How NOT to Become a Millionaire **2**:145
How to Read **3**:305
How to Write Horror Fiction **16**:221
Howard, Alan **2**:329, 331
Howard, Donald **8**:244
Howard, Elizabeth Jane **4**:82-84
Howard, Peter **2**:210
Howard, Richard
  Disch **4**:156
  Taylor **7**:187
Howard University
  Forbes **16**:118
  Killens **2**:282, 286
  Major **6**:190
Howe, Irving
  Higgins **5**:92-93
  Shapiro **6**:306
  Solotaroff **2**:398
  Sukenick **8**:289-90
Howes, Barbara 3:133-47
Howl
  Eshleman **6**:128
  Saroyan **5**:213
  Škvorecký **1**:346
Howland, Llewellyn **3**:431
Hrabal, Bohumil 12:183-95
  Škvorecký **1**:338
Hu Shih **5**:140-41
Hubbard, L. Ron **8**:321, 325
Huckleberry Finn
  Bell **12**:22
  Dennison **6**:121

Van Brunt **15**:371-72
Hudd, Roy **9**:16
Hueffer, Ford Madox See Ford, Ford
    Madox
Huésped de mi tiempo **15**:11
Hugh MacLennan **6**:323
Hughes, A.M.D. **4**:325-26, 328
Hughes, Carol **1**:29
Hughes, Howard **1**:383
Hughes, Langston
    Atkins **16**:10-11, 13
    Forbes **16**:105, 112
Hughes, Ted
    Abse **1**:28, 29
    Booth **2**:52, 54, 55, 59
    Burroway **6**:90, 91, 92
    Davison **4**:134
    Menashe **11**:235
    Stevenson **9**:280
Hugo Award
    Brunner **8**:9, 11
    Gunn **2**:257
    Niven **12**:211, 213
    Pohl **1**:295
    Silverberg **3**:274, 279, 281, 282
    Wilhelm **5**:309
Hugo, Victor **2**:373
Huis Clos (No Exit) **1**:87
Hull, Betty
    Pohl **1**:296
    Wolfe **9**:308
Hull, Cordell **2**:407
Hull, Helen **2**:288
Hull, Tristram **5**:370
Human Comedy, The **2**:267
Human Like Me, Jesus **11**:54-55
Human Voices **10**:105
Humanism
    Lind **4**:200
    Rimmer **10**:303
Humanoids, The **8**:323, 324
Hummer, Terry **7**:164, 165, 166
Humor **12**:201
Humphrey, William **2**:436, 437,
    438-39
Humphreys, Dick **8**:76
Humphries, Rolfe **6**:90
Huncke, Herbert **6**:132
Hundley, Richard **1**:304
Hungarian Revolution, 1956
    Davie **3**:42
    Sinclair **5**:270
Hungary **5**:196, 197, 198
Hungryalist (bulletin) **14**:89-94
Hungryalist (literary movement)
    14:88-94, 98
Hunted, The **2**:223
Hunter College
    Hahn **11**:110
    Inez **10**:189
    Root **11**:329
    Wakoski **1**:363
Hunter, Evan **11**:28
Huntington Hartford Foundation
    8:134
Huntley, Chet **1**:394

Hurst, Maurice (Capitanchick) **5**:261
Huston, John
    Bowles **1**:87
    Wallace **1**:383
Hutchinson, Anne **10**:304
Hutchinson, Mary St. John **5**:371
Huxley, Aldous
    Aldiss **2**:22
    Allen **6**:17, 23
    Dillard **7**:6
    Easton **14**:148, 159
    Ghiselin **10**:133
Hyman, Mac **4**:115, 116
Hyman, Stanley **7**:294, 302-03
Hyman, Stanley Edgar
    Delbanco **2**:159
    Waldman **17**:273
Hyman, Timothy **8**:157, 158, 160
Hymns to the Night **8**:85
"Hypothetical Arbitrary Constant of
    Inhibition, The" **16**:15

I Am a Camera **2**:411
"I Am Lucy Terry" **16**:67
I Am One of You Forever **4**:124-25
*I Am the Babe of Joseph Stalin's
    Daughter* **2**:364
"I Came to See You But You Were
    Asleep" **2**:70
I Ching **15**:159
I, Claudius **4**:29
I Heard My Sister Speak My Name
    15:337, 339, 342
I, Maximus **3**:90
I Refuse **16**:260-61
I Remember Root River **2**:262, 275
I Served the King of England **12**:193
I Walk the Line **11**:182
I Wanted a Year without Fall **1**:133
Ibsen, Henrik
    Blais **4**:75
    Wallace **1**:391
    White **4**:333
Iceland **9**:184
Idaho **14**:168
Idée d'éternité, l' (The concepts of
    eternity) **13**:181
Identities and Other Poems **13**:139
Idiot, The **4**:148
Idle Hands **11**:207
Idol, The **3**:322
If
    Knight **10**:221
    Pohl **1**:292
If I Go Down to Hell **11**:48
If It Moves, Salute It **2**:168
*If Mountains Die: A New Mexico
    Memoir* **2**:335
*If You Don't Like Me You Can Leave
    Me Alone* **5**:165, 166
Ignatow, David 3:149-61
    Bergé **10**:6
Ignoramus **15**:307
*Ikagnak: The North Wind: With Dr.
    Kane in the Arctic* **8**:248
"Illanna Comes Home" **7**:102

Illinois Institute of Technology
    12:230-31
Illot **14**:91
Illusion, The **4**:100
Illustrated London News **1**:392
Illustrated Weekly of India **9**:233
I'm Talking about Jerusalem **7**:249-50
Imaginary Magnitude **1**:262
Immanuel Kant in England **7**:220,
    224
Immaterial Murder Case, The **3**:389
Immoral Reverend, The **10**:285, 303
Immortal, The **2**:254, 255, 256
Immortal Wife **3**:370
Immortals, The **2**:251, 252, 253, 254,
    258
*Impact 20: Excursions into the
    Extraordinary* **16**:215
Impetus **7**:12
Importance of Being Earnest, The
    7:182
Impotence
    Brunner **8**:10
    Kerrigan **11**:218-19
In a Dark Time **15**:23
In a Green Eye **1**:223
In a Lost World **14**:284
In and Out **15**:224
In Broken Country **3**:411
In Chontales **3**:81, 83
"In Darkness and Confusion" **6**:265
In Defence of Art **14**:135
"In Fact" **6**:171
In Good Time **2**:141
"In My Dreaming" **17**:245
In Search of Eros **15**:151, 157, 158-
    59
In Search of History **6**:172
*In Search of Wonder: Essays on Modern
    Science Fiction* **10**:220
In the Beginning **4**:265
"In the House of Double Minds"
    3:283
In the House of the Judge **7**:165
In the Middle Distance **2**:156, 159
"In the South Seas" **6**:325
In the Trojan Ditch **3**:304, 305
In Transit **4**:85
In Watermelon Sugar **7**:107
*Incas and Other Men: Travels in the
    Andes* **6**:321
Income and Employment **3**:238, 243
*Incomparable Aphra: A Life of Mrs.
    Aphra Behn, The* **6**:321
Incubator on the Rock **13**:153
India
    Aldiss **2**:19, 20-21
    Choudhury **14**:81-99
    Hahn **11**:116, 117-18
    Hauser **11**:130-31
    Keating **8**:171, 172, 174
    Kyger **16**:195
    Mahapatra **9**:137-50
    McCord **9**:183
    Ray **7**:145-46
    Rimmer **10**:291-92

Singh   **9**:223-25, 228-29, 232, 233-35
Skelton   **5**:281-82
Van Itallie   **2**:419
Waldman   **17**:279, 282
Woodcock   **6**:321-22, 324-25
Indian Phantom Play   **11**:131
Indiana University
   Barnstone   **15**:107
   Brewster   **15**:155, 157
   Caute   **4**:105
   Eshleman   **6**:129, 130
   Manuel   **9**:166
   Peters   **8**:241
   Solotaroff   **2**:396
   Wagoner   **3**:403
   West   **7**:281-82
Indiana University Press Poetry
   Series   **3**:404
Indianapolis, Ind.   **6**:125-28
Indianapolis Star   **7**:195
"Individual and Mass Psychology"
   3:140
Indonesia
   Morgan   **3**:242
   Raffel   **9**:210-11
   Swenson   **13**:316
Inez, Colette   10:179-97
Inferno (Larry Niven)   **12**:222
Inferno See *Divine Comedy*
Infinite Worlds   **14**:133
Infinity of Mirrors, An   **1**:197
Inge, William   **2**:173
Ingram Merrill Poetry Writing
   Fellowship   **11**:22
Inheritor, The   **10**:26
Inkling, The   **4**:118, 120
Inkster, Tim   **15**:357
Inman, Philip   **5**:260, 261
Inner Weather   **13**:204
Innes, Michael (pseudonym of J.I.M.
   Stewart)   **3**:348, 352, 353, 354,
   355-56, 357
Innocence   **10**:109
Innocence Is Drowned   **6**:20
Innocent, The   **11**:178-80, 181
Innovative Fiction   **9**:113
Inscripts   **11**:153
Insect Societies, The   **16**:302
Inside Linda Lovelace   **5**:127
Insoumise, L'   **4**:73, 76
Inspector Ghote Breaks an Egg   **8**:172
Inspector Ghote Caught in Meshes
   8:172
Inspector Ghote Draws a Line   **8**:175
Inspector Ghote Goes by Train   **8**:173
Inspector Ghote Hunts the Peacock
   8:172
Inspector Ghote Plays a Joker   **8**:172
Inspector Ghote Trusts the Heart
   8:173
Inspector Ghote's Good Crusade   **8**:172
Institute of American Indian Arts
   17:289
Institute of Design, Chicago, Ill.
   12:342

Instituto Americano, Barcelona,
   Spain   **2**:328
"Intellectual, The"   **6**:299
*Intemperance: The Unexpurgated
   Version*   **9**:186
Interlochen Arts Academy   **11**:328
Intermedia
   Higgins   **8**:94
   Kostelanetz   **8**:186
International Commission on English
   in the Liturgy   **3**:64
International News Service   **3**:122,
   123
International Poetry Festival,
   Rotterdam, Holland, 1977
   6:192
International Poetry Festival, Struga,
   Yugoslavia, 1975   **6**:190-91
International Poetry Forum   **11**:149-
   50
International Pushkin Festival   **2**:305
International Who's Who in Poetry
   9:145
International Writers' Program,
   University of Iowa
   Corman   **2**:145
   Mahapatra   **9**:146-47
Interview   **13**:19
Interview: A Fugue for Eight Actors
   2:414
*Intimate Sex Lives of Famous People,
   The*   **1**:378, 384, 401
*Into Tibet: The Early British
   Explorers*   **6**:325
Introduction to Economics (Theodore
   Morgan)   **3**:238, 241
Introduction to Poetry, An   **9**:85
Intruder, The   **16**:214
Invaders from Earth   **3**:276
Inventory, The   **8**:146-47, 156
Invincible, The   **1**:260, 261
Invisible Man, The
   Bennett   **13**:84
   Forrest   **7**:23
Invocations   **8**:187
Ionesco, Eugene   **12**:158
Iovis: All Is Full of Jove   **17**:290
Iowa   **13**:165-66, 167
Iowa Art Project   **1**:164
Iowa Baseball Confederacy, The   **7**:107
Iowa City Creative Reading Series
   7:102-03
Iowa City, Iowa
   Bell   **14**:48
   Grumbach   **2**:212
Iowa Review   **14**:48
Iowa Short Fiction Award   **12**:246
Iowa State Teacher's College   **1**:163
Iowa Writers' Workshop
   Bausch   **14**:8
   Becker   **1**:39
   Bell   **14**:44-45, 48, 49
   Blaise   **3**:25-26
   Bourjaily   **1**:72, 73, 74, 79
   Cassill   **1**:167-68, 171-72
   Dacey   **17**:27-28

   Grumbach   **2**:212
   Hall   **12**:132-33
   Kinsella   **7**:102, 103
   Ray   **7**:143
   Settle   **1**:320
   Sward   **13**:288-89
   Wright   **7**:297-99
IRA See Irish Republican Army
Iran
   Lessing   **14**:184-86
   Rachlin   **17**:215-29
Ireland
   Arden   **4**:31, 43
   Berrigan   **1**:59
   Davie   **3**:38-39, 42
   Dillon   **3**:49-50
   Galvin   **13**:100, 101
   Nichols   **2**:308
   O'Faolain   **2**:339-46, 350
   Skelton   **5**:292-93
Ireland, Kevin   **3**:257-58, 259, 263
Irgun   **4**:355-56
Irish-Americans
   Ciardi   **2**:86-87
   Higgins   **5**:94-95, 99
Irish Renaissance   **5**:285-86
Irish Republican Army   **3**:56
Irish Signorina, The   **2**:352
Irish Strategies   **11**:210
Iron Pastoral, The   **17**:184
Irresponsibles, The   **8**:301, 308
Irving, John
   Becker   **1**:39
   Blaise   **3**:15, 26
Is Skin-deep, Is Fatal   **8**:172
*Isaac Asimov: The Foundations of
   Science Fiction*   **2**:257
Isherwood, Christopher
   Allen   **6**:18, 27
   Barnstone   **15**:62
   Glanville   **9**:21
   Peters   **8**:244, 250
   Weiss   **2**:443
Ishimoto's Land   **1**:208
*Island in the City: The World of
   Spanish Harlem*   **7**:197
Island of Demons, The   **6**:322
Island of Dr. Moreau, The   **3**:271
Islanders, The   **13**:297
Isle of Arran   **4**:43
Israel
   Goldemberg   **12**:98
   Katz   **9**:64
   Markfield   **3**:222
   Raffel   **9**:216
   Silkin   **5**:258
   Wakefield   **7**:196-97
Istanbul   **2**:361, 363
It Is Time, Lord   **4**:115, 116-17
Italian-Abyssinian War   **2**:309
Italian-Americans   **2**:80-86, 87
Italians
   Jennings   **5**:111-12
   Vivante   **12**:284
Italy
   Booth   **2**:60

Davie **3**:39
Ghiselin **10**:140-43
Glanville **9**:21-23, 24
Katz **14**:170, 171-73
Mrozek **10**:272
Parini **16**:238, 239-40
Pellegrini **11**:262, 265-72
Ray **7**:143
Stone **3**:372-73, 374
Van Brunt **15**:376-77
Wright **7**:295-97, 298, 301-02
It's Easy to Fall on the Ice: Ten Stories
15:160
Ivask, Ivar **2**:367
"I've Had My Fun" **7**:33
Iwamoto, Iwao **12**:164

Jabbing the Asshole Is High Comedy
13:25-26
Jackowski, Andrzej **8**:158, 160
Jackson, Charles **2**:329
Jackson, Glenda **5**:126
Jackson, Hilary Hazlewood **1**:197
Jackson, Jesse **11**:193
Jackson, Joseph Henry **3**:375
Jackson, Mahalia **7**:26, 33-35
Jackson, Richard **15**:288-89
Jackson, Robert **14**:272
Jackson, "Shoeless" Joe **7**:103
Jacob Glatstein Memorial Prize
9:146
Jacob, Max **9**:82
Jacobs, Anthony **12**:12
Jacobs, W.W. **6**:34
Jacobson, Lucien **8**:71, 74
Jaffe, James **12**:348, 350, 353
Jaffe, Marc **1**:295
Jagiellonian University **9**:134
Jake and Honeybunch Go to Heaven
6:154-56
Jakobson, Roman **3**:40
Jakobssen, Ejler **12**:218
Jamaica
Forbes **16**:118-19
Simpson **4**:290
"James at 15" **7**:200-01
James, Edwin (pseudonym of James
Gunn) **2**:249
James, Henry
Bourjaily **1**:72
Burroway **6**:91
Gray **3**:109
Honig **8**:113
Kazin **7**:91
Stewart **3**:355
James, John **8**:244-45
James M. Cain **3**:192
James Shirley's Love's Cruelty **17**:178-
79
James V. Mitchell Memorial Award
for Playwriting **11**:142
Jamison, Judith **7**:31
Janes, Alfred **2**:441
"January" **4**:115
January: A Screenplay **7**:19
Japan

Beltrametti **13**:60-62
Burroway **6**:100
Eshleman **6**:134, 135-37
Kirkup **4**:183-88, 190-91
Kyger **16**:193-96
McPherson **17**:133
Japan Foundation Award **9**:148
Japanese-Americans **16**:171-86
Japan's Mein Kampf **1**:386
Japji **9**:231
Jargon Society (publishers) **12**:340,
348, 349, 352
Jarman, Mark **11**:84
Jarrell, Randall
Hassan **12**:149
Kennedy **9**:84
Root **11**:322
Simpson **4**:293
Sinclair **5**:275
Smith **7**:158, 167
Weiss **2**:447
Jarry, Alfred
Kennedy **9**:82, 83
Slavitt **3**:313
Jauss, David **17**:29-30
Jay, Peter **13**:136, 138
Jazz
Ashby **6**:34
Brunner **8**:6
Dillard **7**:6
Eshleman **6**:126-28
Federman **8**:72-73
Fisher **10**:91-92, 93, 99
Forbes **16**:117
Forrest **7**:29, 30, 31
Hentoff **6**:166, 168, 171
Katz **14**:164
Kerrigan **11**:198
Kirkup **4**:190
Klinkowitz **9**:107, 110, 120
Major **6**:182
Rabassa **9**:198, 203
Škvorecký **1**:328, 339, 348
West **7**:285
Jazz Country **6**:169
Jazz hot, Le **10**:92
Jazz Press **8**:246
Jeffers, Robinson
Anderson **2**:46
Broughton **12**:49-50
Jefferson Reporter **1**:143, 144
Jefferson, Thomas **7**:164
Jefferson's Birthday/Postface **8**:87, 88
Jellinek, Ernst **5**:173-74, 175
Jenkins, David **9**:252
Jennings, Elizabeth **5**:103-15
Jensen, Johannes V. **2**:46
Jeremy's Version **1**:303
Jerome, Judson **8**:127-43
Allen **11**:16
Jerusalem
Jones **5**:125
Wiesel **4**:356, 359
Jerusalem Commands **5**:186
Jesuit order (Society of Jesus) **1**:48
Jesus **1**:59

Jesus Christ **4**:196, 197
Jet **3**:424
Jewish Advocate **4**:137
Jewish-Americans
Corman **2**:129-30
Elman **3**:69
Kazin **7**:86
Markfield **3**:209, 219
Silverberg **3**:270
Solotaroff **2**:391
Jewish Daily Forward **4**:357
Jewish University **9**:62
Jews
Barnstone **15**:48, 49, 73, 92, 97-
98
Becker **1**:33
Brown **10**:42
Davison **4**:134
Epstein **12**:59-76
Federman **8**:64-72
Feirstein **11**:75-77
Goldemberg **12**:93-94, 96-101,
102, 103-06
Gray **2**:183, 188, 191
Hamburger **4**:161, 162, 170
Josipovici **8**:146
Katz **9**:51, 58, 63
Kazin **7**:86
Kumin **8**:205, 208-09, 212
Lifshin **10**:237, 247
Lind **4**:195-97
Megged **13**:141-59
Nichols **2**:317
Raffel **9**:209
Rakosi **5**:194, 196, 197
Roditi **14**:253-54, 276
Rosenblum **11**:341
Salisbury **15**:318, 319
Silkin **5**:244, 247
Simpson **4**:286, 287
Solotaroff **2**:397-99
Sward **13**:282, 284
Van Itallie **2**:405
Vivante **12**:287
Weiss **12**:332-33
Wesker **7**:233-34
Wiesel **4**:353-61
Jews of Silence, The **4**:357
Jews See also Anti-Semitism
Jhabvala, Ruth Prawer **8**:171
Jim Fisk **13**:268
Jiménez, Juan Ramón
Alegría **15**:5-6
Cruz **17**:3, 4, 5-6
Olson **12**:234
J'irai cracher sur vos tombes **8**:72
Jo Stern **3**:322
Joad, C.E.M. **5**:313
Joanne **16**:200
Job's Year **17**:64, 71
Joel, George **1**:72
*Joey: The Life and Political Times of
Joey Smallwood* **15**:252-53
Johannesburg, South Africa
Cassity **8**:49, 52-54, 57
Wright **5**:361, 373

John and Mary **5**:125-26, 128, 129, 131
John and Mary (film) **5**:127-28
John Huston: King Rebel **16**:215
John Lee Taylor: Minister and Missionary **7**:3
John of the Cross, Saint See Juan de la Cruz, San
John Paul I, Pope **7**:50
John W. Campbell Award **2**:257
John XXIII, Pope
  Greeley **7**:44
  Morgan **4**:231
Johns Hopkins University **6**:291, 301-02
Johnson, Andrew **1**:394
Johnson, George Clayton **16**:215, 216
Johnson, Herbert (Hoppie) **3**:418, 419
Johnson, Hewlett **4**:305
Johnson, James Weldon **7**:23
Johnson, Johnnie **9**:107, 120
Johnson, Lyndon
  Knebel **3**:178, 181
  Pohl **1**:291
Johnson, Paul **5**:124
Johnson, Ryerson **10**:219
Johnson, Samuel **4**:114, 116
Johnson, Siddie Jo **1**:225
Johnson, Spud **14**:109, 111
Johnson, William Eugene **13**:277
Johnson, William R. **8**:306
Johnston, George
  Brewster **15**:156
  Corman **2**:144
Joint Defense Appeal **3**:220, 221
Jolas, Maria **12**:199
Jolley, Elizabeth 13:105-23
Jones, E.H. **9**:267
Jones, Ernest **5**:117, 118-19, 120, 129, 130
Jones, James
  Bourjaily **1**:71
  Major **6**:187
  Ray **7**:140-42
  Wright **7**:294
Jones, James Earl
  Giovanni **6**:156
  Wallace **1**:394
Jones, L.E. **1**:38
Jones, LeRoi **1**:363-64
  See Baraka, Amiri
Jones, Loyal **15**:288
Jones, Madison 11:171-87
Jones, Mervyn 5:117-32
Jong, Erica **6**:188
Jonson, Ben **3**:408
Jordan, Fred **3**:322
Jordan, Paul **9**:79, 80
Jordan, Richard **2**:411
Joseph and His Brothers **11**:231
Joseph Conrad **2**:221
Joseph, Michael **6**:22
Joseph, Michael (publishers) **6**:20, 25
Josephy, Alvin **6**:56

Josipovici, Gabriel 8:145-61
Joualonais sa Joualonie, Un **4**:78
Jouffroy, Simon-Théodore **5**:314
Jour est Noir, Le **4**:74
Journal American **2**:400
Journal dénoué(Unbound diary) **13**:188
Journal of an Apprentice Cabbalist, The **14**:284
Journalism
  Allen **11**:8
  Bell **14**:40-41
  Boyd **11**:44, 45, 54
  Easton **14**:155-56
  Glanville **9**:17, 19-20, 24, 26, 28
  Green **11**:96, 97
  Hine **15**:225
  Horwood **15**:245
  Houston **16**:178-79
  Kirk **9**:100
  Knebel **3**:169-70, 176-77, 179-80
  Lottman **12**:201-04
  Megged **13**:156
  Morgan **4**:227, 229-31
  Salisbury **15**:311-13, 315, 321-24
  Shadbolt **3**:262
  Sward **13**:286, 287
  Wiesel **4**:356-58
Journalists, The **7**:256, 260-61
Journals and Dreams **17**:283
"Journey Away, A" **5**:209
Journey in the Month of Av **13**:156, 157
Journey to Chaos **8**:77
Journey to the Land of Gomer **13**:153
Journeying Boy, The **3**:348
Jouve, Pierre Jean **13**:183
Jovanovich, William **4**:134
Joy Makers, The **2**:251, 252, 253, 258
"Joy of Living, The" **16**:212, 217-18, 219
Joyce, James
  Becker **1**:36, 43
  Belitt **4**:54
  Booth **5**:44
  Dillard **7**:14
  Forrest **7**:23
  Jones **5**:121
  Lottman **12**:198, 206
  Pinsky **4**:238
  Pohl **1**:285
  Solotaroff **2**:394-95
  Wallace **1**:375, 391, 396
Joyce, William **2**:312
Juan de la Cruz, San **17**:191
Juana La Loca **1**:317
Judaism
  Bell **14**:37-38
  Fuchs **5**:67
  Goldemberg **12**:95-101
  Hentoff **6**:166, 171
  Josipovici **8**:152
  Kazin **7**:86
  Lem **1**:256
  Piercy **1**:269

  Rimmer **10**:296
  Silkin **5**:246-47
  Škvorecký **1**:327, 329
  See also Cabala
Judd, Donald **5**:216
Jude the Obscure **5**:141
Judgment Day **7**:89
Judson Memorial Church, New York City **6**:117
Judson Poets' Theatre, New York City **2**:360
Juice **1**:36
Junction **15**:160
Jung, Carl
  Howes **3**:140, 142
  Schevill **12**:263-64, 273
  Stone **3**:367, 376
Junges Deutschland **6**:192
Jungle Book, The **13**:167
"Jungle Doctor, The" books **2**:50
Jungwirth, Frantisek **1**:338
Junior Bachelor Society, The **3**:422, 431
Jupus Redeye **17**:50-51, 56
Jurassic Shales, The **13**:281, 295, 296
Jurevitch, Juri **1**:79
Just Space **16**:202
"Just William" series **2**:310
Justice, Donald
  Bourjaily **1**:73
  Wright **7**:297, 299

K-Factor, The **4**:109
Kafka, Franz
  Blaise **3**:19
  Brossard **2**:72, 74
  Harris **3**:130
  Honig **8**:122, 123
  Olson **11**:249, 250
  Škvorecký **1**:347
Kaftanikoff, Luba **9**:281
Kagey, Rudolph **2**:207
Kahawa **13**:343
Kahler, Erich **12**:29, 30, 31, 35, 36
Kahn, Joan **15**:194
Kahn, Michael **2**:412
Kahn, Paul **5**:169
Kahn, Wolf **7**:297, 298
Kalstone, David **6**:239, 250
Kama Sutra **10**:291
Kamaike, Susumu **2**:141, 142
Kamo no Chōmei **11**:204
Kampus **2**:258
Kane **8**:248
Kane, Elisha Kent **8**:248
Kanon, Joe **12**:73
Kansas Alumni **2**:256
Kansas City Art Institute **16**:211
Kansas City, Mo. **5**:305
Kansas City Star **7**:195
Kaprow, Allan
  Higgins **8**:87
  Pinsky **4**:244
Karl, Jean **2**:121, 126
Karl Marx Play, The **2**:358, 361, 363-64, 366

Karp, Sol   **9**:67
Kataoka, Akio   **12**:328
Katz, Debbie   **2**:418
Katz, Fred   **2**:418
Katz, Menke   **9:49-71**
Katz, Steve   **14:161-80**
   Klinkowitz   **9**:112, 116
   Sukenick   **8**:294
Kavanagh, Patrick
   O'Faolain   **2**:345
   Rosenthal   **6**:285
   Wright   **5**:370, 371
Kavanaugh, James   **1**:246
Kavya Bharati   **9**:149
Kawabata, Yasunari   **9**:265
Kay, Bud   **2**:120
Kazan, Elia   **1**:92
Kazin, Alfred   **7:85-96**
   Kennedy   **9**:80
   Markfield   **3**:215, 217, 220, 223
Kearney, Lawrence   **13**:11
Keating, H.R.F.   **8:163-78**
Keats, John
   Abse   **1**:21-22
   Belitt   **4**:64-65
   Brown   **6**:66, 71
   Delbanco   **2**:155
   Hall   **7**:61-62
   Jennings   **5**:106
   Kizer   **5**:147
   Thomas   **4**:313
   Van Brunt   **15**:374
Keele University   **10**:99
Keeley, Edmund   **2**:448
Keene, Donald   **5**:251
Kellett Fellowship   **6**:208
Kelley, William Melvin   **7**:297, 298
Kelly, John   **1**:192
Kelly, Judith   **2**:116
Kelly, Nason & Roosevelt (ad
   agency)   **1**:192
Kelly, Robert
   Eshleman   **6**:131, 134, 142, 147
   Wakoski   **1**:363-64, 369
   Weiss   **2**:442, 443
Kelly, Robert Glynn   **6**:132
Kemp, Penny   **13**:297
Kempton, Murray
   Hentoff   **6**:171
   Wakefield   **7**:196
Kennedy, Jacqueline See Onassis,
   Jacqueline Kennedy
Kennedy, John F.
   Allen   **11**:13-14
   Anaya   **4**:24
   Condon   **1**:196
   Easton   **14**:157
   Hazo   **11**:140-41
   Knebel   **3**:179, 180
   Shreve   **5**:235
   Van Itallie   **2**:412
   Wallace   **1**:394
Kennedy, Joseph, Sr.   **3**:179
Kennedy, Laurie   **6**:215, 218-19, 221
Kennedy, William   **2**:212
Kennedy, X.J.   **9:73-88**

Corman   **2**:138, 145
Kenner, Hugh
   Kyger   **16**:188-89
   Menashe   **11**:236
   Pinsky   **4**:247
Kenny, Elizabeth (Sister Kenny)
   5:239
Kenny, Shirley Strum   **9**:199
Kenosha Times   **1**:376
Kent State University   **11**:17
Kent State University Press   **2**:269
Kenya
   Booth   **2**:49-50
   Morgan   **3**:243
Kenyon College
   Mott   **7**:130
   Thayler   **11**:364
   Turner   **10**:318-21
Kenyon, Jane   **7**:64, 65-66
Kenyon Prize in Philosophy   **12**:327
Kenyon Review
   Feirstein   **11**:84
   Mott   **7**:130
   Pinsky   **4**:241
   Slavitt   **3**:315
   Turner   **10**:318, 320
   Wagoner   **3**:403
Kepler, Johannes   **8**:281
*Kerala: A Portrait of the Malabar
   Coast*   **6**:321-22
Kernan, Alvin   **12**:156, 157
Kerouac, Jack
   Bowering   **16**:28
   Enslin   **3**:92
   Saroyan   **5**:213-14, 217, 219
   Waldman   **17**:279, 283
Kerouac, Jack, School of Disembodied
   Poetics   **17**:283
Kerr, Walter   **2**:415
Kerrigan, Anthony   **11:189-221**
Kerrigan, Elaine
   Cela   **10**:45
   Kerrigan   **11**:199-200
"Kerry Drake"   **4**:146
Kersh, Gerald   **9**:19
Kesey, Ken   **10**:252
Kessenich, Larry   **7**:104, 105, 110
Kessler, Jascha   **11**:212-13
Kettering Review   **8**:141
Key to the Door   **2**:380, 381, 383
Key West, Fla.   **4**:78
Keyes, Daniel   **9**:41
Keyes, Sidney   **5**:365, 366
Keynes, Geoffrey   **5**:283, 293
Keynes, John Maynard
   Morgan   **3**:238
   Rowse   **8**:258
Keyser, Tom   **7**:106
KGB   **12**:314-22
Kherdian, David   **2:261-77**
Kherdian, Nonny Hogrogian   **2**:270,
   273, 274, 275, 276
Kicking the Leaves   **7**:65
Kidd, Virginia
   Knight   **10**:209, 211, 212, 213,
      214, 218, 220, 222

Wolfe   **9**:307, 311, 312
Kienbusch, William   **11**:136-37
Kienzle, William   **1:237-54**
Kierkegaard, Soren
   Gray   **2**:192
   Rakosi   **5**:208
   Ray   **7**:145, 149
   Wilson   **5**:323
Kilgore, Bernard   **7**:196
Killdeer Mountain   **6**:58
Killens, John Oliver   **2:279-306**
Killing Everybody   **3**:128
Killing Floor   **13**:12
Killing Ground, The   **1**:317, 321, 322
Killing of the King, The   **3**:321
Kimball, Richard   **3**:414
Kimm, John   **8**:90
Kimmel, Michael   **2**:329-30
Kimmins, John   **2**:175, 176
*Kind and Usual Punishment: The Prison
   Business*   **17**:150
King, Alex   **1**:38
King, Francis   **4**:84-85
King God Didn't Save, The   **3**:431
King Ludd   **5**:274, 276
King, Margie   **1**:38
King, Martin Luther, Jr.
   Forrest   **7**:26-27
   Nichols   **2**:332
King of Hearts   **3**:322
King of Prussia   **13**:27
King of the Jews   **12**:73, 74, 75
King of the Mountain   **7**:14
King of the United States   **2**:416, 418-
   19
King Solomon's Mines   **11**:374
King, Stephen   **9**:5
King Whistle   **15**:307-08
King, Woodie   **13**:251
Kinglake, William   **2**:27
King's College
   Brewster   **15**:155
   Raworth   **11**:308
Kinnell, Galway
   Ai   **13**:6-8, 9, 10, 12
   Bell   **12**:30, 31-32, 33, 36, 38
   Kizer   **5**:155
   Kumin   **8**:215
   Peters   **8**:246
Kinsella, W.P.   **7:97-111**
Kinsey Institute for Sex Research
   1:389
Kinter, Harold (Doc)   **1**:129-30
Kipling, Rudyard
   Anderson   **2**:46
   Morris   **13**:166-67
Kirk, Russell   **9:89-105**
   Kerrigan   **11**:191, 215
Kirkup, James   **4:175-93**
   Ashby   **6**:42
Kirkus Reviews   **5**:77
Kirkwood, Michael   **10**:323
Kirschenbaum, Blossom   **3**:414-15
Kirstein, George   **7**:196
Kisor, Henry   **1**:43
Kiss of Kin, The   **1**:314, 316

Kissing America **9**:23
Kissing the Dancer **13**:288
Kissinger, Henry **1**:376
Kitaj, R.B. **10**:68
Kitchen Book **12**:81
Kite Protection Committee, Wales
    4:309
Kiyooka, Roy **16**:28
Kizer, Carolyn 5:133-56
"Klail City Death Trip" series
    16:141-43, 151-52
Klass, Philip **10**:210-11, 216
Klee, Paul **2**:197
Kleiber, Otto **11**:130, 132
Klein, Roger **2**:410-11, 415, 417,
    419
Kleine Jazzmusik, Eine **1**:344
Klinkowitz, Jerome 9:107-21
    Federman **8**:80
    Major **6**:196
    Sukenick **8**:291-92
Kluger, Richard **2**:400
Knebel, Fletcher 3:163-84
Knight, Damon 10:199-231
    Disch **4**:150
    Gunn **2**:239, 250, 252
    Moorcock **5**:180
    Niven **12**:216, 217
    Wolfe **9**:305, 306, 307
Knight, David **15**:359
Knight, M.L. **15**:359
Knights of Mark Twain **5**:289
*Knock at a Star: A Child's Introduction
    to Poetry* **9**:86
Knopf, Alfred A. **1**:386, 387, 388,
    389
Knopf, Alfred A. (publishers)
    Bowles **1**:82
    Busch **1**:134
    Disch **4**:156
    Jones **5**:129
    Sillitoe **2**:385
    Sukenick **8**:293
Knotting Sequence, The **2**:57
Know-Nothing **1**:317, 319
Know Your Enemy Japan **1**:380
Knowlton, Perry
    Hauser **11**:127
    Kumin **8**:215
    Nichols **2**:331
Known Homosexual See *Pretty Boy Dead*
Knox, Dillwyn **10**:102
Knox, Edmund V. **10**:103, 104
Knox, Rawle **10**:102
Knox, Ronald **10**:103
Knox, Wilfrid **10**:103
Knoxville, Tenn.
    Madden **3**:195
    White **4**:350
Knye, Cassandra (joint pseudonym of
    Thomas M. Disch and John
    Sladek) **4**:151
Koch, Kenneth
    Knight **10**:214
    Mathews **6**:236
    Raworth **11**:303

Koerber, Martin **8**:189
Koestler, Arthur
    Wakefield **7**:196
    Wallace **1**:385
    Wilson **5**:322
Kogawa, Joy **15**:159
Kohout, Pavel **1**:339
Kolář, Jiří **1**:336, 338
Kolatch, Myron **12**:206
Kollár, Jan **1**:349
Koller, James 5:157-72
    Beltrametti **13**:62, 71
    Kolodin, Irving **7**:81
    Kolodney, John **6**:90
    Kolve, Del **8**:157
    Kolyszko, Anna **6**:201
Kontraption **2**:363, 366
Konwicki, Tadeusz 9:123-35
    Koo, T.Z. **5**:140
    Kopecký, Václav **1**:339
    Korea, South **4**:188
*Korean Love Songs from Klail City
    Death Trip* **16**:143, 151
Korean War
    Baumbach **5**:19-20
    Bennett **13**:83
    Cassity **8**:45-46
    Elman **3**:72
    Hazo **11**:143
    Jones **11**:176
    Kherdian **2**:265-66
    McCord **9**:179-80
    Silkin **5**:258, 259
    Sward **13**:280, 286, 287-88
    Wilson **5**:333, 342, 343-45
    Wolfe **9**:301-03
Kornbluth, Cyril M.
    Knight **10**:206, 207, 211, 212,
        215, 220
    Pohl **1**:290, 293
Kornfeld, Lawrence **6**:117
Kosinski, Jerzy **9**:108, 112, 113-14,
    115, 118
Kostelanetz, Richard 8:179-99
    Federman **8**:79
Kouska, Cezar **1**:255
Koval, Alexander **14**:273-74
Kraków, Poland **1**:259-60
Kramer, Sidney **10**:299, 300
Krapf, Norbert **2**:57, 58
Kraulis, Janis **6**:324
Kraus, Arnošt **7**:212
Kress, Nancy **9**:306
Krim, Arthur **1**:196
Krishnamurti, Jiddu **14**:246
Kroetsch, Robert **16**:28, 30
Kroner, Richard **7**:220
Kroupa, Melanie **2**:126
Krutch, Joseph Wood **4**:59
Kumin, Maxine 8:201-17
    Meredith **14**:220, 221
    Miller **15**:282, 283, 284
    Swenson **13**:313
    Weiss **2**:447
Kumming, Waldemar **8**:13
Kundera, Milan

Barnstone **15**:69
Berrigan **1**:57
Brossard **2**:72
Kunen, James **9**:112
Kunitz, Stanley
    Belitt **4**:52, 65
    Davison **4**:135
Kurtz, Gary **1**:292
Kurtz, Paul **10**:303
Kutnik, Jerzy **6**:200, 201-02
Kuznet, Simon **3**:238
Kwame Nkrumah Ideological
    Institute **13**:46
Kyger, Joanne 16:187-203
    Eshleman **6**:135, 137
    Koller **5**:164, 165-66
    Waldman **17**:283
Kyoto, Japan
    Corman **2**:140-41, 142, 144
    Eshleman **6**:135-37
    Kirkup **4**:190
Kyoto University of Foreign Studies
    4:190

La Motta, Jake **2**:268
*La Traviata in Oklahoma: Selected and
    New Poems, 1961–1991* **15**:383-
    84
Labor unions
    Horwood **15**:243-44
    Ignatow **3**:151-52, 155
    Killens **2**:287, 291
Labors of Love **1**:174
Labour party (Great Britain)
    Arden **4**:44, 46
    Caute **4**:102
    Jones **5**:123
    Rowse **8**:255, 258
Labrador, Canada **15**:244-45
Lacotte, Muriel **6**:195-96, 198, 200
Ladies' Home Journal **5**:152
Ladies, The **2**:212-13
Lady Chatterley's Lover
    Jones **5**:127
    Mano **6**:212
Lafayette College **16**:230
Lagerlöf, Selma
    Lind **4**:200
    Wallace **1**:390
Lal, P. **9**:145-46
Lamb, Catherine **5**:263
Lamb, Charles **4**:305
Lambert, Dorothy **8**:212
Lament for a Maker **3**:354
Lament for Arthur O'Leary, The **3**:62-
    63
*L'Amèr ou le Chapitre effrité: Fiction
    théorique* **16**:50
Lamerhav (magazine) **13**:155
Lamont Award
    Ai **13**:12
    Kennedy **9**:84
Lampasas Dispatch **14**:155-56
Lancaster, Osbert **14**:244
Land of Lost Content, The **13**:205,
    211

Land of Manna **9**:51, 55
Landauer, Jerry **7**:195
Landesman, Jay **2**:69
Landfall (David Wagoner) **3**:411
Landis, Jim **2**:156
Landlocked Man, The **9**:5
Landor, Walter Savage **4**:247, 249
Landor's Poetry **4**:247
Landscape in Concrete **4**:202
Landscape of Nightmare, The **5**:23, 24
Landscape of the Mind **10**:121
Lang, Bob **9**:199, 200
Lang, Daniel **2**:63
Lang, Margaret Altschul **2**:63, 64, 65, 76
Language in Thought and Action **8**:132
Lansky, Bruce **1**:252
Laocoön **8**:94
Lardner, Ring **9**:26
Larkin, Philip
    Ashby **6**:42
    Davie **3**:39
    Glanville **9**:25
    Wain **4**:328-29
Lars, Claudia **15**:3
Larsen, Erling **8**:307
Laski, Harold **5**:141
Last and Lost Poems of Delmore Schwartz **13**:212
Last Beautiful Days of Autumn, The **2**:335
Last Dangerous Visions, The **2**:258
Last Good Time, The **14**:12
Last of the Country House Murders, The **9**:291-92
Last of the Just, The **1**:38
Last of the Moccasins, The **11**:278, 287, 291, 295
Last Poems **12**:237
Last Rites: The Death of William Saroyan **5**:217, 218
Last Station, The **16**:240-41
Last Things **11**:185-86
Last White Class, The **1**:278
Laster, Owen **3**:322
Late in the Season **13**:232-33
Late Settings **4**:78
Latimer, Margery **5**:202-03
Latin **6**:226
Latin American Book Fair **12**:105
Latin American Writers Institute **12**:105
Lattimore, Richmond **6**:100
Laughing Lost in the Mountains: Poems of Wang Wei **15**:65, 92
Laughing Stalks **14**:133
Laughlin, Clarence John **12**:346
Laughlin, James
    Allman **15**:25-26, 27, 30
    Brossard **2**:66
    Busch **1**:133
    Cassill **1**:169
    Honig **8**:113
    Major **6**:192
    Olson **11**:257, 259

Purdy **1**:304
    Roditi **14**:269
    Whittemore **8**:310
Laughter! **12**:3
Laurels of Lake Constance, The **6**:242-43
Lauterer, Arch **4**:63, 65
Laval University, Quebec City, Canada **4**:72
L'aviva **16**:54
Lawrence, D.H.
    Allen **6**:17
    Brown **6**:71, 74
    Ghiselin **10**:131, 141, 142
    Jones **5**:127
    Kennedy **9**:73
    Kizer **5**:140
    Mano **6**:212
    Sillitoe **2**:384
    Wallace **1**:396, 397
    Wellek **7**:222
Lawrence, Frieda **10**:131, 133
Lawrence, Judith Ann **10**:225
Lawrence, Seymour
    Davison **4**:135-36
    Wakefield **7**:200
Lawrence, Thomas Edward (Lawrence of Arabia) **2**:56
Layachi, Larbi **1**:92
Laying Down the Tower **1**:276
Layton, Irving
    Dudek **14**:128, 132
    Purdy **17**:204, 205
    Souster **14**:310, 314-15
Lazard, Naomi **5**:155
Le Braz, Anatole **2**:321
le Carré, John **8**:4
Le Rougetel, Yvonne **9**:232
Leadbeater, Mary Shackleton **15**:155
League of Canadian Poets
    Brewster **15**:159
    Sparshott **15**:357-58
League of Nations **5**:247
"Leap Minnows, Leap" **17**:244-45
Lear, Edward
    Broughton **12**:45
    Keating **8**:167
Leary, Timothy **11**:287
Leaves of Grass
    Kennedy **9**:76
    Shapiro **6**:289, 304
Leavis, F.R.
    Davie **3**:35, 36
    Glanville **9**:13
    Gray **3**:108-09
    Mano **6**:209
LeClair, Thomas **8**:293
Lee, Al **7**:297
Lee, Ann **8**:247
Lee, Laurie **1**:28
Leeds, Barry **9**:41
Leeds University
    Kennedy **9**:85
    Skelton **5**:282-83
Leeming, Glenda **7**:227

Left Bank: Writers, Artists, and Politics from the Popular Front to the Cold War, The **12**:208
Left in Europe since 1789, The **4**:105
Legacy of Heorot, The **12**:221
LeGallienne, Eva **2**:206
Legends **5**:325
Legion of Decency **4**:146
Legion of Honor **15**:144
Legouis, Emile **6**:36
Lehman College **15**:26, 28
Lehmann-Haupt, Christopher **6**:186
Lehmann, John
    Allen **6**:21
    Jennings **5**:110
    Raffel **9**:213
    Wright **5**:369
Lehr, Anne **2**:118, 119
Lehrnman, Nat **6**:217
Leiber, Fritz **10**:213
Leicester, England **1**:217-19
Leighton, Martin **2**:299-300, 301-02, 303
LeLionnais, François **6**:247
Lem, Stanislaw **1**:255-66
LeMay, Curtis **3**:179-80
Lemmon, Jack **9**:249, 250
Lenard, Philipp **1**:391
Leningrad, USSR
    Corcoran **2**:123-24
    Salisbury **15**:323-24
Leonard, John **3**:80
Leone, Len **1**:295
"Lepanto" **5**:106
Lessing, Doris **14**:181-204
    Cassity **8**:54-55
    Jones **5**:122-23, 124, 126, 130
Lessing, Gotthold Ephraim **8**:94
Lestriad, The **14**:171, 172, 179
Let Us Now Praise Famous Men **4**:215
"Let's Pretend" (radio program) **4**:144
Letter to the Past **6**:326
Letters from Hollywood **5**:184
Letters Home (Michael Andre) **13**:22
Letters of John Addington Symonds, The **8**:241
Letters to a Young Poet **1**:24, 25
Letters to Five Artists **4**:330
Letters to Louise **15**:177
Letters to Martha **14**:56, 59-60, 62, 63
Lettres Nouvelles Award, Les **1**:212
Levertov, Denise
    Abse **1**:26
    Corman **2**:137
    Inez **10**:191
    Kizer **5**:145
    Peters **8**:242
Lévesque, Georges-Henri **4**:72, 73
Levey, Michael **4**:81, 82, 83, 84, 86, 87, 88, 89, 90, 92, 93
Levin, Harry **8**:214, 215
Levin, Meyer **3**:222
Levin, Yehuda-Leib **4**:358
Levine, Fran **3**:429

Levine, Philip
   Ai **13**:10
   Williams **3**:429
Lewicki, Zbigniew **6**:201
Lewis, Alun **2**:20
Lewis and Clark College, Portland,
      Ore. **3**:334
Lewis and Clark Expedition **6**:47
Lewis, C.S.
   Aldiss **2**:24
   Jennings **5**:108
   St. Clair **8**:280
   Wain **4**:326-27, 328, 329
Lewis, Doc **1**:70
Lewis, Meade Lux **10**:91
Lewis, R.W.B. **11**:51, 52, 53
Lewis, Sinclair
   Booth **5**:35, 40, 49
   Wakefield **7**:194
Lewis, W.H. **4**:328
Lewis, Wyndham
   Allen **6**:23-24
   Symons **3**:384-85, 388
Lexicographic Study of Tayabas Tagalog,
   A **9**:163
Liaison Parisienne, Une **4**:78
Liberaki, Rita **15**:93
Liberal party (Great Britain) **5**:178
Liberated, The **3**:321
Liberation **6**:116, 119
Liberia **3**:181
Liberman, Alexander **2**:187-88, 189,
      191, 192-93, 196, 200
Liberman, Simon **2**:190-93
Libertarian party **8**:191
Liberté **13**:184
Liberty **1**:378
Librarianship **17**:237-39
Library of Congress
   Bowles **1**:92
   Caldwell **1**:154
   Davison **4**:139
   Honig **8**:110
   Meredith **14**:223, 231
   Shapiro **6**:301
   Whittemore **8**:308, 311
"Library, The" **17**:164
Liddell, Alice **3**:322
Liddy, G. Gordon **1**:319
Lieberman, Laurence **7**:164
Lieberman, Saul **4**:357, 358-59
Liebknecht, Karl **5**:194
Life
   Caldwell **1**:149
   Markfield **3**:220
   Slavitt **3**:320
   Wallace **1**:397
   Wilson **5**:321
Life and Times of Major Fiction, The
   5:29
Life Goes On **2**:387
Life in the West **2**:30
Life Is a Dream **8**:117
Life of Fiction, The **9**:113, 117
Life of Jesus, The **11**:242, 247, 257
Life of Madame Rolland, The **1**:116

Life on the Mississippi **1**:316
"Life, People—and Books" **3**:389
Life Sentences **1**:233, 234
Life Signs **9**:148
Lifeitselfmanship, or How to Become a
   Precisely-Because Man **17**:142-43
Lifshin, Lyn **10**:233-63
Lifton, Robert **1**:62
Light in the Dust **7**:236
Light in the West **8**:135
Lillooet **15**:155
Lilly, Doris **3**:318
Lilo's Diary **3**:74
Limners Society of Artists **5**:290
Lincoln, Abraham
   Hentoff **6**:173
   Pinsky **4**:237
Lincoln Memorial University
   17:235-36
Lind, Jakov **4**:195-204
Lindbergh, Charles **3**:193
Lindenberger, Herbert **8**:244
Lindon, Jérôme **4**:357
Lindsay, Vachel
   Harris **3**:122, 126, 127, 132
   Kizer **5**:141-44
Linetsky, Louis **10**:298-99
Ling, Amy **16**:145
Linhartová, Věra **1**:338
Linklater, Eric **6**:67
Lion Books **1**:169
Lion on the Mountain, A **2**:122
Lippincott, J.B. (publishers) **7**:81
Lispector, Clarice **9**:203
Listen: Gerry Mulligan **9**:108, 120
Listen to the Wind **15**:307
Listeners, The **2**:255, 256, 257
Literary criticism
   Hazo **11**:152-53
   Saroyan **5**:219
Literary Disruptions: The Making of a
   Post-Contemporary American
   Fiction **9**:115, 116
Literary Guild
   Wagoner **3**:408
   Wallace **1**:388
Literary Subversions: New American
   Fiction and the Practice of
   Criticism **9**:118
Literatura na Świecie **6**:201
Literature: An Introduction to Fiction,
   Poetry, and Drama **9**:85
Literature of Silence: Henry Miller and
   Samuel Beckett, The **12**:152
Lithuania
   Budrys **14**:65
   Katz **9**:49-53, 65
Little, Brown & Co. (publishers)
   Bowles **1**:92
   Davison **4**:136, 138
   Stegner **9**:264
   Williams **3**:428, 431
"Little Elegy" **8**:227-28
Little Lives **3**:80
Little Night Music, A **2**:419
Little People's Magazine **2**:113

Little Portia **3**:109, 111
Little Review **5**:203
Little Richard **7**:159-60
Little Theater movement **1**:310
Little Time for Laughter, A **9**:5
Little, Vera **6**:195
Little Women **6**:254
Littleton, Taylor **11**:183
Litvinoff, Emanuel **5**:261-62, 263
Liverpool, England **2**:308-09, 313
Lives of Children: The Story of the First
   Street School, The **6**:119
Lives of Riley Chance, The **14**:28-29,
   30
Lives to Give **4**:233
Livesay, Dorothy **8**:219-36
   Brewster **15**:157
Living **6**:18
Living in America **9**:283
Living on the Dead, The **13**:154
Living Shall Praise Thee, The
   11:135-36
Living Space **6**:21
Living Theater **6**:116
Living Upstairs **17**:64, 65, 72
Livingston, Myra Cohn **9**:86
Livingstone, Angela
   Davie **3**:44
   Feinstein **1**:221
Llandaff Theological College, Wales
   4:304
Llewellyn, Richard **3**:403
Lobrano, Gus **2**:65
Local Assays: On Contemporary
   American Poetry **7**:165
Lockwood, Lee **1**:59
Locus Solus **6**:236
Loeff, Ted **1**:388
Loew's Inc./MGM **2**:208
Lofting, Hugh **2**:310
Loftis, Norman **6**:189
Logan, John
   Bell **14**:43-44
   Dacey **17**:23-24, 32
   Heyen **9**:42
   Root **11**:321
Logan's Run **16**:215, 216, 218-21
Logic **10**:328, 330
Logue, Christopher
   Connell **2**:108
   Wright **5**:370
Lohner, Ed **2**:136
Lomax, S.P. **3**:427
London, England
   Abse **1**:24, 27
   Allen **6**:22
   Booth **2**:51
   Cassity **8**:55
   Corcoran **2**:124
   Hamburger **4**:163
   Kazin **7**:93
   O'Faolain **2**:347-48
   Salisbury **15**:322-23
   Settle **1**:313, 314, 315
   Sinclair **5**:271
   Wesker **7**:228, 238-39

Woodcock **6**:318
London, Jack
    Stone **3**:370, 373
    Thayler **11**:359
    Whittemore **8**:310
London School of Economics **16**:278
London University *See* University of
    London
Loneliness of the Long-Distance Runner,
    The **2**:381, 382, 384, 385, 386
Long Branch, N.J. **4**:237-38, 241
Long Hot Summers of Yasha K., The
    12:243, 248
Long Island Light **9**:32
Long Island University
    Olson **11**:255, 256
    Škvorecký **1**:347
Long Journey, The **2**:121
Long Naked Descent into Boston, The
    1:212
Long Road South, A **4**:350
Long Talking Bad Conditions Blues
    8:294
Long Undressing, A **12**:41
Long Walk to Wimbledon, A **8**:175-76
Longest Voyage, The **3**:279
Longfellow, Henry Wadsworth **3**:399
Longing in the Land: Memoir of a
    Quest, A **10**:147, 148, 162
Longinus **6**:280
Longman, Inc. (publishers)
    Stone **3**:369
    Wallace **1**:389
Longview Foundation **11**:231
Look
    Brossard **2**:68, 69, 70
    Elman **3**:74
    Knebel **3**:171, 179
    Settle **1**:315
    Stegner **9**:266
Look at Lightning, A **4**:63
Look Back in Anger **7**:240
Look Homeward, Angel **4**:207
"Look Up and Live" **2**:412
Looking Ahead: The Vision of Science
    Fiction **11**:19
Looking for Philosophy **15**:360
Looking for the Rainbow Sign **2**:60
Looking Over Hills **2**:273
Lopate, Phillip **11**:255-56
Lopez-Morillas, Juan **8**:180
Lord Jim **8**:303-04
Lord, John Vernon **6**:99
Lord of Darkness **3**:285
Lord of the Dance **7**:44
Lord of the Flies **9**:293
Lord of the Hollow Dark **9**:103
Lord of the Rings, The **9**:103-04
Lord Richard's Passion **5**:129
Lord Valentine's Castle **3**:285
Los Angeles, Calif.
    Brown **10**:34-35
    Connell **2**:107
    Corcoran **2**:118-20
    Eastlake **1**:201
    Easton **14**:146

Eshleman **6**:146
O'Faolain **2**:349
Rechy **4**:264
Thayler **11**:355, 360-61
Los Angeles City College **11**:362
Los Angeles Science Fantasy
    Society **12**:213-15
Los Angeles Science Fiction Society
    16:212
Los Angeles Times Book Award
    14:220
Los Angeles Times Book Review **6**:147
Los Angeles Valley College **15**:209
Lost Cities and Vanished Civilizations
    3:277
Lost Horizon **1**:381
Lost Island, The **3**:57
Lost on Twilight Road **17**:67
Lost Race of Mars **3**:277
Lotbinière-Harwood, Susanne de
    16:39-57
Lottman, Eileen **12**:201
Lottman, Evan **12**:197, 201, 203
Lottman, Herbert R. **12**:197-209
Lotus Press **5**:283
Louisiana State University Press
    Chappell **4**:122, 124-25
    Taylor **7**:181
Louisville, Ky. **5**:303, 305
Loup, Le **4**:77
Love and War: Pearl Harbor through
    V-J Day **14**:143-5, 154, 159
Love Comes to Eunice K. O'Herlihy
    2:126
Love Eaters, The **1**:315, 316
Love Explosion, The **10**:302
Love in Amsterdam **12**:83
Love Letter from an Impossible Land
    14:226
Love Letters on Blue Paper **7**:243,
    247-48, 249, 250-51
Love Life **16**:168
Love Me Tomorrow **10**:300, 301
"Love of Life" **1**:231
Love Run, The **16**:236, 237
Lovecraft, H.P.
    Chappell **4**:119
    Silverberg **3**:271, 272, 274
Lovelace, Linda *See* Marciano, Linda
    Boreman
Lovelock, Jim **2**:31
Lovelock Version, The **3**:251, 265
Lover, The **11**:55
Lovers and Tyrants **2**:186, 190, 194,
    195, 198, 199
Loves of Carmen, The **1**:194
Loving Power: Stories **17**:50
Loving Strangers **3**:81, 82
Low Company **5**:56
Lowell, Amy **8**:228
Lowell, Robert
    Chappell **4**:118, 120
    Cruz **17**:9
    Galvin **13**:91, 99
    Ghiselin **10**:133
    Olson **12**:233

Pinsky **4**:245, 248-49
Raffel **9**:219
Rosenthal **6**:276, 284
Simpson **4**:293
Stevenson **9**:283
Weiss **2**:444
Lowen, Alexander **4**:153
Lowenfels, Lillian **6**:187
Lowenfels, Walter **6**:183, 187
Lowenkopf, Shelly **10**:298
Lowes, John Livingston **7**:218
Lowndes, Robert W. **10**:203, 205,
    206, 207-08, 211, 215, 216
Lowrey, Perrin Holmes **7**:23
Lowry, Jane **2**:412
Lowry, Malcolm
    Delbanco **2**:158
    Purdy **17**:203
Loyola University **15**:5
Lucas, John **8**:306
Luce and His Empire **13**:269, 271,
    272, 273
Luce, Henry
    Barrio **15**:124
    Swanberg **13**:269-72
Lucie ou un midi en novembre (Lucie
    or a November afternoon)
    13:186, 189
Lucifer's Hammer **12**:219, 220
Lucky Alphonse, The **8**:176
Ludlum, Robert **9**:4-5
Ludwig **8**:247, 248, 249, 250
Luisa Domic **6**:107-08, 121-22
Luisa in Realityland **15**:1, 2, 13
"Lullaby" **5**:110
Lumpkin, Grace **6**:53
Lumsden, Charles J. **16**:304
Lunar Attractions **3**:18, 22, 24
Lunar Cycle, The **1**:278
Lunn, Brian **4**:338
Lunsford, Bascom Lamar **15**:274,
    278, 287, 288, 290
Lure, The **13**:229-30
Lust for Life **3**:369-70, 373
Lustgarten, Edgar **3**:111
Lusts **3**:18, 22, 26, 29
Lutheranism
    Smith **7**:155
    Wellek **7**:209
Luxemburg, Rosa **5**:194
Lyn Lifshin: A Critical Study **10**:258
Lynds, Dennis **3**:422, 423
Lynn, Margaret **3**:332
Lyon, Elizabeth **10**:4-5
Lyon, George Ella **15**:288-89
Lyrics for the Bride of God **16**:281
Lysenko, Trofim **1**:259
Lytle, Andrew
    Ghiselin **10**:136-37
    Jones **11**:178
    Whittemore **8**:307

Maas, Willard **17**:97, 98, 99
Mabinogion, The **4**:307
Mac Low, Jackson
    Bergé **10**:7

INDEX

Weiss **2**:442
MacArthur, Douglas **2**:168
MacArthur Fellowship **17**:123, 126
MacArthur Foundation **15**:235
MacArthur, Robert H. **16**:299-300
Macauley, Robie
    Mott **7**:130, 132
    Whittemore **8**:307
Macbeth
    Corman **2**:132
    Jennings **5**:108
MacBeth, George **2**:52, 55, 58, 60
MacDiarmid, Hugh
    Rosenthal **6**:285
    Turnbull **14**:333, 336
Macdonald, Ross **3**:204
MacDowell Colony
    Bergé **10**:16
    Peters **8**:247
    Sward **13**:290, 291, 295
MacFadden Publications **1**:378
MacInnes, Helen **9**:5
Maciunas, George **8**:87, 92
Mackay, Shena **4**:87, 88-89, 92
MacKenzie, Rachel **12**:298-99
MacLeish, Archibald
    Becker **1**:41
    Hall **7**:62
    Hazo **11**:149, 150, 152
    Honig **8**:110, 114
    Jerome **8**:138
    Olson **12**:234
    Settle **1**:319
    Swanberg **13**:269, 275
    Whittemore **8**:301, 306, 308
Macleod, Fiona **4**:304
MacManus, Francis **6**:284
Macmillan Publishing Co.
    Rosenthal **6**:277, 279, 285
    Thomas **4**:310
    Weiss **2**:433
MacNeice, Louis
    Allen **6**:20, 21
    Barnstone **15**:75-76, 77
"MacNeil-Lehrer Newshour" **2**:213
Macon Telegraph **1**:142
Macpherson, Jay
    Brewster **15**:156
    Sparshott **15**:356, 362
Macrae, Jack **3**:322
Macrae-Smith (publishers) **6**:54
Mad River Review **11**:15
Madame Bovary **11**:376
Madame Butterfly **10**:158
Madame President **1**:383
Madden, David **3**:185-206
Mademoiselle
    Burroway **6**:87-88, 91
    Grumbach **2**:208
Madison Square Garden, New York
    City **3**:424
Madison, Wis.
    Morgan **3**:244
    Rakosi **5**:204
"Madly to Learn" **17**:246
Madrid, Spain

Condon **1**:195
    Wallace **1**:380
Maeda, Jun **2**:421
Maes-Jelinek, Hena **16**:132, 134-35
Magazine of Fantasy and Science Fiction
    Budrys **14**:70-71, 78
    Malzberg **4**:208, 216
Magellan of the Pacific **14**:283-84
Maggot: A Novel **17**:46, 51, 55, 56
Magic and magicians
    Hitchcock **12**:168, 173-74, 181
    Shadbolt **3**:255
    Wagoner **3**:400
Magic Cup, The **7**:50
Magic Journey, The **2**:335
Magic Mountain, The
    Lem **1**:259
    Turner **10**:318
Magician's Girl, The **2**:213
Magicians, The **2**:258
Magnet
    Ashby **6**:34
    Brown **6**:66
    Nichols **2**:312-13
Magnus **6**:72
Magog **5**:274
Magritte, René-François-Ghislain
    5:195
Mahaffey, Bea **2**:40
Mahapatra, Jayanta **9**:137-50
Maharani's New Wall, The **7**:145-46
Mahler, Gustav **3**:94, 95
Maiden of the Buhong Sky, The **9**:164
Mailer, Norman
    Bourjaily **1**:70-71, 72
    Boyd **11**:51-52, 53
    Caute **4**:103, 105
    Clarke **16**:83, 84
    Garrett **5**:77
    Hassan **12**:159
Mainland **17**:11-13
Mairet, Philip **3**:299, 301
Majestic Theater, New York City
    4:148
Majipoor Chronicles **3**:285
Major, Clarence **6**:175-204
    Baumbach **5**:29
    Katz **14**:176
    Klinkowitz **9**:113, 116
    Sukenick **8**:293
Make No Sound **2**:126
Make, Vusumzi **2**:298-99
Makeup on Empty Space **17**:286
Making of the Popes 1978, The **7**:50
Malacia Tapestry, The **2**:31
Malahat Review **5**:287, 291
Malamud, Bernard
    Baumbach **5**:24
    Becker **1**:40, 41
    Belitt **4**:53, 65
    Blaise **3**:19, 23, 24-25
    Delbanco **2**:159
    Sukenick **8**:285
    Waldman **17**:273
Malanga, Gerard **17**:95-120
Malaya **2**:376-77, 378-79, 380

Malcolm **1**:302, 304
Malcolm Boyd's Book of Days **11**:51
Malcolm, Janet **1**:97
Malcolm X
    Clarke **16**:84, 86
    Killens **2**:296, 297, 303
    Williams **3**:427
Malcolm X City College **13**:248
Malheurs de Sophie, Les **2**:184
Malina, Judith **6**:116
Malinowski, Bronislaw, Marshal
    1:333
Mallorca, Spain
    Alegría **15**:12-13
    Green **11**:87, 99-106
    Sillitoe **2**:382-84
Mallot, Hector **11**:127
Malone Dies **7**:284
Malraux, André
    Becker **1**:40
    Belitt **4**:60
    Brée **15**:137
    Forrest **7**:29
    Morgan **4**:232
Maltese Falcon Award **16**:220
Malzberg, Barry N. **4**:205-22
    Pohl **1**:285
Man and the Future **2**:253, 255
Man-Eaters of Kumaon, The **2**:50
Man from Porlock, The **2**:449
Man in the Cellar **2**:346, 352
Man in the Maze, The **3**:279
Man in Yellow Boots, The **16**:28
*Man of Letters in the Modern World,
    The* **8**:185
Man of the Thirties, A **8**:260
Man Plus **1**:294
Man, The **1**:384, 393-95
Man to Conjure With, A **5**:23-24
Man Who Came to Dinner, The **2**:410
Man Who Cried I Am, The **3**:421,
    427, 428, 429, 430, 431, 432
Man with Blue Eyes, The **4**:152
Manafon, Wales **4**:306-08, 309, 310
Manchester Evening News **3**:389
Manchester Institute of Contemporary
    Arts **5**:284
Manchester University **5**:283, 286
Manchurian Candidate, The **1**:196
Mangione, Jerre **6**:53
Manhattan Carnival **11**:78, 79, 81,
    83, 84
Manhattan Elegy & Other Goodbyes
    11:78, 84-85
Manhattan Theater Club **2**:418
Manhattan Transfer **6**:48
Manhunt **11**:28-29, 30
Manion, Clarence **11**:142, 143
Maniquis, Bob **4**:243, 244, 247
Mankind under the Leash **4**:151
Mann, Thomas
    Becker **1**:36, 43, 45
    Blaise **3**:19
    Disch **4**:157
    Fisher **10**:93
    Konwicki **9**:129

Lem **1**:259
Menashe **11**:227, 230-31
Turner **10**:318
Manning, Gordon **3**:317
Manning, Olivia **6**:20
Manning, Robert **7**:197-98
Manny, Frank A. **2**:135
Mano, D. Keith 6:205-21
Manocalzati, Italy **2**:80, 83
Mansfield, Katherine
Brewster **15**:153, 160
Shadbolt **3**:259
Manual Labor **1**:133
Manuel, Al **1**:150, 151
Manuel, E. Arsenio 9:151-69
Manulis, Martin **7**:200
Manuscrits de Pauline Archange, Les
4:72
Manuvu' Custom Law **9**:168
Manuvu' Social Organization **9**:165
Many Named Beloved, The **11**:233,
235
Manzanar **16**:175-77, 184-85
Mao Tse-tung
Barnstone **15**:70
Wallace **1**:401
Maori **7**:148
Mappin, Hubert **4**:309-10
Maps **11**:256
Maquisard **2**:224-25
Marburg Chronicles, The **9**:5-6, 9-10
Marcel, Gabriel **11**:210
Marciano, Linda Boreman **5**:127-28
Marcus, Mort **13**:300
"Mardi Gras" **4**:260
Marek, Richard **1**:78
Margins
Owens **2**:366
Peters **8**:248
Margolis, Herbert **10**:298
Marie Antoinette **4**:261
"Marie of the Cabin Club" **6**:264
Marilyn's Daughter **4**:265
Marín, Luis Muñoz **17**:3, 4
Mark Lambert's Supper **3**:355, 356
Mark of Vishnu, The **9**:230
Markfield, Wallace 3:207-27
Markish, Peretz **4**:360
Marks, J See Highwater, Jamake
Marlatt, Daphne
Brossard **16**:54
Eshleman **6**:138
Marlborough School, Los Angeles,
Calif. **2**:120
Marlowe, Christopher **10**:285-86
Marquand, John P. **9**:5
Marquette University **9**:110
Marquez, Velia **9**:204
Marquis, Don **8**:131
Married Land, The **12**:19-20, 31, 36,
37, 38
Married to a Stranger **17**:228
Marsh, Edward **5**:255
Marsh, Ngaio **15**:195
Marshall, Robert K. **8**:241
Marshall, William **6**:182

Marteau, Robert **13**:185, 188
Martha's Vineyard, Mass. **2**:158
Martial arts
Hauser **11**:137
Rosenblum **11**:348
Turner **10**:320
Martin, John
Arden **4**:39
Bergé **10**:10
Wakoski **1**:368
Martin, Knox **4**:156
Martin, Sandy **8**:215
Martinelli, Sheri **6**:180, 188
Martines, Lauro **2**:349-51, 352
Martingale **5**:351
Martlet's Tale, The **2**:156, 159
Marvell, Andrew **7**:216
Marvell Press **3**:39
Marx, Harpo **14**:254-55
Marx, Karl
Owens **2**:364
Pohl **1**:286
Marxism
Anaya **4**:26
Caute **4**:102, 105
Davie **3**:43
Fuller **10**:113
Konwicki **9**:126-27, 134
Nichols **2**:332
Rakosi **5**:208
Rowse **8**:255
Shadbolt **3**:258
Solotaroff **2**:394
Wilson **16**:301, 303-04
Zinoviev **10**:329
See also Communism
Mary Myth, The **7**:50
Maryško, Karel **12**:193
Masaccio **14**:170, 171
Masefield, John **11**:90
Mask of Dust **4**:342
Mask, The **11**:304
Masks of Time, The **3**:279, 281
Maslow, Abraham
Rimmer **10**:299
Wilson **5**:324
Mason, Mason Jordan **14**:117
Mason, Ronald **3**:256, 258
Masquerade **11**:83
Massa (magazine) **13**:153
Massachusetts Institute of Technology
Vivante **12**:302
Weiss **2**:447
Massachusetts Review **5**:286
Massachusetts School of Art **2**:132
Masses **7**:91
Massillon, Ohio **3**:397-98
Master and Margarita, The **11**:376
Master Entrick **7**:130
Master Minds **8**:186, 195
Master of Her Fate **11**:104
Master of Life and Death **3**:276
"Master of None" **7**:188
"Masterson and the Clerks" **4**:151
Mataga, William **4**:250
Matera, Italy **2**:139, 140

Materials, The **3**:93
Mathesius, Vilém **7**:214, 222, 223
Matheson, Richard **16**:212, 213
Mathews, Harry 6:223-52
Mathews, Jackson **11**:213
Matos, Luis Pales **17**:7, 12
Matrix **10**:99
Matson, Harold (literary agents) **6**:57
Matsuoka, Yosuke **1**:380
Matthau, Walter **5**:213
"Matthew Scudder" series **11**:35, 38,
39-40
Matthews, Jack 15:255-71
Heyen **9**:41, 42
Smith **7**:163, 164
Matthiessen, F.O. **10**:66, 68
Maugham **4**:234
Maugham, W. Somerset
Green **11**:95-96, 102
Jennings **5**:111
Morgan **4**:234
Settle **1**:315
Sinclair **5**:269
Wakefield **7**:194
Wallace **1**:391
Maule, Harry **1**:167, 168
Mauriac, François
Blais **4**:72
Wiesel **4**:353, 356-57
Mauve Desert **16**:42, 44, 53
Mavericks **1**:27
Maximus Poems, The **3**:45
Maxwell, William **7**:97
May I Cross Your Golden River?
2:125
May, James Boyer **6**:180
May, Samuel **3**:367
May, Val **9**:255
Mayakovsky, Vladimir
Gray **2**:181
Zinoviev **10**:325
Mayer, Bernadette **17**:281, 282-83
Mayer, Peter **3**:430
McAllister, Claire **9**:83
McBride, Mary Margaret **2**:170
McBrien, Dean **6**:51-52
McCaffery, Larry
Federman **8**:80
Sukenick **8**:293
McCarter Theater, Princeton, N.J.
2:417
McCarthy era
Anderson **2**:42
Andre **13**:18, 19
Boyle **1**:120-22
McCarthy, Joseph
Condon **1**:196
Disch **4**:146
McCarthy, Mary **2**:213
McCarthy, Pat **6**:87
McCauley, Kirby **3**:285
McClintic, Guthrie **12**:235
McClure, Michael
Kherdian **2**:268-69
Koller **5**:163
McCord, Howard 9:171-89

Bergé   **10**:13
Choudhury   **14**:92, 93
Raworth   **11**:303
Rosenblum   **11**:348, 353
Thayler   **11**:364
McCord, William   **9**:149
McCoy, Kid   **1**:381
McCreary, Fred   **10**:66
McCullers, Carson
  Highwater   **7**:74
  Kazin   **7**:92-93
McCullough, Frances   **7**:282
McDowell, Robert   **11**:84
McElderry, Margaret K.   **9**:86
McElroy, Joseph   **6**:250
McGill University
  Andre   **13**:17-18
  Blaise   **3**:27
  Dudek   **14**:125, 131
  Hine   **15**:223-25
  Vivante   **12**:291
McGough, Roger   **2**:52
McGraw, DeLoss   **13**:213-14
McGuane, Thomas   **9**:114, 116
McIntosh, Mavis   **6**:53-54
McKain, David   14:205-17
McKenna, Richard
  Disch   **4**:150
  Knight   **10**:213, 221, 223
McKeon, Richard
  Booth   **5**:51
  Olson   **12**:230, 231, 232, 237
McLoughlin, William G.   **8**:180
McMichael, James
  Ai   **13**:8
  Pinsky   **4**:246, 249
  Wright   **7**:299
"McMillan & Wife"   **1**:231
McMurtry, Larry   **7**:185
McNeill, Bill   **16**:192-93, 195, 196, 202
McPherson, James A.   17:121-36
  Forrest   **7**:34
McQueen   **16**:221
McTaggart, Bill   **9**:42
M.D.: A Horror Story, The   **4**:157, 158
MDS   **1**:273, 274
Mead, Margaret
  Bergé   **10**:4
  Kostelanetz   **8**:181
Mead, Matthew   13:125-40
  Turnbull   **14**:335
Mead, Taylor   **11**:284
Mean Rufus Throw Down   **7**: 163
Mean Streets   **5**:218
Meaning of Witchcraft, The   **8**:274
Meanings of Death and Life   **5**:35
Medal of Honor
  Corcoran   **2**:119
  Nichols   **2**:332
Medea   **2**:419
Medek, Mikuláš   **1**:336
Medgar Evers College   **2**:306
Medhar Batanukul Ghungur   **14**:98
Median Flow, The   **3**:87

Meditations in a Graveyard   **3**:307
Medium, The   **2**:436
Meek, Jay   **15**:23
Meet Me at Tamerlane's Tomb   **2**:124
Meet Mr. Miller   **1**:383
Meeting at Jal   **3**:98
Meeting Point, The   **16**:78
Meeting the Snowy North Again   **2**:59
Megged, Aharon   13:141-59
Megged, Amos   **13**:158
Megged, Eyal   **13**:158
Meigs, Mary   **4**:74, 75, 76, 77, 78
Meiji Hotel, Tokyo   **2**:167-69, 176-77
Mein Kampf   **4**:198
Meiselas, Susan   **3**:80, 81
Meltzer, David
  Corman   **2**:142
  Kherdian   **2**:268, 269
  Kyger   **16**:190
Melville, Elizabeth   **3**:121-22
Melville, Herman
  Harris   **3**:121
  Kennedy   **9**:81
Member of the Wedding, The   **7**:74
Memoirs Found in a Bathtub   **1**:256
Memoirs of the Late Mr. Ashley: An American Comedy, The   **11**: 137-38
Memorial, The   **6**:18
Memorial University of Newfoundland   **7**:280
"Memories of an Obedient Childhood"   **17**:52
Memphis, Tenn.   **3**:137-38
Men of Distinction   **1**:194
Men to Match My Mountains   **3**:371
Menashe, Samuel   11:223-39
Mencken, H.L.
  Knebel   **3**:168, 179
  Wallace   **1**:397
Menlo Junior College   **9**:3
Menon, Krishna   **9**:230
Menon, N.C.   **9**:234
Menorah, The   **1**:345
Mental illness
  Allman   **15**:25, 26-27
  Andre   **13**:23-24
  Van Brunt   **15**:379
Mentch in togn, Der   **9**:56
Menton, France   **2**:381-82
Menu Cypher, The   **3**:81
Menzel, Jiří   **1**:348
Merchant, The   **7**:231
Mercier, Vivian   **3**:60, 65, 66
Mercouri, Melina   **2**:361
Meredith, George   **5**:201
Meredith, James   **3**:429
Meredith, Scott
  Knight   **10**:212-13
  Malzberg   **4**:211, 220
  Rimmer   **10**:296, 302-03
  Westlake   **13**:342
Meredith, Scott, Literary Agency, Inc.   **13**:340
Meredith, Sid   **10**:212-13
Meredith, William   14:219-36

Lifshin   **10**:250
Major   **6**:187
Malanga   **17**:97-98, 99
Mathews   **6**:232
Sward   **13**:288
Mérimée, Prosper   **1**:194
Merkin, Barry   **1**:294
Merlin   **2**:383
Merril, Judith
  Aldiss   **2**:28
  Disch   **4**:150, 151
  Knight   **10**:210, 211-12, 213, 215, 218, 220, 222, 223
  Pohl   **1**:289, 291
Merrill Foundation   **1**:320
Merrill, James
  Blais   **4**:78
  Hine   **15**:228-29, 231
Merry Wives of Windsor, The   **3**:404, 405
Merton, Thomas
  Boyd   **11**:57-58
  Galvin   **13**:91
  Mott   **7**:132-34
  Woodcock   **6**:326
Merwin, Sam, Jr.
  Gunn   **2**:247
  Kennedy   **9**:78
Merwin, W.S.   **16**:113
Mesmerist, The   **13**:226
Message from the Eocene   **8**:274
Messerli, Douglas   **14**:178
Metamorphoses   **3**:304
Metamorphosis in the Arts   **8**:184
"Metamorphosis, The"   **11**:249
Metaphysical Society of America   **12**:332
Metcalf, Paul   **12**:348
Metesky, George   **3**:98
Metro-Goldwyn-Mayer
  Allen   **6**:20
  Nolan   **16**:216, 218
  Roditi   **14**:254
  Wallace   **1**:383
Metropolitan Museum of Art, New York City   **2**:266-67
Metropolitan Opera, New York City   **4**:148
Mexican-Americans See Hispanic-Americans
Mexican Stove, The   **1**:198
Mexico
  Alegría   **15**:8-9
  Anaya   **4**:25
  Barnstone   **15**:55-59
  Barrio   **15**:115-17, 121
  Bennett   **13**:84, 85
  Bowles   **1**:85-86
  Delgado   **15**:165-67
  Disch   **4**:150
  Eshleman   **6**:133
  Ghiselin   **10**:142
  Harris   **16**:135-36
  Kyger   **16**:200-01
  Raworth   **11**:304-05
  Turner   **10**:315-16

White   **4**:349
Williamson   **8**:314-15
Mexico & North   **6**:133
Mexico City College   **15**:58
Mexico City, D.F.   **4**:253
Mexico's Art and Chicano Artists   **15**:121
Meyer, Albert   **7**:46-47
Meyer, Thomas   **12**:348, 351, 354
Meynell, Francis   **3**:353
Mezzrow, Milton Mezz   **8**:5, 6
Mia Poems   **9**:216
Miami Beach, Fla.   **1**:287
Miami Beach Mirror   **12**:202
Miami Student (Oxford, Ohio)   **3**:169
Miami University, Oxford, Ohio
   Hall   **12**:117-20, 131
   Jones   **11**:178, 180
   Knebel   **3**:168, 169
Mica   **8**:78-79
Mich, Dan   **3**:172
Michaeljohn, John   **7**:71
Michel, John   **10**:206, 207, 208, 211
Michelangelo Buonarroti   **3**:372-74
Michener, James   **16**:142, 146, 149-50
Michigan   **9**:89, 92-93
Michigan Catholic   **1**:246-48
Michigan State College See Michigan
   State University
Michigan State University
   Kirk   **9**:94-95, 96, 97, 99
   Root   **11**:323
   Rosenthal   **6**:276, 278-79
   Wakoski   **1**:369
Mickiewicz, Adam   **3**:39-40
Mid-American Review   **9**:186
Middlebury College
   Barnstone   **15**:59
   Brée   **15**:136-37
   Parini   **16**:238-39
Middleton, Christopher
   Hamburger   **4**:169, 171
   Lind   **4**:195
   Mead   **13**:130-31
Midquest   **4**:122-23, 124
MidWatch   **5**:345
Midwest   **14**:45
Midwood Symphony   **4**:206
Migrations   **8**:147
"Mike Hammer" series   **7**:6
Milagro Beanfield War, The   **2**:334-35
Miles, Bernard   **2**:157
Miles College   **17**:26
Miles, Elizabeth   **7**:15
Milford Science Fiction Writers'
   Conference
   Budrys   **14**:70
   Disch   **4**:150, 153
   Knight   **10**:220-21, 222
   Moorcock   **5**:180
   Niven   **12**:216-17
   Wolfe   **9**:305-06, 307
Millar, Kenneth   **3**:43, 44
Millay, Edna St. Vincent   **12**:47-48
Miller, Arthur

Slade   **9**:244
Sukenick   **8**:287
Miller, Brown   **10**:255
Miller, Geraldine   **9**:279
Miller, Henry
   Crews   **14**:103, 108-09, 110, 114, 116
   Dillard   **7**:19
   Elman   **3**:81, 83
   Gray   **2**:195
   Horwood   **15**:243
   Kazin   **7**:90
   Major   **6**:179
   Ouellette   **13**:182, 185
   Rimmer   **10**:288
   Sukenick   **8**:284, 287
   Wallace   **1**:397
Miller, Jim Wayne   15:273-93
Miller, Joe   **1**:383
Miller, Kelly   **2**:297
Miller, Milton   **8**:244
Miller, Nolan   **8**:133
Miller, Warren   **1**:345-46
Millett, Fred B.   **12**:157
Milligan, Spike   **1**:28
Millington Army Base, Memphis,
   Tenn.   **1**:140
Mills & Boon   **11**:98-99, 101, 103-04
Mills, C. Wright
   Kostelanetz   **8**:185
   Wakefield   **7**:196
Mills College   **4**:63
Mills, Robert P.
   Budrys   **14**:70-71
   Disch   **4**:151
   Gunn   **2**:256
   Knight   **10**:222
Milner, Ron   **2**:298
Milosz, Czeslaw
   Miller   **15**:290
   Pinsky   **4**:250
Milton, John   **4**:258
Milwaukee, Wis.   **12**:162
Mind Master, The   **2**:258
Mindwheel   **4**:250
mini   **13**:71
Minister Primarily, The   **2**:306
Minneapolis Fantasy Society   **2**:39-40
Minneapolis Journal   **15**:315
Minneapolis, Minn.   **1**:250
Minnesota   **15**:314-21
Minnesota Review   **4**:150
Minsterworth Court   **4**:343-44, 347, 348, 349
Mintoff, Dom   **5**:365
Minute by Glass Minute   **9**:286
Miracle in Bohemia   **1**:349
Miracle Play   **5**:240
Miracle, The   **1**:399
Miron, Gaston   **13**:183
Mirsky, Mark Jay   **11**:200, 212
Misanthrope, The   **4**:134
Misérables, Les   **2**:373
Miss America Pageant   **6**:153-54
Miss Muriel and Other Stories   **6**:256, 259

Miss Peabody's Inheritance   **13**:121-22
Miss Silver's Past   **1**:345
Missile Summer   **2**:60
Missing   **2**:335
Missing Person, The   **2**:212, 213
Mississippi   **5**:186
Mister Roberts   **9**:267
Mists of Avalon, The   **10**:26
Mitchell, Adrian
   Aldiss   **2**:24
   Booth   **2**:52
Mitchell, Burroughs
   Elman   **3**:75, 77
   Swanberg   **13**:268, 269, 272, 273
Mitchell, H.L.   **3**:137-38
Mitchell, Stephen   **4**:250
Mitford, Jessica   17:137-51
Mizener, Arthur   **8**:302, 305, 306
Mizener, Rosemary   **8**:306
Mobile, Ala.   **16**:293
Mobius the Stripper   **8**:152
Moby-Dick   **7**: 23
Moccasin Telegraph, The   **7**:106
Modern Age   **9**:99, 100
Modern art   **15**:118
*Modern Dogma and the Rhetoric of
   Assent*   **5**:41, 45
Modern European Poetry   **15**:80, 92, 94
*Modern Poetic Sequence: The Genius of
   Modern Poetry, The*   **6**: 280
*Modern Poets: A Critical Introduction,
   The*   **6**:280
Modern Screen   **1**:377
Modernism   **7**:6
Modular Poems   **8**:92
Mohandas Gandhi   **6**:321-22
Moholy-Nagy, László   **8**:186, 189
Mohrt, Michel   **2**:67
Molière, Jean-Baptiste   **4**:134
Molly   **3**:111
Molson Award   **6**:323
Molson, Gordon   **2**:171
Moment of True Feeling, A   **9**:119
Moments of Light   **4**:123-24
*Momma As She Became—But Not As
   She Was*   **4**:265
Mommsen, Theodor   **6**:230-32
Mona   **11**:31
Monde, Le   **6**:239
Money Money Money   **3**:405
Monje Blanco, El   **4**:256
Monmouth County, N.J.   **1**:291
Monologue of a Deaf Man   **5**:370
Monroe, Harriet   **12**:228, 229
Monroe, Marilyn
   Rechy   **4**:265
   Wallace   **1**:398
Montag, Tom   **8**:248
Montague, John   **6**:285
Montaigne, Michel de
   Katz   **9**:70
   Stewart   **3**:353
Montale, Eugenio   **7**:297, 298
Montana
   Savage   **15**:329-45

Wright **7**:299-300
Monteith, Charles
    Aldiss **2**:22
    Burroway **6**:92, 93
Monterrey, Mexico **13**:310
Monteverdi, Claudio **3**:95
Montgomery, Wes **6**:128
Montley, Patricia **2**:352
Montreal, Canada
    Blais **4**:77
    Bowering **16**:28-29
    Brossard **16**:39-57
    Dudek **14**:123, 124-25
    Ouellette **13**:177-78
Montreal Gazette **13**:15
Moody, Charlotte **1**:377
Moonstone, The **6**:254
Moorcock, Michael **5:173-92**
    Aldiss **2**:25, 29
    Disch **4**:151-52
    Tennant **9**:291
    Wolfe **9**:305-06
Moore, Barbara **8**:89
Moore, Brew **9**:198
Moore, Brian **3**:219
Moore, Geoffrey **10**:62
Moore, Lazarus **6**:215
Moore, Marianne
    Atkins **16**:12, 13
    Burroway **6**:90
    Corman **2**:136
    Creeley **10**:66-67
    Ghiselin **10**:139
    Gregor **10**:149, 156
    Weiss **2**:435
    Whittemore **8**:306
Moore, Paul, Jr. **11**:47, 59
Moore School of Electrical
    Engineering **12**:149-50
Moore, Ward **11**:203
Moorhead, Alan **4**:231
Moorsom, Sasha **1**:27
Moraff, Barbara **10**:6
Moral Stories **5**:370
Morandi, Giorgio **14**:171
Moravia, Alberto
    Ghiselin **10**:141
    Tennant **9**:291
    Wright **7**:298
Mordecai Richler **6**:323
More Fool, The **1**:79
More, Paul Elmer **7**:220
Morehead State University **17**:246
Morgan, Dan **8**:7
Morgan, Edwin **6**:73
Morgan, Robin **11**:68
Morgan State College **17**:133
Morgan, Ted **4:223-36**
Morgan, Theodore **3:229-48**
Morley, Anthony Jefferson **12**:340-41
Mormon Country **9**:266
Mormonism
    Booth **5**:34, 36-38, 40-42, 46-47,
        49, 50
    Wallace **1**:389-90

Mormons **2**:74
Morocco **2**:385-86
Morris Brown College
    Killens **2**:282, 285-86
    McPherson **17**:133
    Williams **3**:420
Morris, John N. **13:161-75**
Morris, Robert **1**:363
Morris, William **6**:318
Morris, Wright **3**:188
Morrison, Arthur **2**:384
Morrison, Henry
    Block **11**:34, 35, 36
    Silverberg **3**:277
    Westlake **13**:340, 342
Morrison, Theodore
    Ciardi **2**:90, 93, 94
    Stegner **9**:265, 266, 267
Morrison, Toni
    Clarke **16**:84
    Williams **3**:430-31
Morriss, Richard **5**:290
Morrow, William (publishers) **1**:400
Morse, Stearns **9**:198
Mort vive, La (Death alive) **13**:189
Mortal Consequences **3**:390
Mortal Engines **1**:264
Mortimer, John **5**:127, 128
Morwitz, Ernst **2**:434
Moscow Gold **4**:108
Moscow State University **10**: :328-33
Moscow, USSR
    Corcoran **2**:124
    Easton **14**:152
    Shadbolt **3**:261
Moses **11**:173
"Moses Project, The" **6**:268
Moskowitz, Sam **9**:78
Moss, Graydon **9**:149
Moss, Howard
    Fuchs **5**:58
    Smith **7**:163-64
Mosses from an Old Manse **15**:282-83
Mossman, James **4**:133
Mote in God's Eye, A **12**:220
Motel **2**:414-16
Motets **7**:297
Mother Goose **12**:45
Mother London **5**:186
"Mother's Tale, A" **3**:222
Mothersill and the Foxes **3**:417, 422,
    431
Motherwell, Robert **2**:194
Motion Picture Producers
    Association **1**:194
Motive **14**:110
Motley, Archibald **6**:181
Motley, Willard **6**:181-82
Motor Trend **16**:213
Motorcycle Betrayal Poems, The **1**:368
Motorcycles
    McCord **9**:177, 178
    Rosenblum **11**:335, 350, 351, 352
Motown Record Co. **2**:304
Mots, Les (The Words) **5**:117
Mott, Michael **7:113-34**

Mound Builders of Ancient America
    3:278, 279
Mount Allison University **15**:157
Mount Etna **2**:153, 154
Mount Holyoke College **4**:166
Mount Holyoke Poetry Competition
    6:90
Mountain Road, The **6**:326
Mountains Have Come Closer, The
    15:286, 287, 288
"Mountains Like Mice" **9**:304-05
Mountbatten, Edwina **8**:25
Mountbatten, Louis **8**:25
Mountfort, Guy **4**:309
Mourners Below **1**:303
*Mournful Demeanor of Lieutenant
    Borůvka, The* **1**:345
Mousetrap, The **15**:197
Movement, The (English literary
    movement)
    Abse **1**:27
    Davie **3**:36-37, 38, 44
"Movie of the Week" **2**:254
Moving Parts **14**:175
Mowat, Farley **15**:245, 247
Mowat, Frances **15**:247
Moynihan, John **9**:18
Mozart, Wolfgang Amadeus
    Enslin **3**:90
    Ouellette **13**:181
    Wain **4**:328
Mpls. **1**:249-50
Mr. Field's Daughter **14**:13, 14, 15
Mr. Keynes and the Labour Movement
    8:258
"Mr. Mintser" **4**:241-42
Mr. Sammler's Planet **1**:258
Mrozek, Slawomir **10:265-80**
Mrs. Warren's Profession **5**:147
Muckraking **17**:149-50
Muggeridge, Malcolm
    Jones **5**:125
    Kirk **9**:104
Mug's Game, A **4**:159, 160, 162
Muhlenberg College
    Busch **1**:129, 130
    Weiss **2**:428, 429-30
Muir, Edwin
    Abse **1**:27
    Brown **6**:67, 69-70
Muir, Leo J. **5**:37
Mukherjee, Bharati **3**:25, 26-27, 28,
    29
Mules Sent from Chavín **6**:139
Muller, Julian **9**:8-9
Mulligan, Gerry **9**:107, 110, 120
Multiculturalism **16**:162-65, 168
Multiple sclerosis **4**:90-93
Mumford, Lewis
    Jerome **8**:137
    Kizer **5**:140
Mumps **8**:6
Mundo es ancho y ajeno, El (Broad
    and alien is the world) **12**: :100
Munsel, Patrice **5**:152
Murchie, Guy **9**:57

"Murder by Morning" **1**:386
Murder of the Maharajah, The **8**:176
Murdoch, Iris **4**:88
Murphy, Tom **3**:64
Murray, Don **2**:289
Murray, Donald **7**:107
Murrow, Edgar R. **1**:123
Murry, John Middleton
   Ashby **6**:35-36
   Weiss **2**:430
   Woodcock **6**:320
Musgrave, Susan
   Booth **2**:56
   Skelton **5**:292
Music
   Bell **14**:36, 38-39
   Booth **5**:35
   Broughton **12**:47
   Brunner **8**:5-6
   Dudek **14**:126-27
   Enslin **3**:86, 89, 95-97
   Feirstein **11**:77-78
   Fisher **10**:98
   Higgins **8**:83
   Highwater **7**:78
   Hrabal **12**:189
   Josipovici **8**:157-58
   Kerrigan **11**:196-98, 201-02, 210
   Ouellette **13**:178, 179
   Phillips **13**:195, 196, 197-98, 199, 210
   Plymell **11**:277, 279, 280, 281-82, 288
   Rodgers **13**:240
   Simpson **4**:286
   Smith **7**:159-60
   Stevenson **9**:276-77
Music for Several Occasions **3**:98
Music Man, The **4**:148
Musical composition **16**:7, 9-10, 13, 14-15
My Amputations **6**:195, 197, 198, 202
My Aunt Christina **3**:356
My Day in Court **6**:264
My Father More or Less **5**:28
My Father's Moon **13**:111-12, 117
My Fellow Americans **11**:54
My Friend Judas **5**:270
"My Grandfather's Country" **17**:212
My Life **5**:201
"My Living Doll" **9**:244
My Magazine **3**:350
My Next Bride **1**:116
My Regrets **13**:25
My Souths **4**:350
My Voice Because of You **15**:59
Myasthenia gravis **8**:299, 309
Myers, Dorothy **9**:279
Myers, Lucas **9**:280, 281
Myers, Michael **11**:306, 307
Myette, Louise **4**:73
Mystery and Manners **6**:212
"Mystery of Phillis Wheatley, The" **16**:67
Mystery Play **2**:419

Mystery Writers of America
   Anderson **2**:43
   Symons **3**:390, 391

NAACP See National Association for the Advancement of Colored People
Nabokov, Vladimir
   Belitt **4**:51-52, 54
   Blaise **3**:20
   Charyn **1**:183
   Katz **14**:166
   Turner **10**:318
Náchod, Czechoslovakia **1**:325-34
NACLA See North American Congress on Latin America
Nadamas **13**:65
Nagarajan, T.S. **9**:232
Nagasaki, Japan **1**:166
Naipaul, V.S.
   Becker **1**:43
   Keating **8**:172
Najarian, Peter **4**:243, 244, 247
Naked and the Dead, The **4**:103
Naked Ear, The **14**:112-13
Naked Lunch
   Morgan **4**:235
   Plymell **11**:289
Names and Nicknames **15**:307
Naming of the Beasts, The **15**:358
Narayan, R.K. **8**:171
Naropa Institute
   Kyger **16**:201
   Waldman **17**:282-83, 285, 288-89, 291-93
Narrow Rooms **1**:304
Narrows, The **6**:253, 266-67
NASA See National Aeronautics and Space Administration
Nash, Ogden **6**:89
Nassauer, Rudi **1**:24
Nat Turner **16**:83, 84
Nathanael West: The Cheaters and the Cheated **3**:197
Nation
   Barrio **15**:112
   Belitt **4**:60, 62
   Coppel **9**:6
   Eastlake **1**:211
   Elman **3**:74
   Rosenthal **6**:279
   Simpson **4**:293
   Wakefield **7**:196, 197
Nation Poetry Prize **4**:60
National Academy of Letters Award **9**:147-48
National Aeronautics and Space Administration **7**:283
National Association for Health, England **8**:26
National Association for the Advancement of Colored People **2**:291
National Audubon Society **14**:149
National Book Award
   Bourjaily **1**:76

   Kerrigan **11**:213
   Rabassa **9**:203
   Settle **1**:321
   Stegner **9**:269
   Wagoner **3**:409, 410
National Book Critics Circle Award
   Allen **11**:22
   Grumbach **2**:214
National Broadcasting Corp.
   Gunn **2**:251
   Wakefield **7**:200
   Williams **3**:423, 431
National Defense Education Act Fellowship
   Chappell **4**:113
   Miller **15**:282
National Defense Foreign Language Fellowship **13**:5
National Democratic party, Czechoslovakia **1**:329
National Educational Television
   Van Itallie **2**:414
   Williams **3**:428, 430
National Endowment for the Arts
   Allen **11**:22
   Allman **15**:30
   Bergé **10**:11
   Blaise **3**:29
   Bowles **1**:94
   Cassity **8**:58
   Eshleman **6**:147
   Forbes **16**:118
   Hansen **17**:70
   Hearon **11**:169
   Kerrigan **11**:214
   Markfield **3**:221
   McCord **9**:184-85
   Peters **8**:249
   Saroyan **5**:216
   Wilson **5**:353
National Endowment for the Humanities
   Brée **15**:145
   Taylor **7**:187
National Forensic League **1**:375
National Gallery of Scotland **3**:355
National Geographic **3**:271
National Herald (India) **9**:234
National Institute of Arts and Letters
   Chappell **4**:120
   Davison **4**:138
   Williams **3**:414
National Institute of Public Affairs **8**:309
National Labor Relations Board **2**:282
National Medal of Science **16**:306
National Opinion Research Center **7**:47
National Organization of Women **1**:277
National Public Radio
   Elman **3**:82
   Grumbach **2**:213
   Pinsky **4**:244
   Ray **7**:142

National Review
  Kirk **9**:100
  Mano **6**:208, 215, 216
National Science Foundation Grant **16**:98
National Shakespeare Company **6**:209
National Socialism *See* Nazism
National Society of Film Critics **5**:28
National Trust (England) **4**:309
Native Americans
  Awoonor **13**:48
  Brown **6**:55-56
  Clarke **16**:78
  Highwater **7**:72
  Katz **14**:175
  McCord **9**:174, 175, 184
  Purdy **17**:209-10
  Waters **13**:321, 322, 325-27
  West **7**:285
Native Son of the Golden West, A **16**:160
Natural Classicism: Essays on Literature and Science **10**:321
Nausée, La **8**:72
Navajo Community College **9**:184
Naval Air Station, New Orleans, La. **2**:106
Naval Air Station, Olathe, Kan. **2**:106-07
Naylor, Charles **4**:154, 155
Naylors, The **3**:357
Nazi party **4**:162
Nazi-Soviet Pact **3**:42
Nazimova, Alla **2**:206
Nazis
  Brée **15**:133
  Easton **14**:145
  Hauser **11**:129, 132
  Lind **4**:195
  Ouellette **13**:181
  Roditi **14**:270-73
  Samarakis **16**:251-57
  Sisson **3**:297
  Škvorecký **1**:329-34
Nazism
  Hamburger **4**:169, 170
  Schevill **12**:273-78
  Wellek **7**:221
"NBC Matinee Theater" **2**:170
NBC-TV *See* National Broadcasting Corp.
Neal, Larry **16**:86
Neale, J.E. **8**:259
Nebraska Gifford, J. **8**:181
Nebula Award
  Gunn **2**:258
  Knight **10**:225
  Silverberg **3**:279, 281, 282, 283
  Wilhelm **5**:297
Nebula Award Stories Four **2**:255
Neeld, Elizabeth Cowan **6**:250
Neff, Emery **2**:432
Negro Digest **13**:246
Nehru, Jawaharlal **9**:229
Neighborhood Playhouse **2**:411, 418

Neighboring Lives **4**:155, 156
Neill, A.S. **6**:121
Nelbach, Inez **10**:38
Nemerov, Howard
  Belitt **4**:52, 65
  Waldman **17**:272-73
  Weiss **2**:444
  West **7**:285
  Whittemore **8**:306, 308
Neon Poems **11**:293
Neptune Beach **5**:56
Neptune's Daughter **4**:286
Neruda, Pablo
  Belitt **4**:50, 64
  Kerrigan **11**:189
Nesbit, E. **8**:210
NET *See* National Educational Television
Netherlands **4**:200, 201
Neue Gedichte **2**:158
Nevada **14**:167
New Age / Le nouveau siècle, The **17**:83, 89-93
New American Arts, The **8**:184
New American Library (publishers)
  Brossard **2**:67
  Gunn **2**:257
  Raffel **9**:214
  Rimmer **10**:299-300, 301, 302, 303
  Solotaroff **2**:400, 401
  Williams **3**:424, 427, 432
New American Poetry **5**:348
New American Review
  Dennison **6**:121
  Solotaroff **2**:401-03
New American Writing **2**:383
New and Collected Poems, 1934-84 (Roy Fuller) **10**:118
New and Selected Poems (David Wagoner) **3**:408
New and Selected Poems (Donald Davie) **3**:43
New Black Poetry, The **6**:185, 188
New Campus Writing **8**:133
New Criticism
  Enslin **3**:89, 90, 91, 93
  Kazin **7**:92
  Rosenthal **6**:280, 282
New Deal
  Brown **6**:53, 54
  Elman **3**:70
New Delhi **9**:234
New Directions Annual **1**:132
New Directions (publishers)
  Brossard **2**:66, 67
  Cassill **1**:169
  Olson **11**:257
  Purdy **1**:301-02, 304
New England **1**:40-41
New English Weekly
  Sisson **3**:298, 301
  Woodcock **6**:319
New Exile **7**:124, 127
New Frontier **8**:233, 234
New Guinea **16**:295-96

New Jersey **13**:78
New Leader **12**:206
New Left
  Piercy **1**:273
  Solotaroff **2**:399-400
New Letters
  Petesch **12**:248, 249
  Ray **7**:144-45
"New Letters on the Air" **7**:142
New Lincoln School, New York City **6**:183, 186
New Lines **3**:36, 37
New Mexico
  Anaya **4**:15, 25, 27
  Eastlake **1**:209
  McCord **9**:171, 172-77, 184, 186-87
  Wilson **5**:345, 352
New Mexico Military Institute **8**:325
New Mexico Quarterly Review **8**:112
New Mexico Review **2**:333, 334
New Mexico State University **5**:351, 352, 355
"New Mirror, The" **6**:259
New Movement (literary movement) **5**:284
New Orleans, La. **4**:260
New Orleans Poetry Journal **3**:335
"New Orleans Transient Bureau" **5**:207
New Poets: American and British Poetry since World War II, The **6**:280
New Poets of England and America, The **7**:64
New Provinces **14**:128
New Quarterly **15**:251
New Reasoner, The **12**:5
New Republic
  Elman **3**:74
  Grumbach **2**:211-12
  Kazin **7**:88-89, 91, 92-93
  Rosenthal **6**:279
  Whittemore **8**:310
New School for Social Research
  Cassill **1**:169
  Dennison **6**:111
  Forbes **16**:112
  Inez **10**:189, 191
  Malzberg **4**:211
  Olson **11**:256
  Owens **2**:358
New Sharon's Prospect **3**:98
New Statesman
  Allen **6**:23, 24, 25
  Brown **6**:70
  Burroway **6**:99
  Caute **4**:109
  Jones **5**:124-25
New Statesman and Nation **6**:320
New University of Ulster **6**:26
New Verse **3**:385
New Voices of Hispanic America **15**:9-10
New Wave (literary movement) **4**:151
New World, The **10**:320

New World Writing
  Dillard **7**:6
  Solotaroff **2**:400, 401, 402
New Worlds
  Aldiss **2**:25
  Disch **4**:151
  Moorcock **5**:177, 180-81
New York City
  Allen **6**:25
  Andre **13**:25
  Bergé **10**:3, 5-7, 8-9, 11
  Brée **15**:133
  Burroway **6**:87
  Cruz **17**:5-7
  Dennison **6**:117
  Disch **4**:148
  Duncan **2**:170
  Easton **14**:145
  Federman **8**:74
  Feirstein **11**:73-74, 75, 77-78, 84
  Forbes **16**:112
  Gray **2**:193, 194
  Grumbach **2**:203, 204, 205, 208
  Hailey **1**:230
  Higgins **8**:85-86
  Hine **15**:230-31
  Howes **3**:139
  Katz, Menke **9**:54-58, 61-62
  Katz, Steve **14**:163-64, 170-71
  Kazin **7**:86, 88, 91, 94
  Kherdian **2**:266-67
  Kirkup **4**:190
  Kyger **16**:199
  Mano **6**:205, 207
  Menashe **11**:237
  Owens **2**:358-60
  Phillips **13**:203-04
  Piercy **1**:273-75
  Pohl **1**:289
  Purdy **1**:302
  Rechy **4**:259-60
  Rosenthal **6**:279
  Settle **1**:311-312
  Silverberg **3**:278, 282-83
  Simic **4**:278-79
  Sukenick **8**:285-87
  Swenson **13**:310
  Van Itallie **2**:411-12, 419
  Vivante **12**:296
  Wakefield **7**:197
  Wakoski **1**:361-68
  Wallace **1**:378
  Weiss **2**:431-32
  West **7**:277-78, 281
  Williams **3**:423-24
New York City (audiotape) **8**:185-86
New York Daily Mirror **12**:203
New York Daily News **8**:324
New York Drama Critics Circle
    2:363
New York Herald-Tribune
  Lottman **12**:203
  Morgan **4**:229-31
  Rosenthal **6**:279
  Simpson **4**:292
  Slavitt **3**:319

New York Institute for Gestalt
    Therapy **6**:115
New York Jew **7**:91
New York Poetry Center **1**:362
New York Post **7**:196
New York Public Library **7**:90-91
New York School poets
  Disch **4**:153
  Saroyan **5**:215
New York Theatre Strategy **2**:366
New York Times
  Brossard **2**:68, 69, 70
  Elman **3**:76, 80
  Gray **3**:114
  Grumbach **2**:212
  Knebel **3**:180, 181
  Meredith **14**:233
  Nichols **2**:331
  Salisbury **15**:324
  Shapiro **6**:299
  Van Itallie **2**:415, 418
  Wallace **1**:392
  Weiss **2**:436
New York Times Book Review
  Dillard **7**:16
  Kirk **9**:98
New York Times Magazine **7**:201
New York University
  Allen **6**:26
  Baumbach **5**:24
  Bergé **10**:2
  Brée **15**:143-44
  Busch **1**:131
  Caute **4**:105
  Disch **4**:148-49, 152
  Eshleman **6**:140
  Feirstein **11**:79, 80
  Goldemberg **12**:103
  Grumbach **2**:207
  Higgins **8**:90, 91, 92
  Highwater **7**:80
  Inez **10**:190
  Jones **5**:120
  Killens **2**:288
  Lottman **12**:198, 204
  Root **11**:329
  Rosenthal **6**:276, 277, 279, 282
  Slavitt **3**:311
  Van Itallie **2**:421, 422
New Yorker
  Boyle **1**:117, 120, 121
  Brossard **2**:63-64, 65, 76
  Burroway **6**:90
  Ciardi **2**:93
  Gray **2**:198
  Hahn **11**:111, 113, 115, 116
  Hentoff **6**:170, 171, 173
  Kerrigan **11**:209
  Kizer **5**:152-53
  Smith **7**:163-64, 165
  Swenson **13**:313
  Vivante **12**:298-99, 300
New Zealand
  Ray **7**:148
  Shadbolt **3**:249, 250, 254, 255,
    257, 265-66

New Zealand Herald **3**:257
New Zealand Labour Government
    3:256
New Zealand Labour Party **3**:254
New Zealanders, The **3**:259, 263, 264
Newbattle Abbey College **6**:69, 70
Newbery Award **7**:82
Newdigate Prize **7**:63-64
Newfound **15**:274, 288-89
Newfoundland **15**:248, 249
Newfoundland, Canada **15**:243-44
Newman, Barney **6**:113
Newman, John **6**:50-51
Newman, Phyllis **2**:364
Newman, Tom **6**:50-51
Newspaper Enterprise Association
    1:194
Newspaper of Claremont Street, The
    13:110
Newsweek
  Elman **3**:74
  Slavitt **3**:317-19, 321
  Williams **3**:426, 427, 428
Newton, Douglas **1**:314
Niagara Barn Players **9**:241-42
Nibley, Hugh **1**:390
Nicaragua
  Alegría **15**:1-2, 13, 14
  Elman **3**:80-81
  Nichols **2**:337
  Waldman **17**:289-90
*Nice to See You: Homage to Ted
    Berrigan* **17**:289
Nichols, Dudley **1**:201-02
Nichols, Edward J. **3**:402-03
Nichols, J.G. 2:307-19
Nichols, John 2:321-37
Nichols, Robert
  Bergé **10**:8
  Dennison **6**:117
Nichols, Walter J. **7**:10
Nicholson, Ben **5**:288
Nicholson, Norman **14**:336
Nicolson, Marjorie Hope **7**:277
Niedecker, Lorine
  Corman **2**:144, 145-46
  Honig **8**:109
  Williams **12**:346
Niels Holgerson's Miraculous Journey
    4:200
Nieman Fellowship **7**:197
Niente da (Nothing to) **13**:71
Nietzsche, Friedrich
  Nichols **2**:318
  Rakosi **5**:204
  Stafford **3**:338
Nigeria
  Dacey **17**:25-26
  Killens **2**:303
Night **4**:357
Night Journey **2**:221, 224, 225, 228
Night of Camp David **3**:181
Night of Fire and Snow **9**:5
Night Screams **4**:219
Night Song **3**:414, 415, 424, 425,
    427

Nightmare of God, The **1**:54, 57
Nightwings **3**:280-81
Nijinsky, Vaslav **2**:356
Nilon, Charles H. **6**:190
Nimbus **5**:370
Nims, John Frederick 17:153-94
   Kumin **8**:215
Nin, Anaïs
   Crews **14**:103, 111
   Highwater **7**:78, 80
   Major **6**:183
90 Degrees South **1**:36
98.6 **8**:294
Nirvana Blues, The **2**:335
Nisbet, R.A. **9**:99
Niven, Larry 12:211-24
Niven's Laws **12**:222-24
Nixon, Agnes **7**:199
Nixon-Clay Business College **11**:163
Nixon, Richard
   Knebel **3**:178
   Settle **1**:319
   Wallace **1**:376
Nixon vs Nixon **1**:376
Nizan, Paul **8**:179
Nkrumah, Kwame
   Awoonor **13**:35, 46, 50, 51
   Killens **2**:303
No Country for Young Men **2**:351,
   352
No Exit **1**:87
No Gods Are False **17**:182
No High Ground **3**:179
No Is the Night **14**:111
No Jerusalem but This **11**:235, 236
No Time to Be Young **5**:121, 122
Nobel Prize
   Pinsky **4**:250
   Wallace **1**:390-93
Noble, Edward John, Fellowship
   2:158
Noden, William **7**:266, 270
Noise in the Trees **9**:33
Nolan, Cameron **16**:214-15, 217
Nolan, William F. 16:205-26
Nonesuch Library (publishers) **3**:353
Noonday Press **3**:415
NORC See National Opinion
   Research Center
Nordstrom, Ursula **6**:169
Norman Thomas: The Last Idealist
   13:273
Norse legends **7**:78
North American Congress on Latin
   America **1**:273
North American Education, A **3**:18,
   21, 24
North American Review **14**:48
North Carolina
   Morris **13**:167-68
   Wright **7**:289-90, 292
North of Jamaica **4**:296
North of Summer **17**:210
North of the Danube **1**:148
North Point Press **9**:219

Northeastern Illinois University
   11:305
Northeastern News **6**:167
Northeastern University
   Galvin **13**:93
   Hentoff **6**:166-67
Northern House **5**:251
Northern Illinois University
   Klinkowitz **9**:111
   Ray **7**:142
Northern Spring **6**:323
Northern Virginia Community
   College **14**:25-26, 27, 29, 30
Northwest Review **5**:164
Northwestern University
   Brutus **14**:61
   Gunn **2**:246
   Piercy **1**:271
Norton, Alden H. **10**:209
*Norton Anthology of Short Fiction,
   The* **1**:173-74
Norton, Joshua **11**:294, 295
Norton, W.W. (publishers) **8**:247-48
Not Be Essence That Cannot Be
   2:363
*Not in God's Image: Women in History
   from the Greeks to the Victorians*
   2:351, 352
Not Made of Glass **10**:257
Not-Right House, The **1**:303
"Not to Lethe" **4**:58-59
*Notebook of a Ten Square Rush-Mat
   Sized World: A Fugitive Essay*
   11:204
Notebooks of Malte Laurids Brigge, The
   Abse **1**:25
   Gray **2**:194
Notebooks of Susan Berry, The **7**:127,
   128, 130
Notes from Another Country **3**:384,
   386, 392, 394
Notes on the State of Virginia **7**:164
*Notes on Visitations: Poems
   1936–1975* **6**:326
Notes on Writing a Novel **7**:25
Notre Dame University
   Katz **14**:176-77
   Nims **17**:171-74, 175, 177-78,
      180, 187
Nottingham, England **2**:371-75
Nottingham Writers' Club **2**:385
Novices **6**:148
Now (Charles Plymell) **11**:286, 289
NOW (George Woodcock) **6**:320
Now Playing at Canterbury **1**:77, 78
NOW See National Organization of
   Women
Nowhere for Vallejo, A **16**:281
Nowlan, Alden **15**:157
Noyes, Alfred **10**:119
Noyes, George Rapall **3**:39
NPR See National Public Radio
Nuclear disarmament movement
   Brunner **8**:9-10
   Thomas **4**:312
Nuclear weapons **16**:101-02

Nude Descending a Staircase **9**:84, 86
Nuits de l'Underground, Les **4**:77
Numbers
   Rechy **4**:262, 265
   Sisson **3**:305
Nuremberg Laws **1**:329
Nuremberg War Crimes Trial
   14:269-73
Nureyev, Rudolf **1**:60
Nye, Robert **1**:133
Nylon Age, The **1**:334
Nympho and Other Maniacs, The
   1:397

O Beulah Land **1**:307, 317, 319
O Canada **4**:73
O Didn't He Ramble **5**:169
O. Henry Award
   Boyle **1**:117
   Ignatow **3**:156
*O negro na ficção brasileira: Meio século
   de história literária* **9**:202
Oates, Joyce Carol
   Allen **11**:11
   Highwater **7**:82
   Knebel **3**:182
   Phillips **13**:199-200, 201, 205,
      207, 211, 213
   Weiss **2**:449
Obedient Wife, The **2**:352
Oberg, Arthur **6**:180
Oberon Press **7**:102
"Objectivists" Anthology, An **5**:207
O'Briain, Liam **4**:305
O'Brian, Patrick **1**:43
O'Brien, Edward J. **6**:20
O'Brien, John **9**:113
Obscenity **6**:212, 213
Observer (London)
   Owens **2**:361
   Wilson **5**:321
O'Casey, Sean
   Boyle **1**:97
   Raworth **11**:297
Occidental College
   Olson **11**:253-55
   Rechy **4**:263
Occidental Review **11**:253, 254
Occupation, The **4**:100, 106
Oceanside Theatre **2**:116
Ochoterna, Gaudiosa **9**:165
O'Connell, Eileen **3**:62
O'Connor, Edwin **13**:103
O'Connor, Flannery
   Brown **10**:43
   Gray **2**:201
   Mano **6**:212
O'Connor, Frank
   Blaise **3**:19
   O'Faolain **2**:345
O'Connor, John Cardinal **6**:173
Octavian Shooting Targets **10**:148-49
October Blood **2**:200
Oda, Makoto **10**:4
O'Day, Anita **4**:190
Odd John **3**:271

Odds against Tomorrow **2**:303
"Ode to New York" **8**:309
Odense University **1**:156
Odeon (publishers) **1**:345
Odets, Clifford **1**:202
Odrodzenie **9**:123, 134
*Odysseus Ever Returning: Essays on
    Canadian Writers and Writing*
    6:323
Odyssey
    Forrest **7**:21
    Harris **16**:123, 124, 125
    Sinclair **5**:275
Odyssey (literary review) **9**:203
Odyssey of Katinou Kalokovich, The
    12:241, 243
Of Divers Arts **8**:187
*Of Poetry and Power: Poems Occasioned
    by the Presidency and Death of
    JFK* **10**:6
"Of the Wild Man" **17**:240
Of Time, Passion, and Knowledge
    10:318
Of Trees and Stones **13**:157, 158
O'Faolain, Eileen Gould **2**:339-42,
    343, 344, 345, 350
O'Faolain, Julia 2:339-53
O'Faolain, Sean
    Dillon **3**:57, 64
    O'Faolain **2**:339-40, 341, 342-43,
        344, 345, 347, 350
Off-Broadway theatre **2**:413, 414,
    419
*Off the Ground: First Steps to a
    Philosophical Consideration of the
    Dance* **15**:362
Offen, Ron **13**:288-89
Office of Strategic Services **9**:199,
    200
Office of War Information, London
    1:312
Offshore **10**:107
O'Grady, Desmond **7**:298, 301, 302
O'Hara, Frank
    Hall **7**:62, 63
    Waldman **17**:276, 277
O'Hara, John
    Cassill **1**:173
    Higgins **5**:91
O'Higgins, Patrick **4**:233-34
Ohio State University
    Baumbach **5**:23
    Jerome **8**:132, 133
    Matthews **15**:262, 265
    Morgan **3**:232, 233-34, 235
Ohio University
    Heyen **9**:40
    Kirkup **4**:189, 190
    Matthews **15**:268-69
    Shelnutt **14**:301
Ohio University Press **7**:163
Ohio Wesleyan University **8**:240-41
O'Horgan, Tom **2**:362
O'Keeffe, Georgia **1**:110
Okinawa, Japan **1**:166
Oklahoma **7**:135

Oklahoma A. & M. University **2**:244
Oklahoma City, Okla. **2**:169
Oklahoma City University **2**:167,
    169
"Old Alex" **17**:212
"Old Churchyard at St. Austell,
    The" **8**:254
Old Fictions and the New, The **8**:184
Old House of Fear **9**:100
Old Man and the Sea, The **11**:318-19
Old Ones, The **7**:256, 259
Old Poetries and the New, The **8**:184
Old Saybrook, Conn. **6**:254, 255-57
Old Snow Just Melting **14**:49
Old Westbury College **2**:71
"Old Woman" **4**:246
Oldest Confession, The **1**:196
Olitski, Jules **3**:78
Olivant **6**:180
Olivares, Julian **11**:251, 252-53, 258
Oliver, Chad **16**:212
Olsen, Tillie **3**:82
Olson, Charles
    Bowering **16**:29-30
    Corman **2**:135, 136, 137, 138
    Creeley **10**:61, 67, 70, 71, 72,
        73, 74
    Davie **3**:45
    Enslin **3**:90, 91, 94
    Gray **2**:194, 195, 198
    Kyger **16**:200
    Simpson **4**:296
    Souster **14**:315
    Waldman **17**:275
    Williams **12**:347-48
    Wilson **5**:348, 352
Olson, Elder 12:225-38
    Roditi **14**:260
Olson, Toby 11:241-60
    Owens **2**:363
    Rosenblum **11**:345
Olson's Penny Arcade **12**:236
Olympia Press
    Major **6**:185
    Rimmer **10**:297
    Wallace **1**:396
Olympian, The **9**:27
Olympic Games **14**:55-56
Olympic Games, Tokyo, 1964 **4**:188
O'Malley, Walter **4**:210
Ombres sombres, Les **7**:15
Omni **3**:285
*Omnibus of Speed: An Introduction to
    the World of Motor Sport* **16**:213
Omowale: The Child Returns Home
    3:430
On Becoming American **4**:233
On Being a Son **6**:109-10
"On Being Drafted into the U.S.
    Army from My Log Home in
    March 1942" **17**:242
On Glory's Course **1**:303
On Holography **8**:190
On Human Nature **16**:304, 306
On Light **2**:420

*On Native Grounds: An Interpretation
    of Modern American Prose
    Literature* **7**:90-92, 95
"On Saturday the Siren Sounds at
    Noon" **6**:264
On Striver's Row **6**:267
On the Big Wind **3**:200
*On the Composition of Images, Signs,
    and Ideas* **8**:92
On the Death of Archdeacon Broix
    2:55-56
*On the Death of My Father and Other
    Poems* **2**:271-72
On the Way Home **14**:28
Onassis, Jacqueline Kennedy
    Hazo **11**:141
    Slavitt **3**:322
Once for the Last Bandit **11**:150
Once on Chunuk Bair **3**:255
One Day at a Time **5**:170
One-Eyed Man Is King, The **5**:22
One for New York **3**:423-24
One Hundred Years of Solitude **9**:204
ONE (magazine) **17**:66-67
One Nation **9**:266
One of Those Condor People **13**:64
One Winter Night in August **9**:86
O'Neill, Eugene, Jr. **6**:232
Onís, Federico de **9**:202
Onley, Toni **6**:325
Onliness **7**:162, 165
Ono, Yoko **1**:363
Ontario College of Art **9**:217-18
Open Prison, An **3**:357
Open Theater **2**:411, 412, 413, 414,
    415, 416, 418, 419, 421
Opening Nights **6**:96, 102
Opera
    Gregor **10**:157-58
    Highwater **7**:73
    Kizer **5**:151-52
    Mathews **6**:226
    Schevill **12**:266-67, 271, 273-74,
        275-76
    Simpson **4**:285
    Wellek **7**:211
Operation Ares **9**:307
Opium **7**:279
Opium and the Romantic Imagination
    2:55
Oppen, George
    Enslin **3**:93
    Rakosi **5**:207, 208, 209
    Thayer **11**:361
Oppen, Mary **3**:93
Oppenheimer, Joel **12**:347
Oracle of the Thousand Hands **4**:214
Orage, A.R. **6**:319
Oral literature
    Anaya **4**:24, 27
    Awoonor **13**:41-42
    Forbes **16**:106-07
    Forrest **7**:23, 29, 30
Orbit
    Niven **12**:217
    Wolfe **9**:305

"Orbit" anthology series **10**:224
Ordeal **5**:127-28
Order of Battle **9**:5
Order of Canada **15**:251
Order of Saint John of Jerusalem,
    The **8**:24-25
Oregon **12**:169-70
Oresteia **6**:98, 100
Origin
    Enslin **3**:90, 91, 93, 98
    Fisher **10**:96
    Turnbull · **14**:333
    Wilson **5**:350
*Origin: A Biographical Novel of Charles
    Darwin, The* **3**:377
Origins of the Sexual Impulse **5**:324
Origins of Totalitarianism, The **2**:438
Orkney Herald **6**:67, 70
Orkney Islands **6**:61-62, 67-69, 72,
    73
Orkneyinga Saga **6**:61, 67
Orlando, Fla. **1**:308
Orlovsky, Peter
    Malanga **17**:110
    Plymell **11**:287, 288, 289-90, 295
O'Rourke, P.J. **11**:293, 294
O'Rourke, William **11**:206-07
Orphanages
    Green **11**:87-88
    Inez **10**:179-81
    Ray **7**:138
Ortega y Gasset, José
    Kerrigan **11**:213, 214
    Rimmer **10**:304
Orthodox Church
    Gray **2**:187
    Mano **6**:214
Orthodoxy **6**:214-15
Orton, Iris **5**:261
Orwell, George
    Glanville **9**:21
    Nichols **2**:313
    Symons **3**:387-89
    Woodcock **6**:319, 320, 321
*Orwell's Message: 1984 and the
    Present* **6**:326
Osborne, Charles **1**:29
Osborne, John
    Wesker **7**:240
    Wilson **5**:321, 323
Oster, George F. **16**:304
Osterhout, Hilda **1**:69
Osterling, Anders **1**:391
O'Sullivan, Seamus **4**:305
Othello **7**:22-23
Other Alexander, The **15**:93
Other Canadians **14**:128
Other Poetry **9**:285
Other Side of the River, The **7**:295,
    298
Other Skies **2**:93
"Other, The" **11**:211
Otherwise Engaged **3**:114
Ott, John **2**:420
Oublion Project, The **10**:304
Ouellette, Fernand 13:177-92

Oughton, Diana **2**:330
OUI **6**:215, 216, 217, 218
OuLiPo See Ouvroir de littérature
    potentielle
Our England Is a Garden **3**:356
Our Nig **6**:253
Oursler, Fulton **1**:378
Out **8**:294
Out from Ganymede **4**:219
*Out of My Depths: A Swimmer in the
    Universe* **7**:279
Out of the Night **6**:244
Outcasts, The **1**:39
Outer Mongolian, The **3**:321
Outfit, The **13**:342
Outlanders **2**:433, 436, 450
Outsider, The
    Eshleman **6**:129
    Wilson **5**:314, 319, 320, 321-22,
        327
Outward Side, The **17**:69
Ouvertures **13**:190
Ouvroir de littérature potentielle
    6:247-48
Overlay **4**:210, 213
*Overnight in the Guest House of the
    Mystic* **11**:21-22
Overtures to Death **10**:123
Ovid's Heroines **15**:235
Owen, Guy **7**:12
Owens, Rochelle 2:355-69
    Bergé **10**:6
Owlstone Crown, The **9**:86
Owning Jolene **11**:167
Oxford City Library, England **5**:110,
    112
Oxford, England
    Jennings **5**:107
    Sinclair **5**:267-68
Oxford English Dictionary, The **10**:122
Oxford History of English Literature
    3:354
Oxford Mail **2**:23, 24
Oxford Pledge **2**:207, 209
Oxford University
    Bell **12**:24-25, 27
    Booth **2**:56
    Boyd **11**:47
    Brophy **4**:85-86, 90
    Caute **4**:102-05, 106
    Epstein **12**:69-70
    Fitzgerald **10**:104
    Fuller **10**:117
    Ghiselin **10**:131, 138
    Hahn **11**:113
    Hall **7**:63
    Hamburger **4**:164, 165
    Howes **3**:140-41
    Josipovici **8**:154, 155, 156-57
    Megged **13**:157
    Roditi **14**:245, 247
    Rowse **8**:254, 255-57
    Settle **1**:320
    Stevenson **9**:285
    Stewart **3**:345, 350, 351, 354,
        355-56

    Thomas **11**:376-77
    Turner **10**:315, 316-17
    Wain **4**:324-28
    Weiss **2**:439-40
    West **7**:274-75
Oxford University, All Souls College
    Caute **4**:104
    Rowse **8**:256-57
    West **7**:274
Oxford University, Christ Church
    Hamburger **4**:163
    Rowse **8**:255
    Turner **10**:315
Oxford University, Corpus Christi
    College **15**:352, 359
Oxford University, Lincoln College
    7:275
Oxford University, Oriel College
    Mott **7**:121
    Stewart **3**:350
    Wright **5**:363, 364
Oxford University Press **5**:374
Oxford University, St. Anne's
    College **5**:107, 108
Oxford University, St. John's
    College **4**:325, 326, 328
Oz **5**:127
Ozark Folk Festival **2**:170
Ozick, Cynthia **11**:200

Pablo! **4**:261
Pacheco, Jose Emilio **17**:5, 10
Pacific Lutheran University **11**:329
Pacifica Radio Network **3**:76
Pacifism
    Ashby **6**:35-36
    Blais **4**:76
    Grumbach **2**:209
    Highwater **7**:79
    Woodcock **6**:318-19, 320, 323
Pack, Robert **10**:38
Packer, Tina **6**:236-37, 249
Paden, William **6**:135, 136, 142
Padgett, Ron **6**:180
Padilla, Heberto **11**:192
Padma Bhushan Award **9**:233, 234
Pagayaw, Saddani **9**:164
Page of History, A **3**:63
Page, P.K. **15**:153
Paige, D.D. **2**:434
Paik, Nam June **10**:7
Paine, Thomas **9**:177
Painted Bird, The **9**:112, 115
Painted Dresses **11**:165-66, 167
Painted Turtle: Woman with Guitar
    6:197, 198
Paisan **2**:394
Pakistan **9**:228-29
Pakula, Alan **2**:331
Palace of the Peacock **16**:125
Palamountain, Joseph **9**:205
Palestinian movement **11**:68
Paley, Grace **6**:117
Palmer, Mrs. Charles (pseudonym of
    Mary Lee Settle) **1**:314
Palmetto Country **1**:150

Palomar College **2**:121
Palomino **13**:116, 121
Palpable God, A **6**:259
Pan Tadeusz **3**:39
Panassié, Hugues **10**:92
Papadopoulos, Yannis **15**:77-78, 92
Papandreou, Andreas **3**:248
Papanoutsos, Evangelos P. **16**:258-60
Paper Cage, The **5**:291
Paper Soul **13**:248
Paper, The **15**:124
Papo Got His Gun **17**:7, 9
*Paracriticisms: Seven Speculations of the
    Times* **12**:160
Parade **1**:401
Paradise Lost **10**:316
Paradox of Oscar Wilde, The **6**:321
Paralysis **1**:36-38
Paramount Studios
    Gunn **2**:254
    Wallace **1**:387
Paranormal phenomena
    Awoonor **13**:53
    Wilson **5**:325-26
"Pardoner's Tale" **2**:210
Parijat **14**:91
Parini, Jay 16:227-43
    Stevenson **9**:285
Paris, France
    Bergé **10**:4
    Blais **4**:77
    Bowles **1**:82, 83
    Broughton **12**:56
    Burroway **6**:92
    Condon **1**:194, 195, 197
    Connell **2**:107, 108, 109
    Corman **2**:137-39
    Eastlake **1**:208
    Federman **8**:68-70
    Gray **2**:185-86, 194-95
    Guerard **2**:216, 217-19, 220-21
    Hailey **1**:228
    Hall **7**:63
    Hine **15**:227-28
    Kennedy **9**:82
    Klinkowitz **9**:118
    Lottman **12**:197-99, 208
    Menashe **11**:226-27
    Mott **7**:119
    Nichols **2**:328
    O'Faolain **2**:346-47, 349
    Pohl **1**:288
    Rosenthal **6**:285
    Settle **1**:316
    Simic **4**:276-77
    Sisson **3**:298
    Van Itallie **2**:411
    Weiss **2**:439
    Wright **7**:294-95
Paris Review
    Connell **2**:108
    Disch **4**:149
    Kennedy **9**:83
    Settle **1**:315
    Wilson **5**:318
Parker, Charlie **8**:73

Parkinson, Thomas **1**:357, 359, 369
Parkman, Francis **3**:44
Parks, Rosa **2**:294
Parochial education
    Jennings **5**:105-06
    Kienzle **1**:239, 241
    Klinkowitz **9**:109
    Kumin **8**:208
    O'Faolain **2**:342-43, 344-45
Parrish, Robert **12**:9
Parson's School of Fine and Applied
    Arts **1**:113
Parti-Colored Blocks for a Quilt **1**:277
Parti Québecois **13**:186
*Partial Accounts: New and Selected
    Poems* **14**:220
Partisan Review
    Baumbach **5**:26, 28
    Dennison **6**:113
    Lottman **12**:205
    Markfield **3**:212, 220
Pasadena Junior College **17**:62-63
Pascal, Blaise **1**:57
Pascal, Gabriel **14**:258-59
Pasha, Mustafa el-Nahhas **12**:138
Pasmore, Victor **10**:120
Pass, The **15**:333
Passage of Summer **15**:151-52, 156-57
Passage through Gehenna **11**:184
"Passengers" **3**:281
Passions of the Mind, The **3**:367, 376
Passport and Other Stories, The
    16:263-66
Past Must Alter, The **2**:215, 216,
    219, 221, 223
Pasternak, Boris
    Davie **3**:40, 44
    Feinstein **1**:221
    Fuller **10**:123-24
Patch Boys, The **16**:237-38
Patchen, Kenneth
    Souster **14**:311
    Williams **12**:342, 343
Pater, Walter
    Boyle **1**:112
    Weiss **2**:429
    West **7**:274
Paterson (William Carlos Williams)
    3:90
Patmos and Other Poems **5**:284
Patrick, Walton **11**:183
Patrocinio Barela: Taos Woodcarver
    14:112
Patten, Brian **2**:52
Pattern of the Chinese Past, The **9**:284
*Pattern Poetry: Guide to an Unknown
    Literature* **8**:92
Patterns **3**:72
Patterson **16**:192
Pauker, John **8**:306
Paul Robeson Award **14**:57
Paul, Sherman **2**:145
Paulhan, Jean **2**:67
Pavane **2**:414
Payne, Robert **15**:69-70, 71
Paz, Octavio **11**:194

P.D. Kimerakov **12**:73
Peace **9**:311
Peace Corps
    Dacey **17**:24-26
    Knebel **3**:181
Peaceable Kingdom, The **5**:261, 263,
    264
Pearce, Roy Harvey **2**:144
Pearl **7**:221
Pearl, Eric (pseudonym) See Elman,
    Richard
Pearl on the Bottom, The **12**:191,
    193
Pearson, John **1**:74, 77
Pearson, Norman Holmes
    Major **6**:187-88
    Rosenblum **11**:348
Peaslee, Richard **2**:418, 419
Peck, Tom **2**:272
Peel, Alfreda Marion **7**:8
Pegler, Westbrook **3**:177
Peirce, C.S. **12**:329-30
Peixotto, Jessica **3**:367
Peking, China **1**:34-35
Pelieu, Claude **11**:288, 289
Pellegrini, Angelo 11:261-74
PEN
    Kirkup **4**:187
    Megged **13**:158
    Rakosi **5**:198
    Skelton **5**:288, 289
    Swenson **13**:316
    Wallace **1**:402
PEN/Faulkner Award
    Grumbach **2**:214
    Olson **11**:259
    Settle **1**:321
Pendray, G. Edward **10**:3
*Penguin Book of English Romantic
    Verse, The* **5**:373
Penguin Book of Everyday Verse, The
    5:373
Penguin New Writing **6**:21
Penguin (publishers)
    Brunner **8**:11
    Jones **5**:127
Penn, Irving **2**:189
Pennington, Anne **9**:285
Pennsylvania State University
    Wagoner **3**:402-03, 404, 405
    West **7**:280
Penny Links **8**:103
Pensamientos **16**:77, 81
Penthouse **6**:153-54
People Live Here **4**:296
People's Almanac, The **1**:376, 379,
    400
*Peoples of the Coast: The Indians of the
    Pacific Northwest* **6**:324
People's party See Progressive party
People's Voice **6**:264
Père Goriot, Le **2**:385
Perec, Georges **6**:237-39, 245, 247,
    248, 250
Perfect Murder, The **8**:171-72, 174,
    175

Perfect Vacuum, A **1**:255, 262, 263
Perkins, Maxwell
    Bourjaily **1**:68, 69
    Brown **6**:56
Perkins, Tony **9**:251
Perls, Frederick **6**:114-15
Perls, Lore **6**:115
Perry, Anne **7**:292, 293
Perry, Ruth **6**:119
Perry, Shauneille **13**:251
Persephone **8**:278
Persia See Iran
Persky, Stan **16**:196
Personal Accounts **13**:211
Personal and Possessive **11**:373
Personal Voice, The **2**:229
Peru
    Eshleman **6**:138-39
    Goldemberg **12**:91, 94, 98, 103-
        06
Pessoa, Fernando **8**:116, 117
Pétain, Philippe **12**:207, 208
Peter, John **5**:287
*Peters Black and Blue Guides to
    Current Literary Journals* **8**: 248
Peters, Margery **13**:247
Peters, Pete **6**:198
Peters, Robert 8:237-52
Petersen, Will
    Corman **2**:140, 141, 142, 143,
        144
    Eshleman **6**:135-36
Peterson, Emily **1**:106
Petesch, Natalie L.M. 12:239-51
Petrenko, P. **4**:360-61
Petry, Ann 6:253-69
Petry, George **6**:264
Pets
    Dillard **7**:18-19
    Lifshin **10**:240, 250
Pettet, Edwin **8**:306
Pezzati, Albert **2**:117
Pflaum Publishing Co. **8**:273
Phaedra **1**:315
Pharos Press **5**:290, 292
Phelps, Lyon **7**:62
Phenomena **16**:16, 17
Phi Beta Kappa
    Knebel **3**:169
    Rabassa **9**:202
    St. Clair **8**:272
    Stevenson **9**:279
Phil Hill: Yankee Champion **16**:213
Philadelphia, Pa. **16**:59-62
Philippine Magazine **9**:158
Philippines **9**:151-65, 166-68
Philips, Robert **4**:156
Phillabaum, Leslie **4**:122
Phillips Exeter Academy **7**:58, 59-61
Phillips, Judith **13**:199-200, 201,
    202, 203, 204-10
Phillips, Robert 13:193-216
Phillips University **12**:237
Phillips, William **8**:293
Phillis Wheatley Conference **13**:249-
    50

Philosophy
    Matthews **15**:262
    Ouellette **13**:181
    Solotaroff **2**:394
    Weiss **12**:326-27, 334-35
Philosophy of Chance **1**:263
Photography
    Bell **14**:41, 42-43, 44, 45-47
    Malanga **17**:96-97
Photoplay **1**:378
Picano, Felice 13:217-35
Picasso, Pablo
    Caldwell **1**:156
    Fisher **10**:98
    Kerrigan **11**:189, 191, 194, 205,
        206
Piccione, Anthony **9**:41
Picciotto, Robert S. **12**:91-94
Pick, John **6**:230-31
Pick, J.R. **1**:330-31
Pickford, Mary **11**:46-47
Picnic in the Snow, The **8**:247, 248
Picture Theory **16**:52-53
Pictures of the Journey Back **15**:266
Pieratt, Asa **9**:113
Piercy, Marge 1:267-81
    Elman **3**:77
Piero della Francesca **3**:356
Pierre-Joseph Proudhon **6**:322
*Pierre ou la Guerre du Printemps
    '81* **4**:73-74, 77, 78
Pierrot lunaire **8**:159
"Pig Pen" **16**:67
Pigeon Project, The **1**:398
Pilar, Maria **3**:428
Pilgrim Award **2**:257
Pillard, Basil **8**:132
Pindar
    Enslin **3**:90
    Thomas **4**:310
Pineville, Ky. **1**:307
Pinocchio **1**:192, 193
Pinsky, Robert 4:237-51
Pinter, Harold **3**:113, 114
Piper, Dan **9**:80
Piper, Edwin Ford **6**:20
Pissarro, Camille **3**:379
Pit Strike **2**:386
Pittsburgh, Pa. **3**:22, 25
Pius XII, Pope
    Greeley **7**:43
    Kienzle **1**:242
    Stone **3**:373
Place, Francis **5**:276
Place of Birth **2**:275
Place of Love, The **6**:296
Place to Stand, A **3**:407
Places to Go **16**:199, 200
Plague, The **2**:385
Plagued by the Nightingale **1**:115
Planet Stories **2**:40
Plarr, Victor **10**:112
Plath, Sylvia
    Brown **10**:37
    Burroway **6**:87, 91, 92
    Davison **4**:134, 135, 137-38

Rosenthal **6**:283-84
Stevenson **9**:283, 287
Play By Play **12**:95, 99-100, 101-02,
    104-05
Playboy
    Disch **4**:152
    Elman **3**:74
    Mano **6**:216, 218
    Nolan **16**:213, 214, 216
Playground, The (film) **5**:80
Playground, The (James Broughton)
    12:53
Plays & Poems: 1948–1958 **12**:235
Playwriting
    Bullins **16**:67-68
    Hine **15**:226
    Malzberg **4**:208
Pleasure-Dome **3**:199-200
Pleasure Garden, The **12**:54-55
Plimpton, George
    Burroway **6**:90
    Connell **2**:108
Plomer, William **6**:42
Plot, The **1**:384, 385, 395
Plum Plum Pickers, The **15**:119-21
Plume and Sword **7**:180
Plumly, Stanley **9**:41
Plunkett, Joseph **3**:49
Plutarch **6**:34
Plymell, Charles 11:275-96
P.N. Review **3**:307
Po Chu-i **7**:78
Pochoda, Phil **4**:158
Pocket Book of Science Fiction, The
    9:301
Pocket Books
    Bourjaily **1**:70
    Niven **12**:222
    Wallace **1**:385, 393
    Wolfe **9**:311
Pocket Theatre **2**:414, 415, 416
Podhoretz, Norman **2**:398, 399
Poe, Edgar Allan
    Dillard **7**:6, 17
    Forrest **7**:28
    Glanville **9**:19
    Kizer **5**:147
    Rechy **4**:262
    Shapiro **6**:288, 289-90
    Sward **13**:284
    Symons **3**:391, 392
Poemas humanos **6**:137, 138, 144
Poems Are Hard to Read **14**:229-30,
    235
Poems (Elizabeth Jennings) **5**:110
Poems for All the Annettes **17**:207
Poems for Exchange **15**:106
Poems for F. **14**:257
Poems for Spain **1**:18
Poems from the Old English **9**:212,
    213, 215
Poems Made of Skin **10**:6
Poems of a Decade, 1931–1941 **8**:260
Poems of Doctor Zhivago, The **3**:44
Poems of Mao Tse-tung, The **15**:70

Poems 1928–1948 **14**:259, 260, 265, 267
Poet and the Poem, The **8**:135
Poet & the Translator, The **3**:307
Poet as Ice-Skater, The **8**:248
"Poet in the Bank, The" **8**:308
Poet in the Imaginary Museum: Essays of Two Decades, The **11**:236
Poet Santa Cruz **13**:300
Poetic Art of Horace, The **3**:306
Poetic Image in Six Genres, The **3**:195
Poetic Pattern, The **5**:284
Poetry
　Booth **2**:59
　Cassity **8**:58-59
　Forbes **16**:105-19
　Hamburger **4**:167
　Hazo **11**:152
　Heyen **9**:40, 44-45
　Jerome **8**:130-31
　Katz **9**:62-63, 68
　Livesay **8**:223-24
　Nichols **2**:319
　Rosenblum **11**:341-42, 344-45, 348, 352
Poetry and Jazz concerts
　Abse **1**:28-29
　Dacey **17**:34-35
Poetry and the Common Life **6**:280
Poetry Book Society **5**:284
Poetry London **3**:36
Poetry (magazine)
　Allen **11**:19
　Bell **14**:47-48
　Bergé **10**:7
　Ciardi **2**:90
　Forbes **16**:116
　Hine **15**:234, 235
　Jerome **8**:133
　Kerrigan **11**:208
　Mahapatra **9**:146
　Nims **17**:179
　Olson **12**:228-29
　Pinsky **4**:246
　Rakosi **5**:207
　Rosenthal **6**:276
　Saroyan **5**:215
　Shapiro **6**:292, 302
　Stafford **3**:334
　Wagoner **3**:403, 404
　Wilson **5**:351
Poetry Nation Review **3**:46-47
Poetry Northwest **3**:408, 410, 411
Poetry of Dylan Thomas, The **12**:234
Poetry of the Thirties **5**:286
Poetry Society (Great Britain)
　Booth **2**:52
　Hamburger **4**:169
Poetry Taos, Number One **14**:112
Poet's Art, The **6**:280
Poets' Encyclopedia, The **13**:15, 19
Poets-in-the-Schools program
　Root **11**:325-26
　Sward **13**:295, 297
　Swenson **13**:314
Poets of Bulgaria **14**:232

Poets of the Pacific, Second Series **3**:36
Poets of Today
　Simpson **4**:293
　Slavitt **3**:318
Poet's Other Voice: Conversations on Literary Translation, The **8**:120
Poets' Theater, Cambridge, Mass.
　Davison **4**:134
　Hall **7**:62-63
Poet's Tongue, The **10**:121, 123
Poets' Workshop **2**:52
Poets' Yearbook Award **2**:57
Pohl, Frederik 1:283-98
　Aldiss **2**:27, 28, 29
　Bradley **10**:21
　Budrys **14**:66-67, 68, 77-78
　Gunn **2**:239, 248, 249, 253, 258
　Knight **10**:203, 209, 215, 216, 218
　Malzberg **4**:209
　Niven **12**:217
　Silverberg **3**:277
　Williamson **8**:320, 324, 325, 326
　Wolfe **9**:304-05, 308, 311
Point Blank **13**:342
Point Counterpoint **2**:22
Point of Transfer **17**:206
Points on the Grid **16**:24, 31
Poison Pen **5**:77, 80
Poison Penmanship: The Gentle Art of Muckraking **17**:149, 151
Poker Game **3**:182
Poland
　Konwicki **9**:123-34
　Lem **1**:255-56
　Mrozek **10**:266-78
Poles **7**:279
Polio **12**:226
Polish Subtitles: Impressions from a Journey **15**:228
Political Portfolio **15**:124
Politicians, Poets, and Con Men: Emotional History in Late Victorian America **9**:219
Politics **6**:320
Politics and the Younger Generation **8**:257, 258
Pollet, Elizabeth **3**:415
Pomerantz, Edward **11**:255, 256
Pontes, Peter **1**:29
Poole, C.W. **3**:346
Poore, Charles **1**:73
Poorhouse State, The **3**:74, 83
Pope, Theodate **12**:347
Popescu, Petru **2**:58
"Popeye" **2**:37
Popular Culture Explosion, The **3**:196
Popular Publications **10**:209, 217
Pornography
　Giovanni **6**:153, 154
　Jones **5**:127-28
　Rimmer **10**:303-04
Portable Novels of Science **3**:271
Porter, Arabel **13**:10
Porter, Bern **6**:187
Porter, Don **6**:181, 182

Porter, Katherine Anne
　Dillard **7**:14
　Nims **17**:185
　Purdy **1**:302
Porter, Sylvia **1**:293
Portrait and Other Poems, The **5**:258
Portrait of a Wilderness **4**:309
Portrait of an Artist with 26 Horses **1**:210, 212
Portrait of the Artist as a Young Man, A
　Belitt **4**:54
　Forrest **7**:23
　Simpson **4**:290
Possession **2**:156
Postcards: Don't You Just Wish You Were Here! **2**:76-77
Postmodern Turn: Essays in Postmodern Theory and Culture, The **12**:149
"Postscript" **17**:212
Potomac Fever **3**:179
Potter, Beatrix **2**:341
Poulson, M. Wilford **5**:40, 41-42
Pound, Ezra
　Allen **6**:18
　Creeley **10**:70
　Davie **3**:39, 40, 45
　Dudek **14**:126, 130-33
　Enslin **3**:90, 94
　Feinstein **1**:221
　Gregor **10**:149
　Katz **9**:68
　McCord **9**:180
　Morgan **4**:227
　Olson **12**:234
　Pinsky **4**:244
　Raffel **9**:219
　Rakosi **5**:207
　Sisson **3**:305
　Škvorecký **1**:348
　Waldman **17**:273, 276, 277
　Whittemore **8**:306, 308, 310
　Wright **7**:296, 297, 302
Pournelle, Jerry
　Anderson **2**:44, 45
　Niven **12**:212, 215, 217, 218, 219, 220, 221-22
Powell, Bud **6**:182
Powell, Roxie **11**:284, 294
Power and Glory **14**:159
Power of the Dog, The **15**:337, 339, 344
Power of the Pen, The **15**:251
Powers, J.F. **9**:84
Powers, John Robert **1**:192
"Powers of Heaven and Earth, The" **17**:160-61
Powys, John Cowper
　Boyle **1**:99
　Fisher **10**:96
　Purdy **1**:302
Powys, Llewelyn **10**:131
Practical Knowledge for All **5**:313
Practical Pig, The **1**:192, 193
Prague, Czechoslovakia
　Škvorecký **1**:334-48, 350

Wellek **7**:210-11
Prague English Studies **7**:221
Prashker, Betty **12**:207
Pratt, E.J. **8**:220
Pratt, Enoch, Free Library, Baltimore,
    Md. **6**:292
*Praying Wrong: New and Selected
    Poems, 1957-1984* **4**:134, 140,
    141
Precise Fragments **9**:182
Pregnant Man, The **13**:205
Premar Experiments, The **10**:300
Preminger, Otto **1**:181, 182
Premio Quinto Sol Award **4**:24
Presbyterianism
    Brown **6**:73
    Cassity **8**:39
Present Tense prize **13**:158
President, The **1**:172
Presidential Commission on the
    Holocaust **4**:360
President's Lady, The **3**:373
Presley, Elvis **12**:348, 353
Pressed on Sand **17**:204
Pressler, Menahem **2**:162
Pressure of Time, The **4**:152, 157
Preston, Billy **13**:251
Preston, Don **1**:171, 173
Pretoria, South Africa **8**:49, 50-52,
    56
Pretty Boy Dead **17**:68
Preuss, Paul **12**:213, 215, 216
Preview **14**:128
Price, Reynolds
    Chappell **4**:115, 116, 125
    Petry **6**:259
Pride and the Passion, The **1**:195
Priest, Robert **13**:297-98
Primer for Combat **1**:117
*Primer of the Novel: For Readers and
    Writers* **3**:198
Prince, Harold **2**:419
Prince Ishmael **11**:126-27, 134-35
Prince of Darkness and Co., The
    15:227
Princess of All Lands, The **9**:103
Princeton University
    Abse **1**:31
    Bell **12**:29-30, 31, 32-33, 36
    Garrett **5**:79, 88
    Kazin **7**:95
    Mathews **6**:223, 232, 245
    Meredith **14**:225, 226
    Sparshott **15**:351
    Van Itallie **2**:417, 418, 422
    Weiss **2**:448-49
    Wellek **7**:217-20
    Whittemore **8**:304-05, 308
    Williams **12**:350
Princeton University Press
    Kerrigan **11**:213
    Wagoner **3**:411
Principles of English Metre, The
    2:380
Pringle, Val **2**:293
Prison Notes **4**:76

"Prisoner, The" **4**:153
Prisons **1**:309, 314, 319, 320
Pritchett, V.S. **9**:26-27
Private Line **6**:185
Prix de Meilleur des Livres
    Etrangers **4**:117
Prix de Rome
    Simpson **4**:294
    Williams **3**:413-15
Prix Médicis
    Blais **4**:74, 76
    Zinoviev **10**:335
Prize, The **1**:377, 380, 384, 385,
    391-93
Prizewinner, The **9**:242-43
"Problems of Creativeness" **4**:151
Processionals **3**:98
"Prodigal Son" (parable) **2**:155
Progress of a Crime, The **3**:390
Progressive Herald (Syracuse, N.Y.)
    3:421
Progressive party
    Cassill **1**:167
    Ciardi **2**:94
Prohibition
    Condon **1**:187
    Knebel **3**:169
Prohibition **5**:271
Prohibition **3**:364
"Projective Verse" **5**:348
Proletarian Writers of the Thirties
    3:194
Promethean Fire **16**:304
Prometheus Books **10**:303
Pronzini, Bill **4**:219
Propertius, Sextus **8**:280
Property and Value **17**:92
Proposition 31 **10**:295, 299-300
Proselytizer, The **6**:206, 210, 215
Prosody
    Hall **7**:64, 65
    Shapiro **6**:301-02
    Sillitoe **2**:380
Prostitution
    Guerard **2**:220-21
    Rechy **4**:259-60, 263
Protestantism **7**:209
Proust, Marcel
    Becker **1**:36, 43
    Brée **15**:128, 136
    Brossard **2**:74, 76
    Josipovici **8**:152-53, 154-55
    Katz **14**:168
    Konwicki **9**:129
    Rabassa **9**:198
    Van Itallie **2**:411
Providence Journal **5**:97-98
Provocation **1**:261
Pryce-Jones, Alan **1**:318
Prynne, Jeremy **5**:198, 199
Pryor, Richard **3**:432
"Psychic Pretenders, The" **16**:67
Psychoanalysis
    Brophy **4**:86
    Feirstein **11**:83
    Roditi **14**:261, 265

Van Brunt **15**:379, 381
    Williamson **8**:318-19, 321
Psychology of Power, The **1**:102
*Psychovisual Perspective for "Musical"
    Composition, A* **16**:15
Ptáčník, Karel **1**:342
"Pub" **3**:386
Public Affairs Television **2**:414
Public Broadcasting System **3**:74
    See also National Educational
    Television
Public Landing Revisited **13**:211
Public Lending Right **4**:86, 87, 88,
    91
Public speaking **6**:162-63
Publishers Weekly
    Garrett **5**:80
    Lottman **12**:206, 209
    Wallace **1**:395
Puccini, Giacomo **14**:127
Pudney, John **10**:124-26
Pueblo de Dios y de Mandinga **15**:13
Puerto Rico
    Bell **12**:34
    Cassity **8**:44-47
    Cruz **17**:1-5, 11-13, 15-16
Pugh, Lewis **4**:309
Pulitzer **13**:268
Pulitzer, Joseph
    Nims **17**:156
    Swanberg **13**:268
Pulitzer Prize
    Killens **2**:295, 304
    Kizer **5**:156
    McPherson **17**:123, 133
    Meredith **14**:219-20
    Morgan **4**:230
    Shapiro **6**:300-01
    Simpson **4**:293, 294
    Stegner **9**:269
    Swanberg **13**:268, 272
    Taylor **7**:187
    Wilson **16**:306
Pulp magazines
    Bradley **10**:21
    Brown **6**:47, 48
    Higgins **5**:96
    Kennedy **9**:77-78
    Knight **10**:202, 203, 204-05, 209
    Lem **1**:260
    Malzberg **4**:207
    Moorcock **5**:175, 176, 177-78,
        179-81
    St. Clair **8**:273
    Wilhelm **5**:300
    Williamson **8**:316-18, 324
    Wolfe **9**:301, 304-05
Puppies of Terra, The **4**:151
Purdue University
    Cassill **1**:172
    Honig **8**:110
Purdum, Richard **9**:41
Purdy, Al 17:195-214
Purdy, James 1:299-305
Pure Lives **8**:311
Purge, The **12**:208

Purity of Diction in English Verse **3**:37
Purves, Alan **9**:203
Pushcart Award **15**:30
Pushkin, Aleksandr
    Killens **2**:305-06
    Thomas **11**:377
Putnam Creative Writing Award
    2:194
Putnam Prize **2**:331
Putnam Publishing Group
    Grumbach **2**:212
    Nichols **2**:331
Pygmalion **10**:286
Pyle, Howard **2**:323
Pynchon, Thomas **9**:111

Q Document, The **2**:168, 172, 174
Qadir, Manzur **9**:229
Quakers See Friends, Society of
Quarantuno **13**:66, 68
Quarterly Review of Literature
    Busch **1**:132
    Weiss **2**:433-34, 435, 439, 443,
        445, 447
Quartermaine's Terms **3**:109
Quebec, Canada
    Blais **4**:70-73, 74
    Brossard **16**:46-47
    Ouellette **13**:185-86
Queen Mary (ship) **4**:277-78
Queen of Stones **9**:293
Queen's College, Georgetown,
    Guyana **16**:129-32
Queen's University **15**:155
Quena **6**:138
Queneau, Raymond
    Brossard **2**:66, 67-68
    Mathews **6**:247
Quest for Corvo, The **3**:383
"Quetzal Birds" **17**:212
Quicksand **8**:11
Quigley Seminary, Chicago, Ill. **7**:37,
    40-42
Quincy, U.S.D. (pseudonym of Vance
    Bourjaily) **1**:73
Quinn, Anthony **16**:241
Quinn, James L. **10**:221
Quinn, Robert H. **5**:99
Quinn, Rosemary **2**:417, 421
Quinto Sol Publications **4**:24

R Document, The **1**:384, 398
Rabassa, Clara **9**:204-05
Rabassa, Gregory 9:191-206
Race relations **3**:414, 419-20, 422
Rachlin, Nahid 17:215-29
Rachmaninoff, Sergei Vasilyevich
    12:352
Racism
    Ai **13**:2, 3
    Awoonor **13**:38, 43-44, 46-47
    Bennett **13**:74, 81, 83, 84-85, 88
    Booth **5**:40
    Bullins **16**:62
    Dacey **17**:26
    Forbes **16**:119

Garrett **5**:86
Giovanni **6**:159
Hauser **11**:133, 134
Hinojosa-Smith **16**:149
Kerrigan **11**:193
Major **6**:175, 176, 179, 183-84,
    189, 193, 194, 202
Petry **6**:255-56, 258, 266, 268-69
Salisbury **15**:318-19
Smith **7**:161
Still **17**:234
Radcliffe College
    Brewster **15**:155
    Kumin **8**:213-14
Radcliffe College, Bunting Institute
    13:11
*Radical Innocence: Studies in the
    Contemporary American Novel*
    12:149, 161, 164
Radicalism **2**:198
Radiguet, Raymond
    Boyle **1**:116
    Gray **3**:107
Radio
    Boyd **11**:46
    Hoffman **10**:163, 164, 165, 168
    Kostelanetz **8**:187
Radio broadcasting
    Andre **13**:14
    Hine **15**:226
    Roditi **14**:263-65, 267
    Skelton **5**:282
    Wagoner **3**:400
    Williams **3**:421
    Woodcock **6**:322
Radio-Canada **13**:183-84
Radnóti, Miklós **10**:321
RAF See Great Britain, Royal Air
    Force
Raffel, Burton 9:207-21
Ragged Trousered Philanthropists, The
    2:384
Raging Bull **5**:218
Raging Joys, Sublime Violations **2**:71
Ragman's Daughter, The **2**:386
Ragni, Gerry **2**:412
Rago, Henry **14**:47-48
Rahv, Philip **3**:212
Rai, E.N. Mangat **9**:224-25, 228,
    231
Rain of Rites, A **9**:146, 147
Rainbow **6**:32
Raine, Kathleen
    Menashe **11**:232-34, 236
    Weiss **2**:446
*Rainy Hills: Verses after a Japanese
    Fashion, The* **15**:357
Rajneesh, Bhagwan Shree **10**:305
Rakosi, Carl 5:193-210
    Rosenblum **11**:345, 348, 349, 350
Raman, A.S. **9**:233
Ramanujan, A.K. **15**:157
Ramos, Maximo **9**:167
Ramos, Remedios **9**:167
Ramparts **6**:140
Rancho Linda Vista **11**:327

Randall, John Herman **7**:218-19
Randall, Margaret
    Enslin **3**:94
    Major **6**:184
Randolph-Macon Woman's College,
    Lynchburg, Va. **3**:237, 238
*Randolph of Roanoke: A Study in
    Conservative Thought* **9**:95, 97
Randolph, Vance **2**:170
Random House (publishers)
    Becker **1**:42
    Cassill **1**:167
    Mathews **6**:241
Random Walk **11**:39
Rangan, Josephine **5**:151-52
Ranger **3**:95
Ransom, John Crowe
    Abse **1**:27
    Harris **3**:117
    Slavitt **3**:315
    Wagoner **3**:403
Ransome, Arthur **4**:100
Rapf, Matthew **2**:172
Raphael, Frederic **9**:17, 18, 26, 27
Rapids of Time **10**:121
Rasp, Renate **6**:192, 195
Rat Man of Paris **7**:283, 285
Rathbone, Julian **10**:101
Rats, The **2**:385
Rau, Aurel **5**:355
Rausch, Howard **10**:226
Ravagli, Angelo **10**:133
Ravenshaw College **9**:142
Raw Material **2**:381, 387
Raw Silk **6**:87, 99, 101, 102
Rawling, Tom **9**:285
Raworth, Tom 11:297-311
    Beltrametti **13**:68-69
Rawson, Clayton **10**:222
Ray, David 7:135-53
    Mahapatra **9**:146
    Olson **12**:237
    Petesch **12**:247, 248, 249
Ray, Satyajit **3**:27
Raymond, John **2**:348
Read, Herbert
    Fuller **10**:118-19
    Kerrigan **11**:209
    Woodcock **6**:319, 320
Read, Piers Paul **10**:119
Reade, Vivian **12**:296-97
Reader's Digest
    Barrio **15**:124
    Horwood **15**:249
    Knebel **3**:179
    Slavitt **3**:316
Reader's Digest Book Club **1**:395
Reader's Digest Condensed Books
    3:180, 181
Reading, Pa. **2**:426
Readings in Economic Development
    3:245
Reagan, Ronald
    Condon **1**:194, 198
    Fuchs **5**:57
    Kirk **9**:99, 102

Wallace **1**:379
Real Long John Silver, The **12**:11
Real Presence **14**:9-10, 12
Realism **4**:329
    See also Anti-Realism in literature
Reality **12**:331
Really the Blues **8**:5, 6
Really the Blues (musical) **1**:339
Realm of Prester John, The **3**:281
Reaney, James Crerar 15:295-309
Rear Column, The **3**:114
Rebellion of Yale Marratt, The **10**:281,
    285, 286, 288, 289, 291, 296-
    97, 298
Rebetez, René **10**:229
Recapitulation **9**:262, 264, 269
Rechy, John 4:253-66
Recollection of a Visitor on Earth
    1:157
Recoveries **2**:448, 449
Recyclings **8**:188
Red and the Blue, The **5**:276
Red Army **12**:311, 312-13
Red Beans **17**:15-16
Red Cavalry **5**:260
Red-Hot Vacuum, The **2**:400, 403
Red Noses **12**:13
Red Wolf, Red Wolf **7**:107
Redbook **2**:120
Reddaway, Peter **9**:283
Rediscoveries: Informal Essays in Which
    Well-Known Novelists Rediscover
    Neglected Works of Fiction by One
    of Their Favorite Authors **3**:196
Rediscovery **13**:45
Reed, Carol **4**:102
Reed College
    O'Faolain **2**:350
    Ray **7**:143
Reed, Ishmael
    Anaya **4**:26
    Bergé **10**:13
    Klinkowitz **9**:112
    Major **6**:185, 186, 188
    Sukenick **8**:293
Reed, Oliver **5**:274
Reed, Rex **2**:361
Reese, Harry **8**:119
Reflections on the Revolution in
    France **9**:95
Reflex and Bone Structure **6**:191, 194,
    198
Regions with No Proper Names **11**:19
Regnery, Henry **9**:100
Regrets, The **3**:307
Reich, Wilhelm
    Dennison **6**:114-15
    Eshleman **6**:142
Reid, Alastair
    Mathews **6**:235
    Parini **16**:233, 241
    Stevenson **9**:285
Reid, Marguerite **15**:246, 247
Reiter, Thomas **13**:94, 103
Relation Ship, The (Tom Raworth)
    11:302

Relationship (Jayanta Mahapatra)
    9:147-48
Religion
    Allen **11**:7
    Awoonor **13**:53
    Bell **14**:38
    Bennett **13**:86
    Boyd **11**:43, 45, 47
    Bullins **16**:65-66
    Choudhury **14**:85
    Clarke **16**:72
    Hahn **11**:107-08
    Hamburger **4**:170
    Harris **16**:123-24
    Hassan **12**:142-44
    Hitchcock **12**:167-68
    Houston **16**:161-62
    Kerrigan **11**:194-96
    Kizer **5**:145
    Ouellette **13**:178, 179-80
    St. Clair **8**:271
    Salisbury **15**:319
    Shadbolt **3**:258
    Wakefield **7**:201
    Weiss **12**:333-34
    Wilhelm **5**:302-03
    Woodcock **6**:315
Religion: A Secular Theory **7**:49
Religion and the Rebel **5**:322-23, 324
Religion See also Atheism
Religious literature **2**:345
Reluctant Dictator, The **9**:20
Remaking of Sigmund Freud, The
    4:213, 219
Remarkable Case of Burglary, A **8**:172
Remarkable Exploits of Lancelot Biggs:
    Spaceman, The **7**:14
Rembrandt **2**:140
"Remembering Catullus" **17**:177
Remembering James Agee **3**:198
Remembering Laughter **9**:264
Remembering Summer **15**:242-43, 248,
    249-50, 251
Renaissance, The **2**:429
Renato, Amato **3**:264-65
Renfield, Elinor **2**:421
Rensselaer Polytechnic Institute
    12:155, 156
Repertorio Americano **15**:4
Report on Probability A **2**:29
Republic Pictures **1**:382
Republican party **15**:320-21
Reruns **5**:26, 28
Rescue the Dead **3**:152
Reserve Officers' Training Corps
    Highwater **7**:79
    Manuel **9**:155-56
    McCord **9**:178
    Pinsky **4**:243
    Plymell **11**:283
Resident Alien **3**:15, 16, 18, 20, 22,
    26, 29
Residue of Song **14**:50
Resistance **6**:219
Rest Is Prose, The **11**:153

Resurrection of Anne Hutchinson, The
    10:304
Retreat to Innocence **5**:122
Return Engagements **9**:254, 255
Return from the Stars **1**:261, 262,
    264
Return, The **10**:318
Returning: A Spiritual Journey **7**:201,
    202
"Returning to Church" **7**:201-02
Revelations **4**:213
Reversals **9**:284
Review of Metaphysics **12**:332
Revolt in the South **7**:197
Revolt of the Masses, The
    Kerrigan **11**:213-14
    Rimmer **10**:304
Revolt on Alpha C **3**:273
Revolution in European Poetry **14**:131
Rexroth, Kenneth
    Broughton **12**:52
    Feirstein **11**:81
    Hamill **15**:206, 212
    Olson **12**:234
    Roditi **14**:283, 286
    Weiss **2**:445
    Williams **12**:343-44
    Wilson **5**:349
Reyes, Alfonso **15**:5
Reyes, Carlos **5**:351
Reynal & Hitchcock (publishers)
    8:305
Reynolds, Paul
    Duncan **2**:170, 176
    Wallace **1**:386, 389, 401
Reznikoff, Charles **5**:207, 208, 209
Rhodes, Bob **5**:349
Rhodes Scholarship **12**:22
Rhodesia See Zimbabwe
Rhodomagnetic Digest **16**:212
Rhys, Keidrych **4**:306
Rhythm and blues
    Forbes **16**:107
    Smith **7**:159
Ribbentrop-Molotov Pact See Nazi-
    Soviet Pact
Rich, Adrienne **6**:188
Richard Nixon **1**:376
Richards, C.J. **15**:136
Richardson, Elliot **5**:99
Riding, Laura **4**:29, 30, 31-32
Rieser, Max **9**:45
Riesman, David
    Greeley **7**:46
    Jerome **8**:133, 137
Right Promethean Fire: Imagination,
    Science, and Cultural Change,
    The **12**:160
Right Way to Figure Plumbing, The
    4:153, 154
"Rikki-Tikki-Tavi" **13**:166-67
Rilke, Rainer Maria
    Abse **1**:21, 24-26
    Delbanco **2**:158
    Enslin **3**:88-89
    Gray **2**:194

Gregor **10**:148
　Shapiro **6**:295
Rilla, Wolf **4**:341
Rimbaud, Arthur **2**:155
Rimmer, Robert H. 10:281-306
Rinard, Park **1**:164
Rinconete and Cortadillo **1**:299
Rinehart (publishers) **2**:170
Ringer **3**:322
Rinzler, Alan **6**:57
Rio de Janeiro, Brazil **10**:226-27
Rio Grande Writers (literary
　movement) **4**:26
Rios, Herminio **4**:24
Ríos profundos, Los (The deep
　rivers) **12**:101
Ripley, Patricia **6**:233
Riprap **2**:141
Rise of English Literary History, The
　7:225-26
Ritner, Peter
　Caute **4**:106
　Owens **2**:360
Ritsos, Yannis
　Root **11**:328-29
　Samarakis **16**:249
Ritual in the Dark **5**:318, 319, 322,
　324
River of Earth **17**:234, 239, 241,
　246
Rivera, Tomás **16**:150, 151
"Riverboat" **2**:171
Rizzardi, Alfredo **10**:142
Rizzoli International Bookstore
　13:224
RK Editions **8**:182
RKO Studios
　Condon **1**:194
　Wallace **1**:383
Roach, Max
　Hentoff **6**:168
　Killens **2**:295
Road from Home, The **2**:275
"Road or River" **3**:87
Road to Many a Wonder, The **3**:408
Road to Science Fiction, The **2**:257
Road to Volgograd **2**:386
Road to Wigan Pier, The **9**:21
Roanoke College
　Dillard **7**:10-11, 15
　Taylor **7**:182, 183, 186
Robbe-Grillet, Alain **4**:263
Robbins, Henry **2**:212
Robbins, Jerome **2**:415
*Robert Bridges: A Study of
　Traditionalism in Poetry* **2**:223,
　228
Roberts, James Hall (pseudonym) See
　Duncan, Robert L.
Roberts, Jane **10**:220
Roberts, Rachel **2**:385
Robeson, Paul
　Giovanni **6**:156
　Killens **2**:283, 297, 302
Robin Hood
　Charyn **1**:177

Howes **3**:135
Robinson Crusoe
　Allen **6**:15
　Awoonor **13**:40
Robinson, Edward Arlington **8**:42
Robinson, Henry Crabb **7**:220
Robinson, Jackie **1**:393
Robinson, Joan **3**:236, 238
Robinson, Mabel Louise **6**:264, 268
Robinson, Mollie **1**:393
Robinson, Phil **7**:107
Robinson, William Ronald **7**:15
Robinson, William "Smokey" **2**:304
"Roblin's Mill 2" **17**:212
Robson, Flora **11**:232
Robson, Jeremy **1**:28, 29
Rochelle; or Virtue Rewarded **3**:319,
　320
Rock **3**:407
Rock music
　Booth **2**:51, 52-53
　Giovanni **6**:160, 161
　Moorcock **5**:176-77, 182
　Nichols **2**:325-26
　Rosenblum **11**:335-36
　Smith **7**:159
Rockefeller Foundation
　Davison **4**:138
　Olson **12**:232, 235
　Purdy **1**:302
　Stegner **9**:267
Rockefeller Foundation Residency
　Fellowship in the Humanities
　9:149
Rockefeller Grant
　Bowles **1**:92
　Chappell **4**:120
　Root **11**:324
Rockland Community College **15**:30
Rodenbeck, John
　Dillard **7**:15
　Garrett **5**:80
Rodgers, Carolyn M. 13:237-57
Rodin, Auguste **9**:68
Roditi, Edouard 14:237-87
Rodney, Janet **16**:282-86
Roethke, Theodore
　Allman **15**:23
　Heyen **9**:37
　Kizer **5**:152
　Parini **16**:234
　Peters **8**:242
　Shapiro **6**:303-04
　Wagoner **3**:402-04, 405, 406, 407
Rogers, Ginger **5**:57-58
Roget, John L. **3**:136
Roget, Peter Mark **3**:136
Rogoff, Gordon **2**:412
Rogue Elephant **6**:22
Rogue Moon **14**:71-72, 73
Rohmer, Sax (pseudonym of Arthur
　Henry Sarsfield Ward) **2**:37
Roland, Gilbert **11**:316
Rolle, Richard, of Hampole **6**:36
Rolling Stone **5**:217
Rolling Stones **3**:83

Rolo, Charles J. **7**:6
Roman Catholic Church See Catholic
　Church
Roman Marriage, A **9**:27, 28
Romania **5**:353-55
Romano, Octavio **4**:24
Romano, Umberto **8**:84
Romantic Comedy **9**:249, 250-52, 253
Rome, Italy **5**:111-12
Romeo and Juliet **2**:157
Romm, Vladimir **5**:149
Romulo, Carlos P. **9**:157
Ronde, La **2**:411
Rooke, Leon **3**:23
Roosevelt, Eleanor
　Bourjaily **1**:66
　Condon **1**:190
Roosevelt, Franklin D.
　Knebel **3**:177
　Morgan, Ted **4**:234-35
　Morgan, Theodore **3**:231
Roosevelt Hotel, New York City
　1:190
Roosevelt University **13**:244, 245,
　252
Root River Run **2**:262
Root, Robert Kilburn **7**:217
Root, William Pitt 11:313-31
Roots (Arnold Wesker) **7**:249
Rorem, Ned **7**:81
Rosary Murders, The **1**:252-53
Rose of the Desert **11**:98-99
Rose, Stanley **1**:201-02
Rose, The **10**:46-57
Rose, W.K. **6**:25
Rosen, Philip **10**:189, 190
Rosenberg, Ethel **2**:192
Rosenberg, Harold **2**:449
Rosenberg, Isaac **5**:255, 256, 263
Rosenberg, Julius **2**:192
Rosenblum, Martin Jack 11:333-54
　McCord **9**:187
Rosenfeld, Isaac
　Markfield **3**:215-16, 217-18, 219,
　　221, 222, 224
　Solotaroff **2**:396, 397
Rosenthal, M.L. 6:271-86
　Allen **6**:26
　Feirstein **11**:80
　Weiss **2**:433
Ross, Alan **8**:103
Ross, Charles **14**:173
Ross, Harold **2**:65-66
Rossetti, Dante Gabriel **4**:155
Rossi, Pete **7**:47
Rotary International **1**:34-35, 45
Roth, Henry **3**:429, 430
Roth, Muriel **3**:429, 430
Roth, Philip
　Blaise **3**:25, 26, 27
　Solotaroff **2**:397
Roth, Susanna **12**:193-94
Rothenberg, Erika **13**:13-14, 15, 16,
　17, 19, 20, 23
Rothenberg, Jerome
　Awoonor **13**:47

Major **6**:198
  Wakoski **1**:364
Rothko, Mark **6**:113
Rotrosen, Jane **13**:224
Rotsler, William **12**:218
Rottensteiner, Franz **1**:255, 260
Round Table, The **7**:232-33
Roundhouse Voices: Selected and New Poems, The **7**:165
Rounds **1**:135
Rouse, James **8**:136, 137
Roussel, Raymond **6**:245-46
Rousselot, Pierre **7**:43
Routledge & Kegan Paul (publishers) **3**:46
Row of Tigers, A **2**:120
Rowe, Kenneth **9**:82
Rowe, Thomas **11**:204
Rowing **5**:365
Rowse, A.L. 8:253-66
Roxburgh, J.F. **7**:118-19
Roy, Debi **14**:88-89, 90, 94, 98
Royal Court Theatre, London, England **2**:416
Royal Geographical Society **7**:123
Royal Philharmonic Orchestra **8**:26-27
Royal Scottish Academy **3**:355
Royal Shakespeare Company, England **7**:241, 256
Royal Society for the Protection of Birds **4**:309
Royal Society of Literature, England
  Booth **2**:59
  Dillon **3**:66
  Skelton **5**:287
Royal Swedish Academy of Science **1**:390
Royall, Anne **1**:387
Royet-Journoud, Claude **11**:309
Rubaiyat of Omar Khayyam, The
  Kennedy **9**:76
  McCord **9**:177
  Morgan **3**:233
Ruben, Ernestine Winston **9**:279
Rubens, Bernice **5**:122
Rubia Barcia, José **6**:144
Rubin, Louis D., Jr. **7**:182
Rubinstein, Eli A. **15**:122
Rubinstein, Hilary **2**:29
Ruckle, Ernie **4**:243
Rude Awakening, A **2**:29
Rudich, Norman **15**:63, 66, 67, 71
Ruge, Ferdinand **12**:340
Rukeyser, Muriel **6**:279
Ruling Class, The **12**:12
Runner, The **11**:55
Running on Empty **13**:197, 205
Running Sun, The **1**:304
Runyon, Damon **2**:325
Ruopp, Phil **8**:135
Rush, Christopher **6**:75
Rush, Norman **8**:288
Rush on the Ultimate, A **8**:171
Rushdie, Salman **14**:237, 238
Rushes **4**:264

Ruskin, John **10**:103-04
Ruskin, Micky **1**:362
Russ, Joanna
  Piercy **1**:276
  Pohl **1**:295
Russell, Bertrand
  Booth **5**:35, 42, 43, 48
  Grumbach **2**:208
  Parini **16**:232
  Wilson **5**:314
Russell, Charles **8**:293
Russell, Diarmuid
  Bell **12**:38
  Bourjaily **1**:68, 73, 74, 75, 78-79
  Wagoner **3**:404, 405
Russell Kirk: A Bibliography **9**:103
Russell, Lawrence **7**:101
Russell, Peter **14**:333
Russia
  Corcoran **2**:123-24
  Davie **3**:32-33
  Gray **2**:180-81, 191
  Mrozek **10**:271
  Nichols **2**:314
  Salisbury **15**:323-24, 325, 326
  Sillitoe **2**:386
  Simpson **4**:286-87
  Zinoviev **10**:323-38
  See also Soviet Union
Russian-Americans
  Corman **2**:129-30
  Gray **2**:190
Russian Intelligence, The **5**:187-88
Russian literature
  Thomas **11**:376, 377, 379
  Zinoviev **10**:325, 337-38
Russian Poetry under the Tsars **9**:217
Russian Revolution, 1917
  Gray **2**:188
  Lem **1**:255
  Solotaroff **2**:393
Russians
  Garrett **5**:81-82
  Moorcock **5**:183
Russo, Alan **11**:282, 283, 284, 289
Rutgers University
  Forbes **16**:109, 111-12
  Pinsky **4**:243-44
  Tarn **16**:280, 283
  Williams **3**:431
Rybák, Josef **1**:343

Saari, Oliver **2**:41
Sackton, Alexander **12**:246
Sacred Heart Seminary, Detroit, Mich. **1**:239-41
"Sacrifice Hit" **1**:381, 382
Sacrifice, The **3**:322
Sacrilege of Alan Kent, The **1**:156
Saddlemyer, Ann **5**:287
Sade, Donatien-Alphonse-François, Marquis de **9**:129
Sadness and Happiness **4**:244, 246, 248-49, 250
Safad **9**:64
Safe Conduct **1**:221

Sagan, Carl **7**:283
Sagan, Eli **9**:219
Sailing into the Unknown: Yeats, Pound, and Eliot **6**:280
Sailor on Horseback **3**:370
St. Albans News **12**:340
St. Andrews **9**:97
St. Botolph's Review **9**:280
St. Clair, Margaret 8:267-82
"St. Elsewhere" **6**:220
Saint-Exupéry, Antoine de **15**:137
St. John of the Cross See Juan de la Cruz, San
St. John's College, Santa Fe, N.M. **12**:17, 18, 36, 38
St. Joseph College **17**:87-88
St. Louis University **17**:21-24
St. Mark's Church, New York City
  Wakoski **1**:362
  Waldman **17**:276, 278, 280, 287
St. Mark's Poetry Project
  Wakoski **1**:362
  Waldman **17**:276-80
St. Martin's Press **1**:251-52
Saint Mary of the Lake Seminary **7**:42-44
St. Nicholas Magazine **1**:381
Saint-Simon, Count de **4**:231
St. Stephen's College **9**:224
St. Valentine's Night **7**:44
St. Winifred's; or, The World of School **6**:66
Saints in Their Ox-Hide Boat **13**:97, 99
Saison dans la Vie d'Emmanuel, Une **4**:73, 74, 76, 77
Saks, Gene **9**:246
Sakti and Sakta **10**:291
Salam, Nurdin **9**:211
Šalda, F.X. **7**:214
Sale, Faith **2**:212
Salinas, Pedro **15**:59
Salinger, J.D.
  Burroway **6**:87
  Kinsella **7**:104
Salinger, Pierre **1**:394
Salisbury, Harrison E. 15:311-27
Salisbury, John (pseudonym of David Caute) **4**:108
Sallis, James
  Disch **4**:153
  Knight **10**:226
  Wolfe **9**:306
Sallis, Jane **4**:153
Salt and Core **2**:363
Salt Lake Tribune **5**:46
Sam **2**:121
Samal, Mary Hrabik **12**:183-95
Samaraki, Eleni **16**:255, 261-62, 264, 268
Samarakis, Antonis 16:245-70
Samaras, Lucas **4**:244
Same Time Next Year **9**:245-48, 249, 250, 254-55
Samizdat **10**:328, 330, 337
Samperi, Frank **2**:145

Sampson, Roland **1**:102
Samuel French Award **2**:119
Samuel Goldwyn Award **12**:72
San Diego, Calif. **9**:179
San Diego State University **16**:211
San Francisco Art Institute **12**:57
San Francisco, Calif.
  Broughton **12**:51-52, 57
  Caldwell **1**:151, 152
  Connell **2**:110
  Corman **2**:141-42
  Easton **14**:146
  Kyger **16**:189-90
  Stone **3**:361-63, 364
San Francisco Chronicle **1**:70
San Francisco Poetry Center **1**:360,
  362
San Francisco Poets **5**:162
San Francisco State College See San
  Francisco State University
San Francisco State University
  Boyle **1**:123
  Connell **2**:109
  Markfield **3**:221
  Petesch **12**:248
  Roditi **14**:282
San Jose State University
  Houston, James D. **16**:164
  Houston, Jeanne Wakatsuki
    16:179
  Stafford **3**:335
San Juan de la Cruz See Juan de la
  Cruz, San
Sánchez, Luis Rafael **9**:203, 204
Sandburg, Carl
  Harris **3**:121
  Wakefield **7**:194-95
Sanders, Ed **10**:7, 10
Sandford, Jay **9**:243
Sandia Corp. **5**:333, 348, 349
Sandow, Gregory **4**:155
Sans Famille **11**:127
Santa Barbara City College
  Easton **14**:158, 159
  Kyger **16**:188
Santa Fe, N.M.
  Bergé **10**:15-16
  Tarn **16**:285
Santayana, George **8**:299
Santesson, Hans Stefan **4**:209
Sanzenbach, Keith **3**:83
Sapp, Allen **7**:105
Sappho **6**:280
Sarah Lawrence College
  Kizer **5**:152
  Major **6**:186
Sargent, Porter **10**:70
Sarmatische Zeit **13**:125-29, 130, 136
Saroyan, Aram 5:211-23
Saroyan, William
  Bowles **1**:85, 86
  Kazin **7**:90
  Kherdian **2**:267, 269, 270-71, 272
Sarton, May **7**:180-81
Sartre, Jean-Paul
  Belitt **4**:49-50, 51, 54

Bowles **1**:87
  Flanagan **17**:50-51, 54
  Jones **5**:117
  Kerrigan **11**:194
  Mott **7**:119
  Van Itallie **2**:411
Saryan, Martiros **2**:273
Sasaki, Ruth Fuller **16**:193, 194-95
Sasha My Friend **2**:121, 126
Saskatchewan, Canada **9**:260-61
Sassafras **15**:270
Sassoon, Siegfried
  Silkin **5**:259
  Skelton **5**:283
Sastre, Genoveva Forest de **3**:138
Satis **13**:139
Saturday Evening Post
  Boyle **1**:118, 120
  Morgan **4**:231
  Wakefield **7**:194
  Wallace **1**:380
Saturday Night and Sunday Morning
  2:382, 383-85, 386
Saturday Night at the Greyhound **6**:18,
  19
Saturday Review
  Grumbach **2**:212
  Highwater **7**:81
  Jerome **8**:137
  Lottman **12**:206
Saudek, Erik **7**:214-15, 222
Savage, Elizabeth Fitzgerald **15**:333
Savage God, The **2**:412, 414
Savage Key **10**:174
Savage, Thomas 15:329-45
Savannah News **1**:142
Savory, Teo **8**:248
Šavrdová, Marie **1**:345
Saw **14**:175
*Say Goodbye—You May Never See Them
  Again* **7**:243, 244, 246-47
Say, Is This the U.S.A.? **1**:148
Sayers, Dorothy L.
  Gilbert **15**:194
  Keating **8**:166, 169
  Stewart **3**:352
Scannell, Vernon **1**:28
Scapegoat, The **1**:321, 322
Scarfe, Francis **6**:67
Scarlet Letter, The **5**:98
Scars **7**:103
Scenarios for a Mixed Landscape
  15:20
Scented Hills, The **11**:100, 103
Sceptre Press **2**:54-55
Schamberg, Morton **1**:104, 108,
  109, 113
Schapiro, Meyer
  Dennison **6**:111, 112
  Menashe **11**:228
Schattenland Ströme **13**:129, 130, 136
Scheherazade **2**:192
Scheitinger, Tony **2**:421
Schelling, Andrew **17**:291, 292
Scherzo capriccioso **1**:350
Schevill, James 12:253-80

Honig **8**:118, 119, 120
Schevill, Rudolph **12**:253-6, 266,
  267-68, 269, 271, 273
Schiffrin, André **6**:92
Schiller, David **7**:178-79, 185
Schimmel, Harold
  Katz **14**:165-66, 171-72
  Wright **7**:295, 296
Schizophrenia **6**:115
Schlauch, Margaret **5**:120, 121
Schlesinger, Robert **4**:217
Schliemann, Henry **3**:376-77
Schliemann, Sophia **3**:376-77
Schmidt, Michael
  Ashby **6**:43
  Davie **3**:46, 47
  Sisson **3**:304-05, 306, 307
Schmidt, Paul **9**:214
Schmitt, Martin **6**:55-57
Schnall, Herbert **10**:300
Schneeman, George
  Katz **14**:171-72
  Wright **7**:295
Schneider, Allen **2**:412
Schneyder, John **6**:214
Schoenberg, Arnold
  Enslin **3**:95, 96
  Josipovici **8**:159
Scholes, Robert **7**:180
School of Art, Cork, Ireland **3**:56
School of Letters, Bloomington,
  Indiana **12**:155-56
School of the Art Institute of
  Chicago **16**:119
School of the Arts, Cummington,
  Mass. **3**:139
Schopenhauer, Arthur **8**:42
Schörner, Marshal **1**:333
Schorske, Carl **12**:157
Schramm, Richard **7**:164
Schramm, Wilbur **9**:263, 264, 265,
  266
Schrieber, Ron **5**:351
Schryver, Lee **6**:57
Schubert, David **2**:432, 433-34, 440,
  445
Schubert Foundation Playwrighting
  Fellowship **4**:207, 208, 215
Schueller, Herbert M. **8**:241, 244
Schultz, J.W. **2**:263
Schulz, Bruno
  Brossard **2**:72, 74
  Tennant **9**:292
Schulz, Charles **1**:400
Schumann, Peter **6**:117, 118
Schumpeter, Joseph **3**:236
Schütz, Heinrich **3**:95
Schuyler, George **5**:202
Schuyler, James **6**:236
"Schwartz between the Galaxies"
  3:283
Schwartz, Delmore
  Allman **15**:23
  Brossard **2**:67
  Phillips **13**:199, 201-03, 212
Schwartz, Lloyd **4**:249

Schwarzschild, Bettina **1**:303
Science and the Classics **9**:96
Science Fantasy
  Aldiss **2**:25
  Moorcock **5**:177
Science fiction
  Aldiss **2**:23, 28
  Allen **11**:7, 14-15, 19
  Bradley **10**:21
  Brunner **8**:7, 10-11, 12
  Budrys **14**:65-79
  Clement **16**:89-104
  Coppel **9**:2, 4
  Hoffman **10**:169-70
  Kennedy **9**:77-79, 80
  Lem **1**:260-61
  Malzberg **4**:205-06, 207, 212,
    213-14
  Moorcock **5**:176, 177, 181
  Niven **12**:211, 212, 213-22
  Nolan **16**:212, 215
  St. Clair **8**:273, 281-82
  Silverberg **3**:271-78, 279, 280-88
  Tennant **9**:291-92
  Westlake **13**:337
  Williamson **8**:317, 320, 321-22,
    323-24, 325
  Wolfe **9**:308
Science Fiction and Futurology **1**:263
Science Fiction Encyclopedia, The
  4:154
Science Fiction Research
    Association **2**:257
Science Fiction: The Future **11**:19
Science Fiction Writers of America
  Anderson **2**:45
  Gunn **2**:256
  Knight **10**:224-25
  Pohl **1**:292, 295
  Silverberg **3**:282
Scientific American **9**:186
Sclerosis **12**:10
Scopes Trial, The **1**:318
Scorsese, Martin **5**:218
Scotland
  Cartland **8**:20-21, 22
  Kirk **9**:97
  Parini **16**:231-35
  Stewart **3**:343-45
  Tennant **9**:289-91
Scott, Bobby **6**:233-34
Scott, Frank **15**:159
Scott, John **4**:343
Scott-Moncrieff, George **9**:97
Scovel, Carl **7**:201
Screen **4**:213, 214, 217, 218
Screenwriting **4**:345-46
Scribner, Charles (publishers)
  Brown **6**:56
  Disch **4**:156
  Elman **3**:75, 77
  Swanberg **13**:268, 272, 273, 274
Scrutiny **3**:35
Sculling to Byzantium **15**:355, 359
Scuola Interpreti, Florence, Italy
  2:351

SDS See Students for a Democratic
    Society
Sea Gull, The **2**:417-18
Sea of Zanj **11**: 99
Seagull on the Step, The **1**:123
SeaHorse Press **13**:228, 229
Seal, Marilyn See Nolan, Cameron
Searching for the Ox **4**:296
Season of the Jews **3**:250
Season of the Stranger, The **1**:35
Season of the Strangler **11**:185-86
Seattle Post-Intelligencer **3**:407
Seattle Repertory Theatre **3**:407-08
Seaview **11**:253, 259
Secker & Warburg (publishers) **9**:21,
    23-24
Second Home, A **9**:27, 28
Second Lady, The **1**:384, 398
Second Man, The **3**:386
Second Trip, The **3**:281
*Seductio ad Absurdum: The Principles
    and Practices of Seduction—A
    Beginner's Handbook* **11**:111
Seeing the Light **12**:51
Seetee Ship **8**:322
Seetee Shock **8**:322
Seferis, George **15**:93-94
Segregation
  Anderson **2**:35
  Bradley **10**:23
  Dillard **7**:9
  Killens **2**:282, 289
  Major **6**:177
  Nichols **2**:324
  Petry **6**:263, 268
  Shreve **5**:230
  Stafford **3**:332, 333
  Wellek **7**:218
  Williams **3**:417, 419
  See also Civil rights movement
Segues **3**:333
Ségur, Sophie Rostopchine, Comtesse
    de **2**:184
Segura, Andres **4**:24
Seigle, Henri **16**:276
Seigle, No **16**:276
Seldes, George **6**:171
Selected Declarations of Dependence
    6:247, 248
Selected Essays and Criticism (Louis
    Dudek) **14**:135
Selected Poems (Carl Rakosi) **5**:208,
    209
Selected Poems (George Woodcock)
    6:326
Selected Poems (John Frederick
    Nims) **17**:184
Selected Poems (Jon Silkin) **5**:263
Selected Poems (Malay Roy
    Choudhury) **14**:92, 99
Selected Poems of Alexander Pushkin
    9:219
Selected Poems of Ezra Pound **7**:293,
    295
Selected Poems, 1976–1986 (David
    Wagoner) **3**:411

Selected Poems, 1933–1980 (George
    Faludy) **5**:292
Selected Poems (Robert Peters) **8**:248
Selected Poems (Stanley Kunitz) **4**:135
Selected Poems (Yvor Winters) **4**:245
Selected Works of Unamuno **11**:213
*Selected Writings of Guillaume
    Apollinaire* **8**:184
Self-Culture **5**:36
"Self-Defense" **17**:48-49
Self-publishing **15**:118
"Self Reliance" **11**:7
Seligman, Ben **3**:216, 217, 218, 220,
    222, 223
Selling Out **7**:201
Seltzer, Dan **2**:417, 418
Selver, Paul **7**:213
*Selves at Risk: Patterns of Quest in
    Contemporary American Letters*
    12:163-64
Sender, Ramón **8**:112
Senghor, Leopold Sedar **6**:189, 190-
    91, 192
Senior, Charles **6**:71
Senior Fellowship Award **1**:94
Sense of Direction, A **13**:307, 308,
    314, 315, 316
Sense of the Fire, The **4**:218-19
Sense of the World, A **5**:112
Sent to His Account **3**:59
Separate Notebooks, The **4**:250
Séquences de l'aile (The sequences of
    wings) **13**:183
Sereni, Vittorio **10**:141
Sergeant, Howard **1**:27
Serpent, The **2**:411, 416, 417
Serra, Richard **14**:176
Seton Hall University, South Orange,
    N.J. **9**:79-80
Seton Hill College, Greensburg, Pa.
    3:198
Settle, Mary Lee **1**:307-23
Settlers' West, The **6**:57
Sevastyanov, Valentin **1**:286
Seven Days in May **3**:174, 180-81
Seven Minutes, The **1**:384, 385, 395-
    97
*Seven Mountains of Thomas Merton,
    The* **7**:132-34
Seven Serpents and Seven Moons
    9:204
Seven South African Poets **14**:59, 60
Seven Suspects **3**:353, 354
"Seven Who Were Hanged, The"
    2:392
7.7.73 **8**:92
Seventh Seal, The **7**:17
Sewall, Richard **12**:332
Sewanee Review Fellowship **11**:180
Sex **4**:261-62
Sexism
  El Saadawi **11**:63, 65, 67, 68, 70
  Livesay **8**:234
  Owens **2**:364, 367
  See also Women's movement
Sexton, Anne

Davison **4**:137
Jerome **8**:133
Kumin **8**:216
Weiss **2**:447
Sexual Outlaw, The **4**:263, 265
Seymour Lawrence/Delacorte
    (publishers) **1**:318
Shadbolt, Maurice **3**:249-67
Becker **1**:43, 44
*Shadow Land: Selected Poems of
    Johannes Bobrowski* **13**:132, 133
Shadow Lands **13**:138
Shadow of the Torturer, The **9**:299,
    311
Shadow out of Time **3**:271
Shadow People, The **8**:274, 281
Shadrach in the Furnace **3**:284
Shaffer, Peter **4**:133
Shain, Charles **8**:306
Shainberg, Larry **14**:179
*Shake a Spear with Me, John
    Berryman* **8**:118
Shaker Light **8**:247, 248
Shakers
    Lifshin **10**:247
    Peters **8**:247
Shakespeare and the Nature of Time
    10:316
Shakespeare, William
    Aldiss **2**:20
    Anderson **2**:46
    Brewster **15**:151
    Broughton **12**:45-47
    Busch **1**:137
    Corman **2**:132
    Dillon **3**:50, 51, 53
    Forrest **7**:22
    Glanville **9**:18
    Horwood **15**:242
    Jerome **8**:133-34, 135
    Rowse **8**:262
    Schevill **12**:262
Shaman **17**:284
Shamus Award **11**:38
Shanghai Incident **1**:36
Shannon, Who Was Lost Before **5**:163,
    166
Shapiro, Helen **2**:25
Shapiro, Karl **6**:287-309
    Corman **2**:136
    Enslin **3**:89
    Hazo **11**:142
    Phillips **13**:213
    Smith **7**:161
Shapiro, Meyer **2**:432
Sharp, John **9**:181
Sharp Tools for Catullan Gardens
    12:342
Sharpshooter **3**:200, 203, 204
Shattuck, Roger
    Kostelanetz **8**:184
    Settle **1**:322
Shaw, George Bernard
    Allen **6**:17
    Kizer **5**:147
    Rimmer **10**:286

Stewart **3**:355
Shaw, Irwin **11**:230
Shaw, Larry
    Hoffman **10**:171, 172
    Knight **10**:208, 209-10, 211, 217,
        221
Shawn, William
    Boyle **1**:121
    Brossard **2**:63-65, 76
    Gray **2**:198, 199
    Hentoff **6**:171
Shawno **6**:121
Shea, John **7**:49
Sheckley, Robert
    Aldiss **2**:27
    Malzberg **4**:212
Sheed, Wilfrid
    Kumin **8**:201
    West **7**:275
Sheeler, Charles **1**:104, 109, 113
Sheep Look Up, The **8**:15
Sheer Fiction **7**:281
Sheets, Kermit **12**:52-54
Sheffield University **4**:190
Shekeloff, Brian **2**:142
Shekeloff, Mertis **2**:142
Shelley, Percy Bysshe
    Brown **6**:66
    Dudek **14**:123
    Vivante **12**:284
Shelnutt, Eve **14**:289-301
Sheltering Sky, The **1**:88
Shelton, Dick **13**:7, 8, 9
Shenton, Edward **6**:54
Sherbourne Press **10**:298-99, 300
Sherbrookes trilogy **2**:156, 159, 162
Sherburne, N.Y. **1**:134, 135
Sheridan, Paul **8**:101, 104
Sheriff of Bombay, The **8**:176
*Sherlock Holmes: The Man and His
    World* **8**:177
Sherman, Howard **9**:181
Shimpei, Kusano **2**:142, 144
Ship of Death **6**:74
Ship's Orchestra, The **10**:98-99
Shirer, William **1**:123
Shires, The **3**:46
Shirley, James **17**:178
Shlonsky, Avraham **13**:152, 153
Shoeless Joe **7**:104-06, 107, 110
Shoeless Joe Jackson Comes to Iowa
    7:103, 105, 109
Sholokhov, Mikhail **10**:325
Shore, Viola Brothers **2**:288
Short Life, The **13**:154
Short Season and Other Stories **9**:108,
    118, 120
Short Stories (Kay Boyle) **1**:116
Short Story 3 **9**:212-13, 216
Short Throat, the Tender Mouth, The
    2:207, 210
Shoushani, Mordecai **4**:355
Shragge, Elaine **2**:365
Shreve, Susan Richards **5**:225-41
Shylock **7**:231
Si Malakas at Si Maganda **9**:167-68

Sicily
    Delbanco **2**:153
    Vivante **12**:296
Sickles the Incredible **13**:268
Siebner, Herbert **5**:290
Sierra Club **3**:183
Sieveking, Gale **4**:340
Sieveking, Lance **4**:340
Sighet, Romania **4**:353
Sigma Delta Chi **2**:245
Sigma Delta Chi Award **3**:179
Sign of the Labrys **8**:274, 275, 281
*Signet Classic Book of American Short
    Stories, The* **9**:219
Signet Society **2**:411
Significa **1**:401
Sikelianos, Angelos **15**:80-81
Sikhs and Sikhism **9**:223, 227, 229,
    231, 232, 234
Sikhs, The **9**:231, 232
Silber, John **9**:217
Silberman, Jim **1**:72, 74, 75
Silence, The **7**:13
Silkin, Jon **5**:243-65
    Abse **1**:28
Sillitoe, Alan **2**:371-89
Silone, Ignazio **3**:62, 63
Silver Heron, The **9**:279, 282
"Silver Penny a Year Ago" **17**:176
Silver Snaffles **8**:210
Silverberg, Robert **3**:269-91
    Knight **10**:225
    Malzberg **4**:207
Simak, Clifford D.
    Anderson **2**:39
    Silverberg **3**:276
"Simenon and Spillane: Metaphysics
    of Murder for the Millions"
    7:6
Simenon, Georges **8**:170
Simic, Charles **4**:267-84
Simmons, Charles **7**:16
Simmons College **16**:98
Simon & Schuster (publishers)
    Jones **5**:128, 129
    Wallace **1**:385, 389, 393, 396
Simon and the Shoeshine Boy **11**:81,
    83
Simon, Carly **2**:158
Simon, John **2**:437, 444, 445
Simon, Richard **5**:128-29
Simon Says Get Married **9**:243, 244
Simonov, Konstantin **10**:327
*Simple Lust: Collected Poems of South
    African Jail and Exile, A* **14**:57,
    58, 62-63
Simple People **3**:109
Simpson, Don **12**:219
Simpson, Louis **4**:285-99
    Awoonor **13**:47, 48
    Wakoski **1**:362
Simpson, Martha **1**:208, 209
Sims, Mary **7**:297, 298
Sin **13**:10
Sinatra, Frank **1**:196
Sinclair, Andrew **5**:267-77

Sinclair, Upton **8**:310
Singapore **3**:245
Singer, Isaac Bashevis
    Elman **3**:82
    Petry **6**:268
Singh, Khushwant 9:223-36
Sinking of the Odradek Stadium, The
    6:240-41, 247
Sino-Japanese War **5**:141, 150
Sins of Philip Fleming, The **1**:387
Sions, Harry **3**:428, 430, 431
'Sippi **2**:296
Sir George Williams University **3**:27
Sir Richard Grenville of the
    "Revenge" **8**:259, 260
Sir Slob and the Princess **5**:79
Sirens, Knuckles, Boots **14**:56
Sissie **3**:415, 421, 424, 425, 427
Sisson, C.H. 3:293-309
    Ashby **6**:44
    Davie **3**:46
Sisters, The **15**:149, 152, 153-54,
    159
Situation of Poetry, The **4**:249
Sitwell, Edith
    Allen **6**:17
    Fuller **10**:116-17
    Jennings **5**:113
    Purdy **1**:300-301
    Wilson **5**:322
Sitwell, Osbert **6**:17
Six Poets of the San Francisco
    Renaissance **2**:269, 270
Sixties **7**:179
Sixty-eight Publishers **1**:340, 348
63: Dream Palace **1**:300-302
Sjoblom, Jorma **1**:301
Skelton at Sixty **5**:293
Skelton, Robin 5:279-95
    Kinsella **7**:101
Sketches for a New Mexico Hill Town
    5:351, 352
Sketches of the Valley and Other Works
    See *Estampas del valle y otr*
Skidmore College
    Blaise **3**:28
    Delbanco **2**:159
    Morgan **3**:234
Skin Meat Bones **17**:289
Skinner, Walter Jay **5**:99
Škvorecký, Josef 1:325-52
    Hrabal **12**:191
Škvorecký, Zdena
    Hrabal **12**:191
    Škvorecký **1**:338
Slade, Bernard 9:237-56
Sladek, John
    Disch **4**:150-51, 152
    Tennant **9**:291
Slagle, David **5**:349
Slansky, Rudolf **1**:336
Slashed to Ribbons in Defense of Love
    13:233
Slater, Don **17**:66-67
Slater, Joseph Locke **1**:132
Slaughterhouse-Five **9**:111

Slavery **13**:85
Slavitt, David R. 3:311-25
Sleepers in Moon-Crowned Valleys
    1:303
Sleeping Beauty, The (Hayden
    Carruth) **6**:118-19
Slepyan, Norbert **9**:307
Slezak, Walter **1**:178, 179, 183
Slippery Rock State College **11**:323
Sloan, Stephen **2**:174
Sloane, William
    Ciardi **2**:90
    Kumin **8**:215
Slocum, Joshua **3**:94
Slow Fuse, A **2**:449-50
Small Changes **1**:272, 274, 276
Small Desperation, A **1**:30
Small Perfect Things **14**:136
Small Rain **2**:156
Smallbone Deceased **15**:192, 193, 194
Smalls, Robert **17**:127-28
Smallwood, Norah **6**:70, 71, 72
Smart as the Devil **13**:224-25
Smart, Christopher **5**:195
Smart Set **7**:91
Smile in His Lifetime, A **17**:63, 65,
    69, 71
Smiles on Washington Square **8**:75
Smith, A.J.M. **6**:277, 279
Smith, Annette **6**:147
Smith College
    Grumbach **2**:209
    Kazin **7**:94, 95
    Wellek **7**:218
Smith, Dave 7:155-69
    Heyen **9**:41
Smith, D.V. **6**:180
Smith, Egerton **2**:380
Smith, Evelyn **3**:137-38, 139
Smith, Fuller d'Arch (publishers)
    2:54, 59
Smith, Harry **9**:66-67
Smith, Joseph **5**:36, 38, 40, 41
Smith, Martin Seymour **6**:44
Smith, Raymond
    Phillips **13**:211
    Weiss **2**:449
Smith, Roger **12**:206
Smith, Stevie
    Abse **1**:29
    Wright **5**:370, 371
Smith, Warren **3**:403
Smith, William Jay
    Howes **3**:140-41, 142, 145
    Taylor **7**:182
Smithereened Apart **11**:153
Smiths, W.H. **5**:181
"Smoker" **17**:49
Smoke's Way **3**:329
Smoking Mountain, The **1**:120
Snaps **17**:9-10, 11
Snath **2**:57
Snodgrass, W.D.
    Allen **11**:11-12
    Jerome **8**:133
    Katz **14**:166

Kennedy **9**:83, 84
Morris **13**:165
Snow, Carmel **1**:313
Snow, C.P. **9**:13
Snow, Edgar **15**:324
Snow White and the Seven Dwarfs
    Atkins **16**:6
    Rechy **4**:260
Snyder, Gary
    Beltrametti **13**:61, 62
    Bergé **10**:11
    Corman **2**:140, 141
    Enslin **3**:93
    Eshleman **6**:135, 137, 142
    Kherdian **2**:269
    Kyger **16**:191, 192, 193, 194-95,
        196
Sobrevivo **15**:12
Soccer
    Brown **6**:64-65
    Glanville **9**:16, 19
Social work **5**:205-06, 207
Socialism
    Barrio **15**:112
    Caute **4**:101, 102, 105
    Davie **3**:42
    Gray **2**:191-92
    Lind **4**:195, 197, 201
    Miller **15**:290-91
    Shadbolt **3**:249
    Voinovich **12**:306
    White **4**:347
Socialists **3**:254
Socialized medicine **4**:86-87, 92
Society for Creative Anachronism
    2:44-45
Society for the Prevention of Cruelty to
    Animals, The **1**:330-31
Society of Authors, London
    Aldiss **2**:30
    Wallace **1**:402
Society of St. Sulpice **1**:240
Sociobiology: The New Synthesis
    16:302-03
Sociological Imagination, The **8**:185
Soft Press **13**:293, 294
Soho, London, England **5**:359, 367,
    373
Solano Beach, Calif. **1**:367
Solaris **1**:260, 261, 262, 263
Soldier Erect, A **2**:19, 29
Soldier of Arete **9**:309
Soldier of Humour, A **6**:24
Soldier of the Mist **9**:309
Soleil sous la mort, Le (The sun under
    death) **13**:185
Solidarity movement **10**:277
Sölle, Dorothy **1**:53
Solotaroff, Ted 2:391-403
    Dennison **6**:121, 122
    Markfield **3**:219
    Settle **1**:320
    Smith **7**:165
Solt, Mary Ellen **6**:131
Some Angry Angel **1**:196
Some Came Running **7**:141

Some Cows, Poems of Civilization and Domestic Life 5:163-64
Some Deaths in the Delta 10:41
Some Dreams Are Nightmares 2:251, 258
Some Haystacks Don't Even Have Any Needle 5:351
Some Observations of a Stranger at Zuni in the Latter Part of the Century 6:200
some recent snowflakes (and other things) 8:92
Some Tales of La Fontaine 3:306
Some Time 2:140
Some Unease and Angels 1:223
Somer, John 9:113
Somerset Maugham Award 5:111-12
Something about a Soldier 3:123
Something Else Newsletter 8:89, 90, 91
Something Else Press 8:83, 88-90, 92
Sometimes I Live in the Country 1:135-36
Sometimes I Think of Moving 15:159-60
Sommer, Piotr 6:201
Son of Man 3:281
"Song for Miriam, A" 17:175
Song of Roland, The 3:306
Songs for a Son 8:242, 247
Songs for Certain Children 12:52
Songs of a Blackbird 13:248
"Songs of Innocence and Experience" 2:328
Songs w/out Notes 3:98
Sono Nis Press 5:290
Sons and Fathers 5:84
Sons and Lovers 7:222
Sons of Darkness, Sons of Light 3:430, 431
Sontag, David 7:200
Sontag, Susan
  Heyen 9:43
  Highwater 7:78, 79
Soong Sisters, The 11:113-14, 115
"Sophie" series 2:184
Sorbonne, University of Paris
  Barnstone 15:64, 68-69
  Brée 15:132, 134
  Kennedy 9:82
  Knebel 3:168
  Livesay 8:231-32
  Menashe 11:226-27, 228
  Morgan 4:226
  O'Faolain 2:346, 347
Sorrentino, Gilbert 9:113
Sosa, Roberto 3:81
Soul Clap Its Hands and Sing 12:243, 248
Soul of Wood 4:202
Soul on Ice 16:84
Sound and the Fury, The
  Charyn 1:179
  Forrest 7:23
Sounder 6:155

Sounding Brass 1:390
Sourd dans la Ville, Le 4:78
Souster, Raymond 14:303-19
  Dudek 14:132
  Sparshott 15:357
South Africa
  Brutus 14:55-64
  Cassity 8:48-55, 58, 59
  Killens 2:299
  Wright 5:370
South America 11:118
South Sea Journey 6:325
Southam, Brian 3:46
Southampton University 15:188
Southern Cross, The 7:295, 298
Southern Delights 7:166
Southern Illinois University 7:162
Southern States
  Blaise 3:21, 23-24
  Cassity 8:38-39, 43
  Howes 3:137-39
  Jones 11:171-86
Southern Tenant Farmers Union 3:137
Southern Writing in the Sixties: Poetry 7:181
Southport Bugle 1:376
Southwest Minnesota State College
  See Southwest State University
Southwest State University 17:28
Southwestern Bell Telephone Co. 2:170
Soviet literature 10:325
Soviet Union
  Caute 4:107
  Davie 3:42
  Horwood 15:252
  Voinovich 12:303-22
  Zinoviev 10:323-38
  See also Russia
Soviet Writers Union 12:322
Sow's Head and Other Poems, The 8:242, 244, 247
Soyinka, Wole 5:260
Space for Hire 16:217
Space Merchants, The 1:290, 291
Space Science Fiction 14:67
Space, Time, and Nathaniel 2:22
Spackman, Peter 12:206
Spain
  Brossard 2:70
  Cela 10:47, 49
  Nichols 2:327
  Raworth 11:303
  Thomas 4:309
  White 4:345-46
  Williams 3:424
Spain, Nancy 5:323
Spain, Take This Cup from Me 6:144
Spanish Civil War
  Abse 1:18
  Kerrigan 11:204-05
  Mott 7:114
  Nichols 2:309
  Schevill 12:267
  Woodcock 6:319

Spanish Scene, The 2:70
Sparrow, John 7:274
Sparshott, Francis 15:347-63
Spartacus 4:148
Spatola, Adriano 13:64, 65, 70
Speak, Memory 4:51
Spears, Monroe 11:177
Special Occasions 9:252, 253-54
Special Time, A 8:184
Spectator
  Sisson 3:304
  White 4:343
Spectator Bird, The 9:269
Speech dysfunctions
  Gunn 2:242
  Kazin 7:87
  Wilhelm 5:298, 299
Spell for Green Corn, A 6:72
Spellbound: Growing Up in God's Country 14:205-06, 208-10, 213
Spence School 2:189, 190
Spencer, Elizabeth 13:213
Spender, Stephen
  Abse 1:18
  Barnstone 15:75, 76, 77
  Ciardi 2:90
  Heyen 9:46
  Kostelanetz 8:194
  Menashe 11:235
  Taylor 7:180
Spicer, Jack
  Kyger 16:190, 191, 192, 197
  Wakoski 1:360
Spiegel, Sam 5:276
Spielberg, Peter
  Baumbach 5:26
  Sukenick 8:293
Spies, Claudio 3:87
Spillane, Mickey 7:6
Spinrad, Norman 1:290
Spirit Bodies 14:215-16
Spirit of British Administration, with Some European Comparisons, The 3:304
Spirit of the Seas 13:152
Spirit Spirit 8:119
Spirits 14:13, 14
Splinter in the Heart, A 17:211
Split Second 1:383
Spoil of the Flowers, The 2:210
Spoiled 3:114
Spokane, Wash. 5:139-40
Spontaneous Combustion 2:361
Spoon 1:180
Sport (Clark Blaise) 3:19-20
Sport (London) 9:20
Sporty Creek: A Novel about an Appalachian Boyhood 17:234
Spread, The 4:213
Spriggs, Ed 6:188
Spring Again 15:161
Spring Hill School for the Deaf, Northampton, England 5:362-64
Spring Journal: Poems 8:117
"Spring on Little Carr" 17:245

Spyker, John Howland (pseudonym)
  See Elman, Richard
Square Emerald, The **3**:52
Square Pegs, The **1**:386-87
Squares of the City, The **8**:9
Squires, Radcliffe **9**:283
Sri Lanka
  Bowles **1**:88, 89, 91
  Morgan **3**:240
  See also Ceylon
Stadtfeld, Curtis **9**:93
Stafford, William 3:327-41
  Heyen **9**:32
  Shapiro **6**:307
  Sward **13**:293
Staircase in Surrey, A **3**:348, 356
Stalag 17 **1**:194
Stalin, Joseph
  Lind **4**:200
  Pohl **1**:286
  Simic **4**:272
  Škvorecký **1**:336-38
  Voinovich **12**:305, 306
  Zinoviev **10**:325, 326, 328, 329
Stalinism
  Kizer **5**:149-50
  Solotaroff **2**:393
  Zinoviev **10**:328
Stand **5**:251, 261
Stand on Zanzibar **8**:1, 11
Stanford, Ann **13**:315
Stanford University
  Baumbach **5**:23
  Broughton **12**:48
  Connell **2**:107
  Coppel **9**:7
  Dacey **17**:24, 26
  Davie **3**:43, 47
  Easton **14**:144
  Elman **3**:74, 76, 82
  Guerard **2**:220, 222, 228
  Hall **7**:64
  Higgins **5**:92-93, 97, 99
  Houston **16**:158
  Pinsky **4**:244, 245-47
  Rachlin **17**:228
  Root **11**:324
  Stegner **9**:266-69
Stapledon, Olaf
  Anderson **2**:46
  Silverberg **3**:271, 272, 274
Star Bridge
  Gunn **2**:248, 250
  Williamson **8**:322
Star Diaries, The **1**:264
Star Science Fiction #4 **2**:253
Star Trek
  Niven **12**:220
  Pohl **1**:295
Star Wars **1**:292
Stark Electric Jesus **14**:92-93
Stark, Richard (pseudonym of Donald
  E. Westlake) **13**:341-42
Starkey, Jack **7**:6, 18
Stars and Stripes **6**:297, 298
Start in Life, A **2**:387

Starting Out in the Thirties
  Kazin **7**:88, 89, 90
  Markfield **3**:220
Starting Over **7**:200
Startling Stories **2**:37
State and Revolution **10**:113
State University of New York at
  Albany **10**:252-53
State University of New York at
  Binghamton
  Ai **13**:10
  Burroway **6**:94
  Smith **7**:165
  Westlake **13**:339
State University of New York at
  Brockport **9**:39, 42, 45
State University of New York at
  Buffalo
  Federman **8**:79
  Kerrigan **11**:196
  Mott **7**:130
  Raffel **9**:216
  Tarn **16**:280
  Wakoski **1**:364
  Williams **12**:353
State University of New York at
  Cortland **9**:40, 45
State University of New York at
  Stony Brook
  Kazin **7**:95
  Raffel **9**:215-16
  Simpson **4**:295, 296
statements **14**:42, 43, 45
Station in Space **2**:251, 252, 253,
  258
Statue of Liberty **5**:361
Stature of Man, The **5**:324
Stead **2**:138
Stealer of Souls, The **5**:177, 179
Steele, Max
  Connell **2**:107, 108, 109
  Settle **1**:316
Stegner, Wallace 9:257-71
  Baumbach **5**:23
  Connell **2**:107
  Coppel **9**:4
  Houston **16**:168
Stein, Gertrude
  Bowles **1**:83, 84
  Kerrigan **11**:199
  Kizer **5**:146
  Waldman **17**:273, 276
  Weiss **2**:439
Stein, Maurice **6**:143
Steinbeck, John
  Dillard **7**:11
  Houston **16**:158
Steiner, George
  Purdy **1**:303
  Wesker **7**:233-34
Stendahl, Earl **3**:371-72
Stendhal
  Creeley **10**:67
  Wallace **1**:387
Stenger, Harold L., Jr. **1**:129-30
Stephan, Ruth Walgren

Hauser **11**:136
Wilson **5**:349
Stephen Leacock Memorial Medal
  7:107, 110
Stephens, Edward **9**:83
Stephens, Michael **14**:176
Stepinac Case, The **2**:412
Steps **9**:112, 115
Steps Going Down **17**:72
Steps of the Sun **11**:113
Stepsons of Terra **3**:276
Sterile Cuckoo, The **2**:328, 329, 330,
  331, 332, 333
Sterling, Robert **9**:182
Sterne, Laurence
  Booth **5**:46
  Sukenick **8**:284, 287
Stettheimer, Ettie **14**:253
Stevens Institute of Technology
  17:287-88
Stevens, Shane **8**:215
Stevens, Wallace
  Allen **11**:18
  Feinstein **1**:221
  Gregor **10**:148, 149
  Highwater **7**:80-81
  Honig **8**:113-15
  Kennedy **9**:76, 80
  Sukenick **8**:286-87
  Symons **3**:385
  Weiss **2**:446
  Whittemore **8**:306
Stevenson, Anne 9:273-88
Stevenson, Charles L. **9**:273-75, 276,
  277, 278, 279, 281, 283, 284,
  286
Stevenson, Robert Louis
  Brown **6**:45
  Glanville **9**:17
  Hitchcock **12**:179
  Mott **7**:116
  Wain **4**:323
Steward, Pearl Bank **1**:377
Stewart, Ellen **2**:413, 415, 418, 419
Stewart, James **4**:146
Stewart, J.I.M. 3:343-60
Sticks & Stones **16**:28
Stieglitz, Alfred **1**:104, 109, 110
Still, James 17:231-48
  Miller **15**:288, 291
Stillness **2**:156
Stills **11**:153
Stirring Science Stories **10**:205
Stochastic Man, The **3**:283
Stockhausen, Karlheinz **7**:81
Stockholm, Sweden **1**:390, 392
Stockwell, Dean **11**:285
Stoehr, Taylor **6**:119
Stoic, The **2**:265
Stoke-on-Trent, England **4**:316-17,
  321-22, 325
Stokesberry, Jack Elmo **9**:79
Stolen Stories **14**:176, 177
Stolper, Wolfgang **9**:279
Stoltzfus, Ben **8**:244
Stone, I.F. **6**:171

Stone, Irving **3**:361-80
　Wesker **7**:236
Stone, Lawrence **4**:104
Stone, Nancy **4**:123
Stone Roses **5**:355
Stones of the House, The **2**:94
Stories of a Tenor Saxophonist, The
　1:339, 351
Stories That Could Be True **3**:328,
　329, 331, 332, 336
Storm and Other Poems, The (George
　Mackay Brown) **6**:70
Storm and Other Poems, The (William
　Pitt Root) **11**:324
Storm and Other Things, The **7**:298
Storm of Fortune **16**:80
Storm Warning **5**:57
Stormbringer **5**:177, 179
Stormqueen **10**:25
Storms and Screams **15**:359
Stormy Encounter **11**:101, 105
Story **12**:129, 131-32
Story of Flight, The **1**:318
Story of Philosophy **11**:320
Stovall, Floyd **7**:11
Strachey, Lytton
　Brown **6**:73
　Morgan **4**:234
Strachey, Marjorie **5**:141
Strand, Mark
　Baumbach **5**:27
　Wright **7**:297
*Strange Bedfellows: The State and the
　Arts in Canada* **6**:323
Strange Interlude **4**:146
Strange Marriage **17**:67
Strangers **5**:129
Strangers and Journeys **3**:257, 259,
　261, 264, 265
Strangers in the House **7**:46
Strauss, Richard **12**:275
*Street: An Autobiographical Novel,
　The* **5**:217, 218
Street Games **10**:41
Street, James, Jr. **6**:57
Street of Crocodiles, The **2**:72
Street, The **6**:253, 265-66
Strempek, Bernard **11**:15
Strength to Dream, The **5**:324
Striking the Dark Air for Music
　11:324
Strindberg, August
　Highwater **7**:80
　Wallace **1**:391
　White **4**:333
　Wilson **5**:325
String Game, The **2**:359, 360, 361
String Horses **8**:103
String Too Short to Be Saved **7**:65
Strong Brown God, The **4**:233
Strong Man, The **8**:173
*Strong Measures: Contemporary
　American Poetry in Traditional
　Forms* **17**:29-30
Structure of Aesthetics, The **15**:360
Struwwelpeter **8**:167

Stuart, Jesse **9**:40
Stubborn Hope **14**:56, 57, 60
Stubbs, Harry C. See Clement, Hal
Student activism **3**:43
Students for a Democratic Society
　Piercy **1**:273, 274
　Pinsky **4**:246
Studies in Bibliography **7**:12
Studies in the Short Story **3**:202
Studio **2**:76
Study of History, A **5**:325
Studying the Ground for Holes **13**:25
Sturgeon, Theodore
　Gunn **2**:248, 249
　Knight **10**:211, 217
　Pohl **1**:290
Sturgill, Virgil **15**:274, 278, 287,
　290
Styron, William
　Chappell **4**:114, 115, 116
　Clarke **16**:83, 84
Suares, Carlo **14**:246, 251
Substance abuse
　Allman **15**:25
　Garrett **5**:75-76
Such Men Are Dangerous **11**:35
Such Was the Season **6**:197
Suck-Egg Mule: A Recalcitrant Beast
　14:111-12
Suden, Richard Tum **14**:173
Sugar Mother, The **13**:106, 109
Suicide
　Honig **8**:121
　Shapiro **6**:290
Suicide's Wife, The **3**:199
Suite of Love, Anguish, and Solitude
　15:7
Suits for the Dead **3**:318
Sukenick, Ronald **8**:283-95
　Anaya **4**:26
　Federman **8**:80
　Klinkowitz **9**:108, 112, 113, 115,
　　116, 119
　Major **6**:193
Sulfur **6**:146, 148
Sullivan, Eleanor **15**:197
Sullivan, J.W.N. **5**:328
Summa technologiae **1**:263
*Summer Dreams and the Klieg Light
　Gas Company* **7**:107
Summer Fury **12**:51
Summers, Hollis **9**:41
Summing Up, The **1**:375
Sumsion, John **4**:88
Sun, He Dies, The **7**:82
Sun Rock Man **2**:140
Sunday Gentleman, The **1**:395
"Sunday Morning" **11**:18
Sunday Times (London)
　Ashby **6**:43
　Caute **4**:108
　Glanville **9**:26
　Mott **7**:129
　Wilson **5**:321, 322
　Wright **5**:367, 368
"Sundog Society, The" **7**:110

Sunrise North **15**:153, 158, 159
Sunset Freeway **2**:421
Super, R.H. **4**:247
Supreme Doctrine, The **2**:416
Surfaces and Masks **6**:200
Surly Sullen Bell, The **9**:100, 103
Surrealism **14**:246-47, 247, 256-57
Surry Players **2**:116
Survivors (Frederick Feirstein) **11**:76,
　83, 84
Survivors, The (Elaine Feinstein)
　1:223
Susann, Jacqueline **3**:322
Sussex, England **2**:126-27
Sussex University **6**:98
Sutherland, Betty **14**:128
Sutherland, Efua **2**:303
Sutherland, John
　Dudek **14**:127-28
　Souster **14**:310, 312, 315
　Turnbull **14**:333, 335
Sutphen Music School **16**:16, 17
Sutter, John **4**:245
Sutton, Henry (pseudonym) See David
　R. Slavitt
Sutton, Walter **11**:10
Suzuki, D.T. **2**:416
Sváb, Ludvik **1**:339
Svayamvara and Other Poems **9**:146
Švec **1**:336-38
Svejk **1**:340-341
Svevo, Italo **3**:218
Swallow the Lake **6**:185, 187
Swan Lake **4**:148
Swanberg, W.A. **13**:259-77
　Barrio **15**:124
Swanny's Ways **14**:180
Sward, Robert **13**:279-306
Swarthmore College **9**:233
Swastika Poems, The **9**:42-44
Sweden
　McCord **9**:184
　Skelton **5**:293
　Tranströmer **17**:249-65
Swedenborg, Emanuel **8**:302
Sweeney, Francis **5**:97
Sweet Bird of Youth
　Bowles **1**:92
　Cassity **8**:43
Sweet Briar College **1**:310-11
Sweet William **9**:255
Swell Season, The **1**:330
Swenson, Karen **13**:307-17
Swift, James **5**:370
Swift, Jonathan **8**:122
Swift, Patrick
　Sisson **3**:301, 302
　Wright **5**:370, 371, 372, 374
Swift, Peg **5**:167-68, 171
Swinburne, Algernon Charles **8**:241,
　244-45
Swing in the Garden, The **17**:78, 89,
　91
Switzerland **12**:273-74
Symbolic History **12**:26-27, 28, 29,
　31, 39

Symons, A.J.A.   **3**:382-83, 391
Symons, Julian   **3**:381-96
   Fuller   **10**:112, 120, 123, 124, 127
Symptoms & Madness   **6**:185
Synapse Corp.   **4**:250
Synge, John Millington   **5**:285-86
Synthesis   **3**:94, 95
Syracuse Herald-Journal   **3**:422
Syracuse, N.Y.   **3**:416-19, 422
Syracuse Post Standard   **3**:422
Syracuse University
   Allen   **11**:8-9, 10-11
   Allman   **15**:23-24
   Bell   **14**:41-42
   Elman   **3**:72-73
   Lifshin   **10**:234, 246-49
   Malzberg   **4**:206, 207, 208, 209,
      211
   Phillips   **13**:199-202
   Williams   **3**:417, 420-22, 431
Syzathmary, Arthur   **2**:448-49
Sze, Fred   **5**:150
Szegedy-Makas, Mihaly   **5**:198-99
Szilard, Leo   **1**:272

Taft, Robert   **9**:98
Taft School   **3**:313
Taggard, Genevieve   **3**:137
Taine, John   **3**:271
Taizé Community   **11**:48, 57
Taj, Imtiaz Ali   **9**:225
Take Five   **6**:210, 215, 216, 218
Take It or Leave It   **8**:73, 75, 76
Take Me Back   **14**:11-12
Take Off the Masks   **11**:57
"Taking of Miss Janie, The"   **16**:67
Tal Tal, Chile   **3**:186
Tale of Asa Bean, The   **15**:264
Tale of Pierrot, A   **6**:122
Tale of Two Cities, A   **6**:263
Talent for Living, A   **1**:196
Tales of Arthur, The   **7**:236
Tales of Idiots, The   **7**:124, 127
Tales of Mean Streets   **2**:384
Tales of the Labrador Indians   **15**:251
Talisman Press   **3**:335
"Talking of Books"   **6**:23
Talking Room, The   **11**:136-37
Tallents, Martin   **5**:291
Talmud   **4**:358-59
Tambimuttu, Thurairajah
   Davie   **3**:36
   Wright   **5**:366-67, 368, 369
T&T   **1**:167
Tangents (magazine)   **17**:67
Tangier, Morocco
   Bowles   **1**:83-84, 87-88, 90, 91,
      92, 93, 94
   Morgan   **4**:232, 233
Tangled Vines   **10**:257
Tank Corps, The   **1**:339-41
Tanka   **4**:183
Tanner, Tony   **1**:303
Taos: A Deluxe Magazine of the Arts
   14:111
Taos, N.M.

Crews   **14**:109-10
Nichols   **2**:333-34
Tapestry and The Web, The   **16**:190,
   196
Tar Baby   **16**:84
Targets   **5**:349
Tarlin, Bert   **2**:135
Tarn, Jeremy   **14**:179
Tarn, Nathaniel   **16**:271-89
Tarr   **3**:385
Tarzan Adventures (magazine)   **5**:177
Tate, Allen
   Ghiselin   **10**:136-37, 142
   Hauser   **11**:134
   Kazin   **7**:92
   Kostelanetz   **8**:185
   Olson   **12**:233
   Root   **11**:323
   Whittemore   **8**:307, 308, 310
Tate, James   **7**:298-99
Taxi Driver   **3**:77, 83
Taylor, Carl N.   **9**:157
Taylor, Elizabeth   **3**:322
Taylor, Frances Carney   **7**:19
Taylor, Frank   **3**:127
Taylor, Henry   **7**:171-89
   Dillard   **7**:14-15
   Garrett   **5**:75
Taylor, James   **8**:141
Taylor, Lillie Hill   **2**:281
Taylor, Peter
   Chappell   **4**:118, 120, 125
   Root   **11**:322
   Shreve   **5**:237
   Wagoner   **3**:403
Taylor, Robert W.   **16**:296, 300
Taylor, W.C.   **7**:3
Tazewell, William   **1**:321-22
Te Kooti   **3**:250
"Teach Yourself" series   **5**:284
Teachers Union   **2**:207
Teaching
   Beltrametti   **13**:63
   Bergé   **10**:10-11
   Booth   **5**:35
   Chappell   **4**:118-19
   Creeley   **10**:69-70
   Feirstein   **11**:82
   Fisher   **10**:95-96, 97
   Gunn   **2**:233
   Hazo   **11**:145-46
   Thomas   **11**:372-73
Teatro Campesino (artistic
   movement)   **4**:25
Teatro degli Arte   **2**:416
Technology and Culture   **14**:135
Teepee Tales of the American Indians
   6:58
Teichmann, Howard   **6**:90
Teilhard de Chardin, Pierre
   Berrigan   **1**:58
   Greeley   **7**:43
Teilhet, Darwin   **9**:9
Teitlebaum's Window   **3**:221, 223
Tel Aviv, Israel
   Eastlake   **1**:209

Megged   **13**:143-44, 153
Telegram (Newfoundland, Canada)
   15:245, 246
Telephone Spotlight on Missouri   **2**:170
Telephone Spotlight on Texas   **2**:170
Telepower   **10**:174
Television scriptwriting
   Gray   **3**:110-13
   Nolan   **16**:213, 217-18, 219-20,
      222-23
   Slade   **9**:242-43, 244-45
   Wakefield   **7**:200-01
"Tell-Tale Heart, The"   **7**:28
Telluride Association   **8**:288
Tempest in the Tropics   **11**:104
Tempest, The
   Broughton   **12**:45-47
   Van Itallie   **2**:421
Temple   **9**:149
Temple Dogs   **2**:168, 174, 175
Temple University
   Feirstein   **11**:82
   Lifshin   **10**:241, 247
   Olson   **11**:258
   Slavitt   **3**:322
Templeton, Rini   **2**:334
Ten Interiors with Various Figures
   10:98
Ten Ways of Looking at a Bird   **8**:91,
   92
Tenant of San Mateo, The   **11**:100,
   102
Tender Mercies   **10**:41
Tennant, Emma   **9**:289-95
Tennessee   **7**:290, 291
Tennis   **17**:166-67, 168-70, 174
Tennyson, Alfred, Lord   **7**:240
10th Street Coffee House, New York
   City
   Bergé   **10**:5-6
   Wakoski   **1**:362
Terkel, Studs   **7**:142
Terrell, Robert H., Law School
   2:287
Terrorism   **2**:174-75
Testament   **12**:41
Tête Blanche   **4**:72-73
Teter, Holbrook   **11**:306, 307
Têtes de Pioche, Les   **16**:49
Tevis, Walter   **9**:41
Texas
   Hinojosa-Smith   **16**:139-41, 149-52
   Petesch   **12**:247
   Rechy   **4**:255, 257
   White   **4**:349-50
   Wolfe   **9**:300-01
Texas A&I University   **16**:140
Texas A&M University   **9**:301
Thackeray, William Makepeace
   Federman   **8**:72
   Rakosi   **5**:201
Thailand   **13**:316
Thames & Hudson (publishers)
   7:129, 130
That Girl from Boston   **10**:295, 296-97
That Golden Woman   **3**:322

INDEX

That Only a Mother **1**:289
That's My Baby **1**:382
Thayler, Carl **11**:355-65
    Rosenblum **11**:345, 348
Theater
    Feirstein **11**:81-82, 83
    Flanagan **17**:50-51
    Jennings **5**:108-09
    Malzberg **4**:208
    Mano **6**:208, 209
    Slade **9**:239-56
    Wellek **7**:211
Theater for the New City, New York
    City
    Owens **2**:366
    Van Itallie **2**:418-19, 421
Theatre of Mixed Means, The **8**:184
*Their Finest Hours: Narratives of the
    RAF and Luftwaffe in World War
    II* **9**:108, 120
Theocritus: Idylls and Epigrams
    15:235
*Theodore Roethke: An American
    Romantic* **16**:236
Theory of Comedy, The **12**:235
Theory of Island Biogeography, The
    16:299
Theory of the Arts, The **15**:361
There Are Doors **9**:309
*There Is a Tree More Ancient than
    Eden* **7**:32
*Thesaurus of English Words and
    Phrases* **3**:136
These Our Mothers See *L'Amèr ou le
    Chapitre effrité*
These the Companions **3**:32, 33, 35
They Call It the Cariboo **5**:289
Thibaudeau, Colleen **15**:301-02, 303,
    304, 305, 308
Thief Who Couldn't Sleep, The **11**:34
Thieves Carnival **2**:411
Thing of Sorrow **12**:229
Third Kingdom, The **12**:38, 39
Third Man, The **4**:102
Thirteen Clocks **11**:162-63
Thirteenth Immortal, The **3**:276
Thirties, The **3**:391, 392
Thirty-first of February, The **3**:389,
    390
Thirty-four East **9**:5, 8
31 New American Poets **5**:351
This Day's Death **4**:262
This Do **3**:98
This Earth, My Brother **13**:32, 37,
    38, 41
This Fortress World **2**:248, 250
This Green Tide **10**:113-14
This Is a Recording **2**:121
This Is Dinosaur **9**:268
This Is My Country Too **3**:426
"This Is Poetry" (radio program)
    3:91
This Is Which **3**:93
This Month **12**:202-04
This Promised Land **14**:159

This School Is Driving Me Crazy
    6:170, 172
This Singing World **1**:65
This Summer's Dolphin **3**:261
*This Way for the Gas, Ladies and
    Gentlemen* **2**:72
Thole, Karel **8**:13
Thomas Aquinas, St.
    Mott **7**:123
    Silverberg **3**:272
Thomas, Caitlin **3**:141
Thomas, D.M. **11**:367-84
Thomas, Dylan
    Abse **1**:21, 24, 29
    Broughton **12**:54
    Dacey **17**:22, 23
    Ghiselin **10**:139
    Howes **3**:141
    Kerrigan **11**:208
    Lifshin **10**:247, 250, 255
    Nims **17**:187-90, 193
    Olson **12**:234
    Ray **7**:140
    Roditi **14**:259
    Shapiro **6**:303
    Sinclair **5**:272-73, 274
    Wagoner **3**:403, 405
    Weiss **2**:441
    Wright **5**:367, 368
Thomas, Evan **3**:180
Thomas Hardy: The Teller of Tales
    2:221
Thomas Jefferson College **10**:10-11
Thomas Merton, Monk and Poet **6**:326
Thomas, Norman **13**:273
Thomas, R.S. **4**:301-13
Thomas, Theodore L. **10**:223
Thomas, William David **5**:288, 291
Thompson, D'Arcy **9**:96
Thompson, Dunstan **1**:313
Thompson, Mark **11**:58, 59
Thompson, Randall **6**:232
Thomson, Virgil
    Bowles **1**:84, 86, 92
    Purdy **1**:303
Thoreau, Henry David
    Allen **6**:25
    Enslin **3**:88, 94
    Heyen **9**:31
    Petry **6**:267
    Sward **13**:299
Thornhill, Arthur H. **4**:138
Thorns **3**:278, 279, 283
Thornton, John **11**:236
Thorpe, Jim **1**:381
*Those Who Can: A Science Fiction
    Reader* **2**:257
Thoughts Abroad **14**:56-57
Thousand Nights and One Night, The
    1:77
Thread That Runs So True, The **9**:40
"Three Brothers" **2**:398-99
Three from La Mama **2**:414
Three Front **2**:368
365 Days **1**:117
334 **4**:151, 154, 156

Three Lives for Mississippi **2**:419
Three Lovers **2**:351
Three on the Tower **4**:296
Three Roberts on Childhood, The
    13:298-99
Three Roberts on Love, The **13**:298
*Three Roberts, Premiere Performance,
    The* **13**:298
Three Sirens, The **1**:384, 385, 393
Three Sisters, The **2**:418
Thrice Chosen **14**:282
Thrill of the Grass, The **7**:106
Thrilling Wonder Stories **2**:37
Thurber, James **11**:162-63
Thursday, My Love **10**:300
Thus Spake Zarathustra **3**:338
Thy Kingdom Come **2**:245
Tiananmen Square, Beijing, China
    15:325
Tibetan Book of the Dead, The (Jean-
    Claude van Itallie) **2**:421
Tiempo de silencio (Time of silence)
    12:103
Tiger Tim's Weekly **6**:32
Tigers Wild **4**:265
Tilden, Mike **10**:209, 217
Till, Emmett **7**:196
Tille, Václav **7**:214
Timbuktu **2**:299-301
Time
    Dillard **7**:17
    Kirk **9**:98
    Still **17**:241
    Swanberg **13**:269, 270-71, 272
    Van Itallie **2**:415
    Williams **3**:431
    Wilson **5**:321, 323
Time and Tide **6**:320
Time and Western Man **3**:385
Time Hoppers, The **3**:278
Time of Changes, A **3**:281, 282
Time of the Barracudas **12**:10
Time to Keep, A **6**:71-72
*Timeless Stories for Today and
    Tomorrow* **7**:6
Times Literary Supplement (London)
    Symons **3**:386, 387, 389
    Wesker **7**:233-34
Times (London) **8**:167, 171, 177
Tin Toys **8**:103
Tindal-Atkinson, Father **5**:112
Tindall, William York
    Kennedy **9**:80
    Lottman **12**:205
    West **7**:277
Titania's Lodestone **2**:122
Titian **4**:328
Tituba of Salem Village **6**:253
Tlön, Uqbar, Orbis Tertius **1**:263
Tlooth **6**:246
"To a Skylark" **14**:123
"To a Young Poet Who Fled"
    17:24
To an Early Grave **3**:218-20
To Come, To Have Become **3**:98
"To Hear My Head Roar" **7**:177

To Live Again **3**:279
To Open the Sky **3**:278
"To See the Invisible Man" **3**:277, 279
To the Children in Yemen **13**:151
To the City of the Dead: An Account of Travels in Mexico **6**:321
To the Finland Station **7**:236
To the Gods the Shades **5**:373
"To the Point" **9**:100
"To Whom Is the Poet Responsible?" **8**:308
"Toad" **7**:180
Tobacco Road **1**:148, 151
Tobin, Maurice **6**:171
Tocqueville Prize **10**:335
Todd **17**:69-70
Todd, Glen **11**:284, 285
Todd, Ruthven **3**:386, 389
Toer, Pramoedya Ananta **13**:316
Together **9**:38
Toklas, Alice B. **1**:83
Tokyo, Japan
    Federman **8**:75
    Kirkup **4**:187-88
Tolbert, Mildred **14**:109, 112, 113
Toledo News-Bee **3**:176-77
Toledo, Ohio **17**:38-46
Tolkien, J.R.R.
    Kirk **9**:103-04
    Knight **10**:225
    Wain **4**:328, 329
Tolstoy, Ivan
    Dennison **6**:119
    Enslin **3**:97
Tolstoy, Leo
    Bourjaily **1**:70
    Dennison **6**:121
    Forrest **7**:25
    Josipovici **8**:156
    Rakosi **5**:204
    Wallace **1**:387, 391
Tom o' Bedlam **3**:286
Tom Sawyer **6**:244
"Tom Swift" series **7**:56
Tomerlin, John **16**:212, 213, 214
Tomlinson, Charles
    Davie **3**:35, 36
    Rosenthal **6**:284
"Tomorrow for Angela" **3**:403
Tomorrow Will Be Sunday **15**:238, 247, 248
Tonkinson, Mary **5**:238, 239
Too Loud a Solitude **12**:193
Toomer, Jean **7**:32
Toomey, Robert E., Jr. **10**:172, 174
Toronto, Canada
    Nims **17**:183
    Owens **2**:366-68
    Sward **13**:296-97, 298-99
Toronto Islands: An Illustrated History, The **13**:297
Torregian, Sotere **16**:111-13
Torremolinos, Spain **3**:217
Torrents of Spring **11**:376
Tortuga **4**:26

Totalitarianism
    Davie **3**:42
    Samarakis **16**:250, 262-66
Touch of Clay, A **3**:265
Touch of Time: Myth, Memory and the Self, The **2**:216, 217, 220, 224, 225, 226
Tougaloo College **10**:41
Tough Guy Writers of the Thirties **3**:194
Touster, Irwin **8**:306
Tower of Glass **3**:281, 283
Town & Country **1**:192
Town Life **16**:238-39
Town on the Border, The **1**:342
Toyama, Mitsuru **1**:380
Toynbee, Arnold **5**:325
Toynbee, Philip **5**:323, 326
Trace **6**:180
Tracker **3**:408
Tracy, David **7**:49
Trade unions See Labor unions
Tradition and Dream **6**:25
Tragedy and the Theory of Drama **12**:235
Tragic Ground **1**:150
Tragic Sense of Life, The **11**:213
Trail Driving Days **6**:57
Trails **7**:61
Train, Arthur **6**:264
Train to Pakistan **9**:232
Tramp's Cup, The **7**:138
Transatlantic Review
    Busch **1**:132
    Van Itallie **2**:412
transition
    Bowles **1**:82
    Caldwell **1**:147
    Pohl **1**:285
    Symons **3**:385
Translating and interpreting
    Mead **13**:125-31, 132-34, 136-39
    Rabassa **9**:191-92, 197-98, 203-04
    Raffel **9**:213-14, 219
Translation **17**:191-92
Translation **13**:251
Translations from the Chinese **7**:78
Tranströmer, Tomas **17**:249-65
Traub, John **8**:249
Travelling **4**:166
Traverso, Leone **10**:142
Tree of Time, The **10**:223-24
Tree on Fire, A **2**:386
Treichler, Paul **8**:132
Trembling upon Rome, A **1**:197
Trend of Dehumanization in Weapon Systems of the 21st Century, The **1**:263
Tres cuentos **15**:8
Trespass **3**:181
Treuhaft, Bob **17**:142-50
Triada **15**:211, 213
Trial Impressions **6**:247, 248
Trial, The **2**:72
Tribal Justice **3**:18, 22, 23, 24
Tribune

Booth **2**:55
Fuller **10**:125
Jones **5**:123, 124
Tribute **9**:248-50
Trilce **12**:100
Trilling, Lionel
    Kennedy **9**:80
    Simpson **4**:291, 294
    West **7**:277
Trilling, Steve
    Fuchs **5**:57-58
    Wallace **1**:384
Trimble, Bjo **12**:213
Trimble, John **12**:213
Trinity College, Burlington, Vt. **2**:159
Trio **5**:221-22
Triolet, Elsa **14**:273
Tristia of Ovid, The **3**:324
Tristram Shandy **5**:44, 46
Triumph of the Novel: Dickens, Dostoevsky, Faulkner, The **2**: 219, 221, 228, 229
Triumph of Time **8**:147
Trodd, Kenith **3**:110, 111-12
Troll of Surewould Forest, A **4**:157
Trollope, Anthony
    Arden **4**:36
    Gilbert **15**:189, 195-96
Trophées, Les **2**:158
Tropic of Cancer, The **10**:288
Tropic of Capricorn, The
    Rimmer **10**:288
    Wallace **1**:397
Tropicalization **17**:13-14
Troy **3**:377
Troy, William
    Belitt **4**:62, 65
    Dennison **6**:111-12
    Howes **3**:137
Truck on the Track, The **6**:99
True & False Unicorn **12**:49, 57
True Confessions of George Barker, The **6**:42-43
Trueblood, Alan S. **8**:118, 119
Truman Doctrine **2**:226
Truman, Harry
    Charyn **1**:179
    Knebel **3**:178
Trumbull Park **6**:181
Trungpa, Chögyam
    Kyger **16**:201
    Van Itallie **2**:416, 417, 419, 420
    Waldman **17**:279-80, 283
Trust in Chariots **15**:344
Truth of Poetry, The **4**:166
Tsing Hua University, Peking, China **1**:34
"Tsuruginomiya Regeneration, The" **6**:136, 138, 144
Tsvetayeva, Marina
    Feinstein **1**:221
    Thomas **11**:382
Tu regardais intensément Geneviève (You stared fixedly at Geneviève) **13**:189

Tuberculosis
  Brown **6:**66
  Glanville **9:**20, 21
  Samarakis **16:**248
  Sillitoe **2:**378, 379-80
  Wellek **7:**223
Tubman, Harriet **2:**295
Tuck, Les **15:**246
Tudor Cornwall **8:**260
Tufts University
  Ciardi **2:**88-89, 90
  Corman **2:**132-33, 145
  Forbes **16:**117
  Kennedy **9:**85
  Kumin **8:**215
Tuma, Antoinette **11:**61-72
Tunnicliffe, Charles **4:**311
Tunstall, Edward **5:**98
Turbulent Zone, The **13:**156
Turgenev, Ivan **11:**376
Turkey **4:**152
Turks **2:**273
Turnbull, Gael **14:321-37**
  Fisher **10:**94, 96, 97
Turner, Barbara **5:**293
Turner, Frederick **10:307-22**
  Allen **11:**22
  Feirstein **11:**84, 85
Turner, J.M.W. **4:**155
Turner, Tom **1:**78
Turquoise Lake: A Memoir of World War II, The **8:**239
Turret, The **2:**115
Tutola, Amos **3:**427
Tuwaang Attends a Wedding **9:**164
T.V. **2:**414
Twain, Mark
  Anderson **2:**46
  Booth **5:**31, 40
  Wagoner **3:**408
Twelfth Night **2:**157
Twentieth Century **1:**194
Twentieth Century Fox
  Condon **1:**193
  Jones **5:**126-27
  Thayler **11:**362-63
  Wakefield **7:**200
  Wallace **1:**385
Twentieth Century Fund **8:**137-38
Twentieth Century Verse
  Fuller **10:**123
  Symons **3:**385, 386, 388
28th Day of Elul, The **3:**74, 76, 83
Twenty-One Poems **3:**302
Twenty-seventh Wife, The **1:**388, 389-90
Twenty to Thirty **2:**22
Twilight of the Day **5:**128, 129
Two Ballads of the Muse **5:**285
Two Englands: Empiricism and Idealism in English Literature, The **7:**222
Two Friends **9:**66, 67
Two Hands **5:**163, 164
Two, The **1:**379, 400
Two Wings to Veil My Face **7:**27, 30, 32

Two Women and Their Man **5:**130-31
Two Women of London: The Strange Case of Ms. Jekyll and Mrs. Hyde **9:**291, 295
Tygodnik Powszechny **1:**259
Tyler, Anne **4:**115
Tyler, J.E.A. **9:**104
Tynan, Kenneth **4:**30
Typhoon **2:**228
Tyson, Cicely **13:**251

UAW See United Auto Workers
Udall, Stewart **9:**268-69
Uganda **3:**82
Uh-Oh Plutonium! **17:288**
Ul-Haq, Mohammad Zia **9:**235
Ulysses
  Booth **5:**44
  Boyle **1:**99
  Jones **5:**121
  Thomas **11:**376
  Wallace **1:**375
Un-American Activities Committee, U.S. House of Representatives
  Mitford **17:**147
  Williams **3:**424
Unamuno, Miguel de
  Kerrigan **11:**213, 214
  Rabassa **9:**201-02
"Unc" **7:**139
Uncertainties **15:**378
Uncle Dog and Other Poems **13:**280, 283-84, 288
Uncle Vanya **2:**418
Uncollected Stars **4:**208
Under a Monsoon Cloud **8:**165, 173, 176
Under Milk Wood **5:**274
Under the Apple Tree **7:**201
Under the Skin: The Death of White Rhodesia **4:**109
Under the Volcano
  Delbanco **2:**158
  Williams **3:**421
Underground Church, The **11:**54
Underlay **4:**209-10, 213
Underneath the Arches **9:**16, 27
Underside, The **8:**173
Understanding George Garrett **7:**15
Understanding Poetry
  Jerome **8:**133
  Van Brunt **15:**374
Uneasy Chair, The **9:**269
Ungaretti, Giuseppe **10:**141-42
Unger, David **12:**91-106
Unicorn Press **8:**248
Union of Czech Youth **1:**334
Union Theological Seminary **11:**47
Unitarianism **10:**303
United Artists Studios **1:**194, 196
United Auto Workers **3:**137
United Features Syndicate **1:**65
United Federation of Teachers **1:**365
United Nations **9:**231-32
United Press

Gray **2:**194
Hine **15:**225
Salisbury **15:**321, 324
United States
  Hamburger **4:**171
  Hauser **11:**131-33
  Moorcock **5:**187
  Mrozek **10:**271-72
  Rowse **8:**261-62
  White **4:**348
U.S. Air Force
  Bausch, Richard **14:**5-7
  Bausch, Robert **14:**23-24
  Bennett **13:**83
  Smith **7:**163
  Westlake **13:**338-39
  Whittemore **8:**303
U.S. Army
  Baumbach **5:**22-23
  Bell **14:**47-48
  Booth **5:**38-39
  Busch **1:**130, 133
  Cassill **1:**165-67
  Cassity **8:**44-47
  Ciardi **2:**91, 92
  Corcoran **2:**118
  Crews **14:**108
  Davison **4:**133
  Disch **4:**148
  Easton **14:**154-55
  Federman **8:**74-75
  Garrett **5:**71-72, 78, 81-82, 86-87, 88-89
  Hinojosa-Smith **16:**140
  Kerrigan **11:**204
  Kherdian **2:**265-66
  Kirk **9:**95-96
  Lottman **12:**204-05
  Peters **8:**239
  Rabassa **9:**198-201
  Rechy **4:**259
  Rimmer **10:**289-92
  Simpson **4:**291
  Sukenick **8:**290
  Wright **7:**293-97
U.S. Army Air Force
  Ciardi **2:**94
  Clement **16:**89-91, 92-94, 98
  Still **17:**242-44
  Wallace **1:**379
U.S. Army, Special Training Program **9:**266
United States Award **11:**150
U.S. Coast Guard **15:**259-61
U.S. Department of Agriculture **1:**85
U.S. Department of State **14:**267-68, 278-79
U.S. Department of the Army **14:**269-73
U.S. Forest Service **14:**168
U.S. Information Agency
  Anderson **2:**44
  Caldwell **1:**154, 156
  Corman **2:**139
  Eshleman **6:**138
  Guerard **2:**224

Katz **14**:171-72
Knight **10**:229
Purdy **1**:304
Wagoner **3**:408-09
U.S. Information Service *See* U.S.
    Information Agency
U.S. Marine Corps
    Becker **1**:34
    Connell **2**:103
    Flanagan **17**:44
    Hamill **15**:207-08
    Hazo **11**:143-44
U.S. Naval Academy **5**:333, 341-42
U.S. Navy
    Connell **2**:102, 103
    Corcoran **2**:118
    Dennison **6**:110
    Gunn **2**:243-45, 246
    Kennedy **9**:81-82, 87
    Knebel **3**:177-78
    Mathews **6**:223, 228, 231, 240
    McCord **9**:177, 178-80
    Meredith **14**:226, 233
    Olson **11**:250-52
    Sward **13**:280, 286
    Thayler **11**:361-62
    Williams **3**:419-20
    Wilson **5**:343-45
U.S. Navy, WAVES **2**:209
U.S. Office of War Information
    14:263-65, 266
U.S. Post Office **15**:265, 266
"United States Steel Hour" **2**:170
*Universal Baseball Association, J. Henry
    Waugh, Prop., The* **7**:13-14
Universal Press Syndicate **1**:253
Universal Studios **1**:383
"Universe" **2**:248
Universidad de Mexico **2**:207
Université d'Aix-Marseille **8**:226
Université de Nice **6**:194-95
University at Frankfurt am Main
    12:232
University at Rio Piedras **12**:34
University Bookman **9**:100
University College, Cardiff, Wales
    4:190
University College, Dublin, Ireland
    2:346
University College, Galway, Ireland
    4:305
University College, London,
    England **13**:46
University College of North Wales,
    Bangor **4**:302-03
University of Adelaide **3**:354
University of Alabama **16**:293-94
University of Arizona
    Ai **13**:4-5
    Bourjaily **1**:79
    Boyd **11**:46
    Burroway **6**:86
    Greeley **7**:47
    West **7**:283
    Wilson **5**:349, 350
University of Berlin **11**:128

University of Birmingham
    Allen **6**:18
    Brossard **2**:71
    Fisher **10**:93-95
University of Bridgeport **11**:16, 19,
    20
University of Bristol **3**:296, 303-04
University of British Columbia
    Bergé **10**:7
    Bowering **16**:21, 32-33
    Gray **3**:110
    Woodcock **6**:321, 322
University of Buffalo **11**:79-80
University of Cairo
    El Saadawi **11**:65-66
    Hassan **12**:142, 144, 145, 146-47
University of Calgary
    Blaise **3**:23
    Kinsella **7**:104, 106
University of California
    Ghiselin **10**:129-30
    Kyger **16**:189
    Roditi **14**:269
    Schevill **12**:270, 271-73
University of California at Berkeley
    Barrio **15**:115
    Ghiselin **10**:131
    Kherdian **2**:269
    Pinsky **4**:245, 246, 249-50
    Roditi **14**:261
    St. Clair **8**:271-72
    Shapiro **6**:304
    Simpson **4**:294
    Stegner **9**:263
    Stone **3**:363, 364-65, 366-68, 370,
        379
    Wakoski **1**:356, 358-60
University of California at Davis
    Honig **8**:116-17
    Shapiro **6**:304
University of California at Goleta
    2:120
University of California at Irvine
    Ai **13**:8-9
    Duncan **2**:173
    Kennedy **9**:85
    Peters **8**:248
    Wakoski **1**:369
    Wright **7**:299, 300-01
University of California at Los
    Angeles
    Corcoran **2**:119
    Epstein **12**:71
    Federman **8**:77, 78
    Niven **12**:212
    Rechy **4**:263
University of California at Riverside
    8: 242, 243-44
University of California at Santa
    Barbara
    Barrio **15**:117
    Easton **14**:158
    Federman **8**:78
    Hamill **15**:210, 212-13
    Turner **10**:317
University of Cape Coast **13**:50

University of Chicago
    Bell, Charles G. **12**:22, 32-33, 34,
        36
    Bell, Marvin **14**:43-44
    Booth **5**:42, 43-44, 48
    Flanagan **17**:45-46
    Greeley **7**:43, 46-47
    Hine **15**:231, 232-33, 234, 235
    Jerome **8**:130-31
    Manuel **9**:165-66, 167
    Nims **17**:178-79
    Olson **12**:229, 232
    Pinsky **4**:247
    Rakosi **5**:202
    Ray **7**:139-40
    Rodgers **13**:252
    Roditi **14**:254, 257, 259, 260
    Rosenthal **6**:275
    Simic **4**:283
    Solotaroff **2**:396-98
University of Chicago Press **4**:247
University of Cincinnati **17**:97
University of Colorado
    Corcoran **2**:120
    Gunn **2**:244
    Katz **14**:178
    Sukenick **8**:293
    Williamson **8**:325
University of Connecticut
    McKain **14**:215
    Sward **13**:291
University of Copenhagen **16**:117
University of Denver
    Brutus **14**:61
    Corcoran **2**:121
    Raffel **9**:218-19
University of Dublin, Trinity College
    Davie **3**:37-38
    Keating **8**:166, 167
University of Edmonton **15**:157-58
University of Essex
    Davie **3**:40-43
    Feinstein **1**:221, 223
    Raworth **11**:302, 303
University of Exeter
    Sisson **3**:307
    Turner **10**:321
University of Florida
    Jones **11**:178
    Smith **7**:165-66
University of Georgia **1**:157
University of Ghana **13**:44, 46
University of Hawaii
    Hall **12**:121-22
    Meredith **14**:227
    Morgan **3**:235-36
University of Houston
    Brown **10**:41
    Olson **12**:237
    Wolfe **9**:303
University of Idaho **8**:240
University of Illinois
    Bausch **14**:24
    Brown **6**:57
    Burroway **6**:100
    Greeley **7**:47

Hinojosa-Smith **16**:149
Rodgers **13**:244
Still **17**:237
Sward **13**:288
University of Indiana **12**:235
University of Iowa
    Allen **6**:20
    Bell **14**:44-45
    Blaise **3**:25, 26
    Bourjaily **1**:73
    Busch **1**:133
    Cassill **1**:164, 167
    Delbanco **2**:159
    Hall **12**:131-34
    Kinsella **7**:102, 103
    Koller **5**:163
    McPherson **17**:133, 135
    Stafford **3**:334
    Stegner **9**:263, 264
    Sward **13**:288
    Wright **7**:297-99
    See also International Writers
        Program; Iowa Writers
        Workshop
University of Iowa Short-Fiction
    contest **2**:214
University of Kansas
    Allen **6**:25
    Connell **2**:106-07, 112
    Gunn **2**:233, 243, 245-46, 247,
        252, 253-55, 256-57, 259
    Stafford **3**:332-33
University of Kent **2**:125
University of Kentucky **2**:120
University of Leeds **3**:353
University of London
    Gray **3**:109, 110, 111-12, 114-15
    Hamburger **4**:165
    Mott **7**:130
    Sinclair **5**:271
University of Manchester **3**:239, 246
University of Manila **9**:158-59
University of Manitoba **15**:304, 305
University of Maryland
    Weiss **2**:434
    Whittemore **8**:309
University of Massachusetts
    Ai **13**:12
    Galvin **13**:93-94
    Skelton **5**:286
    Wakefield **7**:198
University of Michigan
    Ciardi **2**:89, 90
    Corman **2**:134, 135
    Delbanco **2**:159
    Hall **7**:65, 66
    Kennedy **9**:82-84, 87
    Kizer **5**:136
    Piercy **1**:271, 277
    Solotaroff **2**:393-95
    Stevenson **9**:278-79, 283
    Wagoner **3**:403
University of Minnesota
    Anderson **2**:38-39
    Disch **4**:155
    Harris **3**:130

Salisbury **15**:311, 312, 317, 320,
    321
Swanberg **13**:260-61
University of Missouri
    Ciardi **2**:90, 93
    Dacey **17**:27
    Olson **12**:237
    Ray **7**:144
    Roditi **14**:262-63
University of Montana
    Corcoran **2**:119, 121, 122, 127
    Root **11**:327
University of Montréal
    Brossard **16**:45-47
    Hood **17**:88
University of Nebraska **6**:304, 306
University of Nevada **5**:346
University of New Brunswick
    15:153-55
University of New Mexico
    Anaya **4**:21, 26
    Bergé **10**:11
    Connell **2**:102
    Creeley **10**:69
    McCord **9**:184
    Olson **12**:237
    Williamson **8**:318
    Wilson **5**:340, 341, 346
University of New Mexico Press
    1:212
University of North Carolina
    Chappell **4**:116, 118-19
    Corman **2**:134
    Root **11**:322
    Shelnutt **14**:298
    Vivante **12**:301
    Weiss **2**:434-35
University of North Carolina Press
    2:116
University of Northern Iowa **9**:113-
    14
University of Notre Dame
    Gunn **2**:244
    Hazo **11**:142-43
    Kerrigan **11**:197
University of Notre Dame Press
    11:213-14
University of Oklahoma
    Duncan **2**:169, 173, 176
    Jerome **8**:127
    Owens **2**:368
University of Oregon **14**:168-69
University of Padua **7**:300, 301
University of Paris **4**:292
University of Patna
    Choudhury **14**:87-88
    Mahapatra **9**:142-43
University of Pennsylvania
    Hassan **12**:147-48, 150-51, 153-54
    Rakosi **5**:207
    Turnbull **14**:331, 334
University of Pittsburgh
    Brutus **14**:62
    Shelnutt **14**:300
University of Portland **17**:174
University of Puerto Rico **12**:234

University of Rome
    Vivante **12**:295-96
    Wright **7**:298
University of St. Andrews
    Kirk **9**:96-98
    Parini **16**:231-35
University of Santo Tomas **9**:164-65,
    167
University of Saskatchewan **15**:159
University of Singapore **3**:245
University of Southern California
    Barrio **15**:114
    Rechy **4**:263
    Stone **3**:366, 368
University of Sussex
    Josipovici **8**:147, 148, 154, 155,
        156, 157, 158
    Morgan **3**:239, 246
University of Tennessee
    Jones **11**:180
    White **4**:350
University of Texas
    Bergé **10**:16
    Caute **4**:105
    Charyn **1**:182
    Clarke **16**:86-87
    Crews **14**:114
    Delgado **15**:173-74, 176-77
    Harris **16**:135
    Hearon **11**:160-61
    Hinojosa-Smith **16**:140, 141
    Kostelanetz **8**:182
    Lifshin **10**:247, 254
    McCord **9**:178, 180-81
    Petesch **12**:246, 248
    Raffel **9**:217
    Rakosi **5**:207
    Raworth **11**:305-06
    Turner **10**:321
    Vivante **12**:301
    White **4**:348
University of Texas Press **3**:74
University of the Philippines
    Manuel **9**:156-58, 160, 162-64,
        167
    Olson **12**:235
University of the West Indies
    16:119
University of Tohoku **4**:183
University of Toledo **17**:44
University of Toronto
    Allen **6**:26
    Hood **17**:85-86
    Livesay **8**:220, 232
    Nims **17**:183
    Škvorecký **1**:348
    Sparshott **15**:352, 354, 355, 360,
        363
University of Toronto Library
    School **15**:155
University of Toronto, Trinity
    College
    Clarke **16**:77, 81-82
    Livesay **8**:225
University of Toronto, University
    College **15**:298, 300-04

University of Tours **3**:168
University of Utah
  Ghiselin **10**:130, 131-39
  McCord **9**:181
  Smith **7**:164
  Stegner **9**:262, 264
  Taylor **7**:183
University of Vermont **10**:250
University of Victoria
  Kinsella **7**:101-02, 103
  Skelton **5**:285, 286, 289, 290-91
  Sward **13**:292, 295
University of Virginia
  Belitt **4**:57-58, 59
  Bell **12**:22, 23, 24
  Bowles **1**:82, 83
  Caldwell **1**:144-45, 146, 157
  Dillard **7**:11, 14, 15, 16
  McPherson **17**:123
  Settle **1**:320, 321
  Shreve **5**:237
  Smith **7**:161, 162
  Taylor **7**:176, 178, 179
  Wakoski **1**:369
University of Washington
  Allen **6**:26
  Major **6**:192-93
  Morgan **3**:236
  Root **11**:321
  Wagoner **3**:405, 408
  Wakoski **1**:370
  Woodcock **6**:321
University of Waterloo **15**:251
University of Western Ontario
  Horwood **15**:251
  Reaney **15**:306-07
University of Wisconsin
  Brée **15**:143, 144-45
  Feirstein **11**:81
  Hahn **11**:109-10
  Hassan **12**:151, 156, 162
  Higgins **8**:90
  Honig **8**:109
  Kherdian **2**:266, 267
  Klinkowitz **9**:110-11
  Morgan **3**:238-39, 241, 243, 244
  Peters **8**:239-40
  Rakosi **5**:202, 203, 204, 205
  Rosenblum **11**:338, 341-42, 344-45, 346, 347, 348, 349-50
  Stegner **9**:264-66
  Thayer **11**:364
  Wallace **1**:374
  West **7**:280
University of Zambia **14**:114, 118
Unmuzzled Ox **13**:22
Unnatural Enemy, The **1**:75
Unpublished Editions **8**:90
Unsealed Lips **10**:257
Untermeyer, Jean Starr
  Bourjaily **1**:65
  Inez **10**:189
Untermeyer, Louis
  Bourjaily **1**:65
  Ciardi **2**:90
Unterseher, Fred **8**:190

Up
  Klinkowitz **9**:112
  Sukenick **8**:283-85, 294
Up and Around **3**:403
Up My Coast **16**:201
Up the Line **3**:281
Updike, John **2**:155, 156
Upsala University **1**:156
Upstate Madonna **10**:241
Upward Reach, The **5**:37
Urban Snow **16**:23
Urbana College **15**:266, 268
Urbánek, Zdeněk **1**:338
Urth of the New Sun, The **9**:311
Uschuk, Pamela **11**:328-30
Usher, Abbott Payson **3**:237
USIA See U.S. Information Agency
USSR See Soviet Union
Utah **9**:95-96

V-Letter and Other Poems **6**:300
Vail, Laurence **1**:116-18
Valdez Horses, The **10**:169, 174
Valentine Pontifex **3**:285
Valéry, Paul **4**:248
Valgardson, W.D. **7**:102, 110
Vallejo, César
  Eshleman **6**:131, 137, 147
  Goldemberg **12**:100
Valtin, Jan **6**:244
Valtinos, Thanassis **9**:147
Vampires, The **4**:262
Van Aelstyn, Ed **5**:164
Van Brunt, Lloyd 15:365-86
  Ray **7**:138
Van der Post, Laurens **11**:329
Van Doren, Carl **7**:90
Van Doren, Irita **6**:279
Van Doren, Mark
  Simpson **4**:291
  Van Brunt **15**:373-74
  Wakefield **7**:202
  Weiss **2**:431, 432
Van Druten, John **2**:411
Van Gogh, Vincent
  Kherdian **2**:267
  Stone **3**:368-70
Van Itallie, Jean-Claude 2:405-23
Vance, Jack **2**:42, 43
Vance, Nina **5**:79
Vancouver Award for Fiction
    Writing **7**:110
Vancouver, Canada **16**:34-35
Vancouver Report, The **10**:7, 10
Vančura, Zdeněk **7**:214-15, 222
Vandam Theatre **2**:413
Vanderbilt, Gloria **5**:212, 221, 222
Vanderbilt University
  Jones **11**:176, 177
  Miller **15**:282
  Morgan **3**:241
  Still **17**:236-37
Vangelisti, Paul **8**:249
Vanguard Press **7**:89
Vanished **3**:169, 181
Vanity Fair **8**:72

Varèse, Edgard **13**:184-85
Vas Dias, Robert
  Eshleman **6**:140
  Olson **11**:253, 255, 259
Vas, Robert **4**:107
Vasconcelos, José **15**:2, 4-5, 9
Vassar College **6**:25
Vatican II
  Greeley **7**:43, 46, 49, 50
  Kienzle **1**:241-43
Vaudeville **3**:402
Vaughan, Sam
  Garrett **5**:76
  Slavitt **3**:321, 322
Vaughn-Thomas, Winford **2**:299-300, 301, 302
Vector **3**:321
Vega, Lope de **8**:119
Vegetarianism **2**:420
Vegetti, Ernesto **8**:13
Velez, Clemente Soto **17**:14
Velvet Horn, The **10**:137
Venice Film Festival, Italy
  Caldwell **1**:152
  Sinclair **5**:274
Venice, Italy
  O'Faolain **2**:350
  Vivante **12**:296
Ventura College **15**:117
Venture **14**:71
Verlaine, Paul **6**:281
Vermont **10**:236
Verne, Jules **2**:37
Vers Libre: A Magazine of Free Verse **14**:110
Verschoyle, Derek (publishers) **5**:370
Versions and Perversions of Heine **3**:300
Very Close Family, A **9**:244
Very Fall of the Sun, The **11**:153
Very Rich Hours of Count von Stauffenberg, The **7**:280
Vestal, Stanley See Campbell, Walter
Vía Unica **15**:11
Vian, Boris
  Brossard **2**:67
  Federman **8**:72, 79
"Vichy France and the Jews" **2**:183
Vicious Circle **9**:240
Victor, Ed **1**:401
Victoria University **15**:157
Victoria University, Skelton
  Collection **5**:290
Vida **1**:280
Vida al contado, La (The life paid in cash) **12**:105
Vidal, Gore
  Parini **16**:240
  Purdy **1**:304
  Weiss **2**:443
Videotape **8**:188
Vie Passionée of Rodney Buckthorne, La **1**:173
Vieira, Antônio **9**:204, 205
Vienna, Austria
  Gregor **10**:152-54, 157-58

Wellek **7**:207-10
Viereck, Peter **4**:171
Vietnam War
  Allen **11**:21
  Allman **15**:23, 24-25
  Anaya **4**:24
  Anderson **2**:44
  Becker **1**:40
  Bell **14**:48
  Berrigan **1**:51, 59
  Blais **4**:76
  Brossard **2**:71
  Busch **1**:133
  Cassill **1**:172
  Connell **2**:110
  Davie **3**:43
  Dennison **6**:117
  Eastlake **1**:211-12
  Enslin **3**:94
  Gray **2**:192, 198
  Hauser **11**:137
  Katz **14**:173
  McCord **9**:182-83, 184
  Nichols **2**:331-32
  Piercy **1**:273
  Plymell **11**:288-89
  Ray **7**:143
  Rosenblum **11**:344
  Salisbury **15**:324
  Shreve **5**:236-37
  Simpson **4**:295
  Smith **7**:162
  Stafford **3**:337
  Swanberg **13**:270-71
  Van Itallie **2**:414
  Wakefield **7**:197-98
  Williams **3**:431
  Wright **7**:301
View
  Atkins **16**:11
  Bowles **1**:87
View from the Weaving Mountain
  16:272
View of the North, A **5**:373
Vigée, Claude **8**:290
Vigilias **15**:9
"Viking Grave at Ladby, The"
  13:313
Vilas Research Professorship **12**:162
Villa in France, A **3**:357
Villa, Jose Garcia **16**:112
Villa, Pancho **4**:253
Village: New and Selected Poems, The
  8:141
Village Voice
  Bourjaily **1**:72
  Hentoff **6**:168-69, 171
  Owens **2**:366, 368
  Wakoski **1**:362
Village Voice Obie Award **2**:361,
  363
Villager Award **2**:361
Villon, François
  Howes **3**:144
  Katz **9**:68

"Villon's Straight Tip to All Cross
  Coves" **3**:144
Vinson, Eddie "Cleanhead" **6**:182
Violated, The **1**:72, 73, 74
Violet Quill Club **13**:230-32
Virgin Islands **8**:135-36
Virginia
  Bennett **13**:75
  Dillard **7**:17-18
  Morris **13**:162
  Smith **7**:156-58, 162, 167
Virginia Commonwealth University
  7:165-66
Virginia Reel **1**:145
Virginia Tech. **6**:27
Vision in Motion **8**:186, 189
Vision of India **9**:233
Visions d'Anna **4**:73-74, 76, 78
Visitations **15**:160
Vitamins for Vitality **8**:26
Vivante, Arturo 12:281-302
  Ghiselin **10**:140
Vivante, Cesare **12**:285
Vivante, Leone
  Ghiselin **10**:140
  Vivante **12**:281, 282, 290, 293-94,
    300
Vivas, Eliseo **12**:326-27
Viviani, GianFranco **8**:12, 13
Vladislav, Jan **1**:338
Vogue **2**:421
VOICE **1**:273
*Voices Underground: Poems from
  Newfoundland* **15**:250
Voinovich, Vladimir 12:303-22
Volleys **17**:51
Volpone **3**:408
Von Kant bis Hegel **7**:220
von Trott, Adam **8**:257
von Zelewski, Ottomar **7**:207
Vonnegut, Kurt
  Bourjaily **1**:76, 79
  Klinkowitz **9**:108, 110, 111-12,
    113, 114, 115, 116, 117
  Wakefield **7**:194
Vonnegut Statement, The **9**:113
Voyage au Bout de la Nuit **14**:256
Voyage to Arcturus, A **3**:281
Voyageurs Sacrés, Les **4**:74
Voyeur, The **3**:321

Wachtel, Chuck **14**:179
Wachuku, Jaja **2**:303
WAG See Writers Action Group
Wagner College **17**:97
Wagner, Lindsay **1**:384
Wagner, Richard
  Atkins **16**:9
  Highwater **7**:78
Wagoner, David 3:397-412
  Allman **15**:23-24
  Kizer **5**:154
Wahl, François **4**:355
Wahl, Jean
  Corman **2**:137
  Menashe **11**:228

Wain, John 4:315-32
Waiting for Godot **8**:77
Wakabayashi, Hiro **5**:212-13
Wake Forest University
  Brée **15**:146-47
  Rimmer **10**:290
Wake Up, Stupid **3**:128, 129
Wake Up. We're Almost There **2**:70,
  71
Wakefield, Dan 7:191-203
  Klinkowitz **9**:114, 116, 118
  Kumin **8**:215
Wakoski, Diane 1:353-72
  Bergé **10**:6, 11
  Dillard **7**:18
  Eshleman **6**:134, 140, 145, 147
  Mott **7**:131
  Owens **2**:363
Wald, Jerry **5**:57-58
Waldbauer, Ivan **6**:234
Waldbauer, Suzanne **6**:234
Walden
  Barrio **15**:111
  Petry **6**:267
Waldman, Anne 17:267-94
  Malanga **17**:115
Waldrop, Keith **9**:83-84
Waldrop, Rosmarie **9**:83
Wales **4**:301-13
Wales **4**:306
Waley, Arthur **7**:78
Walker, Alice **16**:84
Walker in the City, A **7**:90, 94, 95
Walking Edges **9**:182
Walking Four Ways in the Wind
  15:22, 30
Walking the Boundaries **4**:139
Walks **6**:139
Walks to the Paradise Garden **12**:346-
  47
Wallace, Amy **1**:377, 378-79, 399,
  400-401
Wallace, David **1**:378-79
  See also Wallechinsky, David
Wallace, Edgar
  Ashby **6**:33-34
  Dillon **3**:52
Wallace, Henry **2**:192
Wallace, Irving 1:373-403
Wallace, Lois **12**:73
Wallace Stegner Fellowship **11**:324
Wallace Stevens: Musing the Obscure
  8:286-87
Wallace, Sylvia **1**:373, 391, 399,
  400-402
  See also Kahn, Sylvia
Wallace, Tom **6**:57
Wallechinsky, David **1**:377, 378,
  399-401
Wallis, Hal **1**:383
Walls of India, The **6**:325
Walpole, Hugh **11**:280, 282, 284
Walsh, Ernest **1**:115
Walton, Eda Lou **4**:59-62
Walton, Francis **3**:377
Wampanoag Traveler **13**:99

Wampeters, Foma, and Granfalloons
　9:113
Wanderer, The **1**:248
Wandering Fool, The **14**:284
Wang, David **6**:180
Wanning, Andrew **10**:66
Wanted: Hope **16**:253, 257-60
Wanton Summer Air, The **11**:153
Wapshot Chronicle, The **1**:36
War **6**:293
War **2**:412-13
War and Peace
　Bourjaily **1**:70, 72
　Wilson **5**:342
War Comes to America **1**:380
War Commentary **6**:320
War Is Heaven! **6**:210, 211
War of the Worlds, The
　Brunner **8**:3
　Lem **1**:258-59
Warburg, Jim **1**:38
Ward, Cornelia, Foundation **4**:215
Warhol, Andy
　Andre **13**:18-19
　Malanga **17**:95, 97, 100-08, 109-
　　10, 112, 113, 115-18
　Saroyan **5**:216
Warner Brothers Studios
　Epstein **12**:60, 61, 63
　Fuchs **5**:56-58
　Wallace **1**:383
Warner, Francis **2**:56
Warner, Fred **6**:239-40
Warner, Jack
　Epstein **12**:60, 65, 67
　Wallace **1**:384
Warren, Earl **3**:371
Warren, Leonard **4**:230
Warren, Robert Penn
　Clarke **16**:82
　Ghiselin **10**:138
　Jerome **8**:133
　Jones **11**:183
　Meredith **14**:228-29, 232
　Parini **16**:239
Warsaw, Poland **9**:123-24
Warsh, Lewis **17**:276
Warshaw, Howard
　Davie **3**:39-40
　Kyger **16**:189
Warshow, Robert **3**:212, 214-15
Warwick Films **12**:8-9
Washburn University **12**:212
Washington, D.C.
　Brossard **2**:74-76
　Brown **6**:52-54
　Grumbach **2**:212, 213
　Morgan **3**:244
　Wilson **16**:292-93
Washington Evening Star **12**:202
Washington Post
　Brossard **2**:63, 64, 76
　Solotaroff **2**:400
　Whittemore **8**:311
Washington School, Missoula, Mont.
　2:125

Washington Square Review **2**:207
Washington (state) **3**:406
Washington State University **9**:182-
　83
Washington University **10**:16
Wasserman, Harriet **14**:10, 12, 15
Wassermann, Marta **15**:156
Waste Land **14**:128
Wastepaper Theatre **8**:120
Watchboy, What of the Night? **8**:56
Water of Light, The **7**:185
Waters, Frank **13:319-28**
　Wilson **5**:345-46
Watkins, Ann **1**:118, 121, 122
Watkins, Vernon **2**:440-41
Watson, Julia **7**:302
Watson, Sheila **16**:22, 36
Watts, Alan **12**:45
Waugh, Evelyn
　Abse **1**:27
　Lottman **12**:205
　Wesker **7**:235
Wave High the Banner **6**:54
Waves and Licenses **9**:67-68
WAVES See U.S. Navy, WAVES
Way the Future Was, The **9**:311
Way to the World's End, A **7**:127
Way Up, The **4**:233
Wayne State University
　Ai **13**:12
　Boyd **11**:48, 49
　Federman **8**:73-74
　Olson **12**:235
　Peters **8**:241
　Petesch **12**:244
Ways of Escape **8**:169
W.B. Yeats International Summer
　School **3**:40, 41
We Danced All Night **8**:20
We Die before We Live **1**:53
*We Might See Sights! and Other
　Stories* **2**:351
We Speak for Ourselves **3**:361
Weather Shelter, The **1**:155
Weaver, Ed **9**:3
Weaver, William **1**:69
Webb, Ann Eliza **1**:388, 389-90
Webber, Frances **5**:285
Weber, Brom **8**:107, 116, 117
Weber, Hugo **12**:342
Webern, Anton von
　Enslin **3**:95, 96
　Hrabal **12**:185-86
*Webster's New International
　Dictionary* **3**:135
Wedding Day **1**:116, 117
Wedding of Cousins, A **9**:294
Wedgwood, Josiah **4**:316
"Wednesday Play, The" **3**:111
Weegies New York **2**:358
Weekly Packet **7**:196
Weeks, Edward **4**:135
Wei, Wang **15**:65
Weidman, Jerome **1**:383
Weight of Antony, The **14**:171
Weil, Jim **3**:93- 94

Weil, Simone
　Berrigan **1**:48
　Blais **4**:72
Weinberg, Bernard **12**:231, 235-36
Weiner, Joyce **4**:103
Weird Tales
　Belitt **4**:56
　Silverberg **3**:271
Weisinger, Mort **8**:318
Weisman, Mort **12**:248
Weiss, Buddy **4**:229
Weiss, Mark **3**:81
Weiss, Paul **12:323-37**
　Slavitt **3**:315, 318
　Weiss **2**:435, 447
Weiss, Renée Karol **2**:432-33, 434,
　435
Weiss, Theodore **2:425-50**
　Settle **1**:317
Weissner, Carl **11**:292
Welch, Lew
　Kyger **16**:192
　McCord **9**:184
　Saroyan **5**:218
Weldon, Fay **10**:101
Well of Loneliness, The **8**:226, 228
Well, The **13**:109-10
Well Wrought Urn, The **8**:133
Wellek, Bronislav **7**:205, 206, 207,
　208, 209, 210, 211, 225
Wellek, René **7:205-26**
Welles, Orson **5**:274
Wellesley College
　Corcoran **2**:115
　Pinsky **4**:244, 248
Wellfleet, Mass. **1**:276
Wellington College **4**:99, 101-02
Wells, H.G.
　Allen **6**:17
　Anderson **2**:37, 46
　Boyle **1**:114
　Lem **1**:258-59
　Rowse **8**:259
　Silverberg **3**:272, 274
　Wallace **1**:391
Wells, Lester G. **13**:200-01
Wells, Somerset, England **1**:204-05
Welsh language
　Thomas **4**:305-06, 307, 310
　White **4**:335
Welty, Eudora **3**:59
Wensberg, Erik **12**:206
Werewolf Sequence, The **11**:345, 347,
　353
Wesker, Arnold **7:227-63**
Wesker on File (chronology and
　bibliographic checklist) **7**:227,
　240-42
Wesleyan College **1**:123
Wesleyan University **12**:157-59, 160-
　61
Wesleyan University Press
　Major **6**:187
　Piercy **1**:274
　Wakoski **1**:365
　Wright **7**:302

West, Jessamyn
  Coppel **9**:9-10
  Nims **17**:185-86, 187
West, Nathanael
  Eastlake **1**:201
  Madden **3**:197
West of Your City **3**:335
West, Paul 7:265-86
  Fisher **10**:95
West Point Story, The **1**:383, 384
West, Ray B., Jr.
  Cassill **1**:167
  Connell **2**:107
Western Kentucky University **15**:283
Western Michigan University
  Shelnutt **14**:300
  Smith **7**:163, 164
Western Printing & Lithographing
  Co. **2**:248
Western Review
  Cassill **1**:167
  Connell **2**:107
  Hassan **12**:156
Western States Book Award **6**:202
Western Writers of America Spur
  Award **10**:174
Westerners, The **6**:58
Westerns **10**:171, 173-74
Westlake, Donald E. 13:329-45
  Block **11**:32-33, 40
Weston, Edward
  Ghiselin **10**:143
  Thayler **11**:361
Wetterzeichen **13**:133, 134, 136
Wevill, David **9**:217
Wexler, Haskell **2**:289
Weybright, Victor **1**:387, 388, 393
Whalen, Philip
  Beltrametti **13**:58, 61
  Corman **2**:142
  Enslin **3**:93
  Kherdian **2**:269
  Kyger **16**:192, 193, 196, 198
  Plymell **11**:286
Whales: A Celebration **2**:368
Wharton County Community
  College **14**:114
Wharton School, University of
  Pennsylvania **1**:145
What Comes Next **5**:25, 26
What Happens in Fort Lauderdale
  9:42
What She Means **6**:146
Whatever Happened to Betty Lemon
  7:256-57, 259-60, 262
Wheel of Stars, The **5**:285
Wheeler, Benjamin Ide **3**:365
Wheeler, Marion **3**:322
Wheeler, Opal **9**:276
Wheelock, John Hall **3**:318, 319
Wheelright, John **2**:135
Wheelwright, Richard **7**:103
*When He Was Free and Young and He
  Used to Wear Silks* **16**:80-81
When the Sacred Ginmill Closes **11**:38
When the War Is Over **1**:36, 39

"When Wounded Sore the Stricken
  Hart" **1**:317
Where Is My Wandering Boy Tonight?
  3:408
Where the Arrow Falls **9**:217
Which Ones Are the Enemy? **5**:80
While Dancing Feet Shatter the Earth
  5:351
Whistler, James
  Boyle **1**:104
  Disch **4**:155
White, Alan **3**:301, 302
White, Antonia **2**:345
White Cad Cross-Up, The **16**:216
White Dove Review **6**:180
White, Eric Walter **10**:116
White Eskimo: A Novel of Labrador
  15:249, 250, 251
"White Fang Goes Dingo" **4**:151
White Figure, White Ground **17**:87, 89
White, George Dewey **7**:25-26
White Goddess, The
  Arden **4**:29
  Mathews **6**:246
White Hotel, The **11**:373, 377
White Island, The **6**:320
White, Jon Manchip 4:333-52
  Delbanco **2**:157
White, Katharine **2**:65
White, Poppy Cannon **2**:295
White Rabbit Press **16**:190-91
White Shadows, Black Shadows **4**:190
White, Theodore E. **10**:173, 174,
  177
White, Theodore H. **6**:172
White, Valerie Leighton **4**:341, 344,
  345, 349, 351
Whitehall Poetry and Literary
  Society **1**:154
Whitehead, Alfred North **12**:327-29,
  331
Whitehead, Evelyn **12**:328-29
Whiting Field (military base) **2**:106
Whitman, George **1**:169
Whitman, Walt
  Awoonor **13**:48
  Broughton **12**:50-51
  Heyen **9**:37
  Pellegrini **11**:274
  Shapiro **6**:304
  Sward **13**:299
Whitney Father, Whitney Heiress
  13:274
Whitsun **7**:253-56, 257-59
Whittemore, Reed 8:297-312
  Plymell **11**:295
Whittier, Calif. **1**:353
Whittier College **1**:358
Whittier, John Greenleaf **3**:399
Who Killed the British Empire? **6**:325
Who Shall Be the Sun? **3**:410
Who Walk in Darkness **2**:66-68, 70,
  72
Who? **14**:69, 76-77
Whole Hog **3**:408
Whole Lives **8**:311

"Why Do You Write about
  Russia?" **4**:287
Why Is the House Dissolving **10**:235,
  253, 254-55
Wichita University **11**:280, 282-84
Wideman, John Edgar **7**:34
Widower's Son, The **2**:388
Wiebe, Dallas **9**:83, 84
Wieners, John **16**:191-92
Wier and Pouce **14**:172, 177, 178
Wier, Dara **7**:18
Wiesel, Elie 4:353-62
  Elman **3**:76
Wiggins, Evelina **4**:58-59
Wilbur, Richard
  Creeley **10**:66-67
  Davison **4**:134-35
  Hall **7**:62
  Wilson **5**:349
Wilcox, Donald **9**:149
Wild Dog **5**:350
Wild Duck, The **4**:75
Wild Nights **9**:292-93
Wild With All Regret **12**:248
Wildcat **4**: 215
Wilde, Oscar **14**:247, 269
Wilder, Charles **9**:198, 201
Wilder, Laura Ingalls **6**:121
Wilder, Thornton
  Boyle **1**:119
  Olson **12**:228, 229-30
  Rosenthal **6**:276
Wilentz, Ted **6**:185
Wiley, Wild Willie **5**:148
Wilhelm, Kate 5:297-310
  Knight **10**:221, 223, 224, 225,
    226-29
  Moorcock **5**:180
  Wolfe **9**:305, 306, 308
Wilhelm, Richard **5**:309
Wilkins, Roy **1**:40
Willamette University **1**:369
William Allen White Award **2**:126
William and Mary, College of **7**:132,
  134
William Godwin **6**:320
William Saroyan **5**:217
William the Conqueror Prize **12**:199
Williams, Bert **6**:258
Williams College
  Clarke **16**:84
  Delbanco **2**:159
  Higgins **8**:91
Williams, Cora **1**:376
Williams, Cratis **15**:287, 288
Williams, Emmett **8**:89, 92
Williams, Flossie **8**:310
Williams, Glenn "Blossom" **2**:102,
  104, 106, 110, 112
Williams, Harrison **1**:291
Williams Institute, Berkeley, Calif.
  1:376, 377
Williams, John A. 3:413-33
  Major **6**:186
Williams, John Henry **3**:417, 418,
  422

Williams, Jonathan 12:339-58
  Broughton 12:56
  Corman 2:140
  Gray 2:194
Williams, Miller 8:215
Williams, Ola Mae Jones 3:417, 418, 420, 422, 423, 425, 428
Williams, Oscar 8:113, 116
Williams, Paul 10:287, 288, 293-94, 295
Williams, Ralph 10:219
Williams, Tennessee
  Bowles 1:86, 88, 90, 91, 92
  Cassity 8:43
  Forrest 7:23-24
  Katz 14:176-77
  Nims 17:180
  Sinclair 5:273
  Weiss 2:443
Williams, Tom 1:73, 74
Williams, Vanessa 6:153-54
Williams, Virginia 10:293-94, 295
Williams, William Carlos
  Bell 12:35-36
  Corman 2:136, 137, 139
  Cruz 17:9, 10-11
  Enslin 3:90, 94
  Eshleman 6:131
  Ghiselin 10:140
  Gregor 10:149
  Kyger 16:192
  Rimmer 10:287
  Rosenblum 11:342, 345
  Souster 14:315
  Thayler 11:359, 360, 363
  Turnbull 14:336
  Weiss 2:445, 446
  Whittemore 8:306, 310
  Williams 12:352
Williamson, Alan 4:249
Williamson, Jack 8:313-27
  Gunn 2:248, 250
  Wolfe 9:305, 311
Willie Masters' Lonesome Wife 9:112
Wilner, Herbert 3:221
Wilson, Adrian 12:52
Wilson, Angus
  Purdy 1:303
  Settle 1:315
  Wilson 5:319, 320
Wilson, Colin 5:311-31
  Eshleman 6:129
Wilson, Edmund
  Blais 4:73, 74
  Kazin 7:92, 93
  Wesker 7:236
Wilson, Edward O. 16:291-308
Wilson, Francis 9:98
Wilson Harris the Uncompromising Imagination 16:134
Wilson, James Southall 4:58
Wilson, Keith 5:333-57
  Enslin 3:98
  McCord 9:187
Wilson, Richard 10:203, 211
Wilson, Richard L. 3:179

Wilson, Robin Scott
  Knight 10:225
  Wolfe 9:306
Wilson, Thomas J. 4:134
Wilson, Woodrow 1:108-09
Wiltwyck School for Boys 3:423, 424
Wimberley, L.C. 8:274
Winchell, Walter 2:104
Wind, Fragments for a Beginning 5:166
Wind Heart, The 2:329
Wind in the Willows, The 1:100, 101
Windrose: Poems 1929–1979 10:135
Winesburg, Ohio
  Brown 6:47-48
  Jones 11:185
Wing Leader 9:107, 108, 120
Winn, Dilys 3:390
Winning Through 12:2
Winstanley 4:105
Winter, Ella 12:49
Winter in the Hills, A 4:330
Winter Kills 1:196
Winter Talent, A 3:38, 39
"Winter Warrior, The" 2:58
Winters, Yvor
  Broughton 12:48-49
  Davie 3:36, 37, 38
  Elman 3:74, 75, 76
  Guerard 2:222, 223, 228
  Hall 7:64
  Pinsky 4:245-47
Wirsen, Carl David af 1:391
Wisconsin News 1:376
Wise Child 3:113-14
Wise, Matthew M. 7:182
Wise, Stephen S. 4:129
Witching Hour, The 2:249, 255, 258
"With Loss of Eden" 7:146
"With Malice Towards One and All" 9:234
With Naked Foot 11:112
"Witness, The" 6:253, 266
Witter Bynner Prize 7:187
Wittgenstein, Ludwig 9:282
Wizard of Loneliness, The 2:330-31
WKY radio, Oklahoma City, Okla. 2:169
WMEX radio, Boston, Mass. 3:91
Wodehouse, P.G.
  Dennison 6:110
  Glanville 9:17
  Konwicki 9:129
Wolf, Dan 6:171
Wolf Willow 9:260, 269
Wolfe, Bernie 2:66
Wolfe, Gene 9:297-313
  Moorcock 5:180
Wolfe, Thomas
  Cassity 8:42
  Eastlake 1:208
  Wolfe 9:298
"Wolfpen Creek" 17:245
Wollheim, Donald A.
  Bradley 10:27

Hoffman 10:173
Kennedy 9:78
Knight 10:203, 205, 206, 207, 208, 211, 214-15, 225
Pohl 1:294
Silverberg 3:271, 276
Woman Beware Woman 9:293
Woman of Independent Means, A 1:226, 232, 233
Woman on the Edge of Time 1:277
Woman on the Shore, The 17:213
Woman Who Escaped from Shame, The 11:248
Woman's College of North Carolina 9:84
Woman's Day 1:314
Woman's Home Companion 1:120
Women and Sex 11:70
Women in the Wall 2:352
Women Writing and Writing about Women 9:285
Women's movement
  El Saadawi 11:68, 70-71
  Enslin 3:94
  Owens 2:361, 368
  Piercy 1:273, 274, 275, 276
  See also Sexism
Women's University, Kyoto, Japan 2:140
Wonderful Focus of You, The 16:201
Wonder's Child 9:311
Wood, Grant 1:164
Wood, Ira 1:278-81
Woodbridge, Conn. 6:271, 272-73
Woodcock, George 6:311-29
  Symons 3:390
Wooden Horse, The 15:228, 230
Woodhull, Victoria 1:383
Woodroffe, John 10:291
Woodrow Wilson National Fellowship
  Busch 1:131
  Delbanco 2:158
  Dillard 7:11
  McCord 9:181
Woolf, Virginia
  Blais 4:79
  Brown 10:37
  Fuller 10:114, 115
Worcester Telegram 4:227-28
Word Prints 8:192-93
Word, The (Irving Wallace) 1:384, 385, 397-98
Wordplays 2 2:361
Words, The (Jean-Paul Sartre) 4:49-50
Wordsand 8:179, 196
Wordsworth, William
  Heyen 9:37
  Jennings 5:106
  O'Faolain 2:344
Working class 6:29, 30, 33, 36
Working Firewood for the Night 15:382-83, 384-85
Works Progress Administration
  Cassill 1:164, 165
  Corcoran 2:116

Honig **8**:109
World According to Garp, The **3**:15, 29
World and Africa, The **2**:300
World and the Book, The **8**:157
World Anthology: Poems from the St. Mark's Poetry Project, The **17**:279
World Between the Eyes, The **4**:122
World Church Service **4**:276, 277
World Federalist Movement **2**:192
World Inside, The **3**:281
World Journal Tribune **2**:401
World Literature **1**:343
World of Canadian Writing, The **6**:323
World of W.B. Yeats, The **5**:287
World Science Fiction Association
    Aldiss **2**:29
    Gunn **2**:248, 257
    Pohl **1**:295-96
World Science Fiction Convention **3**:274, 281
World Telegram **2**:400
World, The
    Hahn **11**:110-11
    Owens **2**:366
    Pinsky **4**:250
    Waldman **17**:279
World War I
    Aldiss **2**:16
    Boyle **1**:103
    Caldwell **1**:140
    Cartland **8**:20
    Cela **10**:53-55
    Corman **2**:129
    Duncan **2**:165
    Gilbert **15**:183-84
    Grumbach **2**:203
    Gunn **2**:237
    Hamburger **4**:161
    Hauser **11**:123, 125, 126
    Howes **3**:133
    Katz **9**:53
    Lem **1**:255
    Lessing **14**:183, 192
    Roditi **14**:240-41
    Rosenthal **6**:278
    Salisbury **15**:314, 315, 317-18, 320, 321
    Settle **1**:307
    Shadbolt **3**:255
    Symons **3**:381
    Thomas **4**:301
    Wagoner **3**:399
    Wain **4**:319
    Wellek **7**:208, 209-10
    West **7**:268, 269-70
    White **4**:339
    Wilson **5**:328
    Woodcock **6**:314, 315
    Wright **5**:360
World War II
    Abse **1**:19-20
    Aldiss **2**:19-21, 23
    Allen, Dick **11**:5-6

Allen, Walter **6**:20-21
Anderson **2**:38-39
Andre **13**:21
Arden **4**:42-43, 44
Ashby **6**:35, 40
Awoonor **13**:39-40
Barnstone **15**:73
Barrio **15**:113-15
Becker **1**:33, 34
Bell **12**:29, 30
Bennett **13**:79, 82-83
Blaise **3**:20
Booth **2**:48
Bourjaily **1**:67-68
Bowles **1**:86
Boyle **1**:117-20
Brée **15**:138-43
Brown, Dee **6**:54-55
Brown, Rosellen **10**:29
Brunner **8**:2-3
Busch **1**:127, 130
Caldwell **1**:148-49
Cartland **8**:24
Cassill **1**:165-67
Caute **4**:97-98, 101
Ciardi **2**:90-93, 95
Clement **16**:92-94
Condon **1**:193
Connell **2**:102-06
Coppel **9**:3
Corcoran **2**:118
Corman **2**:133
Davie **3**:32-34
Davison **4**:130-31
Dennison **6**:110
Dillard **7**:4, 7, 12
Dillon **3**:55-56
Duncan **2**:166-69
Eastlake **1**:202-08, 211
Easton **14**:143, 145, 146, 147, 151-52, 153, 154
Epstein **12**:59-60, 61, 62-63
Federman **8**:69-70
Fisher **10**:90, 92
Fitzgerald **10**:104-05
Freeling **12**:79-80
Fuchs **5**:53-54
Fuller **10**:111-12, 124-25
Ghiselin **10**:133-35
Gilbert **15**:189-91
Glanville **9**:15-16
Gray, Francine du Plessix **2**:183-84, 188-89, 197
Gray, Simon **3**:102
Green **11**:90-94
Gregor **10**:149, 161
Grumbach **2**:203, 207, 208-09
Guerard **2**:224-26
Gunn **2**:239, 243-45, 252
Hahn **11**:114-15
Hall **12**:124, 126-28
Hamburger **4**:163-64
Hassan **12**:145-46
Heyen **9**:33-35
Holden **8**:100
Honig **8**:109-12

Hood **17**:82-83
Houston **16**:175-77
Hrabal **12**:189
Jennings **5**:107
Jolley **13**:113, 114, 117
Jones **5**:120, 121
Josipovici **8**:146, 148-49
Katz **14**:162
Kazin **7**:91-93
Kerrigan **11**:204, 216
Killens **2**:286, 287
Kirk **9**:95-96
Kirkup **4**:183
Knebel **3**:170, 177-78
Koller **5**:158-59
Konwicki **9**:126, 134
Kumin **8**:212-14
Lem **1**:256, 258
Lessing **14**:196, 197, 198-99, 200-01
Lind **4**:196, 201
Livesay **8**:234
Lottman **12**:202, 203, 204
Mahapatra **9**:139-42
Manuel **9**:159-62
Markfield **3**:208, 209, 210
Mathews **6**:230
Matthews **15**:259-61
McCord **9**:172
Megged **13**:142-43, 149, 150
Menashe **11**:226, 228
Meredith **14**:226-27
Moorcock **5**:173
Morgan, Ted **4**:224-25
Morgan, Theodore **3**:237
Morris **13**:171
Mott **7**:115-18, 122
Mrozek **10**:266, 268, 270
Nichols, J.G. **2**:308, 310, 311-12, 313-17
Nichols, John **2**:322
Olson **12**:232
Owens **2**:355
Peters **8**:239
Petesch **12**:242
Plymell **11**:277-78, 279
Pohl **1**:287-89
Rabassa **9**:198-201
Raworth **11**:297, 298
Rimmer **10**:288, 289-92
Roditi **14**:262, 263-65, 266-67
Rosenthal **6**:276, 277, 278-79
Rowse **8**:257, 260
St. Clair **8**:272
Salisbury **15**:314, 321-24
Samarakis **16**:251-57
Schevill **12**:273
Settle **1**:312-313, 318
Shadbolt **3**:255
Shapiro **6**:291, 293, 294-300
Silkin **5**:247-48, 249, 250, 253
Sillitoe **2**:374-75
Silverberg **3**:270
Simic **4**:267-71
Simpson **4**:291
Sinclair **5**:267-68

INDEX

Sisson **3**:299-300
Skelton **5**:280
Škvorecký **1**:330-32
Slade **9**:237
Solotaroff **2**:393
Sparshott **15**:349-50
Stafford **3**:327, 331, 332-33, 337
Stegner **9**:266
Stevenson **9**:277
Still **17**:242-44
Swanberg **13**:264-67
Sward **13**:286
Tarn **16**:272-74
Thayler **11**:357
Thomas, D.M. **11**:381-82
Thomas, R.S. **4**:305, 307
Van Brunt **15**:369
Van Itallie **2**:406-07, 409
Vivante **12**:287, 288-91, 295
Voinovich **12**:307-08, 311-12
Wain **4**:321, 325
Wakoski **1**:354
Wallace **1**:379
Weiss **2**:435
Wellek **7**:224-25
West **7**:268
White **4**:337-39
Whittemore **8**:301-03
Wilhelm **5**:297, 301, 307
Williams **3**:419-20
Williamson **8**:322
Wilson **5**:340, 341
Wolfe **9**:300-01
Woodcock **6**:320-21
Wright, Charles **7**:290
Wright, David **5**:364-65
Zinoviev **10**:326-27
World within World **8**:194
World without End **2**:190, 200-01
World Zionist Federation **4**:196
Worlds Beyond **10**:215-16
World's Fair, Chicago, 1936 **2**:216-17
WOV radio, New York City **3**:424
*W.P. Kinsella: Tall Tales in Various
     Voices* **7**:107
"Wreck" **17**:174
Wright, Charles 7:287-303
  Ai **13**:9
Wright, Charles Stevenson **6**:187
Wright, David 5:359-75
  Ashby **6**:44
  Sisson **3**:301, 302, 304
Wright, Farnsworth **8**:318
Wright, Frank Lloyd **12**:256
Wright, James **9**:44
Wright, Lee **13**:340-41
Wright, R. Glenn **10**:229
Wright, Richard
  Kazin **7**:90
  Major **6**:184, 185, 186, 189
Wright, Sarah Elizabeth **2**:288
Wright State University **11**:14-16
Wright, Stuart **5**:77
*Write On! Notes from a Writers
     Workshop* **2**:306

Writer and Politics, The **6**:321
Writers Action Group **4**:84, 86, 88
Writer's Center, The **15**:379
Writer's Digest
  Block **11**:36
  Jerome **8**:134-35
Writers' Guild (Great Britain)
  Brophy **4**:82, 86, 88
  Caute **4**:109
"Writers Mind, The" **2**:368
Writers' Revisions **3**:203
Writers' Union of Canada
  Horwood **15**:251
  Skelton **5**:291
Writing Crime Fiction **8**:177
Writing Fiction **6**:102
Writing Life of James M. Cain, The
     3:203
Writing of One Novel, The **1**:390,
     392, 395
Writing the Australian Crawl **3**:334
Wrong, Dennis H. **8**:180
Wurlitzer, Rudolph **14**:177
Wuthering Heights **1**:313
Wyatt, Thomas **10**:252
Wylie, Craig **12**:38
Wylie, Dirk **1**:289
Wylie, Elinor **8**:227
Wylie, Max **2**:329
Wynand, Derk **7**:101
Wynne-Tyson, Jon **5**:261
Wynter, Bryan **5**:369

X (magazine)
  Ashby **6**:43-44
  Sisson **3**:302
  Wright **5**:371
X-Rated Videotape Guide, The **10**:303-
     04
X-Rays **7**:144

Yaddo (artists' colony)
  Bell **12**:19, 38
  Nims **17**:190-91
  Peters **8**:247
  Stegner **9**:265
  Wagoner **3**:403, 405
Yale Daily News **3**:315
Yale Literary Magazine **3**:314
Yale Series of Younger Poets
  Competition **4**:137
Yale University
  Barnstone **15**:107
  Boyd **11**:51-52, 54
  Burroway **6**:93
  Clarke **16**:82-83, 85-86
  Epstein **12**:67-68, 69, 72
  Higgins **8**:85
  Morgan **4**:227
  Raffel **9**:211, 212
  Slavitt **3**:311, 312, 314-16, 317,
     321, 324
  Tarn **16**:276
  Van Itallie **2**:422
  Weiss, Paul **12**:331-32
  Weiss, Theodore **2**:435-36

Whittemore **8**:301, 302
Wiesel **4**:359
Yankee Clipper **1**:84
Yankee Pine **2**:118
Yashima, Taro **2**:136
Yates, David **8**:141
Yates, Richard **9**:114, 116
Yawning Heights, The **10**:333-35
Year before Last **1**:115
Year of the Century: 1876, The **6**:57
Yearbook of Jazz **1**:344
Yeats, William Butler
  Becker **1**:37
  Belitt **4**:60
  Connell **2**:97
  Dillon **3**:53, 64
  Howes **3**:142-43
  Kennedy **9**:80, 81
  Nichols **2**:318
  Pinsky **4**:237
  Rosenblum **11**:342
  Stevenson **9**:281
  Van Itallie **2**:412
  Wain **4**:328
  White **4**:333, 336
Yedioth Ahronoth **4**:356, 357
Yellen, Samuel
  Eshleman **6**:131, 132
  Wagoner **3**:404
Yellowhorse **6**:57
Yenching University, Peking, China
     1:34
Yerma **1**:89, 90, 91
"Yesterday in Belize" **17**:244
Yevtushenko, Yevgeny **11**:149
Yiddish language
  Katz **9**:55, 58, 63, 64-65
  Weiss **2**:426-27
Yih Chia-Shun **7**:66
YM-YWHA Poetry Center
  Burroway **6**:90
  Wakoski **1**:362
Ynyshir Nature Reserve **4**:309
Yoga
  Rimmer **10**:291
  Sward **13**:295-96, 300
  Wilson **5**:348
Yojana **9**:232
York, England **4**:39
York University **3**:28
Yorke, Matthew **9**:293
*You and I . . . Searching for
     Tomorrow* **10**:305
You Could Live If They Let You **3**:225
You Have Seen Their Faces **1**:148
Young America Weekly **1**:376
Young, Brigham **1**:388, 389-90
*Young Cherry Trees Secured against
     Hares* **8**:84
Young Communist League **1**:286
Young, Geoffrey **9**:179
"Young Goodman Brown" **11**:181
Young, Izzy **10**:172
Young, Karl **11**:345, 348
Young, Lafayette **9**:179
Young Lonigan **7**:89

Young Lovers, The **5**:79
Young Presidents Organization **1**:40
Young, Stark **7**:92
Young, Vernon **9**:147
Young Wives' Tale, A **1**:382
Youngblood **2**:281, 282, 285, 287, 288, 289, 290-91, 296, 305
Youngest Camel, The **1**:123
Youngstein, Max **1**:194
"Your Place or Mine?" **2**:70
Ysaÿe, Eugène **1**:112-13
Yugoslavia
    Aldiss **2**:26-28
    Dacey **17**:32-33
Yvain (Le Chevalier au lion) **9**: 219

Zakharchenko, Vasili **1**:286
Zalaznick, Sheldon **2**:400
Zalmen; or, The Madness of God **4**:358
Zangwill, Israel **7**:236
Zanuck, Darryl F. **1**:384, 385

Zanuck, Darryl F., Productions **1**:389
Zanuck, Richard D. **1**:384, 385
Zap **11**:293
Zatz, Asa **9**:200
Zavrian, Suzanne **8**:293
Zemach, Margot **6**:154-55
Zembla's Rocks **14**:136
Zen
    Delbanco **2**:156
    Hamill **15**:207-08, 214
    Kirkup **4**:191
    Kyger **16**:192-93, 194, 195
Zen Contemplations **4**:191
Zen There Was Murder **8**:170
Zend, Robert **13**:297-99
Zeromski, Stefan **9**:129
Ziegler, Evarts **1**:384
Zimbabwe **14**:54
Zimbabwe Tapes, The **4**:109
Zimmer, Paul **12**:249, 250
Zinn, Howard **1**:51
Zinoviev, Alexander 10:323-39

Zinzin Road, The **3**:181
Zionism
    Elman **3**:72
    Lind **4**:196-97, 200, 201
    Wiesel **4**:355-56
Zoline, Pamela **4**:152
Zoline, Patsy **5**:164
Zolotov Affair, The **10**:299
Zone Journals **7**:295
Zoo Story, The **5**:217-18
Zoritte, Eda **13**:150, 151, 152, 154, 158
Zukofsky, Celia **3**:92
Zukofsky, Louis
    Corman **2**:138, 140, 142, 144, 145-46
    Creeley **10**:73, 74
    Enslin **3**:92, 93, 94
    Eshleman **6**:140
    Rakosi **5**:207
    Turnbull **14**:335
Zukofsky, Paul **12**:346

INDEX